DYNAMICS OF STRUCTURES
WITH
MATLAB® APPLICATIONS

Ashok K. Jain
Professor of Civil Engineering
Indian Institute of Technology Roorkee
Roorkee

PEARSON

Chennai • Delhi

Associate Editor—Acquisitions: R. Dheepika
Senior Editor—Production: C. Purushothaman

ISBN 978-93-325-5855-7

First Impression

Published by Pearson India Education Services Pvt. Ltd,
CIN: U72200TN2005PTC057128, formerly known as TutorVista Global Pvt. Ltd, licensee of Pearson Education in South Asia.

Head Office: A-8 (A), 7th Floor, Knowledge Boulevard, Sector 62, Noida 201 309, Uttar Pradesh, India.
Registered office: 4th Floor, Software Block, Elnet Software City, TS-140, Block 2 & 9, Rajiv Gandhi Salai, Taramani, Chennai 600 113, Tamil Nadu, India.
Fax: 080-30461003, Phone: 080-30461060
www.pearson.co.in, Email: companysecretary.india@pearson.com

Compositor: SRS Technologies, Puducherry.
Printed in India by Pushp Print Services.

Dedicated to

my grandchildren, Dhruv and Samyukta, who made me
understand energy dissipation mechanisms
in live *dynamic systems*

Brief Contents

Contents

Preface

It is needless to reemphasize the significance and importance of the subject of dynamics of structures when the architects and engineers are constantly craving for lightweight but strong materials, and lean and slim structures. Among the whole family of the subjects on *Structural Engineering*, this is indeed the most mathematical and, therefore, most scary. There are an umpteen number of textbooks available on the subject of Dynamics of Structures that discuss the derivation of equations along with their physical significance. Nevertheless, it is very difficult to visualize these equations. FORTRAN has been the most powerful and preferred programming language of structural engineers, but it was without graphic commands. The subjects of structural dynamics, stiffness matrix method, nonlinear behaviour of members and structures, FORTRAN language, and computer hardware and software have evolved together since early 1960s. There used to be special Tektronix and vt100 graphic terminals, and Calcomp plotters with proprietary graphics software. The biggest hurdle in understanding the subject of dynamics remained the inability of easy graphical representation of equations and dynamic response of structures. Remember SAP IV, DRAIN-2D and SAKE developed in early 1970s? With the beginning of the twenty-first century, all that has changed. The desktop and laptop computers, and colour laser printers with very high resolutions are easily available and affordable. MATLAB is a very powerful and user-friendly software for carrying out solution of extremely complicated mathematical equations with built-in graphic functions. Another very easy and powerful tool is the electronic worksheet such as MS-EXCEL.

The writing of this book was inspired by the following objectives:

- to present the subject matter with utmost ease,
- to provide necessary and detailed mathematical background,
- to introduce more illustrative examples,
- to present the subject matter useful to final year undergraduate and postgraduate students,
- to introduce MS-EXCEL and MATLAB,
- to introduce nonlinear modelling and analysis,
- to introduce special damping devices and their modelling, and
- to introduce practical applications useful to practicing engineers.

During the past few years, my students have greatly appreciated the power and impact of these tools in understanding the subject. An attempt has been made to present both elementary topics as well as advanced topics including acceleration–displacement response spectra (ADRS) and performance-based seismic design of structures. The response of structures with energy dissipating devices subjected to earthquakes is also presented.

ORGANIZATION OF THE BOOK

A genuine effort has been made to develop the subject from the very basics of simple harmonic motion of a pendulum and introduce the concept of equation of motion. The next step is to find its solution. There are several techniques to solve the equations of motion for different types of dynamic loads. The analysis of structures due to different dynamic loads has been carried out in Chapters 3 to 7. The estimation of earthquake force has been discussed in Chapter 8. Analysis of two degrees of freedom system and tuned mass dampers has been developed in Chapter 9, whereas that of multi-degree-of-freedom systems has been developed in Chapters 10 and 11.

The analysis of multistorey reinforced concrete and steel buildings subjected to earthquake loads in accordance with IS:1893 code has been discussed in Chapter 12. Under a severe earthquake loading, a structure is expected to undergo inelastic region. Modelling for nonlinear analysis, hysteresis models, solution algorithms, energy dissipating devices, concept of ductility etc. are discussed in Chapter 13. Nowadays, there is a great emphasis on predicting the performance of a structure under earthquake loads. The intention is to know whether the structure will remain in *immediate occupancy, damage control, life safety, limited safety, or in structural stability states* during an earthquake event. In case there is a downtime for the building after an event, then how much will it be? What it will cost to the owner and its occupants as a result of downtime? What will be the estimated extent and cost of repair? Pushover analysis is used to study the performance-based design. These issues are discussed in Chapter 14. As on today, we may not have all the answers but these do indicate the direction of further research.

Finally, the last Chapter 15 is devoted to the estimation of wind loads based on IS:875-Part 3 and IRC6. Wind may be treated as a static load or dynamic load. The wind loads on various structures are calculated based on exhaustive studies in wind tunnels over an extended period of time in various countries. The concepts of fluid mechanics are involved in the estimation of wind loads. It is important to understand the estimation of drag coefficient for different shape and size of structures and their exposed structural elements. It is interesting to know that the dynamic wind loads are applied statically to a structure to understand its response.

Wherever required, IS:1893, IS:875-part 3, IS:2974, IRC 6, Eurocode 8, ASCE 7, AISC 341, NZS 1170 and ISO codes have been introduced. Federal Emergency Management Agency (FEMA), Washington, D.C., and Pacific Earthquake Engineering Research Center (PEER) have prepared several documents with detailed commentary and background notes including publications under the National Earthquake

Hazards Reduction Program (NEHRP).These publications have been introduced as appropriate. It is recommended that the reader should have a copy of these codes and research reports to understand and appreciate the latest developments.

HOW TO STUDY THE SUBJECT OF DYNAMICS?

As already pointed out, this is a highly mathematical subject. It is recommended that the reader should himself/herself derive each equation and make it a general practice to represent them in graphical form. It will help develop an understanding of the nature of equations, their physical meaning and interpretation, and, therefore, behaviour of the structure under a given dynamic load. MATLAB is a very powerful tool for learning and exploring the subject. MS-EXCEL is another very powerful tool to carry out repetitive calculations and represent the data in graphical form. In addition, the dynamic response of structures subjected to earthquake loading should be understood using commercially available software such as SAP2000 and ETABS. The GUI in all these tools is extremely powerful and helpful in unravelling the mystery of dynamics of structures. All such tools must be fully exploited for effective computer-aided learning.

MATLAB source codes developed in this text can be obtained by requesting at www.pearsoned.co.in/ashokkjain

ACKNOWLEDGEMENTS

I wish to thank the following students with whom I had short but intense brainstorming sessions, *sometimes forced as is natural in dynamics*, on various aspects of structural dynamics while they were working on their research projects during their stay at Roorkee: M. R. Deshpande, S. S. Dasaka, Shri Pal, R. A. Mir, Satish Annigeri, Jainendra Agarwal, J. Satyanarayan, P. Rajeshwari, M. L. Meena, Abhijit S. Niphade, Sourabh Agrawal, Ranjith Shetty, Sujit Ashok Gangal, Payal Thukral, Abhinav Gupta, Shabbir Lokhandwala, Mandakini Dehuri, Pruthvik B. M., Alwin N., Ripu Daman Singh and Saurabh Khandelwal. In addition, there were several other students who worked on static problems and had very stimulating technical sessions with me.

Special thanks to Ashok Mittal for our long-distance telephonic discussions on various aspects of earthquake engineering from the point of view of a structural designer who was chasing deadlines to finalize computer models and issue structural drawings, and there remained a few fundamental issues still unresolved. I must admit that I learnt wind loads from A. K. M. Tripathi who had a deep understanding of wind loads on TV and MW towers. Sincere thanks to Aparna K. P. who worked with me for her Master's thesis with a clean slate and in a very short time picked up the fine points of inelastic response spectra and acceleration–displacement response spectra, and helped produce numerous tables and graphs.

How can I forget my *alma mater*, the erstwhile University of Roorkee and now Indian Institute of Technology Roorkee, situated in a very small and calm town on the banks of Ganga and foothills of Himalaya, for providing an excellent work environment, library and computing facilities to learn, learn and learn? The University of Michigan at Ann Arbor, my another *alma mater*, provided me with excellent laboratory facilities in its North Campus to generate hysteresis loops for steel bracing members, and computing facilities in its main campus to study the inelastic seismic response of concentrically and eccentrically braced steel frames.

I acknowledge the editorial and production teams at Pearson consisting of R. Dheepika, C. Purushothaman and Sojan Jose for their untiring efforts and tolerating my last-minute changes in producing this book in the present form.

Lastly, I wish to thank my wife Sarita, our children Payal and Gaurav, son-in-law Vikash and daughter-in-law Saavy, for their unconditional support and encouragement in writing this book. I also thank my father who constantly advised me to write a book exclusively on earthquake engineering but some how I wasn't convinced.

Ashok K. Jain

About the Author

Dr Ashok K. Jain is Professor of Civil Engineering at the Indian Institute of Technology Roorkee (formerly University of Roorkee), obtained his B.E. and M.E. degrees with honours from the University of Roorkee in 1972 and 1974, and a doctorate degree from the University of Michigan, Ann Arbor, in 1978. His main areas of interest include multistoreyed buildings, concrete and steel bridges, and nonlinear seismic response of structures. Besides teaching and research, he has been a structural consultant to various state and central government agencies as well as many private companies. A recipient of several awards, he has been a research fellow at the University of Michigan; a visiting Professor at the McGill University, Montreal; Director, Malaviya National Institute of Technology, Jaipur; and Head of Civil Engineering Department, I.I.T. Roorkee.

PART

1

SINGLE DEGREE OF FREEDOM SYSTEMS

1 | Introduction to Structural Dynamics

1.1 INTRODUCTION

There are many situations in real life when a structure is subjected to vibrations caused by *dynamic loads* due to machines, road traffic, rail traffic or air traffic, wind, earthquake, blast loading, sea waves, or tsunami. The movement of pedestrians may cause vibrations in a floor of a building and in a suspension bridge. The term *dynamic loads* includes any loading which varies with time. The manner in which a *structure* responds to a given dynamic excitation depends upon the nature of excitation and the dynamic characteristics of the structure, that is, the manner in which it stores and dissipates energy. The energy is stored in the form of potential energy and is dissipated in the form of kinetic energy through vibrations. Some of these loads could lead to catastrophic loss to lives and properties in a very short span of time while the others cause irritation to the users of the facility. If the vibrations are small but persistent, this condition may lead to cracking in joints and members of a structure. In earlier days, a simplified solution was arrived at by treating the *dynamic load* as *equivalent static load*. Under certain conditions, this idealization works quite well. However, with better understanding of dynamics of structures, it is desirable to develop more efficient solutions by realistically modelling the loads taking account of their dynamic nature. When a dynamic load is applied to the structure it produces a time-dependent response in each element of the structure. The organization of structural systems to resist such loadings has a major influence on the overall planning, design and economics of a structure.

The subject of dynamics of structures becomes quite complex because of a large number of variables involved in the problem. The term *structure* encompasses a single-storey building to a multi-storey building, small overhead water tanks to large water tanks of different shapes, small bridges to large bridges of different materials and configurations, viaducts, microwave and TV towers, industrial structures, machine foundations, theatres, stadiums, airports, jetties and so on. Mass and stiffness of a structure along with their spatial distribution define the structure. Material used in structures is another parameter that defines the structure. Damping is generally associated with materials. Finally the *amplitude, frequency* and *duration of load* lead to another complication. Earthquake loading is a complex variant of this. Some of the dynamic loads are *deterministic* while the others are *non-deterministic or probabilistic*. Some of the structures will respond to dynamic loads in *linear and elastic* range while the others may venture into *nonlinear elastic* or *nonlinear inelastic* range. The role of a structural analyst is to identify each of these parameters and determine the response of the structure as accurately as possible. The study of vibrations, that is, their cause, measurement, analysis and effect on the structure is called *dynamics of structures*.

The details of excitation, structure and response are illustrated in Figures 1.1 to 1.5. The excitation shown in Figures 1.2(b) and 1.2(c) may be static or dynamic or even slow dynamic. A slow dynamic load is also called pseudo static load. It is very helpful in conducting tests in laboratory.

Figure 1.1   Cause and effect on a structure.

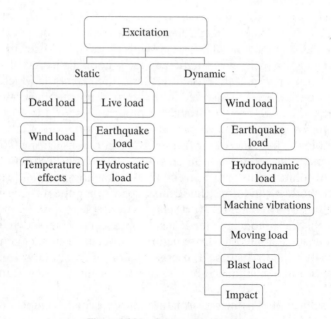

Figure 1.2(a)   Source of excitation.

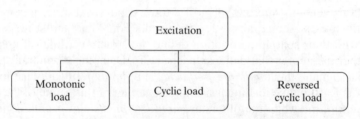

Figure 1.2(b)   Nature of excitation.

structural elements, stiffness is generated from the element level as done in the *matrix method of structural analysis*. The same procedure may be followed for dynamic analysis of structures. Sometimes it may not be easy to find solution of the mathematical model subjected to given loads in the absence of known appropriate boundary conditions. Therefore, it may be necessary to develop a numerical model of the problem and solve it using one or more *numerical techniques*.

Sometimes it is necessary to include soil and foundation in the model to examine the effect of soil–structure interaction. The problem now becomes very complex. The treatment requires advanced treatment that is beyond the scope of the present text.

Let us consider a simple pendulum consisting of a mass suspended from a massless rod as shown in Figure 1.7.

This pendulum can be displaced slightly horizontally and released gently. It sets into simple harmonic motion whose equation is given by the principles of physics, that is, *Newton's second law of motion*:

$$\ddot{x} \propto -x \tag{1.1a}$$

or,
$$\ddot{x} = -\omega^2 x \tag{1.1b}$$

where,
$$\ddot{x} = \frac{d^2x}{dt^2} \text{ acceleration} \tag{1.1c}$$

$$\omega = \sqrt{\frac{k}{m}} \tag{1.1d}$$

k = stiffness of the rod = AE/L
m = total mass
ω = natural frequency of vibration in rad/sec

$$\omega = \frac{2\pi}{T} = 2\pi f \tag{1.1e}$$

f = natural frequency of vibration in cycles/sec or in Hz

$$T = \frac{1}{f} = 2\pi\sqrt{\frac{m}{k}} \tag{1.1f}$$

T = natural period of vibration in sec

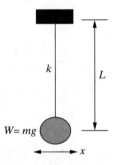

Figure 1.7 Simple pendulum.

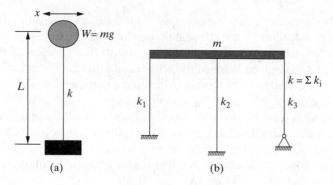

Figure 1.8   Inverted pendulum.

The pendulum has only one degree of freedom in the lateral direction, that is, lateral displacement x. It shows that the acceleration is directed towards the mean position of the pendulum and it is proportional to the displacement.

This pendulum can be inverted upside down as shown in Figure 1.8.

This inverted pendulum still vibrates in simple harmonic motion and its equation of motion remains same as before. In the inverted position, it can simulate the behaviour of an overhead water tank or that of a single-storey building. In case of a water tank, mass m represents the mass of the container and the water, whereas k represents the lateral stiffness of staging of the tank. In case of a building, mass m represents mass lumped at its roof, whereas k represents the lateral stiffness of all the lateral load-resisting elements. These elements may be columns, walls or both. The natural frequency of the pendulum is the most important characteristic of a dynamic system. It is a function of the *mass* and *stiffness* of the system.

Now let us consider a simple portal frame as shown in Figure 1.9(a). There are three degrees of freedom per node: one horizontal translation, one vertical translation and one rotation. Since A and D are fixed supports, the frame has six active degrees of freedom. If axial deformation is neglected, it will have three degrees of freedom: one lateral and two rotational for static analysis. In dynamic analysis, the number of independent displacements required to define the displaced position of all the masses relative to their original position is called *dynamic degrees of freedom*. If mass of the frame is concentrated at one location, that is roof, the frame will have only one degree

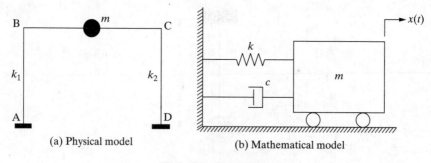

Figure 1.9   Portal frame.

of freedom—lateral displacement. Thus, it is called a SDOF system. Its mathematical model is shown in Figure 1.9(b). Again, natural frequency of the frame is its most important characteristic. It is a function of the mass and lateral stiffness of the system. The lateral stiffness of this rigid jointed frame depends upon the relative stiffness of beams and columns. Let us consider two extreme cases:

Case 1: *Rigid beam, that is, flexural stiffness of beam is infinite.*

The flexural rigidity of each column is EI. Height of each column is L. Therefore, lateral stiffness of each column is given by

$$K = \frac{12EI}{L^3} \tag{1.2a}$$

The total lateral stiffness of the frame =

$$K = 2 \times \frac{12EI}{L^3} \tag{1.2b}$$

Case 2: *Flexible beam, that is, flexural stiffness of beam is very low*

Therefore, lateral stiffness of each column is given by

$$K = \frac{3EI}{L^3} \tag{1.3a}$$

The total lateral stiffness of the frame =

$$K = 2 \times \frac{3EI}{L^3} \tag{1.3b}$$

In case there are three identical columns, the total stiffness of the frame becomes three times the stiffness of a single column. Equations (1.2a) and (1.3a) give range of lateral stiffness of a column.

1.3 DISCRETE AND CONTINUUM MODELLING

In dynamics of structures, the first step is to identify dynamic degrees of freedom. In certain structures these degrees of freedom are obvious and identifiable whereas, in many other structures it is difficult to identify these degrees of freedom. Thus, depending upon the number of degrees of freedom, we may have a multi-degrees-of-freedom system. For example, consider a four-storey moment-resistant frame having rigid floors. It is a skeletal structure and it is referred to as a discrete system in matrix structural analysis terminology. The entire mass of the floor and storey can be lumped at each floor level. It can, therefore, be identified that there is only one lateral displacement at each floor, that is, there is one-degree-of-freedom per floor. Similarly, in an overhead water tank, the entire mass of water is lumped at its top. The mass of water is much more than the mass of the staging. Thus, it can be said that there is only one lateral degree of freedom at the centre of gravity of the mass. This is referred to as a lumped mass approach in a discrete system. A TV tower or a truss steel bridge is an example of discrete structural system having n-degrees-of-freedom as shown in Figure 1.10.

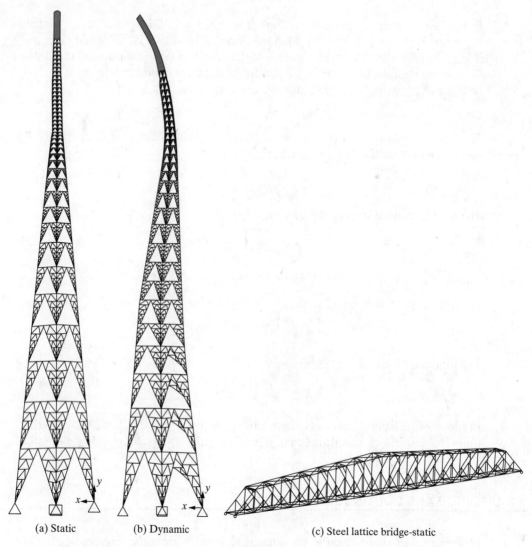

(a) Static   (b) Dynamic   (c) Steel lattice bridge-static

Figure 1.10   (a) Steel TV tower — static; (b) Steel TV tower — dynamic; (c) Steel truss bridge.

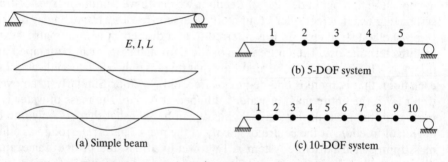

E, I, L

1   2   3   4   5

(b) 5-DOF system

1 2 3 4 5 6 7 8 9 10

(a) Simple beam   (c) 10-DOF system

Figure 1.11   A system with distributed mass and stiffness.

Now consider a simply supported beam under its self-weight having length L as shown in Figure 1.11. Its mass and elasticity or stiffness is distributed along its length. Theoretically, it has infinite degrees of freedom. How do we identify its active degrees of freedom? There are two options. One, make use of generalized displacements. In other words, assume a deflected shape which remains constant along the entire length at any point of time. This is called a *shape function*. It represents one degree of freedom. Similarly, select other shape function compatible with its boundary conditions. It will represent another degree of freedom. Thus, 'n' shape functions can be selected for a system with distributed mass and elasticity representing n-degrees-of-freedom. Other option is to lump its mass at certain locations along its length. If it is lumped at five locations, it will result in a five-degrees-of-freedom system. If it is lumped at 10 locations, it will result in a 10-degrees-of-freedom system. More the number of discretization, better will be the accuracy.

Now consider a retaining wall as shown in Figure 1.12(a). It is again a continuum system having distributed mass and elasticity in its entire body. It has infinite-degrees-of-freedom. How do we identify its active degrees of freedom? The answer lies in making use of the finite element concept. Mesh the wall in appropriate shape and size

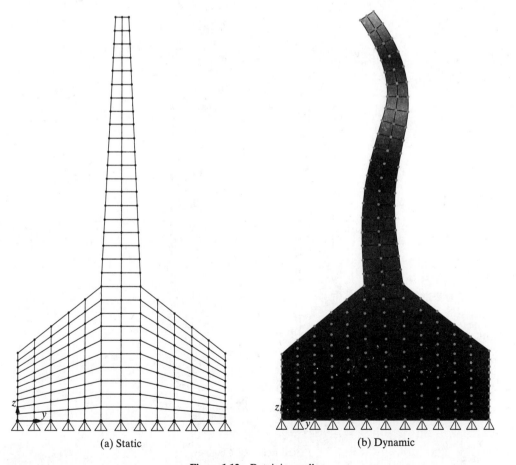

(a) Static   (b) Dynamic

Figure 1.12   Retaining wall.

in each of the two directions in the vertical plane. Identify the degrees of freedom at each node and select appropriate finite element to represent structural characteristics of the wall, that is, *plane stress* element, *plane strain* element, *plate element* or a *shell element*. There are different options to discretize a structure and adopt a finite element depending upon its structural characteristics, desired accuracy and convenience. A typical mode shape under free vibration condition is shown in Figure 1.12(b). The same concept is applicable to chimneys as shown in Figure 1.13.

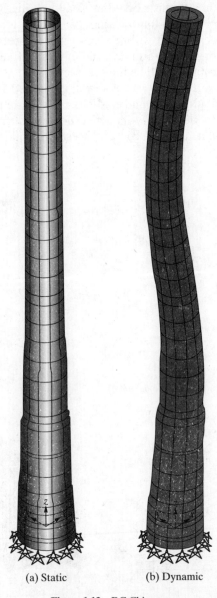

(a) Static   (b) Dynamic

Figure 1.13   RC Chimney.

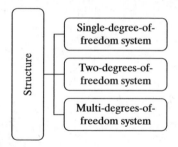

Figure 1.14   Classification of a structure for dynamic analysis.

A structure can be classified according to its degrees-of-freedom for dynamic analysis as shown in Figure 1.14, irrespective of whether it is a discrete system or a distributed system.

1.4 LAWS OF EQUILIBRIUM

In the static analysis of a structure, static equilibrium must be satisfied in order to arrive at a unique solution. It is achieved through the following conditions:

$$\sum F_x = 0, \sum F_y = 0, \sum F_z = 0, \sum M_x = 0, \sum M_y = 0, \sum M_z = 0 \tag{1.4}$$

Similarly, in dynamic analysis of a structure, equilibrium must be satisfied at each time instant. This can be accomplished with the help of *Newton's second law of motion*. The objective of dynamic analysis is to evaluate the displacement–time history of a structure when subjected to a given dynamic load. In most cases, considering only a limited degrees-of-freedom of a structure will give reasonably accurate results. The problem is reduced to the determination of time histories of these selected displacement components. The mathematical equations defining the dynamic displacements are called *equations of motion*. Naturally, these degrees of freedom need to be identified carefully.

1.4.1 Newton's Law of Motion

Consider a mass m attached to a massless spring suspended vertically. It has a vertical stiffness of k. In its unstretched position, the system is shown in Figure 1.15(a). Under its own weight, the system stretches by an amount Δ_{st} as shown in Figure 1.15(b). If the mass is pulled down by an amount x (Figure 1.15(c)) and released, the system will be subjected to vibrations. Let us consider the equilibrium of the system:

For equilibrium of Figure 1.15(b), $k \Delta_{st} = mg = W$ (1.5)

Let us consider the free body diagram of a system shown in Figure 1.15(c), and write the equilibrium equation by making use of Newton's second law, that is, *rate of change of momentum is proportional to the force applied on the body*,

$$\frac{d}{dt}\left(m\frac{dx}{dt} \right) = p(t) \tag{1.6a}$$

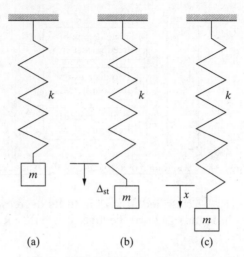

Figure 1.15   Simple spring mass system.

or, for most problems in structural dynamics, it may be assumed that mass m does not vary with time, that is,

$$m\frac{d}{dt}\left(\frac{dx}{dt}\right) = m\frac{d^2x}{dt^2} = p(t) \qquad (1.6b)$$

or, $$m\ddot{x}(t) = p(t) = mg - k\left(\Delta_{st} + x(t)\right) \qquad (1.7)$$

where, $$\ddot{x} = \text{acceleration} = \frac{d^2x}{dt^2}$$

Making use of Equation (1.5), Equation (1.7) can be written as

$$m\ddot{x}(t) + kx(t) = 0 \qquad (1.8)$$

Equation (1.8) can again be written as follows by dividing by m.

$$\ddot{x}(t) + \omega^2 x(t) = 0 \qquad (1.9)$$

where, $$\omega^2 = k/m$$

or, $$\omega = \sqrt{\frac{k}{m}} \qquad (1.1d)$$

ω = undamped natural frequency of vibration in radian/sec

Equation (1.8) shows that 'mg' and $k\,\Delta_{st}$ neutralize at all instants. Therefore, we need to consider only the forces which have come into effect beyond the static equilibrium position. Thus, Equations (1.8) and (1.9) are referred to as the *equations of motion* of an *undamped SDOF system* under *free vibrations*. It is relatively easy to estimate *mass* of a structure. The challenge is to estimate its *stiffness* corresponding to the desired degrees of freedom.

1.4.2 D'Alembert's Principle

The same equation of motion can be obtained by using D'Alembert's principle. It states that:

> *A body which is not in static equilibrium by virtue of some acceleration which it possesses can be brought to static equilibrium by introducing on it the inertia forces which can be considered to be an extra external force. This inertia force is equal to mass times the acceleration of the body and acts through the centre of gravity of the body in the direction opposite to that of the acceleration. That is,*

$$p(t) - f_I = 0 \qquad (1.10a)$$

or,

$$p(t) - m\frac{d^2x}{dt^2} = 0 \qquad (1.10b)$$

The mass develops an inertia force proportional to acceleration and opposes the acceleration of the mass, that is, dynamic motion. It is a very important concept in structural dynamics and permits the equation of motion to be expressed as equations of dynamic equilibrium. The force term $p(t)$ includes many types of forces acting on the mass such as, elastic force that opposes the displacement, viscous force that opposes the velocity, and other such loads. In a free vibration case, damping force is responsible for bringing the system to rest.

Equation (1.10a) may be written as follows:

$$p(t) - f_S - f_D - f_I = 0 \qquad (1.11a)$$

or,

$$f_I + f_D + f_S = p(t) \qquad (1.11b)$$

or,

$$m\frac{d^2x}{dt^2} + f_D + f_S = p(t) \qquad (1.11c)$$

where, f_D = damping force

f_S = elastic force

Equation (1.11b) or (1.11c) is referred to as the *Equation of Motion.*

1.4.3 Principle of Virtual Displacement

Sometimes the structural system is quite complicated and it may be difficult to write equations of equilibrium involving all the forces acting on the system. In such a scenario, it may be helpful to make use of the principle of virtual work or virtual displacement. It may be stated as follows:

> *If a body is in equilibrium under a force system and remains in equilibrium while it is subjected to a small virtual displacement, the virtual work done by the external forces is equal to the virtual work done by the internal stresses due to those forces.*

The imposed virtual displacements have to be compatible with the boundary conditions. Since the net work done due to the virtual displacement is zero, this statement is equivalent to that of a dynamic equilibrium. There is a need to identify all the forces acting on the various masses of the system. Next, equations of motion are obtained by introducing virtual displacements corresponding to each degree of freedom and equating the virtual work to zero. The inherent advantage of this method is that a virtual work is a scalar quantity whereas various forces acting on the structure are vector quantities. It is easy to work with scalars rather than with vectors.

1.5 TYPES OF DYNAMIC LOADING

There can be different types of dynamic loads on any structure such as:

- **(a)** Harmonic load
- **(b)** Periodic load
- **(c)** Impulse load
- **(d)** Earthquake load
- **(e)** Wind load
- **(f)** Blast load
- **(g)** Tornado
- **(h)** Missile or aircraft impact load
- **(i)** Sea wave load

The last four types of loads are not discussed in the present text. Various loads are shown in Figure 1.16. It will be noticed that earthquake and wind loads are essentially

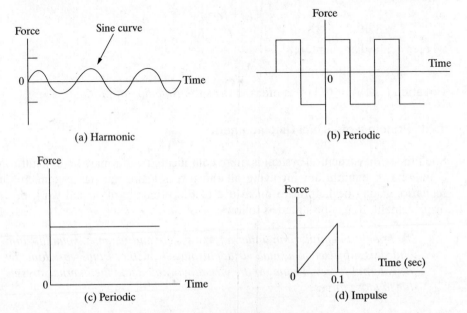

Figure 1.16 Type of dynamic loads.

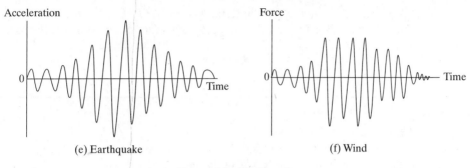

Figure 1.16 (Continued)

random loads. It means these loads are neither repeatable nor it is possible to represent them through a simple mathematical equation. Every time there is a wind load or an earthquake at a given location, it will be different from that recorded previously. Earthquake loads are *transient* in nature. It means it is a short duration load. It may last from a few seconds to a few minutes.

The above description of dynamic loads is very helpful in learning fundamentals of dynamics of structures. Harmonic load is simplest to visualize and understand. It is also easy to understand and appreciate the response of a structure subjected to a harmonic load. The other loads become more complex and, therefore, corresponding response of a structure also becomes more complex and difficult to visualize.

1.6 SOLUTION OF EQUATION OF MOTION

There are various methods to solve a second-order differential equation or a set of such equations depending upon the type of loading. Sometimes, it may be necessary to represent a loading in terms of Fourier series. For simple cases, these equations can be solved using the principles of differential calculus. For other cases, help may be taken from Green's function, Duhamel integral, eigenvalue problems, or various numerical integration schemes. These solution techniques will be discussed throughout the book.

MATLAB, owned by The MathWorks, Inc., USA, is a high-performance language for technical computing which integrates computation, visualization and programming in an easy-to-use environment. Typical uses of MATLAB include

- Mathematics—linear algebra, statistics, differentiation and integrals, Fourier transform, etc.
- Programming scripts and functions
- Data and file management
- Algorithm development
- Data acquisition
- Modelling, simulation and prototyping
- Data analysis, exploration and visualization
- Scientific and engineering graphics (graphical user interface [GUI])
- Application development including GUI building

MATLAB is an interactive system and stands for *MATRIX LABORATORY*. It is the most powerful and user friendly tool to study dynamics of structures and will be discussed in detail.

1.7 ILLUSTRATIVE EXAMPLES

Example 1.1

A simply supported beam of length L carries a mass m at its midspan as shown in Figure 1.17. The beam is massless. Write its equation of motion.

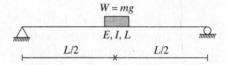

$$W = mg$$
$$E, I, L$$
$$L/2 \qquad L/2$$

Figure 1.17   Simple supported beam.

Solution   Let us determine the flexure stiffness of the beam. It is carrying a load $W = mg$ at its midspan. It is known that under the vertical load W at its midspan, the vertical deflection is given by:

$$\Delta = \frac{WL^3}{48EI}$$

Thus, flexure stiffness of beam is given by

$$k = \frac{W}{\Delta} = \frac{48EI}{L^3}$$

The equation of motion of the beam is

$$m\ddot{x} + kx = 0 \qquad (1.8)$$

or,

$$m\ddot{x} + \frac{48EI}{L^3}x = 0 \qquad \square$$

Example 1.2

A cantilever beam of length L carries a mass m at its free end suspended by a spring of stiffness k as shown in Figure 1.18. The beam and spring are massless. Write the equation of motion.

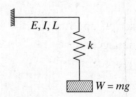

$$E, I, L$$
$$k$$
$$W = mg$$

Figure 1.18   Cantilever beam with loading at free end.

Solution   In this problem, it is important to understand deflected shape of the system under different situations. Under the weight W, the beam will deflect and the spring to which this weight is attached will also elongate. Let the deflection of beam alone is x_1 and that of the spring alone is x_2 due to weight W as shown in Figure 1.19(a). Thus,

$$x_{static} = x_1 + x_2 \qquad (i)$$

The same deflection can be measured from the unstretched position of both beam and spring as shown in Figure 1.19(b) for convenience. Let us now consider the free body diagram of the mass. The equilibrium condition gives

$$W = mg = k_e x_{static} \qquad (ii)$$

where,
k_e = effective vertical stiffness of the beam and spring system

The deflections x_1 and x_2 can be written as follows:

$$x_1 = \frac{W}{k_{beam}} = \frac{W}{\dfrac{3EI}{L^3}} \qquad (iii)$$

and

$$x_2 = \frac{W}{k} \qquad (iv)$$

equation (i) can be written as:

$$\frac{W}{k_e} = \frac{W}{k_{beam}} + \frac{W}{k}$$

or,

$$k_e = \frac{k_{beam}k}{k_{beam} + k} \qquad (v)$$

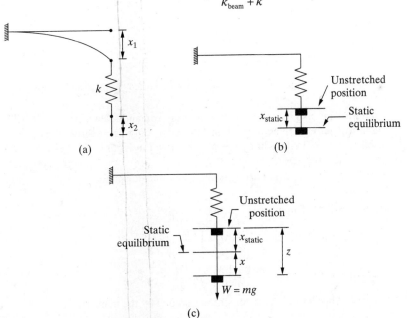

(a)

(b)

(c)

Figure 1.19   Deflected positions under different conditions.

If the mass is given a small displacement x from its static equilibrium position and then released gently, the mass will set in motion and will begin to vibrate. Its free body diagram is shown in Figure 1.19(c). The equation of dynamic equilibrium can be written as follows:

$$m\ddot{x} = mg - k_e z \qquad \text{(vi)}$$

$$m\ddot{x} = mg - k_e(x_{static} + x) \qquad \text{(vii)}$$

Making use of Equation (ii), Equation (vii) can be written as follows:

$$m\ddot{x} + k_e x = 0 \qquad \text{(viii)}$$

This is the equation of motion where the effective stiffness k_e is given by Equation (v). It can be seen that the static displacement under the weight W does not appear in the equation of motion. Same conclusion was arrived at while writing the equation of motion for a simple spring and mass system. ◻

Example 1.3

A rigid thin rod has mass m and is supported on an elastic spring and a viscous damper besides being hinged at end A as shown in Figure 1.20. The viscous damping force is represented by a dash-pot at end C. It is subjected to a triangular load. Derive the equation of motion of a structural system.

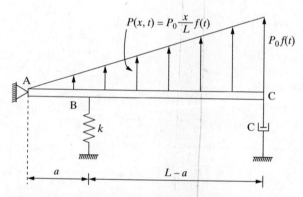

Figure 1.20   A hinged beam supported on spring and damper.

Solution   Let us give a small rotation to the rod and release it gently. It will start vibrating in the vertical plane about hinge A. It has only one-degree-of-freedom, the angular displacement θ. Its free body diagram is shown in Figure 1.21. The various forces generated are as follows:

Mass moment of inertia normal to the rod at its midspan $= \left(\dfrac{mL^2}{12}\right)$

If vertical displacement at C is x, then $x = L\theta$, $\dot{x} = L\dot{\theta}$, $\ddot{x} = L\ddot{\theta}$

1. Rotational inertia force $= M_I = \left(\dfrac{mL^2}{12}\right)\ddot{\theta}$

2. Inertia force $= f_I = \dfrac{m(0 + L\ddot{\theta})}{2} = m\dfrac{L\ddot{\theta}}{2}$

   (average lateral displacement undergone by the mass m)

3. Elastic spring force $= f_S = ka\theta$

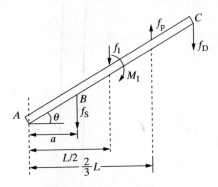

Figure 1.21   Free body diagram.

4. Viscous damping force $= f_D = cL\dot\theta$

5. External force $= f_p = P(x,t) = P_0 f(t)\dfrac{L}{2}$ (= area of the triangle)

The viscous damping force is proportional to velocity. It is a case of damped forced vibrations. Let us consider moment equilibrium by taking moment about A, the centre of rotation:

$$f_P\frac{2L}{3} - f_s a - f_D L - f_1\frac{L}{2} - M_1 = 0$$

or, substituting the values,

$$\frac{mL^2}{12}\ddot\theta + \frac{mL^2}{4}\ddot\theta + cL^2\dot\theta + ka^2\theta = \frac{P_0 L^2}{3}f(t)$$

The equation of motion becomes

$$\frac{mL^2}{3}\ddot\theta + cL^2\dot\theta + ka^2\theta = \frac{P_0 L^2}{3}f(t) \qquad\qquad \square$$

Example 1.4

Consider a structure shown in Figure 1.22. A rigid thin bar is supported on two springs and a dashpot system besides being hinged at end A. The rigid rod has mass m. Determine its equation of motion.

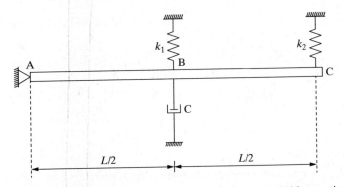

Figure 1.22   A hinged beam supported on damper and suspended from springs.

Solution   Let us give a small rotation to the rod and release it gently. It will start vibrating in the vertical plane about hinge A. It has only one-degree-of-freedom, the angular displacement θ. Its free body diagram is shown in Figure 1.23. The various forces generated are as follows:

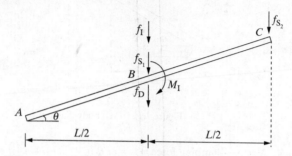

Figure 1.23   Free body diagram.

If the vertical displacement at C is x, then

$$x = L\theta, \quad \dot{x} = L\dot{\theta} \quad \text{and} \quad \ddot{x} = L\ddot{\theta}$$

1. Rotational inertia force $= M_I = \left(\dfrac{mL^2}{12}\right)\ddot{\theta} = \dfrac{mL}{12}\ddot{x}$

2. Inertia force $= f_I = \dfrac{m(0 + L\ddot{\theta})}{2} = \dfrac{mL}{2}\ddot{\theta} = \dfrac{m\ddot{x}}{2}$

3. Elastic spring force $= f_{S_1} = k_1\dfrac{L}{2}\theta = k_1\dfrac{x}{2}$

4. Elastic spring force $= f_{S_2} = k_2 L\theta = k_2 x$

5. Viscous damping force $= f_D = c\dfrac{L}{2}\dot{\theta} = c\dfrac{\dot{x}}{2}$

The rotational inertia force involves mass moment of inertia. The viscous damping force is proportional to velocity. Let us consider moment equilibrium by taking moment about A, the centre of rotation:

$$M_I + f_I\frac{L}{2} + f_D\frac{L}{2} + f_{S_1}\frac{L}{2} + f_{S_2}L = 0$$

There is no external force on the body. It is a case of damped free vibrations.
Substituting the values,

$$\frac{mL}{12}\ddot{x} + \frac{mL}{4}\ddot{x} + c\frac{L}{4}\dot{x} + k_1\frac{xL}{4} + k_2 xL = 0$$

The equation of motion becomes

$$\frac{m}{3}\ddot{x} + \frac{c}{4}\dot{x} + k_1\frac{x}{4} + k_2 x = 0 \qquad \qquad \square$$

Example 1.5

A harmonic oscillation test gave the natural frequency of an overhead water tank to be 0.50 Hz. Given that the weight of the tank is 1000 kN, what deflection will result if a 100 kN horizontal load is applied statically? The mass of the tank staging can be neglected.

Solution   Acceleration due to gravity $g = 980$ cm/sec^2 or, 9.80 m/sec^2

$\therefore$ Mass of tank $= 1000/g = 1000/9.80$ kN-sec^2/m

Natural frequency	$f = 0.50$ Hz
or,	$\omega = 2\pi f$

Natural frequency $\qquad \omega = \sqrt{\dfrac{k}{m}}$

or, $\qquad k = m\omega^2$

or, $\qquad k = \dfrac{1000}{9.80} \times (2 \times 3.14159 \times 0.5)^2 = 1007$ kN/m

$\therefore$ Lateral displacement $\Delta = P/k = 100/1007 = 0.099$ m or 99 mm $\qquad\qquad$ □

Example 1.6

A two-hinged portal frame is shown in Figure 1.24. A mass m has been lumped at the roof level. The frame is massless. Ignore axial deformations and damping. Develop its equation of motion.

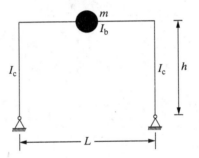

Figure 1.24   Two-hinged portal frame.

Solution   There are three degrees of freedom per node, and therefore, total of eight active degrees of freedom of the frame as shown in Figure 1.25(a). If axial deformations are ignored, the degrees of freedom are reduced to five for static analysis as shown in Figure 1.25(b). A mass has been lumped at the roof level. Therefore, it is a SDOF system for dynamic analysis (Figure 1.25(c)). A lateral load P is applied at its roof level and the corresponding lateral displacement is calculated. Thus, lateral stiffness of the frame can be determined.

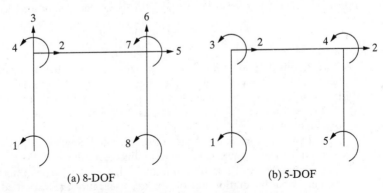

(a) 8-DOF $\qquad\qquad\qquad\qquad\qquad$ (b) 5-DOF

Figure 1.25   Stiffness coefficient computation.

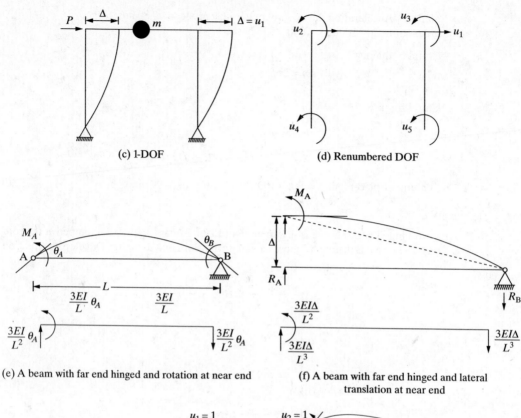

(c) 1-DOF

(d) Renumbered DOF

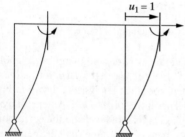

(e) A beam with far end hinged and rotation at near end

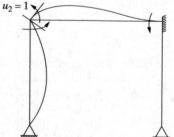

(f) A beam with far end hinged and lateral translation at near end

(g) Frame under deformation due to $u_1 = 1$ (h) Frame under deformation due to $u_2 = 1$

Figure 1.25   (Continued)

Let us determine 3×3 stiffness matrix of the structure with respect to the three degrees-of-freedom u_1, u_2 and u_3 as shown in Figure 1.25(d). The rotational degrees of freedom u_4 and u_5 can be ignored without introducing any significant error in the result.

The following two standard results for a beam can be made use of in the derivation of stiffness coefficients for the frame.

In a beam hinged at far end, if a rotation θ_A is applied at the near end while both its translations are restrained, the forces produced are shown in Figure 1.25(e).

Similarly, in a beam hinged at far end, if a lateral displacement Δ is applied at its near end while its rotation and longitudinal translation are restrained, the forces produced are shown in Figure 1.25(f).

Now, it is easy to generate the stiffness coefficients for the frame due to the following three cases:

Case 1: $u_1 = 1, u_2 = 0$, and $u_3 = 0$ (Figures 1.25(d) and 1.25(g))

Compute the coefficients k_{11}, k_{21} and k_{31} making use of the standard results shown in Figure 1.25(f).
We get,

$$k_{11} = 2 \times \frac{3EI_c}{h^3} = \frac{6EI_c}{h^3}$$

$$k_{21} = \frac{3EI_c}{h^2} = k_{31}$$

Case 2: $u_1 = 0, u_2 = 1$, and $u_3 = 0$ (Figures 1.25(d) and 1.25(h))

Compute the coefficients k_{12}, k_{22} and k_{32} making use of the standard results shown in Figure 1.25(e).
We get,

For beam, $$k_{22} = \frac{4EI_b}{L}$$

For column, $$k_{22} = \frac{3EI_c}{h}$$

Total stiffness $$k_{22} = \frac{4EI_b}{L} + \frac{3EI_c}{h}$$

Similarly, $$k_{32} = \frac{2EI_b}{L}$$

and $$k_{12} = \frac{3EI_c}{h^2}$$

Case 3: $u_1 = 0, u_2 = 0$, and $u_3 = 1$ (Figure 1.25(d))

Compute, the coefficients k_{13}, k_{23} and k_{33} making use of the standard results shown in Figure 1.25(e). These are the same as in Case 2.
We get,

$$k_{13} = \frac{3EI_c}{h^2}$$

$$k_{23} = \frac{2EI_b}{L}$$

$$k_{33} = \frac{4EI_b}{L} + \frac{3EI_c}{h}$$

The total stiffness matrix of the structure can be formulated as follows:

$$[K] = \begin{bmatrix} \dfrac{6EI_c}{h^3} & \dfrac{3EI_c}{h^2} & \dfrac{3EI_c}{h^2} \\[2ex] \dfrac{3EI_c}{h^2} & \dfrac{4EI_b}{L} + \dfrac{3EI_c}{h} & \dfrac{2EI_b}{L} \\[2ex] \dfrac{3EI_c}{h^2} & \dfrac{2EI_b}{L} & \dfrac{4EI_b}{L} + \dfrac{3EI_c}{h} \end{bmatrix}$$

Let us assume:

$$L = 1.5h, I_b = I_c = I$$

The stiffness matrix of the structure can be written as follows:

$$[K] = \frac{EI}{h^3} \begin{bmatrix} 6 & 3h & 3h \\ 3h & 5.67h^2 & 1.34h^2 \\ 3h & 1.34h^2 & 5.67h^2 \end{bmatrix}$$

The force-deformation relation for the portal frame can be written as follows:

$$[K]\{\Delta\} = \{P\}$$

or,

$$\Delta = \begin{Bmatrix} u_1 \\ u_2 \\ u_3 \end{Bmatrix} \text{ and } P = \begin{Bmatrix} P_1 \\ P_2 \\ P_3 \end{Bmatrix} = \begin{Bmatrix} P \\ 0 \\ 0 \end{Bmatrix}$$

Let us solve for Δ.

$$\frac{EI}{h^3} \begin{bmatrix} 6 & 3h & 3h \\ 3h & 5.67h^2 & 1.34h^2 \\ 3h & 1.34h^2 & 5.67h^2 \end{bmatrix} \begin{Bmatrix} u_1 \\ u_2 \\ u_3 \end{Bmatrix} = \begin{Bmatrix} P \\ 0 \\ 0 \end{Bmatrix}$$

The u_2 and u_3 DOFs can be eliminated by static condensation or their values can be determined in terms of u_1.

$$\begin{bmatrix} 5.67 & 1.34 \\ 1.34 & 5.67 \end{bmatrix} \begin{Bmatrix} u_2 \\ u_3 \end{Bmatrix} = -\frac{3}{h} \begin{Bmatrix} 1 \\ 1 \end{Bmatrix} u_1$$

We get,

$$\begin{Bmatrix} u_2 \\ u_3 \end{Bmatrix} = -\frac{0.428}{h} \begin{Bmatrix} 1 \\ 1 \end{Bmatrix} u_1$$

or,

$$3.432 \frac{EI}{h^3} u_1 = P$$

or,

$$k = \frac{P}{u_1} = 3.432 \frac{EI}{h^3}$$

The equation of motion of the portal frame is given by

$$m\ddot{x} + kx = 0$$

or,

$$m\ddot{x} + 3.432 \frac{EI}{h^3} x = 0 \qquad \square$$

PROBLEMS

1.1. A mass of 20 kg when suspended from a spring causes a static deflection of 1 cm. Find natural frequency of the system.

1.2. A spring mass system has spring stiffness of 'k' N/m and mass 'm' kg. Its natural frequency of vibration is 10 Hz. An extra 4 kg mass is coupled to 'm' and the natural frequency reduces by 2 Hz. Determine 'k' and 'm'.

1.3. A mass 'm' is suspended from a spring system as shown in Figure P1.1. Determine natural frequency of the system. Also, derive an expression for equivalent stiffness of the system.

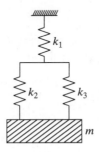

Figure P1.1

1.4. A mass m is suspended through a system of three springs k_1, k_2, and k_3 as shown in Figure P1.2. The spring k_3 is attached to a rigid massless bar A at its midspan. Determine the equivalent stiffness of the system and its natural frequency.

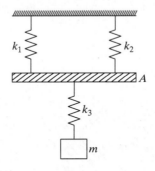

Figure P1.2

Hint: (i) Two springs are in series if each carries the same force.

(ii) Two springs are in parallel if each undergoes the same deformation.

1.5. A spring and mass system is shown in Figure P1.3. Estimate its natural frequency.

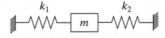

Figure P1.3

1.6. (a) Develop the equation governing the longitudinal motion of the system shown in Figure P1.4. Estimate its natural frequency. Ignore the mass of the rod and measure x from the static equilibrium position.

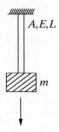

Figure P1.4

(b) If the rod is replaced with a string of length L, estimate the natural frequency of the pendulum.

1.7. Write the equation governing free vibration of the system shown in Figure P1.5, (a) beam is massless and it carries a weight ($W = mg$) at its free end, and (b) beam has a total mass m.

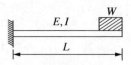

Figure P1.5

1.8. A cylinder of cross-sectional area A and mass m floats in a liquid having a mass density of ρ as shown in Figure P1.6. If the cylinder is pushed by a distance x and released gently, what will be the natural frequency of vibration. Neglect damping effect of the liquid and inertia effect of mass of the displaced liquid.

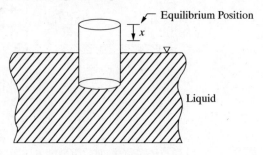

Figure P1.6

1.9. A spring and mass system is shown in Figure P1.7. Determine the effect of gravity on the natural frequency and equation of motion.

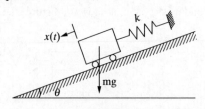

Figure P1.7

1.10. (a) A spring and mass system is shown in Figure P1.8. Assume that the rotation is small so that the spring deflects horizontally and ignore mass of the rod. Determine the frequency of vibration.

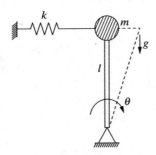

Figure P1.8

(b) If total mass of the rod is m_0, how it will affect the frequency of vibration?

1.11. Write the equation of motion of single-storey portal frame shown in Figure P1.9. Assume that the columns are massless, entire mass of the beam is lumped in the middle as shown and neglect damping.

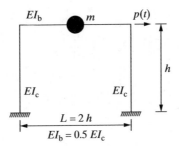

Figure P1.9

Hint: It has three static degrees of freedom and one dynamic degree of freedom. Apply a lateral force P at the beam level and compute lateral sway in the frame using slope–deflection method, or influence coefficient method – generate a 3×3 stiffness matrix corresponding to 3 d.o.f, at the beam level neglecting axial deformations. Finally, eliminate the two rotational degrees of freedom using static condensation.

1.12. A harmonic oscillation test gave the natural frequency of an overhead water tank to be 0.50 Hz. If mass of the tank is 1200 kN, what will be the lateral deflection if a 75 kN horizontal load is applied? You may neglect mass of the staging.

1.13. A 3.5 m high, 6 m wide single-bay single-storey frame is rigidly jointed with a beam of mass 8000 kg and columns of negligible mass and rigidity of $EI_c = 5000$ kNm². Calculate the natural frequency and period. Find the force required to deflect the frame 20 mm laterally.

1.14. A frame is shown in Figure P1.10. Assume that the columns are massless, entire mass of the frame is lumped at the roof level, neglect damping and axial deformations. Determine equation of motion of the frame.

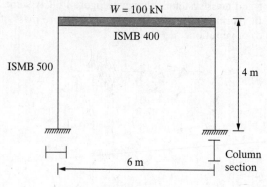

Figure P1.10

Hint: *Get the member properties from Indian Standard steel tables.*

1.15. A RC frame is shown in Figure P1.11. Determine the lateral stiffness of the frame in the lateral direction considering only tension brace. Neglect axial deformations. Column AB = 20 × 30 cm; Column CD = 25 × 35 cm, Brace = 15 × 15 cm. Modulus of elasticity of concrete = 25,000 MPa.

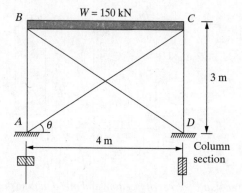

Figure P1.11

Hint: *Lateral stiffness of a diagonal brace* $= \dfrac{AE}{L}\cos^2\theta$, *where A is area of cross-section, L is length of brace, E is modulus of elasticity of the brace material, and θ is the angle a brace makes with horizontal).*

2 | Single Degree of Freedom System: Free Vibrations

2.1 INTRODUCTION

It is interesting to analyse a single-degree-of-freedom (SDOF) system as shown in Figure 2.1 when it vibrates freely under its own characteristics, that is, when external force $p(t)$ is absent. Naturally its motion will not be influenced by the nature, frequency and duration of the external force. It is called a *free vibration* analysis. It is assumed that the spring and damper are massless. A damper is also referred to as a dash-pot system. A SDOF system moves over a smooth and frictionless surface represented by rollers in Figure 2.1. Damping plays a very significant role in the dynamic response of a structure by dissipating vibrational energy. Damping is an inherent property of the material used to construct the structure. It does not depend upon the shape and size of the elements.

There can be different source of energy dissipation in a system, that is, damping. If damping is assumed to be proportional to velocity then it is referred to as *viscous damping*. The concept of viscous damping has been found to be quite satisfactory for structural engineering problems. It is possible to represent any other type of damping as an equivalent viscous damping. A system is said to be *underdamped, critically damped or overdamped* and exhibits characteristic vibrations in each of these three states. In this chapter, we will discuss undamped and damped free vibrations along with viscous and Coulomb damping.

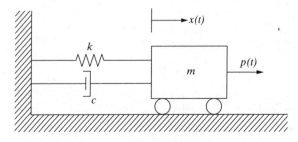

Figure 2.1 A single degree of freedom system.

2.2 SINGLE DEGREE OF FREEDOM SYSTEM (SDOF)

A SDOF system is subjected to an external force $p(t)$ as shown in Figure 2.2(a). The two models shown in Figures 2.1 and 2.2(a) are frequently used to represent the SDOF systems. Its free body diagram is shown in Figure 2.2(b). If this system is subjected to a dynamic force $p(t)$ causing an acceleration $\ddot{x}$, the equation of equilibrium can be written using the Newton's IInd law of motion as follows:

$$f_I = p(t) - f_D - f_S \tag{2.1a}$$

or,
$$f_I + f_D + f_S = p(t) \tag{2.1b}$$

where,

f_I = inertia force = $m\ddot{x}(t)$
f_D = damping force = $c\dot{x}(t)$
f_S = spring force = $kx(t)$
m = mass (in kg)
k = stiffness (in N/m)
c = damping coefficient (in N-sec/m)

It is assumed that the entire mass m is lumped at the floor level in Figure 2.2(a). The damping is represented through a dash-pot system.

Now, Equation (2.1b) can be written as follows:

$$m\,\ddot{x}(t) + c\,\dot{x}(t) + k\,x(t) = p(t) \tag{2.2}$$

This equation is referred to as the general equation of motion of a SDOF system subjected to an external force $p(t)$. Its solution consists of two parts. The first part is known as a complimentary solution or a *transient solution* in structural dynamics problems. The second part is known as a particular integral or a *steady state solution* in structural dynamics problems. The steady state solution depends upon the nature of the forcing function.

For free vibrations, $p(t) = 0$, therefore, the equation of motion becomes:

$$m\ddot{x}(t) + c\,\dot{x}(t) + k\,x(t) = 0 \tag{2.3}$$

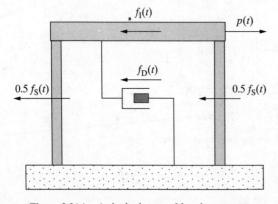

Figure 2.2(a)   A single degree of freedom system.

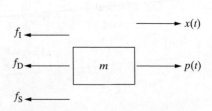

Figure 2.2(b)   Free body diagram of mass.

Let its solution is given by $\qquad x(t) = Ge^{st}$ $\hfill$ (2.4)

Complimentary solution exists but particular integral does not exist for this differential equation because right hand side is zero.

Substituting Equation (2.4) in Equation (2.3) gives,

$$^*(ms^2 + cs + k)Ge^{st} = 0$$

Either $\qquad\qquad\qquad G = 0, \quad \text{or} \quad e^{st} = 0$

or, $\qquad\qquad\qquad s^2 + \dfrac{c}{m}s + \dfrac{k}{m} = 0$

For a non-trivial solution, $Ge^{st} \neq 0$

$\therefore \qquad\qquad\qquad s^2 + \dfrac{c}{m}s + \dfrac{k}{m} \quad$ must be zero

or, $\qquad\qquad\qquad s^2 + \dfrac{c}{m}s + \omega^2 = 0$ $\hfill$ (2.5)

where, $\qquad\qquad\qquad \omega = \sqrt{\dfrac{k}{m}}$ $\hfill$ (2.6)

The term ω represents natural frequency of vibration of a SDOF system in radian/sec. The value of s is obtained by solving the quadratic Equation (2.5).

2.2.1 Undamped Free Vibrations

Let us first consider undamped free vibrations, that is, damping is zero.

$$m\,\ddot{x} + k\,x = 0$$

$\because c = 0$ Hence, Equation (2.5) gives, $s = \pm i\omega$

Equation (2.4) gives, $x(t) = G_1 e^{i\omega t} + G_2 e^{-i\omega t}$

Alternatively, $\qquad e^{\pm i\omega t} = \cos \omega t \pm i \sin \omega t$; Euler's equation $\hfill$ (2.7)

or, $\qquad\qquad\qquad x(t) = A \sin \omega t + B \cos \omega t$ $\hfill$ (2.8)

Constants A and B can be determined knowing the initial conditions, that is, displacement $x(0)$ and velocity $\dot{x}(0)$ at $t = 0$. Substituting the values of initial conditions in Equation (2.8), gives $\qquad x(0) = B$ and $\dot{x}(0) = A\omega$

On substituting the values in Equation (2.8), we get

$$x(t) = \dfrac{\dot{x}(0)}{\omega}\sin \omega t + x(0)\cos \omega t$$ $\hfill$ (2.9a)

where, $\qquad\qquad\qquad w = 2\pi f, \ T = \dfrac{2\pi}{\omega}, \ f = \dfrac{1}{T}$

Upon differentiating Equation (2.9a), velocity can be obtained:

$$\dot{x}(t) = \dot{x}(0) \cos \omega t - x(0) \, \omega \sin \omega t \qquad (2.9b)$$

Upon once again differentiating Equation (2.9b), acceleration can be obtained:

$$\ddot{x}(t) = -\omega^2 x(t) \qquad (2.9c)$$

The displacement, velocity and acceleration terms can be plotted with time to understand the effect of different natural frequencies. Example 2.1 illustrates the vibration characteristics of a system undergoing undamped free vibrations.

2.2.2 Damped Free Vibrations

Let us again consider $\qquad s^2 + \dfrac{c}{m} s + \omega^2 = 0 \qquad\qquad (2.5)$

Solution is:

$$s = -\frac{c}{2m} \pm \sqrt{\left(\frac{c}{2m}\right)^2 - \omega^2} \qquad (2.10)$$

There are three possibilities depending upon the sign of the discriminant;
If the sign is   (i) – ve   the solution is termed as underdamped system
                (ii) 0   the solution is termed as critically damped system
                (iii) + ve   the solution is termed as over damped system
Let us first consider the second case, that is, critically damped system.

Critically Damped System
In this case no oscillations take place and the system quickly returns to its mean position, that is, of rest.

If $\qquad\qquad \left(\dfrac{c}{2m}\right)^2 - \omega^2 = 0$

or, $\qquad\qquad \dfrac{c}{2m} = \omega;$

or, $\qquad\qquad c = c_c = 2m\omega = 2\sqrt{k\,m} \qquad (2.11)$

where, c_c = critical damping

Hence, $\qquad\qquad s = -\dfrac{c}{2m} = -\omega \qquad (2.12)$

Solution is: $\quad x(t) = (G_1 + G_2 t) e^{-\omega t} \qquad$ from Equation (2.4) $\qquad (2.13)$

The second term is multiplied by 't' otherwise only a single value of s is available from Equation (2.12). Introducing initial conditions, that is, displacement $x(0)$ and velocity $\dot{x}(0)$ at $t = 0$, the final solution is

$$x(t) = \left[x(0)(1 + \omega t) + \dot{x}(0)t\right] e^{-\omega t} \qquad (2.14)$$

The critically damped vibrations are shown in Figure 2.3. It can be seen that there are no oscillations about the mean position. So, the system quickly returns to rest.

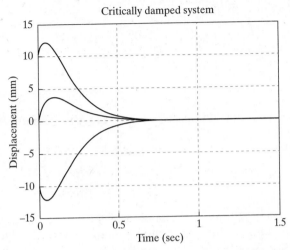

$(m = 1$ kg, $c = 20$ Ns/m, $k = 100$ N/m, (i) $x(0) = 0$, $\dot{x}(0) = 0.1$ m/s;
(ii) $x(0) = 0.01$ m, $\dot{x}(0) = 0.1$ m/s; (iii) $x(0) = -0.01$ m, $\dot{x}(0) = -0.1$ m/s)

Figure 2.3   Critically damped system.

Underdamped System
If damping is less than critical, then it is obvious that $c < 2$ mw and discriminant in
Equation (2.10) is –ve.

Let $$\xi = \frac{c}{c_c} = \frac{c}{2mw} \quad \text{damping ratio} \tag{2.15}$$

∴ Equation (2.10) becomes

$$s = -\xi\omega \pm \sqrt{(\xi\omega)^2 - \omega^2}$$

or, $$s = -\xi\omega \pm i\,\omega_D \tag{2.16a}$$

where, $$\omega_D = \omega\sqrt{1-\xi^2} \tag{2.16b}$$

ω_D is damped frequency of vibration.

For damping ratios to be expected in typical structural systems ($\xi < 20\%$); it differs very little for the undamped frequency as is obvious from Equation (2.16b).

Free vibration response of underdamped system is obtained from Equation (2.4)
by substituting the values of s given by Equation (2.16a).

$$x(t) = G_1 e^{(-\xi\omega + i\omega_D)t} + G_2 e^{(-\xi\omega - i\omega_D)t}$$
$$= e^{-\xi\omega t}(G_1 e^{i\omega_D t} + G_2 e^{-i\omega_D t})$$

It represents a simple harmonic motion

$$x(t) = e^{-\xi\omega t}(A \sin\omega_D t + B\cos\omega_D t) \tag{2.17}$$

If $\dot{x}(0)$ and $x(0)$ are initial velocity and displacement, the constants A and B are given
by:

$$A = \frac{x(0)\,\xi\,\omega + \dot{x}(0)}{\omega_D} \quad \text{and} \quad B = x(0) \tag{2.18a}$$

The final solution is given by

$$x(t) = e^{-\xi\omega t}\left\{\frac{x(0)\xi\omega + \dot{x}(0)}{\omega_D}\sin\omega_D t + x(0)\cos\omega_D t\right\} \tag{2.18b}$$

On differentiating Equation (2.17), the velocity term is obtained:

$$\dot{x}(t) = e^{-\xi\omega t}[-(A\xi\omega + B\omega_D)\sin\omega_D t + (A\omega_D - B\xi\omega)\cos\omega_D t] \tag{2.18c}$$

Upon once again differentiating, the acceleration term is obtained:

$$\ddot{x}(t) = [\{A(\xi^2\omega^2 - \omega_D^2) + B(2\omega\omega_D\xi)\}\sin\omega_D t - \{A(2\omega\omega_D\xi) \\ - B(\xi^2\omega^2 - \omega_D^2)\}\cos\omega_D t] \tag{2.18d}$$

The Equations (2.18b), (2.18c) and (2.18d) can be plotted for different values of the initial conditions and damping ratio ξ to understand the dynamic response of underdamped SDOF systems.

The amplitude of the displacement response can be written as follows:

$$x_0 = \sqrt{\left(\frac{x(0)\xi\omega + \dot{x}(0)}{\omega_D}\right)^2 + \left(x(0)\right)^2} \tag{2.18e}$$

The response of an underdamped system is shown in Figure 2.4 with damping coefficient ($c = 2$ N-s/m). It can be seen that an underdamped system oscillates about its mean position as against no oscillation in a critically damped system.

Overdamped System
Although overdamped systems are not encountered in normal conditions, it is useful to understand thier behaviour:

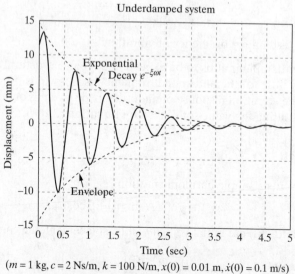

$(m = 1 \text{ kg}, c = 2 \text{ Ns/m}, k = 100 \text{ N/m}, x(0) = 0.01 \text{ m}, \dot{x}(0) = 0.1 \text{ m/s})$

Figure 2.4 Underdamped system

In this case $\xi = \dfrac{c}{c_c} = \dfrac{c}{2m\omega} > 1$

Hence, Equation (2.10) can be written as:

$$s = -\xi\omega \pm \omega\sqrt{\xi^2 - 1} = -\xi\omega \pm \hat{\omega}$$

where, $\hat{\omega} = \omega\sqrt{\xi^2 - 1}$ (2.19)

The solution is given by

$$x(t) = G_1 e^{(-\xi\omega + \hat{\omega})t} + G_2 e^{(-\xi\omega - \hat{\omega})t} \quad \text{from Equation (2.4)}$$

or, $$x(t) = e^{-\xi\omega t}\left(G_1 e^{\hat{\omega}t} + G_2 e^{-\hat{\omega}t}\right)$$

We know that

$$e^x = \sinh x + \cosh x$$

and

$$\sinh x = \left(e^x - e^{-x}\right)/2$$

$\therefore$ $$x(t) = e^{-\xi\omega t}(A \sinh \hat{\omega}t + B\cosh \hat{\omega}t)$$ (2.20a)

where, the constants A and B can be determined using the initial conditions.
On differentiating Equation (2.20a), the velocity term is obtained:

$$\dot{x}(t) = e^{-\xi\omega t}(-\xi\omega)[A \sinh \hat{\omega}t + B \cosh \hat{\omega}t] + e^{-\xi\omega t}(\hat{\omega})[A\cosh \hat{\omega}t + B\sinh \hat{\omega}t]$$ (2.20b)

The motion in over damped systems is not oscillatory, that is, it does not cross the mean position. It is similar to the motion of critically damped system but return towards the mean position is slowed as the damping ratio is increased as shown in Figure 2.5. It can be seen in Figures 2.3 and 2.5 that an over damped system comes to rest very slowly as compared to a critically damped system.

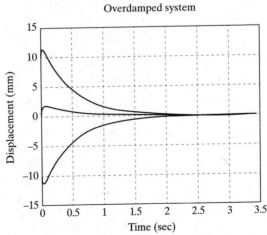

$(m = 1 \text{ kg}, c = 50 \text{ Ns/m}, k = 100 \text{ N/m}, \text{(i) } x(0) = 0, \dot{x}(0) = 0.1 \text{ m/s}; \text{ (ii) } x(0) = 0.01 \text{ m}, \dot{x}(0) = 0.1$
$\text{m/s; (iii) } x(0) = -0.01 \text{ m}, \dot{x}(0) = -0.1 \text{ m/s})$

Figure 2.5   Overdamped system.

2.3 MATLAB APPLICATIONS

Let us arrange the equation of motion for a SDOF system for use with MATLAB. The equation of motion is given by Equation (2.3)

$$m\ddot{x}(t) + c\dot{x}(t) + k x(t) = 0 \tag{2.3}$$

Initial conditions are known through $x(0)$ and $\dot{x}(0)$.

MATLAB requires that the second order differential equation should be rearranged as a set of first order differential equations. Let

$$x(t) = z(1) \text{ and } \dot{x}(t) = z(2) \tag{2.21a}$$

or,

$$\dot{z}(1) = \dot{x}(t) = z(2) \tag{2.21b}$$

$$\dot{z}(2) = \ddot{x}(t) = -\frac{c}{m}z(2) - \frac{k}{m}z(1) \tag{2.21c}$$

$$\begin{Bmatrix} \dot{z}(1) \\ \dot{z}(2) \end{Bmatrix} = \begin{bmatrix} 0 & 1 \\ -\left(\dfrac{k}{m}\right) & -\left(\dfrac{c}{m}\right) \end{bmatrix} \begin{Bmatrix} z(1) \\ z(2) \end{Bmatrix} \tag{2.21d}$$

or,

$$\dot{z} = Az \tag{2.21e}$$

where, $\{z\}$ is a state vector of size 2×1. The matrix A is called the state matrix. The position $z(1)$ and velocity $z(2)$ variables are called the state variables.

Now the set of first order differential equations (2.21a), (2.21b) and (2.21c) can be solved by using the MATLAB function ode23. It is based on Runge – Kutta method. The step size is selected automatically by the program. MATLAB Codes DOS2_1, DOS2_2 and DOS2_3 compute the undamped free response of a SDOF system. The codes have been written in different styles. Code DOS2_4 computes damped free response for underdamped, critically damped or overdamped systems for the given initial conditions. Code DOS2_5 computes damped free response of a SDOF for a given initial conditions.

CODE DOS2_1

```
%    Dynamics of Structures by Ashok K. Jain I.I.T. Roorkee
%    DOS2_1
%    Undamped Free Vibrations of a SDOF System
%    Calls: DOS2_1a          Function: DOS2_1a in a separate file
%    Equation of motion of a SDOF is a second order differential equation
%    The program calls function "ode23" to solve ordinary differential eqn.
%    The program can be modified to read the initial conditions from the
%    command prompt
%
%    m=1;
%    k=10;
ic=[0;0.1];
```

```
tspan=[0 10];
fprintf ('Initial displacement at t=0, is %.3g m\n',ic(1));
fprintf ('Initial velocity at t=0, is %.3g m/s\n',ic(2));
fprintf ('Duration of vibration is %.3g sec\n',tspan(2));
%
[t,y]=ode23(@DOS2_1a,tspan,ic);
subplot 211
plot (t,y(:,1),'.-r');
title ('Displacement vs. time');
xlabel ('Time sec');
ylabel ('Displacement m');
grid on;
subplot 212
plot (t,y(:,2),'.-b');
title ('Velocity vs. time');
xlabel ('Time sec');
ylabel ('Velocity m/s');
grid on;
```

CODE DOS2_1a

```
%    Dynamics of Structures by Ashok K. Jain I.I.T. Roorkee
%    DOS2_1a
%    Called by: DOS2_1
%    Undamped Free Vibrations of a SDOF System
%
function dz = DOS2_1a(t,z)
m=1;
k=10;
w=sqrt(k/m);
if t==0
   fprintf ('\n m = %.3f, k = %.3f\n',m,k);
   fprintf ('\n natural frequency = %.3f rad/s\n',w);
end
dz = zeros(2,1); % initializes the column vector z
dz(1) =  z(2);
dz(2) = -k*z(1)/m;
end
```

CODE DOS2_2   Alternate solution I

```
%    Dynamics of Structures by Ashok K. Jain I.I.T. Roorkee
%    DOS2_2
%    Undamped Free Vibrations of a SDOF System
%    Calls:DOS2_2a
%    Equation of motion of a SDOF is a second order differential equation
%    The program calls function "ode23" to solve ordinary differential eqn.
%    The program can be modified to read the initial conditions
```

```
%          from the command prompt
%    ic=initial conditions: at t=0, x0 and v0
%    t = time duration of vibration - 0 to 5 sec
%    Alternate solution I
%
clear all;
ic=[0.02;0.05];
t=[0; 5];
fprintf('Initial displacement at t=0, is %.3g m\n',ic(1));
fprintf('Initial velocity at t=0, is %.3g m/s\n',ic(2));
fprintf('Duration of vibration is %.3g sec\n',t(2));
%
[t,z]=ode23(@DOS2_2a,t,ic)
plot(t,z(:,1));
xlabel('time');
ylabel('Displacement');
title('Displacement time History');
```

```
-------------------
CODE DOS2_2a
-------------------
```

```
%    Dynamics of Structures by Ashok K. Jain I.I.T. Roorkee
%    DOS2_2a
%    Called by DOS2_2
%    Undamped Free Vibrations of a SDOF System
%    m = 5
%    k = 100
%    The values of mass and stiffnes can be changed as desired
%
function q=DOS2_2a(t,z)
m =5;
k =100;
q=[z(2);(-(k/m)*z(1))]; % column vector
end
```

```
-------------------
CODE DOS2_3    Alternate solution II
-------------------
%    Dynamics of Structures by Ashok K. Jain I.I.T. Roorkee
%    DOS2_3
%    Undamped Free Vibrations of a SDOF System
%    The function to define first order differential equation is builtin here
%        itself.
%    Equation of motion of a SDOF is a second order differential equation
%    The program calls function "ode23" to solve ordinary differential eqn.
%    The program can be modified to read the initial conditions
%        from the command prompt
%    m=1;
%    k=10;
```

```
%    Alternate solution II
%
prompt='Pl enter the value of mass (m):';
m=input (prompt);
prompt='Pl enter the value of stiffness (k):';
k=input (prompt);
omega=sqrt(k/m);
period=2*pi()/omega;
fprintf ('Mass = %.3g kg\n',m);
fprintf ('Stiffness = %.3g N/m\n',k);
fprintf ('Natural frequency = %.3g rad/s.\n',omega);
fprintf ('Period of vibration = %.3g s\n',period);
ic=[0.2;0.1];
fprintf ('Initial displacement at t=0, is %.3g m\n',ic(1));
fprintf ('Initial velocity at t=0, is %.3g m/s\n',ic(2));
%
springmass=@(t,z)[z(2);-k*z(1)/m];
%
tspan=[0 10];
[t,y]=ode23(springmass, tspan,ic);
subplot 211
plot (t,y(:,1),'.-r');
title ('Displacement vs. time')
xlabel ('Time sec');
ylabel ('Displacement m');
grid on;
subplot 212
plot (t,y(:,2),'.-g'); title('Velocity vs. time')
xlabel ('Time sec');
ylabel ('Velocity m/s');
grid on;


--------------------
```

CODE DOS2_4

```
--------------------
%    Dynamics of Structures by Ashok K. Jain I.I.T. Roorkee
%    DOS2_4
%    Damped Free response of a single degree of freedom system.
%    If zai < 1.0, underdamped system
%    If zai = 1.0, critically damped system
%    If zai > 1.0, overdamped system
%    Input parameters are entered at the command prompt
%    m=1;
%    k=100;
%    c=2 for underdamped system;
%    c=20 for critically damped system;
%    c=50 for overdamped system;
%    x0=0.1;
%    v0=0.05;
%    tf=5;
prompt='Pl enter the value of mass (m):';
```

```
m=input(prompt);
prompt='Pl enter the value of stiffness (k):';
k=input(prompt);
prompt='Pl enter the value of damping coeff.(c):';
c=input(prompt);
w=sqrt(k/m);
zai=c/(2*sqrt(k*m));
wd=w*sqrt(1-zai^2);
fprintf ('Mass = %.3g \n',m);
fprintf ('Stiffness = %.3g \n',k);
fprintf ('damping coeff. = %.3g \n',c);
fprintf ('The natural frequency is %.3g rad/s.\n',w);
fprintf ('The damping ratio is %.3g.\n',zai);
fprintf ('The damped natural frequency is %.3g.\n',wd);
prompt='Pl enter initial displacement at t=0; (x0):';
x0=input(prompt);
prompt='Pl enter initial velocity at t=0; (v0):';
v0=input(prompt);
prompt='Pl enter duration of vibrations (tf):';
tf=input(prompt);
fprintf('Initial displacement at t=0, is %.3g m\n',x0);
fprintf('Initial velocity at t=0, is %.3g m/s\n',v0);
fprintf('Duration of vibrations is %.3g \n',tf);
%
t=0:0.01:tf;
if zai < 1
    g0=sqrt(((v0+zai*w*x0)^2+(x0*wd)^2)/wd^2);
    phi=atan2(x0*wd,v0+zai*w*x0);
    x=g0*exp(-zai*w*t).*sin(wd*t+phi);
    fprintf ('Underdamped system\n');
    fprintf ('Amplitude = %.3g\n',g0);
    fprintf ('Phase angle= %.3g radian\n',phi);
  elseif zai==1
    g1=x0;
    g2=v0+w*x0;
    fprintf ('Critically damped system\n');
    fprintf ('g1= %.3g\n',g1);
    fprintf ('g2= %.3g\n',g2);
    x=(g1+g2*t).*exp(-w*t);
else
    wc=w*sqrt(zai^2-1);
    g1=(-v0+(-zai*w+wc)*x0)/(2*wc);
    g2=(v0+(zai*w+wc)*x0)/(2*wc);
    fprintf ('Overdamped system\n');
    fprintf ('constant g1= %.3g\n',g1);
    fprintf ('constant g2= %.3g\n',g2);
    x=exp(-zai*w*t).*(g1*exp(-wc*t)+g2*exp(wc*t));
end
plot (t,x)
xlabel ('Time sec')
```

```
ylabel ('Displacement m')
title ('Displacement versus Time')
grid on


-------------------
CODE DOS2_5
-------------------
%    Dynamics of Structures by Ashok K. Jain I.I.T. Roorkee
%    DOS2_5
%    Damped Free Vibrations of a SDOF System
%    Equation of motion of a SDOF is a second order differential equation
%    The program calls function "ode23" to solve ordinary differential eqn.
%    The program can be modified to read the initial conditions
%                                      from the command prompt
%    Calls DOS2_5a
%    IC=initial conditions at time t=0, x0 and v0
%    t = time duration of vibrations; 0 to 5 sec @ 0.005 sec interval
%
clear all;
clc;
IC =[0.02;0.05];  % Initial conditions x(0) and v(0)
fprintf('\n Initial displacement = %.3f m',IC(1));
fprintf('\n Initial velocity = %.3f m/s',IC(2));
t = [0:0.005:5];
[t,z] = ode23(@DOS2_5a,t,IC);
%
[dismax, maxindex1] = max(z(:,1));
[dismin, minindex1] = min(z(:,1));
dtimemax = (maxindex1-1)*0.005;
dtimemin = (minindex1-1)*0.005;
%
[velmax, maxindex2] = max(z(:,2));
[velmin, minindex2] = min(z(:,2));
vtimemax = (maxindex2-1)*0.005;
vtimemin = (minindex2-1)*0.005;
%
fprintf('\n dismax = %.3f , at time = %.3f sec\n',dismax,dtimemax);
fprintf('\n dismin = %.3f , at time = %.3f sec\n',dismin,dtimemin);
fprintf('\n velmax = %.3f , at time = %.3f sec\n',velmax,vtimemax);
fprintf('\n velmin = %.3f , at time = %.3f sec\n',velmin,vtimemin);
subplot 211
plot(t,z(:,1))
grid on;
xlabel('time sec')
ylabel('displacement m')
title('Displacement time history')
subplot 212
plot(t,z(:,2))
xlabel('time sec')
ylabel('Velocity m/s')
```

```
title('Velocity time history')
grid on;
```

CODE DOS2_5a

```
%    Dynamics of Structures by Ashok K. Jain I.I.T. Roorkee
%    DOS2_5a
%    Called by DOS2_5
%    Damped Free Vibrations of a SDOF System
%    The program can be modified to read mass, stiffness, damping etc.
%                                    from the command prompt
%
function q=DOS2_5a(t,z)
m=5;
k = 100;
zai=0.05; % 5%
w=sqrt(k/m);
c=2*zai*sqrt(k*m);
if t==0
   fprintf ('\n m = %.3f, k = %.3f, zai = %.3f, c  = %.3f\n',m,k,zai,c);
   fprintf ('\n natural frequency = %.3f rad/s\n',w);
end
q=[z(2);(-(c/m)*z(2)-(k/m)*z(1))];
end
```

These MATLAB codes are used to generate results shown in the following examples.

2.4 ILLUSTRATIVE EXAMPLES

Example 2.1

Consider a SDOF system shown in Figure 2.1. It undergoes undamped free vibrations. The mass = 40 kNs²/m, stiffness k = 3500 kN/m. Determine the natural frequency and natural period of vibration. The initial conditions are given as: $x(0) = 0.01$ m, $\dot{x}(0) = 0.1$ m/s. Hence, plot a graph of displacement–time history, and inertia and elastic forces.

Solution The complete solution is given by Equations (2.6) and (2.9). These equations can be plotted either using MS EXCEL or MATLAB.

The frequency of vibration is given by $\omega = \sqrt{\dfrac{k}{m}} = \sqrt{\dfrac{3500}{40}} = 9.3541$ rad/sec

Natural period is given by $T = \dfrac{2\pi}{\omega} = 0.6717$ sec

The plots of displacement, velocity and acceleration are shown in Figure 2.6. Knowing the displacement and acceleration, elastic force ($= kx$) and inertia forces ($= m\ddot{x}$) can be estimated. At any point of time, the sum of elastic and inertia forces is zero to keep the system in equilibrium.   □

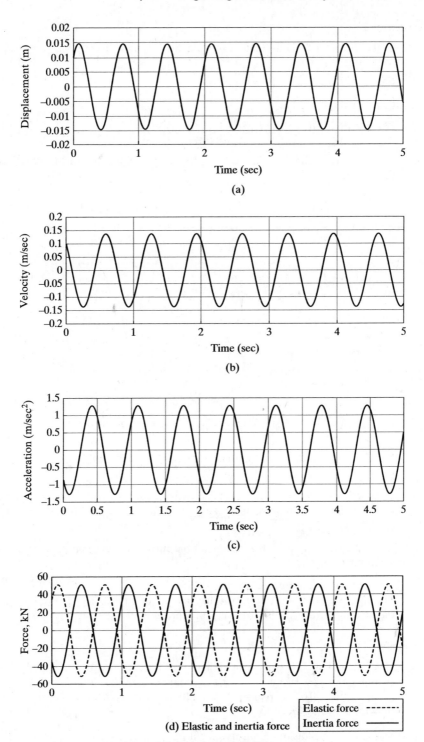

Figure 2.6   Response of SDOF system.

Example 2.2

In the undamped SDOF system of Example 2.1, plot the response for different initial conditions as follows:

Case 1: $x(0) = 0.01$ m, $\dot{x}(0) = 0.1$ m/s

Case 2: $x(0) = 0$, $\dot{x}(0) = 0.1$ m/s

Case 3: $x(0) = 0.01$ m, $\dot{x}(0) = 0$

Solution The solution can be found either using MS EXCEL or MATLAB as shown in Figure 2.7.

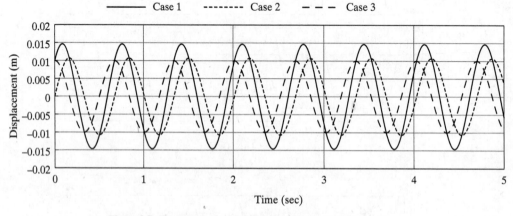

Figure 2.7 Response of a SDOF under different initial conditions.

It is a very interesting problem to understand the effect of initial conditions:

Case 1: $x(0) = 0.01$ m and $\dot{x}(0) = 0.1$ m/s
The curve starts from the initial displacement of 0.01 m and slope of the curve at $x = x(0)$ on the ordinate axis represents initial velocity.

Case 2: $x(0) = 0$ and $\dot{x}(0) = 0.1$ m/s
The curve starts from $x = 0$ and slope of the curve at $x = x(0)$ on the ordinate axis represents initial velocity.

Case 3: $x(0) = 0.01$ m and $\dot{x}(0) = 0$
The curve starts from the initial displacement of 0.01 m and slope of the curve at $x = x(0)$ on the ordinate axis is zero. The tangent is horizontal. □

Example 2.3

Consider a SDOF system shown in Figure 2.1. It undergoes underdamped free vibrations (damping $\xi = 5\%$). The mass = 5 kNs²/m, stiffness $k = 100$ kN/m. The initial conditions are given as: $x(0) = 0.02$ m, $\dot{x}(0) = 0.05$ m/s. Plot the displacement–time history and velocity–time history using MATLAB.

Solution The plots of the displacement response and velocity response obtained using the MATLAB code presented earlier are shown in Figure 2.8. □

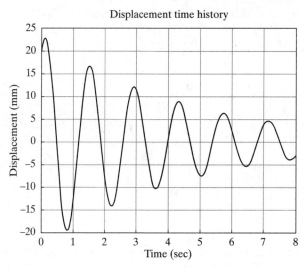

Figure 2.8(a)   Displacement response of an underdamped system.

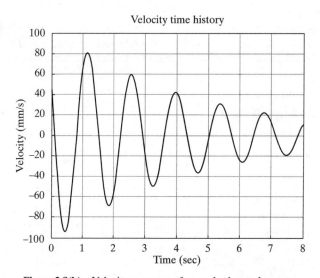

Figure 2.8(b)   Velocity response of an underdamped system.

Example 2.4

Consider a SDOF system shown in Figure 2.2. It undergoes underdamped free vibrations. The mass = 40 kNs²/m and stiffness k = 3750 kN/m. The initial conditions are given as: $x(0)$ = 0.01 m, $\dot{x}(0)$ = 0.1 m/s. Plot the influence of 0, 5% and 10% damping on the displacement–time history.

Solution   The response of a SDOF system can be determined using MATLAB for different damping ratios. The results are plotted in Figure 2.9. The amplitude of displacement decreases with increase in damping. In an undamped system ($\xi = 0\%$), the amplitude remains constant and the system vibrates indefinitely. Even with 5% damping, there is significant drop in the amplitude of vibration.   ☐

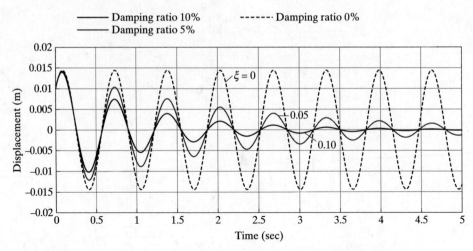

Figure 2.9   Influence of damping ratios on the free response of a SDOF system.

Example 2.5

Consider a SDOF system shown in Figure 2.2. It undergoes underdamped free vibrations. The mass $= 40 \text{ kNs}^2/\text{m}$, stiffness $k = 3750 \text{ kN/m}$ and $c = 50 \text{ kNs/m}$. The initial conditions are given as: $x(0) = 0.01 \text{ m}$, $\dot{x}(0) = 0.1 \text{ m/s}$. Plot the inertia, damping and spring forces.

Solution

Mass $m = 40 \text{ kN s}^2/\text{m}$

Stiffness $k = 3750 \text{ kN/m}$

Damping $c = 50 \text{ kNs/m}$

Natural frequency of vibration $\omega = \sqrt{\dfrac{k}{m}} = 9.6825 \text{ rad/s}$

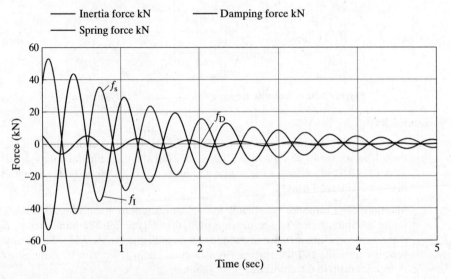

Figure 2.10   Variation of inertia, damping and spring forces.

Period of vibration $T = 2\pi/\omega = 0.6489$ sec

Critical damping $c_c = 774.5967$

Damping ratio $\xi = c/c_c = 6.45\%$

The inertia force $m\ddot{x}(t)$, damping force $c\dot{x}(t)$ and spring force $kx(t)$ are shown in Figure 2.10. The sum of these forces at any instant t is zero. It can be seen that in the present case the damping force is quite small as compared to the other two forces.   □

Example 2.6

A SDOF frame has a mass = 5000 kg, lateral stiffness $k = 4 \times 10^6$ N/m and a damping ratio of 4%. Determine its undamped and damped natural frequency. If the frame is displaced by 25 mm and released suddenly, determine the peak displacements of first five cycles of vibrations.

Solution

Undamped natural frequency $\omega = \sqrt{\dfrac{k}{m}} = \sqrt{\dfrac{4 \times 10^6}{5000}} = 28.28$ rad/sec

$$f = \frac{\omega}{2\pi} = 4.5 \text{ Hz}$$

$$\omega_D = \omega\sqrt{1-\xi^2}$$

ω_D is damped frequency of vibration.

∴ $\omega_D = 28.28\sqrt{1-0.04^2} = 28.257$ rad/sec or, $f_D = 4.496$ Hz

Damped free response of a SDOF system is given by

$$x(t) = e^{-\xi\omega t}\left\{\frac{x(0)\xi\omega + \dot{x}(0)}{\omega_D}\sin\omega_D t + x(0)\cos\omega_D t\right\} \tag{i}$$

If the initial displacement $x(0) = x_0$, and initial velocity $\dot{x}(0) = 0$, damped free response can be written as:

$$x(t) = x_0 e^{-\xi\omega t}(\cos\omega t + \xi\sin\omega t) \text{ if } \omega_D \approx \omega \tag{ii}$$

Differentiating Equation (ii)

$$\frac{dx}{dt} = \dot{x}(t) = -x_0\omega e^{-\xi\omega t}((1+\xi^2)\sin\omega t)$$

For maximum displacement, velocity = 0,

or, $\sin\omega t = 0$

or, $\omega t = n\pi$

or, $t = n\pi/\omega$

For first five peak displacements, time of occurrence is given by

$$t = 0, 2\pi/\omega, 4\pi/\omega, 6\pi/\omega, 8\pi/\omega$$

and $x_{max} = x_0 e^{-2\pi\xi n} = 25 \, e^{-2\pi\xi n} = 25 \, e^{-0.251n}$ where $n = 0, 1, 2, 3$, and 4

∴ Peak displacements are 25, 19.44, 15.12, 9.15 and 7.12 mm as shown in Figure 2.11.   □

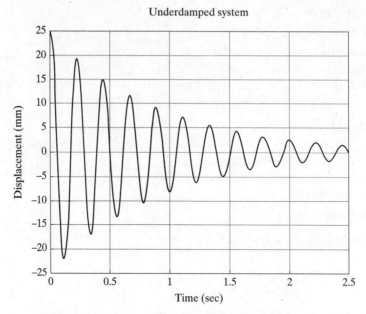

Figure 2.11   Displacement response of an underdamped system.

2.5 VISCOUS DAMPING

The mass and stiffness of a SDOF system can be estimated by static tests. However, the measurement of damping requires a dynamic test. Let us conduct a underdamped vibration test and estimate damping. Its response is given by Equation 2.17 and is shown in Figure 2.12.

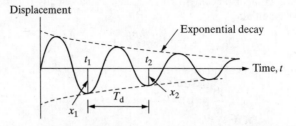

Figure 2.12   Underdamped response for measuring damping.

$$x(t) = e^{-\xi \omega t} (A \sin \omega_D t + B \cos \omega_D t) \tag{2.17}$$

Let x_1 = amplitude of motion at $t = t_1$

and x_2 = amplitude of motion at $t = t_1 + T_D$

where T_D is time period for one cycle

∴ $x_1 = e^{-\xi \omega t_1} (A \sin \omega_D t_1 + B \cos \omega_D t_1) \tag{2.22a}$

$$x_2 = e^{-\xi\omega(t_1+T_D)}\{A\sin\omega_D(t_1+T_D)+B\cos\omega_D(t_1+T_D)\} \qquad (2.22b)$$

$$= e^{-\xi\omega(t_1+T_D)}\{A\sin\omega_D t_1+B\cos\omega_D t_1\} \text{ because } \omega_D=\frac{2\pi}{T_D}$$

Dividing Equations (2.22a) and (2.22b),

$$\frac{x_1}{x_2}=e^{\xi\omega T_D}$$

Taking natural log of both sides,

or, $$\log_e\frac{x_1}{x_2}=\xi\,\omega T_D=\delta= \text{ logarithmic decrement}$$

or, $$\delta = \xi\,\omega\frac{2\pi}{\omega_D} = 2\pi\,\xi\,\frac{\omega}{\omega_D} \qquad (2.23a)$$

or, $$\delta = \frac{2\pi\xi}{\sqrt{1-\xi^2}} \quad \because \omega_D = \omega\sqrt{1-\xi^2} \qquad (2.23b)$$

For low damping $\delta \approx 2\pi\,\xi$ \qquad (2.23c)

Damping is a property of material. Typical values for different materials are as follows:

Material	Damping
Clay Brick	5% to 12%
Concrete	5% to 10%
Earth	20%
Steel	2% to 4%

$$\text{Log decrement} = \log_e\left[\frac{\text{amplitude in cycle } n}{\text{amplitude in cycle}\,(n+1)}\right] = \log_e\frac{x_1}{x_2}=\delta=2\pi\xi \qquad (2.24)$$

For lightly damped system,

$$\frac{x_1}{x_2}=e^{2\pi\xi}=1+2\pi\xi+\frac{(2\pi\xi)^2}{2^2}+\ldots\ldots\ldots\ldots\infty$$

Neglecting higher order terms in ξ

$$\therefore\ \xi = \frac{x_1-x_2}{2\pi\,x_2} \qquad (2.25)$$

A structure whose damping is to be measured is subjected to free vibrations, or 'ambient vibrations'. The free vibrations are recorded as shown in Figure 2.12. The amplitude of vibrations in any two consecutive cycles is measured. The damping ratio is given by Equation (2.25). However, there is a high probability of making an error in measuring the displacement amplitudes in any two consecutive cycles as the difference in these two nearly equal quantities may be very small. Therefore, a greater accuracy can be achieved by considering response peaks which are several cycles apart, say in '*j*' cycles.

The motion decreases from x_i to x_{i+j} over j cycles, that is,

$$\frac{x_i}{x_{i+j}} = \frac{x_i}{x_{i+1}} \frac{x_{i+1}}{x_{i+2}} \frac{x_{i+2}}{x_{i+3}} \cdots\cdots \frac{x_{i+j-1}}{x_{i+j}} = e^{j\delta}$$

Taking natural log of both sides,

$$\delta = \frac{1}{j} \log_e \frac{x_i}{x_{i+j}} \tag{2.26a}$$

but

$$\delta = 2\pi\xi \frac{\omega}{\omega_D} \approx 2\pi\xi$$

∴ For low damping:

$$\xi = \frac{x_i - x_{i+j}}{2 j \pi x_{i+j}} \tag{2.26b}$$

In general for 10% damping, the amplitude is reduced by 50%.

Example 2.7

A displacement–time plot for a free vibration analysis of a SDOF system gives a displacement of 7.5 mm at time t_1 and 1 mm after 7 cycles. Determine logarithmic decrement and damping ratio.

Solution   Logarithmic decrement is given by

$$\delta = \frac{1}{j} \log_e \frac{x_i}{x_{i+j}} = 2 j \pi \xi \frac{\omega}{\omega_D}$$

$$\delta = \frac{1}{7} \log_e \frac{7.5}{1.0} = 0.288$$

∴ Damping ratio $\xi = \delta/2\pi = 0.288/2 \times \pi = 0.046$ or 4.6% □

2.6 COULOMB DAMPING

There are many situations in real life problems where damping results due to looseness of joints, dry friction between components or bolted joints, etc. This situation may lead to non-linear response of the structure. The dry friction damping is also known as Coulomb damping. Let us consider a mass m sliding on a rough surface which produces a force of friction as shown in Figure 2.13.

Its free body diagrams are shown in Figures 2.14(a) when the velocity is negative, and in Figure 2.14(b) when the velocity is positive. During a complete cycle, the velocity changes from zero to maximum positive, then to zero, then to maximum negative, and again to zero.

Damping force $f_D = \mu N = \mu mg$ where N is support reaction

The equilibrium of the mass can be written with respect to Figures 2.14(a) and 2.14(b):

$$f_I + f_D + f_S = 0$$

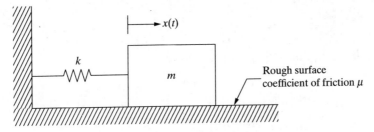

Figure 2.13   SDOF with friction damping.

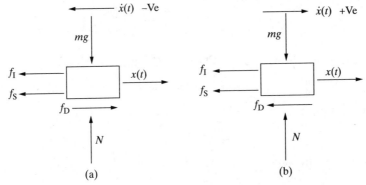

Figure 2.14   Free body diagram of the forces on sliding block.

or,
$$m\ddot{x} + kx \pm f_D = 0 \qquad (2.27a)$$

where, a positive sign before f_D is applicable only when the velocity is positive.

This equation cannot be solved directly using the conventional method of solution of a differential equation. This is because it is a nonlinear equation. Any solution of Equation 2.27a will apply only during a time interval when the sign remains unchanged. Equation 2.27a can be solved by breaking the time interval into two segments corresponding to the changes in the direction of motion in terms of velocity.

Consider Figure 2.14(a)

$$m\ddot{x} + kx - f_D = 0 \quad \text{when the velocity is negative, } \dot{x} < 0 \qquad (2.27b)$$

or,
$$m\ddot{x} + kx = f_D = \mu mg$$

and, consider Figure 2.14(b)

$$m\ddot{x} + kx + f_D = 0 \quad \text{when the velocity is positive, } \dot{x} > 0 \qquad (2.27c)$$

or,
$$m\ddot{x} + kx = -f_D = -\mu mg$$

This block requires non-zero initial conditions to set it in motion. If the initial velocity is zero, then it requires initial displacement so that the spring force exceeds the static frictional force. Naturally, if $x(0)$ is less than the frictional force $f_D = \mu mg$, there will be no motion. If the initial velocity is non-zero, the object will move.

Let

$$x_F = \frac{|f_D|}{k} = \frac{\mu mg}{k} = \frac{\mu g}{\omega^2}$$

(2.28a)

Therefore, Equation (2.27b) can be written as:

$$m\ddot{x} + kx = f_D = m\omega^2 x_F$$

$$\ddot{x} + \omega^2 x = \frac{f_D}{m} = \omega^2 x_F \quad \text{for } \dot{x} < 0$$

(2.28b)

Similarly, Equation (2.27c) can be written as:

$$m\ddot{x} + kx = f_D = -m\omega^2 x_F$$

$$\ddot{x} + \omega^2 x = -\frac{f_D}{m} = -\omega^2 x_F \quad \text{for } \dot{x} > 0$$

(2.28c)

Let us determine the solution of Equation (2.28b).

$$x(t) = A_1 \sin \omega t + B_1 \cos \omega t + x_F$$

(2.29a)

On differentiation,

$$\dot{x}(t) = \omega A_1 \cos \omega t - \omega B_1 \sin \omega t$$

(2.29b)

The initial conditions are as follows:

At $t = 0, \ x = x(0); \text{and } \dot{x}(0) = 0$

Substituting in Equation (2.29a) gives,

$$B_1 = (x(0) - x_F) \text{ and } A_1 = 0$$

$\therefore$ The solution is given by

$$x(t) = (x(0) - x_F)\cos \omega t + x_F \text{ for } 0 \le t \le \frac{\pi}{\omega}$$

(2.30)

First negative peak given by Equation (2.30) is

At $t = \dfrac{\pi}{\omega} = \dfrac{T}{2}$

$\therefore$

$$x\left(\frac{\pi}{\omega}\right) = -x(0) + 2x_F \text{ and } \dot{x}\left(\frac{\pi}{\omega}\right) = 0$$

(2.31)

In the second half cycle, the velocity is positive and the equation of motion is given by Equation (2.28c).

Its solution is given by

$$x(t) = A_2 \sin \omega t + B_2 \cos \omega t - x_F$$

(2.32)

The constants A_2 and B_2 can be determined by using the initial conditions at the beginning of this half cycle given by Equation (2.31).

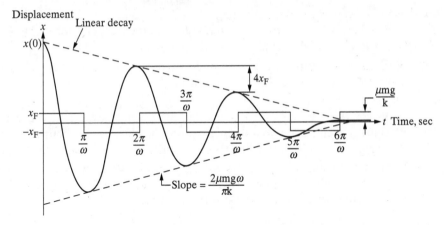

Figure 2.15   Vibrations with Coulomb damping.

Substituting in Equation (2.32) gives,

$$B_2 = (x(0) - 3x_F) \text{ and } A_2 = 0$$

∴ The solution is given by

$$x(t) = (x(0) - 3x_F)\cos\omega t - x_F \quad \text{for} \quad \frac{\pi}{\omega} \le t \le \frac{2\pi}{\omega} \tag{2.33}$$

At $t = \dfrac{2\pi}{\omega}$

or $t = T$ Equation (2.33) gives

$$x\left(\frac{2\pi}{\omega}\right) = x(0) - 4x_F \text{ and } \dot{x}\left(\frac{2\pi}{\omega}\right) = 0 \tag{2.34}$$

Thus, at $t = \dfrac{2\pi}{\omega}$, the motion again reverses. The full motion in a cycle is described by Equations (2.30) and (2.33) and is shown in Figure 2.15. It can be seen that successive peaks are given by $\left[x(0) - 4x_F n\right]$ where n is an integer representing number of complete cycles. The damping envelope is formed by a pair of straight lines and each half cycle is a cosine function.

The solution will stop when the velocity is zero and the spring force (kx) is insufficient to overcome the maximum frictional force (μmg). In other words, the motion stops at the end of the half-cycle for which the amplitude is less than x_F. At that point, the spring force is less than the frictional force.

The amplitude decays linearly. Its slope is given by using its displacement across any one complete cycle, say at 0.5 and 1.5 cycles (Figure 2.15)

$$\tan\theta = \left[(x(0) - 4x_F(1.5)) - (x(0) - 4(0.5)x_F)\right]/\left(\frac{2\pi}{\omega}\right)$$

$$\tan\theta = -\frac{2x_F\omega}{\pi} = -\frac{2\mu mg\omega}{\pi k} = -\frac{2\mu g}{\pi\omega} \tag{2.35}$$

The negative sign shows a decay or decrease in slope.

Coulomb damping vs Viscous damping

A few significant observations can be made for the free response of a SDOF system with these two types of damping:

1. With viscous damping, the amplitude of displacement decays exponentially, whereas with coulomb damping, the same decays linearly and comes to a complete rest.

2. A system with viscous damping continues to vibrate even at a very small displacement amplitude about its mean position, whereas, a system with coulomb damping comes to rest at a different equilibrium position than its mean position.

3. The damped natural frequency is different than the undamped natural frequency in a system with viscous damping, whereas, damped and undamped frequencies in a system with coulomb damping are the same.

Example 2.8

A SDOF system with a friction damper vibrates with an initial displacement of 50 mm. It completes 4 cycles in 0.8 second when its amplitude reduces to 5 mm. Estimate the coefficient of friction and when does the system come to rest.

Solution   Period of vibration T = 0.8/4 = 0.2 sec

Frequency of vibration $\omega = 2\pi/T = \dfrac{2\pi}{0.2} = 31.4$ rad/sec

Slope of the displacement-time envelope curve $= -\dfrac{2\mu g}{\pi\omega}$

or,

$$\text{Slope} = \frac{50-5}{0.8} = -\frac{45}{0.8} = -\frac{2\mu g}{\pi\omega}$$

or,

$$\mu = \frac{\pi\omega}{2g}\left(\frac{45}{0.8}\right) = \frac{\pi \times 31.4 \times 45}{2 \times 9810 \times 0.8} = 0.2828$$

The displacement x_F is given by

$$x_F = \frac{\mu g}{\omega^2} = \frac{0.2828 \times 9810}{31.4^2} = 2.81 \text{ mm}$$

It will come to rest when

$$x(0) - 4x_F n < x_F \text{ and velocity is zero.}$$

or,

$$n = \frac{x(0) - x_F}{4x_F} = \frac{50 - 2.81}{4 \times 2.81} = 4.198 \text{ cycles}$$

It means the system will come to rest at the beginning of next half cycle, that is, 4.5 cycles or at 0.9 sec. The displacement at 0.9 sec will be equal to

$$x(0) - 4x_F \times 4.5 = 50 - 4 \times 2.81 \times 4.5 = -0.58 \text{ mm}$$

The minus sign indicates that 0.58 mm is in a direction opposite to that of the initial displacement.   □

PROBLEMS

2.1 An undamped SDOF system ($m = 30$ kg, $k = 500$ N/m) is given an initial displacement of 10 mm and initial velocity of 75 mm/s. Find
(a) the natural frequency
(b) the period of vibration
(c) the amplitude of vibration
(d) the time at which the second and third maximum peak occurs.

2.2 An undamped SDOF system is set in motion from rest by giving it an initial velocity of 0.1 m/s. It vibrates with a maximum amplitude of 15 mm. Determine its natural frequency.

2.3 The mass of a block shown in Figure P2.1 is 100 kg and the spring stiffness is 1000 N/m. A bullet weighing 250 gm is fired at a speed of 20 m/s into the block and becomes embedded in the block. Determine the resulting undamped motion of the block.

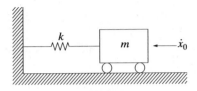

Figure P2.1

2.4 A mass m_1 hangs from a massless spring k and is in static equilibrium. A second mass m_2 drops through a height h and sticks to m_1. Determine the subsequent motion $x(t)$ measured from the static position of m_1 and k.

2.5 Consider a SDOF system having a mass $m = 5$ kg, damping $c = 10$ N-s/m and stiffness $k = 20$ N/m. Determine the values of undamped and damped natural frequency. Is the system overdamped, critically damped or underdamped?

2.6 Consider a SDOF system shown in Figure P2.2 where $m = 20$ kg, $c = 125$ N-s/m, $k_1 = 3000$ N/m, $k_2 = 500$ N/m and $k_3 = 1200$ N/m. Is the system overdamped, critically damped or underdamped?

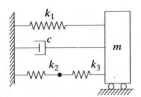

Figure P2.2

2.7 Consider a SDOF system having a mass $m = 30$ kN s²/m, damping $c = 50$ kNs/m and stiffness $k = 4000$ kN/m. Determine natural frequency, damping ratio and critical damping.

For $x(0) = 0.02$ m, and $\dot{x}(0) = 0.1$ m/s. Find the solution of the equation of motion. Hence, plot inertia, damping and spring force vs time for free vibration.

(Hint: Make use of MS-EXCEL)

2.8 A braced portal frame is shown in Figure P2.3. Beam and columns are of concrete of M25 grade. Size of column is 300 × 400 mm. Area of steel brace = 10 cm² and length = 5 m. Determine the natural period of vibration considering only the tension brace. If the initial displacement is 50 mm, and initial velocity is 0.5 m/s, plot the response up to 3 cycles.

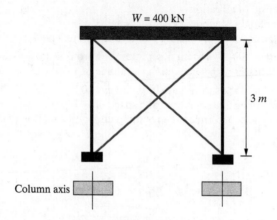

W = 400 kN

3 m

Column axis

Figure P2.3

2.9 It is observed that amplitude of free vibration of a structure reduces from 100 mm to 30 mm in 10 cycles. Determine the viscous damping ratio.

2.10 A sliding block shown in Figure P2.4 has a natural period of 0.3 sec and the coefficient of friction between the block and the sliding surface is 0.25. If the block is given an initial displacement of 150 mm, what is the displacement after one cycle; what is the velocity after one cycle.

2.11 Consider the friction block of Figure P2.4. Mass = 50 kg, stiffness k = 100 kN/m and friction force is 50 N. If the initial displacement is 200 mm, determine the amplitude after two cycles.

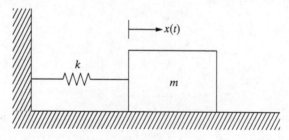

$x(t)$

k

m

Figure P2.4

2.12 Consider a friction block having a mass = 250 kg and stiffness k = 50 kN/m. Coefficient of friction is 0.15 and initial displacement is 25 cm. Plot the displacement–time history. How long does it take for the system to come to rest and what is the amplitude at rest?

MATLAB APPLICATIONS

2.13 Consider a SDOF system with mass m, stiffness k and damping coefficient c. It is given an initial displacement $x(0)$ and initial velocity $\dot{x}(0)$. Write a MATLAB code to plot displacement–time history, velocity–time history, and acceleration–time history. Also plot inertia force, damping force and spring force–time history. Make use of MATLAB functions '*diff*' to differentiate the displacement to obtain velocity and acceleration. Choose appropriate input data to make the system underdamped, critically damped and over damped.

2.14 In problem 2.13, also show the influence of initial conditions by taking: (i) $x(0) = 10$ mm, and $\dot{x}(0) = 0$, (ii) $x(0) = 100$ mm, and $\dot{x}(0) = 0$, (iii) $x(0) = 0$, and $\dot{x}(0) = -10$ mm/sec; (iv) $x(0) = 0$, and $\dot{x}(0) = 100$ mm/sec.

2.15 The solution of an undamped free vibration SDOF system is given by the following equation:

$$x(t) = A\sin(\omega t + \phi)$$

where

$$A = \frac{\sqrt{\omega^2 x_0^2 + v_0^2}}{\omega} \quad \text{and} \quad \phi = \tan^{-1}\frac{\omega x_0}{v_0}$$

Make a 3D surface plot in MATLAB of the amplitude A vs x_0 and v_0 for the range of initial conditions given by $-0.1 \leq x_0 \leq 0.1$ m and $-1 \leq v_0 \leq 1$ m/s for a system with natural frequency of 20 rad/s.

(Hint: Make use of MATLAB functions meshgrid, grid, and mesh or surf.)

2.16 A spring and damper are attached to a mass of 100 kg to obtain a SDOF system. The initial conditions are: $x(0) = 0.1$ m, and $v(0) = 10$ mm/s. Design the spring and the damper such that the system will come to rest in 2 sec and not oscillate more than two complete cycles. Try to keep damping as small as possible.

2.17 A sliding block has a natural period of 0.25 sec and the coefficient of friction between the block and the sliding surface is 0.15. If the block is given an initial displacement of 5 cm and an initial velocity of 50 cm/sec, plot the displacement and velocity – time history.

3 Single Degree of Freedom System: Harmonic Loading

3.1 INTRODUCTION

A harmonic loading or sinusoidal loading is the simplest dynamic force and frequently encountered in vibrations due to machines. The nature of the force is well defined in terms of magnitude, frequency, shape, as well as duration. It is, therefore, customary to begin the study of dynamics of structures with this loading. A single-degree-of-freedom (SDOF) system is subjected to harmonic loading and its response is studied without and with damping. The total response consists of two components: a *transient response*, which dies out quickly and a *steady state response*, which continues till the forcing function continues. The steady state response has a constant amplitude and frequency. The steady state response is of much interest to the analysts. The ratio of frequency of the forcing function and that of the structure plays a very significant role in dynamics. If the forcing frequency is equal to the natural frequency of the SDOF system, a *resonance* is said to have occurred. It is very enlightening to study the response at resonance. It also helps in determining damping in the system.

3.2 UNDAMPED FORCED VIBRATIONS

The general equation of motion of a single degree of freedom system is given by:

$$m\ddot{x}(t) + c\dot{x}(t) + kx(t) = p(t) \tag{3.1}$$

For an undamped system shown in Figure 3.1, $c = 0$

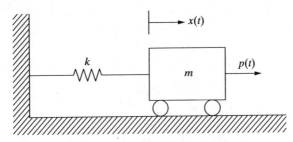

Figure 3.1 Undamped SDOF system.

Let $p(t) = p_0 \sin \bar{\omega} t$ for harmonic loading,
where $p_0 =$ amplitude of harmonic loading,
$\bar{\omega} =$ circular frequency of harmonic loading.

$\therefore$ Equation (3.1) reduces to $\quad m\ddot{x}(t) + k\,x(t) = p_0 \sin \bar{\omega} t$ (3.2)

Its solution consists of the following two components:

(i) Complimentary solution—it is given by the free vibration analysis done earlier
(ii) Particular solution

Particular solution means the specific behaviour generated by the form of the dynamic loading. The response to the harmonic loading can be assumed to be harmonic and in phase with loading. Thus,

$$x_p(t) = G \sin \bar{\omega} t$$

Differentiating twice and substituting in Equation (3.2) gives,

$$-m\bar{\omega}^2 G \sin \bar{\omega} t + kG \sin \bar{\omega} t = p_0 \sin \bar{\omega} t$$

On rearranging the terms,

$$G\left(1 - \frac{\bar{\omega}^2}{\omega^2}\right) = \frac{p_0}{k}$$

$\therefore$ Amplitude of the response becomes,

$$G = \frac{p_0}{k} \cdot \frac{1}{1 - \beta^2}$$

where

$\beta =$ ratio of applied load frequency to the natural free vibration frequency.
$= \bar{\omega} / \omega$ frequency ratio.

Total response is given by $x(t) = x_c(t) + x_p(t)$ (3.3)

$$= \underbrace{A \sin \omega t + B \cos \omega t}_{\text{complimentary solution}} + \underbrace{\frac{p_0}{k} \frac{1}{1 - \beta^2} \sin \bar{\omega} t}_{\text{steady state solution}}$$ (3.4)

The values of A and B depend on the initial conditions.
If the initial conditions are at $t = 0, x = x(0)$ and $\dot{x} = \dot{x}(0)$, the final solution becomes

$$x(t) = \underbrace{x(0)\cos \omega t + \left[\frac{\dot{x}(0)}{\omega} - \frac{p_0}{k}\frac{\beta}{(1-\beta^2)}\right]\sin \omega t}_{\text{Transient solution}} + \underbrace{\frac{p_0}{k}\frac{1}{1-\beta^2}\sin \bar{\omega} t}_{\text{Steady state solution}}$$ (3.5a)

If the system is *at rest* at $t = 0, x(0) = 0$ and $\dot{x}(0) = 0$

then $B = 0$ and $A = -p_0 \beta / (k(1 - \beta^2))$

The final solution of undamped forced vibration becomes

$$x(t) = \frac{p_0}{k}\frac{1}{(1-\beta^2)}(\sin \bar{\omega} t - \beta \sin \omega t)$$ (3.5b)

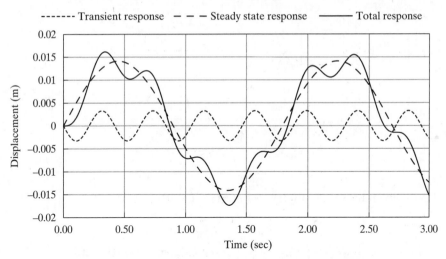

Figure 3.2   Transient, steady state and total response of an undamped SDOF system.
($m = 33.33$ kN-s²/m, $k = 7500$ kN/m, $P_0 = 100$ kN, $\bar{\omega} = 3.5$ rad/sec $x(0) = 0$, $\dot{x}(0) = 0$)

where,

$p_0/k = \Delta_{ST}$, that is, displacement which would be produced by the load p_0 applied statically

$\dfrac{1}{(1-\beta^2)}$ = magnification factor representing dynamic amplification effect of harmonically applied load

$\sin \bar{\omega}t$ = response component at frequency of the applied load
= steady state response directly related to the load

$\beta \sin \omega t$ = response component at natural frequency of vibration
= free vibration effect induced by the initial condition

The last term in Equation (3.5b) is also called *transient response.*

The variation of transient response, steady state response and total response with time is shown in Figure 3.2. It can be seen that in the absence of any damping, the transient response goes on indefinitely.

3.3 DAMPED FORCED VIBRATIONS

A damped SDOF system is shown in Figure 3.3. The dash-pot represents a viscous damper having damping coefficient c.

Equation (3.1) can be rewritten as:

$$\ddot{x}(t) + 2\xi\omega\dot{x}(t) + \omega^2 x(t) = \frac{p_0}{m}\sin\bar{\omega}t \qquad (3.6)$$

where,

$$c/m = 2\xi\omega$$

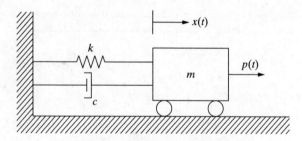

Figure 3.3 Damped SDOF system.

Complimentary solution $x_c(t) = e^{-\xi\omega t}(A\sin\omega_D t + B\cos\omega_D t)$ $\qquad(3.7)$

where, $\qquad\qquad\qquad\qquad \omega_D = \omega\sqrt{1-\xi^2}$

Let $\qquad\qquad$ particular integral $x_p(t) = G_1 \sin\bar{\omega}t + G_2 \cos\bar{\omega}t$ $\qquad(3.8)$

in which the second term is required because, in general, the response of a damped system is not in phase with the loading.

The constants G_1 and G_2 are to be found using the initial conditions. Substitute Equation (3.8) in Equation (3.6) and compare the coefficients of $\sin\bar{\omega}t$ and $\cos\bar{\omega}t$. It gives

$$G_1 = \frac{p_0}{k}\frac{1-\beta^2}{(1-\beta^2)^2 + (2\xi\beta)^2}\qquad(3.9)$$

$$G_2 = \frac{p_0}{k}\frac{-2\xi\beta}{(1-\beta^2)^2 + (2\xi\beta)^2}\qquad(3.10)$$

Final solution becomes

$$x(t) = e^{-\xi\omega t}(A\sin\omega_D t + B\cos\omega_D t)$$
$$+\frac{p_0}{k}\left\{\frac{1}{(1-\beta^2)^2 + (2\xi\beta)^2}\right\}[(1-\beta^2)\sin\bar{\omega}t - 2\xi\beta\cos\bar{\omega}t]\qquad(3.11)$$

The transient response dies quickly and is of little interest. The steady state response will continue till the external force continues to be applied. The variation of transient, steady state and total response for a typical SDOF system is shown in Figure 3.4. The data was as follows:

Undamped natural frequency $\omega = 15$ rad/sec, damping = 5%, force amplitude = 100 kN stiffness $k = 7500$ kN/m, forcing frequency $\bar{\omega} = 5$ rad/sec

The solution given by Equations (3.8), (3.9) and (3.10) is of interest to the analysts. The resultant ρ of the two vectors represent the amplitude of the steady state response.

$$\rho = \frac{p_0}{k}[(1-\beta^2)^2 + (2\xi\beta)^2]^{-0.5}\qquad(3.12)$$

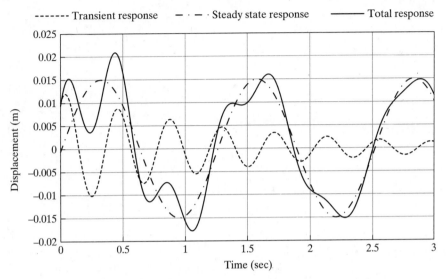

Figure 3.4 Transient, steady state and total response of a damped SDOF system.

and the phase angle θ by which the response lags behind the applied load is given by

$$\theta = \tan^{-1}\frac{2\xi\beta}{1-\beta^2} \qquad 0<\theta<180° \tag{3.13}$$

The steady state response can be written as:

$$x(t) = \frac{p_0}{k}\left\{\frac{1}{\left[(1-\beta^2)^2+(2\xi\beta)^2\right]}\right\}\left[(1-\beta^2)\sin\varpi t-(2\xi\beta)\cos\varpi t\right] \tag{3.14a}$$

or, $$x(t) = \rho\sin(\bar{\omega}t-\theta) \tag{3.14b}$$

The ratio of the resultant response amplitude to the static displacement, which would be produced by the force p_0 is called *dynamic magnification* factor D

$$D = \frac{\rho}{p_0/k} = \frac{x_{\max}}{x_{\text{static}}} \tag{3.15a}$$

or, $$D = [(1-\beta^2)^2+(2\xi\beta)^2]^{-0.5} \tag{3.15b}$$

The variation of magnification factor with the frequency ratio β for a given damping ratio can be plotted as shown in Figure 3.5 using MATLAB.

Similarly, the variation of phase angle with the frequency ratio β for a given damping ratio can be plotted as shown in Figure 3.6 using MATLAB.

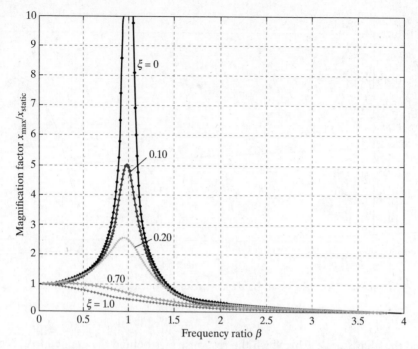

Figure 3.5   Variation of dynamic magnification factor with frequency ratio.

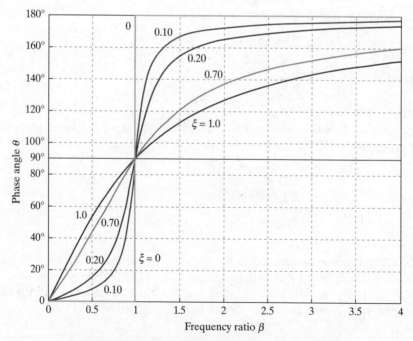

Figure 3.6   Variation of phase angle with frequency ratio.

3.3.1 Dynamic Magnification Factor

It is interesting to understand the behaviour of the dynamic magnification factor as seen in Figure 3.5. The following observations can be made:

1. There is a decrease in amplitude of displacement with increase in damping. It is maximum for 0% damping.
2. For frequency ratio equal to 1, that is, at resonance, the displacement amplitude is maximum.
   At $\beta = 1$ and $\xi = 0$, $D = \infty$
   At $\beta = 1$ and $\xi \neq 0$, D is very high
3. For frequency ratios near 1, the factor is very sensitive to damping. It can be very large depending upon the damping.

$$x_{max} = x_{static} \frac{1}{2\xi}$$

$$x_{max} = \frac{p_0}{k} \frac{1}{2\xi} = \frac{p_0}{c\omega} \tag{3.16a}$$

4. For frequency ratios less than 1 ($\ll 1.0$), the factor is slightly more than 1 and appears to be independent of damping, that is,

$$D \approx 1, \text{ or } x_{max} \approx x_{static} = \frac{p_0}{k} = \frac{p_0}{m\omega^2} \tag{3.16b}$$

5. For frequency ratios greater than 1 ($\gg 1.0$), the factor D tends to be zero and is essentially independent of damping, that is,

$$D \approx \frac{1}{\beta^2} = \frac{\omega^2}{\varpi^2}$$

or,

$$x_{max} \approx x_{static} \times \left(\frac{k}{m}\right)\left(\frac{1}{\varpi^2}\right) = \frac{p_0}{k} \frac{k}{m} \frac{1}{\varpi^2} \tag{3.16c}$$

or,

$$x_{max} \approx \frac{p_0}{m} \frac{1}{\varpi^2} \tag{3.16d}$$

This information is very useful while designing machine foundations or structures against undesirable vibrations.

Behaviour of the Phase Angle with Frequency Ratio
Similarly, the variation of phase angle between the response and the applied force with frequency ratio and damping can be examined:

1. For frequency ratios less than 1 ($\ll 1.0$), the phase angle is close to $0°$ and the displacement is in phase with the force.
2. For frequency ratios greater than 1 ($\gg 1.0$), the phase angle is very close to $180°$ and the displacement is out of phase with the force. The force and the displacement are in opposite directions.
3. For frequency ratios equal to 1 ($= 1.0$), the phase angle is $90°$ irrespective of damping. The displacement attains its peak when the force passes through zero.

3.4 MATLAB APPLICATIONS

Two MATLAB codes have been written. DOS3_1 computes the damped forced response of a SDOF and DOS3_2 computes dynamic magnification factor D and phase angle θ with frequency ratio β

```
------------------
CODE DOS3_1
------------------
%    Dynamics of Structures by Ashok K. Jain I. I. T. Roorkee
%    DOS3_1
%    Damped Forced Vibrations of a SDOF System
%    Calls DOS3_1a
%    The program calls function "ode23" to solve ordinary differential eqn.
%    Initial conditions are defined inside and can be changed.
%    Total duration of sinusoidal force = tf.
%
clear all;
clc;
IC = [0.02;0.05];   % Initial conditions x(0) and v(0)
tf = 15.0;
fprintf('Initial displacement at t=0, is %.3g m\n',IC(1));
fprintf('Initial velocity at t=0, is %.3g m/s\n',IC(2));
fprintf('Total duration of force = %.3g sec\n',tf);
t = [0:0.005:tf];
[t,z] = ode23(@DOS3_1a,t,IC);
% dismax=max((z(:,1)'))   % I need the max. value of displacement
% velmax=max((z(:,2)'))   % I need the maximum value of velocity
% sprintf('%s',dismax, velmax)
plot(t,z(:,1))
grid on;
xlabel('time sec')
ylabel('displacement m')
title('Displacement time history')
figure;
plot(t,z(:,2))
xlabel('time sec')
ylabel('Velocity m/sec')
title('Velocity time history')
grid on;


------------------
CODE DOS3_1a
------------------
%    Dynamics of Structures by Ashok K. Jain I. I. T. Roorkee
%    DOS3_1a
```

```
%     Damped Forced Vibrations of a SDOF System
%     Called by DOS3_1
%     force = f*sin(omegab*t)
%     Input parameters are defined inside function and can be changed
function q=DOS3_1a(t,z)
m=5;
k = 100;
zai=0.05; % 5%
c=2*zai*sqrt(k*m);
omega=sqrt(k/m);
per=2*pi/omega;
omegab=10;
f=10.;
if (t==0)
fprintf('Mass = %.3g kg\n',m);
fprintf('Stiffness = %.3g N/m\n',k);
fprintf('Damping ratio = %.3g \n',zai);
fprintf('Natural frequency = %.3g rad/s.\n',omega);
fprintf('Period of vibration = %.3g s\n',per);
fprintf('Forcing frequency = %.3g rad/s\n',omegab);
fprintf('Amplitude of force = %.3g N\n',f);
end
q=[z(2);((f/m)*sin(omegab*t)-(c/m)*z(2)-(k/m)*z(1))];
end


------------------

CODE DOS3_2
------------------

%     Dynamics of Structures by Ashok K. Jain I. I. T. Roorkee
%     DOS3_2
%     Dynamic magnification factor plot
%     Phase angle plot
%     beta = frequency ratio
clc
clear all;
close all
zai=[ 0.0001 0.10 0.20 0.70 1.0];
beta=[0:0.01:4];
for i=1:length(zai)
    for j=1:length(beta)
        d(i,j)=(1/((1-beta(j)^2)^2+(2*beta(j)*zai(i))^2))^0.5;
    end
end
for i=1:length(zai)
    plot(beta,d(i,:),'.-k')
    hold on
end
grid on
```

```
xlabel('frequency ratio')
ylabel('Magnification factor')
axis([0 4 0 10])
hold on
%
% Alternative way of plotting the same but with different colors
%
figure
plot(beta,d,'.-')
grid on
xlabel('frequency ratio')
ylabel('Magnification factor')
axis([0 4 0 10])
hold on
%
% Calculate phase angle with beta and zai
%
for i=1:length(zai)
    for j=1:length(beta)
        theta(i,j)=mod(atan(2*zai(i)*beta(j)/(1-beta(j)*beta(j))),pi);
    end
end
%
figure
for i=1:length(zai)
    plot(beta,theta*180/pi)
    hold on
end
grid on
xlabel('frequency ratio')
ylabel('Phase angle')
%axis([beta(1) beta(end) 0 180]);
--------------------------
```

These codes have been used to generate results as shown in the following examples.

Example 3.1

Consider a SDOF system shown in Figure 3.3. The mass = 5 kNs²/m, stiffness k = 100 kN/m and damping is 5%. It is subjected to a sinusoidal force having a magnitude of 10 kN and a forcing frequency of 10 rad/sec. Determine the natural frequency and natural period of vibration. The initial conditions are given as: $x(0) = 0.02$ m and $\dot{x}(0) = 0.05$ m/s. Hence, plot its total displacement and total velocity response.

Solution The displacement and velocity response obtained using MATLAB code are shown in Figure 3.7. It can be seen that in the initial seven seconds, the response is a combination of transient and forcing functions; later the transient response dies down and only steady state response is available. Its free damped vibration response was shown in Example 2.3.   □

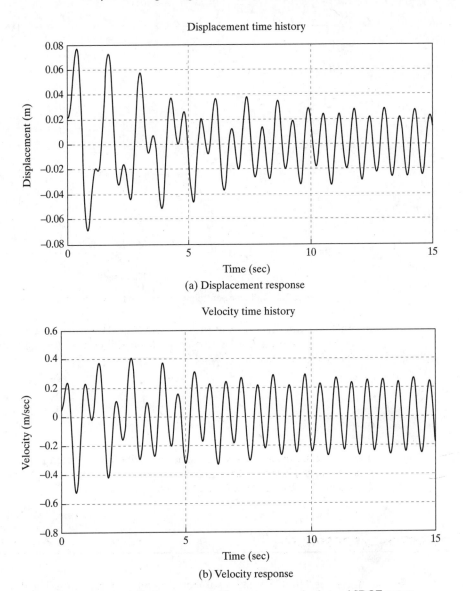

(a) Displacement response

(b) Velocity response

Figure 3.7   Total displacement and velocity response of a damped SDOF system.

Example 3.2

A SDOF system has a stiffness $k = 7500$ kN/m, natural frequency of 15 rad/sec and a damping of 10%. The initial conditions are $x(0) = 0.01$ m and $\dot{x}(0) = 0.1$ m/sec. Plot the variation in steady state response if the frequency ratio $\beta = 0.5, 1.0$ and 2.0.

Solution   The steady state response was determined using Equation (3.14a) in MS-EXCEL for different frequency ratios and the response is plotted in Figure 3.8. It can be seen that the frequency ratio has a significant influence on the response.

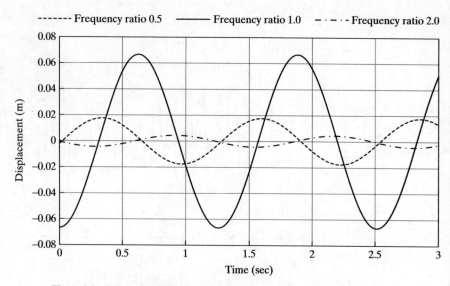

Figure 3.8   Influence of frequency ratio on the steady state response ($\xi = 10\%$).

It would be interesting to know the static response due to the force $p(t)$. It can be determined by applying the force $p(t)$ very slowly instead of at its forcing frequency $\bar{\omega}$ using the following relation:

$$x_{st}(t) = \frac{p_0}{k}\sin\bar{\omega}t$$

or,

$$\frac{x_{st}(t)}{x_0} = \sin\bar{\omega}t$$

The static displacement $x_{st}(t)$ is in phase with the forcing function $p(t)$. By plotting the steady state displacement and static displacement on the same graph for a given forcing frequency, the phase difference can be seen.   ☐

3.5 RESONANT RESPONSE

For an undamped SDOF system subjected to harmonic loading, the dynamic magnification factor D is given by Equation (3.15b) with $\xi = 0$.

$$D = \frac{x_{max}}{x_{static}} = \frac{1}{(1-\beta^2)} \tag{3.16e}$$

At resonance, $\beta = 1, D = \infty$

For a damped system, D is given by Equation (3.15b)

$$D = \frac{1}{\sqrt{(1-\beta^2)^2 + (2\beta\xi)^2}} \tag{3.17}$$

At resonance, $\beta = 1$, that is,

$$D_{max} = \frac{1}{2\xi} \tag{3.18a}$$

Let us differentiate D in Equation (3.17) with respect to β and equate it to zero, it gives, $\beta_{max} = \sqrt{1-2\xi^2}$ and the corresponding D_{max} is given by

$$D_{max} = \frac{1}{2\xi\sqrt{1-\xi^2}} \tag{3.18b}$$

For reasonable amounts of damping, the difference between Equation (3.18a) and (3.18b) is negligible.

Let us consider the nature of resonant response of a SDOF system to harmonic loading. Its total response at $\beta = 1$ is given by Equation (3.11)

$$x(t) = e^{-\xi\omega t}(A\sin\omega_D t + B\cos\omega_D t) - \frac{P_0}{k}\frac{\cos\omega t}{2\xi} \tag{3.19}$$

If the system is *at rest* at $t = 0$, $x(0) = 0$ and $\dot{x}(0) = 0$, then

The constants $\quad A = \dfrac{P_0}{k}\dfrac{1}{2\sqrt{1-\xi^2}}\quad$ and $\quad B = \dfrac{P_0}{k}\dfrac{1}{2\xi} \tag{3.20}$

Equation (3.19) can be re-written as follows:

For $\beta = 1$ means $\omega = \varpi$, and if ξ^2 can be neglected, $\omega = \omega_{D;}$ also the term $(\xi\sin\omega_D t)$ will contribute very little and, therefore, ignored.

$$x(t) = \frac{1}{2\xi}\frac{P_0}{k}(e^{-\xi\omega t}-1)\cos\omega t \tag{3.21}$$

$$\therefore \qquad D(t) = \frac{x(t)}{P_0/k} = \frac{1}{2\xi}(e^{-\xi\omega t}-1)\cos\omega t \tag{3.22}$$

If damping ratio ξ becomes zero, Equation (3.22) becomes indeterminate. Using the principles of differential calculus, the resonant response of an undamped system is given by

$$D(t) = \frac{1}{2}(\sin\omega t - \omega t\cos\omega t) \tag{3.23}$$

A MATLAB code DOS3_3 is written using Equation (3.22) and (3.23). The plots of Equation (3.22) and (3.23) are shown in Figure 3.9.

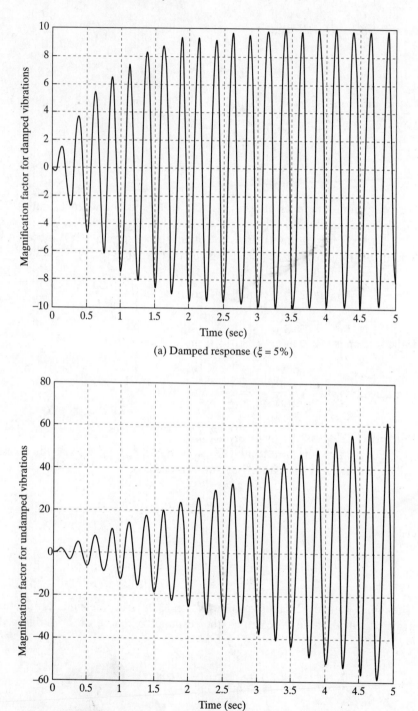

(a) Damped response ($\xi = 5\%$)

(b) Undamped response

Figure 3.9   Resonant response of a SDOF system ($\omega = 25$ rad/sec).

```
------------------
CODE DOS3_3
------------------
%    Dynamics of Structures by Ashok K. Jain I. I. T. Roorkee
%    DOS3_3
%    Dynamic magnification factor for damped/undamped resonant response
%    Damping ratio = 5%
%    Natural frequency = 25 rad/sec - it can be changed in program
%
clc
clear all;
close all
zai=0.05;
omega=25;
t=[0:0.01:5];
yy=length(t);
for i=1:length(t)
    dd(i)=(1/(2*zai))*(exp(-zai*omega*t(i))-1)*cos(omega*t(i));
end
plot(t,dd,'-r')
hold on
grid on
xlabel('Time, sec')
ylabel('Magnification factor for Damped Vibrations')
%
for i=1:length(t)
yy(i)=0.5*(sin(omega*t(i))-omega*t(i)*cos(omega*t(i)));
end
figure;
plot(t,yy,'-b')
grid on
xlabel('Time, sec')
ylabel('Magnification factor for undamped Vibrations')
```

3.6 MEASUREMENT OF VISCOUS DAMPING

The viscous damping in a SDOF system can be measured as follows:

(a) Free vibration analysis—exponent decay or logarithmic decay method
(b) Resonant amplification method
(c) Half power (Bandwidth) method
(d) Resonant testing or energy loss per cycle method

The exponent decay or logarithmic method has already been discussed earlier in Section 2.5. Let us discuss the other methods.

3.6.1 Resonant Amplification Method

A SDOF system can be subjected to a harmonic loading and under steady state, its vibrations can be recorded. The amplitude and frequency of the harmonic loading can be adjusted to obtain the desired response. The forcing frequency can be varied spanning the resonance and the resulting displacement amplitude can be plotted against frequency ratio. At resonance,

$$\text{Dynamic amplification factor } D = \frac{1}{2\xi} \quad \text{or} \quad \xi = \frac{1}{2D} = \frac{x_{\text{static}}}{2x_{\text{max}}} \tag{3.24}$$

where x_{max} is measured at resonance.

Sometimes it may be difficult to subject the SDOF system to resonate. Let us rewrite Equation (3.18b) as follows:

$$D_{\text{max}} = \frac{1}{2\xi} \frac{\omega}{\omega_D} \tag{3.25}$$

Thus, damping can be measured.

3.6.2 Half Power (Bandwidth) Method

In this method, the damping is measured at frequencies at which the amplitude is reduced to $1/\sqrt{2}$ of that at resonance, that is,

$$\text{The displacement amplitude} = \frac{1}{\sqrt{2}} \text{ of } x_{\text{max}} \text{ at } \beta = 1.$$

The corresponding frequency ratio β can be determined using Equation (3.15a), as follows:

$$x_{\text{max}} = x_{\text{static}} \times D = x_{\text{static}} \times \frac{1}{2\xi} \qquad \text{using Equation (3.24)}$$

$$\therefore \quad \frac{x_{\text{max}}}{\sqrt{2}} = \frac{1}{\sqrt{2}} \times x_{\text{static}} \times \frac{1}{2\xi} = x_{\text{static}} \times \frac{1}{\sqrt{(1-\beta^2)^2 + (2\beta\xi)^2}} \qquad \text{using Equation (3.17)}$$

or, $\qquad \beta^2 = 1 - 2\xi^2 \pm 2\xi\sqrt{1+\xi^2}$

Neglecting ξ^2 term being too small,

$$\beta^2 \approx 1 \pm 2\xi \quad \text{or} \quad \beta \approx (1 \pm 2\xi)^{\frac{1}{2}}$$

Expanding using the Taylor series and taking only the first term,

$$\beta_1 \approx 1 - \xi \tag{i}$$

Similarly, $\beta_2 \approx 1 + \xi$ \hfill (ii)

Equations (i) and (ii) give, $\qquad\qquad \xi = (\beta_2 - \beta_1)/2$ \hfill (3.26a)

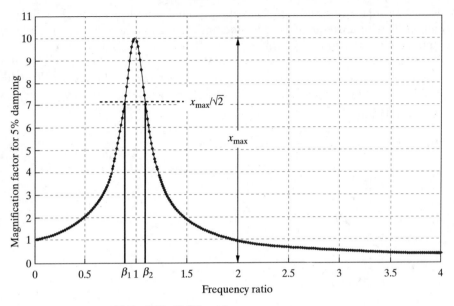

Figure 3.10   Half band frequency response curve.

This can also be written as follows:

$$\xi = \frac{\omega_2 - \omega_1}{2\omega}$$
(3.26b)

This is known as *bandwidth method* or *half power method* as illustrated in Figure 3.10.

3.6.3 Energy Loss per Cycle: Resonant Testing Method

Force-deformation curve for a SDOF system when subjected to a force can be plotted in each cycle. The area under the force-deformation curve represents energy dissipation in each cycle. The shape of the force-deformation curve depends upon the nature of the force and system properties. The energy loss per cycle due to elastic force and damping force are shown in Figure 3.11.

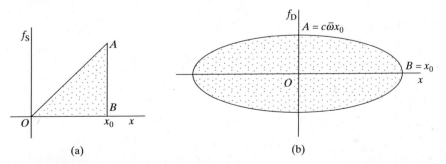

Figure 3.11   (a) Energy loss in elastic force (b) Energy loss in damping force.

Consider the response of a damped SDOF due to sinusoidal loading $p(t) = p_0 \sin \varpi t$. The input frequency is adjusted until the response is 90° out of phase with the applied loading and the system resonates, that is, $\omega = \varpi$. Now the applied load is balanced exactly by the damping force. The relation between the applied load and the resulting displacement in one loading cycle is as shown in Figure 3.11(b). This result can be interpreted as the damping force-displacement diagram.

Viscous damping force $f_D = c \dot{x}(t)$

But $x(t) = x_0 \sin \varpi t$ and $\dot{x}(t) = \varpi x_0 \cos \varpi t$

$\therefore$
$$f_D = c\varpi x_0 \cos \varpi t = c\varpi x_0 \sqrt{1 - \sin^2 \varpi t}$$

or,
$$f_D = c\varpi \sqrt{x_0^2 - x^2(t)} \qquad (3.27a)$$

This equation can be rewritten as follows:

$$\left(\frac{f_D}{c\varpi} \right)^2 = x_0^2 - x^2(t)$$

or,
$$\left(\frac{x(t)}{x_0} \right)^2 + \left(\frac{f_D}{c\varpi x_0} \right)^2 = 1 \qquad (3.27b)$$

This represents an ellipse.

Area of the ellipse $= \pi a b = \pi \,(\text{semi-major axis}) \times (\text{semi-minor axis})$

$$= \pi x_0 c\varpi x_0 = \pi c\varpi x_0^2 \qquad (3.28)$$

Thus, energy loss per cycle in a SDOF due to viscous damping is proportional to:
   (i) Damping coefficient c,
   (ii) Forcing frequency ϖ, and
   (iii) Square of amplitude.

The total spring and damping force $= f_S + f_D = k\,x(t) + c\,\dot{x}(t)$

$$f_S + f_D = k\,x(t) + c\varpi \sqrt{x_0^2 - x^2(t)} \qquad (3.29)$$

Let us compute its ordinates as follows:

If $x(t) = 0$,	$f_S + f_D = \pm c\,\varpi x_0$	(i)
If $x(t) = x_0$,	$f_S + f_D = k\,x_0$	(ii)
If $x(t) = -x_0$,	$f_S + f_D = -k\,x_0$	(iii)

If $f_S + f_D = 0$,

$$(k\,x(t))^2 = (c\varpi)^2 \left(x_0^2 - x^2(t) \right)$$

or, $$(k^2 + (c\varpi)^2)\,x^2(t) = (c\varpi x_0)^2$$

or, $$x(t) = \pm \frac{c\varpi x_0}{\sqrt{k^2 + (c\varpi)^2}}$$

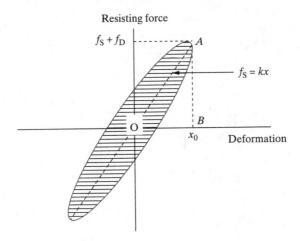

Figure 3.12   Definition of loss of energy E_D and E_S under harmonic vibrations.

$$= \pm \frac{x_0}{\sqrt{1 + \left(\dfrac{k}{c\bar{\omega}}\right)^2}} \qquad\qquad (iv)$$

Knowing the various ordinates, Equation (3.29) can be plotted as shown in Figure 3.12. The elliptic curve represents energy dissipated per cycle by the damping force f_D, that is, work done. Similarly, the area OAB represents the energy dissipated per cycle by the spring force f_S. The ordinate OB represents x_0 while the slope OA represents the elastic stiffness k.

If the structure has linear viscous damping, the curve will be an ellipse as shown in Figure 3.11(b). Damping coefficient is given by

$$f_{D\,max} = c\dot{x}_{max}$$

or,

$$c = \frac{f_{D\,max}}{\dot{x}_{max}} = \frac{p_0}{\bar{\omega}\, x_{max}} \qquad\qquad (3.30)$$

(given that $p(t) = p_0 \sin \bar{\omega}t$, $\dot{x}(t) = \bar{\omega}x_0 \cos \bar{\omega}t$ and $x_{max} = x_0$)

If the damping is not linear viscous damping, the shape of the force-deformation curve will not be elliptic but some other shape. However, it is possible to determine equivalent viscous damping by drawing an elliptic force-displacement diagram having the same area and maximum displacement as that of the original curve as shown in Figure 3.13.

If W_D = area under the non-elliptic force-deformation curve
          = work done by the equivalent damping force

then W_D = area under the elliptic curve = $\pi a\, b$.

where, a = amplitude of equivalent applied force = p_0 (say)
             b = maximum displacement of the actual force-deformation curve
             = x_{max} (say)

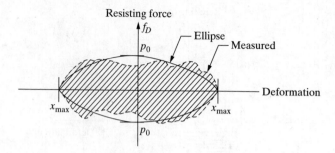

Figure 3.13   Measured and Equivalent damping energy per cycle.

$\therefore$ Amplitude of equivalent applied force $= p_0 = \dfrac{W_D}{\pi\, x_{max}}$ (v)

$\therefore$ Equivalent viscous damping $C_{eq} = \dfrac{p_0}{\varpi\, x_{max}}$ from Equation (3.30)

$$= \dfrac{1}{\varpi\, x_{max}}\, p_0 = \dfrac{1}{\varpi\, x_{max}}\dfrac{W_D}{\pi\, x_{max}} \text{ from (v)}$$

or, $\quad C_{eq} = \dfrac{W_D}{\pi\, \varpi\, x_{max}^2}$ (vi)

If $\quad C_c = 2\, m\, \omega = \dfrac{2k}{\omega}$ (vii)

The equivalent elastic stiffness can be measured by the area under the linear elastic force-deformation curve, that is, work done by the spring force W_S

$$W_S = \dfrac{1}{2}\, x_{max}\, f_S = \dfrac{1}{2}\, k\, x_{max}^2$$

or, $\quad k = \dfrac{2W_S}{x_{max}^2}$ (viii)

The damping ratio is given by $\xi = C_{eq}/C_c$
Making use of Equations (vi) and (vii),

$$\xi = \dfrac{W_D}{\pi\, \varpi\, x_{max}^2}\bigg/\dfrac{2k}{\omega}$$

Again, making use of Equation (viii),

$$\xi = \dfrac{\dfrac{W_D}{\pi\, \varpi\, x_{max}^2}}{\dfrac{2\,2W_S}{\omega\, x_{max}^2}}$$

or, $$\xi = \frac{W_D}{4\pi W_S} \quad \text{where } \omega = \varpi \text{ at resonance} \tag{3.31}$$

Knowing the area under the work done by the damped force and elastic force, the equivalent damping ratio can be determined.

3.7 MEASUREMENT OF COULOMB DAMPING

Let us determine equivalent viscous damping for a system with Coulomb damping. Equation (vi) can be re-written as:

$$W_D = \pi \, \varpi x_{max}^2 C_{eq}$$

or, $$W_D = \pi \, \varpi x_{max}^2 \xi_{eq} 2\frac{k}{\omega} = 2\pi\xi_{eq}\frac{\varpi}{\omega}k\,x_{max}^2 = 4\pi\xi_{eq}\frac{\varpi}{\omega}W_S \tag{3.32}$$

or, $$\xi_{eq} = \frac{1}{4\pi\left(\dfrac{\varpi}{\omega}\right)}\frac{W_D}{W_S} \tag{3.33}$$

Coulomb damping will produce a rectangular hysteresis loop as shown in Figure 3.14. The area under the curve is given by

$$W_D = 4Fx_{max}$$

$$\xi_{eq} = \frac{4Fx_{max}}{4\pi\left(\dfrac{\varpi}{\omega}\right)\dfrac{1}{2}kx_{max}^2} = \frac{2}{\pi}\frac{1}{\left(\dfrac{\varpi}{\omega}\right)}\frac{F}{k}\frac{1}{x_{max}} = \frac{2}{\pi}\frac{1}{\left(\dfrac{\varpi}{\omega}\right)}\frac{x_F}{x_{max}} \tag{3.34}$$

where $$x_F = \frac{F}{k} = \frac{\mu mg}{k}$$

For a system subjected to harmonic loading, the maximum dynamic displacement can be determined from the dynamic amplification factor discussed earlier.

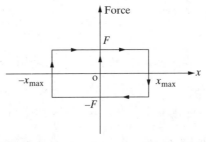

Figure 3.14   Hysteresis loop for Columb friction.

3.8 ILLUSTRATIVE EXAMPLES

Example 3.3

A SDOF system is subjected to a sinusoidal force. At resonance, the displacement amplitude is 70 mm. At an exciting frequency of one-fifth of the natural frequency of the system,
the displacement amplitude was measured to be 10 mm. Determine the damping ratio.

Solution

Dynamic amplification factor $D = \dfrac{1}{\sqrt{(1-\beta^2)^2 + (2\beta\xi)^2}}$

At frequency ratio $\beta = 1$,

$$D = \frac{70}{x_{static}} = \frac{1}{\sqrt{(2\times 1 \times \xi)^2}} \tag{i}$$

At a frequency ratio $\beta = 1/5$,

$$D = \frac{10}{x_{static}} = \frac{1}{\sqrt{(1-0.2^2)^2 + (2\times 0.2 \times \xi)^2}} \tag{ii}$$

Dividing Equations (i) and (ii) and solving for ξ gives, $\xi = 6.85\%$
If at an exciting frequency of 2.5 times natural frequency, the same displacement ampli-
tude of 10 mm is again observed, determine the damping ratio.
At a frequency ratio $\beta = 2.5$

$$D = \frac{10}{x_{static}} = \frac{1}{\sqrt{(1-2.5^2)^2 + (2\times 2.5 \times \xi)^2}} \tag{iii}$$

Dividing Equations (i) and (iii), and solving for ξ gives, $\xi = 0.40$ or 40%.
The damping plays a very significant role on the magnification depending upon the frequency ratio.   ◻

Example 3.4

A SDOF system has a mass $m = 35$ kN s²/m, damping $c = 27.5$ kN s/m and stiffness
$k = 6000$ kN/m. It is subjected to a sinusoidal force having amplitude $p_0 = 100$ kN.
Determine the peak response if the forcing frequency is (i) 12.5 rad/sec and (ii) 3.5 rad/sec.

Solution

Natural frequency of vibration $\omega = \sqrt{\dfrac{k}{m}} = \sqrt{\dfrac{6000}{35}} = 13.09$ rad/sec

or, Period $T = 0.48$ sec

Critical damping $c_c = 2m\omega = 2\sqrt{km} = 2\sqrt{35\times 6000} = 916.5$ kNs/m

Damping ratio $\xi = c/c_c = 27.5/916.5 = 0.03$ or 3%

Case 1: Frequency ratio $\beta = \bar{\omega}/\omega = 12.5/13.09 = 0.955$

Dynamic amplification factor $D = \dfrac{1}{\sqrt{(1-\beta^2)^2 + (2\beta\xi)^2}} = 9.52$

Static displacement $D_{ST} = p_0/k = 100/6000 = 0.0167$ m

$\therefore$ Peak dynamic displacement $= 9.52 \times 0.0167 = 0.159$ m

This is quite close to resonance.

Case 2: Frequency ratio $\beta = \bar{\omega}/\omega = 3.5/13.09 = 0.267$

Dynamic amplification factor $D = \dfrac{1}{\sqrt{(1-\beta^2)^2 + (2\beta\xi)^2}} = 1.077$

$\therefore$ Peak dynamic displacement $= 1.077 \times 0.0167 = 0.018$ m

Thus, there is little amplification as the forcing frequency is quite away from resonance.

$\square$

Example 3.5

A portal frame supports a machine that exerts a sinusoidal force of 8.5 kN at a frequency of 1.75 Hz. The mass of the machine is 4000 kg and is added to that of the frame. The mass of the frame at the floor level is 5000 kg and lateral stiffness of the frame is 4×10^6 N/m.

(a) Determine the steady state amplitude of vibration, if damping ratio is 4%.
(b) What would be the steady state amplitude if the forcing frequency was in resonance with the supporting structure?

Solution

Given $p_0 = 8.5$ kN $= 8500$ N, $\bar{f} = 1.75$ Hz or, $\bar{\omega} = 2\pi 1.75$ rad/sec

Lateral stiffness $k = 4 \times 10^6$ N/m

The applied force $p(t) = p_0 \sin \bar{\omega} t = 8500 \sin (2\pi 1.75\ t)$

or, $p(t) = 8500 \sin 11\ t$

Maximum static deflection $\Delta st = p_0/k = 8500/4 \times 10^6 = 0.002125\ m = 2.125$ mm

Total mass $= 5000 + 4000 = 9000$ kg

Natural frequency of the total system $\omega = \sqrt{\dfrac{k}{m}} = \sqrt{\dfrac{4 \times 10^6}{9000}} = 21.08$ rad/sec

or, $f = \omega/2\pi = 3.356$ Hz

$\therefore$ Frequency ratio $\beta = \bar{\omega}/\omega = \bar{f}/f = 1.75/3.356 = 0.521$

Dynamic amplification factor $D = \dfrac{1}{\sqrt{(1-\beta^2)^2 + (2\beta\xi)^2}} = 1.371$ for $\xi = 4\%$

$\therefore$ Steady state amplitude $= D\ x_{st} = 1.371 \times 2.125 = 2.92$ mm

At resonance, $\beta = 1$

$\therefore$ Dynamic amplification factor $D = \dfrac{1}{2\xi} = 1/0.08 = 12.5$

$\therefore$ Steady state amplitude $= D\ x_{st} = 12.5 \times 2.125 = 26.56$ mm $\square$

Example 3.6

In a SDOF system, the damping force is proportional to the square of speed. Determine the equivalent viscous damping for this system.

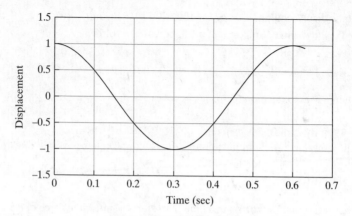

Figure 3.15 Cosine function.

Solution

It is given that $f_D \propto \pm (\dot{x}(t))^2$ or $f_D = \pm \alpha\, (\dot{x}(t))^2$ (i)

where α = damping coefficient

The energy dissipated per cycle $= W_D = 2 \int\limits_{-x_0}^{x_0} (\alpha \dot{x}^2)\, dx$

Let $x(t) = x_0 \cos \varpi t$ (Figure 3.15)

$\therefore$ $dx = -\varpi\, x_0 \sin \varpi t\; dt$

or, $dx = \dot{x}\, dt$

$\therefore$ $W_D = 2 \int\limits_{-x_0}^{x_0} (\alpha \dot{x}^3)\, dt$ (ii)

Let us find the limits in terms of ϖ.

When $x = -x_0$

$\cos \varpi t = -1$

or, $\cos \dfrac{2\pi}{\overline{T}} t = -1$

or, $t = \dfrac{\overline{T}}{2} = \dfrac{\pi}{\varpi}$

When $x = x_0$

$\cos \varpi t = 1$

or, $t = 0$

$\therefore$ $W_D = 2 \int\limits_{\frac{\pi}{\varpi}}^{0} (\alpha \dot{x}^3)\, dt = 2 \int\limits_{\frac{\pi}{\varpi}}^{0} \alpha (-x_0 \varpi \sin \varpi t)^3\, dt$

$= -2\alpha x_0^3 \varpi^3 \int\limits_{\frac{\pi}{\varpi}}^{0} \sin^3 \varpi t\, dt$

$$= -2\alpha x_0^3 \varpi^3 \left.\frac{-1}{3\varpi}\cos\varpi t \; (\sin^2\varpi t + 2)\right|_{\frac{\pi}{\varpi}}^{0}$$

$$= \frac{8}{3}\alpha\varpi^2 x_0^3$$

∴ Equivalent damping $C_{eq} = \dfrac{W_D}{\pi\varpi x_{max}^2} = \dfrac{8/3\alpha\varpi^2 x_0^3}{\pi\varpi x_0^2}$

or, $C_{eq} = \dfrac{8}{3\pi}\alpha\varpi x_0$ ☐

Example 3.7

A system of mass 20 kg and stiffness 15000 N/m is subjected to Coulomb damping. If the mass is driven harmonically by a 100 N force at 6 Hz, determine the equivalent viscous damping coefficient if the coefficient of friction is 0.35.

Solution

Forcing frequency $\varpi = 2\pi f = 2\pi(6) = 37.70$ rad/sec

Natural frequency $\omega = \sqrt{(k/m)} = \sqrt{(15000/20)} = 27.38$ rad/sec

Frequency ratio $\beta = 37.70/27.38 = 1.37$

$$x_F = \frac{F}{k} = \frac{\mu mg}{k} = \frac{0.35 \times 20 \times 9.81}{15000} = 4.578 \times 10^{-3}\,\text{m}$$

$$x_{static} = 100/15000 = 6.666 \times 10^{-3}\text{ m}$$

$$D = [(1-\beta^2)^2 + (2\xi\beta)^2]^{-0.5}$$

$$\frac{x_{max}}{x_{static}} = \frac{1}{\sqrt{(1-\beta^2)^2 + (2\beta\xi)^2}}$$

∴ $$x_{max} = \frac{6.666 \times 10^{-3}}{\sqrt{(1-1.37^2)^2 + \left(2 \times 1.37 \times \xi_{eq}\right)^2}}$$

Also, $$\xi_{eq} = \frac{2}{\pi}\left(\frac{1}{\dfrac{\varpi}{\omega}}\right)\frac{x_F}{x_{max}} = \frac{2 \times 4.578 \times 10^{-3}}{\pi \times 1.37 \times x_{max}}$$

Equating the value of x_{max} from these two equations, we obtain,

$$\xi_{eq} = 0.57 \quad \text{or} \quad \xi_{eq} = 57\%$$ ☐

PROBLEMS

3.1 Consider a SDOF system having a mass $m = 8$ kg and stiffness $k = 3000$ N/m. It is subjected to a harmonic force $p_0 \cos \varpi t$, where $p_0 = 50$ N and forcing frequency is 3 Hz. If the system is initially at rest, plot the steady state response time history.

3.2 How the response will change in problem 3.1, if the initial conditions are $x(0) = 0$ and $\dot{x}(0) = 0.1$ m/s?

3.3 How the response in problem 3.1 will change if the damping ratio is 5%?

3.4 Consider a SDOF system having a mass $m = 30$ kN s²/m, damping $c = 50$ kN s/m and stiffness $k = 4000$ kN/m. It is subjected to a harmonic force having an amplitude of $p_0 = 150$ kN. For $x(0) = 0.02$ m and $\dot{x}(0) = 0.1$ m/s. Plot

(a) the transient response time history

(b) the steady state response time history

(c) total response time history

(d) inertia, damping and spring force time history

(Hint: You may make use of MS-EXCEL worksheet)

3.5 In problem 3.4 determine the magnification factor if (i) $\varpi = 20$ rad/sec and (ii) $\varpi = 5$ rad sec.

3.6 A SDOF system is subjected to a sinusoidal force. At resonance, the displacement amplitude is 100 mm. At an exciting frequency of one-third of the natural frequency of the system, the displacement amplitude was measured to be 25 mm. Determine the damping ratio.

3.7 A SDOF system is subjected to a sinusoidal excitation. It was observed that at resonance the amplitude is eight times of that at a frequency ratio of 3. Estimate the damping ratio.

3.8 The mass m, stiffness k and natural frequency of an undamped SDOF system are unknown. These properties are to be determined by harmonic excitation tests. At an excitation frequency of 4 Hz, the response tends to increase without any bound. Next, a mass $\Delta m = 15$ kg is attached to the mass m and the resonance test is repeated. This time resonance occurs at $f = 3$ Hz. Determine the mass and stiffness of the system.

3.9 A system of mass 12 kg and stiffness 15000 N/m exhibits Coulomb damping. If the mass is driven harmonically by a 120 N force at 25 Hz, determine the equivalent viscous damping coefficient if the coefficient of friction is 0.15.

3.10 In a resonant vibration test, it was noted that at frequency ratios of 0.97 and 1.05, the maximum amplitude was $1/\sqrt{2}$ of that at the resonance. Estimate the damping ratio.

3.11 A SDOF system was subjected to sinusoidal loading at different frequencies and the steady state amplitude of acceleration was recorded as follows:

Frequency Hz	Acceleration amplitude, (10^{-2}) g	Frequency Hz	Acceleration amplitude, (10^{-2})g
2.10	0.55	2.21	7.2
2.11	0.7	2.22	6.2
2.12	0.9	2.23	5.3
2.13	1.3	2.24	4.7
2.14	1.9	2.25	3.95
2.15	2.5	2.26	3.4

(Continued)

Frequency Hz	Acceleration amplitude, (10^{-2}) g	Frequency Hz	Acceleration amplitude, (10^{-2})g
2.16	3.4	2.27	2.7
2.17	6.5	2.28	2.1
2.18	9.4	2.29	1.7
2.19	10.2	2.30	1.6
2.20	8.5		

Determine the natural frequency of vibration and damping ratio.

MATLAB APPLICATIONS

3.12 A single degree of freedom system has a mass of 40 kg, damping ratio of 5% and stiffness of 2000 N/m. It is subjected to a periodic forcing function $P_0 \sin \omega t$, where $P_0 = 1000$ N and forcing frequency $\omega = 10$ rad/sec. Using MATLAB function 'diff' determine

(a) the maximum displacement from rest position, $x(0) = 0$ and $v(0) = 5$ mm/s.

(b) the response of the system at 2 sec.

(c) the maximum force applied to dash pot.

(d) the angle by which the displacement lags the applied force.

3.13 Derive the expressions for magnification factors for velocity and acceleration for a steady state damped vibration. Using MATLAB function 'diff' plot the dynamic magnification factors for displacement, velocity and acceleration vs. frequency ratio and damping ratio.

3.14 A single degree of freedom system has a mass of 75 kg and stiffness of 1500 N/m and exhibits Coulomb damping with coefficient of friction of 0.12. The initial conditions are $x(0) = 0.2$ m, and $\dot{x}(0) = 0$. Plot its response and determine how long does it take for the system to come to rest.

4 Single Degree of Freedom System: Periodic Loading

4.1 INTRODUCTION

Sometimes it is very difficult to express dynamic loading in terms of an equation. If this loading happens to be periodic as shown in Figure 4.1, then it is possible to express it in the form of Fourier trigonometric series. Each term of the Fourier series represents a harmonic component. The response of a SDOF system due to harmonic loading has already been computed earlier. The response to each term of the series is then merely the response to a harmonic loading, and by the principle of superposition the total response is sum of response of each individual harmonic term. The response of a SDOF system to a periodic loading is examined with the help of Fourier series. The load and response terms are expressed in terms of trigonometric series or exponential series. The response of a SDOF system can be studied in frequency domain through a Fourier transform pair. The Fourier series representation involves intensive mathematics and integration. The final expressions may sometimes be quite lengthy. Therefore, it is highly recommended that these equations should be developed in graphics form using MS Excel or MATLAB in order to appreciate the power of the Fourier series.

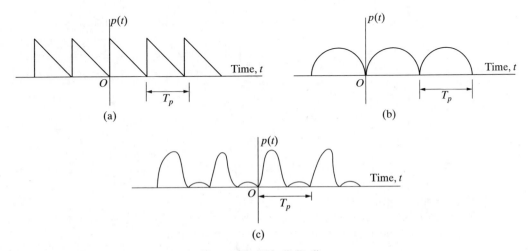

Figure 4.1 Periodic loading.

4.2 FOURIER SERIES

A periodic function $p(t)$ can be expressed by the Fourier series:

$$p(t) = a_0 + \sum_{n=1}^{\infty} a_n \cos n\varpi_1 t + \sum_{n=1}^{\infty} b_1 \sin n\varpi_1 t \qquad (4.1a)$$

or,

$$p(t) = a_0 + \sum_{n=1}^{\infty} a_n \cos \frac{2\pi n}{T_p} t + \sum_{n=1}^{\infty} b_n \sin \frac{2\pi n}{T_p} t \qquad (4.1b)$$

where

n = number of harmonics and varies from 1 to ∞

ϖ_1 = first harmonic frequency of the load function = $\dfrac{2\pi}{T_p}$

$\varpi_n = n\varpi_1$

T_p = period of the load function

The coefficients a_0, a_n and b_n can be expressed in terms of $p(t)$ because the sine and cosine functions are orthogonal:

$$a_0 = \frac{1}{T_p} \int_0^{T_p} p(t)\,dt$$

$$a_n = \frac{2}{T_p} \int_0^{T_p} p(t) \cos \frac{2\pi n}{T_p} t \qquad n = 1, 2, 3 \dots \qquad (4.2)$$

and

$$b_n = \frac{2}{T_p} \int_0^{T_p} p(t) \sin \frac{2\pi n}{T_p} t \qquad n = 1, 2, 3, \dots$$

The orthogonality property of the trigonometric functions can be stated as follows:

$$\int_0^T \sin n\omega_1 t \, \sin m\omega_1 t \, dt = \begin{cases} 0 & m \neq n \\ T/2 & m = n \end{cases}$$

$$\int_0^T \cos n\omega_1 t \, \cos m\omega_1 t \, dt = \begin{cases} 0 & m \neq n \\ T/2 & m = n \end{cases}$$

$$\int_0^T \cos n\omega_1 t \, \sin m\omega_1 t \, dt = 0 \qquad (4.3)$$

where, n and m are integers.

When an arbitrary periodic loading has been expressed in the Fourier series in the form of Equation (4.1), it is apparent that it consists of a

(i) constant load – average load value represented by coefficient a_0, plus

(ii) a series of harmonic loads of frequencies $n\bar{\omega}_1$ and amplitudes a_n and b_n

4.3 UNDAMPED SYSTEM

The total response produced in an undamped SDOF structure by each sine term of the harmonic loading series is given as follows:

$$x(t) = \frac{p_0}{k} \frac{1}{(1-\beta^2)} (\sin \bar{\omega} t - \beta \sin \omega t) \tag{4.4}$$

The steady state response can be determined by omitting the transient term ($\sin \omega t$), as follows:

Sine terms

$$x_n(t) = \frac{b_n}{k} \frac{1}{1-\beta_n^2} \sin n \bar{\omega}_1 t \tag{4.5a}$$

where

$$\beta_n = \frac{n\bar{\omega}_1}{\omega} = \frac{nT}{T_p} \tag{4.5b}$$

Cosine terms

Similarly, the response due to the cosine terms can be determined:

$$x_n(t) = \frac{a_n}{k} \frac{1}{1-\beta_n^2} \cos n \bar{\omega}_1 t \tag{4.5c}$$

Constant term

$$x_0 = a_0/k \tag{4.5d}$$

The total periodic steady state response of the undamped structure can be expressed as follows:

$$x(t) = \frac{1}{k} [a_0 + \sum_{n=1}^{\infty} \frac{1}{1-\beta_n^2} (a_n \cos n\bar{\omega}_1 t + b_n \sin n\bar{\omega}_1 t)] \tag{4.6}$$

where the load amplitude coefficients are given by Equation (4.2).

4.4 DAMPED SYSTEM

To take account of damping in evaluating the response of a SDOF structure to a periodic loading, it is necessary merely to substitute the damped harmonic response expression in the form of Equation (3.11) for the undamped response expressions in Equation (4.6). The total steady state response is given by:

$$x(t) = \frac{1}{k}(a_0 + \sum_{n=1}^{\infty} \frac{1}{(1-\beta_n^2)^2 + (2\xi\beta_n)^2}$$

$$\{[a_n 2\xi \beta_n + b_n(1-\beta_n^2)]\sin n\bar{\omega}_1 t$$

$$+ [a_n(1-\beta_n^2) - b_n 2\xi\beta_n]\cos n\bar{\omega}_1 t\} \tag{4.7}$$

4.5 EXPONENTIAL FORM OF FOURIER SERIES SOLUTION

The Fourier series expressions of Equations (4.1) and (4.2) can also be written in exponential form by substituting for the trigonometric functions, the corresponding exponential terms given by Euler's equation, namely

$$\sin x = -i\frac{(e^{ix} - e^{-ix})}{2}$$

$$\cos x = \frac{(e^{ix} + e^{-ix})}{2} \tag{4.8}$$

The result is

$$p(t) = \sum_{n=-\infty}^{\infty} C_n e^{in\bar{\omega}_1 t} \tag{4.9a}$$

where,

$$C_n = \frac{1}{T_p} \int_0^{T_p} p(t) e^{-in\bar{\omega}_1 t} dt \tag{4.9b}$$

Having expressed the arbitrary periodic loading in the exponential Fourier series form, by means of Equations (4.9a) and (4.9b), let us write the response in the exponential form.

The equation of motion can be written as follows:

$$m\ddot{x}(t) + c\dot{x}(t) + kx(t) = p(t) = e^{i\bar{\omega}t} \tag{4.10}$$

↑ unit complex forcing function

Its steady state solution is of the form

$$x(t) = H(\bar{\omega})p(t) \tag{4.11a}$$

$$x(t) = H(\bar{\omega})e^{i\bar{\omega}t} \tag{4.11b}$$

where $H(\bar{\omega})$ = complex frequency response function.
Let us differentiate Equation (4.11b) twice

$$\dot{x}(t) = i\bar{\omega}H(\bar{\omega})e^{i\bar{\omega}t} \tag{4.11c}$$

and

$$\ddot{x}(t) = -\bar{\omega}^2 H(\bar{\omega})e^{i\bar{\omega}t} \tag{4.11d}$$

Substituting Equations (4.11c) and (4.11d) in Equation (4.10) gives

$$\left(-\bar{\omega}^2 m + i\bar{\omega}c + k\right)H(\bar{\omega})e^{i\bar{\omega}t} = e^{i\bar{\omega}t}$$

or,

$$H(\bar{\omega}) = \frac{1}{-\bar{\omega}^2 m + i\bar{\omega}c + k} \tag{4.12a}$$

$$= \frac{1}{k(-\beta^2 + 2i\xi\beta + 1)} \tag{4.12b}$$

Consequently, the complex frequency response to a forcing frequency $\bar{\omega} = n\bar{\omega}_1$ will be

$$H(n\bar{\omega}_1) = \frac{1}{k(-n^2\beta_1^2 + 2in\beta_1\xi + 1)} \tag{4.13}$$

where, $\beta_1 = \bar{\omega}_1 / \omega$

Equation (4.13) shows that $H(n\bar{\omega}_1)$ is complex conjugate of $H(-n\bar{\omega}_1)$. Hence, it is possible to express the steady state response of a SDOF system to the forcing function which represents each term of the Fourier series. From the principle of superposition, it follows that the total steady state response of the system to any periodic forcing function can be written as:

$$x(t) = \sum_{n=-\infty}^{\infty} H(n\bar{\omega}_1) C_n e^{in\bar{\omega}_1 t} \tag{4.14}$$

where $H(n\bar{\omega}_1)$ is given by Equation (4.13) and C_n is given by Equation (4.9b).

Physical Significance of $H(\bar{\omega})$

Let us substitute Equation (4.12b) in Equation (4.11a),

$$x(t) = \frac{1}{k(1-\beta^2 + 2i\beta\xi)} \cdot p(t)$$

$$= \frac{1}{(1-\beta^2 + 2i\beta\xi)} \frac{p(t)}{k}$$

$$= \frac{1}{(1-\beta^2 + 2i\beta\xi)} x'(t)$$

or, $x(t) = H'(\bar{\omega}) \, x'(t)$ (4.15a)

where,

$$H'(\varpi) = \frac{1}{(1-\beta^2 + 2i\beta\xi)} \tag{4.15b}$$

$$x'(t) = \frac{p(t)}{k} \tag{4.15c}$$

It means when a periodic force $p(t)$ is applied statically to the SDOF system, the resulting displacement becomes $x'(t)$. Hence, $H(\bar{\omega})$ can be assumed to be a magnification factor representing the complex ratio of the steady state dynamic displacement to the displacement which results when the exciting force is applied statically.

The frequency response $H'(\bar{\omega})$ contains information regarding the phase lag of the response with respect to the exciting force function. The term $H'(\bar{\omega})$ can be written as the vector sum of the real part $R(\bar{\omega})$ and imaginary part $I(\bar{\omega})$

$$H'(\bar{\omega}) = R(\bar{\omega}) + I(\bar{\omega}) \tag{4.16a}$$

or, $$H'(\bar{\omega}) = |H(\bar{\omega})| \, e^{i\psi} \tag{4.16b}$$

where $|H(\bar{\omega})|$ and ψ are the amplitude and phase of the response $x(t)$ of the SDOF when it is excited by the simple harmonic forcing function $f(t) = k\ f'(t)$

$$\therefore \qquad x(t) = |H(\bar{\omega})|e^{i(\bar{\omega}t+\psi)} \qquad (4.17)$$

Multiplying both the numerator and denominator in Equation (4.15b) by $(1 - \beta^2 - 2i\beta\xi)$, we get

$$H'(\bar{\omega}) = \frac{1}{[(1-\beta^2)^2 + (2\beta\xi)^2]}(1-\beta^2 - i2\beta\xi)$$

The amplitude $|H(\bar{\omega})|$ is found to be

$$|H(\bar{\omega})| = \{(1-\beta^2)^2 + (2\xi\beta)^2\}^{-0.5} \qquad (4.18a)$$

and phase angle

$$\psi = \tan^{-1}\frac{2\xi\beta}{1-\beta^2} \qquad (4.18b)$$

4.6 FREQUENCY DOMAIN ANALYSIS

In the preceding sections, the force was known in the time domain, that is, the variation of the force with time was known. The response was also formulated in the time domain, that is, variation of response with time was determined. This is referred to as the *time-domain* analysis. The time-domain analysis described so far is completely general and can be used to evaluate the response of any linear SDOF system to any arbitrary input. Sometimes, the force function is arbitrary or random and it is not possible to determine its frequency. Moreover, it may have a variable frequency over its duration. It is sometimes convenient to perform the analysis in the frequency domain. The force and response are expressed in terms of frequency varying from 0 to 2π or 0 to $2n\pi$. It means both the force and the response will repeat after one complete 2π cycle. The frequency domain approach is similar in concept to the Fourier analysis procedure. Both these methods involve:

(i) expressing the applied loading in terms of harmonic components,
(ii) evaluating the response of the structure to each component and
(iii) superposing the harmonic responses to obtain the total structural response.

However, to apply the periodic load technique to arbitrary loadings, it is necessary to extend the Fourier series concept to the representation of non-periodic functions. Consider non-periodic loading shown by a solid line in Figure 4.2. If this function were to be represented by a Fourier series, the coefficients C_n obtained by Equation (4.9b) over the interval $0 < t < T_p$ would actually define the periodic function shown in the figure by the dash as well as solid lines. As a matter of fact, the loading in dash lines does not exist and must be eliminated. It is possible to eliminate the spurious repetitive loadings by extending loading period to infinity. Thus, there is a need to reformulate the Fourier series expression so that it extends over an infinite time range.

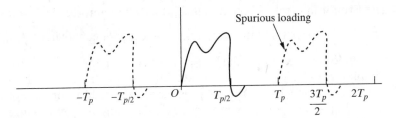

Figure 4.2 Non-periodic loading.

Let us rewrite Equations (4.9a) and (4.9b) in a slightly modified form using a notation defined as follows:

$$\frac{1}{T_p} = \frac{\bar{\omega}_1}{2\pi} \equiv \frac{\Delta\bar{\omega}}{2\pi}$$

$$n\bar{\omega}_1 = n\Delta\bar{\omega} \equiv \bar{\omega}_n \tag{4.19}$$

$$C_n \equiv \frac{1}{T_p}C(\bar{\omega}_n) = \frac{\Delta\bar{\omega}}{2\pi}C(\bar{\omega}_n)$$

The Fourier series Equations (4.9a) and (4.9b) now become:

$$p(t) = \frac{\Delta\bar{\omega}}{2\pi}\sum_{n=-\infty}^{\infty}C(\bar{\omega}_n)e^{i\bar{\omega}_n t} \tag{4.20}$$

$$C(\bar{\omega}_n) = T_p C_n = \int_{-T_p/2}^{T_p/2} p(t)e^{-i\bar{\omega}_n t}dt \tag{4.21}$$

Here advantage has been taken of the fact that the limits of the integral are arbitrary so long as they span one complete loading period. Now, if the loading period is extended to infinity $(T_p \to \infty)$ the frequency increment becomes an infinitesimal $(\Delta\bar{\omega} \to d\bar{\omega})$ and the discrete frequencies $\bar{\omega}_n$ become a continuous function $\bar{\omega}$.

Thus, in the limit, the Fourier series expression of Equation (4.20) becomes the following Fourier integral:

$$p(t) = \frac{1}{2\pi}\int_{-\infty}^{\infty} C(\bar{\omega})e^{i\bar{\omega}t}\,d\bar{\omega} \tag{4.22a}$$

in which the harmonic amplitude function is given by

$$C(\bar{\omega}) = \int_{-\infty}^{\infty} p(t)e^{-i\bar{\omega}t}\,dt \tag{4.22b}$$

The two integrals of Equations (4.22a) and (4.22b) are called a *Fourier Transform Pair* because the time function can be derived from the frequency function or vice versa by equivalent processes. A necessary condition for the existence of the Fourier Transform is that

The integral $I = \int_{-\infty}^{\infty} |p(t)|\,dt$ should be finite $\tag{4.23}$

The Fourier integral of Equation (4.22a) may be interpreted as representing an arbitrary loading as an infinite sum of harmonic component, where $\dfrac{1}{2\pi}C(\bar{\omega})$ defines the amplitude per unit of $\bar{\omega}$ of the load component at frequency $\bar{\omega}$. Multiplying this by the complex frequency response function, $H(\bar{\omega})$ yields the amplitude per unit $\bar{\omega}$ of the response component at frequency $\bar{\omega}$. Hence, the total response can be obtained by summing these response components over the entire frequency range

$$x(t) = \frac{1}{2\pi} \int\limits_{-\infty}^{\infty} H(\bar{\omega})C(\bar{\omega})e^{i\bar{\omega}t}\, d\bar{\omega} \tag{4.24}$$

where $C(\bar{\omega})$ is given by Equation (4.22b)
and $H(\bar{\omega})$ is given by Equation (4.12).

4.7 ILLUSTRATIVE EXAMPLES

Example 4.1

A square pulse is shown in Figure 4.3. Develop the Fourier series representation of $p(t)$.

Solution   The square pulse is having a period of T_p. It can be assumed to vary from $-T_p/2$ to $T_p/2$ for convenience. The Fourier series constants can be evaluated as follows:

$$a_0 = \frac{1}{T_p} \int\limits_{-T_p/2}^{T_p/2} p(t)\, dt \tag{i}$$

$$a_n = \frac{2}{T_p} \int\limits_{-T_p/2}^{T_p/2} \cos(n\bar{\omega}_1 t)\, dt \tag{ii}$$

and

$$b_n = \frac{2}{T_p} \int\limits_{-T_p/2}^{T_p/2} \sin(n\bar{\omega}_1 t)\, dt \tag{iii}$$

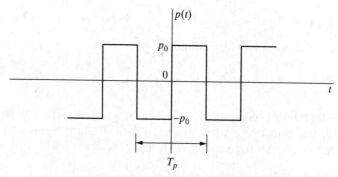

Figure 4.3   Square pulse loading.

where $\qquad p(t) = -P_0 \qquad$ for $-T_p/2 < t < 0$

$\qquad\qquad\qquad = P_0 \qquad\qquad$ for $0 < t < T_p/2$ $\qquad\qquad$ (iv)

Substituting the value of $p(t)$ from Equation (iv) in Equations (i) and (ii), gives $a_0 = 0$ and $a_n = 0$ because $p(t)$ is an odd function of t, that is, $p(t) = -p(-t)$ while a_0 and a_n are coefficients of even terms in the Fourier series.

Equations (iii) and (iv) give

$$b_n = \frac{4P_0}{T_p} \int_0^{T_p/2} \sin(n\varpi_1 t)\,dt$$

But $\qquad\qquad\qquad \varpi_1 = \frac{2\pi}{T_p}$

$\therefore \qquad\qquad\qquad b_n = -\frac{2P_0}{n\pi}(\cos(n\pi) - 1)$

or, $\qquad\qquad\qquad b_n = \frac{4P_0}{n\pi}$ for $n = 1, 3, 5,$ etc.

The Fourier series representation of the square pulse is given by

$$p(t) = \frac{4P_0}{\pi} \sum_{n=1,3,5,}^{\infty} \frac{1}{n}\sin(n\varpi_1 t)$$

It can be plotted for different values of $n = 1, 3, 5,$ etc. in MS-EXCEL. The convergence of different harmonic components of sine to the square pulse can be seen in Figure 4.4. The convergence will improve further by taking more number of harmonic terms. □

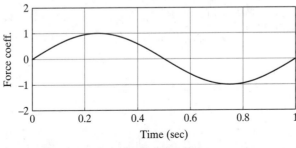

(a) First harmonic

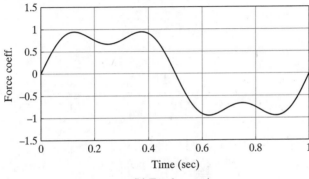

(b) Two harmonics

Figure 4.4 Fourier representation of the square pulse loading.

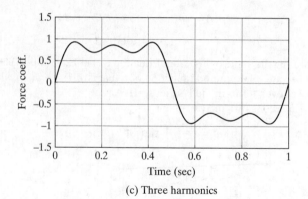

(c) Three harmonics

(d) Four harmonics

Figure 4.4   (Continued)

Example 4.2

Find the steady state response of an undamped SDOF system to a square pulse. Given $\omega = 4\,\varpi_1$.

Solution   The steady state response of an undamped SDOF subjected to a harmonic excitation $p_0 \sin \varpi t$ is given as follows:

$$x(t) = \frac{p_0}{k} \frac{1}{\left(1 - \beta^2\right)} \sin \varpi t$$

where $\beta = \varpi / \omega = n\,\varpi_1 / \omega = \beta_n$
The load term can be written as follows:

$$p(t) = \frac{4 p_0}{\pi} \sum_{n=1,3,5,}^{\infty} \frac{1}{n} \sin\left(n \varpi_1 t\right) \quad \text{for } n = 1, 3, 5, \text{etc.}$$

$$= 0 \qquad \text{for } n = 0, 2, 4, \text{etc.}$$

The nth term of the steady state response is of the form:

$$x_n = \frac{4 p_0}{n\pi}\left(\frac{1}{k}\right)\frac{\sin\left(n\varpi_1 t\right)}{\left(1 - \beta_n^2\right)}$$

Hence, the steady state response is given by

$$x(t) = \sum_{n=1,3,5}^{\infty} \frac{4 p_0}{k \pi} \frac{1}{n} \frac{\sin(n\varpi_1 t)}{\left(1 - \left(\dfrac{n\varpi_1}{\omega}\right)^2\right)}$$

Let us plot the amplitude of each harmonic term of load as well as displacement versus frequency.

$$p_n = \frac{4 p_0}{n\pi} \quad \text{or} \quad \frac{p_n}{p_0} = \frac{4}{n\pi}$$

or

$$\frac{p_n}{p_0} \frac{\pi}{4} = \frac{1}{n}, \quad \text{where } n = 1, 3, 5, \text{ etc.}$$

$$= 0 \quad n = 0, 2, 4, \text{ etc.}$$

Its plot is shown in Figure 4.5(a).

Similarly, the amplitude of each harmonic of the response term can be plotted as follows:

$$\frac{x_n}{\dfrac{p_0}{k}} = \frac{4}{n\pi\left(1 - \left(\dfrac{n\varpi_1}{\omega}\right)^2\right)} \quad \text{for } n = 1, 3, 5$$

$$= 0 \quad \text{for } n = 0, 2, 4, 6$$

Given $\varpi_1/\omega = \frac{1}{4}$,

$$\therefore \qquad \frac{x_n}{\dfrac{p_0}{k}} = \frac{4}{n\pi\left(1 - \left(\dfrac{n}{4}\right)^2\right)} \quad \text{for } n = \text{odd}$$

Its plot is shown in Figure 4.5(b).   □

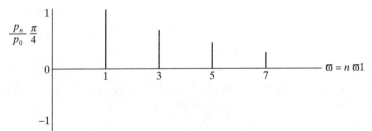

Figure 4.5(a)   Amplitude of Fourier force function.

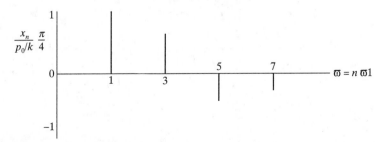

Figure 4.5(b)   Amplitude of Fourier response function.

Example 4.3

Express the square pulse of Example (4.1) in exponential form.

Solution   The Fourier pair is given by Equation (4.9):

$$p(t) = \sum_{n=-\infty}^{\infty} C_n e^{in\bar{\omega}_1 t} \qquad (4.9a)$$

where,

$$C_n = \frac{1}{T_p} \int_0^{T_p} p(t) e^{-in\bar{\omega}_1 t} dt \qquad (4.9b)$$

The constant term C_n can be written as follows:

$$C_n = \frac{1}{T_p} \int_0^{T_{p/2}} p_0 e^{-i\bar{\omega}t} dt + \frac{1}{T_p} \int_{T_{p/2}}^{T_p} (-p_0) e^{-i\bar{\omega}t} dt$$

$$= \frac{-p_0}{i\bar{\omega}T_p} \left[\left| e^{-i\bar{\omega}t} \right|_0^{T_{p/2}} + \left| -e^{-i\bar{\omega}t} \right|_{T_{p/2}}^{T_p} \right]$$

But

$$\bar{\omega} = n\,\bar{\omega}_1 = n\,\frac{2\pi}{T_p}$$

∴

$$e^{-in\bar{\omega}_1 T_p/2} = e^{-in\pi} = 1 \qquad \text{for } n \text{ even}$$

and

$$e^{-in\bar{\omega}_1 T_p} = e^{-i2\pi n} = -1 \qquad \text{for } n \text{ odd}$$

Hence,

$$C_n = \frac{i p_0}{2\pi n} \left[2e^{-in\pi} - 2 \right]$$

or,

$$C_n = \frac{-2 p_0 i}{n\pi} \qquad \text{for } n \text{ odd}$$

$$= 0 \qquad \text{for } n \text{ even}$$

This can also be written as follows as amplitude of imaginary and real terms:

$$I(C_n) = \frac{-2 p_0}{n\pi} \qquad \text{for } n \text{ odd} \qquad (i)$$

$$R(C_n) = 0 \qquad \text{for } n \text{ even} \qquad (ii)$$

The expression (i) and the amplitude of the Fourier force function can be depicted as shown in Figures 4.6(a) and 4.6(b). □

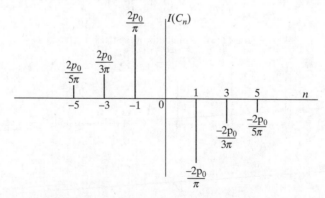

Figure 4.6(a)   Amplitude of imaginary harmonic terms.

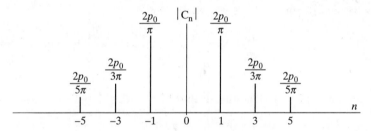

Figure 4.6(b)   Amplitude of Fourier force function.

Example 4.4

Determine an expression for steady state response of an undamped SDOF system subjected to a square pulse with $\omega = 4\,\omega_1$ in exponential form.

Solution   Let us write the expression for the steady state response of SDOF system as given in Equations 4.10(a) and 4.10(b).

$$x(t) = H(\omega)p(t)$$

or,

$$x(t) = H(\omega)C_n e^{i\omega t}$$

where,

$$H(\omega) = \frac{1}{k\left(1 - \beta^2 + i2\beta\xi\right)}$$

For an undamped system, $\xi = 0$,

$$\therefore \qquad H(\omega) = \frac{1}{k\left(1 - \beta^2\right)} = \frac{1}{k\left[1 - \left(\dfrac{n\omega_1}{\omega}\right)^2\right]}$$

or,

$$H(\omega) = \frac{1}{k\left[1 - \left(\dfrac{n}{4}\right)^2\right]}$$

Also, derived earlier, $\qquad C_n = 0$ $\qquad\qquad\qquad$ for n even

$$C_n = \frac{-2\,p_0 i}{n\pi} \qquad\qquad\qquad \text{for } n \text{ odd}$$

$\therefore$ n^{th} term of response can be written as $x_n = H(\omega)C_n$

or,

$$x_n = \frac{-i2\,p_0}{n\pi k\left[1 - \left(\dfrac{n}{4}\right)^2\right]} \qquad\qquad \text{for } n \text{ odd}$$

$$= 0 \qquad\qquad\qquad\qquad \text{for } n \text{ even}$$

$$\therefore \qquad |x_n| = \left|\frac{2\,p_0/\pi k}{n\left[1 - \left(\dfrac{n}{4}\right)^2\right]}\right| \qquad\qquad \text{for } n \text{ odd}$$

Alternatively, this can be re-written as follows:

$$\frac{x_n \pi/2}{p_0/k} = \frac{1}{n\left[1-\left(\dfrac{n}{4}\right)^2\right]} = \alpha \qquad \text{for } n \text{ odd}$$

This can be plotted as shown in Figure 4.7. ◻

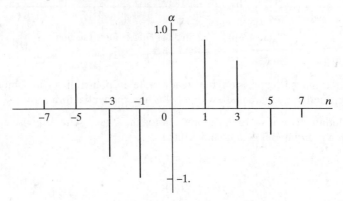

Figure 4.7 Amplitude of Fourier response function.

Example 4.5

Determine the Fourier Transform of the rectangular pulse, which is symmetric about $t = 0$ as shown in Figure 4.8(a) in frequency domain.

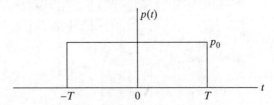

Figure 4.8(a) Square pulse

Solution The Fourier transform pairs are as follows:

$$p(t) = \frac{1}{2\pi} \int_{-\infty}^{\infty} C(\bar{\omega})e^{i\bar{\omega}t}\, d\bar{\omega} \qquad (4.22a)$$

in which the harmonic amplitude function is given by,

$$C(\bar{\omega}) = \int_{-\infty}^{\infty} p(t)e^{-i\bar{\omega}t}\, dt \qquad (4.22b)$$

Equation (4.22b) gives,

$$C(\bar{\omega}) = \int_{-T}^{T} p_0 e^{-i\bar{\omega}t}\, dt$$

or,

$$= \left. -\frac{p_0}{i\bar{\omega}}\left(e^{-i\bar{\omega}t} - e^{i\bar{\omega}t}\right)\right|_{-T}^{T}$$

or,
$$= \frac{i p_0}{\varpi}((\cos\varpi T - i\sin\varpi T) - (\cos\varpi T + i\sin\varpi T))$$

or,
$$C(\varpi) = 2 p_0 T\left(\frac{\sin\varpi T}{\varpi T}\right) \quad \text{Real function}$$

It can be plotted as shown in Figure 4.8(b). ☐

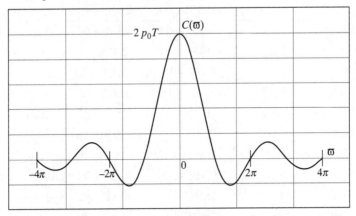

Figure 4.8(b)   Plot of Fourier transform pair $C(\varpi)$.

Example 4.6

A SDOF system has a mass of 100 kg, stiffness of 100 kN/m and a damping of 10 per cent. It is subjected to a force as shown in Figure 4.9. Period of the forcing function is 0.12 sec and its duration is also 0.12 sec. Determine the Fourier constants of force and displacement up to 20 terms. Also, plot the steady state response.

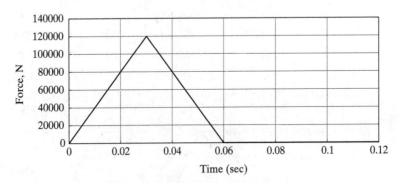

Figure 4.9   Forcing function

Solution

Natural frequency of SDOF = 31.623 rad/sec
Forcing frequency = $2\pi/0.12$ = 52.36 rad/sec
    A computer code was written in FORTRAN using Equations (4.2) and (4.7), and the results are shown in Table 4.1.
    Fourier force coefficient $A_0 = 30000.000$
    Fourier displacement coefficient $X_0 = 0.300$
    The plot of the Fourier periodic force due to first 20 terms is shown in Figure 4.10 and that of the response in Figure 4.11. ☐

TABLE 4.1 FOURIER CONSTANTS FOR FORCE AND DISPLACEMENT TERMS

N	Frequency	Frequency Ratio	Fourier Force Coeff.		Fourier Displacement Coeff.	
			A(N) COS term	B(N) SINE term	X1(N) COS term	X2(N) SINE term
1	52.36	1.656	−2.13E − 03	4.86E + 04	−2.70E − 01	−5.12E − 02
2	104.72	3.312	−2.43E + 04	−2.13E − 03	−1.61E − 03	2.43E − 02
3	157.08	4.967	7.09E − 04	−5.40E + 03	2.28E − 03	9.56E − 05
4	209.44	6.623	0.00E + 00	0.00E + 00	0.00E + 00	0.00E + 00
5	261.799	8.279	−4.25E − 04	1.95E + 03	−2.88E − 04	−7.06E − 06
6	314.159	9.935	−2.70E + 03	−7.09E − 04	−5.62E − 06	2.76E − 04
7	366.519	11.59	3.04E − 04	−9.93E + 02	7.44E − 05	1.29E − 06
8	418.879	13.246	0.00E + 00	0.00E + 00	0.00E + 00	0.00E + 00
9	471.239	14.902	−2.36E − 04	6.00E + 02	−2.72E − 05	−3.66E − 07
10	523.599	16.558	−9.73E + 02	−4.25E − 04	−4.32E − 07	3.56E − 05
11	575.959	18.213	1.93E − 04	−4.02E + 02	1.22E − 05	1.34E − 07
12	628.319	19.869	0.00E + 00	0.00E + 00	0.00E + 00	0.00E + 00
13	680.678	21.525	−1.64E − 04	2.88E + 02	−6.22E − 06	−5.80E − 08
14	733.038	23.181	−4.96E + 02	−3.04E − 04	−8.00E − 08	9.25E − 06
15	785.398	24.836	1.42E − 04	−2.16E + 02	3.51E − 06	2.83E − 08
16	837.758	26.492	0.00E + 00	0.00E + 00	0.00E + 00	0.00E + 00
17	890.118	28.148	−1.25E − 04	1.68E + 02	−2.13E − 06	−1.51E − 08
18	942.478	29.804	−3.00E + 02	−2.36E − 04	−2.27E − 08	3.38E−06
19	994.838	31.46	1.12E − 04	−1.35E + 02	1.36E − 06	8.67E − 09
20	1047.198	33.115	0.00E + 00	0.00E + 00	0.00E + 00	0.00E + 00

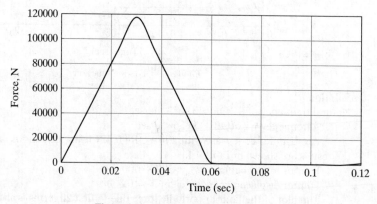

Figure 4.10 Fourier periodic force.

Displacement response

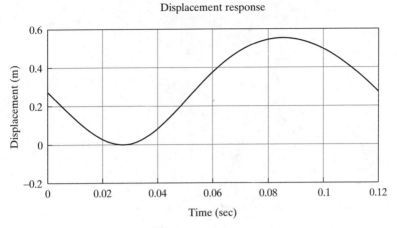

Figure 4.11   Steady state response.

4.8 MATLAB APPLICATIONS

MATLAB codes are written to represent periodic loading using Fourier series. Thereafter, response of a SDOF system can be obtained by using the results obtained in Chapter 3.

Example 4.7

Represent the triangular function shown in Figure 4.12 in terms of Fourier series using MATLAB.

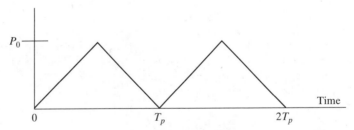

Figure 4.12   Triangular function.

Solution   The MATLAB code is written in the following parts:

Main module DOS4_1 calls MATLAB function 'quad'. The function 'quad' numerically evaluates an integral using Simpson rule.

Function curve1 calculates the constant term a_0

Function curve1c calculates the a_n coefficients of cosine terms

Function curve1s calculates the b_n coefficients of sine terms

The Fourier representation with 15 terms is shown in Figure 4.13.

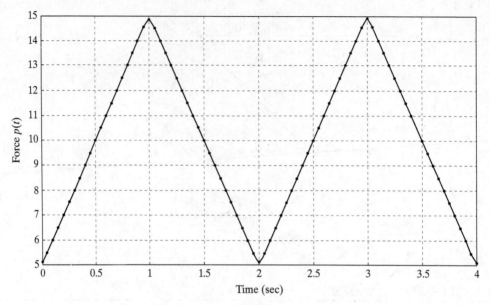

Figure 4.13 Fourier representation of triangular pulse.

```
-------------------
CODE DOS4_1     Triangular Function
-------------------


%    Dynamics of Structures by Ashok K. Jain I. I. T. Roorkee
%    DOS4_1
%    Fourier representation of a periodic force: Triangular function
%    Calls: curve1, curve1c and curve1s
%    curve1c: cosine constants; curve1s: sine constants
%    The program calls function "quad" to integrate and find Fourier constants
%    N: total number of terms to be included
%    T: period of periodic force
%    P: Amplitude of periodic force
%
close all;
clear all;
clc;
P = 10;
T = 2;
fprintf('Amplitude of periodic force = %.3g N\n',P);
fprintf('Period of force = %.3g sec\n',T);
a0 = quad(@(t)curve1(t,T,P),0,T,1e-9);
% for N=15:15
for N=1:10
    for n=1:N
        a(n)  = quad(@(t)curve1c(t,n,T,P),0,T,1e-9);
        b(n)  = quad(@(t)curve1s(t,n,T,P),0,T,1e-9);
    end
```

```
        Outp = 0;
        x=1;
        for  t=0:0.05:T*2
             c=0;
             s=0;
             for  n=1:N
                   c=c+a(n)*cos(t*2*pi*n/T);
                   s=s+b(n)*sin(t*2*pi*n/T);
             end
             Outp(x)=s+c+a0;
             x=x+1;
        end
        subplot (5,2,N)
        plot(0:0.05:T*2,Outp,'.-')
        grid on
        pause(1);
end
```

CODE CURVE1

```
%    curve1
%    Called by: DOS4_1
%    Fourier representation of a periodic force: Triangular function
%
function a = curve1(t,T,P)
w = 2*pi/T;
for d=1:length(t)
    if t(d)<=T/2
        p1(d)  = 2*t(d)*P/T;
    else
        p1(d)  = 2*(T-t(d))*P/T;
    end
end
a = (1/T)*p1;
end
```

CODE CURVE1C

```
%    curve1c
%    Called by: DOS4_1
%    Fourier representation of a periodic force: Triangular function
%    Computes constants for cosine terms
%
function a = curve1c(t,n,T,P)
```

```
w = 2*pi/T;
for d=1:length(t)
    if t(d)<=T/2
        p1(d) = 2*t(d)*P/T;
    else
        p1(d) = 2*(T-t(d))*P/T;
    end
end
a = (2/T)*p1.*cos(w*t*n);
end
```

```
-------------------
CODE CURVE1S
-------------------

%    curve1s
%    Called by: DOS4_1
%    Fourier representation of a periodic force: triangular function
%    Computes constants for sine terms
%
function b = curve1s(t,n,T,P)
w = 2*pi/T;
for d=1:length(t)
    if t(d)<=T/2
        p1(d) = 2*t(d)*P/T;
    else
        p1(d) = 2*(T-t(d))*P/T;
    end
end
b = (2/T)*p1.*sin(w*t*n);
end
----------------------
```

Example 4.8

Represent the ramp function shown in Figure 4.14 in terms of Fourier series using MATLAB.

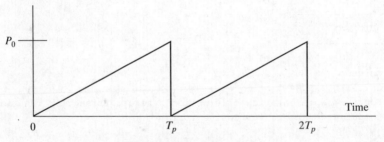

Figure 4.14   Ramp function.

Solution
The MATLAB code for ramp function is written in the following parts:

Main module DOS4_2 calls MATLAB function 'quad'. The function 'quad' numerically evaluates an integral using Simpson rule.

Function curve2 calculates the constant term a_0

Function curve2c calculates the a_n coefficients of cosine terms

Function curve2s calculates the b_n coefficients of sine terms

The Fourier representation of the ramp function with 15 terms is shown in Figure 4.15.

□

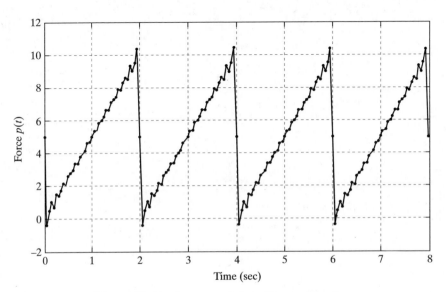

Figure 4.15   Fourier representation of the ramp function.

```
--------------------
CODE DOS4_2    RAMP Function
--------------------


%    Dynamics of Structures by Ashok K. Jain I. I. T. Roorkee
%    DOS4_2
%    Fourier representation of a periodic force: Ramp function
%    Calls: curve2, curve2c and curve2s
%    curve2c: cosine constants; curve2s: sine constants
%    The program calls function "quad" to integrate and find Fourier constants
%    N: total number of terms to be included
%    T: period of periodic force
%    P: Amplitude of periodic force
%
close all;
clear all;
```

```
clc;
P = 10;
T = 2;
fprintf('Amplitude of periodic force = %.3g N\n',P);
fprintf('Period of force = %.3g sec\n',T);
a0 = quad(@(t)curve2(t,T,P),0,T,1e-9);
for N=1:15
    for n=1:N
        a(n)  = quad(@(t)curve2c(t,n,T,P),0,T,1e-9);
        b(n)  = quad(@(t)curve2s(t,n,T,P),0,T,1e-9);
    end
    Outp = 0;
    x=1;
    for t=0:0.05:T*4
        c=0;
        s=0;
        for n=1:N
            c=c+a(n)*cos(t*2*pi*n/T);
            s=s+b(n)*sin(t*2*pi*n/T);
        end
        Outp(x)=s+c+a0;
        x=x+1;
    end

    plot(0:0.05:T*4,Outp,'.-')
    pause(1);
end

grid on;

--------------------
CODE CURVE2
--------------------


%    curve2
%    Called by: DOS4_2
%    Fourier representation of a periodic force: Ramp function
%
function a = curve2(t,T,P)
%
% Ramp function
%
w = 2*pi/T;
for d=1:length(t)

    if t(d)<=T
        p1(d) = t(d)*P/T;
    else
```

```
        p1(d) = 0;
    end
end
a = (1/T)*p1;
end
```

CODE CURVE2C

```
%    curve2c
%    Called by: DOS4_2
%    Fourier representation of a periodic force: Ramp function
%    Computes constants for cosine terms
%
function a = curve2c(t,n,T,P)
w = 2*pi/T;
for d=1:length(t)

    if t(d)<=T
        p1(d) = t(d)*P/T;
    else
        p1(d) = 0;
    end
end
a = (2/T)*p1.*cos(w*t*n);
end
```

CODE CURVE2S

```
%    curve2s
%    Called by: DOS4_2
%    Fourier representation of a periodic force: Ramp function
%    Computes constants for sine terms
%
function b = curve2s(t,n,T,P)
w = 2*pi/T;
for d=1:length(t)
    if t(d)<=T
        p1(d) = t(d)*P/T;
    else
        p1(d) = 0;
    end
end
b = (2/T)*p1.*sin(w*t*n);
end
```

4.9 HUMAN-INDUCED VIBRATIONS IN STRUCTURES

With the development of new materials, improvement in understanding of the behaviour of structures, construction technologies, and development of GUI-based analysis and design software, there is a demand for more slender and lighter structures such as large span building floors and footbridges. Forces are induced due to movement of the pedestrians. They may be walking slowly, normally or faster. They may be walking, running, jumping or dancing. There may be a single person or a group of persons (density) irrespective of age and built-up. The other feature is the synchronization of the walking pattern among the pedestrians and synchronization of human with the structure. The mass and damping of thin and slender structures can have significant influence due to human loading.

The human response to floor vibrations is a very complex phenomenon depending upon the magnitude and frequency of the motion, the environment and the human sensor itself. A continuous motion (steady state) may be more disturbing than an intermittent impact (transient). The reaction of a person depends very strongly as to what he was doing. The vibration frequencies between 2 and 8 Hz are more annoying. People sitting in offices or at home do not like vibrations having peak accelerations of about 0.5 per cent due to gravity. People engaged in some activity may accept vibrations about 10 times greater, that is 5 per cent of the acceleration due to gravity. People dining besides a dance floor, or exercising in a gym, or enjoying in a shopping mall will accept about 1.5 per cent of the acceleration due to gravity. The sensitivity within each occupancy also depends upon the duration of the vibration and remoteness of the source. Outside the frequency range of 2–8 Hz, people accept higher vibration accelerations.

4.9.1 Forces While Walking and Running

The human-induced force has three components: vertical, longitudinal, and lateral. The vertical component is about 40 per cent of the weight of the body. It is the largest component. The lateral component is much smaller while the longitudinal component is the least. During normal walking, the vertical forces have a frequency in the range of 1.3–2.4 Hz depending on the pace; while running, the frequency is in the range of 2–3.5 Hz. During walking, at least one foot is always in contact with the ground. While running, both foot may be off the ground at the same instant; also, the duration of contact while a foot is on the ground is relatively small.

During walking, the vertical component shows a typical double hump as shown in Figures 4.16(a) and 4.16(b). The first hump is the result of impact of the heel on the ground; while the second hump is due to push off by the toe. The amplitude of the force increases with the step frequency. Also, the next footfall begins just before the earlier one has finished. The load model for running or jumping can be represented by a half sine curve as shown in Figure 4.16(c). The net force during walking is shown in Figure 4.17. The walking load is much more complex than the running load. Both are periodic forces. The vertical component of the walking or running loads due to a single pedestrian can be represented by the Fourier series. The building floor or a

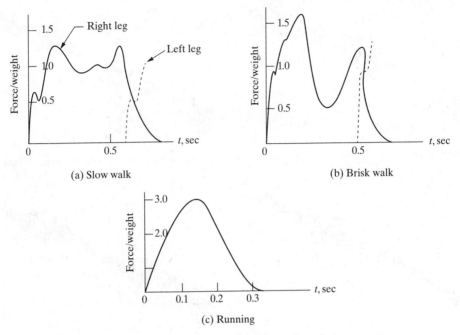

Figure 4.16   Force due to walking and running.

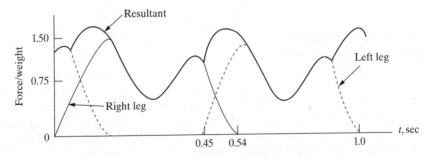

Figure 4.17   Combined force due to both legs while walking.

pedestrian bridge can be represented by a single degree of freedom system. The steady state response can be determined using the equations derived earlier.

4.9.2 Vibration Modes of a Bridge Deck

The modes of vibration of a RC bridge deck supported along the two opposite short supports are shown in Figure 4.18. The deck vibrates in vertical (flexure), lateral and torsional modes due to its flexibility. These vibration modes are very critical for its safety. The frequency of vibration for this deck varies from 0.33 Hz in the first mode to 8 Hz in the 12th mode. In 1940, the Tacoma Narrows bridge in the State of Washington, USA, collapsed within four months of its opening under a wind speed of only 64 kmph because of flexure – torsional mode also known as flutter mechanism.

Figure 4.18(a)   Mode 3 – Frequency = 1.75 Hz.

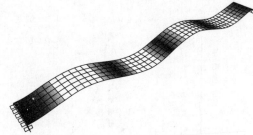

Figure 4.18(b)   Mode 5 – Frequency = 3 Hz.

Figure 4.18(c)   Mode 10 – Frequency = 6 Hz.

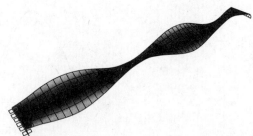

Figure 4.18(d)   Mode 12 – Frequency = 8 Hz.

The London Millennium footbridge spans over 332 m divided into a north span of 80 m, a central span of 144 m and a southern span of 108 m. On the opening day in June 2000, unexpected large lateral vibrations occurred mainly in the south span of the bridge and the bridge had to be closed. The frequencies of the movements were around 0.8 Hz, the first lateral mode of the south span. In the central span, movements took place at barely 0.5 Hz and 1.1 Hz, respectively, the first and second lateral modes. At the north side, movements occurred at a frequency around 1.0 Hz, the first lateral mode of the north span. The maximum lateral acceleration on the south and north span was about 2.5 m/s². Later special dampers were fitted to control the undesirable vibrations. Therefore, it is important to examine the frequencies and modes of vibrations of slender bridge decks.

4.9.3 Fourier Representation of Running Load

It is a periodic load as shown in Figure 4.19. It can be represented as follows:

$$p(t) = p_0 \sin\left(\frac{\pi}{t_d} t\right) \quad t \le t_d \tag{4.25a}$$

$$= 0 \qquad t_d \le t \le T_p \tag{4.25b}$$

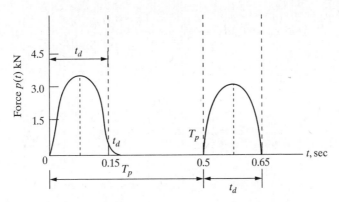

Figure 4.19   Force due to running.

The first part will lead to forced vibrations, whereas the second part will lead to free vibrations. The first part can be represented by the Fourier series, and the Fourier constants can be evaluated as follows:

$$p(t) = a_0 + \sum_{n=1}^{\infty} a_n \cos\varpi t + \sum_{n=1}^{\infty} b_n \sin\varpi t \tag{4.1a}$$

or,

$$p(t) = a_o + \sum_{n=1}^{\infty} a_n \cos\frac{2\pi n}{T_p}t + \sum_{n=1}^{\infty} b_n \sin\frac{2\pi n}{T_p}t \tag{4.1b}$$

where T_p represents period of the load function and the coefficients can be evaluated using Equation (4.2).
The coefficient a_0 is determined as follows:

$$a_0 = \frac{1}{T_p}\int_0^{t_d} p_0 \sin\left(\frac{\pi}{t_d}t\right)dt$$

Upon integration and simplification,

$$a_0 = \frac{2p_0}{\pi}\frac{t_d}{T_p} \tag{4.26a}$$

The coefficient a_n is determined as follows:

$$a_n = \frac{2p_0}{T_p}\int_0^{t_d} \sin\left(\frac{\pi}{t_d}t\right)\cos(n\varpi t)\,dt$$

or,

$$a_n = \frac{2p_0}{T_p}\int_0^{t_d} \sin\left(\frac{\pi}{t_d}t\right)\cos\left(\frac{2\pi n}{T_p}t\right)dt$$

By making use of the following trigonometric relations,

$$\int \sin mx \cos nx\,dx = -\frac{\cos(m-n)x}{2(m-n)} - \frac{\cos(m+n)x}{2(m+n)}$$

$$\int \sin mx \sin nx \, dx = \frac{\sin(m-n)x}{2(m-n)} - \frac{\sin(m+n)x}{2(m+n)}$$

$$\cos(\pi - x) = -\cos x; \; \sin(\pi - x) = \sin x$$

$$\cos(\pi + x) = -\cos x; \; \sin(\pi + x) = -\sin x$$

$$\cos 2x = 2\cos^2 x - 1 = 1 - 2\sin^2 x$$

We get,

$$a_n = \frac{4 p_0 \left(\dfrac{t_d}{T_p}\right) \cos^2\left(n\pi \dfrac{t_d}{T_p}\right)}{\pi \left[1 - 4n^2 \left(\dfrac{t_d}{T_p}\right)^2\right]} \tag{4.26b}$$

Similarly, the coefficient b_n is determined as follows:

$$b_n = \frac{2 p_0}{T_p} \int_0^{t_d} \sin\left(\frac{\pi}{t_d} t\right) \sin\left(\frac{2\pi n}{T_p} t\right) dt$$

Upon integration and simplification, we get,

$$b_n = \frac{4 p_0 \left(\dfrac{t_d}{T_p}\right) \sin\left(n\pi \dfrac{t_d}{T_p}\right) \cos\left(n\pi \dfrac{t_d}{T_p}\right)}{\pi \left[1 - 4n^2 \left(\dfrac{t_d}{T_p}\right)^2\right]} \tag{4.26c}$$

Now, it is possible to plot harmonics of the periodic force. The steady state response of the damped SDOF system can be determined using the equations derived from Chapter 3.

Steady State Response to Sine Force

The equation of motion is given by

$$m\ddot{x}(t) + c\dot{x}(t) + kx(t) = p_0 \sin \varpi t \tag{3.6}$$

Its particular solution was given by Equations (3.8), (3.9) and (3.10)

$$\text{Particular integral } x_p(t) = G_1 \sin \varpi t + G_2 \cos \varpi t \tag{3.8}$$

where,

$$G_1 = \frac{p_0}{k} \frac{1 - \beta^2}{(1 - \beta^2)^2 + (2\xi\beta)^2} \tag{3.9}$$

$$G_2 = \frac{p_0}{k} \frac{-2\xi\beta}{(1 - \beta^2)^2 + (2\xi\beta)^2} \tag{3.10}$$

The steady state response could be re-written as:

$$x(t) = \rho \sin(\bar{\omega}t - \theta) \tag{3.14b}$$

where

$$\rho = \frac{p_0}{k}[(1-\beta^2)^2 + (2\xi\beta)^2]^{-0.5} \tag{3.12}$$

and the phase angle θ by which the response lags behind the applied load is given by

$$\theta = \tan^{-1}\frac{2\xi\beta}{1-\beta^2} \qquad 0 < \theta < 180° \tag{3.13}$$

Steady State Response to Cosine Force

The equation of motion is given by

$$m\ddot{x}(t) + c\dot{x}(t) + kx(t) = p_0\cos\bar{\omega}t \tag{3.6}$$

Its particular solution is given by Equation (3.8), where

$$G_1 = \frac{p_0}{k}\frac{2\xi\beta}{(1-\beta^2)^2 + (2\xi\beta)^2} \tag{4.27a}$$

$$G_2 = \frac{p_0}{k}\frac{1-\beta^2}{(1-\beta^2)^2 + (2\xi\beta)^2} \tag{4.27b}$$

The steady state response is given by

$$x(t) = \rho\cos(\bar{\omega}t - \theta) \tag{4.27c}$$

where amplitude ρ and phase angle θ remain same as given by Equations (3.12) and (3.13).

The response of the SDOF system due to the running force consists of two parts:

Forced response for $t \le t_d$: The total steady state response due to various Fourier terms can now be obtained by superimposition. The velocity can be obtained by differentiating the displacement response term.

Free response for $t_d \le t \le T_p$: The free response can be obtained by using the equations derived in Chapter 2, Equation (2.18b).

$$x(t) = e^{-\xi\omega(t-t_d)}\left\{\frac{x(0)\xi\omega + \dot{x}(0)}{\omega_D}\sin\omega_D(t-t_d) + x(0)\cos\omega_D(t-t_d)\right\} \tag{4.28}$$

The vibrations after the loading has ceased to zero may be found by the response of the free vibration analysis with proper boundary conditions. It means we need to know the displacement $x(0)$ and velocity $\dot{x}(0)$ at the end of the force function, at time t_d. These can be obtained by substituting $t = t_d$ in the displacement response terms and differentiating them to get the velocity and substituting $t = t_d$.

A MATLAB code can be written to plot different harmonics of the load and response functions.

4.9.4 Fourier Representation of Walking Load

The walking load can be represented by the Fourier series in the same manner. Alternatively, It may be convenient to carry out numerical integration to determine the Fourier constants.

4.10 CODAL PROVISIONS FOR HUMAN INDUCED VIBRATIONS

AISC Design Guide 11, Eurocode 1990, 1991 and 1993, ISO 2631, ISO 10137 and IS : 800 codes have detailed provisions for measurement and estimating the human-induced vibrations as well as comfort and performance criteria in structures. These manuals/codes should be referred for details.

4.10.1 Natural Frequency of Steel Framed Floor System

The following simplified procedure is suggested by Murray et. al. in AISC Steel Design Guide Series 11 (1997) for determining the fundamental frequency of vertical vibration of a steel frame floor system.

A floor is assumed to consist of concrete deck supported on steel beams which are supported on walls or steel girders between columns. The natural frequency is estimated by first considering a 'beam or joist panel' mode and a 'girder panel' mode separately and then combining them. Alternatively, finite element method can be used to estimate the natural frequency. The beam or joist and girder panel mode natural frequency can be estimated from the fundamental natural frequency of a uniformly loaded simply supported beam:

$$f = \frac{\pi}{2}\left[\frac{gE_sI}{wL^4}\right]^{0.5}$$

(4.29)

where

E_s = modulus of elasticity of steel
I = effective moment of inertia
w = uniformly distributed load per unit length
L = member span
G = acceleration due to gravity
f = fundamental natural frequency, Hz

The combined mode or system frequency can be estimated using the Dunkerley relationship:

$$\frac{1}{f^2} = \frac{1}{f_j^2} + \frac{1}{f_g^2}$$

(4.30)

where
f_j = beam or joist panel mode frequency
f_g = girder panel mode frequency

Equation (4.29) can be written as follows:

$$f = \frac{\pi}{2} \times \sqrt{\frac{5}{384}} \sqrt{\frac{g}{\Delta}} = 0.18\sqrt{\frac{g}{\Delta}} \qquad (4.31a)$$

where
Δ = midspan deflection of the member due to the uniform weight w per unit length

$$= \frac{5wL^4}{384E_sI} \qquad (4.31b)$$

4.10.2 IS : 800 – 2007 Code Provisions

Annexure C deals with the design against floor vibration due to pedestrian loads. It makes use of the Equations (4.29), (4.30) and (4.31).

4.10.3 ISO 2631 – 1997 Provisions

Part 1 of this code defines methods for the measurements of periodic, random and transient whole body vibration. It provides guidance on the possible effects of the vibration on health, comfort, and perception and motion sickness. The frequency range considered is 0.5 Hz to 80 Hz for health, comfort and perception; and 0.1 Hz to 0.5 Hz for motion sickness. The code considers motions transmitted to the human body as a whole through the supporting surface: the feet of a standing person, the buttocks, back and seat of a seated person or the supporting area of a recumbent person. This type of vibration is found in vehicles, machinery, buildings and in the vicinity of a machinery in running state. It requires that weighted root mean square acceleration should be measured in m/s² for translational vibration and radians per sec² for rotational vibration as follows:

$$a_w = \left[\frac{1}{T}\int_0^T a_w^2(t)\,dt\right]^{0.5} \qquad (4.32)$$

T = duration of the measurement, in seconds

Comfort Reactions to Vibration Environments

Clause C.2.3 specifies acceptable values of vibration magnitude for comfort in public transport. It should be noted that the reactions at various magnitudes depend on passenger expectations with regard to trip duration and the type of activities passengers expect to accomplish (e.g. reading, eating, writing, etc.) and many other factors such as acoustic noise, temperature, etc.

TABLE 4.2 VIBRATION MAGNITUDE FOR COMFORT

Acceleration in m/s^2	Reaction
Less than 0.315	Not comfortable
0.315 to 0.63	A little uncomfortable
0.5 to 1	Fairly uncomfortable
0.8 to 1.6	Uncomfortable
1.25 to 2.5	Very uncomfortable
> 2	Extremely uncomfortable

ISO 2631-Part 2 specifies a method for measurement and evaluation, comprising the determination of the measurement direction and measurement location.

4.10.4 ISO 10137 2007 Provisions

ISO 10137 deals with serviceability criteria for buildings subjected to vibrations. The standard covers various aspects of serviceability of buildings and walkways against vibrations. The design or evaluation criteria employed for achieving satisfactory vibration behaviour of buildings and walkways in the serviceability limit state should consider, among others, the following aspects:

- variability of tolerance of human occupants due to cultural, regional or economic factors;
- sensitivity of building contents to vibrations and changing use and occupancy;
- emergence of new dynamic loadings which are not explicitly addressed by this international standard;
- use of materials whose dynamic characteristics may change with time;
- impracticality of analysis due to the complexity of the structure or complexity of the loading and
- social or economic consequences of unsatisfactory performance.

4.10.5 Eurocode Provisions

There are three Eurocodes that deal with pedestrian loads and structural requirements:

Eurocode 1990 – It deals with the comfort criteria for pedestrians

Eurocode 1991 – Part 2 – It deals with pedestrian loads on bridges

Eurocode 1993 – Part 2 – It deals with performance criteria for pedestrian bridges

Eurocode 1990

Annexure A2 deals with bridges while Annexure A2.4.3 deals with verifications concerning vibration for footbridges due to pedestrian traffic. Pedestrian comfort criteria are dealt in Annexure A2.4.3.2. The comfort criteria should be defined in terms of maximum acceptable acceleration of any part of the deck. The following accelerations (m/s^2) are the recommended maximum values for any part of the deck:

- 0.70 m/s^2 for vertical vibrations
- 0.20 m/s^2 for horizontal vibrations due to normal use
- 0.40 m/s^2 for horizontal vibrations under exceptional crowd conditions

A verification of the comfort criteria should be performed if the fundamental frequency of the deck is:

- < 5 Hz for vertical vibrations
- < 2.5 Hz for horizontal (lateral) and torsional vibrations

Eurocode 1991 – Part 2

Section 5 of this code deals with actions on footways, cycle tracks and footbridges. Depending on the dynamic characteristics of the structure, the relevant natural frequencies (corresponding to vertical, horizontal, torsional vibrations) of the main structure of the bridge deck should be determined from an appropriate structural model. Vibrations of footbridges may be caused by pedestrians, who can walk, run, jump or dance and wind.

The forces exerted by pedestrians with a frequency identical to one of the natural frequencies of the bridge can result into resonance and need to be taken into account for limit state verifications in relation with vibrations. The effects of pedestrian traffic on a footbridge depend on various factors. For example, the number and location of people likely to be simultaneously on the bridge, and also on external circumstances, more or less linked to the location of the bridge. A pedestrian exerts the following simultaneous periodic forces while walking normally:

- in the vertical direction, with a frequency range of between 1 and 3 Hz.
- in the horizontal direction, with a frequency range of between 0.5 and 1.5 Hz.
- Groups of joggers may cross a footbridge with a frequency of 3 Hz.

Eurocode 1991 – Part 2 National Annex (UK)

Clause NA.2.44 *Dynamic models for pedestrian actions on footbridges*
Dynamic models for pedestrian loads and associated comfort criteria are specified. Two distinct analyses are required:

- the determination of the maximum vertical deck acceleration and its comparison with the comfort criteria and
- analysis to determine the likelihood of large synchronized lateral responses.

For unusual bridges, or in circumstances where other responses or response mechanisms are likely to cause discomfort (e.g. the wind buffeting of pedestrian bridges over railways), the effects of actions other than those described should be considered. The following activities are not included and any associated requirements should be determined for the individual activities:

- mass gathering (e.g. marathons, demonstrations)
- deliberate pedestrian synchronization
- vandal loading

TABLE 4.3 BRIDGE CLASSIFICATION – EN1991-2-UK NATIONAL ANNEX

| | | Group Size | | Crowd Density Persons/m² |
		Walking	Jogging	Walking
Bridge Class	Bridge Usage	Walking	Jogging	Walking
A	Rural locations used and in sparsely populated area	$N = 2$	$N = 0$	0
B	Suburban location likely to experience slight variations in pedestrian loading intensity on an occasional basis	$N = 4$	$N = 1$	0.4
C	Urban routes subject to significant variation in daily usage	$N = 8$	$N = 2$	0.8
D	Primary access to major public assembly facilities such as sports stadiums or major public transportation services	$N = 16$	$N = 4$	1.5

The UK National Annex describes three main load models: two of these load models concern vertical vibrations and one horizontal vibration.

Dynamic actions representing the passage of single pedestrians and pedestrian groups (vertical)

The design maximum vertical accelerations that result from single pedestrians or pedestrian groups should be calculated by assuming that these are represented by the application of a vertical pulsating force $F(N)$, moving across the span of the bridge at a constant speed v_t, as follows:

$$F = F_0 k(f_v)\sqrt{1+\gamma(N-1)}\sin(2\pi f_v t) \tag{4.33}$$

where

$N =$ number of pedestrians in the group, as shown in Table 4.3.

$F_0 =$ reference amplitude of the applied fluctuating force given in Table 4.4 (and represents the maximum amplitude of the applied pedestrian force at the most likely pace frequency).

$f_v =$ natural frequency (Hz) of the vertical mode under consideration.

$k(f_v) =$ a combined factor to deal with (a) the effects of a more realistic pedestrian population, (b) harmonic responses and (c) relative weighting of pedestrian sensitivity to response. Refer Figure 4.20.

$\gamma =$ for the unsynchronized combination of actions in a pedestrian group, is a function of damping and effective span, refer code.

TABLE 4.4 REFERENCE AMPLITUDE OF FORCE

Load Parameter	Walking	Jogging
Reference load F_0	280 N	910 N
Pedestrian crossing speed v_t	1.7 m/s	3 m/s

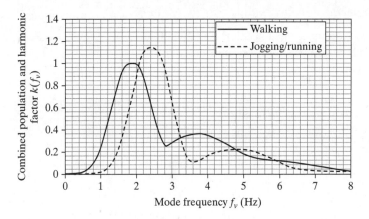

Figure 4.20   Relation between $k(f_v)$ and f_v

Steady state modelling of pedestrians in crowded conditions
The design maximum vertical accelerations that result from pedestrians in crowded conditions may be calculated by assuming that these are represented by a vertical pulsating distributed load w (N/m²), applied to the deck for a sufficient time so that steady state conditions are achieved as follows:

$$w = 1.8 \frac{F_0 k(f_v)}{A} \sqrt{\frac{\gamma N}{\lambda}} \sin(2\pi f_v t) \tag{4.34}$$

where
  N = total number of pedestrians distributed over the span S
  $N = \rho A = \rho S b$
  ρ = the required crowd density obtained from Table 4.3 but with a maximum value of 1.0 persons/m². (This is because crowd densities greater than this value produce less vertical response as the forward motion slows).
  b = the width of the bridge subject to pedestrian loading.
  γ = factor to allow for the unsynchronized combination of actions in a crowd
  λ = factor that reduces the effective number of pedestrians when loading from only part of the span contributes to the mode of interest $\lambda = 0.634 \, (S_{eff}/S)$.

For other symbols used in Equations (4.33) and (4.34), the code should be referred.

In order to obtain the most unfavourable effect, this loading should be applied over all relevant areas of the footbridge deck with the direction of the force varied to match the direction of the vertical displacements of the mode for which responses are being calculated.

Lateral responses due to crowd loading

  • Structures should be designed to avoid unintended unstable lateral responses.
  • If there are no significant lateral modes with frequencies below 1.5 Hz, it may be assumed that unstable lateral responses will not occur.
  • For all other situations, it should be demonstrated that unstable lateral responses due to crowd loading will not occur.

Recommended serviceability limits for use in design

The maximum vertical acceleration calculated from the above actions should be less than the design acceleration limit given by:

$$a_{\text{limit}} = 1.0\,k_1 k_2 k_3 k_4 \text{ m/s}^2 \quad 0.5\,\text{m/s}^2 \le a_{\text{limit}} \le 2.0\,\text{m/s}^2 \qquad (4.35)$$

where

k_1 = site usage factor
k_2 = route redundancy factor
k_3 = height of structure factor
k_4 = exposure factor = 1.0 unless determined otherwise

Eurocode 1993 – Part 2

Performance criteria for road bridges: The natural frequencies of vibrations and deflections of the bridge should be limited to avoid discomfort to users as specified in Clause 7.8.

Performance criteria for pedestrian bridges: The footbridges and cycle track bridges with excessive vibrations could cause discomfort to the users. Clause 7.9 requires that measures should be taken to minimize such vibrations by designing the bridge with an appropriate natural frequency or by providing suitable damping devices. Tuned mass dampers discussed in Chapter 9 can provide possible solutions.

PROBLEMS

MATLAB APPLICATIONS

4.1 (a) Represent the triangular periodic loading shown in Figure 4.1(a) having an amplitude p_0 and period T_p by Fourier series using MATLAB.

    (b) How many terms are necessary to obtain a reasonable convergence? Show the plots for different number of terms.

    (c) Find the steady state response of an undamped SDOF system having a frequency ratio of (i) 0.5 and (ii) 2. Show the plots for different number of terms.

4.2 Repeat Problem 4.1 for the half sine wave shown in Figure 4.1(b).

4.3 (a) Represent the periodic loading shown in Figure 4.1(a) having an amplitude of p_0 and period T_p using the exponential form of Fourier series. Show the amplitude of real and imaginary Fourier terms.

    (b) Find the steady state response of an undamped SDOF system having a frequency ratio of (i) 0.5 and (ii) 2 using the exponential form of Fourier series. Show the amplitude of real and imaginary Fourier terms.

4.4 Determine the Fourier transform of a triangular pulse which is symmetric about $t = 0$ as shown in Figure 4.12 in frequency domain.

4.5 A SDOF system has a mass of 100 kg, stiffness of 250 kN/m and a damping of 5 per cent. It is subjected to a force as shown in Figure P4.1. The amplitude and period of the periodic forcing function is 100 kN and 0.20 sec, respectively. Determine the Fourier constants of displacement and response up to 25 terms. Also, plot the steady state response.

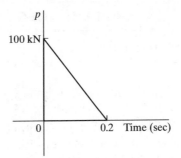

Figure P4.1

4.6 The force due to one leg of a person walking on a floor is shown in Figure P4.2. Discretize the load function so as to capture its salient features. Illustrate the first four Fourier harmonics using MATLAB or MS-EXCEL.

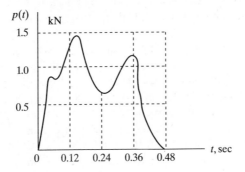

Figure P4.2

4.7 The force due to both legs of a person walking on a floor is shown in Figure P4.3. Discretize the load function so as to capture its salient features. Illustrate the first four Fourier harmonics using MATLAB or MS-EXCEL.

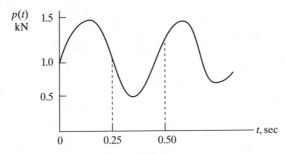

Figure P4.3

4.8 Determine the response of a damped SDOF system due to the force shown in Figure P4.2, if natural frequency of vibration of the system is 2Hz and damping is 1.5 per cent. Illustrate the first four Fourier harmonics using MATLAB or MS-EXCEL.

4.9 Determine the response of a damped SDOF system due to the force shown in Figure P4.3, if natural frequency of vibration of the system is 2.5 Hz and damping is 1.5 per cent. Illustrate the first four Fourier harmonics using MATLAB or MS-EXCEL.

REFERENCES

Bachmann, H. (2002) Lively Footbridges a Real Challenge, Proceedings of the International Conference on the Design and Dynamic Behaviour of Footbridges, Paris, France, November 20–22, pp. 18–30.

Ellis, B.R. (2004) The Response of Structures to Dynamic Crowd Loads, BRE Digest 426, London.

Eurocode 1990 (2002) Basis of Structural Design, European Standard, Brussels.

Eurocode 1991- part 2 (2003) Actions on structures – Part 2: Traffic loads on bridges, and UK National Annex, European Standard, Brussels.

Eurocode 1993-part 2 (2004): Design of Steel Structures – Part 2: Steel Bridges, European Standard, Brussels.

IS:800 (2007) General Construction in Steel – Code of Practice, Bureau of Indian Standards, New Delhi.

ISO 2631-part 1 (1997) Mechanical Vibration and Shock — Evaluation of Human Exposure to Wholebody Vibration — Part 1: General Requirements, International Standardization Organization, Geneva.

ISO 2631-part 2 (2003) Mechanical Vibration and Shock — Evaluation of Human Exposure to Wholebody Vibration — Part 2: Vibration in buildings (1 Hz to 80 Hz), International Standardization Organization, Geneva.

ISO 10137 (2007)Bases for Design of Structures: Serviceability of Buildings and Pedestrian Walkways against Vibration, International Standardization Organization, Geneva.

Kala, J., Salajka, V. and Hradil, P. (2009) Footbridge Response on Single Pedestrian Induced Vibration Analysis, International Science Index, Vol 3, No.2, pp. 548–559.

Murray, T.M., Allen, D.E., and Ungar, E.E. (1997) Floor Vibrations Due to Human Activities, Steel Design Guide Series-11, American Institute of Steel Construction, Chicago.

SETRA (2006) Footbridges, Assessment of Vibrational Behaviour of Footbridges Under Pedestrian Loading, *Technical guide SETRA*, Paris.

5 | Single Degree of Freedom System: Impulse Loading

5.1 INTRODUCTION

In many practical situations, the forcing function is neither harmonic nor periodic. It may be a single impulse loading having a very large magnitude but a very short duration t_d. It may be a sine impulse, a rectangular impulse, a ramp impulse or any other similar impulse having a total duration of t_d as shown in Figure 5.1. Such impulses may be produced by a blast loading. The response of such an impulse depends upon the ratio t_d/T, where T is a natural period of the SDOF system. The response of such arbitrary single impulse excitation is presented for an undamped SDOF system because the effect of damping on the response of a SDOF system due to single impulse excitation is usually not significant. The maximum response to an impulse force will be reached in a very short time. The damping force will not be able to absorb energy from the structure during this time. Duhamel integral is used to determine the response of a SDOF system subjected to such loadings. The concept of *shock spectrum* is introduced to represent the response in graphical form, which is very easy to understand.

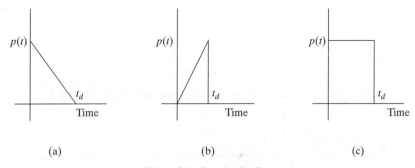

(a)   (b)   (c)

Figure 5.1 Impulse loading.

5.2 DUHAMEL INTEGRAL

Consider a unit impulse shown in Figure 5.2(a) and an impulse momentum relationship gives:

$$\text{Impulse} = P \, dt \text{ and momentum} = m\dot{x}$$

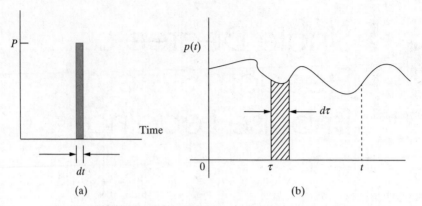

Figure 5.2 (a) Unit impulse; (b) Impulse loading.

or, $$P \, dt = m\dot{x} \tag{5.1}$$

or, $$\dot{x} = P \, dt/m \tag{5.2}$$

For undamped free vibrations in a SDOF, it was shown in Chapter 2 that:

$$x(t) = A \sin \omega t + B \cos \omega t$$

Constants A and B can be expressed in terms of initial conditions, that is, $x(0)$ and $\dot{x}(0)$ at $t = 0$.

$$x(t) = \frac{\dot{x}(0)}{\omega} \sin \omega t + x(0) \cos \omega t \tag{5.3}$$

The initial displacement is zero prior to and up to the impulse, therefore,

$$x(t) = \frac{\dot{x}(0)}{\omega} \sin \omega t'$$

where t' is time after impulse is zero.

or, $$x(t) = \frac{Pdt}{m\omega} \sin \omega t' \tag{5.4}$$

The impulse imparts initial velocity to the mass given by Equation (5.2).

5.3 UNDAMPED SYSTEM

An impulse is shown in Figure 5.2(b). It can be assumed to consist of a series of short impulses of duration $d\tau$ each producing its own response. Using Equation (5.4), response of a SDOF can be written as follows:

$$dx(t) = \frac{p(\tau) \, d\tau}{m\omega} \sin \omega(t - \tau) \tag{5.5}$$

$dx(t)$ represents differential response to the differential impulse over the entire response history, for $t > \tau$, it is not change of x during a time interval $d\tau$. The total steady state response can be obtained by integration

$$x(t) = \frac{1}{m\omega} \int_0^t p(\tau) \sin \omega(t-\tau) d\tau \qquad (5.6)$$

It is called Duhamel integral. It can also be written as

$$x(t) = \int_0^t p(\tau) h(t-\tau) d\tau \qquad (5.7a)$$

where

$$h(t-\tau) = \frac{1}{m\omega} \sin \omega(t-\tau) \qquad (5.7b)$$

Equation (5.7) is called the convolution integral. The function $h(t-\tau)$ is called unit impulse response for undamped systems. Equation (5.6) or (5.7) can be evaluated using numerical integration. In these equations, it is implicit that the initial conditions of the SDOF system is at rest, that is, $x(0) = 0$ and $\dot{x}(0) = 0$. If not, then the resulting free vibration response given by Equation (5.3) should also be considered.

5.4 DAMPED SYSTEM

The steady state response of a damped SDOF system for a single pulse of magnitude p and duration $d\tau$ at instant τ can be written as follows:

$$x(t) = \frac{p d\tau}{m\omega_D} e^{-\xi\omega(t-\tau)} \sin \omega_D (t-\tau) \qquad (5.8a)$$

Unit impulse response for a damped system is given by the convolution integral

$$h(t-\tau) = \frac{1}{m\omega_D} e^{-\xi\omega(t-\tau)} \sin \omega_D (t-\tau) \qquad (5.8b)$$

or, for the single pulse, the total response is given as

$$x(t) = p_0 h(t-\tau) \qquad (5.8c)$$

where $p_0 = p\, d\tau =$ magnitude of impulse.
For a series of three impulses of magnitude p_1, p_2 and p_3 at different instants τ_1, τ_2 and τ_3, respectively, the response can be written as:

$$x(t) = p_1 h(t-\tau_1) + p_2 h(t-\tau_2) + p_3 h(t-\tau_3) \qquad (5.8d)$$

or, $$x(t) = \sum_i p_i h(t-\tau_i) \qquad (5.8e)$$

Similarly, if a continuous function can be finely divided, its total response can be written in terms of an integral

$$x(t) = \frac{1}{m\omega_D} \int_0^t p(\tau) e^{-\xi\omega(t-\tau)} \sin \omega_D (t-\tau) d\tau \qquad (5.8f)$$

or, $$x(t) = \int_0^t p(\tau) h(t-\tau) d\tau \qquad (5.8g)$$

The unit impulse response function $h(t-\tau)$ can be evaluated using the convolution function CONV in MATLAB.

5.5 SHOCK SPECTRA

If a SDOF system is subjected to an impulse of duration t_d, its maximum response can be obtained using the Duhamel's integral. The dynamic magnification factor can be computed. By changing the duration of the impulse of a given shape, different values of the dynamic magnification factor can be obtained. A plot can be made between dynamic magnification factor and t_d/T for a given shape of the impulse. Such a plot is referred to as *shock spectra*. Similar plots can be made for other shapes of the impulse function. Shock spectra is very useful in designing SDOF systems subjected to impulse loading. The Duhamel integral can be easily evaluated using MATLAB.

5.6 ILLUSTRATIVE EXAMPLES

Example 5.1

Find the steady state response of an undamped SDOF system subjected to a constant step impulse as shown in Figure 5.3.

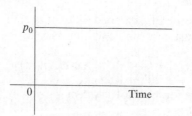

Figure 5.3   Step impulse.

Solution   The steady state response can be written as follows:

$$x(t) = \frac{1}{m\omega} \int_0^t p(\tau)\sin\omega(t-\tau)\,d\tau \tag{1}$$

$$x(t) = \int_0^t \frac{p_0}{m\omega} \sin\omega(t-\tau)\,d\tau$$

Upon integration,

$$x(t) = \frac{p_0}{m\omega^2}(1-\cos\omega t) = \frac{p_0}{k}(1-\cos\omega t) \tag{2}$$

It is implicit that the initial conditions $x(0)$ and $\dot{x}(0)$ are zero.
Equation (2) leads to a very important conclusion.
The maximum value of $x(t)$ is equal to

$$x_{max} = \frac{2p_0}{k} \quad \text{when } \cos\omega t = -1$$

It shows that if a constant load p_0 is applied suddenly, the maximum dynamic displacement is twice that of the static displacement.   □

Example 5.2

An undamped SDOF system is subjected to a ramp impulse as shown in Figure 5.4. Find (a) steady state response in the forced and free vibration states using Duhamel integral and (b) shock spectra.

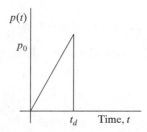

Figure 5.4   Ramp impulse.

Solution
(a) Steady State Response
The forcing function can be expressed as

$$p(\tau) = \frac{\tau}{t_d} p_0 \qquad 0 \le t \le t_d \tag{1a}$$

and

$$= 0 \qquad t \ge t_d \tag{1b}$$

Duhamel integral of Equation (1a) gives,

$$x(t) = \frac{p_0}{m\omega} \int_0^t \frac{\tau}{t_d} \sin\omega(t-\tau)d\tau \tag{2}$$

On integration, $$x(t) = \frac{p_0}{m\omega t_d} \left| \tau \cos\omega(t-\tau) - \sin\omega(t-\tau) \right|$$

or, $$x(t) = x_{st}\left[\frac{t}{t_d} - \frac{\sin\omega t}{\omega t_d} \right] \quad \text{for} \quad t \le t_d \tag{3}$$

and velocity is given by $$\dot{x}(t) = x_{st}\left[\frac{1}{t_d} - \frac{\cos\omega t}{t_d} \right] \quad \text{for} \quad t \le t_d \tag{4}$$

The vibrations after the loading has ceased to zero may be found by the response of the free vibration analysis with proper boundary conditions. It means we need to know the displacement and velocity at the end of the force function, at time t_d. These can be obtained by substituting $t = t_d$ in Equations (3) and (4).

Free vibration response is given by

$$x(t) = \frac{\dot{x}(t_d)}{\omega} \sin\omega(t-t_d) + x(t_d)\cos\omega(t-t_d) \quad \text{for} \quad t > t_d \tag{5}$$

Upon substituting the values of initial conditions at $t = t_d$ from Equations (3) and (4) in Equation (5), we obtain

$$x(t) = \frac{x_{st}}{\omega t_d}\left[\sin\omega(t-t_d)(1-\cos\omega t_d) + \cos\omega(t-t_d)(\omega t_d - \sin\omega t_d) \right] \quad \text{for} \quad t > t_d \tag{6}$$

It is now possible to plot $x(t)/x_{st}$ vs t_d/T for the ramp impulse for a SDOF system and develop a shock spectra using Equations (3) and (6).

Let us rewrite Equation (3) as follows:

$$\frac{x(t)}{x_{st}} = \left[\frac{t}{T}\frac{T}{t_d} - \frac{\sin 2\pi \frac{t}{T}}{2\pi \frac{t_d}{T}} \right] \quad \text{for} \quad t \le t_d \tag{7}$$

Similarly, Equation (6) can be re-written as follows:

$$\frac{x(t)}{x_{st}} = \frac{T}{2\pi t_d} \left[\sin \frac{2\pi}{T}(t - t_d)\left(1 - \cos 2\pi \frac{t_d}{T}\right) + \cos \frac{2\pi}{T}(t - t_d)\left(2\pi \frac{t_d}{T} - \sin 2\pi \frac{t_d}{T}\right) \right] \tag{8}$$

$$\text{for } t \ge t_d$$

Now a plot can be drawn between the steady state response $x(t)/x_{st}$ and (t/T) for given value of (t_d/T) using Equations (7) and (8) using MATLAB code DOS5_1.

The maximum response may occur either in the forced vibration phase or in the free vibration phase depending up on the ratio t_d/T.

The static displacement at any instant t can be estimated as follows:

$$x_{st}(t) = \frac{p(t)}{k} = \frac{p_0}{k}\frac{t}{t_d} = x_{st}^0 \frac{t}{t_d} \quad \text{for} \quad t < t_d \tag{9}$$

where x_{st}^0 is maximum static displacement due to p_0.

This equation can also be plotted on the dynamic response graphs in order to compare static and dynamic displacements.   ☐

```
------------------
CODE DOS5_1
------------------
%   Dynamics of Structures by Ashok K. Jain I. I. T. Roorkee
%   DOS5_1                  Calls: calc_x
%   Increasing ramp force impulse
%   Effect of td/T on the response - (free and forced vibrations)
%   x1 = displacement for ramp part
%   x2 = displacement for the free vibrations
%   td = duration of ramp force
%   T = Period of vibration of a SDOF system
%   plot between D vs t/T for a given td/T
%
clear all;
close all;
clc;
dt = 0.01;
tmax = 2.5;
%   First define a row vector x, x1, x2 and then transpose to get column
%   vectors
x=[0,1,tmax/dt];
   x=x';
x1 = [0,1,tmax/dt];
   x1=x1';
x2 = [0,1,tmax/dt];
   x2=x2';
```

```
%   t1 = [0,dt,tmax/dt];
%   t1=t1';
    td = 0.5;
    T  = 5;
    w = 2*pi/T;
    xst = 1; %static
    k=0;
    for t =0:dt:tmax
      k=k+1;
      [x(k),x1(k),x2(k)] = calc_x(td,t,T,xst);
    end
    t=0:dt/T:tmax/T;
    t=t';
%
%   t=0:tmax/T;
    plot(t,x,'.-k');
    grid on;
    legend('Constant td/T')
    xlabel('t/T')
    ylabel('x(t)/xst')

%   figure;
%   plot(t,x1','.-k');
%   grid on;
%   legend('Constant td/T')
%   xlabel('t/T')
%   ylabel('Forced Vibrations x1(t)/xst')
%
%   figure;
%   plot(t,x2,'.-k');
%   grid on;
%   legend('Constant td/T')
%   xlabel('t/T')
%   ylabel('Free Vibrations x2(t)/xst')


    -----------------
CODE calc_x
    -----------------
%   calc_x              Called by : DOS5_1
%   Increasing ramp force impulse
%
    function [x,x1,x2] = calc_x(td,t,T,xst)
%   compute maximum response
%   x1 for ramp force function (forced vibration)
%   x2 for zero force function (free vibration)
    t1 = t/T;
    t2 = td/T;
    x1 = xst*(t1/t2 - sin(2*pi*t1)/(2*pi*t2));
    x2 = xst/(2*pi*t2)*(sin(2*pi*(t1-t2))*(1-cos(2*pi*t2))+ cos(2*pi*
    (t1-t2))*(2*pi*t2-sin(2*pi*t2)));
```

```
    if t1 <= t2
        x=x1;
    else
        x=x2;
    end
end
```

The net dynamic response for t_d/T = 0.1, 0.2, 0.5, 1, 2, 3 and 4.0 are shown in Figures 5.5(a) to 5.5(g); respectively. The arrow in these graphs indicates the demarcation between forced and free vibrations. The following observations can be made in these plots:

1. The dynamic response consists of two parts: forced response and free response. The forced response acts till the duration of the ramp force, after this, it undergoes free vibrations.

2. The dynamic response depends upon the ratio t_d/T and not on the individual values of t_d and T because of the presence of the term $\omega t_d = 2\pi(t_d/T)$ in the expression for dynamic response.

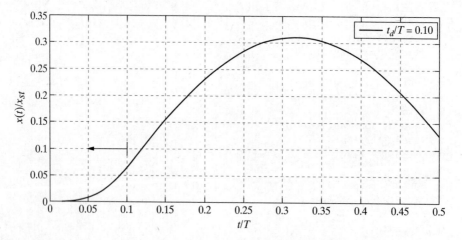

Figure 5.5(a)   Dynamic response for $t_d/T = 0.1$.

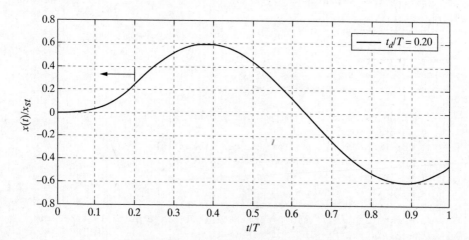

Figure 5.5(b)   Dynamic response for $t_d/T = 0.2$.

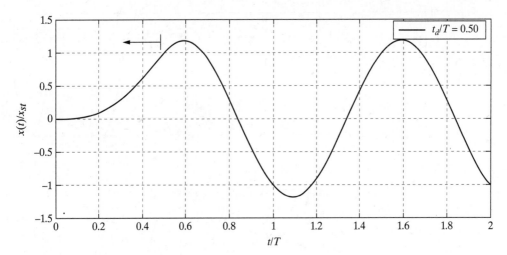

Figure 5.5(c)   Dynamic response for $t_d/T = 0.5$.

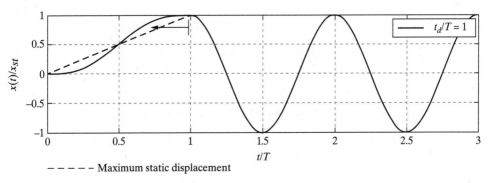

Figure 5.5(d)   Dynamic response for $t_d/T = 1.0$.

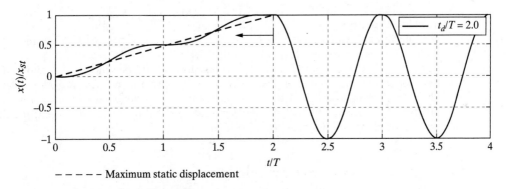

Figure 5.5(e)   Dynamic response for $t_d/T = 2.0$.

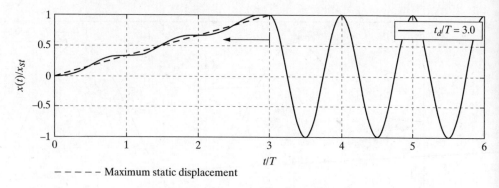

Figure 5.5(f)   Dynamic response for $t_d/T = 3.0$.

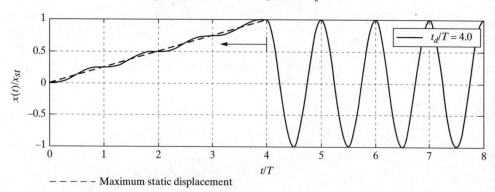

Figure 5.5(g)   Dynamic response for $t_d/T = 4.0$.

3. During the forced response phase, the system oscillates about its static solution. During the free vibration phase, the SDOF system vibrates about its mean zero position.

4. As t_d/T increases from 0.1 to 1.0, the ratio of dynamic displacement to static displacement increases up to 1.0, thereafter, with the increase in t_d/T, there is no further increase in the magnitude of $x_{dynamic}/x_{static}$. It means there is no dynamic effect in the present pulse loading.

(b) Shock Spectra
The maximum response of a SDOF system is obtained for a given t_d/T value. The MATLAB code developed earlier is modified. Using the MATLAB code DOS5_2, shock spectra is plotted in Figure 5.6(a) and (b) on semi-log and normal scales. It shows the ratio of absolute maximum displacement and static displacement versus t_d/T. For short duration pulse up to $t_d/T \le 0.5$, there is an increase in the maximum displacement ratio up to about 1.25, thereafter, the dynamic magnification factor reduces continuously, and the system vibrates about its mean static position.

```
--------------------
CODE DOS5_2      Shock Spectra for Ramp Force
--------------------

%   Dynamics of Structures by Ashok K. Jain I. I. T. Roorkee
%   DOS5_2                   Calls calc_x2
```

```
%    Undamped Forced Vibrations of a SDOF System - Impulse loading
%    increasing ramp force impulse - Compute Shock Spectra
%    x = displacement for ramp part
%    td = duration of impulse loading
%    R=td/T
%
clear all;
close all;
clc;
%
r=0;
Rmin = 0.01;
Rstep = 0.01;
dT = 0.01;
Rmax = 50;
tmax = 30.;
x = zeros(Rmax/Rstep,tmax/dT);

for R = Rmin:Rstep:Rmax
    r=r+1;
    %R  = td/T
    td  = 20;
    T = td/R;
    w = 2*pi/T;
    xst =   1; %static
    k=0;
    for t = 0:dT:tmax
        k=k+1;
        [x(r,k)] = calc_x2(td,t,w,xst);
    end
end
%subplot 211
R = Rmin:Rstep:Rmax;
xmax = max(x');
semilogx(R,xmax,'.-k');
grid on;
legend('xmax/xst')
xlabel('td/T')
ylabel('Maximum response ratio')
figure
%subplot 212
plot(R,xmax,'.-k');
grid on;
legend('xmax/xst')
xlabel('td/T')
ylabel('Maximum response ratio')
```

```
-------------------
CODE calc_x2
-------------------


%  calc_x2            Called by : DOS5_2
%  Increasing ramp force impulse
%

function [x] = calc_x2(td,t,w,xst)

%  compute maximum response
%  x1 for ramp force function (forced vibration)
%  x2 for zero force function (free vibration)

    x1 = xst*(t/td - sin(w*t)/(w*td));
    x2=xst/(w*td)*(sin(w*(t-td))*(1-cos(w*td))+cos(w*(t-td))*(w*td-
    sin(w*td)));
    if t <= td
       x = x1;
    else
       x = x2;
    end
end
```

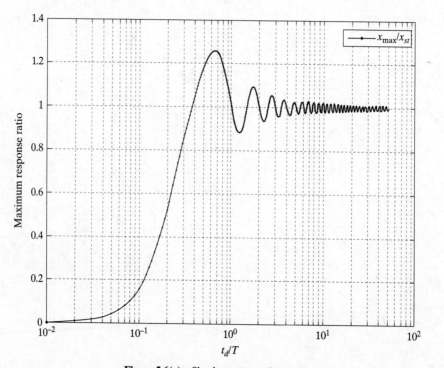

Figure 5.6(a)   Shock spectra on log scale.

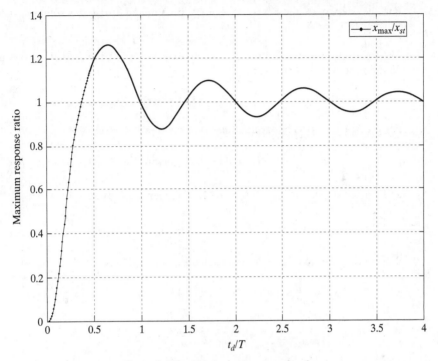

Figure 5.6(b) Shock spectra-normal scale.

Example 5.3

An undamped SDOF system is subjected to a ramp + step impulse as shown in Figure 5.7. Find (a) steady state response in the forced and free vibration states using Duhamel integral and (b) shock spectra.

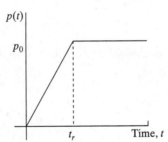

Figure 5.7 Ramp + step impulse.

Solution
(a) Steady State Response
For the first part when $t \leq t_r$, the solution was obtained in Example 5.2 through Equation (1).

$$x(t) = x_{st}\left[\frac{t}{t_r} - \frac{\sin \omega t}{\omega t_r}\right] \qquad \text{for } t \leq t_r \qquad (1)$$

For the step part, the response can be determined using the solution obtained in Example 5.1.

For $t \geq t_r$

The total response consists of two components: free vibration response $x_1(t)$ and forced vibration response $x_2(t)$, that is,

$$x(t) = x_1(t) + x_2(t) \tag{2}$$

For the free vibration part, Equation (6) of Example 5.2 gives,

$$x_1(t) = \frac{x_{st}}{\omega t_r}[\sin\omega(t - t_r)(1 - \cos\omega t_r) + \cos\omega(t - t_r)(\omega t_r - \sin\omega t_r) \tag{3a}$$

and, for the step force part, Equation (2) of Example 5.1 gives,

$$x_2(t) = \frac{P_0}{k}(1 - \cos\omega(t - t_r)) = x_{st}(1 - \cos\omega(t - t_r)) \tag{3b}$$

Substituting the values of $x_1(t)$ and $x_2(t)$ in Equation (2), gives

$$x(t) = \frac{x_{st}}{\omega t_r}[\sin\omega(t - t_r)(1 - \cos\omega t_r) + \cos\omega(t - t_r)(\omega t_r - \sin\omega t_r) +$$

$$\omega t_r(1 - \cos\omega(t - t_r))] \tag{4}$$

This can be simplified to

$$x(t) = x_{st}\left[1 + \frac{1}{\omega t_r}\left[\sin\omega(t - t_r)(1 - \cos\omega t_r) - \cos\omega(t - t_r)(\sin\omega t_r)\right]\right.$$

or,

$$x(t) = x_{st}\left[1 - \frac{1}{\omega t_r}\{\sin\omega t - \sin\omega(t - t_r)\}\right] \qquad t \geq t_r \tag{5}$$

It is possible to generate the dynamic response as well as shock spectra using Equations (1) and (5).

The maximum response may occur either in the ramp phase or in the step phase. ☐

```
--------------------
CODE DOS5_3      Ramp and step force
--------------------

%   Dynamics of Structures by Ashok K. Jain I. I. T. Roorkee
%   DOS5_3       Calls: calc_x3
%   Effect of tr/T on the response - (free and forced)
%
%   increasing ramp force + constant impulse
%   x1 = displacement for ramp part + step force part
```

```
%  x2 = displacement for the free vibrations
%  plot between D vs t/T for a given tr/T
%  tr = rise time of the ramp force
%  T = natural period of SDOF system
clear all;
close all;
clc;
dt = 0.01;
tmax = 20;
%  First define a row vector x, x1, x2 and then transpose to get column
%  vectors
x = [0,1,tmax/dt];
  x=x';
x1 = [0,1,tmax/dt];
   x1=x1';
x2 = [0,1,tmax/dt];
   x2=x2';
%t1 = [0,dt,tmax/dt];
%t1 = t1';

  tr = 15;
  T  = 5;
  w = 2*pi/T;
  xst = 1; %static
  k=0;
  for t = 0:dt:tmax
    k = k+1;
    [x(k),x1(k),x2(k)] = calc_x3(tr,t,T,xst);
  end
  t=0:dt/T:tmax/T;
  t=t';
%
%t=0:tmax/T;
plot(t,x,'.-k');
grid on;
legend('tr/T=3.0')
xlabel('tr/T')
ylabel('x(t)/xst')

%  figure;
%  plot(t,x1','.-k');
%  grid on;
%  legend('Constant tr/T')
%  xlabel('tr/T')
%  ylabel('Ramp-Forced Vibrations x1(t)/xst')
```

```
%
%  figure;
%  plot(t,x2,'.-k');
%  grid on;
%  legend('Constant tr/T')
%  xlabel('tr/T')
%  ylabel('Step-Forced Vibrations x2(t)/xst')
```

```
--------------------
CODE calc_x3
--------------------

function [x,x1,x2] = calc_x3(tr,t,T,xst)
%
%  calc_x3     called by    DOS5_3
%
%  compute maximum response
%  x1 for ramp force (forced vibration)
%  x2 for step force (forced vibration)
%
t1 = t/T;
t2 = tr/T;
x1=xst*(t1/t2 - sin(2*pi*t1)/(2*pi*t2));
x2=xst/(2*pi*t2)*(2*pi*t2-(sin(2*pi*t1)- sin(2*pi*(t1-t2))));
if t1 <= t2
    x=x1;
else
    x=x2;
end
end
```

The response of a SDOF system subjected to the ramp + step force impulse using Equations (1) and (5) in MATLAB code DOS5_3 are shown in Figures 5.8(a) to 5.8(f) for $t/T = 0.2, 0.5, 1.0, 1.5, 2.0$ and 3.0. The following observations can be made:

1. For short duration pulse $t/T = 0.2$ and 0.5, the system achieves maximum response in its step force phase.
2. During the ramp phase, the system oscillates at its natural period about the static solution.
3. During the step force phase, the system oscillates at the natural period about its static solution.
4. If the velocity is zero at the end of ramp, the system does not oscillate during the constant force phase (Figures 5.8(c), 5.8(e) and 5.8(f)).
5. For large t_d/T, the dynamic displacement is close to its static displacement. It shows that dynamic effect is small.

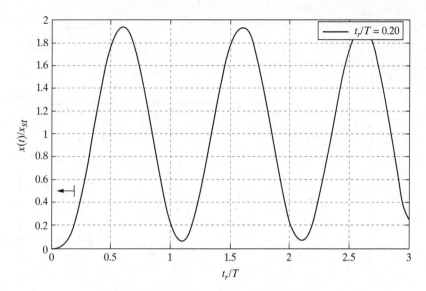

Figure 5.8(a)   Dynamic response for $t_r/T = 0.20$.

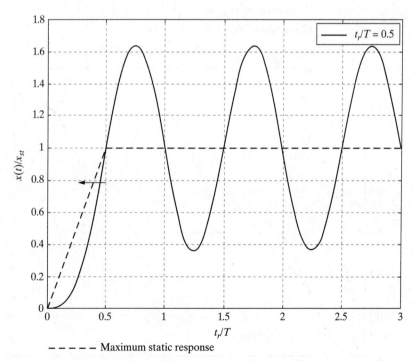

- - - - - Maximum static response

Figure 5.8(b)   Dynamic response for $t_r/T = 0.5$.

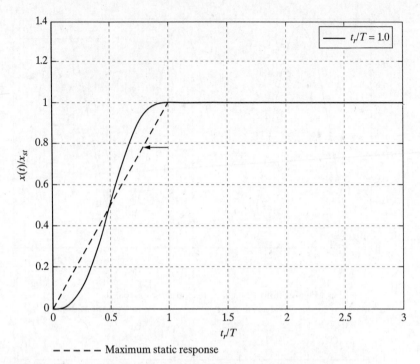

Figure 5.8(c) Dynamic response for $t_r/T = 1.0$.

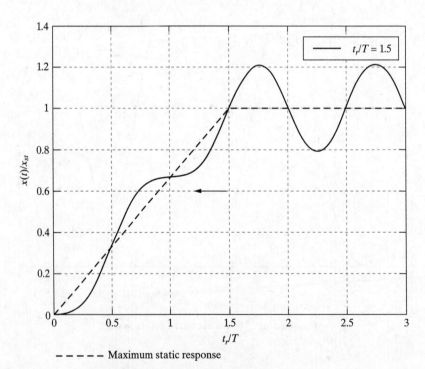

Figure 5.8(d) Dynamic response for $t_r/T = 1.5$.

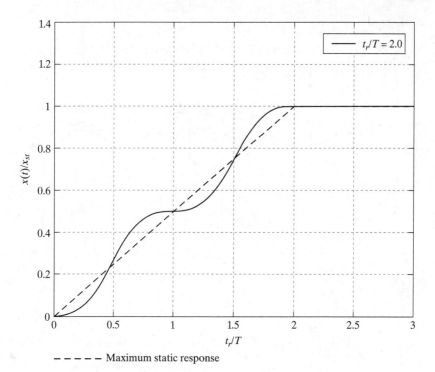

Figure 5.8(e) Dynamic response for $t_r/T = 2.0$.

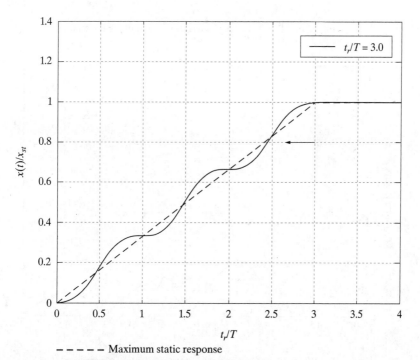

Figure 5.8(f) Dynamic response for $t_r/T = 3.0$.

(b) Shock Spectra

The shock spectra is generated by slightly modifying the MATLAB code DOS5_3 as DOS5_4. The shock spectra is shown in Figures 5.9(a) and 5.9(b) on log and normal scales.

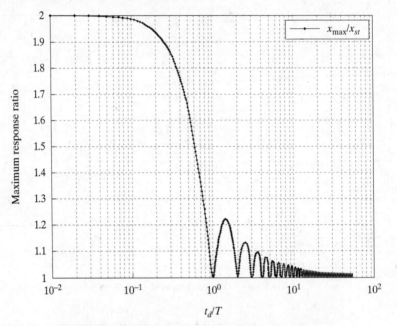

Figure 5.9(a)   Dynamic response factor for impulse – log scale.

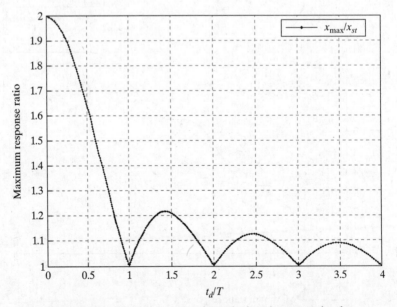

Figure 5.9(b)   Dynamic response factor for impulse – normal scale.

```
------------------
CODE DOS5_4    Shock Spectra for Ramp and step Force
------------------


%  Dynamics of Structures by Ashok K. Jain I. I. T. Roorkee
%  DOS5_4
%       Calls calc_x4 and calc_xdot4 if desired
%  Undamped Forced Vibrations of a SDOF System - Impulse loading
%
%  Determine shock spectra for ramp plus step force impulse
%  x1 = displacement for ramp part
%  x2 = displacement for constant force part
%  x = governing displacement depending upon the values of td and t.
%  R = td/T
%  td = duration of ramp part
%  T = period of SDOF system
%
clear all;
close all;
clc;
%
r=0;
Rmin = 0.01;
Rstep = 0.01;
dT = 0.01;
Rmax = 50;
tmax = 30;
x = zeros(Rmax/Rstep ,tmax/dT );
x1 = zeros(Rmax/Rstep ,tmax/dT );
x2 = zeros(Rmax/Rstep ,tmax/dT );

%xdot = zeros(Rmax/Rstep,4/dT);

for R = Rmin:Rstep:Rmax
   r=r+1;
   %R   = td/T
   td  = 0.1;
   T = td/R;
   w = 2*pi/T;
   xst =   1; %static
   k=0;

  for t =0:dT:tmax
    k=k+1;
    [x(r,k) x1(r,k) x2(r,k)] = calc_x4(td,t,w,xst);
%   xdot(r,k) = calc_xdot4(td,t,w,xst);
    end
end
R = Rstep:Rstep:Rmax;
% Print values to check results
```

```
xmax = max(x');
%x1max = max(x1');
%x2max = max(x2');
%xdotmax = max(xdot');

semilogx(R,xmax,'.-k');
grid on;
legend('xmax/xst')
xlabel('td / T ')
ylabel('Maximum response ratio')

figure;
plot(R,xmax,'.-');
legend('xmax/xst')
xlabel('td / T ')
ylabel('Maximum response ratio')
%plot(R,xdotmax,'.-');
%semilogx(R,xdotmax,'.-r');
% grid on;
%legend('velmax')
```

CODE calc_x4

```
%    Calc_x4          Called by : DOS5_4
function [x x1 x2] = calc_x4(td,t,w,xst)
% compute shock spectra
% ramp function and step function
    x1 = xst*(t/td - sin(w*t)/(w*td));
    x2 = xst*(1 - 1/(w*td)*(sin(w*t) -sin(w*(t-td))) );
    if t <= td
        x = x1;
    else
        x = x2;
    end
end
```

CODE calc_xdot4

```
%  Calc_xdot4        called by : DOS5_4
%
function xdot = calc_xdot4(td,t,w,xst)
% velocity function : ramp + step phase
if t <= td
        xdot = xst/td*(1 - cos(w*t));
    else
        xdot = -1*xst/td*(cos(w*t) - cos(w*(t-td)));
    end
end
```

Example 5.4

An undamped SDOF system is subjected to a down ramp impulse as shown in Figure 5.10. Find its steady state response in the forced and free vibration states. Determine the maximum response if peak load is 50 kN and duration of the impulse is 0.16 sec, stiffness $k = 4000$ kN/m and natural frequency of vibration is 4.5 Hz. Also, determine the maximum spring force.

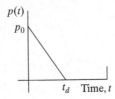

Figure 5.10   Down ramp impulse.

Solution
(a) Steady State Response
The forcing function can be written as follows:

$$p(t) = p_0\left(1 - \frac{t}{t_d}\right) \qquad 0 \le t \le t_d \tag{1}$$

$$= 0 \qquad t \ge t_d \tag{2}$$

Duhamel integral gives

$$x(t) = \int_0^t \frac{p_0}{m\omega}\left(1 - \frac{\tau}{t_d}\right)\sin\omega(t-\tau)d\tau \tag{3}$$

Upon integration,

$$x(t) = x_{st}\left(1 - \frac{t}{t_d} + \frac{1}{\omega t_d}\sin\omega t - \cos\omega t\right) \qquad 0 \le t \le t_d \tag{4}$$

where, $\qquad x_{st} = \dfrac{p_0}{k} = \dfrac{p_0}{m\omega^2}$

The vibrations after the loading has ceased to zero may be found by the response of the free vibration analysis with proper boundary conditions. It means we need to know the displacement and velocity at the end of the force function, at time t_d.
Displacement at $t = t_d$ is given by

$$x(t_d) = x_{st}\left(\frac{1}{\omega t_d}\sin\omega t_d - \cos\omega t_d\right) \tag{5a}$$

Similarly, the velocity at $t = t_d$ is given by

$$\dot{x}(t_d) = x_{st}\left(\omega\sin\omega t_d + \frac{1}{t_d}\cos\omega t_d - \frac{1}{t_d}\right)$$

or,

$$\dot{x}(t_d) = x_{st}\omega\left(\sin\omega t_d + \frac{1}{\omega t_d}\cos\omega t_d - \frac{1}{\omega t_d}\right) \tag{5b}$$

Free vibration response is given by

$$x(t) = \frac{\dot{x}(0)}{\omega}\sin\omega(t - t_d) + x(0)\cos\omega(t - t_d) \quad \text{for} \quad t > t_d \tag{6}$$

where, $x(0) = x(t_d)$ given by Equation (5a)

           $\dot{x}(0) = \dot{x}(t_d)$ given by Equation (5b)

Upon substituting the values of initial conditions at $t = t_d$ in Equation (6), we obtain

$$x(t) = \frac{x_{st}}{\omega t_d}[\sin\omega(t - t_d)\times(\omega t_d \sin\omega t_d + \cos\omega t_d - 1) + \cos\omega(t - t_d)\times$$

$$(\sin\omega t_d - \omega t_d \cos\omega t_d)] \quad \text{for} \quad t > t_d \tag{7}$$

It is now possible to plot the steady state response $x(t)/x_{st}$ versus t_d/T for the down ramp impulse for a SDOF system and develop a shock spectra using Equations (4) and (7). The MATLAB code DOS5_5 is written to compute it. The shock spectra is shown in Figures 5.11(a) and 5.11(b) on log and normal scales.

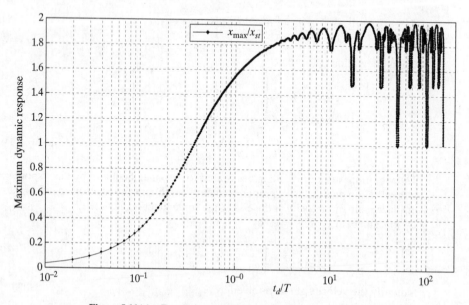

Figure 5.11(a)   Dynamic response factor for impulse – log scale.

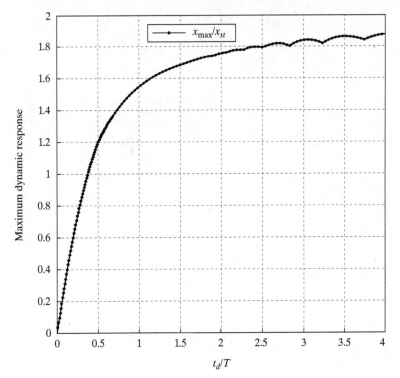

Figure 5.11(b)   Dynamic response factor for impulse – normal scale.

```
--------------------
CODE DOS5_5    Down Ramp force
--------------------

%   Dynamics of Structures by Ashok K. Jain I. I. T. Roorkee
%   DOS5_5              Calls: calc_x5
%   Undamped Forced Vibrations of a SDOF System - Impulse loading
%   Decreasing ramp force impulse
%   x = displacement for ramp part
%   Determine shock spectra
%   td = duration of impulse loading
%   R=td/T
%
clear all;
close all;
clc;

r=0;
Rmin = 0.01;
Rstep = 0.01;
dT = 0.01;
Rmax = 50;
tmax = 10.;
```

```
x = zeros(Rmax/Rstep,tmax/dT);
for R = Rmin:Rstep:Rmax
   r=r+1;
   %R = td/T
   td = 0.50;
   T = td/R;
   w = 2*pi/T;
   xst =    1; %static
   k=0;
   for t =0:dT:tmax
      k=k+1;
      [x(r,k)] = calc_x5(td,t,w,xst);
    end
end
R = Rmin:Rstep:Rmax;
xmax = max(x');
semilogx(R,xmax,'.-k');
grid on;
legend('xmax/xst')
xlabel('td / T ')
ylabel('Maximum dynamic response')
figure;
plot (R,xmax,'.-k');
grid on;

legend('xmax/xst')
xlabel('td / T ')
ylabel('Maximum dynamic response')


-------------------
CODE calc_x5
-------------------
%  calc_x5     called by:DOS5_5
%  Undamped Forced Vibrations of a SDOF System - Impulse loading
%  Decreasing ramp force impulse
%
function [x] = calc_x5(td,t,w,xst)

% compute shock spectra
% ramp decreasing function

   x1 = xst*(1 - t/td + sin(w*t)/(w*td) - cos(w*t));
   x2 = xst*(sin(w*(t-td))*(w*td*sin(w*td) +cos(w*td) -1) + cos(w*(t-
       td))*(sin(w*td) -w*td*cos(w*td)))/(w*td);

   if t <= td
      x = x1;
   else
      x = x2;
    end
end
```

(b)

Given: spring stiffness $k = 4 \times 10^6$ N/m, natural frequency $f = 4.5$ Hz, peak force = 50 kN and duration of triangular impulse = 0.16 sec.

Period of vibration $T = 1/f = 1/4.5 = 0.22$ sec

$$\frac{t_d}{T} = \frac{0.16}{0.22} = 0.72$$

∴ The dynamic amplification factor for the down ramp impulse for the given $t_d/T = 1.40$.

Static displacement $x_{st} = \dfrac{P_0}{k} = \dfrac{50}{4000} = 0.0125$ m = 12.5 mm

∴ Dynamic displacement $x_{max} = D x_{st} = 1.40 \times 12.5 = 17.5$ mm

Elastic spring force = $k x_{max} = 4000 \times 0.0175 = 70$ kN   ☐

Example 5.5

An undamped SDOF system is subjected to a down ramp impulse as shown in Figure 5.12. The maximum amplitude of the force is 5 kN and its duration is 0.04 sec. Estimate the elastic force developed in the system. If the duration of the impulse is reduced to 0.01 sec only, what is the elastic force?

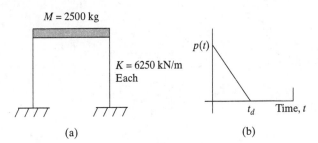

$M = 2500$ kg

$K = 6250$ kN/m Each

$p(t)$

t_d Time, t

(a)   (b)

Figure 5.12   (a) SDOF system; (b) Down ramp impulse.

Solution

(a) For two columns, the total lateral stiffness = $2 \times 6250 \times 10^3 = 12500000$ N/m

Natural frequency $\omega = \sqrt{\dfrac{k}{m}} = \sqrt{\dfrac{125 \times 100000}{2500}} = 70.70$ rad/sec

Period $\qquad T = \dfrac{2\pi}{\omega} = \dfrac{2\pi}{70.70} = 0.0888$ sec

∴ $\qquad \dfrac{t_d}{T} = \dfrac{0.04}{0.0888} = 0.45$

Shock spectra for down ramp impulse (Figure 5.11(b)) gives, $D = 1.12$

Static deflection $\Delta_{st} = \dfrac{P_0}{k} = \dfrac{5000}{125 \times 10^5} = 0.4$ mm

∴ Dynamic displacement amplitude $x_{max} = 0.4 \times 1.12 = 0.448$ mm

Corresponding maximum elastic force produced = $k x_{max} = 125 \times 10^5 \times (0.448 \times 10^{-3})$

= 5600 N

(b) If duration of the impulse loading was only 0.01 sec, then

$$\frac{t_d}{T} = \frac{0.010}{0.0888} = 0.11$$

$$\therefore \qquad D = 0.38$$

$\therefore$ Dynamic displacement amplitude $x_{max} = 0.40 \times 0.38 = 0.152$ mm

Corresponding maximum elastic force produced $= k\, x_{max} = 125 \times 10^5 \times (0.152 \times 10^{-3})$

$$= 1900 \text{ N}$$

$$\ll 5650 \text{ N in case (a)}$$

For an impulse of very small duration, a large part of the load is resisted by inertia of the system. ☐

Example 5.6

An overhead water tank (Figure 5.13(a)) has an effective weight of 1800 kN at its top when filled with water. Its lateral stiffness is 20000 kN/m. Estimate the maximum lateral displacement of its top when it is subjected to a dynamic force as shown in Figure 5.13(b) and Figure 5.13(c). Maximum amplitude of force $p(t) = 200$ kN and duration of impulse is 0.15 sec.

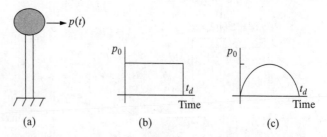

Figure 5.13   Overhead water tank under impulse loading.

Solution

For the water tank, lateral stiffness = 20000 kN/m

$$\text{Natural frequency of the OHT } \omega = \sqrt{\frac{k}{m}} = \sqrt{\frac{20000}{1800/10}} = 10.54 \text{ rad/sec}$$

$$\text{Period T} = \frac{2\pi}{\omega} = \frac{2\pi}{10.54} = 0.60 \text{ sec}$$

There is a need to develop shock spectra for the impulse loading shown in Figures 5.13(b) and 5.13(c). Alternatively, standard results are available in the literature.

(a) When subjected to the step impulse shown in Figure 5.13(b)

$p_0 = 200$ kN and duration of impulse $t_d = 0.15$ sec.

$$\text{For} \qquad \frac{t_d}{T} = \frac{0.15}{0.60} = 0.25$$

Shock spectra gives amplification factor $D = 1.25$

$$\therefore \text{ Dynamic displacement} = \Delta_{st} \times D = \frac{200}{20000} \times 1.25 = 0.0125 \text{ m} \quad \text{or,} \quad 12.50 \text{ mm}$$

(b) When subjected to the half sine impulse shown in Figure 5.13(c)

For $t_d/T = 0.25$, amplification factor $D = 0.86$ by making use of shock spectra

$\therefore$ Dynamic displacement $= \Delta_{st} \times D = \dfrac{200}{20000} \times 0.86 = 0.0086$ m   or,   8.60 mm $\square$

PROBLEMS

MATLAB APPLICATIONS

5.1 An undamped system is subjected to a rectangular impulse force of amplitude p_0 and duration t_d as shown in Figure P5.1. Derive the equations for the response to this impulse starting from rest during the forced vibration phase and free vibration phase.

Figure P5.1

(a) Plot the response $x(t)/x_{st}$ vs. t/T for various values of t_d/T.

(b) Plot the maximum response ratio x_{max}/x_{st} against t_d/T, where x_{max} is defined as the absolute value of $x(t)$ during (i) the forced vibration phase and (ii) the free vibration phase.

(c) Plot the shock spectra.

5.2 An undamped system is subjected to a symmetric triangular impulse force as shown in Figure P5.2. Derive the equations for the response to this impulse starting from rest during the forced vibration phase and free vibration phase.

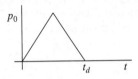

Figure P5.2

(a) Plot the response $x(t)/x_{st}$ vs. t/T for various values of t_d/T.

(b) Plot the maximum response ratio x_{max}/x_{st} against t_d/T, where x_{max} is defined as the absolute value of $x(t)$ during (i) the forced vibration phase and (ii) the free vibration phase.

(c) Plot the shock spectra.

5.3 An undamped system is subjected to a half sine impulse force as shown in Figure P5.3. Derive the equations for the response to this impulse starting from rest during the forced vibration phase and free vibration phase. Plot the maximum response ratio against t_d/T.

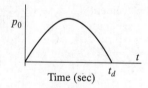

Figure P5.3

(a) Plot the response $x(t)/x_{st}$ vs t/T for various values of t_d/T.

(b) Plot the maximum response ratio x_{max}/x_{st} against t_d/T, where x_{max} is defined as the absolute value of $x(t)$ during (i) the forced vibration phase and (ii) the free vibration phase.

(c) Plot the shock spectra.

5.4 An undamped system is subjected to a full sine impulse force as shown in Figure P5.4. Derive the equations for the response to this impulse starting from rest during the forced vibration phase and free vibration phase. Plot the maximum response ratio against t_d/T.

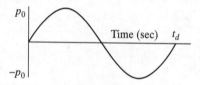

Figure P5.4

(a) Plot the response $x(t)/x_{st}$ vs t/T for various values of t_d/T.

(b) Plot the maximum response ratio x_{max}/x_{st} against t_d/T, where x_{max} is defined as the absolute value of $x(t)$ during (i) the forced vibration phase and (ii) the free vibration phase.

(c) Plot the shock spectra.

5.5 A damped SDOF system with mass = 1 kg, natural frequency = 10 rad/sec, and damping = 10% is subjected to a set of three impulses each having a duration of 0.1 sec as shown in Fig. P5.5. Determine the response of the SDOF system due to each impulse separately and combined response up to 10 sec using an EXCEL sheet.

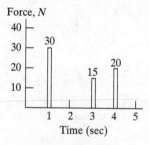

Figure P5.5

5.6 A damped system with $\xi = 5\%$ and mass = 1 kg is subjected to an impulse force as shown in Figure P5.6. Derive the equations for the response to this impulse starting from rest and valid for $t > t_d$

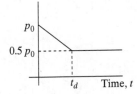

Figure P5.6

Plot the response $x(t)/x_{st}$ vs t/T for various values of t_d/T using MATLAB.

5.7 A damped system with $\xi = 10\%$ and mass = 1 kg is subjected to an impulse force as shown in Figure P5.7. Derive the equations for the response to this impulse starting from rest during the forced vibration phase and free vibration phase. Plot the maximum response ratio against t_d/T using MATLAB.

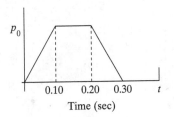

Figure P5.7

REFERENCES

Biggs, J.M. (1964) Introduction to Structural Dynamics, Mc Graw Hill Book Co., New York.

Chopra, A.K. (2001) Dynamics of Structures, 3rd ed., Pearson Education Inc., New Delhi.

Clough, R.W. and Penzien, J. (1993) Dynamics of Structures, Mc Graw Hill Book Co., 2nd ed., New York.

6 | Single Degree of Freedom System: Machine Vibrations

6.1 INTRODUCTION

There are two types of problems in the design of machine foundations. First, there may be undesirable vibrations induced due to base excitation. The base is excited due to either a machine operating in nearby room or building or due to nearby road or rail traffic. Second, the vibrations are caused due to the presence of rotating unbalance mass of the machine. These vibrations are transmitted through its foundation to adjoining areas. Both of these situations are unwelcome. In terms of displacements, the permissible displacements may be as low as about 10^{-4} mm at between 0.1 and 10 Hz for very delicate electronic or medical components, or CNC machine foundations, to several cm (say 10 cm to 50 cm) in tall buildings at between 0.05 and 0.50 Hz. Machine vibrations can range between 10 and 1000 Hz. Vibrations of the foundation may be injurious to the safety and working of the machine as well as foundation itself. Therefore, there is a need to isolate such undesirable vibrations. This isolation is achieved by suitably designing the stiffness and damping of the foundation.

These vibrations can be measured with the help of very tiny but powerful sensors in three orthogonal directions simultaneously and the real time data can be easily recorded in a laptop. These sensors are based on the micro-electro-mechanical sensor (MEMS) technology. A triaxial accelerometer is small and thin, it is only 5 mm × 3 mm × 1 mm or even smaller (2 mm × 2 mm × 1 mm) in size; has low power consumption, variable range, and high resolution characteristics. It is capable of measuring vibrations in various selectable ranges: ± 2, ± 4, ± 8 g and up to ± 400 g as well as different frequency range.

Here, it is important to understand the term *machine foundation*. Generally, in the civil engineering terminology, a foundation is understood to be below the ground level. But in the case of machines, a machine foundation is usually above the ground. A machine foundation may be in the shape of a simple 3D reinforced concrete block as shown in Figure 6.1(a). There may be some openings or cut-outs as per the requirements of the machine. Alternatively, a machine foundation may be in the form of a space frame consisting of beams, columns, and slabs as shown in Figure 6.1(b). A turbo generator foundation in a power plant consists of a space frame. Both the RC block and the space frame may have a conventional foundation below the ground level in the form of a raft or pile foundation depending upon the geotechnical considerations.

A machine foundation can be modeled as a single-degree-of-freedom system or a multi-degree-of-freedom system depending upon the type of machine and its foundation. In certain situations, it may be necessary to incorporate soil–structure interaction, especially in the case of soft soils. The discussion in this chapter covers only single-degree-of-freedom systems but without soil–structure interaction. The analysis of a multi-degree-of-freedom system will be discussed in Chapters 9 and 10.

There are five parts to the Indian standard IS : 2974 for different types of machine foundations. Salient features of these specifications are also discussed.

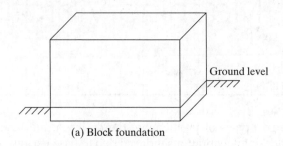

(a) Block foundation

Figure 6.1 (a)   Machine foundation.

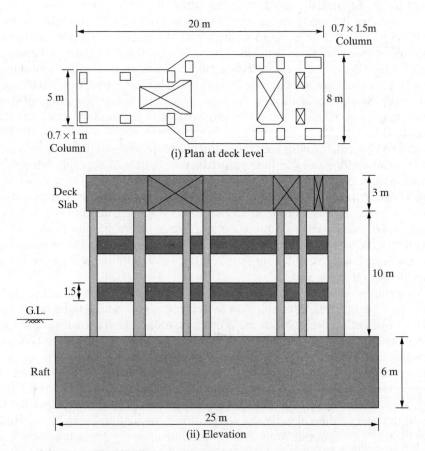

(ii) Elevation

Figure 6.1 (b)   A typical turbogenerator foundation.

6.2 VIBRATION ISOLATION DUE TO BASE EXCITATION

Let us consider a single-degree-of-freedom system as shown in Figure 6.2(a). Let the motion of the mass be $x(t)$ and that of the base be $y(t) = y_0 \sin \bar{\omega} t$. The free body diagram of the system is shown in Figure 6.2(b) The equation of motion can be written by taking into account the relative motion between the mass and the base, that is,

$$m\ddot{x} + c(\dot{x} - \dot{y}) + k(x - y) = 0 \tag{6.1a}$$

The force of inertia is not dependent on the ground motion. That is why it is taken as its absolute value. Equation (6.1a) can be re-written as follows:

$$m\ddot{x} + c\dot{x} + kx = c\dot{y} + ky \tag{6.1b}$$

where,
$$y = y_0 \sin \bar{\omega} t \tag{6.1c}$$

Substituting the values of $y(t)$ and $\dot{y}(t)$, we get

$$m\ddot{x} + c\dot{x} + kx = c\bar{\omega} y_0 \cos \bar{\omega} t + k y_0 \sin \bar{\omega} t \tag{6.2}$$

The right-hand side term can be re-written in terms of its amplitude

$$= y_0 \sqrt{(c\bar{\omega})^2 + k^2} \, \sin(\bar{\omega} t + \varphi) \tag{6.3a}$$

or,
$$m\ddot{x} + c\dot{x} + kx = p_0 \sin(\bar{\omega} t + \phi) \tag{6.3b}$$

where,
$$p_0 = y_0 \sqrt{(c\bar{\omega})^2 + k^2} \qquad \text{It has the unit of force}$$

$$\phi = \tan^{-1} \frac{c\bar{\omega}}{k} \tag{6.3c}$$

= phase lag between ground motion and system response

Equation (6.3a) is similar to the equation of a forced vibration problem derived in Chapter 3. The only difference is the amplitude of the forcing function and the existence of a phase difference ϕ. The phase difference can be ignored if we choose to measure time from a different origin. Thus, the amplitude of vibration of the motion can be obtained. The equation of motion, Equation (6.3b), can be written as follows:

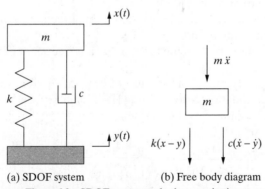

(a) SDOF system   (b) Free body diagram

Figure 6.2   SDOF system under base excitation.

$$m\ddot{x} + c\dot{x} + kx = p_0 \sin \bar{\omega}t' \tag{6.4}$$

The time t' is measured from a different origin so that the phase difference ϕ is zero. Let us drop the symbol (') for ease while retaining its definition.

The steady state solution can be written as follows:

$$x = y_0 \sin \bar{\omega}t \; \frac{\sqrt{k^2 + c^2\bar{\omega}^2}}{\sqrt{(k - m\bar{\omega})^2 + c^2\bar{\omega}^2}} \tag{6.5a}$$

Phase difference $\qquad\qquad \phi = \tan^{-1} \dfrac{c\bar{\omega}}{(k - m\bar{\omega})} \tag{6.5b}$

Dividing by m in denominator as well as numerator and taking maximum displacement

$$\frac{x_{max}}{y_0} = \frac{\sqrt{\dfrac{k^2}{m^2} + \dfrac{c^2\bar{\omega}^2}{m^2}}}{\sqrt{\left(\dfrac{k}{m} - \bar{\omega}\right)^2 + \dfrac{c^2\bar{\omega}^2}{m^2}}}$$

or, $\qquad\qquad \dfrac{x_{max}}{y_0} = \dfrac{\sqrt{\omega^4 + (2\xi\omega\bar{\omega})^2}}{\sqrt{(\omega^2 - \bar{\omega}^2)^2 + (2\xi\omega\bar{\omega})^2}} \tag{6.6}$

$$\frac{x_{max}}{y_0} = \frac{\sqrt{1 + (2\beta\xi)^2}}{\sqrt{(1 - \beta^2)^2 + (2\beta\xi)^2}} \tag{6.7}$$

or, $\qquad\qquad TR = D\sqrt{1 + (2\beta\xi)^2} \tag{6.8}$

where,

$$TR = \text{Transmissibility ratio} = \frac{\text{amplitude of motion of mass}}{\text{amplitude of ground motion}} \tag{6.9}$$

D = dynamic magnification factor obtained earlier for steady state response due to harmonic loading.

β = ratio of the frequency of the forcing function to that of the natural vibration of the foundation.

The frequency of the forcing function means frequency of vibration of the ground motion or ground vibrations.

Transmissibility ratio is a measure of how much vibration is transmitted to the mass from the foundation below. Thus, $(1 - TR)$ is a measure of effectiveness of the isolation system. A plot of TR vs. frequency ratio β is shown in Figure 6.3 for different damping ratios.

If TR = 1,

$$\sqrt{1 + (2\beta\xi)^2} = \sqrt{(1 - \beta^2)^2 + (2\beta\xi)^2}$$

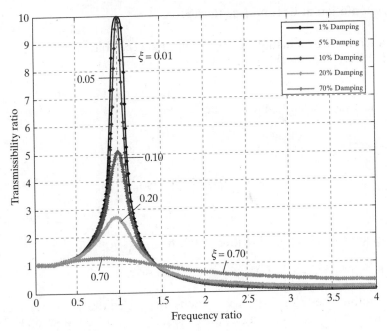

Figure 6.3   Transmissibility ratio vs. frequency ratio for different damping.

or,
$$1 = \left(1-\beta^2\right)^2$$

or,
$$1-\beta^2 = \pm 1$$

or,
$$\beta = 0 \text{ or } \sqrt{2} \tag{6.10}$$

It can be seen in Figure 6.3 that for a frequency ratio β greater than $\sqrt{2}$, TR is always less than 1. Hence there is no magnification of the ground vibrations.

It is interesting to understand the curves of Figure 6.3. The following observations can be made:

(a) For a frequency ratio $\beta > \sqrt{2}$, the transmissibility ratio TR is always less than 1 irrespective of damping ξ.

(b) For a frequency ratio $\beta < \sqrt{2}$, increase in damping reduces the displacement amplitude. However, for a frequency ratio $\beta > \sqrt{2}$, increase in damping increases the displacement amplitude.

(c) For TR < 1, the frequency ratio β should be >> 1. It means the natural frequency of the foundation should be very small, that is, it should have a very low stiffness. Again, damping should also be very low in this region.

There is a need to carefully choose the stiffness and damping parameters in order to arrive at a satisfactory solution meeting all the specified design criteria under static and dynamic operating conditions.

6.2.1 Isolation of Ground Acceleration

An alternative formulation in terms of ground acceleration can also be derived. If the SDOF system is subjected to harmonic ground motion, that is,

$$\ddot{y}(t) = \ddot{y}_0 \sin(\bar{\omega}t) \tag{6.11}$$

and the total acceleration of the mass is given by

$$\ddot{x}^t(t) = \ddot{x}(t) + \ddot{y}(t) \tag{6.12}$$

where,

$$x(t) = \frac{p_0}{k} D \sin(\bar{\omega}t - \phi) \tag{6.13a}$$

and

$$p_0 = \left| -m\,\ddot{y} \right|_{max} \tag{6.13b}$$

∴ Equation (6.13a) can be written as follows:

$$x(t) = \frac{-m\ddot{y}_0}{k} D \sin(\bar{\omega}t - \phi) \tag{6.13c}$$

Substituting the values of accelerations from Equations (6.13c) and (6.11) into Equation (6.12), and rearranging the equation leads to Equation (6.7). Thus,

$$TR = \frac{\ddot{x}_0^t}{\ddot{y}_0} = \frac{\text{acceleration transmitted to the mass}}{\text{amplitude of ground acceleration}} \tag{6.14}$$

The transmissibility is defined in terms of displacement transmitted to the mass or acceleration transmitted to the mass. The undesirable ground vibrations can be isolated by properly designing the vertical stiffness and damping of the foundation system, that is, k and c. The expression given by Equation (6.14) is significant while designing vibration measuring instruments.

6.3 VIBRATION ISOLATION DUE TO ROTATING UNBALANCE

A machine is mounted on a foundation as shown in Figure 6.4. It is quite possible that when the machine is in motion at $\bar{\omega}$ rotations per minute (rpm), it may transmit vibrations through its foundation to the adjoining areas. The machine has an unbalanced mass of m' acting at a radius of r from its center of rotation. It will produce a centrifugal force equal to $m'\,r\,\bar{\omega}^2$. Even though a machine is always designed to be balanced, there may still be some small unbalance causing significant vibrations. This is a problem of designing a machine foundation.

$$\text{Vertical component of centrifugal force} = m'r\,\bar{\omega}^2 \sin\bar{\omega}\,t \tag{6.15}$$

Therefore, the equation of motion of a SDOF system is given by

$$m\ddot{x} + c\,\dot{x} + k\,x = m'r\,\bar{\omega}^2 \sin\bar{\omega}\,t \tag{6.16a}$$

$$= p_0 \sin(\bar{\omega}t) \tag{6.16b}$$

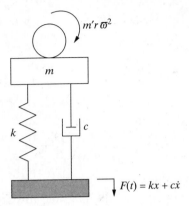

Figure 6.4   A machine foundation under rotating unbalance.

Steady state response $x(t) = \dfrac{p_0}{k} D \sin(\varpi t - \phi)$ (6.13a)

The amplitude of the motion is given by

$$x_{max} = \frac{p_0}{k} D = \frac{m' r \varpi^2}{m \varpi^2} D \qquad (6.17a)$$

$$= \left(\frac{m'}{m}\right) r \left(\frac{\varpi}{\omega}\right)^2 \frac{1}{\sqrt{\left(1 - \left(\frac{\varpi}{\omega}\right)^2\right)^2 + \left(2\xi \frac{\varpi}{\omega}\right)^2}}$$

or, $$x_{max} = \frac{(m'/m) r \beta^2}{\sqrt{\left(1 - \beta^2\right)^2 + \left(2\xi\beta\right)^2}} \qquad (6.17b)$$

At resonance, $$x_{max} = \frac{m' r}{2 m \xi} \qquad (6.17c)$$

For very large values of the frequency ratio β, Equation (6.17b) reduces to

$$x_{max} = \frac{m' r}{m} \qquad (6.17d)$$

Force transmitted to foundation through the spring and dash-pot system is equal to

$$F_t = c\dot{x} + kx \qquad (6.18a)$$

$\therefore$ $$\dot{x}(t) = \frac{p_0}{k} D \cos(\varpi t - \phi) \varpi \qquad (6.18b)$$

The spring force $f_s = k\,x(t)$ and damping force $f_d = c\dot{x}(t)$
Total force transmitted to the foundation is given by

$$f(t) = f_s(t) + f_d(t) \qquad (6.19a)$$

or,
$$= p_0 D \sin(\varpi t - \phi) + 2\beta\xi\, p_0 D \cos(\varpi t - \phi) \tag{6.19b}$$

Its amplitude is given by

$$F_{t\,max} = \sqrt{(p_0 D)^2 + (2\beta\xi p_0 D)^2}$$

or,
$$= p_0 D \sqrt{1 + (2\beta\xi)^2} \tag{6.20}$$

or,
$$\frac{F_{t\,max}}{m' r \bar{\varpi}^2} = \frac{\sqrt{1 + (2\beta\xi)^2}}{\sqrt{(1 - \beta^2)^2 + (2\beta\xi)^2}} \tag{6.21}$$

This is same as Equation (6.7).

β is ratio of forcing frequency of the machine to natural frequency of the system. Transmissibility ratio is defined as follows:

$$TR = \frac{\text{Maximum force applied on the base}}{\text{amplitude of the force}} \tag{6.22}$$

or,
$$TR = D\sqrt{1 + (2\xi\beta)^2}$$

The undesirable vibrations are isolated from being transmitted to the foundation by designing the vertical stiffness k and damping c of the foundation.

The effectiveness for zero damping is given by Equation (6.21):

$$TR = \pm\frac{1}{(1 - \beta^2)}$$

For β greater than 1, it can be written as follows:

$$TR = \frac{1}{\beta^2 - 1} \tag{6.23a}$$

or,
$$1 - TR = \frac{\beta^2 - 2}{\beta^2 - 1} = E, \text{ say (where } \beta > \sqrt{2}\,) \tag{6.23b}$$

The term $(E = 1 - TR)$ is a measure of effectiveness of the vibration isolation system, that is, degree of vibration cut-off. If TR is 15%, it means 85% vibrations were isolated or cut-off.

If frequency ratio $\beta = \dfrac{\varpi}{\omega} = \dfrac{\varpi}{\sqrt{\dfrac{k}{m}}}$

Equation (6.23b) can be re-written as follows:

$$\beta^2 = \frac{2 - E}{1 - E} \tag{6.24a}$$

or,
$$\beta = \frac{\varpi}{\omega} = \frac{\varpi}{\sqrt{\dfrac{k}{m}}} = \sqrt{\frac{2 - E}{1 - E}} \tag{6.24b}$$

or,

$$\varpi = \sqrt{\frac{k}{m}\left(\frac{2-E}{1-E}\right)} \qquad (6.25)$$

Stiffness is given by $k = \dfrac{mg}{\Delta_{st}}$ where Δ_{st} is static deflection

The forcing frequency, that is, frequency of rotation of the machine in rpm $(\bar{f})$ can be written as follows:

$$\varpi = 2\pi\,\bar{f}$$

and

$$\bar{f} = \frac{1}{2\pi}\sqrt{\frac{g}{\Delta_{st}}\frac{2-E}{1-E}} \qquad (6.26)$$

If $g = 980$ cm/sec², Equation (6.26) can be written as follows:

$$\bar{f} = 4.98\sqrt{\frac{1}{\Delta_{st}}\frac{2-E}{1-E}} \qquad (6.27)$$

The static displacement is given in cm and the machine frequency is in radians per sec or in rotation per second. For a given percentage reduction of force transmitted E, a plot can be drawn between frequency of rotation and static displacement. This plot can be used for design of such foundations. For a given machine frequency and desired effectiveness, the support deflection can be estimated from the graph. These curves can also be plotted on a log-log scale.

$$\log \bar{f} = -\frac{1}{2}\log\Delta_{st} + \log\left(4.98\sqrt{\frac{2-E}{1-E}}\right) \qquad (6.28)$$

The design curves are shown in Figure 6.5.

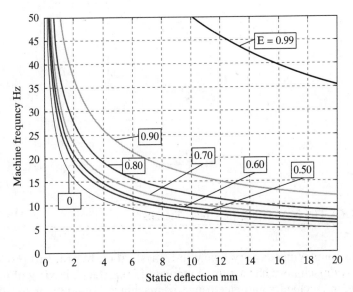

Figure 6.5   Effectiveness of vibration isolation system.

6.4 APPLICATION TO EARTHQUAKE ENGINEERING

In Equation (6.1a), the base motion could be due to an earthquake. This equation can be modified to model the earthquake motion. In vibrations due to earthquakes, we are more interested in the relative displacement of a mass with respect to ground rather than its absolute displacement as shown in Figure 6.6.

Let us re-write Equation (6.1a)

$$m\ddot{x} + c(\dot{x} - \dot{y}) + k(x - y) = 0 \tag{6.1a}$$

Thus, taking $x_r = x - y$, $\dot{x}_r = \dot{x} - \dot{y}$ and $\ddot{x}_r = \ddot{x} - \ddot{y}$ $\tag{6.29a}$

where $x_r, \dot{x}_r$ and $\ddot{x}_r$ are relative displacement, relative velocity and relative acceleration, respectively, of the mass m.

Substituting Equation (6.29a) in Equation (6.1a) gives,

$$m\ddot{x}_r(t) + c\dot{x}_r(t) + k x_r(t) = -m\ddot{y}(t) \tag{6.29b}$$

or, for convenience, the subscript r is dropped, and $\ddot{y}$ is replaced with $\ddot{y}_g$

Thus, we get $\qquad m\ddot{x}(t) + c\dot{x}(t) + k x(t) = -m\ddot{y}_g(t) \tag{6.30a}$

or, $\qquad\qquad\qquad m\ddot{x} + c\dot{x} + k x = -m\ddot{y}_g \tag{6.30b}$

This is the equation of motion of a SDOF system subjected to ground motion $\ddot{y}_g(t)$. It's solution is discussed in Chapters 7 and 8.

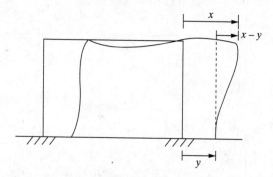

Figure 6.6   A SDOF system under ground displacement.

6.5 I.S. CODE ON MACHINE FOUNDATIONS

The country needs very heavy industrialization in order to progress. Installation of heavy machinery has assumed increased importance in view of increased sophistication in mechanics and electronics of machines. Foundations for these machines have to be specially designed taking into consideration the impact and vibration character-istics of the load and the properties of soil under dynamic conditions. IS: 2974 code on machine foundations has five parts for different kinds of machines. These codes give the data on machines to be provided by the machine manufacturer, data required for the site, mass and geometric constraints on the foundation, desirable static and dynamic characteristics, modeling, limiting deflection and frequency ratios, load com-binations, damping, minimum grade of concrete and minimum reinforcement. Salient features for various kinds of machine foundations as specified in each of the five parts are as follows:

Part 1: Foundation for reciprocating type machines

The following data needs to be provided by the machine manufacturer:
- Description of driving and driven machinery
- Operating speed or speed ranges
- Number and arrangement of cylinders
- Distance between axis of main shaft of the machine and the top face of foundation
- Maximum rated output
- Gear box ratio where applicable
- Maximum operating temperature in the bases of the machine

For Static Design: A detailed loading diagram comprising plan, elevation and section showing details of communication and point of all loads on foundation.

For Dynamic Design: Details of out-of-balance forces and couples should be given, together with associated frequencies for all possible modes of vibration for driving and driven machinery. These include the following:
- External forces
- External primary couples
- External secondary couples
- Harmonic torques

Mass moments of inertia of driving and driven machine about three principal axes should be indicated. Additional information relating to specific machines, as given below, should be provided where necessary:
- (a) Loads due to dynamic short circuit conditions
- (b) Loads due to an abnormal sudden stoppage

Part 2: Foundations for impact type machines (Hammer foundations)

The machine foundation system should be analysed as a two-degree-of-freedom system, with anvil forming one mass and the foundation block as the second mass. For analysis the dynamic force is calculated on the basis of momentum equation. The dynamic analysis of a two-degree-of-freedom system is explained in Chapter 9. Selected results are also available in Appendix A of IS: 2974-Part 2.

Part 3: Foundation for rotary type machines with medium and high frequency machine data

The following data must be made available to the designer by the machine manufacturer:

- Loading diagram of the machine showing the location, magnitude and direction of all loads including dynamic loads
- Speed of the machine
- Critical speeds of the machine
- Outline dimensions of the foundation
- Mass moment of inertia of the machine components
- Details of inserts and embedments
- Layout of piping, ducting and their supporting details
- Temperatures in various zones during operation
- Allowable displacements at the machine bearing points during normal operation

The following loads should be considered for the foundation design:

- Dead loads which include the self-weight of the foundation and dead weight of the machine;
- Operation loads supplied by the machine manufacturer which include friction forces, power torque, thermal elongation forces, vacuum in the condenser, piping forces, etc;
- Unbalance forces during normal operation;
- Temperature forces caused by uniform temperature change and gradient temperature;
- Short circuit breaker;
- Loss of blade unbalance forces/bearing failure load;
- Seismic forces; and
- Erection loads.

Modeling of Foundation

The following points needs to be considered while developing model for dynamic analysis of machine foundation:

- The foundation should be modelled as a three-dimensional space frame. Slabs and walls, if present, may be modelled using thin shell (plate bending) elements.
- The columns should be assumed to be fixed at the base disregarding the base mat.
- Lumped-mass approach should be used for computing modal masses of the foundation. The machine should be modelled to lump its mass together with the mass of the foundation. The stiffness and damping of the shaft and casing can be disregarded.
- Soil–structure interaction must be accounted for in the dynamic analysis.
- Uncracked sections may be used for calculating moments of inertia of the members. The rotational inertia may be disregarded. However, shear rigidity should be considered.

The code gives further guidelines on how to size the foundation, top deck, girders, columns and base mat.

Part 4: Foundations for rotary type machines of low frequency

The code specifies machine data, design data, load combinations and other details. As a rule, the equipment foundation should not be allowed to serve as a support for other structures or for machineries not related to the particular equipment.

Isolation: To avoid transmission of vibration to adjoining parts of buildings or other foundations, it is necessary to provide a suitable isolation between the equipment foundation and the adjoining structures. This may commonly be achieved by providing sand trench or a vertical sheet of thermocole around the foundation block, the thickness and depth of which should be determined for each individual case.

The natural frequencies of the foundation depend upon the size of foundation in terms of total mass and contact area. Therefore, the mass and contact area should be decided taking into consideration the dynamic characteristics. The mass of the foundation should be at least 2.5 times the mass of the whole machine.

Part 5: Foundations for impact machines other than hammer (forging and stamping press, pig breaker, drop crusher and jolter)

6.5.1 General Requirements

All machine foundations must satisfy *two criteria*:
  (i) that resonance does not occur between the frequencies of the pulsating loads and natural frequency of foundation/soil system
  (ii) the amplitude of vibration does not exceed safe limits as prescribed by the machine manufacturer

The foundation of machine needs to be isolated at all levels from the main building and from other foundations as far as possible. In case there are any overhanging cantilevers, they should be designed to ensure rigidity against vibration. Design criteria based on frequency and amplitude limits can be classified as follows:

  (a) Limits set by the possibility of damage or uneconomic wear to machinery or associated equipment or both,
  (b) Limits set by the possibility of damage to building structures,
  (c) Limits of structural borne vibrations to ensure comfort of person, and
  (d) Limits set by possibility of disturbance of ground resulting in unacceptable settlement of foundation.

Frequency Ratio
The natural frequency of the foundation-soil system should be higher than the highest disturbing frequency. Alternatively, natural frequency of the foundation-soil system should be kept lower than the lowest disturbing frequency. It is important to know that even though a machine may be balanced, minor disturbing forces can occur due to manufacturing tolerances and other causes; for sensitive installations, the frequencies arising from these may have to be considered. The natural frequency should be computed corresponding to the longitudinal, transverse and vertical modes. The transmissibility ratio should be checked accordingly.

A set of vibration isolation devices are placed at the top of each column supporting the turbo generator base slab for a 500 MW power project at Jharli, Haryana, as shown in Figures 6.7. The number of such devices at each column top depends upon the total load acting on the base slab.

More details on vibration isolation can be seen in IS: 13301, ISO: 10811 and ISO:10816 codes.

Figure 6.7(a) Vibration isolators.

Figure 6.7(b) A view of TG foundation block showing vibration isolators below deck slab.

Figure 6.7(c)   A close-up view of TG foundation block showing vibration isolators below deck slab.

Figure 6.7(d)   A view of vibration isolators below deck slab from top.

6.6 ILLUSTRATIVE EXAMPLES

Example 6.1

A machine is supported on a pedestal which can tolerate a vertical deflection of 1×10^{-3} mm under operating conditions. It is subjected to a forcing function causing a base displacement amplitude of 20×10^{-3} mm at a frequency of 10 Hz. Damping may be taken as 2%.

(a) Determine the natural frequency of the system.

(b) If the mass of the machine including platform is 1500 kg, what will be its static deflection?

Solution

(a) Transmissibility ratio (TR) $= \dfrac{\text{amplitude of motion of mass}}{\text{amplitude of ground motion}} = \dfrac{1 \times 10^{-3}}{20 \times 10^{-3}} = \dfrac{1}{20}$

$$= \frac{\sqrt{1+(2\beta\xi)^2}}{\sqrt{(1-\beta^2)^2+(2\beta\xi)^2}} \qquad (6.7)$$

For damping ratio $\xi = 2\%$, β can be estimated from Equation (6.7).

It gives frequency ratio $\beta = 4.62 = \dfrac{\varpi}{\omega} = \dfrac{\bar{f}}{f} = 4.62$

The natural frequency ω or $f = 10/4.62 = 2.16$ Hz

(b) Stiffness of the foundation $k = m\,\omega^2 = 1500 \times (2\,\pi f)^2 = 276.3$ kN/m

Hence, static deflection under self-weight $\Delta_{st} = mg/k = \dfrac{1500 \times 9.8}{276.3 \times 10^3} = 53.1 \times 10^{-3}$ m

or, $\Delta_{st} = 53.1$ mm ◻

Example 6.2

A foundation block is to be installed in a plant such that the vibration from the adjacent areas will not affect it. The mass of the foundation system is 2000 kg and the surrounding floor vibrates at 2500 cycles per minute. Estimate the stiffness of the foundation so that the transmissibility ratio is not more than 10%, if

(a) Damping is ignored

(b) Damping is taken as 30%

Solution

(a) Damping is zero

$$TR = \pm \frac{1}{1-\beta^2} = 10\%$$

or, $\qquad 0.1 - 0.1\,\beta^2 = -1$, or, $\beta = \pm 3.32 > \sqrt{2}$ OK

Frequency ratio $\beta = \varpi/\omega = 3.32$

But forcing frequency $= \bar{f} = 2500$ c.p.m. $= 41.67$ Hz or, $\varpi = 6.63$ rad/sec

$\therefore$ Natural frequency $\omega = 6.63/3.32 = 2$ rad/sec

$\therefore$ Stiffness of the isolated system $= k = m\,\omega^2 = 2000 \times 2^2 = 8000$ N/m

(b) Damping is 30%

$$TR = \frac{\sqrt{1+(2\beta\xi)^2}}{\sqrt{(1-\beta^2)^2+(2\beta\xi)^2}}$$

For TR $= 0.1$, and damping ratio 30%, frequency ratio β is calculated as 6.33

Frequency ratio $\beta = \varpi/\omega = 6.33$

But forcing frequency = $\bar{\omega} = 6.63$ rad/sec

∴ Natural frequency $\omega = 6.63/6.33 = 1.047$ rad/sec

∴ Stiffness of the isolated system $= k = m\ \omega^2 = 2000 \times 1.047^2 = 2192$ N/m

It shows that if a highly damped isolation system such as a rubber pad or rubber tyre is used to isolate the vibrations, it will require a very low stiffness. □

Example 6.3

A machine foundation has a mass of 500 kg with a vertical stiffness of 400 kN/m. If the base displacement amplitude is 5 mm, the displacement amplitude of the mass is 10 mm while it is vibrating at its natural frequency. Calculate the damping ratio and damping coefficient.

Solution   It is a problem of base excitation.

$$TR = \frac{\sqrt{1+(2\beta\xi)^2}}{\sqrt{(1-\beta^2)^2+(2\beta\xi)^2}}$$

At resonance, $\beta = 1$,

$$TR = \frac{\sqrt{1+(2\xi)^2}}{2\xi} = \frac{10}{5} = 2$$

or, $1 + (2\xi)^2 = (4\ \xi)^2$

or, $\xi = 0.288$ or 28.8%

Natural frequency of the system $\omega = \sqrt{\dfrac{k}{m}} = \sqrt{\dfrac{400 \times 1000}{500}} = 63.24$ rad/sec

Damping coefficient $c = 2\ m\ \omega\ \xi = 2 \times 500 \times 63.24 \times 0.288 = 18213$ kg/sec □

Example 6.4

In Example 6.3, also calculate the force transmitted to the base.

Solution   The force acting at the base $F_t = k(x-y) + c(\dot{x}-\dot{y})$

At equilibrium,

$$m\ddot{x} + c(\dot{x}-\dot{y}) + k(x-y) = 0$$

∴ $F_t = -m\ddot{x}$

Let us find the acceleration of the mass by twice differentiating its displacement. The steady state solution is given by Equation (6.5a),

$$x = y_0 \sin\bar{\omega}t\frac{\sqrt{k^2+c^2\bar{\omega}^2}}{\sqrt{(k-m\bar{\omega})^2+c^2\bar{\omega}^2}}$$

∴ $$\ddot{x}(t) = -\bar{\omega}^2 y_0 \sin\bar{\omega}t\frac{\sqrt{k^2+c^2\bar{\omega}^2}}{\sqrt{(k-m\bar{\omega})^2+c^2\bar{\omega}^2}}$$

Thus, force acting at its base $F(t)$ is given by

$$F(t) = -m\ddot{x}(t) = m\omega^2 y_0 \sin\omega t \frac{\sqrt{k^2 + c^2\omega^2}}{\sqrt{(k - m\omega)^2 + c^2\omega^2}}$$

or,

$$F(t) = k\,\beta^2 y_0 \sin\omega t \frac{\sqrt{k^2 + c^2\omega^2}}{\sqrt{(k - m\omega)^2 + c^2\omega^2}}$$

The amplitude of the force transmitted to the base is given by

$$F = k y_0 \beta^2 \frac{\sqrt{k^2 + c^2\omega^2}}{\sqrt{(k - m\omega)^2 + c^2\omega^2}}$$

This can be rearranged as follows:
Force transmissibility

$$\frac{F}{k y_0} = \beta^2 \frac{\sqrt{k^2 + c^2\omega^2}}{\sqrt{(k - m\omega)^2 + c^2\omega^2}}$$

$$\frac{F}{k y_0} = \beta^2 \frac{\sqrt{1 + (2\beta\xi)^2}}{\sqrt{(1 - \beta^2)^2 + (2\beta\xi)^2}}$$

In the present example, $\beta = 1$, $\xi = 0.288$, $k = 400$ kN/m and $y_0 = 5$ mm
$\therefore$ Amplitude of force transmitted

$$F = 400 \times (5/1000) \times \frac{\sqrt{1 + (2 \times 0.288)^2}}{2 \times 0.288}$$

or, $F = 4$ kN   □

Example 6.5

A SDOF system is subjected to base excitation. At a frequency ratio of 2.5, it is desired to keep the transmissibility ratio to less than 0.40. Determine the damping ratio.

Solution
The displacement transmissibility ratio (TR)

$$\text{TR} = \frac{x_{max}}{y_0} = \frac{\sqrt{1 + (2\beta\xi)^2}}{\sqrt{(1 - \beta^2)^2 + (2\beta\xi)^2}}$$

$$0.40 = \frac{\sqrt{1 + (2 \times 2.5 \times \xi)^2}}{\sqrt{(1 - 2.5^2)^2 + (2 \times 2.5 \times \xi)^2}}$$

or, $\xi = 0.40$ or 40%

Any damping ratio less than 40% will ensure a transmissibility ratio of less than 0.40 because the frequency ratio is more than $\sqrt{2}$.   □

Example 6.6

A building is modeled as a SDOF system having a mass of 250 kN and a lateral stiffness of 5000 kN/m. If the base amplitude is 0.20 m at a frequency of 10 rad/sec during an earthquake, estimate the lateral displacement at its top.

Solution

Natural frequency of the building $\omega = \sqrt{\dfrac{k}{m}} = \sqrt{\dfrac{5000 \times 1000}{250 \times 1000 / 9.8}} = 14$ rad/sec

Period of vibration $T = \dfrac{2\pi}{\omega} = 0.448$ sec

$$TR = \frac{x_{max}}{y_0} = \frac{\sqrt{1 + (2\beta\xi)^2}}{\sqrt{(1 - \beta^2)^2 + (2\beta\xi)^2}}$$

Frequency ratio $\beta = 10/14 = 0.714$
Let us assume a damping ratio of 2% for a steel building,

$$\therefore TR = \frac{\sqrt{1 + (2 \times 0.714 \times 0.02)^2}}{\sqrt{(1 - 0.714^2)^2 + (2 \times 0.714 \times 0.02)^2}} = 1.96$$

$\therefore$ Displacement at the top of the building $= 1.96 \times 0.20 = 0.392$ m   □

Example 6.7

A machine is mounted on a foundation and rotates at 1250 rpm, its unbalance mass is 15 kg (10% of the total mass) at an eccentricity of 50 mm from its centre. The stiffness of the foundation is 250000 N/m and damping is 10%. Determine the amplitude of vertical vibrations.

Solution

Natural frequency of the foundation $\omega = \sqrt{\dfrac{k}{m}} = \sqrt{\dfrac{250000}{(150 + 15)}} = 38.90$ rad/sec

Forcing frequency $\varpi = 1250$ rpm $= 1250/60 = 20.83$ cps $= 20.83$ Hz
$\therefore \varpi = 2\,\pi\,20.83 = 130.90$ rad/sec
$\therefore$ Frequency ratio $\beta = 130.90/38.90 = 3.36$
Its steady state response is given by

$$x(t) = \frac{p_0}{k} D \sin(\varpi t - \phi) \tag{6.13a}$$

Its amplitude $\quad x_0 = \dfrac{p_0}{k} D = \dfrac{p_0}{k} \dfrac{1}{\sqrt{(1 - \beta^2)^2 + (2\beta\xi)^2}}$

$$x_0 = \frac{m' r \varpi^2}{k} \frac{1}{\sqrt{(1 - \beta^2)^2 + (2\beta\xi)^2}}$$

$$x_0 = \frac{15 \times 50 / 1000 \times 130.9^2}{250000} \frac{1}{\sqrt{(1 - 3.36^2)^2 + (2 \times 3.36 \times 0.10)^2}}$$

$$x_0 = 0.00494 \text{ m} = 4.94 \text{ mm} \qquad\qquad □$$

Example 6.8

A machine is mounted on a framed foundation whose 2D model is shown in Figure 6.8. The mass at the deck level is 750 kN and the three columns are rigidly connected at top and bottom with the slabs. The column size is 30 cm × 50 cm and a clear height is 3 m. The machine has an unbalanced mass of 40 kg acting at a radius of 25 cm and operates at 3000 rpm. Determine the amplitude of vertical vibrations neglecting damping. Grade of concrete = M30.

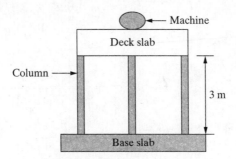

Figure 6.8 Machine foundation.

Solution

Modulus of elasticity of concrete = $5000 \sqrt{f_{ck}} = 5000 \times \sqrt{30} = 27380$ MPa

$$= 27380 \times 10^3 \text{ kN/m}^2$$

Vertical stiffness of columns = $3\dfrac{AE}{L} = \dfrac{3 \times 0.30 \times 0.50 \times 27380 \times 10^3}{3} = 4107000 \text{ kN/m}$

Natural frequency of the foundation $\omega = \sqrt{\dfrac{k}{m}} = \sqrt{\dfrac{4107000 \times 1000}{750 \times 1000 / 9.80}} = 231$ rad/sec

Period of vibration in vertical direction $T = \dfrac{2\pi}{\omega} = \dfrac{2\pi}{231} = 0.027$ sec

Forcing frequency $\varpi = 3000$ rpm = $\dfrac{3000}{60} \times 2\pi = 314$ rad/sec

Frequency ratio $\beta = 314/231 = 1.36$

Centrifugal force $p_0 = m'r\varpi^2 = 40 \times 0.25 \times 314^2 = 985960 \, N$

Steady state displacement amplitude x_0 is given by

$$\frac{p_0}{k} D = \frac{p_0}{k} \frac{1}{\sqrt{\left(1 - \beta^2\right)^2 + \left(2\beta\xi\right)^2}}$$

$$x_0 = \frac{985960}{4107000 \times 10^3} \times \frac{1}{\left(1 - 1.36^2\right)} = 204 \times 10^{-6} \, m$$

or, amplitude of vertical vibrations = 0.204 mm ☐

Example 6.9

A machine foundation is supporting a machine. It exhibits an amplitude of 20 mm at resonance. At very high machine frequencies, an amplitude of 2.5 mm is observed. Estimate the damping in the system.

Solution

At resonance

$$x_{max} = \frac{m'r}{2m\xi} = 20$$ (6.17c)

At very high frequencies,

$$x_{max} = \frac{m'r}{m} = 2.5$$ (6.17d)

∴ Dividing Equation (6.17d) by Equation (6.17c) gives

$$2\xi = \frac{2.5}{20} \quad \text{or} \quad \xi = 0.0625 \quad \text{or} \quad 6.25\% \qquad \square$$

Example 6.10

A motor weighing 10 kN is supported by four springs each of stiffness 5000 N/m. The system has a viscous damping. Estimate the minimum damping coefficient such that there is no oscillation.

Solution

For no oscillation, minimum damping = critical damping C_c

Critical damping $C_c = 2\sqrt{km}$

Mass $m = 10 \times 1000/9.81 = 1019.37$ kg

Stiffness $k = 4 \times 5000 = 20000$ N/m

Natural frequency $\omega = \sqrt{\dfrac{k}{m}} = \sqrt{\dfrac{20000}{1019.37}} = 4.43$ rad/sec

Period $T = \dfrac{2\pi}{\omega} = 1.42$ sec

Critical damping $C_c = 2\sqrt{20000 \times 1019.37} = 4515$ Ns / m

or, $C_c = 4.52$ kNs/m $\square$

Example 6.11

An instrument weighs 0.1 kN and mounted on a base having spring stiffness of 5 kN/m and damping of 15%. The ground is transmitting a vertical acceleration of 0.1 g at a frequency of 50 rad/sec.

(a) What acceleration is transmitted to the instrument?

(b) If the instrument can tolerate an acceleration of 0.004 g, advice how to modify the foundation using the same support system.

Solution

(a) Natural frequency of the base $\omega = \sqrt{\dfrac{k}{m}} = \sqrt{\dfrac{5000}{0.1 \times 1000 / 9.80}} = 22.14$ rad/sec

The frequency ratio $\beta = \omega/\omega = 50/22.14 = 2.258$

$$TR = \frac{\ddot{x}'_{max}}{\ddot{y}_0} = \frac{\sqrt{1+(2\beta\xi)^2}}{\sqrt{(1-\beta^2)^2 + (2\beta\xi)^2}}$$

$$= \left[\frac{1+(2\times 2.258\times 0.15)^2}{(1-2.258^2)^2 + (2\times 2.258\times 0.15)^2} \right]^{0.50}$$

$$\frac{\ddot{x}^t_{max}}{\ddot{y}_0} = 0.29$$

$\therefore$ $\ddot{x}^t = 0.29\times 0.1g = 0.029\,g$

(b) The machine can tolerate a transmissibility ratio given by

$$TR = 0.004\,g\,/\,0.1\,g = 0.04$$

In order to achieve such a low TR ratio, the frequency ratio β needs to be very high, that is, the natural frequency of the supporting system needs to be very low since the base excitation frequency cannot be controlled.

(i) Let us try and add a mass of 0.3 kN on to the foundation
Revised natural frequency of the base is given by

$$\omega_1 = \sqrt{\frac{k}{m+m'}} = \sqrt{\frac{5}{(0.1+0.3)/g}} = 11.068\,\text{rad/sec}$$

Revised frequency ratio $\beta = \omega/\omega_1 = 50/11.068 = 4.52$
Let us calculate revised damping ratio for the system with added mass
Earlier damping ratio $\xi = c/c_c$

Revised damping ratio $\xi' = \dfrac{c}{c'_c}$

$\therefore$ $\dfrac{\xi}{\xi'} = \dfrac{c'_c}{c_c} = \dfrac{2(m+m')\omega_1}{2m\omega}$

$$\xi' = \frac{m\omega\xi}{(m+m')\omega_1} = \frac{0.1\times 22.14\times 0.15}{(0.1+0.3)\times 11.068} = 0.075$$

$$TR = \frac{\ddot{x}^t_{max}}{\ddot{y}_0} = \frac{\sqrt{1+(2\beta\xi)^2}}{\sqrt{(1-\beta^2)^2 + (2\beta\xi)^2}}$$

$$= \left[\frac{1+(2\times 4.52\times 0.075)^2}{(1-4.52^2)^2 + (2\times 4.52\times 0.075)^2} \right]^{0.50} = 0.062$$

$$\ddot{x}^t = 0.062\times 0.1\,g = 0.0062\,g > 0.004g \qquad No\ Good$$

(ii) Therefore, there is a need to revise the design. Let us add a mass of 0.6 kN
Revised natural frequency of the base

$$\omega_1 = \sqrt{\frac{k}{m+m'}} = \sqrt{\frac{5}{(0.1+0.6)/g}} = 8.36\,\text{rad/sec}$$

Revised frequency ratio $\beta = \omega/\omega_1 = 50/8.36 = 5.98$
Revised damping ratio ξ' is given by

$$\xi' = \frac{m\omega\xi}{(m+m')\omega_1} = \frac{0.1\times 22.14\times 0.15}{(0.1+0.6)\times 8.36} = 0.0567$$

$$TR = \frac{\ddot{x}^t_{max}}{\ddot{y}_0} = 0.0348$$

$$\ddot{x}^t = 0.0348 \times 0.1\ g = 0.00348\ g < 0.004\ g \qquad OK$$

Therefore, there is a need to add a mass of 0.6 kN to the base in order to control the acceleration transmitted to the instrument. □

PROBLEMS

6.1 A machine is supported on a pedestal which can tolerate a vertical deflection of 1×10^{-3} mm under operating conditions. It is subjected to a forcing function causing a base displacement of amplitude 50×10^{-3} mm at a frequency of 15 Hz. Damping may be taken as 4%.

(a) Determine the natural frequency of the system.

(b) If the mass of the machine including platform is 2500 kg, what will be its static deflection?

6.2 A foundation block is to be installed in a plant such that the vibration from the adjacent areas will not affect it. The mass of the foundation system is 3000 kg, and the surrounding floor vibrates at 2500 cycles per minute. Estimate the stiffness of the foundation so that the transmissibility ratio is not more than 5%, if

(a) Damping is ignored and

(b) Damping is taken as 20%.

6.3 A machine foundation has a mass of 1500 kg with a vertical stiffness of 650 kN/m. If the base displacement amplitude is 10 mm, the displacement amplitude of the mass is 20 mm while it is vibrating at its natural frequency. Calculate the damping ratio and damping coefficient. Also, calculate the force transmitted to the base.

6.4 A SDOF system is subjected to base excitation. At a frequency ratio of 2.75, it is desired to keep the transmissibility ratio to less than 0.30. Determine the damping ratio.

6.5 A building is modelled as a SDOF system having a mass of 350 kN, damping 5%, and a lateral stiffness of 5000 kN/m. If the base amplitude is 0.10 m at a frequency of 12.5 rad/sec during an earthquake, estimate the lateral displacement at its top.

6.6 A machine is mounted on a foundation and rotates at 1800 rpm, its unbalance mass is 25 kg (10% of the total mass) at an eccentricity of 35 mm from its center. The stiffness of the foundation is 350000 N/m and damping is 15%. Determine the amplitude of vertical vibrations.

6.7 An instrument weighs 0.25 kN and mounted on a base having spring stiffness of 10 kN/m and damping of 10%. The ground is transmitting a vertical acceleration of 0.3 g at a frequency of 50 rad/sec.

(a) What acceleration is transmitted to the instrument?

(b) If the instrument can tolerate an acceleration of 0.005 g, advice how to modify the foundation using the same support system.

REFERENCES

IS: 2974

Part 1: Foundation for reciprocating type machines

Part 2: Foundations for impact type machines (Hammer foundations)

Part 3: Foundation for rotary type machines with medium and high frequency

Part 4: Foundations for rotary type machines of low frequency

Part 5: Foundations for impact machines other than hammer (forging and stamping press, pig breaker, drop crusher and jolter)

Bureau of Indian Standards, New Delhi.

IS: 13301 (1992) Vibration Isolation for Machine Foundation – Guidelines, Bureau of Indian Standards, New Delhi.

FURTHER READING

ISO 2631 (1997) Mechanical Vibration and Shock – Evaluation of Human Exposure to Whole-Body Vibration – Part 1: General Requirements, ISO, Geneva.

ISO 2631 (2003) Mechanical Vibration and Shock – Evaluation of Human Exposure to Whole-Body Vibration – Part 2: Vibration in Buildings (1 Hz to 80 Hz), ISO, Geneva.

ISO/TS 10811:2000 Mechanical Vibration and Shock – Vibration and Shock in buildings with Sensitive Equipment – Part 1: Measurements and Evaluation, Part 2: Classification, International Organization for Standardization, Geneva.

ISO 10816:1995 to 2014 Mechanical Vibrations – Evaluation of Machine Vibrations by Measurements on Non-rotating Parts, Parts 1 to 8, International Organization for Standardization, Geneva.

Murray, T. M., Allen, D. E., and Ungar, E. E. (1997) Floor Vibrations Due to Human Activity, Steel Design Guide 11, AISC, Chicago.

7 | Direct Integration of Equation of Motion

7.1 INTRODUCTION

In the previous chapters, the second-order differential equation of motion has been solved using the basic principles of calculus. The forcing function had a simple nature and it was convenient to solve the differential equation. In case a single-degree-of-freedom (SDOF) system or a multi-degree-of-freedom (MDOF) system is subjected to a random acceleration-time history or if the system is nonlinear, it will be very difficult to solve its differential equation using the methods discussed so far. Direct integration methods or step-by-step integration methods are used for the solution of such problems as illustrated in Figure 7.1. A very small time step Δt is chosen and the solution is obtained from one step to the next step. The force is linearly interpolated as shown in Figure 7.2. The term direct means prior to numerical integration no transformation of the equations of motion has been carried out. These methods are based on two essential features:

1. Variation of displacement, velocity and acceleration is assumed within each time step. Hence, the accuracy and stability of the final solution depends upon this variation.
2. The equilibrium is satisfied at all discrete time points within the interval of solution instead of at any time t.

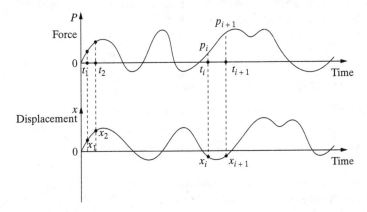

Figure 7.1 Force and displacement variation with time stepping.

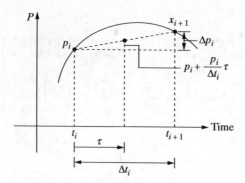

Figure 7.2 Interpolation of force.

The main advantage of these methods is that they are applicable to linear as well as nonlinear analysis of SDOF systems as well as MDOF systems. A very large number of algorithms are available in the literature for the solution of various types of differential equations. The mathematical development, accuracy, convergence and stability criteria of these methods are discussed in the literature. In the present study, only a few commonly used algorithms will be discussed in order to make the reader familiar and aware of these procedures.

7.2 ALGORITHMS

The solution is obtained step-by-step starting from the initial condition at time $t = t_0$. The most critical factor is the selection of the time step 'h'. The solution is known at a time step t, and the problem is to obtain the solution at the next time step $(t + h)$. The expressions at time step $(t + h)$ may be either entirely in terms of the quantities at time step t or both at time step t and $(t + h)$. This gives rise to two types of algorithms: *explicit algorithm* and *implicit algorithm*. In the former, the expressions at time step $(t + h)$ are in terms of time step t only, whereas, in the latter, the expressions at time step $(t + h)$ are in terms of both at time t and $(t + h)$. The solution using the explicit algorithms is easy as compared to those using the implicit algorithms.

These methods may be classified as follows:

1. Conditionally stable

2. Unconditionally stable

These numerical methods are based on any of the three approaches:

1. Numerical interpolation of the excitation function,

2. Finite difference expressions for velocity and acceleration, and

3. Assumed variation of acceleration in a time step.

Notation The solution at the current time step is denoted by either t or t_n, and the solution at next time step is denoted by $(t + h)$ or t_{n+1}. The time step is denoted by h or Δt, and it is taken as a very small value for better accuracy, stability and fast convergence.

Explicit Algorithms   The response at time t_{n+1} is known in terms of the known variables at time t_n. Thus, the response values displacement, velocity and acceleration can be determined directly.

$$x_{n+1} = f(x_n)$$
$$\dot{x}_{n+1} = f(\dot{x}_n)$$
$$\ddot{x}_{n+1} = f(\ddot{x}_n) \tag{7.1}$$

There are two methods for the solution:

1. Euler method or constant acceleration method
2. Central difference method

Implicit Algorithms   The response at time t_{n+1} is known in terms of the known variables at time t_n and unknown variables at time t_{n+1}. Such algorithms involve either an iterative scheme or solution of linear simultaneous equations because the unknown quantities are appearing on both sides of the equations.

$$x_{n+1} = f(x_n, x_{n+1})$$
$$\dot{x}_{n+1} = f(\dot{x}_n, \dot{x}_{n+1})$$
$$\ddot{x}_{n+1} = f(\ddot{x}_n, \ddot{x}_{n+1}) \tag{7.2}$$

Some of these algorithms are as follows:

1. Linear acceleration method
2. Newmark β method
3. Wilson θ method
4. Houbolt method
5. Hilber–Hughes–Taylor method

Convergence means the solution should approach the exact solution with the decrease in time step.

Stability means the solution should not destabilize in the presence of numerical round-off errors. Any error in displacement, velocity and acceleration at time t do not grow in integration due to numerical round-off error.

Accuracy means a numerical method should provide an accurate solution which is close enough with the exact solution. It is measured in terms of amplitude accuracy or amplitude decay or period accuracy or period elongation.

7.3 CONSTANT ACCELERATION METHOD

The equation of motion of a SDOF system at time step t or t_n is given as follows:

$$m\ddot{x}(t) + c\dot{x}(t) + kx(t) = p(t) \tag{7.3}$$

or, it may be written for convenience as follows:

$$m\ddot{x} + c\dot{x} + kx = p(t)$$

or,

$$\ddot{x} = \frac{1}{m}\left[p(t) - c\dot{x} - kx\right] \tag{7.4}$$

Let us write the Taylor's series:

$$x(t+h) = x(t) + h\dot{x}(t) + \frac{h^2}{2}\ddot{x}(t) + \frac{h^3}{6}\dddot{x}(t) + \dots \quad h \ll 1 \tag{7.5}$$

On differentiating Equation (7.5),

$$\dot{x}(t+h) = \dot{x}(t) + h\ddot{x}(t) + \frac{h^2}{2}\dddot{x}(t) + \dots \tag{7.6}$$

Since time increment h is small, and we are interested in $\ddot{x}$, dropping all the terms higher than $\ddot{x}$,
  we get,

$$x(t+h) = x(t) + h\dot{x}(t) + \frac{h^2}{2}\ddot{x}(t) \tag{7.7}$$

$$\dot{x}(t+h) = \dot{x}(t) + h\ddot{x}(t) \tag{7.8}$$

$$\ddot{x}(t+h) = \frac{1}{m}\left[p(t+h) - c\dot{x}(t+h) - kx(t+h)\right] \tag{7.9}$$

The new response values at time $(t+h)$ can be obtained directly from Equations (7.7), (7.8) and (7.9) knowing the displacement, velocity and acceleration values at the previous time step. The dynamic equilibrium of the system is satisfied through Equation (7.9) at each time step. The variation of acceleration, velocity and displacement is shown in Figure 7.3.

  This method is called constant acceleration method because in Equation (7.8), the term $\dddot{x}(t)$ is taken as zero, that is, the acceleration $\ddot{x}(t)$ is constant, therefore, its derivative is zero. It is essential to keep the time step size small in order to get good results from the constant acceleration method. It is recommended that

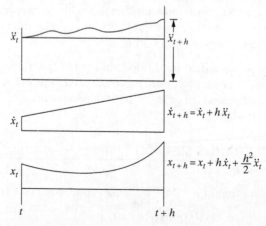

Figure 7.3   Variation of response parameters – constant acceleration method.

$$\frac{\Delta t}{T} \leq \frac{1}{10} \tag{7.10}$$

Typically, Δt is chosen as 0.01 sec or 0.02 sec or sometimes even still smaller, say 0.005 sec.

7.4 CENTRAL DIFFERENCE METHOD

This method is based on the finite difference approximation of the time derivative of displacement, that is, velocity and acceleration. The central finite difference expressions for velocity and acceleration at time i are as follows:

$$\dot{x}_i = \frac{x_{i+1} - x_{i-1}}{2\Delta t} \tag{7.11}$$

and

$$\ddot{x}_i = \frac{x_{i+1} - 2x_i + x_{i-1}}{(\Delta t)^2} \tag{7.12}$$

Both velocity and acceleration terms are now expressed in terms of displacement terms. The equation of motion can be written as:

$$m\frac{x_{i+1} - 2x_i + x_{i-1}}{(\Delta t)^2} + c\frac{x_{i+1} - x_{i-1}}{2\Delta t} + kx_i = p_i \tag{7.13}$$

Equation (7.13) is in terms of displacements only. The values x_i and x_{i-1} are known, and x_{i+1} is unknown. Let us re-write this equation in terms of known and unknown quantities:

$$\left[\frac{m}{(\Delta t)^2} + \frac{c}{2\Delta t}\right]x_{i+1} = p_i - \left[\frac{m}{(\Delta t)^2} - \frac{c}{2\Delta t}\right]x_{i-1} - \left[k - \frac{2m}{(\Delta t)^2}\right]x_i \tag{7.14}$$

Or,

$$\bar{k}x_{i+1} = \bar{p}_i \tag{7.15}$$

where,

$$\bar{k} = \left[\frac{m}{(\Delta t)^2} + \frac{c}{2\Delta t}\right] \tag{7.16a}$$

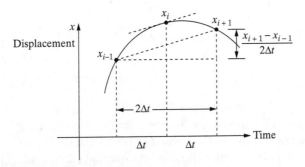

Figure 7.4   Variation of displacement – central difference method.

and

$$\bar{p}_i = p_i - \left[\frac{m}{(\Delta t)^2} - \frac{c}{2\Delta t}\right]x_{i-1} - \left[k - \frac{2m}{(\Delta t)^2}\right]x_i \qquad (7.16b)$$

or,

$$\bar{p}_i = p_i - ax_{i-1} - bx_i \qquad (7.16c)$$

where,

$$a = \left[\frac{m}{(\Delta t)^2} - \frac{c}{2\Delta t}\right] \qquad (7.16d)$$

$$b = \left[k - \frac{2m}{(\Delta t)^2}\right] \qquad (7.16e)$$

The unknown displacement x_{i+1} is given by Equation (7.15).

In this approach, the problem will arise at the first time step to determine x_{i-1}. The initial displacement must be known, that is, x_0. To determine x_{-1}, Equations (7.11) and (7.12) give for $i = 0$,

$$\dot{x}_0 = \frac{x_1 - x_{-1}}{2\Delta t}$$

and

$$\ddot{x}_0 = \frac{x_1 - 2x_0 + x_{-1}}{(\Delta t)^2}$$

The first equation will give x_1 and the second equation will give x_{-1}, that is,

$$x_{-1} = x_0 - \Delta t \, \dot{x}_0 + \frac{(\Delta t)^2}{2} \ddot{x}_0 \qquad (7.17a)$$

In this equation, initial displacement x_0 and initial velocity $\dot{x}_0$ are known. The initial acceleration $\ddot{x}_0$ can be determined from the equation of motion at time $t = 0$:

$$\ddot{x}_0 = \frac{p_0 - c\dot{x}_0 - kx_0}{m} \qquad (7.17b)$$

Again, for stability, the time step should be chosen small as follows:

$$\frac{\Delta t}{T} < \frac{1}{\pi} \qquad (7.17c)$$

Equation (7.10) gives still smaller step size.

Algorithm:

Step 1: Initial displacement and velocity are known as initial conditions of the problem at time $t = 0$

Step 2: Damping c and stiffness k are computed from the system properties

Step 3: Acceleration at time $t = 0$ is computed from Equation (7.17b)

Step 4: Compute equivalent stiffness $\bar{k}$ from Equation (7.16a)

Step 5: Compute constants a and b from Equation (7.16d) and (7.16e)

Step 6: For time step i, compute equivalent force $\bar{p}_i$ from Equation (7.16c)

Step 7: Solve for new displacement x_{i+1} from Equation (7.15)

$$x_{i+1} = \frac{\overline{p}_i}{\overline{k}}$$

Step 8: Compute velocity and acceleration at time step i from Equations (7.11) and (7.12)

Step 9: Repeat Steps 6 to 8 for the next time step

Example 7.1

An undamped SDOF system has a mass of 4900 N and stiffness of 20 kN/m. It is subjected to a triangular force as shown in Figure 7.5. The initial displacement and velocity are zero. Determine the displacement-time history.

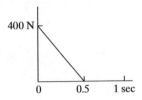

Figure 7.5 Triangular force.

Solution   Acceleration due to gravity = 9.8 m/sec²

$$\text{Mass} = W/g = 4900/9.8 = 500 \text{ kg}$$

Natural frequency of vibration $\omega = \sqrt{\dfrac{k}{m}} = \sqrt{\dfrac{20000}{500}} = 6.32$ rad/sec

Therefore, period of vibration $T = 0.994 \approx 1$ sec

$$m\ddot{x} + c\dot{x} + kx = p(t)$$

or,
$$\ddot{x} = \frac{1}{m}\big[p(t) - c\dot{x} - kx\big] \tag{7.4}$$

Since it is an undamped system, $c = 0$,

$$\ddot{x}(t) = \frac{1}{m}\big(p(t) - kx(t)\big)$$

$$x(t+h) = x(t) + h\dot{x}(t) + \frac{h^2}{2}\ddot{x}(t) \tag{7.7}$$

$$\dot{x}(t+h) = \dot{x}(t) + h\ddot{x}(t) \tag{7.8}$$

Equations (7.4), (7.7) and (7.8) can also be written as follows:

$$\ddot{x}_n = \frac{1}{m}\big(p_n - kx_n\big)$$

$$\dot{x}_{n+1} = \dot{x}_n + h\ddot{x}_n$$

$$x_{n+1} = x_n + h\dot{x}_n + \frac{h^2}{2}\ddot{x}_n$$

Equation (7.4) is valid for time t_n as well as t_{n+1}.

Step size $h = T/10 = 0.1$ sec

It is convenient to solve these equations in tabular form in MS-EXCEL as shown in Table 7.1.

TABLE 7.1 CONSTANT ACCELERATION METHOD

t	x_n	$20000x_n$	p	$\ddot{x}_n$	$\dot{x}_n$	$h\dot{x}_n$	$h\ddot{x}_n$	$\dfrac{h^2}{2}\ddot{x}_n$	x_{n+1}	$\dot{x}_{n+1}$
sec	m		N	m²/s	m/s				m	m/s
(1)	(2)	(3)	(4)	(5)	(6)	(7)	(8)	(9)	(10)	(11)
0	0.0000	0.00	400.00	0.8000	0.0000	0.0000	0.0800	0.0040	0.0040	0.0800
0.1	0.0040	80.00	320.00	0.4800	0.0800	0.0080	0.0480	0.0024	0.0144	0.1280
0.2	0.0144	288.00	240.00	-0.0960	0.1280	0.0128	-0.0096	-0.0005	0.0267	0.1184
0.3	0.0267	534.40	160.00	-0.7488	0.1184	0.0118	-0.0749	-0.0037	0.0348	0.0435
0.4	0.0348	696.32	80.00	-1.2326	0.0435	0.0044	-0.1233	-0.0062	0.0330	-0.0797
0.5	0.0330	660.10	0.00	-1.3202	-0.0797	-0.0080	-0.1320	-0.0066	0.0184	-0.2118
0.6	0.0184	368.59	0.00	-0.7372	-0.2118	-0.0212	-0.0737	-0.0037	-0.0064	-0.2855
0.7	-0.0064	-128.66	0.00	0.2573	-0.2855	-0.0285	0.0257	0.0013	-0.0337	-0.2597
0.8	-0.0337	-673.89	0.00	1.3478	-0.2597	-0.0260	0.1348	0.0067	-0.0529	-0.1250
0.9	-0.0529	-1058.61	0.00	2.1172	-0.1250	-0.0125	0.2117	0.0106	-0.0548	0.0867
1	-0.0548	-1096.83	0.00	2.1937	0.0867	0.0087	0.2194	0.0110	-0.0352	0.3061

The displacement-time history, velocity-time history and acceleration-time history are shown in Figure 7.6.

The problem is again solved using a smaller time step $h = 0.05$ sec to see the effect of step size. The results are shown in the same figure. It can be seen that there is appreciable difference in the two sets of results. It means a smaller time step is more desirable.   □

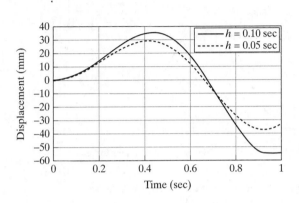

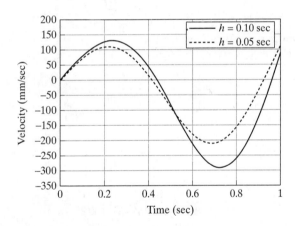

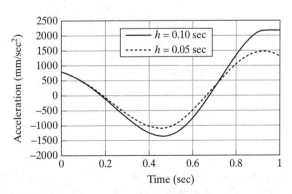

Figure. 7.6   Response of an undamped system using constant acceleration method.

Example 7.2

A damped SDOF system has a mass of 4900 N, stiffness of 20 kN/m and damping ratio of 5%. It is subjected to a triangular force as shown in Figure 7.7. The initial displacement and velocity are zero. Determine the displacement-time history using central difference method.

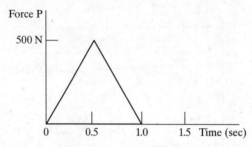

Figure 7.7   Triangular force.

Solution   Acceleration due to gravity = 9.8 m/sec^2

Mass = W/g = 4900/9.8 = 500 kg

Natural frequency of vibration $\omega = \sqrt{\dfrac{k}{m}} = \sqrt{\dfrac{20000}{500}} = 6.32$ rad/sec

Therefore, period of vibration $T = 1$ sec

Damping $c = 2\, m\omega\xi = 2 \times 500 \times 6.32 \times 0.05 = 316$ kg/sec

$$x_0 = 0 \text{ and } \dot{x}_0 = 0$$

$$\ddot{x}_0 = \frac{p_0 - c\dot{x}_0 - kx_0}{m} = 0$$

$$x_{-1} = x_0 - \Delta t\, \dot{x}_0 + \frac{(\Delta t)^2}{2}\ddot{x}_0 = 0$$

$$\bar{k} = \left[\frac{m}{(\Delta t)^2} + \frac{c}{2\Delta t}\right] = \frac{500}{0.1^2} + \frac{316}{0.20} = 51580$$

$$a = \left[\frac{m}{(\Delta t)^2} - \frac{c}{2\Delta t}\right] = 48240$$

$$b = \left[k - \frac{2m}{(\Delta t)^2}\right] = 20000 - \frac{2 \times 500}{0.1^2} = -80000$$

$$\bar{p}_i = p_i - ax_{i-1} - bx_i = p_i - 48240x_{i-1} + 80000x_i$$

$$x_{i+1} = \frac{\bar{p}_i}{\bar{k}} = \frac{\bar{p}_i}{51580}$$

Rest of the calculations can be done in tabular form in MS-EXCEL for convenience as shown in Table 7.2. The displacement response is shown in Figure 7.8.   □

TABLE 7.2   CENTRAL DIFFERENCE METHOD

t	p_i	x_{i-1}	x_i	$\bar{p}_i$	x_{i+1}
sec	N	m	m	N	m
0	0	0.0000	0.0000	0.0000	0.0000
0.1	100	0.0000	0.0000	100.0000	0.0019
0.2	200	0.0000	0.0019	355.0989	0.0069
0.3	300	0.0019	0.0069	757.2297	0.0147
0.4	400	0.0069	0.0147	1242.3499	0.0241
0.5	500	0.0147	0.0241	1718.6745	0.0333
0.6	400	0.0241	0.0333	1903.7418	0.0369
0.7	300	0.0333	0.0369	1645.2982	0.0319
0.8	200	0.0369	0.0319	971.3718	0.0188
0.9	100	0.0319	0.0188	67.8277	0.0013
1	0	0.0188	0.0013	−803.2717	−0.0156
1.1	0	0.0013	−0.0156	−1309.3010	−0.0254
1.2	0	−0.0156	−0.0254	−1279.4544	−0.0248
1.3	0	−0.0254	−0.0248	−759.9005	−0.0147
1.4	0	−0.0248	−0.0147	18.0078	0.0003
1.5	0	−0.0147	0.0003	738.6239	0.0143

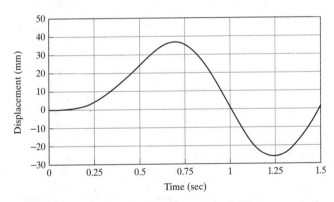

Figure 7.8   Displacement-time history – central difference method.

7.5 INCREMENTAL EQUATION OF MOTION

Let us rewrite the equation of motion in the incremental form for convenience in the solution of implicit algorithms. The equation of motion is written at time steps t_n and t_{n+1}

$$m\ddot{x}_n + c_n\dot{x}_n + k_n x_n = p_n \tag{7.18}$$

and

$$m\ddot{x}_{n+1} + c_{n+1}\dot{x}_{n+1} + k_{n+1} x_{n+1} = P_{n+1} \tag{7.19}$$

where,

$$x_{n+1} = x_n + \Delta x \tag{7.20a}$$

$$\dot{x}_{n+1} = \dot{x}_n + \Delta\dot{x} \tag{7.20b}$$

$$\ddot{x}_{n+1} = \ddot{x}_n + \Delta\ddot{x} \tag{7.20c}$$

$$c_{n+1} = c_n + \Delta c \tag{7.20d}$$

$$k_{n+1} = k_n + \Delta k \tag{7.20e}$$

Δx = displacement increment in a time step
$\Delta\dot{x}$ = velocity increment in a time step
$\Delta\ddot{x}$ = acceleration increment in a time step

In nonlinear problems, the damping c and stiffness k may vary with each time step. However, in linear problems, the increments Δc and Δk will be zero. The mass term will always remain constant.

Let us substitute terms from Equation (7.20) in Equation (7.19) and then subtract Equation (7.18), we get

$$m\Delta\ddot{x} + c_n \Delta\dot{x} + k_n \Delta x + P_2 = P_1 \tag{7.21}$$

where,

$$P_1 = P_{n+1} - m\ddot{x}_n - c_n\dot{x}_n - k_n x_n \tag{7.22a}$$

$$P_2 = \Delta c\,(\dot{x}_n + \Delta\dot{x}) + \Delta k(x_n + \Delta x) \tag{7.22b}$$

For a linear system, $P_2 = 0$ because Δc and Δk are zero. The damping and stiffness terms will remain constant in a linear system.

In general, it is possible to express incremental velocity and acceleration in terms of incremental displacement.

7.6 LINEAR ACCELERATION METHOD

In this method, $\dddot{x} \neq 0$ in the Taylor's series, that is,

$$x(t+h) = x(t) + h\dot{x}(t) + \frac{h^2}{2}\ddot{x}(t) + \frac{h^3}{6}\dddot{x}(t) + \dots \qquad h \ll t \tag{7.23}$$

This equation can be re-written by changing symbols as follows:

$$x_{n+1} = x_n + h\dot{x}_n + \frac{h^2}{2}\ddot{x}_n + \frac{h^3}{6}\dddot{x}_n \tag{7.24}$$

On differentiating Equation (7.24),

$$\dot{x}_{n+1} = \dot{x}_n + h\ddot{x}_n + \frac{h^2}{2}\dddot{x}_n \tag{7.25}$$

On differentiating Equation (7.25),

$$\ddot{x}_{n+1} = \ddot{x}_n + h\dddot{x}_n \tag{7.26a}$$

or,

$$\dddot{x}_n = \frac{\ddot{x}_{n+1} - \ddot{x}_n}{h} \tag{7.26b}$$

$$= \frac{\Delta\ddot{x}}{h} \tag{7.26c}$$

or, Equation (7.26a) becomes $\ddot{x}_{n+1} = \ddot{x}_n + \Delta\ddot{x}$ $\tag{7.26d}$

Equation (7.24) can be written making use of Equation (7.26b) as:

$$x_{n+1} = x_n + h\dot{x}_n + \frac{h^2}{3}\ddot{x}_n + \frac{h^2}{6}\ddot{x}_{n+1} \tag{7.27a}$$

or,

$$x_{n+1} = x_n + h\dot{x}_n + \frac{h^2}{3}\ddot{x}_n + \frac{h^2}{6}(\ddot{x}_n + \Delta\ddot{x}) \tag{7.27b}$$

and Equation (7.25) as:

$$\dot{x}_{n+1} = \dot{x}_n + \frac{h}{2}(\ddot{x}_n + \ddot{x}_{n+1}) \tag{7.28a}$$

or,

$$\dot{x}_{n+1} = \dot{x}_n + \frac{h}{2}(\ddot{x}_n + \ddot{x}_n + \Delta\ddot{x}) \tag{7.28b}$$

Equations (7.27), (7.28) and (7.26d) are shown in Figure 7.9.
    It is now possible to express either

(a) $\Delta\dot{x}$ and Δx in terms of $\Delta\ddot{x}$
(b) $\Delta\dot{x}$ and $\Delta\ddot{x}$ in terms of Δx

    In either case, only one unknown quantity remains in the incremental equations of equilibrium. It is preferred to express incremental velocity and acceleration in terms of incremental displacement. So far, we have not enforced the condition of dynamic equilibrium. Let us write the equation of motion for time step t_{n+1} as follows:

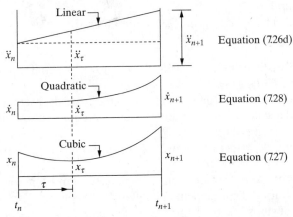

Figure 7.9   Variation of response – linear acceleration method.

$$\ddot{x}_{n+1} = \frac{1}{m}\left[p_{n+1} - c\dot{x}_{n+1} - kx_{n+1}\right] \tag{7.29}$$

Making use of the relations:

$$\Delta x = x_{n+1} - x_n$$

$$\Delta\dot{x} = \dot{x}_{n+1} - \dot{x}_n$$

$$\Delta\ddot{x} = \ddot{x}_{n+1} - \ddot{x}_n \tag{7.30}$$

Equation (7.27b) can be re-written as follows:

$$\Delta\ddot{x} = -3\ddot{x}_n - \frac{6}{h}\dot{x}_n + \frac{6}{h^2}\Delta x \tag{7.31}$$

and Equation (7.28b) can be re-written as follows:

$$\Delta\dot{x} = -\frac{h}{2}\ddot{x}_n - 3\dot{x}_n + \frac{3}{h}\Delta x \tag{7.32}$$

Now, the equation of motion can be written in the incremental form:

$$m\Delta\ddot{x} + c\Delta\dot{x} + k\Delta x = P_{n+1} - P_n = \Delta P \tag{7.33}$$

Let us substitute Equations (7.31) and (7.32) into Equation (7.33), we get

$$\bar{k}\Delta x = \overline{\Delta P} \tag{7.34}$$

where,

$$\bar{k} = \frac{6m}{h^2} + \frac{3c}{h} + k \tag{7.35a}$$

and

$$\overline{\Delta P} = \Delta P + 3m\left(\ddot{x}_n + \frac{2}{h}\dot{x}_n\right) + c\left(\frac{h}{2}\ddot{x}_n + 3\dot{x}_n\right) \tag{7.35b}$$

h = time interval
All values in R.H.S. of Equation (7.35b) are known

Algorithm:
Step 1: Initial displacement and velocity are known as initial conditions of the problem at time $t = 0$
Step 2: Damping c and stiffness k are computed from the system properties
Step 3: Initial acceleration is computed from the equation of motion, Equation (7.29) at time step $t = n$
Step 4: Effective load increment and stiffness increment are computed using Equations (7.35a) and (7.35b)
Step 5: Compute Δx from Equation (7.34) and $\Delta\dot{x}$ from Equation (7.32)
Step 6: Finally total displacement and velocity are computed from Equation (7.30)
Step 7: Repeat steps 3 to 6 for the next time step

7.6.1 Selection of the Time Increment h

1. It depends up on the rate of variation of the applied load or ground motion $p(t)$
2. Period of vibration of the structure
3. Accuracy and stability criteria
4. Complexity of nonlinear behaviour of the structure, that is, stiffness K and damping C, if applicable

The linear acceleration method is conditionally stable. It means the step size is governed by Equation (7.10). It is stable only if this equation is satisfied. The implicit schemes require triangularization of the stiffness matrix for solution of a MDOF system.

Example 7.3

An undamped SDOF system has a mass of 4900 N and stiffness of 20 kN/m. It is subjected to a triangular force as shown in Figure 7.5. The initial displacement and velocity are zero. Determine the displacement-time history using linear acceleration method.

Solution This is the same problem that was solved earlier by constant acceleration method.

$$\Delta \bar{P} = \Delta P + 3m\left(\ddot{x}_n + \frac{2\dot{x}_n}{h} \right) + 0$$

$$= \Delta P + 1500\ddot{x}_n + 30000\dot{x}_n$$

$$\bar{k} = \frac{6m}{h^2} + \frac{3c}{h} + k = 320000 \text{ N/m}$$

$$\Delta x = \Delta \bar{P}/\bar{k}$$

$$\ddot{x}_n = \frac{1}{m}(p_n - c\dot{x}_n - kx_n) = \frac{1}{m}(p_n - 20000x_n)$$

$$\dot{x}_{n+1} = -\frac{h}{2}\ddot{x}_n - 2\dot{x}_n + \frac{3}{h}\Delta x = -0.05\ddot{x}_n - 2\dot{x}_n + 30\Delta x$$

Now it is convenient to carry out the calculations in a tabular form in MS-EXCEL as shown in Table 7.3. Again, the calculations are repeated for a smaller step size $h = 0.05$ sec. The displacement-time history, velocity-time history and acceleration-time history are shown in Figure 7.10. It can be seen that effect of reducing the time step is insignificant in this case.   □

TABLE 7.3   LINEAR ACCELERATION METHOD – UNDAMPED SDOF SYSTEM

t	p	x_n	$\dot{x}_n$	$\ddot{x}_n$	Δp	$\overline{\Delta p}$	Δx	$\dot{x}_{n+1}$	x_{n+1}
sec	N	m	m/sec	m/sec²	N	N	m	m/sec	m
(1)	(2)	(3)	(4)	(5)	(6)	(7)	(8)	(9)	(10)
0	400.00	0.0000	0.0000	0.8000	−80	1120.0000	0.0035	0.0650	0.0035
0.1	320.00	0.0035	0.0650	0.5000	−80	2620.0000	0.0082	0.0906	0.0117
0.2	240.00	0.0117	0.0906	0.0125	−80	2657.5000	0.0083	0.0673	0.0200

(Continued)

TABLE 7.3 (CONTINUED)

t	p	x_n	$\dot{x}_n$	$\ddot{x}_n$	Δp	$\overline{\Delta p}$	Δx	$\dot{x}_{n+1}$	x_{n+1}
0.3	160.00	0.0200	0.0673	−0.4797	−80	1218.4375	0.0038	0.0037	0.0238
0.4	80.00	0.0238	0.0037	−0.7920	−80	−1157.5391	−0.0036	−0.0763	0.0202
0.5	0.00	0.0202	−0.0763	−0.8073	0.00	−3499.4385	−0.0109	−0.1351	0.0092
0.6	0.00	0.0092	−0.1351	−0.3699	0.00	−4609.0485	−0.0144	−0.1433	−0.0052
0.7	0.00	−0.0052	−0.1433	0.2063	0.00	−3990.2653	−0.0125	−0.0978	−0.0176
0.8	0.00	−0.0176	−0.0978	0.7050	0.00	−1875.1326	−0.0059	−0.0155	−0.0235
0.9	0.00	−0.0235	−0.0155	0.9394	0.00	943.1748	0.0029	0.0725	−0.0205
1	0.00	−0.0205	0.0725	0.8215	0.00	3407.7916	0.0106	0.1334	−0.0099

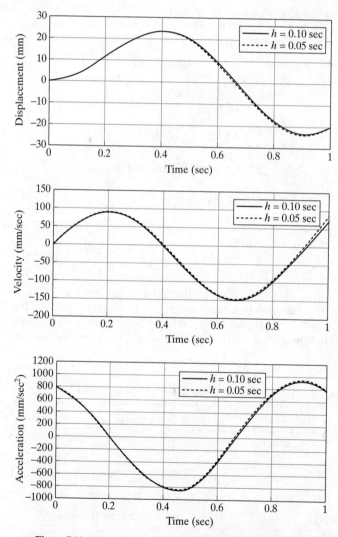

Figure 7.10   Response history – linear acceleration method.

Example 7.4

Let us solve Example 7.3 again by taking 5% damping.

Solution   Damping coefficient $c = 2m\omega\xi = 2 \times 500 \times 6.32 \times 0.05 = 316$ kg/m

$$\Delta\bar{P} = \Delta P + 3m\left(\ddot{x}_n + \frac{2\dot{x}_n}{h}\right) + c\left(\frac{h}{2}\ddot{x}_n + 3\dot{x}_n\right)$$

$$= \Delta P + 1500\ddot{x}_n + 30000\dot{x}_n + 15.8\ddot{x}_n + 948\dot{x}_n$$

$$= \Delta P + 1515.8\ddot{x}_n + 30948\dot{x}_n$$

$$\bar{k} = \frac{6m}{h^2} + \frac{3c}{h} + k = 329480$$

$$\Delta x = \Delta\bar{P}/\bar{k}$$

$$\ddot{x}_n = \frac{1}{m}\left(p_n - c\dot{x}_n - kx_n\right) = \frac{1}{m}\left(p_n - 316\dot{x}_n - 20000x_n\right)$$

$$\dot{x}_{n+1} = -\frac{h}{2}\ddot{x}_n - 2\dot{x}_n + \frac{3}{h}\Delta x = -0.05\ddot{x}_n - 2\dot{x}_n + 30\Delta x$$

The calculations are shown in Table 7.4. The effect of 5% damping is shown in Figure 7.11.
□

TABLE 7.4   LINEAR ACCELERATION METHOD – DAMPED SDOF SYSTEM

t	p	x_n	$\dot{x}_n$	$\ddot{x}_n$	Δp	$\overline{\Delta p}$	Δx	$\dot{x}_{n+1}$	x_{n+1}
sec	N	m	m/sec	m/sec²	N	N	m	m/sec	m
(1)	(2)	(3)	(4)	(5)	(6)	(7)	(8)	(9)	(10)
0	400.00	0.0000	0.0000	0.8000	−80	1132.6400	0.0034	0.0631	0.0034
0.1	320.00	0.0034	0.0631	0.4626	−80	2574.9429	0.0078	0.0851	0.0113
0.2	240.00	0.0113	0.0851	−0.0239	−80	2516.4274	0.0076	0.0602	0.0189
0.3	160.00	0.0189	0.0602	−0.4737	−80	1064.7706	0.0032	0.0003	0.0221
0.4	80.00	0.0221	0.0003	−0.7250	−80	−1171.1507	−0.0036	−0.0709	0.0186
0.5	0.00	0.0186	−0.0709	−0.6979	0	−3251.8603	−0.0099	−0.1194	0.0087
0.6	0.00	0.0087	−0.1194	−0.2724	0	−4108.4741	−0.0125	−0.1216	−0.0038
0.7	0.00	−0.0038	−0.1216	0.2277	0	−3419.4454	−0.0104	−0.0794	−0.0142
0.8	0.00	−0.0142	−0.0794	0.6162	0	−1524.6698	−0.0046	−0.0107	−0.0188
0.9	0.00	−0.0188	−0.0107	0.7579	0	816.3708	0.0025	0.0579	−0.0163
1	0.00	−0.0163	0.0579	0.6154	0	2725.3652	0.0083	0.1015	−0.0080

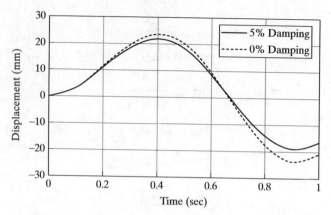

Figure 7.11 Effect of damping – linear acceleration method

7.7 NEWMARK β METHOD

Prof. N. M. Newmark, University of Illinois, Urbana, Champaign in 1959 proposed the following equations for displacement and velocity:

$$x_{n+1} = x_n + \Delta t \dot{x}_n + (0.5 - \beta)(\Delta t)^2 \ddot{x}_n + \beta(\Delta t)^2 \ddot{x}_{n+1} \qquad (7.36)$$

and

$$\dot{x}_{n+1} = \dot{x}_n + (1 - \gamma)\Delta t \ddot{x}_n + \gamma \Delta t \ddot{x}_{n+1} \qquad (7.37)$$

β and γ can be selected suitably based on the accuracy and stability criteria.

It is interesting to see that this formulation represents a family of algorithms depending upon the values of γ and β.

$\gamma = 0.5$ and $\beta = 1/6$ leads to linear acceleration method (Figure 7.9)
$\beta = \frac{1}{4}$ leads to constant average acceleration method (Figure 7.12)
$\beta = 0$ leads to explicit method
For $\gamma = 0.5$, Equation (7.37) can be written as:

$$\dot{x}_{n+1} = \dot{x}_n + 0.5 \, \Delta t (\ddot{x}_n + \ddot{x}_{n+1}) \qquad (7.38)$$

and

$$\ddot{x}_{n+1} = \frac{1}{m}\left[p_{n+1} - c\dot{x}_{n+1} - kx_{n+1} \right] \qquad (7.39)$$

Iterative Algorithm

Since the new values occur on both sides of the equation, an iterative solution is preferred.

Step 1: Initial displacement and velocity are known as initial conditions of the problem at time $t = 0$

Step 2: Damping c and stiffness k are computed from the system properties

Step 3: Initial acceleration is computed from the equation of motion, Equation (7.39) at time step $t = n$

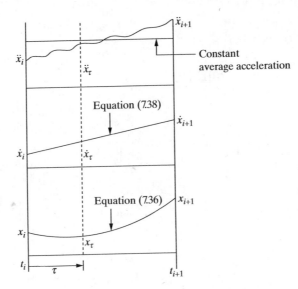

Figure 7.12   Variation of response–Newmark method.

Step 4: Assume a value of acceleration at time step $n + 1$

Step 5: Solve for new displacement and velocity using Equations (7.36) and (7.38)

Step 6: Solve for new acceleration at time $n+1$ from Equation (7.39)

Step 7: If $\ddot{x}_{n+1}$ from Steps 4 and 6 compare within acceptable accuracy, go to the next time step and repeat Steps 4 to 7; otherwise, revise the assumption for $\ddot{x}_{n+1}$ and repeat Steps 5 to 7

The basic difference between the linear acceleration method and Newmark method is that in the former, acceleration is computed from the incremental equation of equilibrium while in the latter the acceleration is computed from the total equation of equilibrium. In this manner, the former method may accumulate more errors than the latter.

Non-iterative Algorithm

It is possible to re-formulate the Newmark's equations such that there is no need for any iteration.

Step 1: Let us express acceleration $\ddot{x}_{n+1}$ in terms of displacement x_{n+1} and previous values of displacement, velocity and acceleration using Equation (7.36)

$$\ddot{x}_{n+1} = \frac{1}{\beta \Delta t^2}(x_{n+1} - x_n) - \frac{1}{\beta \Delta t}\dot{x}_n - \left(\frac{1}{2\beta} - 1\right)\ddot{x}_n \tag{7.40}$$

Step 2: Substitute it in Equation (7.37) and the velocity $\dot{x}_{n+1}$ can be obtained in terms of displacement x_{n+1}

$$\dot{x}_{n+1} = \dot{x}_n + \Delta t(1-\gamma)\ddot{x}_n + \gamma \Delta t \ddot{x}_{n+1} \tag{7.41}$$

Step 3: Now substitute the values of acceleration $\ddot{x}_{n+1}$ and velocity $\dot{x}_{n+1}$ in terms of displacement x_{n+1} in Equation (7.39). This is now in terms of displacement only, and its value can be determined without any iteration. We get,

$$\bar{k}x_{n+1} = \bar{P} \quad \text{or,} \quad x_{n+1} = \frac{\bar{P}}{\bar{k}} \tag{7.42}$$

where

$$\bar{k} = k + \frac{1}{\beta \Delta t^2} m + \frac{\gamma}{\beta \Delta t} c \tag{7.43}$$

and

$$\bar{P} = P_{n+1} + m \left(\frac{1}{\beta \Delta t^2} x_n + \frac{1}{\beta \Delta t} \dot{x}_n + \left(\frac{1}{2\beta} - 1 \right) \ddot{x}_n \right)$$

$$+ c \left(\frac{\gamma}{\beta \Delta t} x_n + \left(\frac{\gamma}{\beta} - 1 \right) \dot{x}_n + \frac{\Delta t}{2} \left(\frac{\gamma}{\beta} - 2 \right) \ddot{x}_n \right) \tag{7.44}$$

All values in R.H.S. of Equation (7.44) are known.

Step 4: The acceleration $\ddot{x}_{n+1}$ and velocity $\dot{x}_{n+1}$ can be determined using Equations (7.40) and (7.41), respectively

This algorithm can be summarized as follows:

Algorithm:

Step 1: Compute m, c and k for the system

Step 2: Initialize $x(0)$, $\dot{x}(0)$ and $\ddot{x}(0)$, that is, initial displacement and velocity are known. Acceleration at $t = 0$ can be obtained from the equation of motion

Step 3: Select time step Δt, β and γ. Define the following constants:

For γ.GE. 0.50 and β.GE. 0.25$(0.50 + \gamma)^2$

$$a_0 = \frac{1}{\beta \Delta t^2}, \; a_1 = \frac{\gamma}{\beta \Delta t}, \; a_2 = \frac{1}{\beta \Delta t}, \; a_3 = \frac{1}{2\beta} - 1$$

$$a_4 = \frac{\gamma}{\beta} - 1, \; a_5 = \frac{\Delta t}{2} \left(\frac{\gamma}{\beta} - 2 \right), \; a_6 = \Delta t (1 - \gamma), \; a_7 = \gamma \Delta t \tag{7.45}$$

Step 4: Form $\bar{k} = k + a_0 m + a_1 c$ (7.46)

Step 5: For each time step

$$\bar{P} = P_{n+1} + m \, (a_0 x_n + a_2 \dot{x}_n + a_3 \ddot{x}_n) + c \, (a_1 x_n + a_4 \dot{x}_n + a_5 \ddot{x}_n) \tag{7.47}$$

Determine, $x_{n+1} = \bar{P}/\bar{k}$ (7.42)

Step 6: Now determine the new acceleration and velocity using the following equations:

$$\ddot{x}_{n+1} = a_0 \, (x_{n+1} - x_n) - a_2 \dot{x}_n - a_3 \ddot{x}_n \tag{7.48}$$

$$\dot{x}_{n+1} = \dot{x}_n + a_6 \ddot{x}_n + a_7 \ddot{x}_{n+1} \tag{7.49}$$

7.7.1 Stability of the Newmark Method

The Newmark method is stable if,

$$\frac{\Delta T}{T} \le \frac{1}{\pi\sqrt{2}\sqrt{\gamma-2\beta}} \tag{7.50a}$$

For $\gamma = 0.5$ and $\beta = \frac{1}{4}$, this condition becomes,

$$\frac{\Delta T}{T} \le \infty \tag{7.50b}$$

This implies that the constant average acceleration method is stable for any h (or Δt) no matter how large it may be. However, for accuracy, Δt should be small enough.

For $\gamma = 0.5$ and $\beta = 1/6$ (i.e. linear acceleration method), $\dfrac{\Delta T}{T} \le 0.551$

Again a shorter time step is desirable for obtaining accurate solutions.

7.7.2 Newmark Method in Incremental Form

It is more convenient to arrange the Newmark's equations in incremental form.
    Consider Equation (7.33)

$$m\Delta\ddot{x} + c\Delta\dot{x} + k\Delta x = P_{n+1} - P_n = \Delta p \tag{7.33}$$

It can be written as

$$m\Delta\ddot{x}_i + c\Delta\dot{x}_i + k\Delta x_i = \Delta p_i \tag{7.51}$$

We know that

$$x_{n+1} = x_n + \Delta t\,\dot{x}_n + (0.5 - \beta)(\Delta t)^2\ddot{x}_n + \beta(\Delta t)^2\ddot{x}_{n+1} \tag{7.36}$$

and

$$\dot{x}_{n+1} = \dot{x}_n + (1 - \gamma)\,\Delta t\,\ddot{x}_n + \gamma\Delta t\,\ddot{x}_{n+1} \tag{7.37}$$

Making use of the relations:

$$\Delta x = x_{n+1} - x_n$$
$$\Delta\dot{x} = \dot{x}_{n+1} - \dot{x}_n$$
$$\Delta\ddot{x} = \ddot{x}_{n+1} - \ddot{x}_n \tag{7.30}$$

Equation (7.37) can be written as:

$$\Delta\dot{x}_i = \Delta t\,\ddot{x}_i + \gamma\,\Delta t\Delta\ddot{x}_i \tag{7.52a}$$

Equation (7.36) can be written as:

$$\Delta x_i = \Delta t\,\dot{x}_i + \frac{(\Delta t)^2}{2}\ddot{x}_i + \beta(\Delta t)^2\,\Delta\ddot{x}_i \tag{7.52b}$$

This gives

$$\Delta\ddot{x}_i = \frac{1}{\beta(\Delta t)^2}\Delta x_i - \frac{1}{\beta\Delta t}\dot{x}_i - \frac{1}{2\beta}\ddot{x}_i \tag{7.53}$$

Substituting Equation (7.53) in Equation (7.52a)

$$\Delta \dot{x}_i = \frac{\gamma}{\beta \Delta t} \Delta x_i - \frac{\gamma}{\beta} \dot{x}_i + \Delta t \left(1 - \frac{\gamma}{2\beta} \right) \ddot{x}_i \tag{7.54}$$

Equation (7.53) and (7.54) can be substituted in Equation (7.51)

$$\overline{k} = \frac{\Delta \overline{p}}{\Delta x_i} \tag{7.55}$$

where,

$$\overline{k} = k + \frac{\gamma}{\beta \Delta t} c + \frac{1}{\beta (\Delta t)^2} m \tag{7.56}$$

and

$$\Delta \overline{p}_i = \Delta p_i + \left(\frac{1}{\beta \Delta t} m + \frac{\gamma}{\beta} c \right) \dot{x}_i + \left[\frac{1}{2\beta} m + \Delta t \left(\frac{\gamma}{2\beta} - 1 \right) c \right] \ddot{x}_i \tag{7.57}$$

Once Δx_i is known, $\Delta \dot{x}_i$ and $\Delta \ddot{x}_i$ can be computed from Equations (7.54) and (7.53), respectively. The total displacement, velocity and acceleration can be computed from Equation (7.30). Alternatively, the total acceleration can also be computed from Equation (7.39) instead of using Equations (7.53) and (7.30). It should be remembered that Equation (7.39) is required to start the process from the beginning.

Example 7.5

Solve Example 7.3 using Newmark method for $\beta = 1/4$ and $\beta = 1/6$.

Solution   Mass = 500 kg, stiffness = 20000 N/m, damping = 0
Period $T = 1.0$ sec, step size $\Delta t = 0.10$ sec
Newmark constants are:

$$a_0 = \frac{1}{\beta \Delta t^2}, \ a_1 = \frac{\gamma}{\beta \Delta t}, \ a_2 = \frac{1}{\beta \Delta t}, \ a_3 = \frac{1}{2\beta} - 1$$

$$a_4 = \frac{\gamma}{\beta} - 1, \ a_5 = \frac{\Delta t}{2} \left(\frac{\gamma}{\beta} - 2 \right), \ a_6 = \Delta t (1 - \gamma), \ a_7 = \gamma \Delta t$$

Newmark integration constants:

For $\beta = 0.25$

$a_0 = 400.0000$	$a_4 = 1.0000$
$a_1 = 20.0000$	$a_5 = 0.0000$
$a_2 = 40.0000$	$a_6 = 0.0500$
$a_3 = 1.0000$	$a_7 = 0.0500$

For $\beta = 0.16667$

$a_0 = 600.2401$	$a_4 = 2.0012$
$a_1 = 30.0120$	$a_5 = 0.0501$
$a_2 = 60.0240$	$a_6 = 0.0500$
$a_3 = 2.0012$	$a_7 = 0.0500$

The calculations can be carried out either in MS-EXCEL, MATLAB or in Fortran. The results are shown in Figure 7.13. Since the step size was taken as T/10, the results are very close to each other.   □

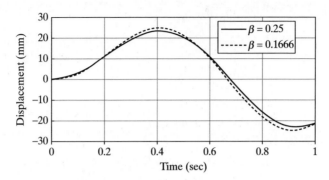

Figure 7.13   Effect of Newmark constant β

Example 7.6

A damped SDOF system has a mass of 10 kg, stiffness of 175 N/m and damping of 2%. It is subjected to a reversed cyclic acceleration force as shown in the table. The initial displacement and velocity are zero. Determine the displacement-time history using Newmark β method.

Acceleration, g	0	0.2	– 0.2	0.4	– 0.4	0.6	– 0.6	0.2	– 0.2	0.1	0	0
Time, sec	0	0.1	0.2	0.3	0.4	0.5	0.6	0.7	0.8	0.9	1.0	5.0

Solution   Let us take $\gamma = 0.5$ and $\beta = 1/4$, $\Delta t = 0.10$ sec
Mass = 10 kg; stiffness = 175 N/m; Natural frequency = 4.18 rad/sec and period $T = 1.5$ sec
Acceleration due to gravity $g = 980$ cm/sec²
The input ground excitation is shown in Figure 7.14. It needs to be multiplied by mass to get force.

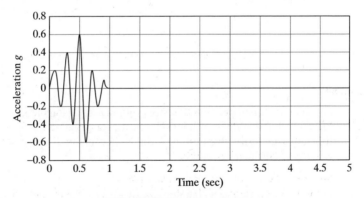

Figure 7.14   Ground acceleration.

$$a_0 = \frac{1}{\beta \Delta t^2}, \ a_1 = \frac{\gamma}{\beta \Delta t}, \ a_2 = \frac{1}{\beta \Delta t}, \ a_3 = \frac{1}{2\beta} - 1$$

$$a_4 = \frac{\gamma}{\beta} - 1, \ a_5 = \frac{\Delta t}{2}\left(\frac{\gamma}{\beta} - 2\right), \ a_6 = \Delta t (1 - \gamma), \ a_7 = \gamma \Delta t$$

The integration constants are:
$$a_0 = 400.0000$$
$$a_1 = 20.0000$$

$$a_2 = 40.0000$$
$$a_3 = 1.0000$$
$$a_4 = 1.0000$$
$$a_5 = 0.0000$$
$$a_6 = 0.0500$$
$$a_7 = 0.0500$$
$$\bar{k} = k + a_0 m + a_1 c$$

For each time step,

$$\bar{P} = P_{n+1} + m(a_0 x_n + a_2 \dot{x}_n + a_3 \ddot{x}_n) + c(a_1 x_n + a_4 \dot{x}_n + a_5 \ddot{x}_n)$$
$$x_{n+1} = \bar{P}/\bar{k}$$

The detailed calculations can be done in MS-Excel, MATLAB or in Fortran. The displacement response is shown in Figure 7.15. The same problem was again solved with $\xi = 10\%$. The results are shown in the same figure. ☐

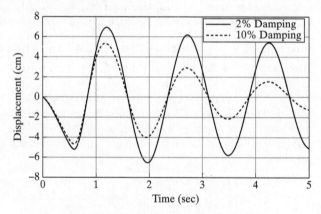

Figure 7.15 Newmark method with $\beta = 0.25$.

Example 7.7

Consider an undamped SDOF system with the following data:
Mass = 2000 kg, stiffness = 20000 N/m, initial displacement = 0, velocity = 0
It is subjected to a constant force = 100 N throughout. Illustrate the effect of step size on stability of Newmark β method.

Solution Period of vibration = 1.987 sec
Let us find its response with a step size $\Delta t = 0.25$ sec and again with 2.5 sec. The results are shown in Table 7.5. Two observations can be made from this table:

- The numerical values do not grow with increase in step size from 0.25 sec to 2.5 sec.
- In the first step, the displacement increases to a very high value from 1.35 mm to 9.4 mm and then it keeps oscillating.
- The maximum displacements in the two cases are 9.96 mm and 9.93 mm.
- The results with step size = 2.5 are not accurate, but it shows that the method is stable and does not depend upon the step size. The values do not grow.

The results are also shown in Figure 7.16. ☐

TABLE 7.5 EFFECT OF STEP SIZE ON STABILITY OF NEWMARK METHOD

	$\Delta t =$	0.250										
Time	Δt	$2\,\Delta t$	$3\,\Delta t$	$4\,\Delta t$	$5\,\Delta t$	$6\,\Delta t$	$7\,\Delta t$	$8\,\Delta t$	$9\,\Delta t$	$10\,\Delta t$	$11\,\Delta t$	$12\,\Delta t$
Displacement	1.35	4.67	8.17	9.96	9.06	5.97	2.35	0.168	0.595	3.4	7.07	9.62
	$\Delta t =$	2.500										
Displacement	9.4	2.26	5.42	7	1.06	9.93	0.266	8.4	3.75	3.8	8.37	0.28

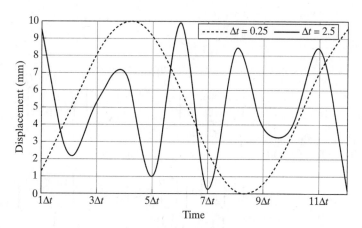

Figure 7.16 Effect of step size on the stability of Newmark β method.

Example 7.8

A two DOF system is subjected to a constant force P. The initial displacement and velocity are zero. Determine the response-time history using Newmark β method.

$$M = \begin{bmatrix} 4 & 0 \\ 0 & 1 \end{bmatrix} \quad K = \begin{bmatrix} 8 & -2 \\ -2 & 6 \end{bmatrix} \quad C = \begin{bmatrix} 0.53 & 0 \\ 0 & 0.25 \end{bmatrix} \quad P = \begin{Bmatrix} 0 \\ 2.5 \end{Bmatrix}$$

Initial conditions are: $\begin{Bmatrix} x_{10} \\ x_{20} \end{Bmatrix} = \begin{Bmatrix} 0 \\ 0 \end{Bmatrix}$ and $\begin{Bmatrix} \dot{x}_{10} \\ \dot{x}_{20} \end{Bmatrix} = \begin{Bmatrix} 0 \\ 0 \end{Bmatrix}$

Solution The natural frequency and periods for the two DOF system can be computed as discussed in Chapters 9 and 10 and are shown as follows:

$$\begin{Bmatrix} \omega_1 \\ \omega_2 \end{Bmatrix} = \begin{Bmatrix} 1.328 \\ 2.497 \end{Bmatrix} \text{ and } \begin{Bmatrix} T_1 \\ T_2 \end{Bmatrix} = \begin{Bmatrix} 4.73 \\ 2.51 \end{Bmatrix}$$

Newmark β method with $\beta = \frac{1}{4}$ is unconditionally stable. Any step size can be chosen. Let us choose a step size of $\Delta t = 0.25$ sec and $\beta = 1/4$.
Newmark integration constants are:

$$a_0 = \frac{1}{\beta \Delta t^2}, \ a_1 = \frac{\gamma}{\beta \Delta t}, \ a_2 = \frac{1}{\beta \Delta t}, \ a_3 = \frac{1}{2\beta} - 1$$

$$a_4 = \frac{\gamma}{\beta} - 1, \ a_5 = \frac{\Delta t}{2}\left(\frac{\gamma}{\beta} - 2\right), \ a_6 = \Delta t(1 - \gamma), \ a_7 = \gamma \Delta t$$

$$a_0 = 64.0$$
$$a_1 = 8.0$$
$$a_2 = 16.0$$
$$a_3 = 1.0$$
$$a_4 = 1.0$$
$$a_5 = 0.0$$
$$a_6 = 0.125$$
$$a_7 = 0.125$$

The effective stiffness matrix can be written as follows:

$$\left[\bar{K}\right] = \begin{bmatrix} 8 & -2 \\ -2 & 6 \end{bmatrix} + a_0 \begin{bmatrix} 4 & 0 \\ 0 & 1 \end{bmatrix} + a_1 \begin{bmatrix} 0.53 & 0 \\ 0 & 0.25 \end{bmatrix} \tag{7.46}$$

For each time step:
The effective load vector can be written as follows:

$$\{\bar{P}\} = \begin{Bmatrix} 0 \\ 2.5 \end{Bmatrix} + \begin{bmatrix} 4 & 0 \\ 0 & 1 \end{bmatrix}\left(a_0 \begin{Bmatrix} x_{1n} \\ x_{2n} \end{Bmatrix} + a_2 \begin{Bmatrix} \dot{x}_{1n} \\ \dot{x}_{2n} \end{Bmatrix} + a_3 \begin{Bmatrix} \ddot{x}_{1n} \\ \ddot{x}_{2n} \end{Bmatrix} \right)$$
$$+ \begin{bmatrix} 0.53 & 0 \\ 0 & 0.25 \end{bmatrix}\left(a_1 \begin{Bmatrix} x_{1n} \\ x_{2n} \end{Bmatrix} + a_4 \begin{Bmatrix} \dot{x}_{1n} \\ \dot{x}_{2n} \end{Bmatrix} + a_5 \begin{Bmatrix} \ddot{x}_{1n} \\ \ddot{x}_{2n} \end{Bmatrix} \right) \tag{7.47}$$

Solve for
$$\begin{Bmatrix} x_{1n+1} \\ x_{2n+1} \end{Bmatrix} = \left[\bar{K}\right]^{-1}\{\bar{P}\}$$

or,
$$\{\bar{P}\} = \left[LDL^T\right]\{x_{n+1}\}$$

There is no need to determine inverse of effective stiffness matrix. Instead, effective stiffness matrix can be decomposed in a lower triangular matrix, and by using back substitution, a solution for displacement vector can be estimated.

Now, the acceleration and velocity vectors can be estimated at $t + \Delta t$ step as follows:

$$\begin{Bmatrix} \ddot{x}_{1n+1} \\ \ddot{x}_{2n+1} \end{Bmatrix} = a_0 \begin{Bmatrix} x_{1n+1} - x_{1n} \\ x_{2n+1} - x_{2n} \end{Bmatrix} - a_2 \begin{Bmatrix} \dot{x}_{1n} \\ \dot{x}_{2n} \end{Bmatrix} - a_3 \begin{Bmatrix} \ddot{x}_{1n} \\ \ddot{x}_{2n} \end{Bmatrix} \tag{7.48}$$

and

$$\begin{Bmatrix} \dot{x}_{1n+1} \\ \dot{x}_{2n+1} \end{Bmatrix} = \begin{Bmatrix} \dot{x}_{1n} \\ \dot{x}_{2n} \end{Bmatrix} + a_6 \begin{Bmatrix} \ddot{x}_{1n} \\ \ddot{x}_{2n} \end{Bmatrix} + a_7 \begin{Bmatrix} \ddot{x}_{1n+1} \\ \ddot{x}_{2n+1} \end{Bmatrix} \tag{7.49}$$

The calculations were carried out in MS-EXCEL and the results are shown in Table 7.6. The displacement response for the two DOF system is shown in Figure 7.17. Similarly, this method can be used for the solution of any MDOF system. The displacement is quite high because of the selection of the data. Normally such a large displacement would be expected if the system becomes inelastic. □

TABLE 7.6 TWO DOF SYSTEM NEWMARK β METHOD

t	x_{1n}	x_{2n}	$\dot{x}_{1n}$	$\dot{x}_{2n}$	$\ddot{x}_{1n}$	$\ddot{x}_{2n}$	Re1	Re2	x_{1n+1}	x_{2n+1}	$\ddot{x}_{1n+1}$	$\ddot{x}_{2n+1}$	$\dot{x}_{1n+1}$	$\dot{x}_{2n+1}$
(1)	(2)	(3)	(4)	(5)	(6)	(7)	(8)	(9)	(10)	(11)	(12)	(13)	(14)	(15)
Δt	0.00	0.00	0.00	0.00	0.00	10.00	0.00	40.00	0.00	0.56	0.27	25.56	0.03	4.45
$2\,\Delta t$	0.00	0.56	0.03	4.45	0.27	25.56	4.24	134.75	0.03	1.87	0.85	-12.42	0.17	6.09
$3\,\Delta t$	0.03	1.87	0.17	6.09	0.85	-12.42	22.01	207.33	0.10	2.88	1.12	-20.35	0.42	1.99
$4\,\Delta t$	0.10	2.88	0.42	1.99	1.12	-20.35	57.76	198.49	0.24	2.76	0.66	-19.14	0.64	-2.94
$5\,\Delta t$	0.24	2.76	0.64	-2.94	0.66	-19.14	104.07	113.12	0.40	1.58	-0.43	-9.36	0.67	-6.51
$6\,\Delta t$	0.40	1.58	0.67	-6.51	-0.43	-9.36	143.46	-9.69	0.53	-0.12	-1.69	4.53	0.40	-7.11
$7\,\Delta t$	0.53	-0.12	0.40	-7.11	-1.69	4.53	155.76	-114.39	0.57	-1.57	-2.53	16.22	-0.12	-4.52
$8\,\Delta t$	0.57	-1.57	-0.12	-4.52	-2.53	16.22	127.61	-154.21	0.46	-2.13	-2.47	20.45	-0.75	0.07
$9\,\Delta t$	0.46	-2.13	-0.75	0.07	-2.47	20.45	59.92	-112.22	0.21	-1.55	-1.42	15.35	-1.24	4.54
$10\,\Delta t$	0.21	-1.55	-1.24	4.54	-1.42	15.35	-30.56	-8.84	-0.11	-0.13	0.29	3.28	-1.38	6.87
$11\,\Delta t$	-0.11	-0.13	-1.38	6.87	0.29	3.28	-116.43	107.64	-0.42	1.48	2.04	-10.21	-1.09	6.00
$12\,\Delta t$	-0.42	1.48	-1.09	6.00	2.04	-10.21	-169.72	183.28	-0.61	2.53	3.14	-18.96	-0.44	2.36

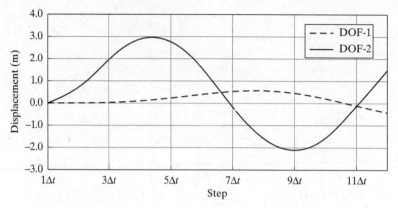

Figure 7.17   Variation of displacement with time step.

7.8 WILSON θ METHOD

This is another algorithm for the solution of incremental equation of equilibrium developed by Prof. E. L. Wilson, University of California, Berkeley. The calculations are carried out over an extended time step $\tau = \theta \Delta t$, where θ is an amplifier for the time step. It assumes that the variation of acceleration over the extended time step remains unchanged, that is, it is still the same as that of the original time step Δt, that is, a linear variation (Figure 7.18).

At time t, acceleration $\qquad = \ddot{x}(t)$
At time $t + \Delta t$, the acceleration $\quad = \ddot{x}(t) + \Delta \ddot{x}$ over the normal time step
At time $t + \tau$, the acceleration is $\; = \ddot{x}(t) + \overline{\Delta \ddot{x}}$ over the extended time step
The equation of motion at the end of $t + \tau$ can be written as follows:

$$m\ddot{x}_{t+\tau} + c_n \dot{x}_{t+\tau} + k_n x_{t+\tau} = R \tag{7.58}$$

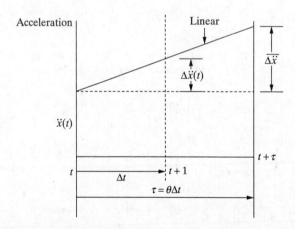

Figure 7.18   Linear acceleration assumption over extended time τ.

where R is the projected load vector given as follows:

$$R = P_n + \theta(P_{n+1} - P_n) \qquad (7.59)$$

$$x_{t+\tau} = x_n + \Delta x_\tau$$
$$\dot{x}_{t+\tau} = \dot{x}_n + \Delta \dot{x}_\tau \qquad (7.60)$$
$$\ddot{x}_{t+\tau} = \ddot{x}_n + \Delta \ddot{x}_\tau$$

Therefore, Equation (7.58) becomes,

$$m\Delta\ddot{x}_\tau + c_n\Delta\dot{x}_\tau + k_n\Delta x_\tau = R - m\ddot{x}_n - c_n\dot{x}_n - k_n x_n \qquad (7.61)$$

Thus, by analogy with Equations (7.24, 7.27a) and (7.28b) of the linear accelera-tion method,

$$\Delta x_\tau = \tau\dot{x}_n + \frac{\tau^2}{2}\ddot{x}_n + \frac{\tau^2}{6}\Delta\ddot{x}_\tau \qquad (7.62a)$$

$$\Delta\dot{x}_\tau = \tau\ddot{x}_n + \frac{\tau}{2}\Delta\ddot{x}_\tau \qquad (7.62b)$$

Rearranging these equations to express each of them in terms of incremental displace-ment Δx_τ, we get,

$$\Delta\ddot{x}_\tau = \frac{6}{\tau^2}\Delta x_\tau - \frac{6}{\tau}\dot{x}_n - 3\ddot{x}_n \qquad (7.63a)$$

$$\Delta\dot{x}_\tau = \frac{3}{\tau}\Delta x_\tau - 3\dot{x}_n - \frac{\tau}{2}\ddot{x}_n \qquad (7.63b)$$

Substituting Equation (7.63) in Equation (7.61) yields,

$$\left[\frac{6}{\tau^2}m + \frac{3}{\tau}c_n + k_n\right]\Delta x_\tau = R - k_n x_n + m\left[\frac{6}{\tau}\dot{x}_n + 2\ddot{x}_n\right] + c_n\left[2\dot{x}_n + \frac{\tau}{2}\ddot{x}_n\right] \qquad (7.64a)$$

$$\bar{k}\,\Delta x_\tau = \overline{\Delta P} \qquad (7.64b)$$

This gives Δx_τ.

Finally, the acceleration, velocity and displacement at the end of the normal time step Δt are calculated as follows:

$$\ddot{x}_{n+1} = \frac{1}{\theta}\left[\frac{6}{\tau^2}\Delta x_\tau - \frac{6}{\tau}\dot{x}_n + \theta\left(1 - \frac{3}{\theta}\right)\ddot{x}_n\right] \qquad (7.65)$$

The velocity and displacements can be computed using Equations (7.28a) and (7.27a) derived for the linear acceleration method, where h is the same as Δt, that is,

$$x_{n+1} = x_n + \Delta t\,\dot{x}_n + \frac{(\Delta t)^2}{3}\ddot{x}_n + \frac{(\Delta t)^2}{6}\ddot{x}_{n+1} \qquad (7.66)$$

$$\dot{x}_{n+1} = \dot{x}_n + 0.5\,\Delta t\,(\ddot{x}_n + \ddot{x}_{n+1}) \qquad (7.67)$$

Alternatively,
Equation (7.64a) can be re-written as follows:
Let us add and subtract $m\ddot{x}_n$ and $c_n\dot{x}_n$ on the right-hand side of Equation (7.64a) and re-write as follows:

$$\left[\frac{6}{\tau^2}m+\frac{3}{\tau}c_n+k_n\right]\Delta x_\tau = R-m\ddot{x}_n-c_n\dot{x}_n-k_nx_n$$

$$+m\left[\frac{6}{\tau}\dot{x}_n+3\ddot{x}_n\right]+c_n\left[3\dot{x}_n+\frac{\tau}{2}\ddot{x}_n\right]$$

or, $\quad\left[\frac{6}{\tau^2}m+\frac{3}{\tau}c_n+k_n\right]\Delta x_\tau = R_1+m\left[\frac{6}{\tau}\dot{x}_n+3\ddot{x}_n\right]+c_n\left[3\dot{x}_n+\frac{\tau}{2}\ddot{x}_n\right]$ \hfill (7.68a)

$$\bar{k}\,\Delta x_\tau = \overline{\Delta P} \hfill (7.68b)$$

This gives Δx_τ.

Alternatively,

Equation (7.64a) can again be re-written by adding the following term on both sides:

$$\left[\frac{6}{\tau^2}m+\frac{3}{\tau}c_n+k_n\right]x_n$$

The final equation becomes as follows:

$$\left[\frac{6}{\tau^2}m+\frac{3}{\tau}c_n+k_n\right]x_{t+\tau} = R+m\left[\frac{6}{\tau^2}x_n+\frac{6}{\tau}\dot{x}_n+2\ddot{x}_n\right]+c_n\left[\frac{3}{\tau}x_n+2\dot{x}_n+\frac{\tau}{2}\ddot{x}_n\right] \hfill (7.69a)$$

or, $\qquad\qquad \bar{k}\,x_{t+\tau} = \overline{\Delta P}$ \hfill (7.69b)

This gives $x_{t+\tau}$.

Algorithm:

Step 1: Compute $\bar{k}$ from $\left[\dfrac{6}{\tau^2}m+\dfrac{3}{\tau}c_n+k_n\right]$

Step 2: For each time step

Form $\overline{\Delta P}$

Solve for Δx_τ using Equation (7.64b), or (7.68b), or $x_{t+\tau}$ using Equation (7.69b)

Step 3: Calculate $x_{n+1}, \dot{x}_{n+1}$ and $\ddot{x}_{n+1}$ using Equations (7.65), (7.66) and (7.67).

Step 4: Update c and k.

Step 5: Repeat steps 1 to 4.

It should be noted that in this method, k and c are assumed to remain constant during the extended time step and are updated at the end of the real-time increment Δt.

$\theta = 1$ leads to the linear acceleration method.

It is recommended that θ is taken > 1.37.

7.9 NONLINEAR PROBLEMS

The algorithms for linear acceleration method, Newmark method and Wilson method are capable of analysing nonlinear problems due to material nonlinearity. There is a need to track the system displacement, member spring force and spring stiffness. Appropriate stiffness should be considered in the calculations. The time step needs to be chosen very carefully so that the change in stiffness occurs at the selected time interval. Otherwise, a correction will have to be applied. A detailed treatment of non-linear analysis is presented in Chapter 13.

PROBLEMS

7.1 A SDOF system has a mass $=100$ kg, stiffness $= 4000$ N/m and damping $\xi = 5\%$. Determine the response of this system when it is subjected to a triangular pulse force as defined in the table using (a) Constant acceleration method and (b) Central difference method. Take step size $= 0.1$ sec and plot the displacement, velocity and acceleration time history.

Time, sec	0	0.1	0.2	0.3	0.4	0.5	0.6	1.0
Force, N	0	100	150	90	40	10	0	0

7.2 Solve Problem 7.1 again with a step size $= 0.05$ sec and comment on the accuracy and stability of the solution.

7.3 Solve Problem 7.1 again using the linear acceleration method with a step size $= 0.1$ sec and compare the results obtained by using the Constant acceleration and central difference method.

7.4 A SDOF system has a mass $m = 125$ kg and stiffness $= 2000$ N/m and damping $= 7\%$. Determine the response of this system when it is subjected to a half sine pulse force $= 50 \sin (3t)$ N using (a) Constant acceleration method and (b) Central difference method. Take (i) step size $= 0.1$ sec and (ii) step size $= 0.2$ sec. Plot the displacement, velocity and acceleration time history, and comment on the stability and accuracy.

7.5 Solve Problem 7.4 using the Newmark β method with $\beta = 0.25$ and compare the results with those obtained in Problem 7.4.

7.6 Solve Problem 7.4 again using the Wilson θ method. Comment on the results.

7.7 A two DOF system has the following properties (kg-N-m units):

$$M = \begin{bmatrix} 5 & 0 \\ 0 & 1 \end{bmatrix}, \quad K = \begin{bmatrix} 10 & -2 \\ -2 & 4 \end{bmatrix}, \quad C = \begin{bmatrix} 0.53 & 0 \\ 0 & 0.25 \end{bmatrix}, \quad P = \begin{Bmatrix} 0 \\ 5 \end{Bmatrix}$$

Initial conditions are: $\begin{Bmatrix} x_{10} \\ x_{20} \end{Bmatrix} = \begin{Bmatrix} 0.05 \\ 0 \end{Bmatrix}$ and $\begin{Bmatrix} \dot{x}_{10} \\ \dot{x}_{20} \end{Bmatrix} = \begin{Bmatrix} 0 \\ 0.01 \end{Bmatrix}$

Determine its response up to 5 sec using the linear acceleration method and Newmark β method with $\beta = \frac{1}{4}$. Compare the results.

8 Elastic Response Spectra

8.1 INTRODUCTION

One of the top priorities of researchers in early 1900s was to develop a methodology to analyse and design buildings that are resistant to earthquakes. But how to estimate the earthquake force was a moot point. How to get the accelerogram of '*the earthquake*' that is likely to occur at a given location? The problem became quite complicated for the following reasons:

(a) Earthquakes do not occur frequently.

(b) Earthquakes cannot be predicted.

(c) It is not possible to instrument each and every possible location to record the earthquake ground motion and maintain these instruments over a period of several decades -24×7.

(d) Very meagre database on earthquakes.

(e) An earthquake is a random natural phenomenon. Each earthquake occurring even at the same site is expected to be different.

An earthquake excitation may be described in terms of ground displacement, velocity or acceleration varying with time. The most important characteristics of an earthquake include its magnitude, frequency content, peak ground acceleration and duration. An earthquake motion is recorded in terms of ground acceleration using accelerometers at any location in three mutually perpendicular directions (x, y and z). It is called accelerogram. This accelerogram after applying some corrections can be integrated to get ground velocity-time history and again integrated to obtain ground displacement-time history. The North–South component of the El Centro or Imperial Valley, California earthquake of 18 May 1940, Koyna earthquake of 11 December 1967, Mexico earthquake of 19 September 1985 and Kobe earthquake of 17 January 1995 were some of the very strong earthquakes ever recorded in different continents and were selected for illustration in this chapter. The El Centro earthquake of May 1940 was the first strongest earthquake ever recorded till that point of time and became the natural choice of the researchers all over the world to study the dynamic response of various structures as a bench mark. The main features of these four earthquakes are shown in Table 8.1 and the estimated damage in Table 8.2. The accelerograms of these earthquakes are shown in Figures 8.1 to 8.4. The data for different strong earthquakes is available from

TABLE 8.1   DATA OF THE EARTHQUAKES CONSIDERED

Earthquake	Date	Magnitude	MM Intensity	Epicenter	Depth	Soil type	Peak ground acceleration
El Centro or Imperial valley, USA	19 May 1940	6.9	X	8 km North of Calexico, California	16 km	hard	0.33 g
Koyna, India	11 Dec 1967	6.5	V	1–5 km	27 km	hard	0.67 g
Mexico City	19 Sept 1985	8.1	IX	350 km west of city	20 km	soft	0.18 g
Kobe, Japan or Great Hanshin earthquake	17 Jan 1995	6.9	X	20 km	17 km	hard	0.35 g

TABLE 8.2   ESTIMATED LOSS TO LIFE AND BUILDINGS

Earthquake	Estimated loss and damage
El Centro	9 dead, 25% residential buildings and about 50% commercial buildings collapsed/severely damaged
Koyna	180 dead, 2000 injured, 80% houses damaged, minor cracks in a dam
Mexico	9500 dead, 30,000 injured, 3500 buildings collapsed/demolished and 100,000 seriously damaged
Kobe	6000 dead, 45,000 injured, 200,000 buildings collapsed or severely damaged, 1 km long Hanshin expressway collapsed

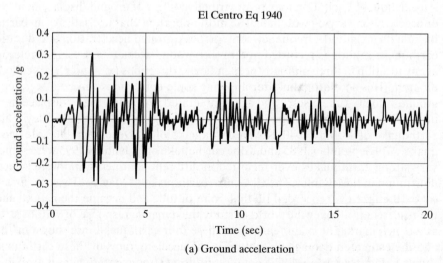

(a) Ground acceleration

Figure 8.1   N–S component of El Centro earthquake, May 1940.

El Centro Eq 1940

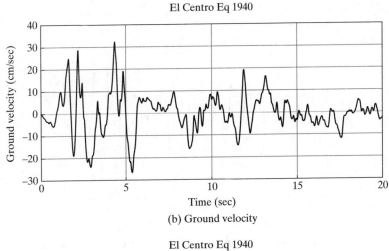

(b) Ground velocity

El Centro Eq 1940

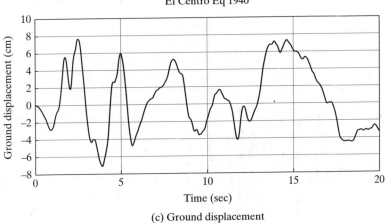

(c) Ground displacement

Figure 8.1   (Continued)

Koyna Eq 1967

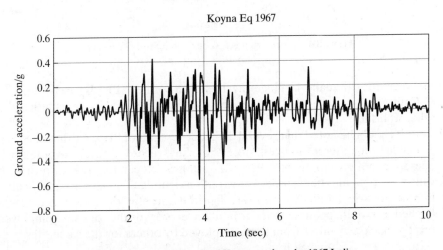

Figure 8.2   Accelerogram of Koyna earthquake 1967, India.

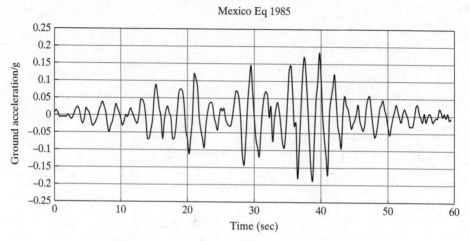

Figure 8.3 Accelerogram of Mexico earthquake 1985, Mexico.

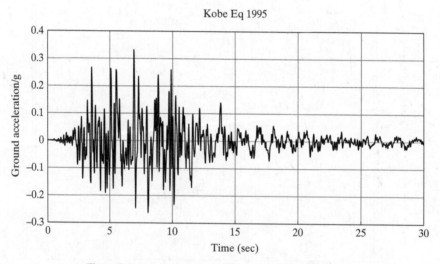

Figure 8.4 Accelerogram of Kobe earthquake 1995, Japan.

the Pacific Earthquake Engineering Research Center (PEER) web site, University of California, Berkeley, USA (peer.berkeley.edu) and USGS web site besides many other web sites.

It should be noted that several different versions of these earthquake records are available from different sources. An earthquake is recorded at several different stations operating in a given region. A variation will arise depending upon which record and which component is being used. The variations among them also arise from differences in how the original analog data was digitized and how the base line correction was applied. It is quite possible that earthquake records for the four sites employed in the present book may differ from those employed by others for the same sites.

In the early 1900s, the dynamic behaviour of structures was being explored. The behaviour of a single-degree-of-freedom (SDOF) system was understood quite well. The researchers focused on developing a methodology to analyse and design a SDOF system for different damping ratio and period of vibration. This chapter deals with the development of elastic response spectra, design response spectra, tripartite graph and tripartite design spectra. The spectra developed for SDOF systems became the basis for design of MDOF systems. It was a revolutionary concept and the structures designed using this concept have performed quite well in severe seismic zones all over the world.

8.2 MATHEMATICAL BACKGROUND

When earthquake excitation is applied to the base of a structure, it produces a time-dependent response in each element of the structure which may be described in terms of displacement, velocity or acceleration. Consider a SDOF system which consists of mass 'm' attached to the ground through a spring of stiffness 'k' and a damper having a coefficient of viscous damping 'c' as shown in Figure 8.5. If such a system is subjected to a ground motion, its equation of motion is given by:

$$m\ddot{x}(t) + c\dot{x}(t) + kx(t) = -m\ddot{y}_g(t) \tag{6.26}$$

where $\ddot{y}_g(t)$ = ground acceleration

$x(t)$, $\dot{x}(t)$, $\ddot{x}(t)$ = relative displacement, relative velocity and relative acceleration of the mass with respect to ground, respectively.

The solution of the above equation for the relative displacement x at any time t is given by Duhamel's integral as follows:

$$x(t) = (-)\frac{1}{\omega_D}\int_0^t \ddot{y}_g(\tau)e^{-\omega\xi(t-\tau)}\sin\omega_D(t-\tau)\,d\tau \tag{8.1a}$$

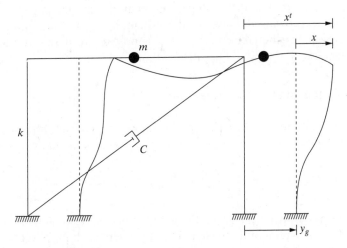

Figure 8.5   A SDOF system subjected to ground excitation.

or,

$$x(t)=(-)\frac{1}{\omega\sqrt{1-\xi^2}}\int_0^t \ddot{y}_g(\tau)e^{-\omega\xi(t-\tau)}\sin\omega\sqrt{1-\xi^2}(t-\tau)d\tau \qquad (8.1b)$$

where,

$\omega = \sqrt{\dfrac{k}{m}}$ = undamped circular frequency of the system.

$\xi = \dfrac{c}{2m\omega}$ = damping ratio.

t and τ are the time parameters.

It is possible to determine the absolute maximum values of the displacement, velocity and acceleration for a given damping and natural frequency of a SDOF system using the above equations. Similarly, a set of such data can be generated for different damping ratios and natural frequencies. Alternatively, any of the direct integration methods discussed earlier can be used to solve the equation of motion for any set of input data, and the absolute maximum response can be estimated.

8.3 ELASTIC RESPONSE SPECTRA

Each of the three plots consisting of peak relative displacement versus natural frequency, peak relative velocity versus natural frequency and peak acceleration versus natural frequency of a SDOF system for a given damping is referred to as the *elastic response spectrum*. Alternatively, the plots can be drawn with respect to natural periods instead of natural frequency of a SDOF system. A spectrum provides a convenient means of presenting the peak response of all possible linear SDOF systems to a given component of earthquake motion.

For a given SDOF system, knowing its natural frequency or period, and damping, the response spectrum curve will provide peak displacement, peak velocity or peak acceleration. Knowing the mass of the system, it is easy to estimate its acceleration and, therefore, earthquake force. Now it is possible to design the SDOF system to resist this force.

8.3.1 Displacement Response Spectra

The maximum value of relative displacement x of the system with respect to the ground is termed as the *Peak Relative Displacement* and it is denoted by x_0. It is given by

$$x_0(\omega,\xi)=\frac{1}{\omega\sqrt{1-\xi^2}}\left|\int_0^t \ddot{y}_g(\tau)e^{-\omega\xi(t-\tau)}\sin\omega\sqrt{1-\xi^2}(t-\tau)d\tau\right|_{max} \qquad (8.2)$$

x_0 depends not only on the ground motion history but also on the frequency of vibration and the damping of the system. For any given earthquake record, by assuming a suitable value of damping in the structure, it is possible to calculate values of x_0 for a full range of vibration frequencies. A graph showing these peak displacement values plotted as a function of frequency (or its reciprocal quantity, period of vibration) for different damping ratios is called a *Relative Displacement Response Spectrum*. Such a spectrum is very useful in assessing the internal forces in various members of a structure. The internal forces such as bending moment, shear force and axial force, etc. are related to the relative displacements through member stiffness matrix.

8.3.2 Velocity Response Spectra

For the maximum value of $\dot{x}$ the relative velocity of the system with respect to the ground is denoted by $\dot{x}_0$ and it is termed as the *peak relative velocity*. When this is plotted as a function of period of vibration of a system, the plot is known as *Relative Velocity Response Spectrum*.

Upon differentiating Equation (8.1) under the integral sign gives,

$$\dot{x}(t) = -\xi\omega x(t) - \int_0^t \ddot{y}_g(\tau)e^{-\xi\omega(t-\tau)}\cos\omega_D(t-\tau)d\tau \tag{8.3}$$

In Equation (8.2), the term $\left|\int_0^t \ddot{y}_g(\tau)e^{-\omega\xi(t-\tau)}\sin\omega_D(t-\tau)d\tau\right|_{\max}$ can be re-written by replacing ω_D by ω

$$\left|\int_0^t \ddot{y}_g(\tau)e^{-\omega\xi(t-\tau)}\sin\omega(t-\tau)d\tau\right|_{\max} \tag{8.4}$$

This equation has the units of velocity. It may be denoted by S_v and is called *peak pseudo velocity*. The prefix *pseudo* is used because it is not the same as $\dot{x}_0$.

We can calculate the peak relative velocity either from Equation (8.3), which is the exact value or by Equation (8.4) which will be an approximate value. However, for small damping, these two equations are expected to give fairly close results. The comparison between the maximum velocity given by these two methods is shown in Figure 8.6 for the El Centro and Koyna earthquakes for 2% and 20% damping. It can

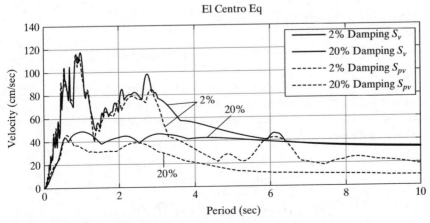

Figure 8.6(a)   El Centro earthquake — velocity and pseudo velocity spectra.

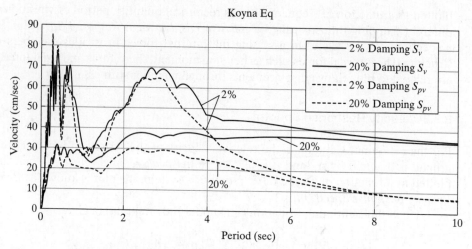

Figure 8.6(b)   Koyna earthquake—velocity and pseudo velocity spectra.

be seen that for 2% damping and small periods, the difference in velocity spectra and pseudo velocity spectra is quite small. The difference gets magnified at large damping and longer periods.

Naturally, it is convenient to use Equation (8.4) instead of Equation (8.3). Thus,

$$\dot{x}_0 \approx S_v = \omega S_d \tag{8.5a}$$

or,

$$S_d = \frac{S_v}{\omega} \tag{8.5b}$$

Therefore, it we plot S_v instead of $\dot{x}_0$ as a function of period, for different values of damping, the plot is known as *Pseudo Velocity Response Spectra.*

8.3.3 Acceleration Response Spectra

Let us consider Equation (8.3).

$$\dot{x}(t) = -\xi\omega x(t) - \int_0^t \ddot{y}_g(\tau) e^{-\xi\omega(t-\tau)} \cos \omega_D (t-\tau) d\tau \tag{8.3}$$

An equation for relative acceleration $\ddot{x}(t)$ can be obtained by differentiating Equation (8.3). Total acceleration can be obtained by adding the ground acceleration $\ddot{y}_g(t)$. Alternatively, the total acceleration can be obtained by writing the equation of motion as follows:

$$m\ddot{x}_r(t) + c\dot{x}_r(t) + kx_r(t) = -m\ddot{y}_g(t) \tag{6.25}$$

or,

$$m\ddot{x}_r(t) + m\ddot{y}_g(t) + c\dot{x}_r(t) + kx_r(t) = 0$$

or,

$$m\ddot{x}^t(t) + c\dot{x}_r(t) + kx_r(t) = 0$$

or,

$$m\ddot{x}^t(t) = -c\dot{x}_r(t) - kx_r(t)$$

or,

$$\ddot{x}^t(t) = -2\omega\xi\dot{x}_r(t) - \omega^2 x_r(t) \tag{8.6}$$

where,

$\ddot{x}^t(t)$ = absolute acceleration of the SDOF system ($x_r = x - y$ used in Equation (6.25a))

The maximum value of absolute acceleration or total acceleration of the system $\ddot{x}^t = \ddot{x}_r + \ddot{y}_g$ denoted by $\ddot{x}_0$ is termed as *peak acceleration* and when it is plotted against natural period of vibration of the system, for different damping values, the plot obtained is termed as the *Acceleration Response Spectra*. However, instead of $\ddot{x}_0$, we plot $\omega^2 S_d$ denoted by S_a which has the units of acceleration. Such a response spectra is called *Pseudo Acceleration Response Spectra*. Again for small values of damping $\ddot{x}_0 \approx S_a$. A comparison of maximum acceleration as obtained by these two methods is shown in Figure 8.7 for El Centro and Koyna earthquakes for 2% and 20% damping. It can be seen that the difference in total acceleration and pseudo acceleration spectra for both these earthquakes for 2% damping is very small and is slightly more for 20% damping. This observation is very significant in developing pseudo acceleration spectra for earthquakes.

Most often the dimensionless quantity S_a/g is plotted for acceleration spectra where g denotes acceleration due to gravity. It most of the civil engineering structures the value of damping ratio ξ is very low (normally less than 20%) and therefore, we have the following simple relationships between the three spectral quantities (displacement, velocity and acceleration):

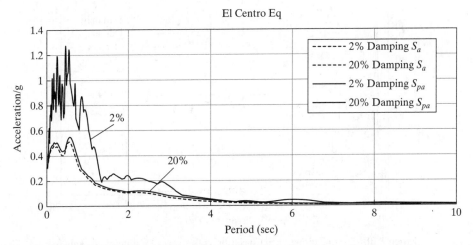

Figure 8.7(a)   El Centro earthquake—acceleration and pseudo acceleration spectra.

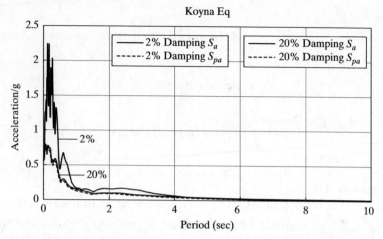

Figure 8.7(b)   Koyna earthquake—acceleration and pseudo acceleration spectra.

$$S_v = \omega S_d = \frac{2\pi}{T} S_d \tag{8.7}$$

$$S_a = \omega S_v = \omega^2 S_d = \frac{4\pi^2}{T^2} S_d \tag{8.8a}$$

or,

$$S_v = \frac{S_a}{\omega} = \frac{T}{2\pi} S_a \tag{8.8b}$$

The spectral displacement, pseudo velocity and pseudo acceleration response spectra for 0%, 2%, 5%, 10% and 20% damping for El Centro earthquake (N–S Component)

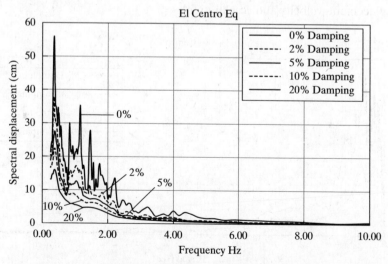

Figure 8.8(a)   Spectral displacement spectrum vs. frequency for different damping— El Centro Earthquake.

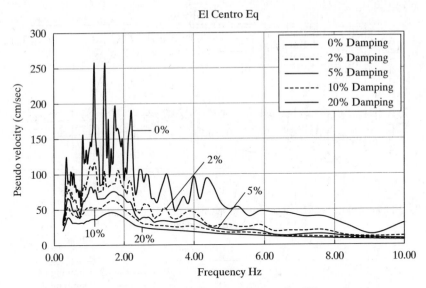

Figure 8.8(b)   Pseudo velocity spectrum vs. frequency for different damping—
El Centro Earthquake.

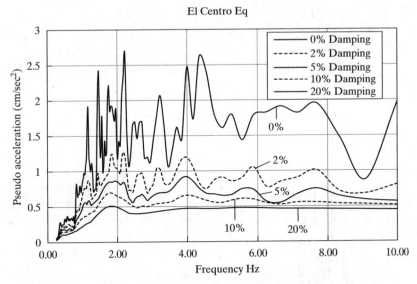

Figure 8.8(c)   Pseudo acceleration spectrum vs. frequency for different damping—
El Centro Earthquake.

are shown in Figure 8.8 with natural frequency and in Figure 8.9 with natural period.
The two plots are mirror image of each other since frequency and period are inverse
of each other. The pseudo velocity spectra and pseudo acceleration spectra for Koyna
earthquake of 11 December 1967, Mexico earthquake of 19 September 1985 and Kobe
earthquake of 17 January 1995 are shown in Figures 8.10 to 8.12.

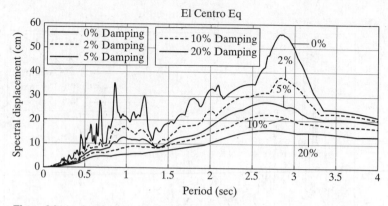

Figure 8.9(a)   Spectral displacement spectrum vs. period for different damping—
El Centro earthquake.

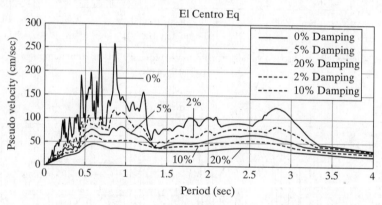

Figure 8.9(b)   Pseudo velocity spectrum vs. period for different damping—
El Centro earthquake.

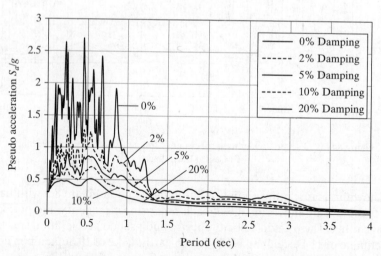

Figure 8.9(c)   Pseudo acceleration spectrum vs. period for different damping—
El Centro earthquake.

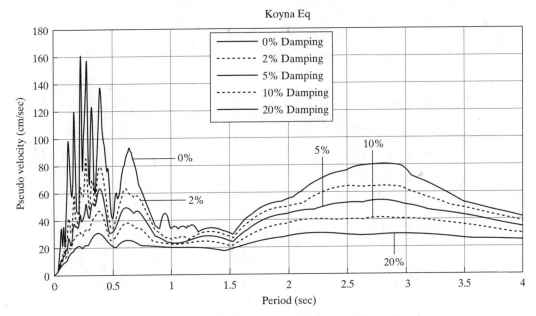

Figure 8.10(a)   Pseudo velocity spectrum vs. period for different damping—
Koyna earthquake.

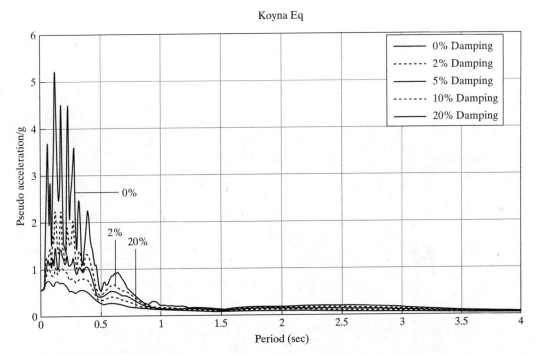

Figure 8.10(b)   Pseudo acceleration spectrum vs. period for different damping—
Koyna earthquake.

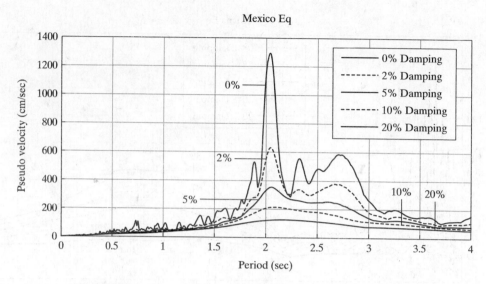

Figure 8.11(a) Pseudo velocity spectrum vs. period for different damping—
Mexico earthquake.

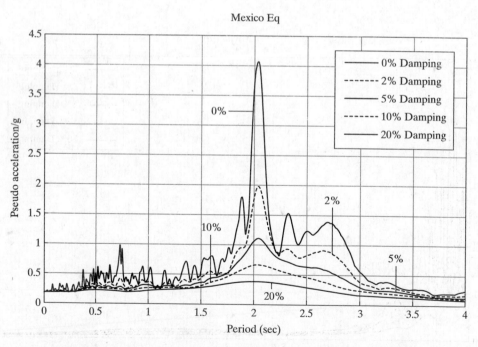

Figure 8.11(b) Pseudo acceleration spectrum vs. period for different damping—
Mexico earthquake.

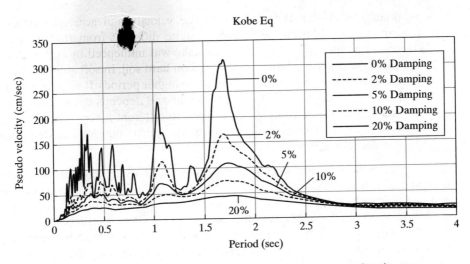

Figure 8.12(a)   Pseudo velocity spectrum vs. period for different damping—
Kobe earthquake.

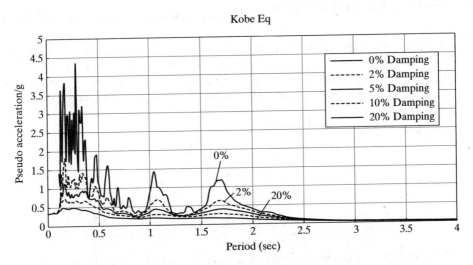

Figure 8.12(b)   Pseudo acceleration spectrum vs. period for different damping—
Kobe earthquake.

In all these response spectra, the following common features can be seen:

1. There are too many sharp peaks for zero damping.
2. For a slight damping of 2%, the oscillations start becoming less violent. With further increase in damping to 20%, the curves became quite smooth.
3. The acceleration response spectrum has three distinct segments: initial increasing segment, near plateau segment and decreasing segment.

4. Another observation is that peak in the velocity and acceleration response spectra for the Mexico earthquake is quite different from that of the other three earthquakes. The Mexico earthquake was influenced by soft alluvial soil, whereas the other earthquakes occurred on hard soil. In soft soils, the dominating period of an earthquake gets shifted to higher periods. It is quite natural and well expected. Each earthquake is different and depends upon several seismological and geotechnical features. It leads to different *power spectral density* in each earthquake. Therefore, each earthquake spectra may have its own dominating frequency or period.

In practice, commonly used structural materials such as steel and concrete exhibit a damping of 2% and 5%, respectively. At these damping, the zig-zag pattern in the response curves became a big hurdle in design. It was not possible to take an average as the variation was too much, and the number of strong motion records available in the 1950s were very few. If there was an ensemble of 50 or 100 records of earthquakes, then it was possible to draw statistical elastic response spectra for different confidence and damping levels.

8.4 FOURIER AMPLITUDE SPECTRA

Another approach for characterizing the response of a system for a ground motion is provided by Fourier amplitude spectrum, which is a measure of the total energy of an undamped system evaluated at the end of the earthquake (i.e., at time $\tau = t_1$ where duration of earthquake is from $\tau = 0$ to $\tau = t_1$). The Fourier spectrum of a ground motion is defined as:

$$F(\omega) = \int_{\tau=-\infty}^{\infty} \ddot{y}(\tau)\, e^{-i\omega\tau}\, d\tau \tag{8.9}$$

where

$\ddot{y}(\tau)$ = ground motion acceleration

ω = natural frequency of the system

τ = time parameter

If the duration of the ground motion is from $\tau = 0$ to $\tau = t_1$, this can be written as:

$$F(\omega) = \int_0^{t_1} \ddot{y}(\tau)\cos\omega\tau\, d\tau - i\int_0^{t_1} \ddot{y}(\tau)\sin\omega\tau\, d\tau$$

The amplitude of the Fourier Spectrum termed as *Fourier amplitude spectrum* $|F(\omega)|$ will be given by:

$$|F(\omega)| = \left[\left\{\int_0^{t_1} \ddot{y}(\tau)\cos\omega\tau\, d\tau\right\}^2 + \left\{\int_0^{t_1} \ddot{y}(\tau)\sin\omega\tau\, d\tau\right\}^2\right]^{1/2} \tag{8.10}$$

The total energy of a structural system can be obtained by combining expressions for the strain energy and the kinetic energy, that is,

$$E(t) = \frac{1}{2}m\{\dot{x}(t)\}^2 + \frac{1}{2}k\{x(t)\}^2 \tag{8.11}$$

where $x(t)$, $\dot{x}(t)$ can be determined from Equation (8.2) for undamped system ($\xi = 0$). In practice, it is convenient to express the energy in terms of the square root of twice its value per unit mass, that is:

$$\sqrt{\frac{2E(t)}{m}} = [\{\omega x(t)\}^2 + \{\dot{x}(t)\}^2]^{1/2} \tag{8.12}$$

The maximum value of this quantity clearly provides an upper bound to both the pseudo-velocity response spectrum and the time-velocity response spectrum, each of which is represented by one of the terms under the square root sign above. By substituting the values of $x(t)$ and $\dot{x}(t)$ for *undamped case* from Equation (8.2), Equation (8.12) is reduced to:

$$\sqrt{\frac{2E(t)}{m}} = \left[\left\{\int_0^t \ddot{y}(\tau)\cos\omega\tau \ d\tau\right\}^2 + \left\{\int_0^t \ddot{y}(\tau)\sin\omega\tau \ d\tau\right\}^2\right]^{1/2} \tag{8.13}$$

Comparison of Equations (8.10) and (8.13) shows that the Fourier amplitude spectrum is a measure of the total energy of an undamped system evaluated at the end of an earthquake as shown in Figure 8.13 for El Centro and Mexico earthquakes. But the maximum response due to a ground motion may occur sometime before the end of the earthquake, therefore, the Fourier amplitude spectrum is not a good approach for design than the response spectrum which represents the maximum response of the structure during the ground motion.

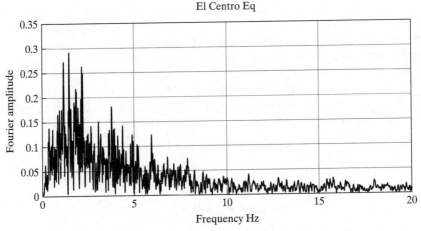

Figure 8.13(a)   Fourier amplitude spectra for El Centro earthquake.

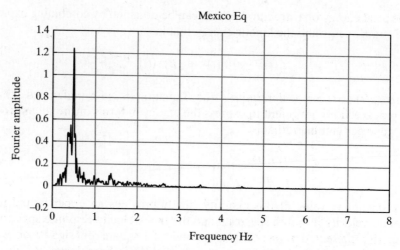

Figure 8.13(b) Fourier amplitude spectra for Mexico earthquake.

8.5 DESIGN RESPONSE SPECTRA

A response spectra is different from a design response spectra. A response spectra represents peak response of a SDOF system for various natural frequencies or periods of vibrations and damping values for a given component of earthquake motion at a given site. Each curve has too many zig-zags. A response value may lie in a valley or a peak of a curve depending upon how accurately natural frequency of the SDOF system has been computed. Moreover, if there are more than one earthquake record for a given site, each record may provide different peak-response value for a given natural frequency and damping. The question arises as to how to use this information in design of a structure? Moreover, there may not be any earthquake data available for a given site. Thus, the question arises as to how to design a structure for earthquake resistance under these circumstances? There is a need to arrive at an average and smoothened response spectrum which exhibits all the basic characteristics and can be adopted in design with reasonable confidence in the absence of realistic data. Such a spectrum is called a *design spectrum*.

For aseismic design of structures, the maximum force experienced by the structure due to the effect of ground motion is required. This maximum force for a SDOF system is given by:

$$\text{Design force} = m \, |\ddot{x}|_{\max}$$

$$= m S_a = \frac{W}{g} S_a$$

or
$$\text{Design Force} = W \cdot \alpha_0 \tag{8.14}$$

where $\alpha_0 = \dfrac{S_a}{g}$ and it is termed as *seismic coefficient*

$W = mg = $ weight of the system

For a structural system, the seismic coefficient S_a/g for a given earthquake can be directly read from the acceleration response spectra of that earthquake corresponding to the natural period of vibration and damping ratio of the system, and when it is multiplied by the weight of the system, the design seismic force is obtained. If a spectra is generated for different earthquake records for a given site, it can be noticed that there is a difference in the peak ground acceleration, velocity and displacement for various earthquake records as shown in Figures 8.9 to 8.12. The computed response cannot be averaged on an absolute basis.

The pseudo acceleration spectra for 5% damping for the El Centro, Koyna, Mexico and Kobe earthquakes are shown in Figure 8.14. These four earthquakes were recorded in four different continents of the world at different points of time. The Mexico response spectra is different than the rest of the three due to its frequency contents and soft soil attenuation. Figure 8.14 highlights the variations in the response spectra. A zig-zag spectra can be very inconvenient and impractical. The zig-zag in lower damping ratio spectra is very high. It is possible to draw a smooth curve through these data and avoid the zig-zag pattern. A smooth curve can be drawn either by simple inspection and judgement or by using some statistical parameter. It can follow more or less a set pattern in three segments, that is, a smooth curve, a straight line and another smooth curve. A smoothened curve is also shown in Figure 8.15. This appeared to be a reasonable compromise except of course for the Mexico earthquake. Studies have been carried out by several researchers in the past to develop a simplified elastic spectrum, which can be used for designing. The following are the most popular spectra:

(a) Housner's average spectra
(b) Newmark and Hall's spectra

Such spectra are termed as the smoothened response spectra and makes things easier for a designer. These spectra will be discussed next.

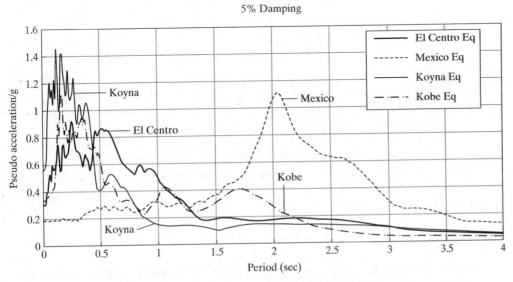

Figure 8.14   Comparison of different earthquake spectra.

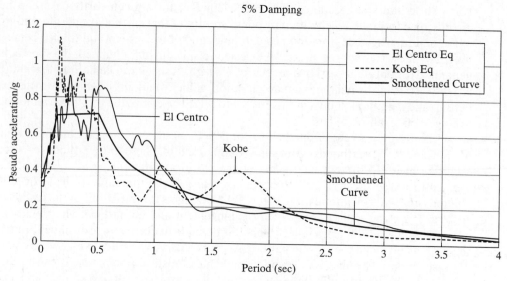

Figure 8.15   El Centro and Kobe pseudo acceleration spectra for 5% damping.

8.6 HOUSNER'S AVERAGE SPECTRA

Each earthquake is different in terms of its frequency content, magnitude and duration. Different earthquakes can be combined by normalizing them to the same scale. Various procedures were used to normalize response spectra before averaging is carried out. Among these procedures, two have been most commonly used:

1. *normalization* according to spectrum intensity where the areas under the spectra between two given frequencies or periods are set equal to each other

2. normalization to peak ground motion where the spectral ordinates are divided by peak ground acceleration, velocity or displacement for the corresponding region of the spectrum.

Normalization to other parameters such as effective peak acceleration and effective peak velocity-related acceleration has also been suggested and used in development of design spectra for seismic codes.

Prof. G. W. Housner, at the CalTech, Pasedena, California, chose to normalize the spectra by keeping the area under the velocity spectrum for 20% damping to be the same. At this damping, the velocity spectrum curve becomes nearly a straight line and the shape between any two period limits becomes a trapezoid. The spectral intensity was computed as follows:

$$SI = \int_{0.1}^{2.5} S_v(T, \xi) \, dt \qquad (8.15)$$

For example, let A_1 and A_2 be the areas under the velocity spectrum curves of two different accelerograms. In that case, if the ordinates of the second accelerogram are multiplied by A_1/A_2, then the modified second and the original first record are considered to have been normalized to the same scale. If we plot the response spectra for the above two normalized accelerograms, both the response spectra will be running very close to each other, and the average of these two can be conveniently considered as the spectra depicted by either of the normalized accelerograms. This type of response spectra is termed as *Averaged Spectra*.

Prof. G.W. Housner developed a design spectrum by computing the spectra for two components of each of the four different earthquakes that occurred in the Western USA, and then *normalizing, averaging, scaling and smoothening* the resulting curves. The four earthquake records studied by Housner were:

(a) El Centro earthquake of 1934

(b) El Centro earthquake of 1940

(c) Olympia earthquake of 1949

(d) Taft earthquake of 1952

The spectra were scaled so that the long period value of the undamped spectral velocity was 1 ft/sec (30 cm/sec) at 0% damping. The average smoothened velocity and acceleration spectra obtained by Housner are shown in Figures 8.16(a) and 8.16(b), respectively. It should be noted that the maximum spectral accelerations in this average smoothened spectra are much lower than those obtained in these real earthquakes. It was done purposely in view of a lower probability of occurrence of a strong earthquake in any given zone. This spectrum was used and is still being used as a design response spectrum in many countries even today. It was used in the Indian Code IS:1893 till 2002 when it was replaced with the spectra based on an ensemble of Indian earthquakes.

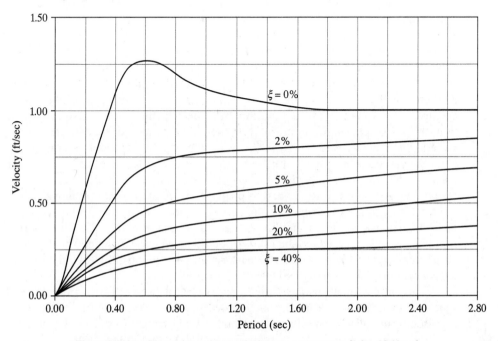

Figure 8.16(a)   Housner's average velocity response spectra (1 ft = 30.48 cm).

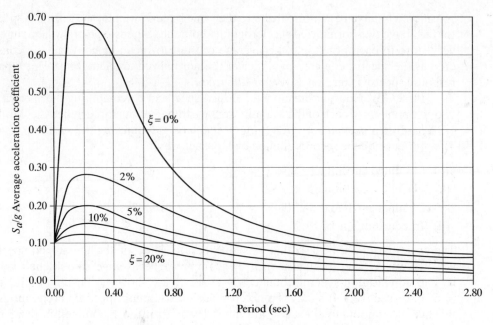

Figure 8.16(b)   Housner's average acceleration response spectra.

8.7 TRIPARTITE GRAPH

The displacement, pseudo velocity and pseudo acceleration response spectra for a given earthquake motion virtually provides the same information. The three spectra are different ways to present the same information for a SDOF system. The obvious question is why do we need three spectra? The plots show how each quantity varies with natural frequency of a SDOF directly. Although these three quantities are mathematically related, a plot gives much more clarity directly without having to go through the mathematical equations. The displacement spectra shows the variation of peak displacement of a SDOF system, the pseudo velocity spectra shows the variation of peak kinetic energy ($=1/2\ mv^2$), whereas the pseudo acceleration spectra gives the variation of peak seismic force (mass times acceleration) or base shear. Thus, each spectra contributes to the total response in its own way. Prof. A. S. Veletsos and Prof. N. M. Newmark were the first to propose the concept of combining all the three spectra into a single spectrum in 1960.

A response spectrum should cover a wide range of natural vibration periods or frequencies and several damping ratios so that it provides peak response of all possible structures – very short period as well as very long period, on different soil and geological conditions. Choice of logarithmic scales was obvious.

The simple relationships Equations (8.7) and (8.8) existing among the three spectral quantities (i.e. displacement, velocity and acceleration) make it possible to represent them all in a simple plot on four way log paper. This type of plot is known as *tripartite* plot. The maximum displacement (relative to ground) is designated by the symbol D, the maximum pseudo-velocity (relative to ground) by the symbol V, and the maximum pseudo-acceleration (representing the force in the spring) by the symbol A.

Construction of tripartite spectra with natural frequency as abscissa   It has already been shown earlier Equations (8.7) and (8.8b) that:

$$S_v = \omega S_d \tag{8.7a}$$

and

$$S_v = \frac{S_a}{\omega} \tag{8.8b}$$

Taking log of both the above equations,

$$\log S_v = \log \omega + \log S_d \tag{8.7b}$$

and

$$\log S_v = -\log \omega + \log S_a \tag{8.8c}$$

Comparing these two equations with that of a straight line, that is, $y = mx + C$.

In Equation (8.7b), if $\log S_v$ is taken as ordinate and $\log \omega$ is taken as abscissa, and the remaining term $\log S_d$ is taken as constant, then the straight line makes an angle of 45° with the abscissa. Similarly, in Equation (8.8c), the straight line makes an angle of –45° with the abscissa. First the coordinates of the origin are decided, that is, the values of S_v and T or ω along with their maximum values. It will decide the number of log cycles along the period (or frequency) and pseudo velocity axes. For the purpose of plotting the graph, the minimum values of T or ω and S_v may be taken as equal, say 0.01 and 0.01 each. Then, the point of intersection of S_d curve with T or ω is computed using Equation (8.7b). Similarly, the point of intersection of S_a curve with T or ω is computed using Equation (8.8b). The coordinates of the four corners of the graph may be taken as shown in Figures 8.17(a) and 8.17(b) for use in MATLAB code.

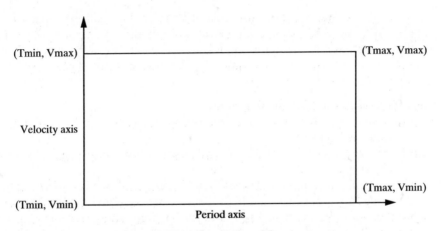

Figure 8.17(a)   Coordinates of the corners.

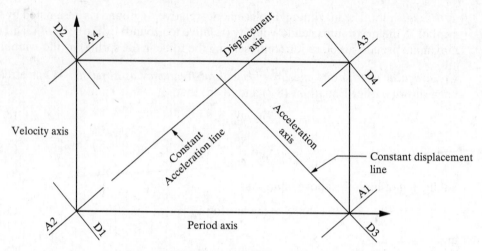

Figure 8.17(b)   Coordinates of the corners for diagonals.

Construction of tripartite spectra with natural period as abscissa

It has already been shown earlier Equations (8.7) and (8.8b) that:

$$S_v = \omega S_d = \frac{2\pi}{T} S_d \tag{8.7b}$$

$$S_v = \frac{S_a}{\omega} = \frac{T}{2\pi} S_a \tag{8.8b}$$

Taking log of both the above equations,

$$\log S_v = -\log T + \log S_d + \log 2\pi \tag{8.7d}$$

and

$$\log S_v = \log T + \log S_a - \log 2\pi \tag{8.8d}$$

Comparing these two equations with that of a straight line, that is, $y = mx + C$.

In Equation (8.7d), if $\log S_v$ is taken as ordinate and $\log T$ is taken as abscissa, and the remaining terms 2π and $\log S_d$ are taken as constants, then the straight line makes an angle of $-45°$ with the abscissa. Similarly, in Equation (8.8d), the straight line makes an angle of $45°$ with the abscissa.

Steps for Generating a Tripartite Graph

Step 1: Generate vertical grid lines, that is lines of constant period or frequency in terms of log cycles.

Step 2: Generate horizontal grid lines, that is lines of constant pseudo velocity in terms of log cycles.

Step 3: Compute the limiting values of S_a and S_d at each of the four corners of the graph using Equations (8.7) and (8.8) knowing the coordinates of these corners.

Step 4: Compute the coordinates (T, S_v) corresponding to each of the diagonal grids parallel to acceleration or displacement axes at the two ends of each grid line.

A computer code can be written in MATLAB to generate the tripartite graph. A four-way log scale is plotted as shown in Figure 8.18 with period as absicca. The displacement axis is right angles to the acceleration lines, whereas the acceleration axis is right angles to the displacement lines.

The tripartite spectra for any earthquake can be plotted in MATLAB by importing the pseudo velocity versus period or frequency data for a given set of damping ratio as shown in Figures 8.19 to 8.22 for the four different earthquakes. The response spectra data should be made available in MS-Excel sheet, which will be read by MATLAB.

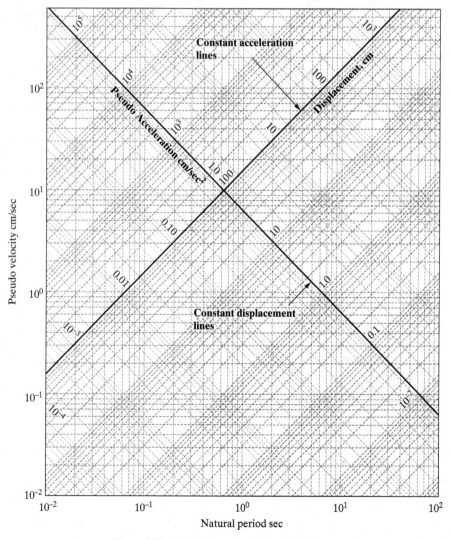

Figure 8.18   Tripartite graph—Period as abscissa.

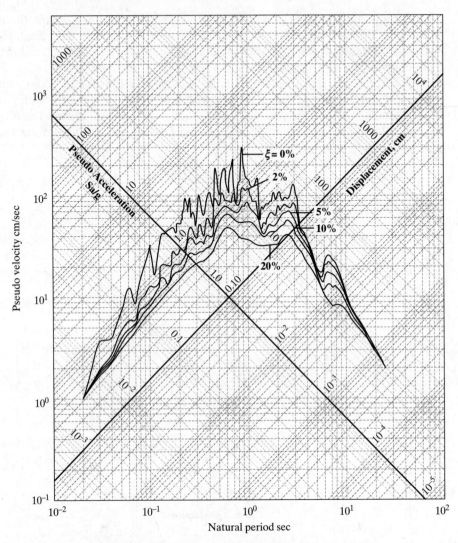

Figure 8.19   Tripartite spectra for El Centro earthquake, 1940.

8.7.1 MATLAB Code

```
%    Dynamics of Structures by Ashok K. Jain I.I.T. Roorkee
%    DOS8_1
%    Tripartite Graph Paper
%
clear all;
close all;
%
```

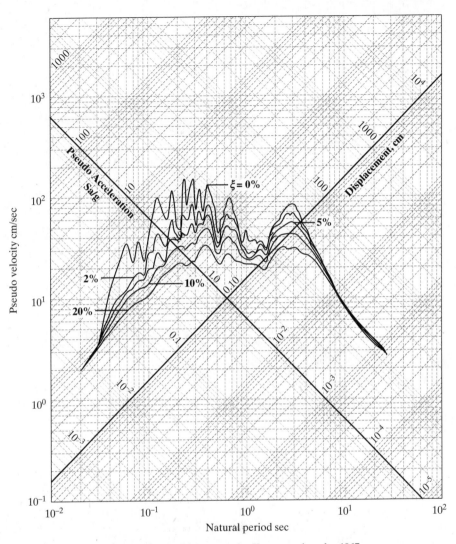

Figure 8.20   Tripartite spectra for Koyna earthquake, 1967.

```
Tmin=0.01;
Tmax=600.;
t(1)=Tmin;
t(32)=Tmax;
Vmin=0.01;
Vmax=600.;
Agmin=0.0001;
Agmax=90;
Dmin=0.001;
```

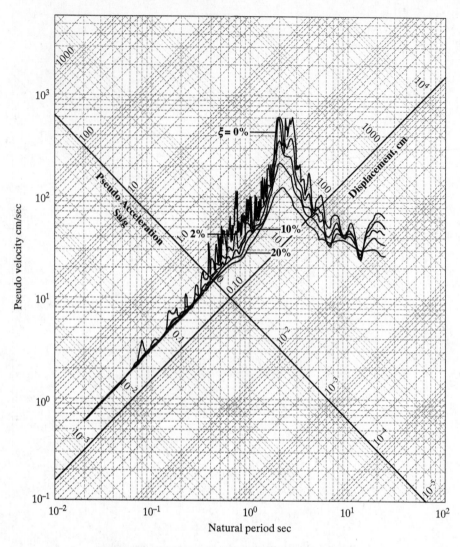

Figure 8.21 Tripartite spectra for Mexico earthquake, 1985.

```
Dmax=10000;
%
% Compute vertical grid
%
k=1;
fori=1:4
for j=1:9
if (k <=36)
t(k)=j*10^(i-3);
```

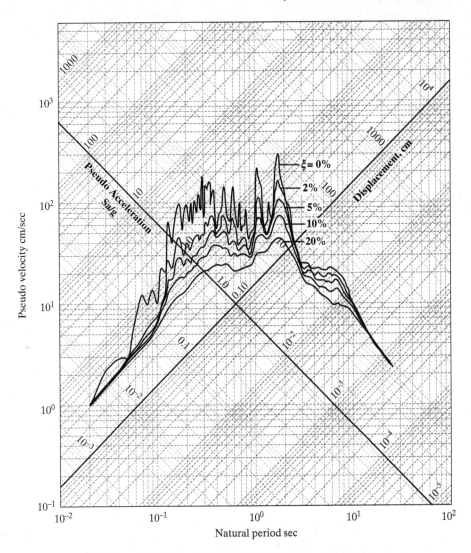

Figure 8.22   Tripartite spectra for Kobe earthquake, 1995.

```
        k=k+1;
end;
end;
end;
%
% Compute horizontal Grid
%
k=1;
for i=1:4
```

```
for j=1:9
if (k <=36)
v(k)=j*10^(i-2);
     k=k+1;
end;
end;
end;
%
% Compute Acceleration Grid
k=1;
for i=-1:7
for j=1:9
a(k)=j*10^(i-5);
     k=k+1;
end;
end;
k=1:72;
a(k);
%
% Compute Displacement Grid
k=1;
for i=-1:8
for j=1:9
d(k)=j*10^(i-4);
     k=k+1;
end;
end;
k=1:81;
d(k);
loglog(t,v,'w')
set(gca,'LineWidth',0.5)
holdon;
%
% Compute Acceleration Grid
%
g=981.0
A1=2*pi()*Vmin/(Tmax*g);
A2=2*pi()*Vmin/(Tmin*g);
A3=2*pi()*Vmax/(Tmax*g);
A4=2*pi()*Vmax/(Tmin*g);
ta1i  = 1;
ta3i  = 1;
for i=1:72
if (a(i)>= A1) & (a(i)<= A3)
ta(i)=2*pi*Vmin/(g*a(i));
va(i)=Tmax/(2*pi)*a(i)*g;
line([ta(i) Tmax],[Vminva(i)])
%    (X1:td1(i) Y1:Vmax X2:td2(i) Y2:Vmin)
end
```

```
%     Plot this grid - part 1
if (A2 > A3) & (a(i)>= A3) & (a(i) <= A2)
ta1(ta1i)=2*pi*Vmin/(a(i)*g);
ta2(ta1i)=2*pi*Vmax/(a(i)*g);
line([ta1(ta1i) ta2(ta1i)],[VminVmax]);
       ta1i = ta1i+1;
end
%     Plot this grid - Part 2
if (a(i)>= A2) & (a(i)<= A4)
va3(ta3i)=Tmin/(2*pi)*a(i)*g;
ta3(ta3i)=2*pi*Vmax/(a(i)*g);
line([Tmin ta3(ta3i)],[va3(ta3i) Vmax]);
ta3i  = ta3i +1;
% Plot this grid - Part 3
end
end
%
%Plot Displacement grid
D1=Tmin*Vmin/(2*pi);
D2=Tmin*Vmax/(2*pi);
D3=Tmax*Vmin/(2*pi);
D4=Tmax*Vmax/(2*pi);
tdi = 1;
td1i = 1;
td3i = 1;
fori=1:81
if (d(i)>= D1) & (d(i)<= D2)
td(tdi)=2*pi*d(i)/Vmin;
vd(tdi)=2*pi*d(i)/Tmin;
line([Tminvd(tdi)],[td(tdi) Vmin]);
tdi =tdi +1;
end
%
%     Plot this grid - part 1
%     (X1:Tmin Y1:vd(i) X2:td(i) Y2:Vmin)
%
if (D3 > D2) & (d(i)>= D2) & (d(i) <= D3)
td1(td1i)=2*pi*d(i)/Vmax;
td2(td1i)=2*pi*d(i)/Vmin;
line([td1(td1i) Vmax],[td2(td1i) Vmin]);
td1i = td1i +1;
end
%
%     Plot this grid - Part 2
%     (X1:td1(i) Y1:Vmax X2:td2(i) Y2:Vmin)
%
if (d(i)>= D3) & (d(i)<= D4)
td3(td3i)=2*pi*d(i)/Vmax;
vd3(td3i)=2*pi*d(i)/Tmax;
```

```
line([td3(td3i) Vmax],[Tmax vd3(td3i)]);
td3i = td3i +1;
%
%  Plot this grid - Part 3
%  X1:td3(i) Y1:Vmax X2:Tmax Y2:vd3(i)
%
end
end


axis([0.01 100 0.1 600])
gridon
xlabel('Period/sec');
ylabel('Pseudo Velocity cm/sec');
```

How to Read the Tripartite Graph?

Let us draw a tripartite graph and consider two points P and Q as shown in Figure 8.23. The period coordinate of P is 0.70 sec and V ordinate point Q is 200 cm/sec. It should be remembered that diagonal grid lines correspond to a constant displacement or constant acceleration value. The diagonal lines passing through point P can be read at P1 and P2 for displacement and acceleration values, respectively. Line P–P1 is parallel to the constant displacement lines and line P–P2 is parallel to the constant acceleration lines. Similarly, diagonal lines passing through point Q can be read at Q1 and Q2 for displacement and acceleration values, respectively. Line Q–Q1 is parallel to the constant displacement lines and line Q–Q2 is parallel to the constant acceleration lines. The steps to read the displacement D, velocity V and acceleration A coordinates of P and Q are as follows:

Step 1: Draw a vertical line from the time axis at 0.7 sec and then a horizontal line at P to V axis. Read V ordinate as 0.9 cm/sec. The true value is 0.897 cm/sec.

Step 2: Now draw a line normal to the displacement axis through P and read D ordinate as 0.1 cm.

Step 3: Now draw a line normal to the acceleration axis through P and read A ordinate as 8 cm/sec². The true value is 8.056 cm/sec².

Step 4: Similarly, draw a horizontal line from the V axis at 200 cm/sec and then a vertical line at Q to the time axis. Read T ordinate as 3 sec.

Step 5: Now draw a line normal to the displacement axis through Q and read D ordinate as 95 cm. The true value is 95.49 cm.

Step 6: Now draw a line normal to the acceleration axis through Q and read A ordinate as 420 cm/sec². The true value is 418.90 cm/sec².

The T, D, V and A coordinates of P and Q are as follows:

Point	T sec	D cm	V cm/sec	A cm/sec²
P	0.7	0.10	0.90	8
Q	3	95	200	421

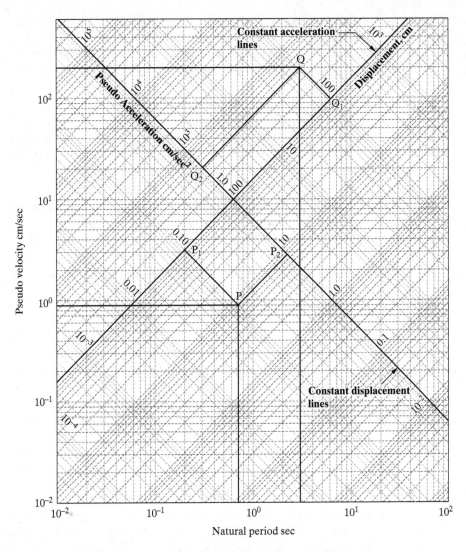

Figure 8.23 Tripartite graph.

8.8 ELASTIC DESIGN TRIPARTITE SPECTRA

Prof. N. M. Newmark and W. J. Hall studied the characteristics of tripartite response spectra of several earthquakes recorded at different sites in different countries having different seismological parameters and noted some common key features. They observed the following characteristics in the response spectra of the horizontal component of the North–South component of El Centro earthquake of 1940 for systems having 0, 2, 5, 10 and 20% of critical damping (Figure 8.19):

1. For high frequency systems, higher than about 2 cycles/sec (or low period systems having T < 0.5 sec), the maximum acceleration response is nearly constant but is a function of damping. The amplification of the response acceleration as compared to the ground acceleration is quite large for lightly damped systems.

2. For extremely high frequency systems (or very low periods), the maximum response acceleration is same as the maximum ground acceleration.

3. For relatively low frequency systems, having frequencies less than about 0.3 cycles/sec (or for high period systems having T > 3 sec), the maximum displacement response is nearly constant and maximum displacement shows only a slight amplification over the maximum ground displacement.

4. For extremely low frequency systems (or extremely high period systems having T > 10 sec), the maximum displacement response is exactly the same as the maximum ground displacement.

5. In the intermediate range of frequencies, the maximum pseudo velocity response is nearly constant, indicating constant energy absorption over the entire range of frequencies from 0.3 to 3 cycles/sec (or T between 0.33 sec and 3 sec). The amplifications are strongly influenced by damping.

A tripartite spectra for El Centro earthquake, Koyna earthquake, Mexico earthquake and Kobe earthquakes for 5% damping is shown in Figure 8.24. These curves also exhibit a behaviour similar to those noticed in Figure 8.19.

Procedure to Generate Simplified Elastic Design Response Spectra   Based on these characteristics, they proposed a much simpler method to construct them using the peak values of ground displacement, ground velocity and ground acceleration. It is possible to draw the tripartite response spectra using these three parameters without any more knowledge about the time history of that component of the ground motion. The response spectra for an earthquake can be approximated by using straight line segments in the response spectrum plot, having for the different degrees of damping about the same ratio to the ground motions as the El Centro response spectrum or that of an ensemble of ground motions. The important question was if a normalized, averaged, and smoothened response spectra based on eight components of four earthquakes recorded in USA is acceptable for design, why not make it simpler while retaining the most significant characteristics? They identified three sensitive regions in any tripartite spectra: *acceleration sensitive region, velocity sensitive region* and *displacement sensitive region.*

Region 1a: Maximum acceleration of the SDOF system is equal to maximum ground acceleration.

Region 1b:

   (i) Maximum acceleration response of a SDOF system is constant for a given damping.

   (ii) It varies with damping—higher for lightly damped system.

Region 2: Constant energy absorption, that is, constant velocity amplification and a function of damping.

Region 3: Maximum displacement response of a SDOF is equal to maximum ground displacement.

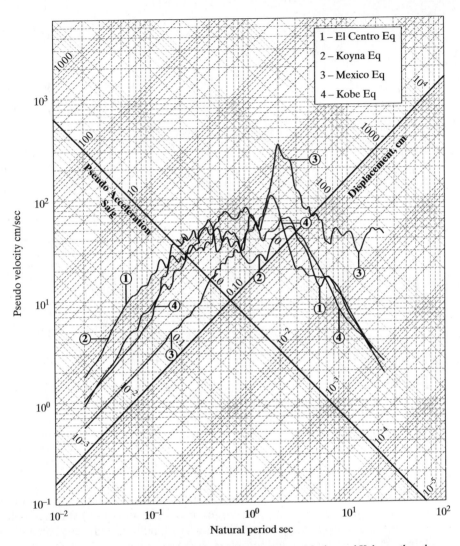

Figure 8.24 Tripartite response spectra for El Centro, Koyna, Mexico and Kobe earthquakes for 5% damping.

The maximum values of ground acceleration $\ddot{x}_{g0}$, velocity $\dot{x}_{g0}$ and displacement x_{g0} are sketched on the tripartite logarithmic chart shown in dash lines in Figure 8.25. These plots give a polygonal curve representing the maximum ground motion values only. The response of items or of equipment, components of structures and complete structures is then determined by amplifying the ground motion values to obtain response spectrum values using amplification factors for various degrees of damping.

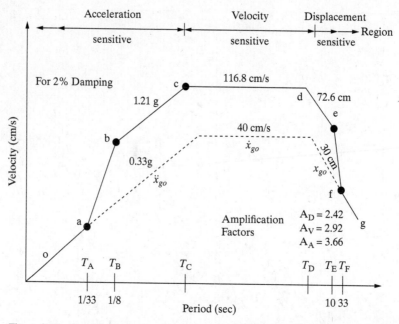

Figure 8.25 Simplified smoothened elastic response spectra for El Centro earthquake for 84.1% non-exceedance probability—Newmark and Hall.

Newmark and Hall carried out statistical analysis of a very large number of earthquake records and computed the probability distributions in each of the three sensitive regions for the spectra ordinate, its mean value and its standard deviation at each period. These used lognormal probability distributions. Based on these data, they generated amplification factors in each of the three sensitive regions for different damping ratio (1%, 2%, 5%, 10% and 20%) two different non-exceedance probabilities of 50% (representing mean value of spectra ordinates) and 84.1 per cent (representing mean plus one standard deviation of spectra ordinates) as shown in Table 8.3. Thus, they developed mean response spectrum (having 50% non-exceedance probability) and mean plus one standard deviation response spectrum (having 84.1% non-exceedance probability).

In the delineation of the complete response spectrum, straight line bounds are used. The procedure for generating a simplified response spectrum is as follows (Figure 8.25):

TABLE 8.3 NEWMARK AND HALL AMPLIFICATION FACTORS

Damping	Median (50%)			Mean + SD (84.1%)		
	A	V	D	A	V	D
1%	3.21	2.31	1.82	4.38	3.38	2.73
2%	2.74	2.03	1.63	3.66	2.92	2.42
5%	2.12	1.65	1.39	2.71	2.30	2.01
10%	1.64	1.37	1.20	1.99	1.84	1.69
20%	1.17	1.08	1.01	1.26	1.37	1.38

1. A line c-d is drawn parallel to the horizontal axis by amplifying the ground velocity by factor V from Table 8.3.

2. A line b-c is drawn parallel to the peak ground acceleration line by amplifying the peak ground acceleration by factor A from Table 8.3. The intersection of lines b-c and c-d gives point c.

3. A line d-e is drawn parallel to the peak ground displacement line by amplifying the peak ground displacement by factor D from Table 8.3. The intersection of lines c-d and d-e give point d.

4. Point b is located corresponding to 1/8 sec period. Similarly, point 'a' is located corresponding to 1/33 sec period. Line a-b is transition line in the acceleration-sensitive region.

5. Point 'e' is located corresponding to 10 sec period. Similarly, point 'f' is located corresponding to 33 sec period. Line e-f is transition line in the displacement sensitive region.

The resulting response spectrum o-a-b-c-d-e-f-g is shown in solid lines in Figure 8.25.

Example 8.1

A SDOF system was subjected to the N–S component of the El Centro accelerogram of May 1940. Determine the spectral ordinates for 5% damping if its period was (i) 0.5 sec, (ii) 1 sec and (iii) 3 sec.

Solution   Its solution can be obtained in any of the following three ways:

(i) The set of three spectra—displacement, velocity and acceleration can be used to determine the ordinates corresponding to three different periods for 5% damping.
(ii) The tripartite spectra can be used to determine these ordinates.
(iii) A time history analysis can be carried out for each of the three SDOF systems for the given accelerogram having a period of 0.5, 1 or 3 sec.

Each of these methods will produce nearly the same results as shown in Table 8.4.   □

TABLE 8.4   SPECTRAL ORDINATES

Period, sec	Displacement, cm	Velocity, cm/sec	Acceleration, g
0.5	4.43	55.68	0.71
1.0	12.08	75.89	0.48
3.0	22.2	46.5	0.10

8.9 INDIAN CODE:1893 PART 1-2002

In the 1960s, the Housner's average smoothened response spectra had become available. This spectra was adopted in many countries as well as in the Indian Standard IS:1893 till it was revised in 2002. IS:1893-2002 adopted an average spectra based on a series of Indian earthquakes as shown in Figure 8.26. This is based on strong motion records of eight Indian earthquakes: Himachal Pradesh 26 April 1986 and 24 March 1995 earthquakes; UP Hills 20 October 1991 and 26 March 1996 earthquakes; N.E. India 10 September 1986, 19 May 1987, 6 February 1988 and 6 August 1988 earthquakes.

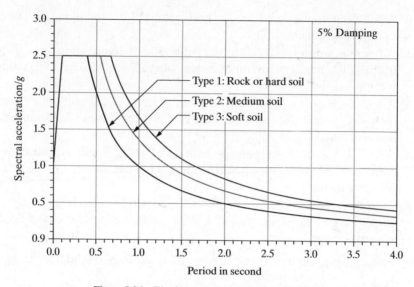

Figure 8.26   Elastic response spectra IS:1893-2002.

The average shape of the response spectra was arrived at from an ensemble of total of 92 records (46 sites × 2 components) for rocky sites and 114 records (57 sites × 2 components) for stiff soil. The mean spectra so obtained were smoothened for convenience of use in design. It was called response spectra for Maximum Considered (or Credible) Earthquake (MCE) condition. This elastic response spectrum is divided by a factor 2 to get a Design Basis Earthquake (DBE) response spectra.

For rocky or hard soils:

$$
S_a/g = \begin{cases} 1 + 15\,T & \text{for} \quad 0 \leq T \leq 0.10 \\ 2.50 & \text{for} \quad 0.10 \leq T \leq 0.40 \\ 1.0/T & \text{for} \quad 0.40 \leq T \leq 4.0 \end{cases} \tag{8.16a}
$$

For medium soils

$$
S_a/g = \begin{cases} 1 + 15\,T & \text{for} \quad 0 \leq T \leq 0.10 \\ 2.50 & \text{for} \quad 0.10 \leq T \leq 0.55 \\ 1.36/T & \text{for} \quad 0.55 \leq T \leq 4.0 \end{cases} \tag{8.16b}
$$

For soft soils

$$
S_a/g = \begin{cases} 1 + 15\,T & \text{for} \quad 0 \leq T \leq 0.10 \\ 2.50 & \text{for} \quad 0.10 \leq T \leq 0.67 \\ 1.67/T & \text{for} \quad 0.67 \leq T \leq 4.0 \end{cases} \tag{8.16c}
$$

The Indian code defines these two terms as follows:

MCE: The most severe earthquake effects considered by this standard

DBE: It is the earthquake which can reasonably be expected to occur at least once during the design life of the structure

The UBC 1997 defined these two terms as follows:

MCE: Largest reasonably conceived earthquake in any zone that appears possible along a recognized fault. It has a 10% probability of being exceeded in 100 years (i.e., a return period = 1000 years)

DBE: Reasonably expected to occur at least once in the design life of the structure. It has a 10% probability of being exceeded in 50 years (i.e., a return period = 475 years)

The IBC 2006 defines these two terms as follows:

MCE: The most severe earthquake effects considered by this code

DBE: The earthquake ground motion that buildings and structures are specifically proportioned to resist

The ASCE 7 2010 defines these two terms as follows:

MCE Ground Motion: The most severe earthquake effects considered by this standard more specifically defined in the following two terms:

Maximum Considered Earthquake Geometric Mean (MCE_G) Peak Ground Acceleration: The most severe earthquake effects considered by this standard determined for geometric mean peak ground acceleration and without adjustment for targeted risk. The MCE_G peak ground acceleration adjusted for site effects (PGA_M) is used in this standard for evaluation of liquefaction, lateral spreading, seismic settlements and other soil related issues.

Risk-Targeted Maximum Considered Earthquake (MCE_R) Ground Motion Response Acceleration: The most severe earthquake effects considered by this standard determined for the orientation that results in the largest maximum response to horizontal ground motions and with adjustment for targeted risk.

Design Earthquake Ground Motion: The earthquake ground motions that are two-thirds of the corresponding MCE_R ground motions.

There is a need to be very careful while using these terms as they may vary from code to code. Nevertheless, the concept behind using these terms remains same. Many countries have developed probability-based response spectra depending upon the risk of earthquakes at a given site.

8.9.1 Eurocode: EC8-part 1-2004

The Eurocode-8 on earthquake actions provides horizontal design action coefficients using elastic response spectrum for five different types of soils. Two types of response spectrum curves are provided: Type 1 and Type 2. If the earthquakes that contribute most to the seismic hazard defined for the site for the purpose of probabilistic hazard assessment have a surface-wave magnitude M_s, not greater than 5.5, Type 2 response spectrum is recommended, otherwise Type 1 is recommended. The shape of the elastic response spectrum is taken as being the same for the two levels of seismic action for the *no-collapse requirement*, that is, *ultimate limit state*, and for the *damage limitation requirement*.

The elastic spectra prescribed in Eurocode 1998-part 1-2004 is shown in Figure 8.27. The values of periods T_B, T_C, T_D and soil factor S depends upon the ground type. Each response spectrum curve is divided in four zones and equations are provided to estimate the design seismic coefficient in different soil conditions.

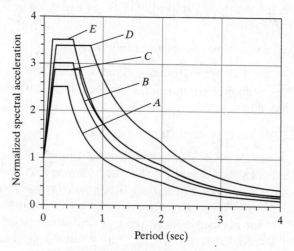

Figure 8.27(a)   Recommended Type 1 elastic response spectra for ground types A to E.

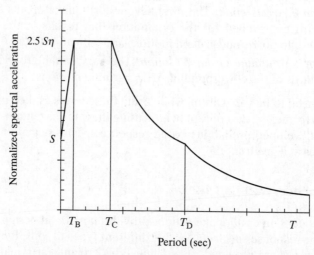

Figure 8.27(b)   Shape of the elastic response spectrum – Eurocode 1998-part 1-2004.

Horizontal elastic response spectrum   For the horizontal components of the seismic action, the elastic response spectrum $S_a(T)$ is defined by the following expressions:

$$S_a(T) = a_g S \left[1 + \frac{T}{T_B}(2.5\eta - 1) \right] \qquad \text{for} \quad 0 < T < T_B \qquad (8.17a)$$

$$S_a(T) = a_g S 2.5\eta \qquad \text{for} \quad T_B < T < T_C \qquad (8.17b)$$

$$S_a(T) = a_g S \eta \frac{T_C}{T} \qquad \text{for} \quad T_C < T < T_D \qquad (8.17c)$$

$$S_a(T) = a_g S \eta \frac{T_C T_D}{T^2} \qquad \text{for} \quad T_D < T < 4.0 \text{ sec} \qquad (8.17d)$$

where

a_g = design ground acceleration on type A ground
T = period of a linear SDOF system
T_B = lower limit of the period of the constant spectral acceleration branch
T_C = upper limit of the period of the constant spectral acceleration branch
T_D = value defining beginning of the constant displacement response range of the spectrum
S = soil factor
η = damping correction factor with a reference value of $\eta = 1$ for 5% viscous damping

More details can be seen in the Eurocode-8-part 1.

8.9.2 Design Spectrum

The elastic response spectra for El Centro and Kobe earthquakes and that given in IS:1893-2002 code for 5% damping are compared in Figure 8.28. It can be seen that the codal spectrum is well below what was obtained during real earthquakes. This is a very

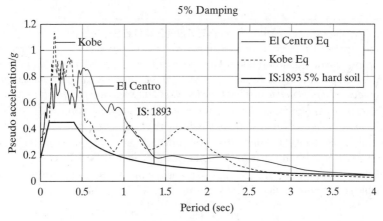

Figure 8.28   El Centro, Kobe and IS:1893–2002 spectra for 5% damping.
(Z = 0.36, I = 1 and R = 1 on hard soil)

significant observation. It shows that the code has intentionally provided a spectrum which is well below the forces recorded during real earthquakes. The question arises as to what is the reason behind such a decision? The answer lies in the probability of occurrence of an earthquake of given magnitude and return period at a given site. Depending upon the probability of occurrence of an earthquake in a given region, it is desirable to design the building for a lesser force and allow the building to undergo inelastic deformations. This requires provision of sufficient ductility in the structure at all possible locations of the formation of plastic hinges to take care of inelastic deformations. The intention is to design a safe and economical structure.

PROBLEMS

8.1 Explain the terms elastic response spectra and design response spectra. Differentiate between velocity response spectra and pseudo velocity response spectra. Get any accelerogram component from the PEER or any other web site, compute and plot these two velocity spectra for 0%, 5% and 20% damping.

8.2 For the accelerogram procured in Problem 8.1, compute and plot acceleration spectra and pseudo acceleration spectra for 0%, 5% and 20% damping.

8.3 (a) Explain the difference between elastic spectra and smoothened elastic spectra. How do you normalize a set of spectra?

  (b) Procure a set of five accelerograms from the PEER or any other web site. Generate elastic response spectra and try to normalize those using different criteria and plot to illustrate salient features of normalization.

8.4 Write a computer code to generate a plot of tripartite graph.

8.5 Discuss the salient features of the various regions in a tripartite elastic response spectrum. How is this information useful to the designers?

8.6 Develop an elastic tripartite response spectrum for the following peak ground parameters using the Newmark and Hall amplification factors: maximum ground acceleration, velocity and displacement equal to 0.45 g, 40 cm/sec, and 25 cm, respectively. Use a damping factor of 5%. Plot the graph with frequency as abscissa and again with period as abscissa.

REFERENCES

Seismosoft <www.seismosoft.com> *Very powerful programs are available to compute and plot elastic response spectra, Fourier spectra, Ground motion parameters, inelastic constant ductility spectra, and generate artificial earthquakes and spectrum compatible earthquakes etc.*

ASCE 7 (2010) Minimum Design Loads for Buildings and other Structures, ASCE/SEI Standard ASCE 7–10, American Society of Civil Engineers, Reston, VA.

Eurocode 1998 (2004) Design of Structures for Earthquake Resistance — Part 1: General Rules, Seismic Actions and Rules for Buildings, European Standard, Brussels.

Housner, G.W. (1941) Calculating the Response of an Oscillator to Arbitrary Ground Motion, Bulletin of Seismological Society of America, Vol 31, pp. 143–149.

IS 1893:1962 Recommendations for Earthquake Resistant Design of Structures, Bureau of Indian Standards, New Delhi.

IS 1893:1966 Criteria for Earthquake Resistant Design of Structures, Bureau of Indian Standards, New Delhi.

IS 1893:1970 Criteria for Earthquake Resistant Design of Structures, Bureau of Indian Standards, New Delhi.

IS 1893:1975 Criteria for Earthquake Resistant Design of Structures, Bureau of Indian Standards, New Delhi.

IS 1893:1984 Criteria for Earthquake Resistant Design of Structures, Bureau of Indian Standards, New Delhi.

IS 1893:2002 (Part 1) Criteria for Earthquake Resistant Design of Structures, Part 1 General Provisions and Buildings, Bureau of Indian Standards, New Delhi.

Newmark, N.M. and Hall, W.J., (1973) A Rational Approach to Seismic Design Standards for Structures, Proc., V[th] World Conference on Earthquake Engg, Rome, Vol. 2, pp. 2266–2275.

Newmark, N.M. and Hall, W.J., (1969) Seismic Design Criteria for Nuclear Reactor Facilities, Proc., IVth World Conference on Earthquake Engg, Santiago, Chile, Vol. 2, pp. 37–50.

PART 2

MULTI-DEGREE OF FREEDOM SYSTEMS

9 | Two-degree of Freedom Systems

9.1 INTRODUCTION

A study of a two degree of freedom (DOF) system explores how to write and solve the equation of motion, find frequencies and mode shapes and interpret its results. It leads to a very special area of highly practical importance known as *vibration absorbers*. These vibration absorbers are mounted in all kinds of structures where vibrations are a problem, for example, buildings, theater floors, bridges, automobile parts, aircrafts and machines. Tuned mass dampers are special cases of the vibration absorbers. The theory of vibration absorbers and tuned mass dampers are discussed along with real-life applications.

9.2 UNDAMPED FREE VIBRATIONS

Let us consider an undamped two-degree of freedom system as shown in Figure 9.1. Its free body diagrams for the mass m_1 and mass m_2 are also shown. Equations of motion for the two masses can be written as follows:

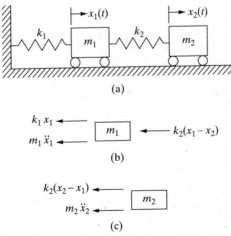

Figure 9.1 Two degree of freedom system – undamped.

$$m_1 \ddot{x}_1 + k_1 x_1 + k_2 (x_1 - x_2) = 0 \tag{9.1a}$$

and
$$m_2 \ddot{x}_2 + k_2 (x_2 - x_1) = 0 \tag{9.1b}$$

Let us assume that the masses vibrate in phase with each other. That is, they follow an identical variation with time but with their own characteristic amplitudes.

Let
$$\left. \begin{aligned} x_1 &= X_1 \sin \omega_1 t \\ x_2 &= X_2 \sin \omega_2 t \end{aligned} \right\} \tag{9.2}$$

∴ Substituting Equation (9.2) in Equation (9.1a) gives,

$$-m_1 X_1 \omega_1^2 \sin \omega_1 t + k_1 X_1 \sin \omega_1 t + k_2 (X_1 \sin \omega_1 t - X_2 \sin \omega_2 t) = 0$$

or,
$$-m_1 X_1 \omega_1^2 \sin \omega_1 t + (k_1 + k_2) X_1 \sin \omega_1 t = k_2 X_2 \sin \omega_2 t$$

or,
$$\frac{X_1}{X_2} = \frac{k_2 \sin \omega_2 t}{[(k_1 + k_2) - m_1 \omega_1^2] \sin \omega_1 t} \tag{9.3}$$

Since X_1 and X_2 are the amplitudes of two harmonic motions, these ratios must be constant and independent of time.

∴
$$\frac{\sin \omega_2 t}{\sin \omega_1 t} = \text{constant} = c \text{ say} \tag{9.4}$$

This should be true at all times

Let us see what happens if $c > 1$

At
$$t = \frac{\pi}{2\omega_1}, \ \sin \omega_1 t = \sin \frac{\omega_1 \pi}{2\omega_1} = 1$$

∴
$$\frac{\sin \omega_2 t}{\sin \omega_1 t} = \sin \omega_2 t = c > 1$$

or $\sin \omega_2 t > 1$, which is not possible.

Therefore c cannot exceed 1. Similarly, it can be shown that c cannot be less than 1.

Hence, $c = 1$ always

∴
$$\frac{\sin \omega_2 t}{\sin \omega_1 t} = 1 \quad \text{or} \quad \omega_1 = \omega_2 \tag{9.5}$$

Thus, the two harmonic motions, if at all they exist, have to be of same frequency. Let us modify the assumed solution as follows:

$$\left.\begin{array}{l} x_1 = X_1 \sin \omega t \\ x_2 = X_2 \sin \omega t \end{array}\right\} \tag{9.6}$$

Substituting in Equation (9.1), we get

$$\left[-m_1\omega^2 + (k_1 + k_2)\right]X_1 = k_2 X_2 \tag{9.7a}$$

and

$$\left(-m_2\omega^2 + k_2\right)X_2 = k_2 X_1 \tag{9.7b}$$

Equation (9.7a) can be written as:

$$\therefore \quad \frac{X_1}{X_2} = \frac{k_2}{-m_1\omega^2 + (k_1 + k_2)} = \frac{k_2}{(k_1 + k_2) - m_1\omega^2}$$

and Equation (9.7b) can be written as:

$$\frac{X_1}{X_2} = \frac{k_2 - m_2\omega^2}{k_2}$$

or,

$$\frac{k_2}{(k_1 + k_2) - m_1\omega^2} = \frac{k_2 - m_2\omega^2}{k_2}$$

or,

$$k_2^2 = [(k_1 + k_2) - m_1\omega^2][k_2 - m_2\omega^2]$$

$$= m_1 m_2 \omega^4 - m_1 k_2 \omega^2 - (k_1 + k_2)m_2\omega^2 + (k_1 + k_2)k_2$$

or,

$$m_1 m_2 \omega^4 - [m_1 k_2 + m_2 (k_1 + k_2)]\omega^2 + k_1 k_2 = 0 \tag{9.8}$$

This gives two positive roots of ω^2, hence two positive values of ω, that is, ω_1^* and ω_2^*. Equation (9.8) is referred to as the characteristic equation of vibration of a two DOF system.

Let us re-write Equation (9.1) in matrix form as follows:

$$\begin{bmatrix} m_1 & 0 \\ 0 & m_2 \end{bmatrix}\begin{Bmatrix} \ddot{x}_1 \\ \ddot{x}_2 \end{Bmatrix} + \begin{bmatrix} k_1 + k_2 & -k_2 \\ -k_2 & k_2 \end{bmatrix}\begin{Bmatrix} x_1 \\ x_2 \end{Bmatrix} = \begin{Bmatrix} 0 \\ 0 \end{Bmatrix} \tag{9.9}$$

Upon substituting the values of x_1 and x_2 from Equation (9.6), we get

$$\begin{bmatrix} k_1 + k_2 - m_1\omega^2 & -k_2 \\ -k_2 & k_2 - m_2\omega^2 \end{bmatrix}\begin{Bmatrix} X_1 \\ X_2 \end{Bmatrix} = \begin{Bmatrix} 0 \\ 0 \end{Bmatrix} \tag{9.10}$$

Since the vector $\{X_1\ X_2\}$ cannot be zero, the determinant of the term inside the square bracket must be zero. That is,

$$\det \begin{vmatrix} k_1 + k_2 - m_1\omega^2 & -k_2 \\ -k_2 & k_2 - m_2\omega^2 \end{vmatrix} = 0 \tag{9.11a}$$

or,
$$[(k_1+k_2)-m_1\omega^2][k_2-m_2\omega^2]-k_2^{\;2}=0 \qquad (9.11b)$$

or it can be written as:

$$\omega^4-\left(\frac{k_2}{m_2}+\frac{k_1+k_2}{m_1}\right)\omega^2+\frac{k_1}{m_1}\frac{k_2}{m_2}=0 \qquad (9.12)$$

This is the same equation as Equation (9.8).

Equation (9.12) can be written as follows:

$$\omega^4-\left(\frac{k_2}{m_1}+\frac{k_1}{m_1}+\frac{k_2}{m_2}\right)\omega^2+\frac{k_1}{m_1}\frac{k_2}{m_2}=0$$

$$\omega^4-\left(\frac{k_1(m_1+m_2)}{m_1(m_1+m_2)}+\frac{k_2}{m_1}+\frac{k_2}{m_2}\right)\omega^2+\frac{k_1}{m_1}\frac{k_2}{m_2}=0$$

or,
$$\omega^4-\left(\frac{k_1}{m_1+m_2}+\frac{k_2}{m_2}\right)\left(\frac{m_1+m_2}{m_1}\right)\omega^2+\frac{k_1}{m_1+m_2}\frac{k_2}{m_2}\frac{m_1+m_2}{m_1}=0 \qquad (9.13)$$

If
$$\bar\omega_1^{\;2}=\frac{k_1}{m_1+m_2} \quad\text{and}\quad \bar\omega_2^{\;2}=\frac{k_2}{m_2}$$

Let
$$\mu=\frac{m_2}{m_1}=\text{mass ratio} \qquad (9.14)$$

Equation (9.13) can be written as follows:

$$\omega^4-\omega^2[(\bar\omega_1^{\;2}+\bar\omega_2^{\;2})(1+\mu)]+\bar\omega_1^{\;2}\bar\omega_2^{\;2}(1+\mu)=0 \qquad (9.15)$$

It again gives four roots of ω, two positive and two negative. Each positive value of ω will give the values of X_1 and X_2 known as eigenvectors.

9.3 UNDAMPED FORCED VIBRATIONS

Now let us consider forced vibrations of undamped two DOF systems as shown in Figure 9.2.

Equations of motion become:

$$m_1\ddot{x}_1+k_1x_1+k_2(x_1-x_2)=P_0\sin\bar\omega t \qquad (9.16a)$$

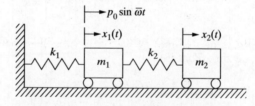

Figure 9.2   Two degree of freedom system.

and
$$m_2\ddot{x}_2 + k_2(x_2 - x_1) = 0 \tag{9.16b}$$

Let us rewrite Equation (9.16) in matrix form:

$$\begin{bmatrix} m_1 & 0 \\ 0 & m_2 \end{bmatrix} \begin{Bmatrix} \ddot{x}_1 \\ \ddot{x}_2 \end{Bmatrix} + \begin{bmatrix} k_1 + k_2 & -k_2 \\ -k_2 & k_2 \end{bmatrix} \begin{Bmatrix} x_1 \\ x_2 \end{Bmatrix} = \begin{Bmatrix} P_0 \sin \bar{\omega}t \\ 0 \end{Bmatrix} \tag{9.17}$$

Let
$$\left. \begin{aligned} x_1 &= X_1 \sin \bar{\omega}t \\ x_2 &= X_2 \sin \bar{\omega}t \end{aligned} \right\} \quad \text{for a steady state solution} \tag{9.18}$$

It is known from the differential equations that the forced response of an undamped system is of the form of a harmonic function of the same frequency as the driving force with different amplitude but in phase. $\bar{\omega}$ is the forcing frequency in Equation (9.18). Substituting in Equation (9.16), we have for steady state response

$$[-m_1\bar{\omega}^2 + (k_1 + k_2)]X_1 - k_2X_2 = P_0 \tag{9.19a}$$

and
$$-m_2\bar{\omega}^2 X_2 + k_2 X_2 - k_2X_1 = 0 \tag{9.19b}$$

or,
$$k_2X_1 + (m_2\bar{\omega}^2 - k_2)X_2 = 0 \tag{9.19c}$$

These equations can be written in matrix form as follows:

$$\begin{bmatrix} k_1 + k_2 - m_1\bar{\omega}^2 & -k_2 \\ -k_2 & k_2 - m_2\bar{\omega}^2 \end{bmatrix} \begin{Bmatrix} X_1 \\ X_2 \end{Bmatrix} = \begin{Bmatrix} P_0 \\ 0 \end{Bmatrix}$$

or,
$$\begin{Bmatrix} X_1 \\ X_2 \end{Bmatrix} = \begin{bmatrix} k_1 + k_2 - m_1\bar{\omega}^2 & -k_2 \\ -k_2 & k_2 - m_2\bar{\omega}^2 \end{bmatrix}^{-1} \begin{Bmatrix} P_0 \\ 0 \end{Bmatrix}$$

or,
$$\begin{Bmatrix} X_1 \\ X_2 \end{Bmatrix} = \frac{1}{(k_1 + k_2 - m_1\bar{\omega}^2) \times (k_2 - m_2\bar{\omega}^2) - k_2^2)} \begin{bmatrix} k_2 - m_2\bar{\omega}^2 & k_2 \\ k_2 & k_1 + k_2 - m_1\bar{\omega}^2 \end{bmatrix} \begin{Bmatrix} P_0 \\ 0 \end{Bmatrix}$$

or,
$$\begin{Bmatrix} X_1 \\ X_2 \end{Bmatrix} = \frac{1}{(k_1 + k_2 - m_1\bar{\omega}^2) \times (k_2 - m_2\bar{\omega}^2) - k_2^2)} \begin{Bmatrix} P_0(k_2 - m_2\bar{\omega}^2) \\ P_0 k_2 \end{Bmatrix} \tag{9.20}$$

Solving Equation (9.20) gives,

$$X_1 = \frac{[k_2 - m_2\bar{\omega}^2]P_0}{[m_1m_2\bar{\omega}^4 - \{m_1k_2 + m_2(k_1 + k_2)\}\bar{\omega}^2 + k_1k_2]} \tag{9.21a}$$

$$X_2 = \frac{k_2 P_0}{[m_1m_2\bar{\omega}^4 - \{m_1k_2 + m_2(k_1 + k_2)\}\bar{\omega}^2 + k_1k_2]} \tag{9.21b}$$

The determinant given by Equation (9.11b) can be written as follows:

$$\det = \left(k_1 - m_1\bar{\omega}^2\right)\left(k_2 - m_2\bar{\omega}^2\right) - k_2 m_2\bar{\omega}^2$$

Equating the determinant to zero, leads to the natural frequencies of the two DOF system ω_1^* and ω_2^*. The amplitude of vibrations is given by Equation (9.21).

9.4 DAMPED FORCED VIBRATIONS

Let us consider a two-degree-of-freedom system as shown in Figure 9.3(a).
    The free body diagrams of the two masses are shown in Figure 9.3(b). The equation of motion for the two masses can be written as follows:

$$m_1\ddot{x}_1 + c_1\dot{x}_1 + k_1 x_1 - k_2\left(x_2 - x_1\right) - c_2\left(\dot{x}_2 - \dot{x}_1\right) - p_1 = 0 \tag{9.22a}$$

or,

$$m_1\ddot{x}_1 + \left(c_1 + c_2\right)\dot{x}_1 - c_2\dot{x}_2 + \left(k_1 + k_2\right)x_1 - k_2 x_2 = p_1 \tag{9.22b}$$

and

$$m_2\ddot{x}_2 + c_2\left(\dot{x}_2 - \dot{x}_1\right) + k_2\left(x_2 - x_1\right) = p_2 \tag{9.22c}$$

In matrix form,

$$\begin{bmatrix} m_1 & 0 \\ 0 & m_2 \end{bmatrix}\begin{Bmatrix} \ddot{x}_1 \\ \ddot{x}_2 \end{Bmatrix} + \begin{bmatrix} c_1 + c_2 & -c_2 \\ -c_2 & c_2 \end{bmatrix}\begin{Bmatrix} \dot{x}_1 \\ \dot{x}_2 \end{Bmatrix} + \begin{bmatrix} k_1 + k_2 & -k_2 \\ -k_2 & k_2 \end{bmatrix}\begin{Bmatrix} x_1 \\ x_2 \end{Bmatrix} = \begin{Bmatrix} p_1 \\ p_2 \end{Bmatrix} \tag{9.23}$$

These are coupled equations and need to be solved simultaneously.

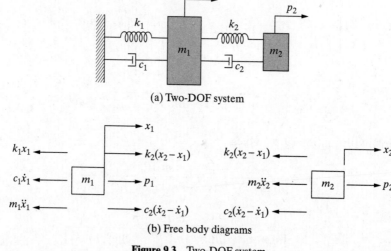

(a) Two-DOF system

(b) Free body diagrams

Figure 9.3   Two-DOF system.

9.5 UNDAMPED VIBRATION ABSORBER

Let us again consider two DOF undamped system of Figure 9.2. Equation (9.21a) can be written as:

$$X_1 = \frac{P_0 k_2 \left[1 - \dfrac{m_2}{k_2}\bar{\omega}^2\right]}{k_1 k_2 \left[1 - \dfrac{\bar{\omega}^2}{\omega_1^2}\right]\left[1 - \dfrac{\bar{\omega}^2}{\omega_2^2}\right] - k_2 m_2 \bar{\omega}^2}$$

or,

$$X_1 = \frac{\dfrac{P_0}{k_1}\left[1 - \dfrac{\bar{\omega}^2}{\omega_2^2}\right]}{\left[1 - \dfrac{\bar{\omega}^2}{\omega_1^2}\right]\left[1 - \dfrac{\bar{\omega}^2}{\omega_2^2}\right] - \dfrac{m_1}{m_1}\dfrac{m_2}{k_1}\bar{\omega}^2}$$

or,

$$D_1 = \frac{\left[1 - \dfrac{\bar{\omega}^2}{\omega_2^2}\right]}{\left[1 - \dfrac{\bar{\omega}^2}{\omega_1^2}\right]\left[1 - \dfrac{\bar{\omega}^2}{\omega_2^2}\right] - \mu\dfrac{\bar{\omega}^2}{\omega_1^2}} \tag{9.24}$$

where

$$\omega_1^2 = \frac{k_1}{m_1} \quad \text{and} \quad \omega_2^2 = \frac{k_2}{m_2}$$

$$X_{st} = P_0/k_1$$

$$\omega_1 = \sqrt{\frac{k_1}{m_1}}, \quad \omega_2 = \sqrt{\frac{k_2}{m_2}}, \quad \mu = \frac{m_2}{m_1} \tag{9.25}$$

μ = Mass ratio

and D_1 is the dynamic magnification factor for mass m_1.

It is assumed that ω_1 is the natural frequency of a SDOF system consisting of mass m_1 and spring k_1 only. Similarly, ω_2 is the natural frequency of a SDOF system consisting of mass m_2 and spring k_2 only.

It is interesting to know that the denominator of Equation (9.21) is same as the frequency equation of undamped-free vibrations. These two DOF systems will have two roots or two natural frequencies, ω_1^* and ω_2^*. If the exciting frequency $\bar{\omega}$ is equal to ω_1^* or ω_2^*, the natural frequency of the two DOF system, there is resonance. The denominator vanishes and the amplitude becomes infinity, that is, $X_1 = \infty = X_2$.

Further, the numerator of X_1 vanishes, when

$$k_2 - m_2\bar{\omega}^2 = 0$$

or, if forcing frequency

$$\bar{\omega} = \omega_2 = \sqrt{\frac{k_2}{m_2}}$$

(9.26)

Then $X_1 = 0$

Thereby, making the mass m_1 motionless at this frequency ($X_1 = 0$).

At this condition, there is no resonance because ω_2 is not a natural frequency of the two mass system. As stated earlier, ω_2 is the natural frequency of a SDOF system consisting of mass m_2 and spring stiffness k_2 only. No such stationary condition (zero displacement) occurs for mass m_2. This formulation gives rise to the concept of *vibration absorber*. Let us assume there is a primary SDOF system consisting of mass m_1 and spring k_1. It will vibrate at its natural frequency ω_1. It is subjected to a forcing function $P(t)$ having a frequency of $\bar{\omega}$. It is now desired to control the vibrations of this primary system. Let us attach another SDOF system called secondary system consisting of mass m_2 and spring k_2 as shown in Figure 9.4. The vibrations of this secondary system are of no consequence to our problem. The object is to control the vibrations of the primary SDOF system. Let the frequency ω_2 be adjusted in such a manner that $\bar{\omega} = \omega_2$. In such a situation, the mass m_1 will have zero vibrations as $X_1 = 0$. Only mass m_2 will vibrate.

The fact that a mass which is being excited can have zero amplitude of vibration under certain conditions by coupling it to another spring mass system, forms the *basis of vibration absorbers*. The second mass continues to vibrate. This type of absorber is extremely effective at one speed only and this is suitable only for constant speed machines or for wind or seismic force acting at a certain frequency.

At

$$\bar{\omega} = \omega_2$$

(9.27)

$$X_2 = -\frac{X_{st}}{\mu \dfrac{\omega_2^2}{\omega_1^2}} = -\frac{P_0}{k_2}$$

or,

$$P_0 = -k_2 X_2$$

(9.28)

This equation shows that spring force $k_2 X_2$ on the main mass due to the amplitude X_2 of the absorber mass is equal and opposite to the exciting force on the main mass resulting in no motion of the main system. The absorber system exerts a force equal and

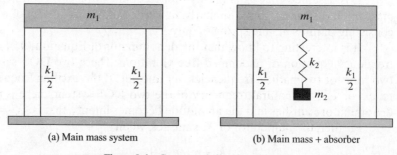

(a) Main mass system   (b) Main mass + absorber

Figure 9.4   Concept of vibration absorber.

opposite to that of the applied force. The main system vibrations have been reduced to zero and these vibrations have been taken up by the absorber system. Hence, the name *vibration absorber.*

The analysis used to design a vibration absorber assumes that it can be constructed without introducing any appreciable damping. If damping is introduced, the equations can not necessarily be decoupled and the magnitude of the displacement of the primary mass will not be zero.

9.6 TUNED VIBRATION ABSORBER

The concept of vibration absorber developed earlier can be further refined. The auxiliary system is much more effective, if the main system is operating at resonance. That is, $\varpi = \omega_1$

But for absorber to be effective, we have $\varpi = \omega_2$

that is,

$$\varpi = \omega_1 = \omega_2 \quad \text{or} \quad \frac{k_2}{m_2} = \frac{k_1}{m_1} \tag{9.29}$$

When this condition is fulfilled, this absorber is known to be a *tuned vibration absorber or tuned mass damper.*

Equations (9.21a) and (9.21b) can be written as follows:

$$\frac{X_1}{X_{ST}} = \frac{1 - \dfrac{\bar{\varpi}^2}{\omega_2^2}}{\dfrac{\bar{\varpi}^4}{\omega_2^4} - (2 + \mu)\dfrac{\bar{\varpi}^2}{\omega_2^2} + 1} \tag{9.30a}$$

and

$$\frac{X_2}{X_{ST}} = \frac{1}{\dfrac{\bar{\varpi}^4}{\omega_2^4} - (2 + \mu)\dfrac{\bar{\varpi}^2}{\omega_2^2} + 1} \tag{9.30b}$$

To get resonant frequencies, the denominator of Equations (9.30a) or (9.30b) must be zero,

$$\left(\frac{\bar{\varpi}}{\omega_2}\right)^4 - (2 + \mu)\left(\frac{\bar{\varpi}}{\omega_2}\right)^2 + 1 = 0$$

or,

$$\left(\frac{\bar{\varpi}}{\omega_2}\right)^2 = \left(1 + \frac{\mu}{2}\right) \pm \sqrt{\mu + \frac{\mu^2}{4}} \tag{9.31}$$

This equation can be plotted as shown in Figure 9.5. At a given mass ratio, it gives two resonant frequencies corresponding to the two degrees of freedom.

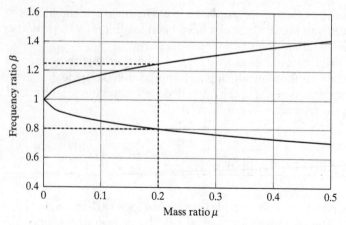

Figure 9.5 Mass ratio vs. resonant frequency ratio (ϖ/ω_2).

9.6.1 Effect of Mass Ratio on the Amplitude of Primary Mass

In Equation (9.30a), at a frequency ratio of 1.0 ($\beta = \varpi / \omega_2$) and mass ratio $\mu = 0$, there is resonance and its denominator is zero. The amplitude of primary mass is infinity. This is a highly undesirable situation. If a small mass is attached having a mass ratio equal to 2% only, it is possible to reduce the amplitude of mass m_1 to zero or less than the static displacement. However, it will be very difficult to design a vibration absorber with a frequency ratio equal to 1.0 at which the response of the primary mass will be exactly zero because of the practical difficulties. Therefore, an obvious choice will be to design a vibration absorber such that the amplitude of the primary mass is less than 1.0, that is $(x_1/x_{st} \leq 1.0)$. Because the system has two DOF, there will be two frequencies within which this criteria can be satisfied. This bandwidth is known as *operating frequency* of the vibration absorber.

Let us re-write Equation (9.30a) as follows:

$$1 - \frac{\varpi^2}{\omega_2^2} \leq \frac{\varpi^4}{\omega_2^4} - (2 + \mu)\frac{\varpi^2}{\omega_2^2} + 1$$

or,

$$\frac{\varpi^4}{\omega_2^4} - (1 + \mu)\frac{\varpi^2}{\omega_2^2} \geq 0$$

or,

$$\frac{\varpi^2}{\omega_2^2} \geq (1 + \mu) \qquad (9.32)$$

Equation (9.32) gives only one positive value of the frequency ratio, while the second value gets lost in simplification. It gives the upper frequency ratio. To get the other frequency ratio at which the normalized response of primary mass is less than 1.0, graphical solution is adopted.

Let us examine the effect of different mass ratios ($\mu = 0.02, 0.05, 0.25, 0.5$ and 2.0) on the normalized amplitude of the primary mass m_1 and secondary mass m_2 as shown in Figures 9.6 to 9.10 by plotting Equation (9.30). The combined response of primary mass and secondary mass for different mass ratio $\mu = 0.02, 0.05, 0.50$ and 2.0 are shown in Figures 9.11(a) to 9.11(d).

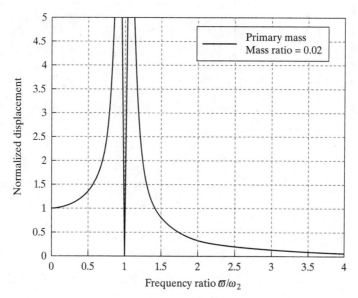

Figure 9.6(a)   Normalized amplitude of primary mass vs. normalized driving frequency for $\mu = 0.02$.

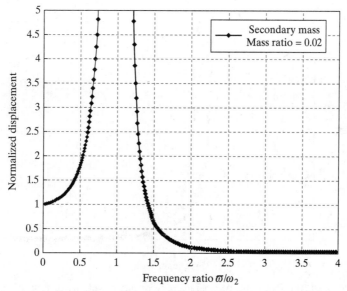

Figure 9.6(b)   Normalized amplitude of secondary mass vs. normalized driving frequency for $\mu = 0.02$.

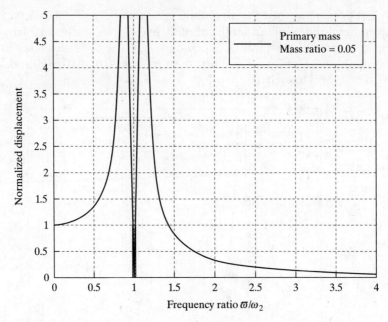

Figure 9.7(a)   Normalized amplitude of primary mass vs. normalized driving frequency for $\mu = 0.05$.

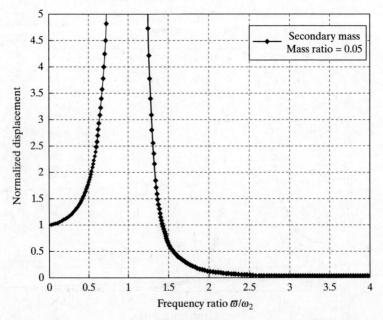

Figure 9.7(b)   Normalized amplitude of secondary mass vs. normalized driving frequency for $\mu = 0.05$.

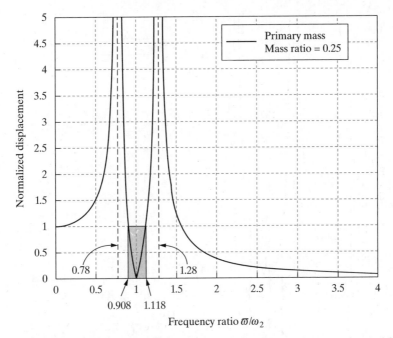

Figure 9.8(a)   Normalized amplitude of primary mass vs. normalized driving frequency for $\mu = 0.25$. The shaded area shows the frequency ratios for which the displacement magnification is less than 1.0.

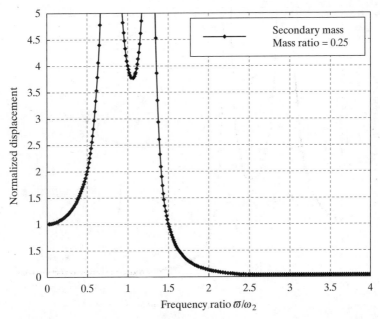

Figure 9.8(b)   Normalized amplitude of secondary mass vs. normalized driving frequency for $\mu = 0.25$.

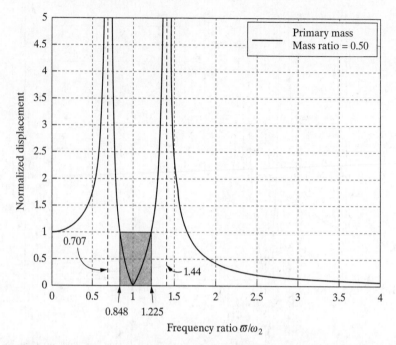

Figure 9.9(a)   Normalized amplitude of primary mass vs. normalized driving frequency for $\mu = 0.50$. The shaded area shows the frequency ratios for which the displacement magnification is less than 1.0.

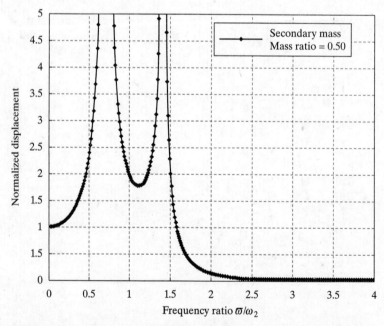

Figure 9.9(b)   Normalized amplitude of secondary mass vs. normalized driving frequency for $\mu = 0.50$.

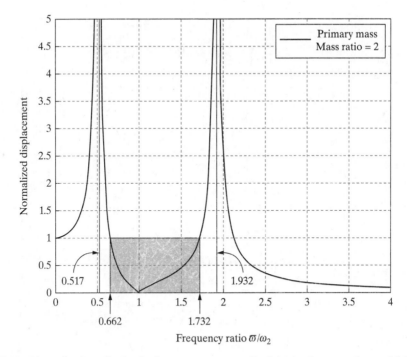

Figure 9.10(a)   Normalized amplitude of primary mass vs. normalized driving frequency for $\mu = 2.0$. The shaded area shows the frequency ratios for which the displacement magnification is less than 1.0.

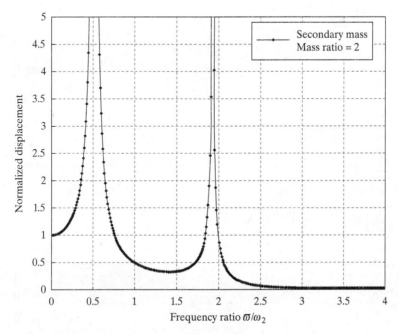

Figure 9.10(b)   Normalized amplitude of secondary mass vs. normalized driving frequency for $\mu = 2.0$.

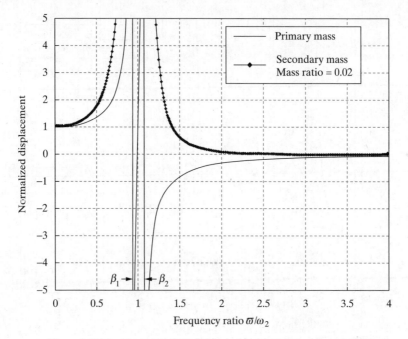

Figure 9.11(a)   Normalized amplitude vs. frequency ratio for $\mu = 0.02$.

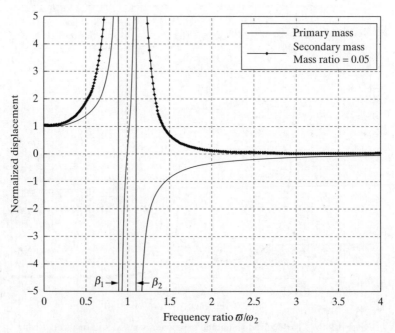

Figure 9.11(b)   Normalized amplitude vs. frequency ratio for $\mu = 0.05$.

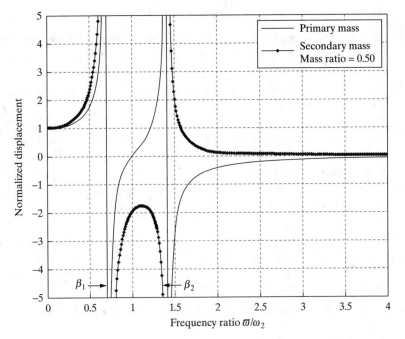

Figure 9.11(c)   Normalized amplitude vs. frequency ratio for $\mu = 0.50$.

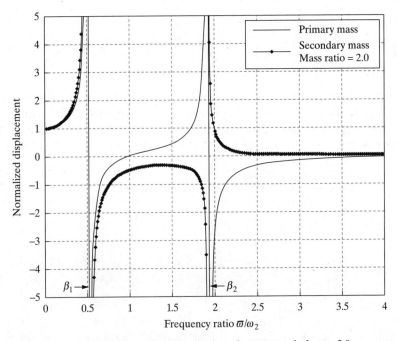

Figure 9.11(d)   Normalized amplitude vs. frequency ratio for $\mu = 2.0$.

The following observations can be made in these figures:

- The effect of attaching a secondary mass to the primary mass is to split a single resonant frequency in two resonant peaks corresponding to two natural frequencies of the two DOF systems.
- The spread between the two resonant frequencies keeps increasing with the increase in mass ratio.
- The main purpose of attaching a secondary mass is to reduce the displacement of primary mass. It means the normalized displacement should be less than 1.0. The figures for primary mass show the operating frequency range for which the amplification is less than 1.0.
- Figures 9.6(a) to 9.10(a) give both lower and upper values of the operating frequency ratio. The range of operating frequencies can be seen clearly in Figures 9.8(a), 9.9(a) and 9.10(a).
- The advantage of a higher mass ratio is a larger spread in resonant frequencies. It helps in choosing a larger range of operating frequency. However, a higher mass ratio means larger space is required for accommodating the secondary mass, which may not be practically feasible.

The resonant frequencies and operating frequencies for different mass ratios are shown in Table 9.1.

The stiffness ratio of primary mass and secondary mass is given by the following relation:

$$\mu = \frac{m_2}{m_1} \text{ and } \beta^2 = \frac{\omega_2^2}{\omega_1^2} = \frac{k_2}{k_1}\frac{m_1}{m_2}$$

or,

$$\frac{k_2}{k_1} = \mu\beta^2 \qquad (9.33)$$

Stiffness of the secondary mass also plays a significant role in selecting an absorber. The displacement of mass m_2 will depend upon its stiffness k_2. If the stiffness k_2 is low, it will undergo very large displacements which again may not be acceptable. There is a need to arrive at a compromise value for the mass ratio as well as stiffness k_2. Mass

TABLE 9.1 RESONANT AND OPERATING FREQUENCY RATIO

Mass Ratio	Resonant Frequency Ratio		Operating Frequency Ratio	
	β_1	β_2	ω_1/ω_2	ω_2/ω_2
0.02	0.931	1.073	0.990	1.010
0.05	0.894	1.118	0.977	1.025
0.25	0.780	1.280	0.908	1.118
0.50	0.707	1.414	0.848	1.225
2.0	0.517	1.932	0.662	1.732

ratio μ is usually kept between 0.02 and 0.25. A mass ratio above 0.50 may not be practically feasible. Charts shown in Figures 9.6 to 9.11 will help arrive at a reasonable and acceptable solution.

9.6.2 Secondary mass with viscous damping

The design of the vibration absorber can be made more efficient under certain conditions by incorporating damping in the secondary mass system as shown in Figure 9.12(a). The free body diagrams of the two masses are shown in Figure 9.12(b). The equation of motion for the two masses can be written as follows:

$$m_1\ddot{x}_1 + k_1 x_1 - k_2 (x_2 - x_1) - c_2 (\dot{x}_2 - \dot{x}_1) - p = 0 \tag{9.34a}$$

or,

$$m_1\ddot{x}_1 + c_2 (\dot{x}_1 - \dot{x}_2) + (k_1 + k_2)x_1 - k_2 x_2 = p \tag{9.34b}$$

and

$$m_2\ddot{x}_2 + c_2 (\dot{x}_2 - \dot{x}_1) + k_2 (x_2 - x_1) = 0 \tag{9.34c}$$

In matrix form,

$$\begin{bmatrix} m_1 & 0 \\ 0 & m_2 \end{bmatrix}\begin{Bmatrix} \ddot{x}_1 \\ \ddot{x}_2 \end{Bmatrix} + \begin{bmatrix} c_2 & -c_2 \\ -c_2 & c_2 \end{bmatrix}\begin{Bmatrix} \dot{x}_1 \\ \dot{x}_2 \end{Bmatrix} + \begin{bmatrix} k_1 + k_2 & -k_2 \\ -k_2 & k_2 \end{bmatrix}\begin{Bmatrix} x_1 \\ x_2 \end{Bmatrix} = \begin{Bmatrix} p \\ 0 \end{Bmatrix} \tag{9.35}$$

These are coupled equations and can be solved for steady state condition. The damping of the secondary mass plays a significant role in optimizing the design of vibration absorber. Further discussion is beyond the scope of the present text.

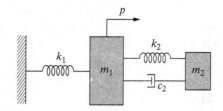

Figure 9.12(a)   Tuned mass damper with viscous damping.

x_1

$m_1\ddot{x}_1$

$k_1 x_1$

$k_2(x_2 - x_1)$ $k_2(x_2 - x_1)$

x_2

m_1 p $m_2\ddot{x}_2$ m_2

$c_2(\dot{x}_2 - \dot{x}_1)$ $c_2(\dot{x}_2 - \dot{x}_1)$

Figure 9.12(b)   Free body diagrams.

9.6.3 Applications

Burj-al-Arab, Dubai

It is a hotel building in Dubai built in 1999 as shown in Figure 9.13(a). Its height is 322 m. It is located 230 m into the sea from the shore and is supported by 40 m deep 230 concrete piles. One of the main problems was to mitigate the vibrations due to strong wind. It is fitted with tuned mass dampers to absorb vibrations due to wind at frequencies varying from 0.75 Hz to 2 Hz. Weight of each damper is 5000 kg. These absorbers were placed inside the vertical steel arms of the building as shown in Figure 9.13(b).

Taipei 101, Taiwan

It is the tallest building in Taipei, Taiwan, built in 2004 as shown in Figure 9.14(a). Its height is 509 m. There are 101 floors above ground and 5 floors below ground. The top floor is at an elevation of 439 m and the roof top is at 448 m. The building was designed to resist a very strong earthquake as well as vibrations due to very strong winds. It is fitted with a 662 metric ton steel pendulum that serves as a tuned mass damper. Suspended from the 92nd to the 88th floor, the pendulum sways to offset movements in the building caused by strong gusts. Its sphere, the largest damper sphere in the world, consists of 41 layered steel plates, each with a height of 125 mm being welded

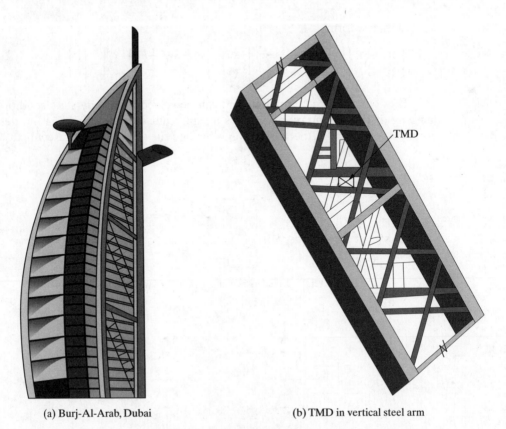

(a) Burj-Al-Arab, Dubai   (b) TMD in vertical steel arm

Figure 9.13   TMD in Burj-Al-Arab, Dubai

together to form a 5.5 m diameter sphere as shown in Figures 9.14(b) and 9.14(c). Another two tuned mass dampers, each weighing 4.5 tons, sit at the tip of the spire. These prevent cumulative damage to the structure due to strong wind loads.

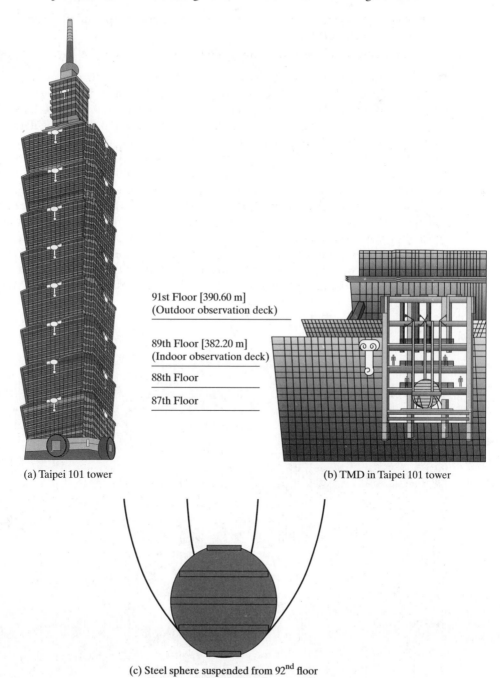

(a) Taipei 101 tower

91st Floor [390.60 m]
(Outdoor observation deck)

89th Floor [382.20 m]
(Indoor observation deck)

88th Floor

87th Floor

(b) TMD in Taipei 101 tower

(c) Steel sphere suspended from 92nd floor

Figure 9.14   TMD in Taipei 101 tower.

London Millennium Footbridge

The London Millennium footbridge is sited on the River Thames, London. There were two design constraints:

- maximum height limitation so that tourists would be provided an unobstructed view of the river front
- requirement of the head room to allow marine traffic on the River Thames.

It is a three span bridge with the end span of 80 m on the north, central main span of 144 m between the piers, and end span of 108 m on the south. The bridge deck is 4 m wide, and uses articulated sliding joints spaced at regular intervals along its length. In the bridge lateral suspension cables are located at the level of the bridge deck in view of the constraints. The bridge exhibited severe lateral sway in a frequency band of 0.5 to 1.1 Hz, with lateral accelerations of up to 0.25 g. As many as five natural modes were being excited, and pedestrians found it virtually impossible to walk on the bridge. It was baffling that resonance was occurring without any intentional or expected forced motion or synchronous marching. Extensive investigations revealed a unique phenomenon *synchronous lateral footfall* which resulted in seemingly random walking motions becoming synchronized over time, among members of an unrelated group of people on the bridge. A series of vertical and lateral TMDs were employed to mitigate the problem. There were 50 Vertical TMD, weight @ 1000 to 2000 kg, and frequency 1.20 to 2.2 Hz; and 8 Horizontal TMD weight @ 2500 kg, and frequency 0.45 Hz. TMDs used in this bridge are shown in Figure 9.15.

Figure 9.15   TMD in London Millennium bridge

9.7 ILLUSTRATIVE EXAMPLES

Example 9.1

An undamped two DOF system shown in Figure 9.1 has mass $m_1 = m_2 = m$ and stiffness $k_1 = k_2 = k$. Determine its frequencies and mode shapes.

Solution   Let us make use of Equations (9.14) and (9.15).

$$\omega^4 - \omega^2 \left[\left(\bar{\omega}_1^2 + \bar{\omega}_2^2 \right)(1+\mu) \right] + \bar{\omega}_1^2 \bar{\omega}_2^2 (1+\mu) = 0 \qquad (9.15)$$

where

$$\bar{\omega}_1^2 = \frac{k_1}{m_1 + m_2}, \quad \text{and} \quad \bar{\omega}_2^2 = \frac{k_2}{m_2}$$

$$\mu = \frac{m_2}{m_1} = \text{mass ratio} \qquad (9.14)$$

$$\therefore \qquad \bar{\omega}_1^2 = \frac{k_1}{m_1 + m_2} \quad \text{or} \quad \bar{\omega}_1^2 = \frac{k}{2m}$$

$$\bar{\omega}_2^2 = \frac{k_2}{m_2} \quad \text{or} \quad \bar{\omega}_2^2 = \frac{k}{m} = 2\bar{\omega}_1^2$$

Mass ratio $\mu = 1$

∴ frequency equation is written as follows:

$$\omega^4 - 6\bar{\omega}_1^2 \omega^2 + 4\bar{\omega}_1^2 = 0$$

Or, its roots are $\qquad \omega_1^{*2} = 0.764\,\bar{\omega}_1^2 \quad \text{or} \quad \omega_2^{*2} = 5.236\,\bar{\omega}_1^2$

$$\therefore \qquad \omega_1^* = 0.874\,\bar{\omega}_1 \quad \text{and} \quad \omega_2^* = 2.288\,\bar{\omega}_1$$

Mode shapes can be determined using Equation (9.10)

$$\begin{bmatrix} k_1 + k_2 - m_1\omega^2 & -k_2 \\ -k_2 & k_2 - m_2\omega^2 \end{bmatrix} \begin{Bmatrix} X_1 \\ X_2 \end{Bmatrix} = \begin{Bmatrix} 0 \\ 0 \end{Bmatrix} \qquad (9.10)$$

Substituting $\omega^2 = 0.764\,\bar{\omega}_1^2$
Equation (9.10) can be written as:

$$\begin{bmatrix} 3.236 & -2 \\ -2 & 1.236 \end{bmatrix} \begin{Bmatrix} X_{11} \\ X_{21} \end{Bmatrix} = \begin{Bmatrix} 0 \\ 0 \end{Bmatrix}$$

or,

$$3.236\,X_{11} - 2\,X_{21} = 0 \quad \text{or} \quad X_{11} = 0.618\,X_{21}$$

Similarly, substituting $\omega^2 = 5.236\,\bar{\omega}_1^2$
Equation (9.10) can be written as:

$$\begin{bmatrix} -1.236 & -2 \\ -2 & -3.236 \end{bmatrix} \begin{Bmatrix} X_{12} \\ X_{22} \end{Bmatrix} = \begin{Bmatrix} 0 \\ 0 \end{Bmatrix}$$

or, $-1.236\, X_{12} - 2\, X_{22} = 0$ or, $X_{12} = -1.618\, X_{22}$

The mode shapes can be plotted as shown in Figure 9.16.   □

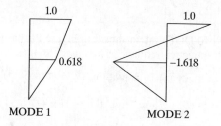

MODE 1   MODE 2

Figure 9.16   Mode shape in two-DOF system.

Example 9.2

An undamped two DOF system is shown in Figure 9.17. Determine its frequencies and mode shapes.

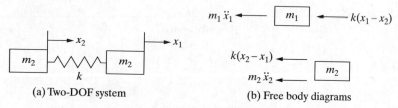

(a) Two-DOF system   (b) Free body diagrams

Figure 9.17   Two-DOF system.

Solution   The free body diagrams of the mass m_1 and m_2 are shown in Figure 9.17(b). The equations of motion can be written as:

$$m_1\ddot{x}_1 + k(x_1 - x_2) = 0$$

and $$m_2\ddot{x}_2 + k(x_2 - x_1) = 0 \tag{i}$$

Let $$x_1 = x_{10}\sin\omega t \qquad x_2 = x_{20}\sin\omega t \tag{ii}$$

Substituting these values in Equation (i) gives,

$$(-)\begin{bmatrix} m_1\omega^2 & 0 \\ 0 & m_2\omega^2 \end{bmatrix}\begin{Bmatrix} x_{10} \\ x_{20} \end{Bmatrix} + \begin{bmatrix} k & -k \\ -k & k \end{bmatrix}\begin{Bmatrix} x_{10} \\ x_{20} \end{Bmatrix} = \begin{Bmatrix} 0 \\ 0 \end{Bmatrix}$$

or,

$$\begin{bmatrix} k - m_1\omega^2 & -k \\ -k & k - m_2\omega^2 \end{bmatrix}\begin{Bmatrix} x_{10} \\ x_{20} \end{Bmatrix} = \begin{Bmatrix} 0 \\ 0 \end{Bmatrix} \tag{iii}$$

It can be written in short as follows:

$$\big[[K] - [M]\omega^2\big]\{X_0\} = \{0\} \tag{iv}$$

where $[K]$ and $[M]$ are stiffness and mass matrices of the system.

Its solution is given by setting the determinant to zero,

$$\det|K - M\omega^2| = 0 \qquad (v)$$

This is referred to as the characteristic equation.
Equations (iv) and (v) are very important for eigenvalue analysis.

or,
$$m_1 m_2 \omega^4 - (m_1 + m_2) k \omega^2 = 0$$

Its roots are given by $\omega_1^{*2} = 0$ or $\omega_2^{*2} = \dfrac{(m_1 + m_2)k}{m_1 m_2}$

or, the frequencies are given by $\omega_1^* = 0$ and $\omega_2^* = \sqrt{\left(\dfrac{m_1 + m_2}{m_1 m_2}\right)k}$

Mode shapes
Mode shapes can be obtained by substituting the value of ω in Equation (iii).
Substituting $\omega^2 = 0$ in Equation (iii) gives

$$x_{10} = x_{20} = 1 \quad \text{say}$$

Similarly, substituting the other value,

$$\omega^2 = \frac{(m_1 + m_2)k}{m_1 m_2}$$

$$(k - m_1\omega^2)x_{10} - kx_{20} = 0$$

or,
$$\frac{x_{20}}{x_{10}} = 1 - \frac{m_1}{k}\,\omega^2 = 1 - \frac{m_1 + m_2}{m_2} = -\frac{m_1}{m_2}$$

Thus, if
$$x_{10} = 1, x_{20} = -\frac{m_1}{m_2}$$

Now the mode shapes can be plotted as shown in Figure 9.18. It can be seen that the spring remain undeformed in Mode 1, that is, Mode 1 is a rigid body displacement mode. ☐

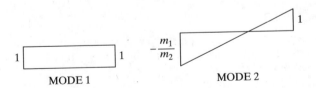

MODE 1   MODE 2

Figure 9.18 Mode shapes.

Example 9.3

A 4000 kg machine operates at a frequency of 130 Hz. A mass of 500 kg is attached to absorb the vibrations at the operating frequency. Calculate the frequency range at which the vibration absorber is very effective.

Solution The main mass $m_1 = 4000$ kg; auxiliary mass $m_2 = 500$ kg, operating frequency $\bar{f} = 130$ Hz.

Mass ratio $\mu = 500/4000 = 0.125$

$$\left(\frac{\bar{\omega}}{\omega_2}\right)^2 = (1 + \frac{\mu}{2}) \pm \sqrt{\mu + \frac{\mu^2}{4}} \qquad (9.31)$$

$\therefore$

$$\beta^2 = \left(1 + \frac{500}{2 \times 4000}\right) \pm \sqrt{0.125 + \frac{0.125^2}{4}}$$

$$\beta^2 = 0.703 \quad \text{or} \quad 1.421$$

or,

$$\beta = 0.838 \quad \text{or} \quad 1.192$$

but

$$\beta = \bar{\omega}/\omega_2$$

$\therefore$ The frequency range at which the absorber is most effective is between $130/0.838 = 155.13$ Hz and 109.06 Hz.

The displacement magnification factor for the absorber mass X_2

$$\frac{X_2}{X_{ST}} = \frac{1}{\dfrac{\bar{\omega}^4}{\omega_2^4} - (2 + \mu)\dfrac{\bar{\omega}^2}{\omega_2^2} + 1}$$

It can be re-written as follows:

$$\frac{X_2}{X_{st}} = \frac{1}{(1 - \beta^2)^2 - \mu\beta^2} \approx \frac{1}{-\mu\beta^2}$$

For $\beta = 0.838$,

$\therefore$

$$\frac{X_2}{X_{st}} = \frac{1}{0.125 \times 0.838^2} = 11.40$$

For $\beta = 1.192$,

$$\frac{X_2}{X_{st}} = \frac{1}{0.125 \times 1.192^2} = 5.63$$

At these frequencies, the amplitude ratio of the secondary mass will vary between 5.63 and 11.40. The amplitude ratio of the machine vibration will be zero or nearly zero. □

Example 9.4

A machine operates at a frequency of 5000 rpm, exerts a force of 140 N and produces excessive vibrations. Design a vibration absorber having a maximum displacement of 3.5 mm only.

Solution $P_0 = 140$ N, operating frequency $\bar{\omega} = 5000$ rpm $= 5000/60 = 83.33$ rad/sec

$$P_0 = -k_2 X_2$$

The spring stiffness $k_2 = 140/(3.5/1000) = 40000$ N/m

$$\left(\frac{\bar{\omega}}{\omega_2}\right)^2 = (1 + \frac{\mu}{2}) \pm \sqrt{\mu + \frac{\mu^2}{4}}$$

If the mass ratio = 0.10, let us determine the frequency range in which the absorber will be effective.

$$\beta^2 = (1 + 0.10/2) \pm \sqrt{0.10 + \frac{0.10^2}{4}} = 1.05 \pm 0.32$$

$$\beta^2 = 0.73 \text{ or } 1.37$$

or, $\beta = 0.854 \text{ or } 1.170$

∴ The frequency range at which the absorber is most effective is between 83.33/0.854 = 97.58 rad/sec and 71.22 rad/sec. The vibration absorber will have a mass ratio of 0.10 and a stiffness of 40000 N/m. The nearest resonance will be about 15% away from the operating frequency.   □

Example 9.5

A steel box girder foot bridge may be assumed to be represented by a SDOF system with a mass of 17500 kg and a stiffness of 3×10^6 N/m. The worst case of dynamic loading occurs when two people walk across the bridge in steps in tune with its natural frequency. This is almost equivalent to a sinusoidal loading with a constant amplitude of 0.48 kN. Design a suitable tuned vibration absorber.

Solution

$$m_1 = 17500 \text{ kg}, \quad k_1 = 3 \times 10^6 \text{ N/m}$$

∴ $\omega_1 = \sqrt{\dfrac{k_1}{m_1}} = 13.09$ rad/sec

or, $f_1 = 2.08$ Hz

Let mass ratio

$$\mu = 0.01$$

∴ $m_2 = 175$ kg – It can be easily accommodated in the box girder.

∴ $\omega_2 = \omega_1 = 13.09$ rad/sec

or, $k_2 = \omega_2^2 m_2 = 13.09^2 \times 175 = 30000$ N/m

Resonant frequencies:

$$\left(\frac{\bar{\omega}}{\omega_2}\right)^2 = \left(1 + \frac{0.01}{2}\right) \pm \sqrt{0.01 + \frac{(0.01)^2}{4}}$$

$$= 1.005 \pm 0.100 \quad \text{or} \quad 0.905 \quad \text{and} \quad 1.105$$

Taking square roots

∴ $\bar{\omega}_1 = 0.951\, \omega_2 = 12.45$ rad/sec

and $\bar{\omega}_2 = 1.051\, \omega_2 = 13.76$ rad/sec

For these frequencies, $X_1 = 0$

and $X_2 = \dfrac{F_0}{k_2} = \dfrac{480}{30000} = 0.016$ m $= 16$ mm

This motion can be easily accommodated within the box girder using coil springs.   □

Example 9.6

A two storey portal frame is shown in Figure 9.19. Develop its equation of motion if it is subjected to an undamped-free vibration. EI_c is the flexural rigidity of the upper storey columns, and $2EI_c$ is the flexural rigidity of the lower storey columns. The flexural rigidity of beams may be treated as very high. Axial deformation in columns can be neglected.

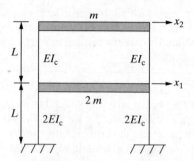

Figure 9.19   Two-DOF portal frame.

Solution   It can be treated as a two DOF system having lateral displacements of the floors x_1 and x_2. The lateral stiffness of each storey can be determined from the basic definition of stiffness. The lateral displacement at the roof level is restrained, that is, $x_2 = 0$, and a unit displacement is given to x_1. Now determine the forces produced in the upper and lower storey columns. Similarly, the first floor lateral displacement is restrained, that is, $x_1 = 0$, and a unit displacement is given to x_2. Now determine the forces produced in the upper storey columns. This can also be explained with the help of diagrams shown in Figure 9.20.

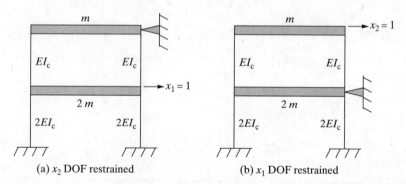

(a) x_2 DOF restrained   (b) x_1 DOF restrained

Figure 9.20   Storey lateral stiffness.

The lateral stiffness of each column can be obtained as follows using slope – deflection method:

$$k = \frac{12EI}{L^3} \text{ and the total lateral stiffness of a storey can be taken as } 2k.$$

Thus, lateral stiffness of upper storey

$$k_2 = \frac{24EI_c}{L^3}$$

and
lateral stiffness of lower storey

$$k_1 = \frac{2 \times 24 EI_c}{L^3}$$

Now this two storey portal frame can be replaced with a spring mass system having two-degrees of freedom as shown in Figure 9.21(a). Its free body diagram is also shown in Figures 9.21(b) and 9.21(c).

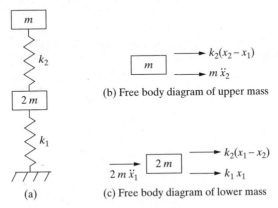

(b) Free body diagram of upper mass

(a)　　　　(c) Free body diagram of lower mass

Figure 9.21　Two-DOF spring-mass system

The equations of motion of undamped vibrations can be written as follows:

$$2m\ddot{x}_1 + k_1 x_1 + k_2 (x_1 - x_2) = 0$$

and

$$m\ddot{x}_2 + k_2 (x_2 - x_1) = 0$$

or,
in matrix notation

$$\begin{bmatrix} 2m & 0 \\ 0 & m \end{bmatrix} \begin{Bmatrix} \ddot{x}_1 \\ \ddot{x}_2 \end{Bmatrix} + \begin{bmatrix} k_1 + k_2 & -k_2 \\ -k_2 & k_2 \end{bmatrix} \begin{Bmatrix} x_1 \\ x_2 \end{Bmatrix} = \begin{Bmatrix} 0 \\ 0 \end{Bmatrix}$$

Stiffness matrix will always be a symmetric matrix. On substituting the values of stiffness coefficients, we get

$$\begin{bmatrix} 2m & 0 \\ 0 & m \end{bmatrix} \begin{Bmatrix} \ddot{x}_1 \\ \ddot{x}_2 \end{Bmatrix} + \frac{24 EI_c}{L^3} \begin{bmatrix} 3 & -1 \\ -1 & 1 \end{bmatrix} \begin{Bmatrix} x_1 \\ x_2 \end{Bmatrix} = \begin{Bmatrix} 0 \\ 0 \end{Bmatrix}$$

Its frequency and mode shapes can be determined as shown in Example 9.2 using Equations (iv) and (v).

$$\left[[K] - [M]\omega^2 \right]\{X_0\} = \{0\} \qquad (iv)$$

$$\begin{bmatrix} \dfrac{72 EI_c}{L^3} - 2m\omega^2 & -\dfrac{24 EI_c}{L^3} \\ -\dfrac{24 EI_c}{L^3} & \dfrac{24 EI_c}{L^3} - m\omega^2 \end{bmatrix} \begin{Bmatrix} X_{10} \\ X_{20} \end{Bmatrix} = \begin{Bmatrix} 0 \\ 0 \end{Bmatrix}$$

Its solution is given by Equation (v), that is,

$$\det |K - M\omega^2| = 0 \quad \text{the characteristic equation} \qquad (v)$$

$$\begin{vmatrix} \dfrac{72EI_c}{L^3} - 2m\omega^2 & -\dfrac{24EI_c}{L^3} \\ -\dfrac{24EI_c}{L^3} & \dfrac{24EI_c}{L^3} - m\omega^2 \end{vmatrix} = 0$$

The frequencies and mode shapes can be determined by substituting the numerical values. $\square$

Example 9.7

A cantilever portal frame is shown in Figure 9.22. Develop its equation of motion for undamped-free vibration. *EI* is the flexural rigidity of the beam as well as that of the column. Axial deformation in the beam and column can be neglected.

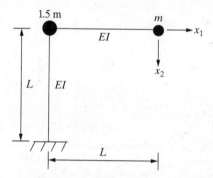

Figure 9.22 Cantilever portal frame.

Solution Let us derive the stiffness matrix of this cantilever portal frame. It can be derived from its flexibility matrix. There are two degrees of freedom – lateral displacement x_1 at the floor level and vertical displacement x_2 at the free end. The flexibility coefficients f_{ij} can be derived using the influence coefficient method as follows:

$$F = \begin{bmatrix} f_{11} & f_{12} \\ f_{21} & f_{22} \end{bmatrix}$$

Let us first draw bending moment diagram due to a unit force f_1 applied at the free end alone as shown in Figure 9.23. This diagram is known as h_{11} diagram. Now draw bending moment diagram due to a unit force f_2 applied at the free end alone. This diagram is known as h_{12} diagram. The influence coefficients can be computed as follows:

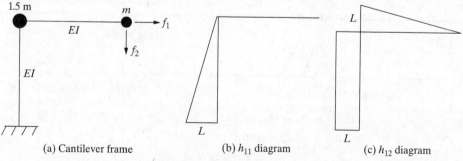

(a) Cantilever frame   (b) h_{11} diagram   (c) h_{12} diagram

Figure 9.23 h-diagram.

$$f_{11} = \int \frac{h_{11}h_{11}\,dy}{EI} = \frac{L^3}{3EI}$$

$$f_{12} = \int \frac{h_{11}h_{12}\,dy}{EI} = \frac{L^3}{2EI}$$

$$f_{22} = \int \frac{h_{12}h_{12}\,dy}{EI} = \frac{L^3}{3EI} + \frac{L^3}{EI} = \frac{4L^3}{3EI}$$

The flexibility matrix can be written as follows:

$$[F] = \frac{L^3}{6EI}\begin{bmatrix} 2 & 3 \\ 3 & 8 \end{bmatrix}$$

The flexibility matrix is always a symmetric matrix. The stiffness matrix is the inverse of the flexibility matrix, that is,

$$[K] = [F]^{-1}$$

or,

$$[K] = \frac{6EI}{7L^3}\begin{bmatrix} 8 & -3 \\ -3 & 2 \end{bmatrix}$$

The stiffness matrix is always a symmetric matrix. The mass matrix can be written as follows:

$$[M] = \begin{bmatrix} 2.5m & 0 \\ 0 & m \end{bmatrix}$$

It should be noted that for vibration along the x_1 direction, the two masses will add up. The equation of motion of undamped-free vibrations can be written as follows:

$$[M]\{\ddot{X}\} + [K]\{X\} = \{0\}$$

or,

$$\begin{bmatrix} 2.5m & 0 \\ 0 & m \end{bmatrix}\begin{Bmatrix} \ddot{x}_1 \\ \ddot{x}_2 \end{Bmatrix} + \frac{6EI}{7L^3}\begin{bmatrix} 8 & -3 \\ -3 & 2 \end{bmatrix}\begin{Bmatrix} x_1 \\ x_2 \end{Bmatrix} = \begin{Bmatrix} 0 \\ 0 \end{Bmatrix}$$

Its frequency and mode shapes can be determined as shown in Example 9.2 using Equations (iv) and (v).

$$\left[[K] - [M]\omega^2\right]\{X_0\} = \{0\}$$

Let us denote

$$\frac{6EI}{7L^3} = C, \text{ a constant}$$

or,

$$\begin{bmatrix} 8C - 2.5m\omega^2 & -3C \\ -3C & 2C - m\omega^2 \end{bmatrix}\begin{Bmatrix} x_{10} \\ x_{20} \end{Bmatrix} = \begin{Bmatrix} 0 \\ 0 \end{Bmatrix}$$

Its solution is given by Equation (v), that is,

$$\det|K - M\omega^2| = 0$$

$$\begin{vmatrix} 8C - 2.5m\omega^2 & -3C \\ -3C & 2C - m\omega^2 \end{vmatrix} = 0$$

By substituting the numerical values, frequency and mode shapes can be determined.   □

Example 9.8

A rigid bar of total mass m is supported on two springs as shown in Figure 9.24. Write the equations of motion in terms of end displacements and find natural frequencies and mode shapes.

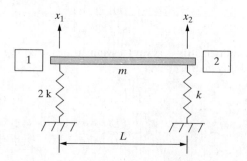

Figure 9.24   Rigid bar on two springs.

Solution   Consider the deflected shape of the bar shown in Figure 9.25. The left spring will have a deflection x_1 and the right spring will have a deflection x_2. Since stiffness of the left spring is higher than that of the right spring, the mass will rotate anti-clockwise. This system has the following independent two degrees of freedom:

1. Translational deformation at node 1
2. Translational deformation at node 2

Alternatively, it can have the following independent two degrees of freedom at the center of mass:

1. Translational deformation at the midspan
2. Rotational deformation at the midspan

Yet there can be another alternative,

1. Translational deformation at node 1
2. Rotational deformation at the node 1

The similar two DOFs can be written at node 2 also.

The equations of motion will depend upon the selection of the independent two degrees of freedom. The frequencies and mode shapes will always correspond to the independent degrees of freedom. It means they will change depending upon the selection of the two degrees of freedom. However, final forces in various members to a given set of force will always remain unchanged.

Let us first consider the two translational degrees of freedom x_1 and x_2. At the center of the bar, a rotational inertia force will act in clockwise direction.

$$\text{Inertia force} = \frac{mL^2\ddot{\theta}}{12} = \frac{mL^2(\ddot{x}_2 - \ddot{x}_1)}{12L}$$

It can be resolved as a couple acting on the two springs across a length L. The free body diagram of the two springs is shown in Figures 9.25(b) and (c).

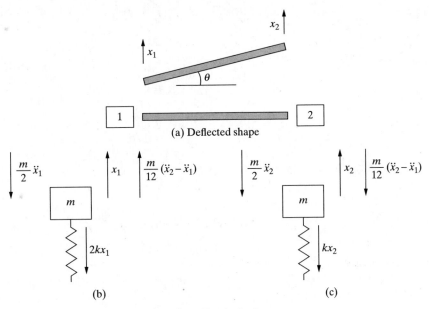

(a) Deflected shape

(b)   (c)

Figure 9.25   Free body diagrams.

∴ The equation of motion at the left spring can be written as follows:

$$\frac{m\ddot{x}_1}{2} - \frac{m}{12}(\ddot{x}_2 - \ddot{x}_1) + 2kx_1 = 0$$

Similarly, the equation of motion at the right spring can be written as follows:

$$\frac{m\ddot{x}_2}{2} + \frac{m}{12}(\ddot{x}_2 - \ddot{x}_1) + kx_2 = 0$$

These equations can be re-written as follows:

$$\frac{m}{12}\begin{bmatrix} 7 & -1 \\ -1 & 7 \end{bmatrix}\begin{Bmatrix} \ddot{x}_1 \\ \ddot{x}_2 \end{Bmatrix} + \begin{bmatrix} 2k & 0 \\ 0 & k \end{bmatrix}\begin{Bmatrix} x_1 \\ x_2 \end{Bmatrix} = \begin{Bmatrix} 0 \\ 0 \end{Bmatrix}$$

Two important observations can be made in this equation:

1. The mass matrix is not a diagonal matrix. Rather it is a coupled matrix. The rotational inertia force is acting at the center of the bar and not at the two nodes where degrees of freedom are identified.
2. The stiffness matrix is a diagonal matrix.

The solution is given by the following equation:

$$[[K]-[M]\omega^2]\{X_o\}=\{0\}$$

or,

$$\begin{bmatrix} 2k-7m'\omega^2 & m'\omega^2 \\ m'\omega^2 & k-7m'\omega^2 \end{bmatrix}\begin{Bmatrix} x_{10} \\ x_{20} \end{Bmatrix} = \begin{Bmatrix} 0 \\ 0 \end{Bmatrix}$$

where $m' = m/12$

Its solution is given by the equation:

$$\det|K - M\omega^2| = 0$$

$$\left(2k - 7m'\omega^2\right)\left(k - 7m'\omega^2\right) - m'^2\omega^4 = 0$$

or,

$$48m'^2\omega^4 - 21km'\omega^2 + 2k^2 = 0$$

Solving it, we get, $\omega_1^{*2} = 0.297\dfrac{k}{m'}$ or $\omega_1^{*2} = 3.57\dfrac{k}{m}$

Similarly, $\omega_2^{*2} = 0.140\dfrac{k}{m'}$ or $\omega_2^{*2} = 1.68\dfrac{k}{m}$

Mode shape 1 is given by

$$\left(2k - 7m'\omega^2\right)x_{11} + m'\omega^2 x_{21} = 0$$

On substituting $\omega^2 = \omega_1^{*2} = 0.297\dfrac{k}{m'}$

$$\frac{x_{11}}{x_{21}} = \frac{0.297}{0.079} = 3.76$$

Mode shape 2 is given by substituting $\omega^2 = \omega_2^{*2} = 0.140\dfrac{k}{m'}$

$$\frac{x_{12}}{x_{22}} = \frac{-0.14}{1.02} = -0.137$$

The mode shapes are shown in Figure 9.26.

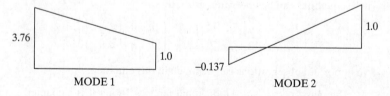

Figure 9.26   Mode shapes.

Alternatively, it can have the following independent two degrees of freedom at the center of mass:

1. Translational deformation at the midspan, x_0
2. Rotational deformation at the midspan, θ

The stiffness coefficients for this system can be determined by drawing free body diagrams for the two cases shown in Figure 9.27 as follows:

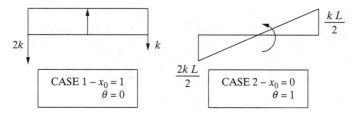

Figure 9.27   Stiffness coefficients.

For Case 1,

Give the unit deformation $x_0 = 1$ keeping $\theta = 0$, the spring forces will develop as shown. Now consider the static equilibrium, we get the stiffness coefficients:

$$k_{xx} = 2k + k = 3k, \quad \text{and} \quad k_{x\theta} = 2k\frac{L}{2} - k\frac{L}{2} = k\frac{L}{2}$$

and,

For Case 2,

Give the unit deformation $\theta = 1$ keeping $x_0 = 0$, the spring forces will develop as shown. Now consider the static equilibrium, we get the stiffness coefficients:

$$k_{\theta\theta} = \left(2k\frac{L}{2} + k\frac{L}{2}\right)\frac{L}{2} = 3k\frac{L^2}{4}$$

and

$$k_{x\theta} = 2k\frac{L}{2} - k\frac{L}{2} = k\frac{L}{2}$$

The 2×2 stiffness matrix can be written as follows:

$$K = \begin{bmatrix} k_{xx} & k_{x\theta} \\ k_{x\theta} & k_{\theta\theta} \end{bmatrix} = \begin{bmatrix} 3k & k\dfrac{L}{2} \\ k\dfrac{L}{2} & 3k\dfrac{L^2}{4} \end{bmatrix}$$

An important observation can be made in this equation:

The stiffness matrix is not a diagonal matrix unlike in the first case. Rather it is a coupled matrix. The two springs are located at the two ends that resist the translational as well as rotational forces acting at the center of the bar. Had there been a translational spring and a rotational spring each located at the center of the bar, the stiffness matrix would have been a diagonal matrix.

Similarly, the mass matrix can be generated directly.

The inertia force will be generated along the two degrees of freedom as identified. The translational inertia force will be $m\ddot{x}$ and the rotational inertia force will be $m'\ddot{\theta}$, where m' is mass moment of inertia given as:

$$m' = \frac{mL^2\ddot{\theta}}{12}$$

The mass matrix can be written as follows:

$$[M] = \begin{bmatrix} m & 0 \\ 0 & \dfrac{mL^2}{12} \end{bmatrix}$$

The mass matrix is a diagonal matrix. It means it has uncoupled terms since the inertia forces have been written directly in terms of the degrees of freedom of the midspan node.

☐

Example 9.9

A two degrees of freedom system is shown in Figure 9.28. Estimate its natural frequencies of vibrations.

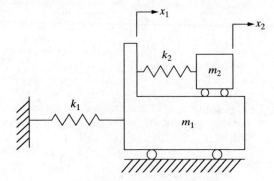

Figure 9.28   Two-DOF system.

Solution   The free body diagrams of the mass m_1 and m_2 can be drawn as shown in Figure 9.29.

$$k_2 (x_2 - x_1) \longleftarrow \boxed{m_2}$$
$$m_2 \ddot{x}_1 \longleftarrow$$

(a)

$$(m_1 + m_2)\ddot{x}_1 \longleftarrow \boxed{m_1 + m_2} \longrightarrow k_2 (x_2 - x_1)$$
$$k_1 x_1 \longleftarrow$$

(b)

Figure 9.29   Free body diagrams.

Considering the equilibrium of mass m_2 and m_1 gives,

$$m_2 \ddot{x}_2 + k_2 (x_2 - x_1) = 0$$

or,
$$m_2 \ddot{x}_2 + k_2 x_2 = k_2 x_1 \tag{i}$$

and
$$(m_1 + m_2)\ddot{x}_1 + k_1 x_1 - k_2 (x_2 - x_1) = 0$$

or,
$$(m_1 + m_2)\ddot{x}_1 + (k_1 + k_2)x_1 = k_2 x_2 \tag{ii}$$

These can be arranged as follows:

$$\begin{bmatrix} m_1 + m_2 & 0 \\ 0 & m_2 \end{bmatrix} \begin{Bmatrix} \ddot{x}_1 \\ \ddot{x}_2 \end{Bmatrix} + \begin{bmatrix} (k_1 + k_2) & -k_2 \\ -k_2 & k_2 \end{bmatrix} \begin{Bmatrix} x_1 \\ x_2 \end{Bmatrix} = \begin{Bmatrix} 0 \\ 0 \end{Bmatrix} \tag{iii}$$

The solution is given by the following equation:

$$[[K] - [M]\omega^2]\{X_0\} = \{0\}$$

or,

$$\begin{bmatrix} (k_1 + k_2) - (m_1 + m_2)\omega^2 & -k_2 \\ -k_2 & k_2 - m_2\omega^2 \end{bmatrix} \begin{Bmatrix} x_{10} \\ x_{20} \end{Bmatrix} = \begin{Bmatrix} 0 \\ 0 \end{Bmatrix}$$

Its solution is given by the equation:

$$\det|K - M\omega^2| = 0$$

or,

$$\left[(k_1 + k_2) - (m_1 + m_2)\omega^2 \right] \times \left(k_2 - m_2\omega^2 \right) - k_2^2 = 0 \tag{iv}$$

On simplification,

$$(m_1 + m_2)m_2\omega^4 - \left[m_1 k_2 + m_2 (k_1 + 2k_2) \right]\omega^2 + k_1 k_2 = 0 \tag{v}$$

This equation gives two positive roots of the natural frequency ω.
If $m_1 = 250$ kg, $k_1 = 50000$ N/m, $m_2 = 75$ kg and $k_2 = 20000$ N/m
The characteristic equation can be written as:

$$24375w^4 - 1175 \times 10^4 \omega^2 + 10^9 = 0$$

The frequencies are 19.27 and 10.50 rad/sec.
For a higher degree polynomial, MATLAB function ROOTS can be used to find its roots.
□

Example 9.10

Consider the system shown in Figure 9.30. The supports A and B also move by x_a and x_b, respectively. Write its equation of motion.

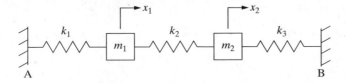

Figure 9.30   Two-DOF system.

Solution   The free body diagrams of the mass m_1 and m_2 can be drawn as shown in Figure 9.31.

$$k_2(x_2 - x_1) \longleftarrow \boxed{m_2} \longrightarrow k_3(x_b - x_2)$$
$$m_2\ddot{x}_2 \longleftarrow$$
(a)

$$m_1\ddot{x}_1 \longleftarrow \boxed{m_1} \longrightarrow k_2(x_2 - x_1)$$
$$k_1(x_1 - x_a) \longleftarrow$$
(b)

Figure 9.31   Free body diagrams.

Considering the equilibrium of mass m_1,

$$m_1\ddot{x}_1 + k_1(x_1 - x_a) - k_2(x_2 - x_1) = 0$$

or,

$$m_1\ddot{x}_1 + (k_1 + k_2)x_1 - k_2 x_2 = k_1 x_a$$

Similarly, the equilibrium of mass m_2 gives

$$m_2\ddot{x}_2 + k_2(x_2 - x_1) - k_3(x_b - x_2) = 0$$

or,

$$m_2\ddot{x}_2 - k_2 x_1 + (k_2 + k_3)x_2 = k_3 x_b$$

The equation of motion can be written in matrix form

$$\begin{bmatrix} m_1 & 0 \\ 0 & m_2 \end{bmatrix}\begin{Bmatrix} \ddot{x}_1 \\ \ddot{x}_2 \end{Bmatrix} + \begin{bmatrix} k_1 + k_2 & -k_2 \\ -k_2 & k_2 + k_3 \end{bmatrix}\begin{Bmatrix} x_1 \\ x_2 \end{Bmatrix} = \begin{bmatrix} k_1 & 0 \\ 0 & k_3 \end{bmatrix}\begin{Bmatrix} x_a \\ x_b \end{Bmatrix}$$

If the supports are fixed, the right-hand side becomes zero.

In case the system moves statically, the inertia term becomes zero, that is,

$$\begin{bmatrix} k_1 + k_2 & -k_2 \\ -k_2 & k_2 + k_3 \end{bmatrix}\begin{Bmatrix} x_1 \\ x_2 \end{Bmatrix} = \begin{bmatrix} k_1 & 0 \\ 0 & k_3 \end{bmatrix}\begin{Bmatrix} x_a \\ x_b \end{Bmatrix}$$

The solution of this equation yields x_{10} and x_{20}, the static displacements of mass 1 and 2,

$$x_{10} = \frac{\left(\dfrac{1}{k_2} + \dfrac{1}{k_3}\right)x_a + \dfrac{1}{k_1}x_b}{\dfrac{1}{k_1} + \dfrac{1}{k_2} + \dfrac{1}{k_3}}$$

and

$$x_{20} = \frac{\dfrac{1}{k_3}x_a + \left(\dfrac{1}{k_1} + \dfrac{1}{k_2}\right)x_b}{\dfrac{1}{k_1} + \dfrac{1}{k_2} + \dfrac{1}{k_3}}$$

In case the two supports move by an equal amount in the same direction, then

$$x_a = x_b$$

∴

$$x_{10} = x_{20} = x_a = x_b$$

It means, there will be a rigid body motion under static conditions. ☐

Example 9.11

A two DOF system is shown in Figure 9.32. Write its equations of motion.

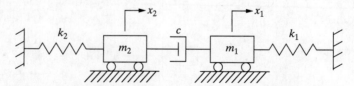

Figure 9.32   Two-DOF systems with a common damper.

Solution The free body diagrams of the mass m_1 and m_2 can be drawn as shown in Figure 9.33.

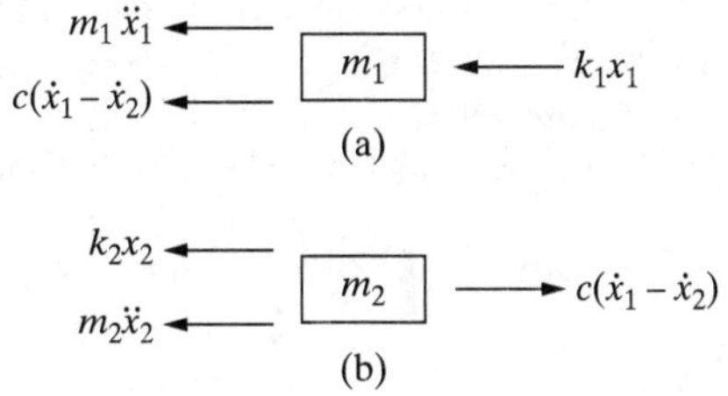

Figure 9.33 Free body diagrams.

Considering the equilibrium of mass m_1,

$$m_1\ddot{x}_1 + k_1 x_1 + c(\dot{x}_1 - \dot{x}_2) = 0 \qquad \text{(i)}$$

Similarly, the equilibrium of mass m_2 gives

$$m_2\ddot{x}_2 + k_2 x_2 - c(\dot{x}_1 - \dot{x}_2) = 0 \qquad \text{(ii)}$$

The equations of motion can be written in matrix form as follows:

$$\begin{bmatrix} m_1 & 0 \\ 0 & m_2 \end{bmatrix} \begin{Bmatrix} \ddot{x}_1 \\ \ddot{x}_2 \end{Bmatrix} + \begin{bmatrix} c & -c \\ -c & c \end{bmatrix} \begin{Bmatrix} \dot{x}_1 \\ \dot{x}_2 \end{Bmatrix} + \begin{bmatrix} k_1 & 0 \\ 0 & k_2 \end{bmatrix} \begin{Bmatrix} x_1 \\ x_2 \end{Bmatrix} = \begin{Bmatrix} 0 \\ 0 \end{Bmatrix} \qquad \text{(iii)}$$

Its solution is assumed as follows:

$$x_1 = D_1 e^{\omega^* t} \quad \text{and} \quad x_2 = D_2 e^{\omega^* t} \qquad \text{(iv)}$$

Differentiating these equations twice and substituting in Equations (i) and (ii) gives,

$$\left[m_1 D_1 \omega^{*2} + k_1 D_1 + c\omega^* (D_1 - D_2) \right] e^{\omega^* t} = 0 \qquad \text{(v)}$$

and

$$\left[m_2 D_2 \omega^{*2} + k_2 D_2 - c\omega^* (D_1 - D_2) \right] e^{\omega^* t} = 0 \qquad \text{(vi)}$$

For a non-trivial solution,

$$e^{\omega^* t} \neq 0$$

$$\therefore \qquad m_1 D_1 \omega^{*2} + k_1 D_1 + c\omega^* (D_1 - D_2) = 0$$

or,

$$m_1 \omega^{*2} + c\omega^* + k_1 = c\omega^* \frac{D_2}{D_1} \qquad \text{(vii)}$$

and

$$m_2 D_2 \omega^{*2} + k_2 D_2 + c\omega^* (D_2 - D_1) = 0$$

or,

$$m_2 \omega^{*2} + c\omega^* + k_2 = c\omega^* \frac{D_1}{D_2} \qquad \text{(viii)}$$

Equations (vii) and (viii) can be written as:

$$\frac{D_1}{D_2} = \frac{c\omega^*}{m_1 \omega^{*2} + c\omega^* + k_1} = \frac{m_2 \omega^{*2} + c\omega^* + k_2}{c\omega^*} \qquad \text{(ix)}$$

Equations (ix) yields the characteristic eigenvalue equation, that is,

$$\left(m_1\omega^{*2} + c\omega^* + k_1\right) \times \left(m_2\omega^{*2} + c\omega^* + k_2\right) = \left(c\omega^*\right)^2 \tag{x}$$

This gives four roots of ω^* – two positive and two negative. The natural frequencies of the two DOF system can be obtained.

If $m_1 = m_2 = m$ and $k_1 = k_2 = k$, Equation (x) can be written as

$$\left(m\omega^{*2} + k\right) \times \left(m\omega^{*2} + 2c\omega^* + k\right) = 0 \tag{xi}$$

Therefore,

$$\left(m\omega^{*2} + k\right) = 0,$$

It gives

$$\omega^* = \pm i\sqrt{\frac{k}{m}} \tag{xii}$$

and

$$\left(m\omega^{*2} + 2c\omega^* + k\right) = 0$$

or,

It gives

$$\omega^* = -\frac{c}{m} \pm \sqrt{\left(\frac{c}{m}\right)^2 - \frac{k}{m}} \tag{xiii}$$

Using the relations

$$\omega = \sqrt{\frac{k}{m}} \quad \text{and} \quad \xi = \frac{c}{c_c} = \frac{c}{2m\omega}$$

Equation (xiii) can be written as

$$\omega^* = -2\xi\omega \pm \sqrt{(2\xi\omega)^2 - \omega^2}$$

or,

$$\omega^* = \left(-2\xi \pm i\sqrt{1 - (2\xi)^2}\right)\omega \quad \text{for low damping} \tag{xiv}$$

The solution of the equations of motion can be given by both Equations (xii) and (xiv). The most general solution can be written as follows:

$$x_1(t) = D_{11}e^{\pm i\omega t} + D_{12}e^{\left(-2\xi \pm i\sqrt{1-(2\xi)^2}\right)\omega t}$$

This can be simplified and written as follows:

$$x_1(t) = A_1 \sin(\omega t + \theta_1) + A_2\, e^{-2\xi\omega t}\sin\left(\sqrt{1-(2\xi)^2}\,\omega t + \theta_2\right) \tag{xv}$$

Similarly,

$$x_2(t) = A_3 \sin(\omega t + \theta_1) + A_4\, e^{-2\xi\omega t}\sin\left(\sqrt{1-(2\xi)^2}\,\omega t + \theta_2\right) \tag{xvi}$$

The constants need to be evaluated using the initial conditions. ☐

PROBLEMS

9.1 An undamped two DOF system shown in Figure 9.1 has a mass $m_1 = m$, mass $m_2 = 2$ m, stiffness $k_1 = k$, and stiffness $k_2 = 2$ k. Determine its natural frequencies and mode shapes.

9.2 An undamped two DOF system has a mass $m_1 = m_2 = 2$ kg, and for the first mode $\omega_1 = 50$ rad/sec and mode shapes $\phi_{11} = 0.6$ and $\phi_{21} = 1.0$. Determine the mode shape and natural frequency of the second mode.

9.3 A machine operates at a frequency of 2000 rpm, exerts a force of 350 N and produces excessive vibrations. Design a vibration absorber having a maximum displacement of 3 mm only.

9.4 Plot the frequency response curve for the system shown in Figure 9.2 with $m_1 = 3$ m, $m_2 = m, k_1 = 3$ k and $k_2 = k$ subjected to a harmonic force p_0 applied on mass m_1.

9.5 What do you understand by vibration absorber? Derive the expression for the amplitude of the absorber mass when the main mass is at rest.

9.6 What do you mean by a tuned mass damper? Derive the expression for resonant frequencies for a given mass ratio and plot it. For a mass ratio of $\mu = 0.3$, compute the resonant frequencies and the frequency range for which the displacement amplification is less than 0.5.

9.7 A steel box girder foot bridge may be assumed to be represented by a SDOF system with a mass of 25000 kg and a stiffness of 5×10^6 N/m. The worst case of dynamic loading occurs when five people walk across the bridge in steps in tune with its natural frequency. This is almost equivalent to a sinusoidal loading with a constant amplitude of 0.75 kN. Design a suitable tuned vibration absorber so that its displacement does not exceed 10 cm.

9.8 A machine weighing 50 kg runs at a constant speed of 5000 rpm. At this speed, it is known to resonate with the foundation. Design an absorber such that its nearest resonance is at least 20% away from the operating frequency.

9.9 A balcony floor of a theater experiences excessive vibrations when 50 persons walk over it. This is equivalent to a sinusoidal loading with a constant amplitude of 25 kN. Design a suitable tuned vibration absorber so that its displacement does not exceed 5 cm. The balcony floor may be assumed to be represented by a SDOF system with a mass of 50000 kg and a stiffness of 15000 kN/m.

9.10 A two degree freedom system shown in Figure 9.29 has $m_1 = 50$ kg, $m_2 = 75$ kg, $k_1 = 20000$ N/m, $k_2 = 30000$ N/m and $k_3 = 15000$ N/m. Estimate its natural frequencies and mode shapes if the supports are rigid.

10 Multi-degree of Freedom Systems

10.1 INTRODUCTION

If the physical properties of a system are such that its motion can be described by a single coordinate and no other motion is possible, then it is a SDOF system and its solution can be obtained using any method discussed so far. If, however, the structure has more than one possible mode of displacement and it is reduced mathematically to a SDOF approximation, the solution of the equation of motion is only an approximation to the true dynamic behaviour. The quality of results obtained with a SDOF model depends on several factors, such as, the spatial distribution of mass and stiffness. In general, dynamic response of a flexible structure cannot be determined adequately by a SDOF model. Behaviour of such a structure can be described by more than one degree of freedom, that is, displacement amplitudes of certain selected points in the structure. The number of degrees of freedom (DOF) or displacement components to be considered is left to the judgement of the analyst; greater numbers provide better approximation to the true behaviour. A structure may consist of a discrete system or a distributed mass and elasticity system. Its DOF needs to be identified. If it is a discrete system, it may be analysed using the standard matrix analysis methods. In case, it is a distributed system, it may be analysed using the finite element method. The equations of motion remain same in either case.

The object of this chapter is to develop the equation of motion of a general *multi-degree-of-freedom system* (MDOF) subjected to *forced vibrations*. The MDOF system may be a multi-storey building, a TV tower, a flexural member, a machine foundation, a water retaining structure, a bridge including its super-structure and/or sub-structure, an underground metro station or parking structure or an off-shore oil platform. The forced vibrations may be due to any possible source. Once the equation of motion of a MDOF system is constituted, its solution can be easily obtained using the solution algorithms discussed in Chapter 7 on direct integration methods. However, the direct integration methods have their own limitations. They need time-history of the external loading. This is itself a very challenging problem. Most of the time, such time-histories are not available or not available in sufficient number. Therefore, there is a need to develop other solution techniques that give solutions with reasonable accuracy for any MDOF system. One such solution is called *modal analysis* or *response spectrum analysis*. This method is discussed in detail in this chapter.

There are certain methods that are applicable exclusively to discrete systems. One such method is Holzer's method applicable for the analysis of a simple spring-mass system or a lumped-mass system such as a multi-storey building or a steel TV tower. It is a very powerful method for understanding the physical concept of frequency and mode shapes in MDOF systems and is also discussed.

10.2 SPRING MASS MODEL: MDOF SYSTEM

A multistorey building may be represented by a series of springs and masses as shown in Figure 10.1. This is also referred to as a *lumped mass system*. All the masses on a given floor are lumped together. Similarly, stiffness of all the lateral load resisting system in one storey are lumped together. Damping is neglected in the present formulation. It is assumed that there is only one lateral degree of freedom per floor. If there are 20 storeys in the building, it will have 20-degrees of freedom. If there are n-storeys, there will be n-degrees of freedom. If this system is allowed to vibrate freely, it will vibrate in *natural mode or normal mode*. It means the system has exactly the same number of normal modes as the DOF. A *natural frequency* and a *characteristic shape* is associated with each normal mode. A salient feature of this normal mode is that the system could under certain conditions vibrate freely in that mode alone, and during such vibration, the ratio of the displacement of any two masses is constant with time. The complete motion of the system can be obtained by superimposing the independent motions of the individual modes. This forms the basis of the solution of the MDOF system.

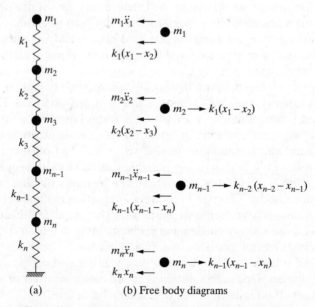

(a)   (b) Free body diagrams

Figure 10.1   An undamped multi-degree of freedom system.

Free body diagram of each mass can be considered and equation of dynamic equilibrium may be written for each mass as follows:

For mass m_1,

$$m_1\ddot{x}_1 + k_1(x_1 - x_2) = 0 \tag{A.1}$$

For mass m_2,

$$m_2\ddot{x}_2 + k_2(x_2 - x_3) + k_1(x_2 - x_1) = 0 \tag{A.2}$$

Similarly, for other masses,

$$m_3\ddot{x}_3 + k_3(x_3 - x_4) + k_2(x_3 - x_2) = 0 \tag{A.3}$$

and so on

$$m_n\ddot{x}_n + k_n(x_n) + k_{n-1}(x_n - x_{n-1}) = 0 \tag{A.n}$$

Let this set of n Equations be (A).

This set of n equations can be arranged in matrix form as follows:

$$[M]_{n\times n}\{\ddot{X}\}_{n\times 1} + [K]_{n\times n}\{X\}_{n\times 1} = \{0\}_{n\times 1} \tag{10.1a}$$

where,

$$[M]_{n\times n} = \text{mass matrix of size } n \times n$$
$$[K]_{n\times n} = \text{stiffness matrix of size } n \times n$$
$$\{X\}_{n\times 1} = \text{displacement vector of size } n \times 1$$
$$\{\ddot{X}\}_{n\times 1} = \text{acceleration vector of size } n \times 1$$
$$n = \text{DOF of the system}$$

A square bracket represents a matrix of size $m \times n$, whereas a curly bracket represents a column vector of size $m \times 1$. If it is a square matrix, then rows are equal to columns, that is, $m = n$.

Equation (10.1a) can also be written as follows:

$$M\ddot{X} + KX = 0 \tag{10.1b}$$

Bold and capital letters are used to represent a matrix. Thus, M and K each represent a matrix. A bold and capital letter X and P represent a column vector.

It can be shown that vibration in a normal mode must always be harmonic. It was already stated earlier that during vibration in a single mode, the displacements of several masses are always in the same proportion, that is, all possible positions are geometrically similar. All masses vibrate in phase with the same natural frequency.

Let us assume that:

$$x_1 = \phi_1 \sin \omega t \quad \text{or} \quad \ddot{x}_1 = -\omega^2 \phi_1 \sin \omega t \tag{B.1}$$

$$x_2 = \phi_2 \sin \omega t \quad \text{or} \quad \ddot{x}_2 = -\omega^2 \phi_2 \sin \omega t \tag{B.2}$$

and so on,

$$x_n = \phi_n \sin \omega t \quad \text{or} \quad \ddot{x}_n = -\phi^2 \phi_n \sin \omega t \tag{B.n}$$

Let this set of n Equations be (B).

This set of n equations can be arranged in matrix form as follows:

$$\{X\}_{n\times 1} = \{\phi\}_{n\times 1} \sin \omega t = \sin \omega t \{\phi\}_{n\times 1} \tag{10.2}$$

and

$$\{\ddot{X}\}_{n\times 1} = -\omega^2 \sin \omega t \{\phi\}_{n\times 1} = -\omega^2 \{X\} \tag{10.3}$$

Now let us substitute Equations of set B in set A, and for $\sin \omega t \neq 0$.

For mass m_1

$$-m_1 \omega^2 \phi_1 + k_1(\phi_1 - \phi_2) = 0$$

or

$$\phi_1(k_1 - m_1\omega^2) - \phi_2 k_1 = 0 \tag{C.1}$$

for mass m_2

$$-k_1 \phi_1 + (k_1 + k_2 - m_2\omega^2)\phi_2 - k_2 \phi_3 = 0 \tag{C.2}$$

for mass m_3

$$-k_2 \phi_2 + (k_2 + k_3 - m_3\omega^2)\phi_3 - k_3 \phi_4 = 0 \tag{C.3}$$

and so on, for mass m_n

$$-k_{n-1}\phi_{n-1} + (k_{n-1} + k_n - m_n\omega^2)\phi_n = 0 \tag{C.n}$$

Let this set of n equations be (C).

The set of Equations (C) can be re-written as follows:

$$\begin{bmatrix} (k_1 - m_1\omega^2) & -k_1 & 0 & 0 & 0 \\ -k_1 & (k_1 + k_2 - m_2\omega^2) & -k_2 & 0 & 0 \\ 0 & -k_2 & (k_2 + k_3 - m_3\omega^2) & -k_3 & 0 \\ 0 & 0 & & & \\ 0 & 0 & 0 & -k_{n-1} & (k_{n-1} + k_n - m_n\omega^2) \end{bmatrix} \begin{Bmatrix} \phi_1 \\ \phi_2 \\ \phi_3 \\ \phi_n \end{Bmatrix} = \{0\}$$

$$\tag{10.4}$$

This set of equations can be arranged in matrix notation as follows:

$$\left[[K] - \omega^2[M]\right]_{n\times n} \{\phi\}_{n\times 1} = \{0\}_{n\times 1} \tag{10.5}$$

There are $(n + 1)$ unknowns: n values of ϕ's and one ω^2. However, there are only n-equations. Thus, it is an under-determined system. The solution of Equation (10.4) or (10.5) gives n-values of ω^2. Each of the frequency ω_1, ω_2, ω_3, etc. is substituted in Equation (10.4) one-by-one, and the corresponding values of vector $\{\phi\}_{n\times 1}$ is determined in terms of any one vector component ϕ_i. Thus, vector $\{\phi\}_{n\times 1}$ is determined as a relative value because this system of equations happen to be an under-determined system. The vector $\{\phi\}_{n\times 1}$ is called *mode shapes*.

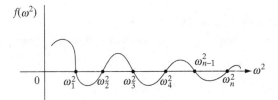

Figure 10.2   Roots of a polynomial.

For a non-trivial solution, vector $\{\phi\}_{n \times 1} \neq 0$, therefore, determinant of matrix of Equation (10.5) must be zero. This is referred to as the *frequency determinant or characteristic equations*. Upon simplification, it yields a polynomial equation of order n in ω^2, that is,

$$a_n(\omega^2)^n + a_{n-1}(\omega^2)^{n-1} + a_{n-2}(\omega^2)^{n-2} + ... + a_0 = 0 \tag{10.6}$$

This gives n values of ω^2, that is, n eigenvalues or n natural frequencies of vibration. A plot of this polynomial is shown in Figure 10.2. The problem is to find these roots at which this polynomial has zero values. This n^{th} order equation can be solved in several ways.

10.3 HOLTZER METHOD

This is an iterative method for computing frequencies of vibration of a MDOF spring mass system. Let us rearrange equations in set C.
Equation (C.1) gives,

$$\phi_2 = \phi_1 - \frac{\omega^2}{k_1} m_1 \phi_1 \tag{D.1}$$

Equation (C.2) gives,

$$\phi_3 = \phi_2 - \frac{\omega^2}{k_2}(m_1 \phi_1 + m_2 \phi_2) \tag{D.2}$$

after substituting for k_1 from Equation (C.1) in Equation (C.2).
Similarly,

$$\phi_n = \phi_{n-1} - \frac{\omega^2}{k_{n-1}} \left(\sum_{i=1}^{n-1} m_i \phi_i \right) \tag{D.n-1}$$

By similarity, the following additional equation can be written:

$$\phi_{n+1} = \phi_n - \frac{\omega^2}{k_n} \left(\sum_{i=1}^{n} m_i \phi_i \right) = 0 \quad \text{since base is fixed.} \tag{D.n}$$

There are n equations. Let this set of n equations be (D). These equations can be solved iteratively using a very simple logic.

Algorithm:
Step 1: Write equations of motion, set A
Step 2: Write set of equations B
Step 3: Write set of equations C

Step 4: Write set of equations D

Step 5: Choose ω^2 (say $= 0.1$ k/m)

Step 6: Work out ϕ_2 from Equation (D.1) in terms of ϕ_1; then ϕ_3 from Equation (D.2) in terms of ϕ_1; then ϕ_4 from Equation (D.3) in terms of ϕ_1 and so on. Remember that ϕ represents displacement.

Step 7: Compute ϕ_{n+1} from the last equation.

The displacement given by ϕ_{n+1} must turn out to be zero since the base is fixed. If not, choose another value of ω^2 and iterate on ω^2 till ϕ_{n+1} is zero.

It is a very easy, convenient and powerful manual method for estimating eigenvalues and eigenvectors for a MDOF-lumped mass system.

10.4 DYNAMIC EQUILIBRIUM CONDITION: MDOF SYSTEM

The equations of motion of the system shown in Figure 10.3 can be formulated by expressing the equilibrium of the effective forces associated with each of its n-degrees of freedom. It is a general MDOF system. It may be any discrete or distributed system. The choice of selection of DOF depends upon the characteristics of the structure under consideration and the experience and judgement of the structural analyst. The formulation is concerned only with the total DOF 'n'. There are four types of forces acting at any i^{th} degree of freedom:

1. externally applied load $p_i(t)$
2. elastic force f_{si}
3. damping force f_{di}
4. inertia force f_{ii}

For each of the n-degrees of freedom, the dynamic equilibrium equations may be expressed as:

$$f_{i1} + f_{d1} + f_{s1} = p_1(t)$$
$$f_{i2} + f_{d2} + f_{s2} = p_2(t)$$
$$f_{i3} + f_{d3} + f_{s3} = p_3(t)$$

and so on

$$f_{in} + f_{dn} + f_{sn} = p_n(t) \tag{10.7}$$

Rearranging these n-equations in matrix form:

$$\{f_I\}_{n\times1} + \{f_D\}_{n\times1} + \{f_S\}_{n\times1} = \{p(t)\}_{n\times1} \tag{10.8}$$

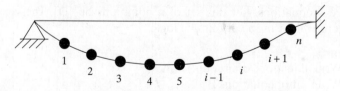

Figure 10.3 A MDOF system.

Each of the resisting forces is expressed most conveniently by means of an appropriate set of influence coefficients. In a MDOF system, any displacement applied at i^{th} degree-of-freedom will influence all the remaining $n-1$ DOF. There is a need to evaluate all these influence coefficients using the standard procedure adopted for the static analysis of a structure using matrix method, that is, *matrix structural analysis*. These coefficients will be determined separately for the inertia, damping and elastic forces. Let us first find the influence coefficients for elastic forces with which we are already familiar in the matrix analysis method.

10.4.1 Elastic Force (Spring Force)

At node 1, let us apply a unit displacement and determine the force produced at each of the remaining $(n-1)$ degrees of freedom. That is, let us determine the *influence coefficients for stiffness k_{ij}*

where k_{ij} = force produced at node i due to unit displacement applied at node j.

Similarly, let us apply a unit displacement at node 2 and determine the force produced at each of the remaining $(n-1)$ degrees of freedom. And so on.

If the final displacement at node 1 is x_1, at node 2 is x_2, at node 3 is x_3 and so on, we can get the total spring force produced at each of the n nodes.

Finally, let us collect all the forces acting at node 1, node 2, node 3, etc.

At node 1,

$$f_{s1} = k_{11}x_1 + k_{12}x_2 + k_{13}x_3 + k_{14}x_4 + \cdots + k_{1n}x_n$$

At node 2,

$$f_{s2} = k_{21}x_1 + k_{22}x_2 + k_{23}x_3 + k_{24}x_4 + \cdots + k_{2n}x_n$$

At node 3

$$f_{s3} = k_{31}x_1 + k_{32}x_2 + k_{33}x_3 + k_{34}x_4 + \cdots + k_{3n}x_n$$

and, in general

$$f_{sn} = k_{n1}x_1 + k_{n2}x_2 + k_{n3}x_3 + k_{n4}x_4 + \cdots + k_{nn}x_n$$

In these expressions, it has been assumed that the structural behaviour is linear so that the principle of superposition is applicable.

Let us arrange these n–equations in matrix form:

$$
\begin{Bmatrix} f_{s1} \\ f_{s2} \\ \vdots \\ f_{sn} \end{Bmatrix} =
\begin{bmatrix}
k_{11} & k_{12} & \cdots & x_{1n} \\
k_{21} & \cdots & \cdots & \cdots \\
\cdots & \cdots & \cdots & \cdots \\
k_{n1} & \cdots & \cdots & k_{nn}
\end{bmatrix}
\begin{Bmatrix} x_1 \\ x_2 \\ \vdots \\ x_n \end{Bmatrix}
\tag{10.9a}
$$

or,

$$\{f_s\}_{n\times 1} = [K]_{n\times n}\{X\}_{n\times 1} \tag{10.9b}$$

where

       $[K]$ is matrix of stiffness influence coefficients of size $n \times n$.

       $\{X\}$ is a displacement vector of size $n \times 1$

10.4.2 Damping Force

If it is assumed that damping depends on the velocity, that is, if it is a viscous type damping, the influence coefficients for damping force can be evaluated in the same manner as for the elastic force.

At node 1, let us apply a unit velocity and determine the damping force produced at each of the remaining $(n - 1)$ degrees of freedom. That is, let us determine the *influence coefficients for damping* c_{ij}

where c_{ij} = force produced at node i due to unit velocity imposed at node j.

The same procedure is repeated at each of the remaining $(n - 1)$ nodes. The final expression can be written in matrix form similar to Equation (10.9).

$$\begin{Bmatrix} f_{d1} \\ f_{d2} \\ f_{d3} \\ \vdots \\ f_{dn} \end{Bmatrix} = \begin{bmatrix} c_{11} & c_{12} & c_{13} & \cdots & c_{1n} \\ c_{21} & \cdots & \cdots & \cdots & \cdots \\ \vdots & \cdots & \cdots & \cdots & \cdots \\ \vdots & \cdots & \cdots & \cdots & \cdots \\ c_{n1} & \cdots & \cdots & \cdots & c_{nn} \end{bmatrix} \begin{Bmatrix} \dot{x}_1 \\ \dot{x}_2 \\ \dot{x}_3 \\ \vdots \\ \dot{x}_n \end{Bmatrix} \tag{10.10a}$$

Or,

$$\{f_D\}_{n \times 1} = [C]_{n \times n} \{\dot{X}\}_{n \times 1} \tag{10.10b}$$

where

[C] is matrix of damping influence coefficients of size $n \times n$.

$\{\dot{X}\}$ is a velocity vector of size $n \times 1$

10.4.3 Inertia Force

The inertia forces may also be expressed by a set of influence coefficients similar to elastic force and damping force coefficients. At node 1, let us apply a unit acceleration and determine the inertia force produced at each of the remaining $(n - 1)$ degrees of freedom. That is, let us determine the *influence coefficients for inertia* m_{ij}
where

m_{ij} = force corresponding to node i due to unit acceleration imposed at node j.

By analogy with damping forces:

$$\begin{Bmatrix} f_{i1} \\ f_{i2} \\ \vdots \\ f_{in} \end{Bmatrix} = \begin{bmatrix} m_{11} & m_{12} & m_{13} & \cdots m_{1n} \\ m_{21} & \cdots & \cdots & \cdots \\ \cdots & \cdots & \cdots & \cdots \\ m_{n1} & \cdots & \cdots & \cdots m_{nn} \end{bmatrix} \begin{Bmatrix} \ddot{x}_1 \\ \ddot{x}_2 \\ \vdots \\ \ddot{x}_n \end{Bmatrix} \tag{10.11a}$$

where

$$\{f_I\}_{n \times 1} = [M]_{n \times n} \{\ddot{X}\}_{n \times 1} \tag{10.11b}$$

where

$[M]$ is matrix of mass influence coefficients of size $n \times n$.

$\{\ddot{X}\}$ is acceleration vector of size $n \times 1$

By substituting the values in Equation (10.8), the equation of motion becomes:

$$[M]_{n \times n} \{\ddot{X}(t)\}_{n \times 1} + [C]_{n \times n} \{\dot{X}(t)\}_{n \times 1} + [K]_{n \times n} \{X(t)\}_{n \times 1} = \{p(t)\}_{n \times 1} \qquad (10.12a)$$

This equation can also be written as follows:

$$M\ddot{X} + C\dot{X} + KX = P(t) \qquad (10.12b)$$

where, the capital and bold letters M, C and K represents matrices, bold and capital letters X, $\dot{X}$ and $\ddot{X}$ represents displacement, velocity and acceleration vectors; and P represents a force vector.

The nature of mass matrix, damping matrix and stiffness matrix, whether they are diagonal, banded, full, and real or complex, will depend upon the physical problem. In any case, one thing is for certain. The stiffness matrix will always be a coupled matrix. The mass and damping matrices may be coupled or uncoupled. The solution of equation of motion will depend upon the nature of its constituents and size 'n'. Therefore, there are several algorithms available in the literature for the solution of this equation. One has to select the most efficient algorithm to suit the given problem.

The first step in any MDOF problem is to determine its frequencies or periods and mode shapes in various modes. It should be remembered that size 'n' of the problem may vary from two to several thousand. Depending upon the problem, it may not be necessary to determine all the n-frequencies and mode shapes. The fundamental frequency or fundamental periods are the most significant parameters. Next, it may be sufficient to determine a few lowest frequencies and also a few highest frequencies along with the corresponding mode shapes. Thus, a complete band of frequencies will be available.

The determination of natural frequencies and mode shapes of a MDOF system will be discussed in the next section.

10.5 UNDAMPED FREE VIBRATION ANALYSIS

The equation of motion for a freely vibrating undamped system can be obtained by omitting the damping matrix and applied load vector.

$$[M]_{n \times n} \{\ddot{X}\}_{n \times 1} + [K]_{n \times n} \{X\}_{n \times 1} = \{0\}_{n \times 1} \qquad (10.13a)$$

or,

$$M\ddot{X} + KX = 0 \qquad (10.13b)$$

The problem of vibration analysis consists of determining the condition under which Equation (10.13) will permit motion to occur. By analogy with SDF systems, it will be assumed that the free vibration motion is simple harmonic, that is

$$\{X(t)\} = \{X_0\} \cos(\omega t + \theta) \tag{10.14a}$$

$$\therefore \qquad \{\ddot{X}(t)\} = -\omega^2 \{X_0\} \cos(\omega t + \theta) = -\omega^2 \{X(t)\} \tag{10.14b}$$

Equation (10.13) can be written as

$$-\omega^2 M \{X_0\} \cos(\omega t + \theta) + K \{X_0\} \cos(\omega t + \theta) = \{0\}$$

or, $$\big[[K] - \omega^2 [M]\big]\{X_0\} = \{0\} \tag{10.15}$$

since $\cos(\omega t + \theta) \neq 0$

Hence, non-trivial solution of Equation (10.15) is possible only if determinant $|K - \omega^2 M|$ vanishes.

or, $$\det \big\|[K] - \omega^2 [M]\big\| = 0 \tag{10.16}$$

Re-writing Equation (10.15) as

$$[K]_{n \times n} \{X_0\}_{n \times 1} = \omega^2 [M]_{n \times n} \{X_0\}_{n \times 1} \tag{10.17}$$

or, $$[M]^{-1}_{n \times n} [K]_{n \times n} \{X_0\}_{n \times 1} = \omega^2 \{X_0\}_{n \times 1} \tag{10.18}$$

or, $$[A]_{n \times n} \{\phi\}_{n \times 1} = \lambda \{\phi\}_{n \times 1} \tag{10.19a}$$

or, $$A\phi = \lambda\phi \tag{10.19b}$$

where

$$[A]_{n \times n} = [M]^{-1}_{n \times n} [K]_{n \times n} \text{ and } \lambda = \omega^2 \tag{10.20}$$

$[A] = $ coefficient matrix of size $n \times n$
$\lambda = $ eigenvalue, a scalar quantity, size 1×1
$\{\phi\} = $ eigenvector corresponding to eigenvalue λ.

Equation (10.19) is known as the *characteristic eigenvalue equation*.
Alternatively, consider Equation (10.17)

$$[K]_{n \times n} \{X_0\}_{n \times 1} = \omega^2 [M]_{n \times n} \{X_0\}_{n \times 1}$$

or, $$\{X_0\}_{n \times 1} = \omega^2 [K]^{-1}_{n \times n} [M]_{n \times n} \{X_0\}_{n \times 1}$$

or, $$[K]^{-1}_{n \times n} [M]_{n \times n} \{X_0\}_{n \times 1} = \frac{1}{\omega^2} \{X_0\}_{n \times 1} \tag{10.21}$$

$$[A]_{n \times n} \{\phi\}_{n \times 1} = \lambda \{\phi\}_{n \times 1} \tag{10.22a}$$

or, $$A\phi = \lambda\phi \tag{10.22b}$$

where

$$[A]_{n \times n} = [K]_{n \times n}^{-1} [M]_{n \times n} \text{ and } \lambda = \frac{1}{\omega^2} \tag{10.23}$$

$[A]$ = coefficient matrix of size $n \times n$
λ = eigenvalue, a scalar quantity, size 1×1
$\{\phi\}$ = eigenvector corresponding to eigenvalue λ.

Equation (10.22) is known as the *characteristic eigenvalue equation*.

There are several standard solutions for this equation depending upon the characteristics of [A]. In Equation (10.19a), the coefficient matrix A consists of product of stiffness matrix K pre-multiplied by the inverse of mass matrix M; and the eigenvalue λ consists of ω^2. In Equation (10.22a), the coefficient matrix A consists of product of mass matrix M pre-multiplied by the inverse of stiffness matrix K; and the eigenvalue λ consists of $1/\omega^2$. Again, matrix A may be symmetric or unsymmetric, full or sparse, real or complex, banded or tri-diagonal, etc. It may be positive definite or not.

The solution of the characteristic eigenvalue problem, Equations (10.19) or (10.22), provides 'n' eigenvalues and corresponding to each eigenvalue λ_i, an eigenvector $\{\phi\}_{n \times 1}$. In turn, eigenvalue λ leads to natural frequency ω and eigenvector $\{\phi\}$ leads to mode shapes of free vibration of the MDOF system. If there are n eigenvalues, λ_1, λ_2, λ_3, etc., there will be 'n', eigenvectors $\{\phi\}$ each of size $n \times 1$. Let us write each of these n-eigenvectors column-wise in a single matrix Φ as follows:

$$[\Phi]_{n \times n} = \left[\{\phi_1\}_{n \times 1} \quad \{\phi_2\}_{n \times 1} \quad \{\phi_3\}_{n \times 1} \quad \cdots \quad \{\phi_n\}_{n \times 1} \right]_{n \times n} \tag{10.24}$$

Thus, Equation (10.24) is a square matrix of size $n \times n$.

It can be shown that for *real, symmetric, positive definite* mass and stiffness matrices which pertain to a stable structural system, all roots of the characteristic equation will always be real and positive. It is only then the frequency, which is given by square root of the eigenvalue λ, will be real and positive.

The solution of Equation (10.19) by power method leads to the highest eigenvalue, that is, highest frequency of vibration or lowest period. Similarly, the solution of Equation (10.22) by the power method leads to the highest eigenvalue, that is, lowest frequency of vibration or highest period. The lowest frequency of vibration is referred to as the *fundamental frequency of vibration*. Similarly, the highest period is referred to as the *fundamental period of vibration*.

10.5.1 Solution of Eigenvalue Problem

There are several algorithms for the solution of an eigenvalue problem depending upon the characteristics of the coefficient matrix A. Some of these algorithms are as follows:

1. Iterative Methods
   (a) Power method
   (b) Matrix deflation method
   (c) Inverse iteration method

2. Transformation-cum-Iterative Methods
   (a) Jacobi method
   (b) Given's method
   (c) Householder method
   (d) LR or QR method
3. For Very Large Systems
   (a) Determinant search technique
   (b) Subspace iteration method

Given's method and Householder method transform an $n \times n$ coefficient matrix in a tri-diagonal matrix. The eigenvalues of a tri-diagonal matrix are same as those of the original matrix. However, its eigenvectors are different. The eigenvalues of a tri-diagonal matrix are determined using Sturm sequence method along with Bisection or Secant iteration method.

Some of these methods will be discussed through examples in this chapter.

Basic Theorems

There are some basic theorems that are very useful in the solution of eigenvalue problems.

1. If $\lambda_1, \lambda_2, \lambda_3, ..., \lambda_n$ are eigenvalues of coefficient matrix A, then eigenvalues of A^k are $\lambda_1^k, \lambda_2^k, \lambda_3^k, ..., \lambda_n^k$

2. If coefficient matrix A is real and symmetric, all eigenvalues and eigenvectors are real. Moreover, eigenvectors corresponding to distinct eigenvalues are orthogonal.

3. If matrix A is real and positive definite, its eigenvalues will be positive.

4. Any similarity transformation PAP^{-1} or $P^{-1}AP$ applied to coefficient matrix A leaves the eigenvalues of the matrix A unchanged.

5. If A is any coefficient matrix, whose eigenvalues are all distinct, then there exists a similarity transformation such that

$$X^{-1}AX = D$$

where,

D = diagonal matrix whose diagonal elements are the eigenvalues of matrix A.
X = orthogonal matrix

10.5.2 Rayleigh's Quotient

Consider the Characteristic equation

$$A\phi = \lambda\phi$$

Pre-multiply with ϕ^T

$$\phi^T A\phi = \lambda\phi^T\phi$$

or,

$$\lambda = \frac{\phi^T A \phi}{\phi^T \phi} \qquad (10.25a)$$

Alternatively,

$$KX = \lambda MX$$

Pre-multiplying by X^T gives

$$X^T KX = \lambda X^T MX$$

or,

$$\lambda = \frac{X^T KX}{X^T MX} \qquad (10.25b)$$

The quotient λ is called *Rayleigh's quotient*. The positive definiteness of M guarantees that the denominator is non-zero.

If vector ϕ or X is an eigenvector of the problem, the Rayleigh's quotient is equal to its eigenvalue λ. Moreover, the Rayleigh's quotient is bounded between its minimum and maximum eigenvalues λ_1 and λ_n.

10.5.3 Orthogonality Condition of Modes

Free vibration mode shapes $[\Phi]$ have certain special properties which are very useful in structural dynamics. These are called *orthogonality conditions*.

$$\{\phi_r\}_{1 \times n}^T [M]_{n \times n} \{\phi_s\}_{n \times 1} = 0 \qquad \text{for} \qquad \omega_r \neq \omega_s \qquad (10.26)$$

and

$$\{\phi_r\}_{1 \times n}^T [K]_{n \times n} \{\phi_s\}_{n \times 1} = 0 \qquad \text{for} \qquad \omega_r \neq \omega_s \qquad (10.27)$$

where

$\{\phi_r\}$ = r^{th} mode shape

$\{\phi_s\}$ = s^{th} mode shape

It can be seen that these equations lead to a scalar product.

These two equations represent that vibrating shapes are orthogonal with respect to the mass matrix as well as stiffness matrix. It means, if mass matrix M is pre-multiplied by mode shape vector in r^{th} mode and post-multiplied by mode shape vector in the sth mode, this scalar product will be a zero. Similarly, if stiffness matrix K is pre-multiplied by mode shape vector in r^{th} mode and post-multiplied by mode shape vector in the sth mode, this scalar product will be a zero.

Proof

Let us consider Equation (10.17)

$$[K]_{n \times n} \{X_0\}_{n \times 1} = \omega^2 [M]_{n \times n} \{X_0\}_{n \times 1} \qquad (10.17)$$

Let us write it for the rth mode

$$[K]\{\phi_r\} = \omega_r^2 [M]\{\phi_r\} \qquad (10.28)$$

where

$\phi_r = r^{th}$ mode shape

$\omega_r = r^{th}$ frequency

Pre-multiply Equation (10.28) by s^{th} mode shape vector ϕ_s^T, that is, by transposing dimensional compatibility,

$$\{\phi_s\}^T [K]\{\phi_r\} = \omega_r^2 \{\phi_s\}^T [M]\{\phi_r\} \tag{10.29}$$

Similarly, let us consider Equation (10.17) for the sth mode shape and pre-multiply it by r^{th} mode shape vector

$$\{\phi_r\}^T [K]\{\phi_s\} = \omega_s^2 \{\phi_r\}^T [M]\{\phi_s\} \tag{10.30}$$

Let us re-write Equation (10.29) by taking transpose of both sides as follows:

$$\left[\{\phi_s\}^T [K]\{\phi_r\}\right]^T = \omega_r^2 \left[\{\phi_s\}^T [M]\{\phi_r\}\right]^T \tag{10.31}$$

or, it can be written as

$$\{\phi_r\}^T [K]^T \{\phi_s\} = \omega_r^2 \{\phi_r\}^T [M]^T \{\phi_s\} \tag{10.32}$$

In structural engineering problems, mass matrix and stiffness matrix are always symmetric for a stable structural system, therefore, Equation (10.32) can be written as:

$$\{\phi_r\}^T [K]\{\phi_s\} = \omega_r^2 \{\phi_r\}^T [M]\{\phi_s\} \tag{10.33}$$

Therefore, Equations (10.30) and (10.33) must be equal

$$\omega_s^2 \{\phi_r\}^T [M]\{\phi_s\} = \omega_r^2 \{\phi_r\}^T [M]\{\phi_s\}$$

or,

$$\left(\omega_s^2 - \omega_r^2\right)\left[\{\phi_r\}^T [M]\{\phi_s\}\right] = 0$$

If the frequencies ω_r and ω_s are not equal, then it follows that

$$\{\phi_r\}^T [M]\{\phi_s\} = 0 \qquad \text{for} \qquad \omega_r \neq \omega_s \tag{10.34}$$

This proves orthogonality of mode shapes in r^{th} and s^{th} modes with respect to mass matrix.

Similarly, orthogonality of mode shapes in r^{th} and s^{th} modes with respect to stiffness matrix can be proved. This is a very crucial property for decoupling the equations of motion in a MDOF system.

The orthogonality of natural modes implies that the following matrices are diagonal:

$$[\Phi]^T [K][\Phi] = [\bar{K}]$$

also

$$[\Phi]^T [M][\Phi] = [\bar{M}]$$

where the diagonal elements are given by

$$k_r = \phi_r^T [K]\phi_r \tag{10.35a}$$

and

$$m_r = \phi_r^T [M] \phi_r \tag{10.35b}$$

Since both mass and stiffness matrices are positive definite, the diagonal elements of K and M are positive. They are related by

$$k_r = m_r \omega_r^2 \tag{10.35c}$$

10.5.4 Normalization of Modes

It should be noted that the vibration mode shapes or mode amplitudes obtained from eigen problem solution are arbitrary; any amplitude will satisfy the characteristic of Equation (10.19) or (10.22). The eigen solution is usually carried out iteratively, and in this process, the eigenvectors keep growing due to numerical calculations. If not checked, it may lead to numerical instability of the solution. It also follows that if any vector ϕ satisfies Equation (10.19) or (10.22), any other vector which is proportional to ϕ will also satisfy it.

Hence, it is usual to normalize mode shapes so that

$$\{\phi_r\}^T [M] \{\phi_r\} = 1 \tag{10.36}$$

It can be done by computing a scale factor S_r for r^{th} mode,

$$\{\hat{\phi}_r\}^T [M] \{\hat{\phi}_r\} = S_r \tag{10.37}$$

where $\{\hat{\phi}_r\}$ represents an arbitrarily determined r^{th} modal amplitude.

Now, normalized mode shape is given as

$$\{\phi_r\} = \frac{\{\hat{\phi}_r\}}{\sqrt{S_r}} \tag{10.38}$$

Thus,

$$[\Phi]^T [M] [\Phi] = I \tag{10.36}$$

where, $I =$ identity matrix

Equation (10.36) states that the natural modes are not only orthogonal but also normalized with respect to mass. Mode shapes normalized in this fashion are said to be *orthonormal* relative to the mass matrix. These are called *orthonormal mode shapes*.

When the modes are normalized in this manner, Equation (10.35c) can be written as follows:

$$k_r = m_r \omega_r^2 = \omega_r^2 \tag{10.39}$$

10.6 TRANSFORMATION OF EIGENVALUE PROBLEM TO STANDARD FORM

Let us again consider Equations (10.19) and (10.20)

$$A\phi = \lambda\phi \tag{10.19b}$$

where

$$[A]_{n \times n} = [M]_{n \times n}^{-1}[K]_{n \times n} \text{ and } \lambda = \omega^2 \tag{10.20}$$

The mass matrix M and the stiffness matrix K are generally both symmetric in structural engineering problems but the product A given by Equation (10.20) or (10.23) in general is not symmetric. Although Equation (10.19b) or Equation (10.22b) is a standard eigenvalue problem for which many computer codes are readily available, due to unsymmetric nature of matrix A, the computational efforts are increased significantly. Let us try to arrive at a symmetric matrix A. Consider a diagonal mass matrix M which is positive definite. It means its inverse exists.

Define $M = M^{1/2}M^{1/2}$ (10.40)

or,

$$I = M^{1/2}M^{-1/2} = M^{-1/2}M^{1/2} \tag{10.41}$$

Consider Equation (10.17)

$$[K]_{n \times n}\{X_0\}_{n \times 1} = \omega^2[M]_{n \times n}\{X_0\}_{n \times 1} \tag{10.17}$$

or,

$$K\phi = \omega^2 M\phi \tag{10.42}$$

This can be re-written as follows:

$$KM^{-1/2}M^{1/2}\phi = \omega^2 M^{1/2}M^{1/2}\phi$$

Pre-multiplying both sides by $M^{-1/2}$ gives

$$M^{-1/2}KM^{-1/2}M^{1/2}\phi = \omega^2 M^{-1/2}M^{1/2}M^{1/2}\phi \tag{10.43}$$

or,

$$By = \lambda y \tag{10.44}$$

where

$$B = M^{-1/2}KM^{-1/2} \tag{10.45a}$$

$$y = M^{1/2}\phi \tag{10.45b}$$

and

$$\lambda = \omega^2$$

Equation (10.44) is a standard eigenvalue problem and coefficient matrix B is now symmetric.

10.7 NORMAL COORDINATES

For most applications, there is no need to compute all the n frequencies as well as mode shapes as it may be computationally very expensive. The determination of first few lowest frequencies is generally sufficient in many cases. The normal coordinates serve to uncouple the damped MDOF equations of motion. Let us assume that we need to consider only the lowest p modes out of total n modes in any MDOF system. These p modes will be sequential from mode 1 to p.

Let us consider Equation (10.12b)

$$M\ddot{X} + C\dot{X} + KX = P(t) \qquad (10.12b)$$

The displacement vector $\{X\}_{n\times 1}$ can be written as follows:

$$\{X\}_{n\times1} = [\Phi]_{n\times p}\{Y\}_{p\times1} \qquad (10.46)$$

where
  $\{X\}$ = displacement vector of size $n \times 1$
  Φ = mode shape matrix of size $n \times p$
  $\{Y\}$ = vector of size $p \times 1$
  p = number of desired modes $\leq n$

Thus, the total displacement $\{X\}$ is obtained as the sum of the modal components. In this equation, the mode shape matrix Φ serves to transform *generalized coordinates* $\{Y\}_{p\times1}$ to the *geometric coordinates* $\{X\}_{n\times1}$. The generalized coordinates $\{Y\}$ are called the *normal coordinates* of the structure.

10.8 UNCOUPLED EQUATIONS OF MOTION

The equation of motion of a MDOF system is given by Equation (10.12a)

$$[M]_{n\times n}\{\ddot{X}(t)\}_{n\times1} + [C]_{n\times n}\{\dot{X}(t)\}_{n\times1} + [K]_{n\times n}\{X(t)\}_{n\times1} = \{P(t)\}_{n\times1} \qquad (10.12a)$$

or,

$$M\ddot{X} + C\dot{X} + KX = P(t) \qquad (10.12b)$$

The influence coefficients for stiffness, damping and inertia forces derived earlier indicate that this equation has coupled terms. Therefore, Equation (10.12a) will have to be solved simultaneously, which is a very tedious task. It is possible to decouple this equation with the help of normal coordinates and orthogonality conditions derived in the previous sections. These decoupled equations essentially represent a set of SDOF systems that can be solved using the results derived in Chapters 2, 3 and 7.

Let us write Equation (10.46) as:

$$\{X\}_{n\times1} = [\Phi]_{n\times p}\{Y\}_{p\times1} \qquad (10.46)$$

or,

$$X = \Phi Y$$

where
    $\{X\}$ = displacement vector in geometric coordinates, size $n \times 1$

    $\{Y\}$ = displacement vector in generalized or normal coordinates, size $p \times 1$

Let us substitute Equation (10.46) in Equation (10.12b)

$$M\Phi\ddot{Y} + C\Phi\dot{Y} + K\Phi Y = P(t)$$

Pre-multiply it by the transpose of the modal shape vector Φ^T,

$$\Phi^T M\Phi\ddot{Y} + \Phi^T C\Phi\dot{Y} + \Phi^T K\Phi Y = \Phi^T P(t) \qquad (10.47a)$$

where

$$\Phi^T M\Phi = \Phi^T_{p\times n} M_{n\times n} \Phi_{n\times p} = M_{p\times p}$$

Similarly, damping and stiffness terms can be written.

$$M_{p\times p}\ddot{Y}_{p\times 1} + C_{p\times p}\dot{Y}_{p\times 1} + K_{p\times p}Y_{p\times 1} = \Phi^T_{p\times n}P(t)_{n\times 1} \qquad (10.47b)$$

The set of n equations of motion are now reduced to a set of p equations, where p is the desired number of modes considered for the reduced MDOF system. This is referred to as the modal equation of motion.

Orthogonality condition gives

$$\phi^T_r M\phi_s = 0 \quad \text{for} \quad \omega_r \neq \omega_s \qquad (10.26)$$

and

$$\phi^T_r K\phi_s = 0 \quad \text{for} \quad \omega_r \neq \omega_s \qquad (10.27)$$

$\phi_r = r^{\text{th}}$ mode shape vector, size $n \times 1$
$\phi_s = s^{\text{th}}$ mode shape vector, size $n \times 1$

It is assumed that similar orthogonality relation applies to damping also, provided it is a classical damping

$$\phi^T_r C\phi_s = 0 \quad \text{for} \quad \omega_r \neq \omega_s \qquad (10.48)$$

After applying all the orthogonality conditions Equations (10.26), (10.27) and (10.48) in Equation (10.47b), all the terms for mass, stiffness and damping in Equation (10.47b) for which $r \neq s$ will vanish. Therefore, Equation (10.47b) will be reduced to equation of a SDOF system for r^{th} mode:

$$m_r\ddot{y}_r + c_r\dot{y}_r + k_r y_r = p_r(t) \qquad (10.49)$$

where

$$m_r = \phi^T_r M\phi_r$$

Similarly,

$$k_r = \phi^T_r K\phi_r = \omega^2_r m_r$$

m_r = generalized mass
c_r = generalized damping
k_r = generalized stiffness
p_r = generalized force $= \phi^T_r P(t)_{n\times 1}$

Equation (10.49) is the decoupled modal equation of motion of the MDOF system for r^{th} mode. This is equation of a SDOF system since all quantities are scalar. This equation of motion can also be written as:

$$\ddot{y}_r + 2\xi_r \omega_r \, \dot{y}_r + \omega_r^2 y_r = \frac{p_r(t)}{m_r}$$ (10.50)

where ξ_r = modal damping

Thus, we get p decoupled or independent equations of motion for the p modes. These SDOF equations of motion can be solved by any method discussed earlier. Knowing the generalized displacement in each mode, the geometric displacements can be obtained by making use of normal coordinate transformation in Equation (10.46).

The method to obtain the response is referred to as the *Mode Superposition Method*. For most structures, the contributions of the various modes generally are greatest for the lowest frequencies and tend to decrease for the higher frequencies except under certain conditions. Consequently, it is not necessary to include all modes of vibration in the superposition process. The series of Equation (10.46) can be truncated when the response has been obtained to any desired degree of accuracy.

10.9 SOLUTION OF UNDAMPED FREE VIBRATION ANALYSIS

Once the equations of motion of a MDOF system have been decoupled, it is convenient to determine the solution for undamped free vibration analysis. It was shown in Chapter 2 that for a SDOF system,

$$x(t) = A \sin \omega t + B \cos \omega t$$

or, $$x(t) = \frac{\dot{x}(0)}{\omega} \sin \omega t + x(0) \cos \omega t$$

These equations can be written for the decoupled equations of motion for a set of 'n' SDOF systems.

Let us consider $$\{X\}_{n \times 1} = [\Phi]_{n \times p} \{Y\}_{p \times 1}$$ (10.46)

It is possible to evaluate $\{Y\}_{p \times 1}$. Let us multiply both sides by $\phi_r^T m$

$$\{\phi_r\}^T [M]\{X\} = \{\phi_r\}^T [M]_{n \times n} [\Phi]_{n \times p} \{Y\}_{p \times 1}$$

Due to orthogonality condition, this equation will be reduced to

$$\{\phi_r\}^T [M]\{X\} = \{\phi_r\}^T [M]_{n \times n} \{\phi_r\} y_r$$

Thus, $$y_r = \frac{\{\phi_r\}^T [M]\{X\}}{\{\phi_r\}^T [M]_{n \times n} \{\phi_r\}}$$ (10.51)

For initial conditions, it can be written as:

$$y_r(0) = \frac{\phi_r^T [M]\{x(0)\}}{\phi_r^T M \phi_r}$$ (10.52a)

and

$$\dot{y}_r(0) = \frac{\phi_r^T [M]\{\dot{x}(0)\}}{\phi_r^T M \phi_r}$$ (10.52b)

By making use of Equation (10.46), the initial displacement and velocity can also be written as:

$$x(0) = \sum_{r=1}^{n} \phi_r y_r(0) \tag{10.53a}$$

and

$$\dot{x}(0) = \sum_{r=1}^{n} \phi_r \dot{y}_r(0) \tag{10.53b}$$

Final solution is given by

$$x(t) = \sum_{r=1}^{n} \phi_r y_r(t) \tag{10.54a}$$

where

$$y_r(t) = y_r(0)\cos\omega_r t + \frac{\dot{y}_r(0)}{\omega_r}\sin\omega_r t \tag{10.54b}$$

10.10 RESPONSE SPECTRUM ANALYSIS

Let us develop the response spectrum analysis procedure to determine the response of a structure due to earthquake ground motion *identical at all supports*. The decoupled equation of motion can be written as follows:

$$m_r \ddot{y}_r + c_r \dot{y}_r + k_r y_r = \phi_r^T p(t) = -\phi_r^T MI\ddot{y}_g(t) \tag{10.55}$$

where $\ddot{y}_g(t)$ is ground acceleration– time history

$$p(t) = -MI\ddot{y}_g(t) \tag{10.56}$$

Equation (10.55) can be re-written as follows:

$$\ddot{y}_r + 2\xi_r \omega_r \dot{y}_r + \omega_r^2 y_r = \frac{\bar{m}}{m_r}\ddot{y}_g(t) \quad \text{neglecting sign}$$

Term $\bar{m}$ is defined as follows:

$$\bar{m} = \phi_r^T [M]\{I\} \tag{10.57}$$

I = identity vector, size $n \times 1$

The ratio $\dfrac{\bar{m}}{m_r}$ is defined as follows:

$$\Gamma_r = \frac{\phi_r^T [M]\{I\}}{\phi_r^T M\phi_r} \tag{10.58}$$

where

Γ_r = modal participation factor in r^{th} mode
The symbol Γ is pronounced as Gamma.

For a lumped mass system or a system having diagonal mass matrix, Equation (10.58) can be written as follows:

$$\Gamma_r = \frac{\sum_{i=1}^{n} m_i \phi_i}{\sum_{i=1}^{n} m_i \phi_i^2} \tag{10.59}$$

It gives the contribution of each mode.

$$y_r = \Gamma_r S_d \qquad (10.60)$$

It gives modal displacement for the rth mode.

For a SDOF, the Duhamel's integral gives (Equation (8.5b), Chapter 8)

$$|y(t)|_{max} = \frac{1}{\omega}|S_v| = S_d$$

$$S_v = \omega S_d \quad \text{and} \quad S_a = \omega^2 S_d$$

∴ The geometric displacement vector for the rth mode is given by

$$\{x_r\} = \{\phi_r\}y_r = \{\phi_r\}\Gamma_r S_d \qquad (10.61)$$

By modal superposition, the final displacement vector can be obtained.

$$\{X(t)\}_{n\times1} = [\Phi]_{n\times p}\{Y(t)\}_{p\times1} = [\Phi]_{n\times p}\{\Gamma_r S_d\}_{p\times1} \qquad (10.62)$$

10.10.1 Member Forces

Elastic forces in members of the structure are given by

$$\{f_s(t)\} = [K]\{X(t)\} = [K][\Phi]\{Y(t)\} \qquad (10.63)$$

Also, we know that $[K][\Phi] = [M][\Phi][\Omega^2]$

∴ $$\{f_s(t)\} = [M][\Phi][\Omega^2]\{Y(t)\}$$

or, $$\{f_s\} = [M]_{n\times n}[\Phi]_{n\times p}\{\Gamma_r \omega_r^2 S_d\}_{p\times1} \qquad (10.64)$$

or, for each mode,

$$\{f_{s,r}(t)\}_{n\times1} = [M]_{n\times n}\{\phi_r\}_{n\times1}\Gamma_r \omega_r^2 S_d \qquad (10.65)$$

For each ith dof in the rth mode,

$$f_{i,r} = m_i \phi_r^i \Gamma_r \omega_r^2 S_d \qquad (10.66a)$$

or,

$$f_{i,r} = m_i g \phi_r^i \Gamma_r \frac{S_a}{g} \qquad (10.66b)$$

$$= \frac{S_a}{g}\phi_r^i \Gamma_r W_i \qquad (10.67)$$

where

W_i = weight at the ith DOF

ϕ_r^i = r^{th} mode shape ordinate for the ith DOF

This is the same equation as that of Clause 7.8.4.5 (c) of IS:1893 Code to compute force at the ith floor in the rth mode of a building. The code accounts for seismicity, importance and ductile behaviour of a structure and modifies S_a/g with these dimensionless parameters while retaining its units.

10.10.2 Modal Mass

Let us re-consider Equation (10.64)

$$\{f_s\}_{n\times1} = [M]_{n\times n}[\Phi]_{n\times p}\{\Gamma_r\omega_r^2 S_d\}_{p\times1}$$

where, n = total degrees of freedom
p = number of modes considered in analysis $\leq n$
It can be written as follows:

$$\{f_s\}_{n\times1} = [M]_{n\times n}[\Phi]_{n\times p}\{\Gamma_r S_a\}_{p\times1} \qquad (10.68)$$

Let us expand only $[M]_{n\times n}[\Phi]_{n\times p}$ for convenience

$$[M]_{n\times n}[\Phi]_{n\times p} = \begin{bmatrix} m_1 & 0 & 0 & 0 & 0 & 0 \\ 0 & m_2 & 0 & 0 & 0 & 0 \\ 0 & 0 & m_3 & 0 & 0 & 0 \\ 0 & 0 & 0 & m_i & 0 & 0 \\ 0 & 0 & 0 & 0 & m_r & 0 \\ 0 & 0 & 0 & 0 & 0 & m_n \end{bmatrix} \times \begin{bmatrix} \phi_{11} & \phi_{12} & \phi_{13} & \phi_{1i} & \phi_{1r} & \phi_{1p} \\ \phi_{21} & \phi_{22} & \phi_{23} & \phi_{2i} & \phi_{2r} & \phi_{2p} \\ \phi_{31} & \phi_{32} & \phi_{33} & \phi_{3i} & \phi_{3r} & \phi_{3p} \\ \phi_{i1} & \phi_{i2} & \phi_{i3} & \phi_{ii} & \phi_{ir} & \phi_{ip} \\ \phi_{r1} & \phi_{r2} & \phi_{r3} & \phi_{ri} & \phi_{rr} & \phi_{rp} \\ \phi_{n1} & \phi_{n2} & \phi_{n3} & \phi_{ni} & \phi_{nr} & \phi_{np} \end{bmatrix}$$

Due to the diagonal nature of mass matrix with all off-diagonals being zero, this product can be written as follows:

$$[M]_{n\times n}[\Phi]_{n\times p} = \begin{bmatrix} m_1\phi_{11} & 0 & 0 & 0 & 0 & 0 \\ 0 & m_2\phi_{22} & 0 & 0 & 0 & 0 \\ 0 & 0 & m_3\phi_{33} & 0 & 0 & 0 \\ 0 & 0 & 0 & m_i\phi_{ii} & 0 & 0 \\ 0 & 0 & 0 & 0 & m_r\phi_{rr} & 0 \\ 0 & 0 & 0 & 0 & 0 & m_n\phi_{np} \end{bmatrix}$$

Thus, Equation (10.68) becomes

$$\{f_s\}_{n\times1} = \begin{Bmatrix} f_1 \\ f_2 \\ f_3 \\ f_i \\ f_r \\ f_n \end{Bmatrix}_{n\times1} = \begin{bmatrix} m_1\phi_{11} & 0 & 0 & 0 & 0 & 0 \\ 0 & m_2\phi_{22} & 0 & 0 & 0 & 0 \\ 0 & 0 & m_3\phi_{33} & 0 & 0 & 0 \\ 0 & 0 & 0 & m_i\phi_{ii} & 0 & 0 \\ 0 & 0 & 0 & 0 & m_r\phi_{rr} & 0 \\ 0 & 0 & 0 & 0 & 0 & m_n\phi_{np} \end{bmatrix}_{n\times p} \left\{\sum_{i=1}^{p}\Gamma_i S_{ai}\right\}_{p\times1}$$

The base shear can be determined by adding all the lateral forces from top downwards:

$$V_{\text{Bi}} = \sum_{i=1}^{n} f_i = \left(\sum m_i\phi_i\right)\left(\Gamma_i S_{ai}\right)$$

$$V_{Bi} = \left(\sum_{i=1}^{n} m_i \phi_i \right) \left(\frac{\sum_{i=1}^{n} m_i \phi_i}{\sum_{i=1}^{n} m_i \phi_i^2} (S_{ai}) \right)$$

or

Base shear in i^{th} mode $V_{Bi} = \left(\frac{\left(\sum_{i=1}^{n} m_i \phi_i \right)^2}{\sum_{i=1}^{n} m_i \phi_i^2} \right) (S_{ai})$ (10.69a)

S_{ai} = Spectral acceleration in i^{th} mode corresponding to natural frequency ω_i and damping ξ.

The modal mass in each mode is given by

$$\left(\frac{\left(\sum_{i=1}^{n} m_i \phi_i \right)^2}{\sum_{i=1}^{n} m_i \phi_i^2} \right)$$ (10.69b)

10.10.3 Mode Superposition

In the response spectrum method, there are two distinct stages to get the response. First, to determine the response in a given r^{th} mode. Second, to determine the final or total response. This second stage is referred to as the *mode superposition*. The term response refers to any parameter of interest such as displacement, axial force, shear force, bending moment, storey shear and support reactions. The response spectrum method gives the maximum response or value of a given parameter for each mode. It must then be super-imposed to get the total response. The time variation of a real earthquake at a given location is unknown. Therefore, it is not possible to determine the time variation of response either for a modal component or for the total value. If the absolute value of each modal maxima is added numerically, obviously, it will lead to a very conservative upper bound.

$$\Lambda = |\Lambda_1| + |\Lambda_2| + |\Lambda_3| + |\Lambda_4| + \ldots + |\Lambda_n|$$ (10.70)

Therefore the absolute sum ABSSUM modal combination rule is not used in structural dynamics

The other alternative is to make use of a probable value of the maximum response, which can be obtained by taking the *square root of the sum of the squares* (SRSS) of a given parameter.

$$\Lambda = \sqrt{\Lambda_1^2 + \Lambda_2^2 + \Lambda_3^2 + \ldots \Lambda_n^2}$$ (10.71)

where the symbol Λ is read as lambda.

This is also referred to as the SRSS value of a given parameter. This is based on the assumption that modal components are random variables which is consistent with the random nature of the input, that is earthquake motion. The accuracy of the SRSS value will increase with the increase in number of modes. The SRSS value is recommended by most building codes.

10.10.4 Closely Spaced Modes

In many practical situations, it has been observed that natural frequencies in any two consecutive modes may be equal or very close to each other. The SRSS method of superposition does not give correct estimation of the total response in such situations. Therefore, another method known as *complete quadratic combination* (CQC) method is used. It can be stated as follows:

$$\Lambda = \sqrt{\sum_{i=1}^{r}\sum_{j=1}^{r}\Lambda_i \rho_{ij}\Lambda_j} \tag{10.72}$$

where

r = number of modes being considered
Λ_i = response quantity in i^{th} mode with sign
Λ_j = response quantity in j^{th} mode with sign
ρ_{ij} = cross-correlation coefficient

$$\rho_{ij} = \frac{8\xi^2\left(1+\beta\right)\beta^{1.5}}{\left(1-\beta^2\right)^2 + 4\xi^2\beta(1+\beta)^2} \tag{10.73}$$

β = frequency ratio = ω_i/ω_j
ξ = damping ratio

Any two consecutive modes are treated as closely spaced if the difference in the frequencies is less than 10%.

A plot of the cross-correlation parameter is shown in Figure 10.4 to demonstrate its physical meaning. The CQC method is recommended by most building codes for closely spaced modes.

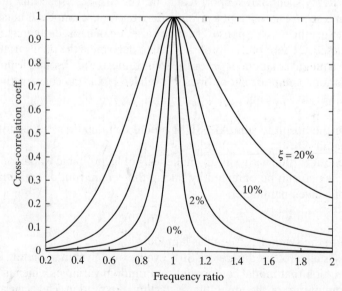

Figure 10.4   Variation of cross-correlation coefficient with frequency ratio and damping.

10.10.5 Minimum Number of Modes

Ideally the response contribution of all the modes must be accounted for in the mode superposition method to obtain an accurate result. The question is how many minimum modes would be sufficient for the modal analysis? In many structures, the contribution of the first p modes would give sufficiently accurate result. The numerical value of p depends upon the dynamic characteristics of a structure. In typical regular symmetric multistoried buildings the response contribution from the first 3 to 5 modes is usually sufficient. In cable roofs the number of modes required is usually very large. The contribution of higher modes is quite significant in many structures and needs to be incorporated. The minimum number of modes may be decided such that the total modal mass considered in any modal analysis is at least 90%.

10.11 ILLUSTRATIVE EXAMPLES

Example 10.1

Consider a three-DOF spring mass system shown in Figure 10.5. Determine its frequencies and mode shapes. Given: $m_1 = 2$ m, $m_2 = 3$ m, $m_3 = 2$ m; $k_1 = k$, $k_2 = 2$ k, $k_3 = 2$ k.

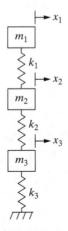

Figure 10.5   Three DOF spring – mass system.

Solution   The equations of motion can be written by considering the dynamic equilibrium of each mass:

$$m_1\ddot{x}_1 + k_1(x_1 - x_2) = 0$$

$$m_2\ddot{x}_2 + k_2(x_2 - x_3) + k_1(x_2 - x_1) = 0 \tag{i}$$

$$m_3\ddot{x}_3 + k_3x_3 + k_2(x_3 - x_2) = 0$$

It may be noted that the DOF may be numbered either from top or from bottom. In the present case, these have been numbered from top. The equations will change accordingly. The mass matrix can be written as follows:

It is given that: $m_1 = 2$ m, $m_2 = 3$ m, and $m_3 = 2$ m

$$[M] = \begin{bmatrix} 2m & 0 & 0 \\ 0 & 3m & 0 \\ 0 & 0 & 2m \end{bmatrix}$$

The stiffness matrix can be written as follows by rearranging Equation (i) in matrix form:

$$[K] = \begin{bmatrix} k_1 & -k_1 & 0 \\ -k_1 & k_1 + k_2 & -k_2 \\ 0 & -k_2 & k_2 + k_3 \end{bmatrix}$$

Given $k_1 = k$, $k_2 = 2$ k and $k_3 = 2$ k
On substitution, we get

$$[K] = k \begin{bmatrix} 1 & -1 & 0 \\ -1 & 3 & -2 \\ 0 & -2 & 4 \end{bmatrix}$$

$$\det\left|K - m\omega^2\right| = \begin{vmatrix} k - 2m\omega^2 & -k & 0 \\ -k & 3k - 3m\omega^2 & -2k \\ 0 & -2k & 4k - 2m\omega^2 \end{vmatrix}$$

Let $k/m = \beta$
The expression for determinant can be written as follows:

$$\det\left|k - m\omega^2\right| = \begin{vmatrix} \beta - 2\omega^2 & -\beta & 0 \\ -\beta & 3\beta - 3\omega^2 & -2\beta \\ 0 & -2\beta & 4\beta - 2\omega^2 \end{vmatrix}$$

Or, it can be expanded as follows:

$$6(\omega^2)^3 - 21\beta(\omega^2)^2 + 16\beta^2(\omega^2) - 2\beta^3 = 0$$

Its three positive roots are given as follows:

$$\{\omega^2\} = \begin{bmatrix} 2.477\beta \\ 0.866\beta \\ 0.155\beta \end{bmatrix} \quad \text{or} \quad \{\omega\} = \begin{bmatrix} 1.574 \\ 0.93 \\ 0.394 \end{bmatrix} \sqrt{\frac{k}{m}}$$

Now mode shapes can be determined for each frequency using the following expression:

$$\left[K - m\omega^2\right]\{X\} = \{0\}$$

$$\begin{bmatrix} \beta - 2\omega^2 & -\beta & 0 \\ -\beta & 3\beta - 3\omega^2 & -2\beta \\ 0 & -2\beta & 4\beta - 2\omega^2 \end{bmatrix} \begin{Bmatrix} x_1 \\ x_2 \\ x_3 \end{Bmatrix} = \begin{Bmatrix} 0 \\ 0 \\ 0 \end{Bmatrix} \quad \text{(ii)}$$

Let us obtain the eigenvector corresponding to $\lambda_3 = \omega_3^2 = 2.477 \beta$. Its value is substituted in Equation (ii), we get

$$\begin{bmatrix} -3.954 & -1 & 0 \\ -1 & -4.431 & -2 \\ 0 & -2 & -0.954 \end{bmatrix} \begin{Bmatrix} x_{13} \\ x_{23} \\ x_{33} \end{Bmatrix} = \begin{Bmatrix} 0 \\ 0 \\ 0 \end{Bmatrix}$$

Upon simplification,

$$-3.954x_{13} - x_{23} + 0 = 0 \qquad \text{(iii)}$$

$$-x_{13} - 4.431x_{23} - 2x_{33} = 0 \qquad \text{(iv)}$$

$$-2x_{23} - 0.954x_{33} = 0 \qquad \text{(v)}$$

Equation (iii) and Equation (v) give,

$$\frac{x_{13}}{x_{23}} = \frac{-1}{3.954} \text{ and } \frac{x_{23}}{x_{33}} = \frac{-0.954}{2} = \frac{-0.477}{1}$$

If the value of x_{33} in terms of x_{23} is substituted in Equation (iv), it gives the same ratio of x_{13} and x_{23} as before.

∴ In such cases, only the ratio of the elements is determined. A numerical value for each element of the eigenvector $\{x_3\}$ may be obtained by arbitrarily assigning any one element as unity. For example, if x_{13} is assigned a unity, then

$$x_{23} = -3.954 \text{ and } x_{33} = 8.289$$

This procedure is repeated for other eigenvalues as well.
For first mode, $\omega_1^2 = 0.155\,\beta$, and $x_{11} = 1$

$$\begin{Bmatrix} x_{11} \\ x_{21} \\ x_{31} \end{Bmatrix} = \begin{Bmatrix} 1.000 \\ 0.689 \\ 0.374 \end{Bmatrix}$$

For second mode, $\omega_2^2 = 0.866\,\beta$, and $x_{12} = 1$

$$\begin{Bmatrix} x_{12} \\ x_{22} \\ x_{32} \end{Bmatrix} = \begin{Bmatrix} 1.364 \\ -1 \\ -0.882 \end{Bmatrix}$$

For third mode $\omega_3^2 = 2.477\,\beta$, and $x_{13} = 1$

$$\begin{Bmatrix} x_{13} \\ x_{23} \\ x_{33} \end{Bmatrix} = \begin{Bmatrix} 1.0 \\ -3.954 \\ 8.289 \end{Bmatrix}$$

Alternatively, it can be normalized with respect to $x_{33} = 1$ instead of $x_{13} = 1$

or,

$$\begin{Bmatrix} x_{13} \\ x_{23} \\ x_{33} \end{Bmatrix} = \begin{Bmatrix} 0.1206 \\ -0.477 \\ 1.0 \end{Bmatrix}$$

The mode shape matrix can be written as follows by arranging them column-wise or row-wise. In this case they have been arranged column-wise.

$$[\Phi] = \begin{bmatrix} \phi_{11} & \phi_{12} & \phi_{13} \\ \phi_{21} & \phi_{22} & \phi_{23} \\ \phi_{31} & \phi_{32} & \phi_{33} \end{bmatrix}$$

where in ϕ_{ij}, i represents DOF and j represents mode number

$$[\Phi] = \begin{bmatrix} 1.000 & 1.364 & 0.121 \\ 0.689 & -1 & -0.477 \\ 0.374 & -0.882 & 1.0 \end{bmatrix}$$

The mode shapes are shown in Figure 10.6.

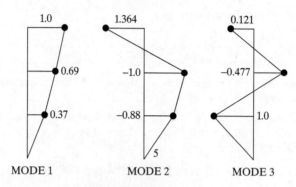

Figure 10.6 Mode shapes.

Let us verify the results using MATLAB.

The command eig(K, M) gives two matrices V and D. Matrix V is for eigenvectors arranged column-wise and matrix D is a diagonal matrix consisting of eigenvalues on the diagonal. The frequencies are obtained as follows:

$$\lambda = \omega^2$$

>>$[V, D] = \text{eig}(K, M)$
$V =$

$$\begin{matrix} -0.5195 & -0.4741 & 0.0734 \\ -0.3582 & 0.3476 & -0.2902 \\ -0.1942 & 0.3066 & 0.6069 \end{matrix}$$

$D =$

$$\begin{matrix} 0.1552 & 0 & 0 \\ 0 & 0.8665 & 0 \\ 0 & 0 & 2.4782 \end{matrix}$$

$$\therefore \qquad \omega^2 = \begin{Bmatrix} 0.1552 \\ 0.8665 \\ 2.4782 \end{Bmatrix} \frac{k}{m} \quad \text{or} \quad \omega = \begin{Bmatrix} 0.394 \\ 0.930 \\ 1.574 \end{Bmatrix} \sqrt{\frac{k}{m}}$$

In this option, the eigenvalues are obtained in increasing order.

Alternatively, the following command can be given in MATLAB.

>> $[V, D] = \text{eig}(M, K)$

It again generates two matrices V and D. Matrix V is for eigenvectors arranged column-wise and matrix D is a diagonal matrix consisting of eigenvalues on the diagonal. The frequencies are obtained as follows:

$$\lambda = 1/\omega^2$$

```
>>[V, D] = eig(M, K)
V =
      -0.0466    0.5093    1.3185
       0.1844   -0.3734    0.9092
      -0.3855   -0.3294    0.4928
D =
       0.4035       0           0
          0       1.1540        0
          0          0       6.4425
```

$$\omega^2 = \begin{cases} \dfrac{1}{0.4035} \\ \dfrac{1}{1.1540} \\ \dfrac{1}{6.4425} \end{cases} \dfrac{k}{m} \quad \text{or} \quad \omega = \begin{cases} 1.574 \\ 0.93 \\ 0.394 \end{cases} \sqrt{\dfrac{k}{m}}$$

In this option, the eigenvalues are obtained in decreasing order.   □

Example 10.2

Determine the eigenvalues of the matrix A using the power method and matrix deflation method.

$$[A] = \begin{bmatrix} 11 & 5 & 2 \\ 5 & 5 & 2 \\ 2 & 2 & 2 \end{bmatrix}$$

Background
The characteristic eigenvalue problem is defined as follows:

$$[A]_{n \times n} \{X\}_{n \times 1} = \lambda \{X\}_{n \times 1} \tag{10.19a}$$

where,

λ = eigenvalue, a scalar quantity
X = eigenvector

In this equation, λ may be considered as a scale factor. Let us assume that it is unity. We can write it as follows:

$$[A]\{X\}^i = \{X\}^{i+1}$$

The power method is an iterative method. It always converges to the highest eigenvalue of the coefficient matrix [A]. In this method, a value of the vector $\{X\}^i$ on the left-hand side is assumed, it is pre-multiplied with [A] and the right-hand side vector $\{X\}^{i+1}$ is obtained. The right-hand side vector $\{X\}^{i+1}$ is normalized with respect to any term, say $x(1)$. It means, $x(1)$ is taken as a common factor and the remaining vector is expected to be close to the assumed left-hand side vector $\{X\}^i$. The next iteration is carried out with this normalized vector on the left-hand side. The iteration is continued till the two consecutive values of the common factor $x(1)$ are close enough. The common factor $x(1)$ is the eigenvalue. The vector $\{X\}$ is the eigenvector.

The second and subsequent eigenvalues and eigenvectors are obtained after carrying out deflation operation on the coefficient matrix [A] by making use of the orthogonality condition. The entire process is illustrated in the following example.

Solution
Power Method
Let us assume $\{X\} = \{I\}$ unity vector
Now we operate on the left side of the characteristic equation and determine vector on the right side.

$$[A]\{X\} = \begin{bmatrix} 11 & 5 & 2 \\ 5 & 5 & 2 \\ 2 & 2 & 2 \end{bmatrix}\begin{Bmatrix} 1 \\ 1 \\ 1 \end{Bmatrix} = \begin{Bmatrix} 18 \\ 12 \\ 6 \end{Bmatrix} = 18\begin{Bmatrix} 1 \\ 0.6667 \\ 0.3334 \end{Bmatrix}$$

Let us carryout the iterations in tabular form for convenience.

I Eigenvalue

Iteration	$\{X\}^T$	$\{X\}^T = \{[A]_{n\times n}\{X\}_{n\times 1}\}^T$	λ
1	$\{1 \quad 1 \quad 1\}$	$\{18 \quad 12 \quad 6\}$	18
2	$\{1 \quad 0.666 \quad 0.333\}$	$\{15 \quad 9 \quad 4\}$	15
3	$\{1 \quad 0.600 \quad 0.266\}$	$\{14.533 \quad 8.533 \quad 3.733\}$	14.533
4	$\{1 \quad 0.587 \quad 0.257\}$	$\{14.45 \quad 8.45 \quad 3.68\}$	14.45
7	$\{1 \quad 0.58424 \quad 0.25489\}$		14.4314

Thus, 7th iteration gives eigenvector and the corresponding eigenvalue.

II Eigenvalue

The second eigenvalue can be obtained using the *matrix deflation method*. It makes use of orthogonality condition.

$$\sum x_i^{(r)} x_i^{(s)} = 0$$

where $r \neq s$ mode

Let us assume that II mode eigenvector is $\{x_1 \quad x_2 \quad x_3\}$.

Therefore, let us apply orthogonality condition between mode 1 and mode 2, we get

$$1 \times x_1 + 0.58424 x_2 + 0.25489 x_3 = 0$$

$$\therefore \qquad x_1 = -0.58424 x_2 - 0.25489 x_3$$

$$x_2 = x_2$$

$$x_3 = x_3$$

Let us write these equations in matrix form:

$$\begin{Bmatrix} x_1 \\ x_2 \\ x_3 \end{Bmatrix} = \begin{bmatrix} 0 & -0.58424 & -0.25489 \\ 0 & -1 & 0 \\ 0 & 0 & 1 \end{bmatrix}\begin{Bmatrix} x_1 \\ x_2 \\ x_3 \end{Bmatrix}$$

or,

$$\{x\}_{3\times 1} = [R_1]_{n\times 1}\{x\}_{3\times 1}$$

$[R_1]$ = rotation matrix

$$[A][R_1] = [A_1]$$

$$\begin{bmatrix} 11 & 5 & 2 \\ 5 & 5 & 2 \\ 2 & 2 & 2 \end{bmatrix}\begin{bmatrix} 0 & -0.58424 & -0.25489 \\ 0 & -1 & 0 \\ 0 & 0 & 1 \end{bmatrix} = \begin{bmatrix} 0 & -1.4266 & -0.80379 \\ 0 & 2.0788 & 0.72555 \\ 0 & 0.83152 & 1.49022 \end{bmatrix}$$

Let us now iterate on A_1 as done earlier on A.

Iteration	$\{X\}^T$	$\{X\}^T = \{[A]_{n\times n}\{X\}_{n\times 1}\}^T$	λ
1	$\{1 \quad 1 \quad 1\}$	$\{-2.30 \quad 2.8043 \quad 2.3217\}$	2.23
2	$\{-1 \quad 1.2573 \quad 1.0409\}$	$\{-2.6304 \quad 3.3689 \quad 2.5966\}$	2.63
3	$\{-1 \quad 1.2807 \quad 0.98716\}$	$\{-2.62 \quad 3.3787 \quad 2.5966\}$	2.62
6	$\{-1 \quad 1.2934 \quad 0.9579\}$		2.6158

Thus, 6th iteration gives eigenvector and the corresponding eigenvalue.

III Eigenvalue

III eigenvector is orthogonal to both first and second eigenvectors.

Let III eigenvector be $\{x_1 \quad x_2 \quad x_3\}$.

Therefore, let us apply orthogonality condition between mode 3 and mode 1, we get

$$1\times x_1 + 0.58424x_2 + 0.25489x_3 = 0$$

or, $\qquad\qquad x_1 = -0.58424x_2 - 0.25489x_3$ $\qquad\qquad$ (i)

Between mode 3 and mode 2, we get

$$x_1 = 1.29348x_2 + 0.95797x_3 \qquad\qquad \text{(ii)}$$

Solving Equations (i) and (ii), in terms of x_3,

$$\begin{bmatrix} x_1 \\ x_2 \\ x_3 \end{bmatrix} = \begin{bmatrix} 0 & 0 & 0.12249 \\ 0 & 0 & -0.64593 \\ 0 & 0 & 1 \end{bmatrix} \begin{bmatrix} x_1 \\ x_2 \\ x_3 \end{bmatrix}$$

$$\{x\}_{3\times 1} = [R_2]_{n\times 1}\{x\}_{3\times 1}$$

$[R_2]$ = rotation matrix

$$[A_1][R_2] = [A_2]$$

or,

$$[A][R_1][R_2] = [A_2]$$

$$\therefore \qquad [A_2] = \begin{bmatrix} 0 & -1.4266 & -0.80379 \\ 0 & 2.0788 & 0.72555 \\ 0 & 0.83152 & 1.49022 \end{bmatrix} \begin{bmatrix} 0 & 0 & 0.12249 \\ 0 & 0 & -0.64593 \\ 0 & 0 & 1 \end{bmatrix}$$

or,

$$[A_2] = \begin{bmatrix} 0 & 0 & 0.1177 \\ 0 & 0 & -0.6172 \\ 0 & 0 & 0.9531 \end{bmatrix}$$

Let us now iterate on A_2 as done earlier on A and A_1.

Iteration	$\{X\}^T$	$\{X\}^T = \{[A]_{n \times n} \{X\}_{n \times 1}\}^T$	λ
1	$\{1 \quad 1 \quad 1\}$	$\{0.1177 \quad -0.6172 \quad 0.9531\}$	0.1177
2	$\{1 \quad -5.2438 \quad 8.0977\}$	$\{0.953 \quad -4.9979 \quad 7.7179\}$	0.953
3	$\{1 \quad -5.2443 \quad 8.0985\}$		0.953

The eigenvalues and eigenvectors are as follows:

$$\{\lambda\} = \begin{Bmatrix} 14.4314 \\ 2.6158 \\ 0.953 \end{Bmatrix} \text{ and } [\Phi] = \begin{bmatrix} 1 & -1 & 1 \\ 0.58424 & 1.2934 & -5.2443 \\ 0.25489 & 0.9579 & 8.0985 \end{bmatrix}$$

The eigenvalues so obtained are not frequencies of the matrix $[A]$.
The eigenvectors are arranged column-wise.   ☐

Example 10.3

Determine the eigenvalues of the Matrix $[A]$ using inverse iteration method.

$$[A] = \begin{bmatrix} 2 & 2 \\ 2 & 5 \end{bmatrix}$$

Background
The characteristic equation of eigenvalue can be written as follows:

$$[A]_{n \times n} \{X\}_{n \times 1} = \lambda \{X\}_{n \times 1} \tag{i}$$

Inverse Iteration Method
The eigenvalue term λ is treated as a scale factor and may be taken as unity. This equation can now be written as:

$$[A]\{X\}^{i+1} = \{X\}^i \tag{ii}$$

In this iterative method, the right-hand side vector $\{X\}^i$ is assumed and the left-hand side vector $\{X\}^{i+1}$ is determined. This equation is similar to the solution of linear simultaneous equation

$$[A]\{X\} = \{b\} \tag{iii}$$

where

$\{b\}$ = known R.H.S. vector
$\{x\}$ = unknown L.H.S. vector

We can make use of any method used to solve the set of linear simultaneous equations. Knowing the left-hand side vector, it is normalized with respect to any term, say, $x(1)$. In the subsequent iteration, this normalized vector is assumed on the right-hand side, and the un-normalized vector on the left-hand side is determined. The iterations are repeated till the two consecutive values of the normalized vector $x(1)$ are close enough. This is called *inverse iteration method* because the iterations are carried out in a direction opposite to that used in the power method.

Inverse Iteration Method with Shift

This is a very powerful iterative procedure as it improves the rate of convergence as well as it makes it converge to an eigenpair other than (λ_1, X_1). Let p be the shift in the origin of the eigenvalue axis.

Let $\bar{\lambda} = \lambda - p$, that is, shifted eigenvalue measured from the shifted origin   (iv)

Equation (i) can be written as follows:

$$\left([A] - (\bar{\lambda} + p)[I]\right)\{X\} = \{0\}$$

or,

$$\left([A] - p[I]\right)\{X\} = \bar{\lambda}\{X\}$$ (v)

or,

$$[B]_{n \times n}\{X\}_{n \times 1} = \bar{\lambda}\{X\}_{n \times 1}$$ (vi)

This method is based on the property that eigenvectors of Equations (i) and (vi) are the same. Knowing the eigenvector, the eigenvalue of Equation (vi) can be obtained using the Rayleigh quotient. Thus, eigenvalue of Equation (i) can be obtained using Equation (iv). The value of shift p can be obtained using Sturm sequence or the Gerschgorin's theorem.

Solution   Let us assume that a root of this matrix lies in the vicinity of 0.9. That is, shift $p = 0.9$

Then

$$\left(\begin{bmatrix} 2 & 2 \\ 2 & 5 \end{bmatrix} - 0.9 \begin{bmatrix} 1 & 0 \\ 0 & 1 \end{bmatrix}\right) \begin{Bmatrix} x_1 \\ x_2 \end{Bmatrix}^{(1)} = \begin{Bmatrix} x_1 \\ x_2 \end{Bmatrix}^{(0)}$$

$$\begin{bmatrix} 1.1 & 2 \\ 2 & 4.1 \end{bmatrix} \begin{Bmatrix} x_1 \\ x_2 \end{Bmatrix} = \begin{Bmatrix} x_1 \\ x_2 \end{Bmatrix}^{(0)}$$

$$\begin{Bmatrix} x_1 \\ x_2 \end{Bmatrix}^{(0)} = \text{normalized vector}$$

and

$$\begin{Bmatrix} x_1 \\ x_2 \end{Bmatrix}^{(1)} = \text{un-normalized vector}$$

Let us assume

$$\begin{Bmatrix} x_1 \\ x_2 \end{Bmatrix}^{(0)} = \begin{Bmatrix} 1 \\ 1 \end{Bmatrix} \text{ and solve for the left-hand side vector } \{x\}.$$

$$\text{Matrix } B = \begin{bmatrix} 1.1 & 2 \\ 2 & 4.1 \end{bmatrix}$$

Let us carry out the iterations as shown in the table. β is the common factor $x(1)$.

Iteration	Assumed $\{b\}$	$\{x\}=[B]^{-1}\{b\}$	β	Normalized vector
1	$\{1 \quad 1\}$	$\{4.14 \quad -1.17\}$	4.14	$\{1 - 0.428\}$
2	$\{1 \quad -0.428\}$	$\{9.766 \quad -4.870\}$	9.766	$\{1 \quad -0.498\}$
3	$\{1 \quad -0.498\}$	$\{10.021 \quad -5.020\}$	10.021	$\{1 \quad -0.50\}$
4	$\{1 \quad -0.50\}$		10.021	

It should be noted that in determining the L.H.S. vector $\{x\}$, inverse of B was not computed. Instead, Gauss elimination method was used.

$$\beta = (\lambda - p)^{-1} = 10.021$$

or,

$$(\lambda - p) = 10.021^{-1} = 0.10$$

or, eigenvalue $\lambda = 0.9 + 0.1 = 1.0$

This can also be verified using the Rayleigh quotient method:

$$\lambda = \frac{\{x\}^T [A]\{x\}}{\{x\}^T \{x\}} = \frac{\{1 \quad -0.5\}\begin{bmatrix} 2 & 2 \\ 2 & 5 \end{bmatrix}\begin{Bmatrix} 1 \\ -0.5 \end{Bmatrix}}{\{1 \quad -0.5\}\begin{Bmatrix} 1 \\ -0.5 \end{Bmatrix}} = 1.0$$

II Eigenvalue

Let second eigenvalue be in the vicinity of 4.

$$\left(\begin{bmatrix} 2 & 2 \\ 2 & 5 \end{bmatrix} - 4\begin{bmatrix} 1 & 0 \\ 0 & 1 \end{bmatrix}\right)\begin{Bmatrix} x_1 \\ x_2 \end{Bmatrix}^{(1)} = \begin{Bmatrix} x_1 \\ x_2 \end{Bmatrix}^{(0)}$$

Let us assume

$$\begin{Bmatrix} x_1 \\ x_2 \end{Bmatrix}^{(0)} = \begin{Bmatrix} 1 \\ 1 \end{Bmatrix}$$ and solve for the left hand side vector $\{x\}$.

Matrix $B = \begin{bmatrix} -2 & 2 \\ 2 & 1 \end{bmatrix}$

Let us again carry out the iterations in the table. In this case β is the common factor $x(2)$. Any element of $\{x\}$ can be taken as common.

Iteration	Assumed $\{b\}$	$\{x\}=[B]^{-1}\{b\}$	β	Normalized vector
1	$\{1 \quad 1\}$	$\{0.166 \quad 0.667\}$	0.667	$\{0.25 \quad 1.0\}$
2	$\{0.25 \quad 1.0\}$	$\{0.292 \quad 0.416\}$	0.416	$\{0.702 \quad 1.0\}$
3	$\{0.702 \quad 1.0\}$	$\{0.216 \quad 0.567\}$	0.567	$\{0.381 \quad 1.0\}$
10	$\{0.506 \quad 1.0\}$		0.496	

$$\beta = (\lambda - p)^{-1} = 0.496$$

or,

$$(\lambda - p) = 0.496^{-1} = 2.0$$

or, eigenvalue $\lambda = 2.0 + 4.0 = 6.0$

This can also be verified using the Rayleigh quotient method:

$$\lambda = \frac{\{x\}^T [A]\{x\}}{\{x\}^T \{x\}} = \frac{\{0.506 \quad 1.0\} \begin{bmatrix} 2 & 2 \\ 2 & 5 \end{bmatrix} \begin{Bmatrix} 0.506 \\ 1.0 \end{Bmatrix}}{\{0.506 \quad 1.0\} \begin{Bmatrix} 0.506 \\ 1.0 \end{Bmatrix}} = 5.99$$

The eigenvalues and eigenvectors are as follows:

$$\{\lambda\} = \begin{Bmatrix} 1 \\ 6 \end{Bmatrix} \quad \text{and} \quad [\Phi] = \begin{bmatrix} 1.0 & 0.506 \\ -0.5 & 1.0 \end{bmatrix} \qquad \square$$

Example 10.4

Consider a four-DOF undamped lumped mass system as shown in Figure 10.7. Determine its frequencies and mode shapes using Holtzer method.

Solution   It is given that all masses are equal ($= m$) and all spring stiffness are also equal ($= k$).

The DOF are numbered from the top as shown in the figure.

The Holtzer expression can be written as follows:

$$\phi_{n+1} = \phi_n - \frac{\omega^2}{k_n}\left(\sum_{i=1}^{n} m_i \phi_i\right) = 0 \quad \text{since base is fixed.} \qquad \text{(D.n)}$$

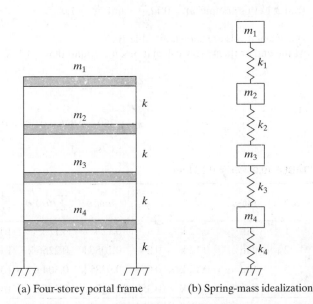

(a) Four-storey portal frame   (b) Spring-mass idealization

Figure 10.7   Four-DOF system.

Trial 1: Let $\omega^2 = 0.1\dfrac{k}{m}$ and $\phi_1 = 1.0$

At the beginning of a trial, it is not possible to predict the mode corresponding to the assumed value of ω^2. It will be known only when the final mode shape in available at the end of the trial.

Let us carryout the calculations shown in Equation (D.n) in tabular form for convenience. The calculations are carried out row-wise in the Table 10.1.

At the end of first row,

$$\phi_2 = \phi_1 - \frac{1}{k}\sum m_i \omega^2 \phi_i = 1.0 - 0.10 = 0.90$$

Now the calculations in row 2 can be done.

At the end of the 4th row calculations, it is found that

$$\phi_s = \phi_4 - \frac{1}{k}\sum m_i \omega^2 \phi_i \quad (\phi_s = \text{displacement of support})$$

Or,

$\therefore$ $\qquad\qquad\qquad \phi_s = 0.449 - 0.306 = 0.143 \neq 0$ Hence revise the calculations.

TABLE 10.1 $\omega^2 = 0.10$ k/m

S. No	mass	$m\omega^2$	ϕ	$m\omega^2\phi$	$\sum m_i\omega^2\phi_i$	$\dfrac{1}{k}$	$\dfrac{1}{k}\sum m_i\omega^2\phi_i$
1	m	0.1 k	1	0.1 k	0.1 k	1/k	0.10
2	m	0.1 k	0.9	0.09 k	0.19 k	1/k	0.19
3	m	0.1 k	0.71	0.071 k	0.261 k	1/k	0.261
4	m	0.1 k	0.449	0.0449 k	0.36 k	1/k	0.306

Trial 2: Let us assume $\omega^2 = 0.12\dfrac{k}{m}$ and $\phi_1 = 1.0$

The calculations are shown in Table 10.2.

At the end of the 4th row calculations, it is found that

$$\phi_s = \phi_4 - \frac{1}{k}\sum m_i \omega^2 \phi_i$$

or,

$$\phi_s = 0.350 - 0.346 = 0.004 \approx 0 \qquad \text{Hence OK}$$

TABLE 10.2 $\omega^2 = 0.12$ k/m

S. No	mass	$m\omega^2$	ϕ	$m\omega^2\phi$	$\sum m_i\omega^2\phi_i$	$\dfrac{1}{k}$	$\dfrac{1}{k}\sum m_i\omega^2\phi_i$
1	m	0.12 k	1	0.12 k	0.12 k	1/k	0.12
2	m	0.12 k	0.88	0.1056 k	0.2256 k	1/k	0.2256
3	m	0.12 k	0.654	0.0785 k	0.304 k	1/k	0.304
4	m	0.12 k	0.350	0.042 k	0.346 k	1/k	0.346

Thus, frequency is given by

$$\omega_1 = 0.346\sqrt{\frac{k}{m}}$$

and the mode shape is given by column 4. Its plot shows that it corresponds to the first mode.

Trial 3: Let us assume $\omega^2 = 1.0\dfrac{k}{m}$ and $\phi_1 = 1.0$

The calculations are shown in Table 10.3.
At the end of the 4th row calculations, it is found that

$$\phi_s = \phi_4 - \frac{1}{k}\sum m_i \omega^2 \phi_i$$

or, $\phi_s = -1 + 1 = 0$ Hence OK

The mode shapes are given by column 4 of Table 10.3. Its plot shows that it corresponds to the second mode.

The frequency is given by $\omega_2 = \sqrt{\dfrac{k}{m}}$

Trial 4: Let us assume $\omega^2 = 3.50\dfrac{k}{m}$ and $\phi_1 = 1.0$

The calculations are shown in Table 10.4.

At the end of the 4th row calculations, it is found that

$$\phi_s = \phi_4 - \frac{1}{k}\sum m_i \omega^2 \phi_i$$

TABLE 10.3 $\omega^2 = k/m$

S. No	mass	$m\omega^2$	ϕ	$m\omega^2\phi$	$\sum m_i\omega^2\phi_i$	$\dfrac{1}{k}$	$\dfrac{1}{k}\sum m_i\omega^2\phi_i$
1	m	k	1	k	k	1/k	1
2	m	k	0	k	k	1/k	1
3	m	k	−1	−k	0	1/k	0
4	m	k	−1	−k	−k	1/k	−1

TABLE 10.4 $\omega^2 = 3.50\, k/m$

S. No	mass	$m\omega^2$	ϕ	$m\omega^2\phi$	$\sum m_i\omega^2\phi_i$	$\dfrac{1}{k}$	$\dfrac{1}{k}\sum m_i\omega^2\phi_i$
1	m	3.50 k	1.0	3.5 k	3.5 k	1/k	3.5
2	m	3.50 k	−2.5	−8.75 k	−5.25 k	1/k	−5.25
3	m	3.50 k	2.75	9.625 k	4.375 k	1/k	4.375
4	m	3.50 k	−1.625	−5.6875 k	−1.3125 k	1/k	−1.3125

or, $\qquad \phi_s = -1.625 + 1.3125 = -0.3125 \neq 0$ $\qquad$ Hence revise it.

Trial 5: Let us assume $\omega^2 = 3.60\dfrac{k}{m}$ and $\phi_1 = 1.0$

The calculations are shown in Table 10.5.
At the end of the 4th row calculations, it is found that

$$\phi_s = \phi_4 - \frac{1}{k}\sum m_i\omega^2\phi_i$$

or, $\qquad \phi_s = -2.456 + 3.2256 = 0.7696 \neq 0$ $\qquad$ Hence revise it.

TABLE 10.5 $\quad \omega^2 = 3.60$ k/m

S. No	mass	$m\omega^2$	ϕ	$m\omega^2\phi$	$\sum m_i\omega^2\phi_i$	$\dfrac{1}{k}$	$\dfrac{1}{k}\sum m_i\omega^2\phi_i$
1	m	3.60 k	1.0	3.6 k	3.6 k	1/k	3.6
2	m	3.60 k	−2.6	−9.36 k	−5.76 k	1/k	−5.76
3	m	3.60 k	3.16	11.376 k	5.616 k	1/k	5.616
4	m	3.60 k	−2.456	−8.8416 k	−3.2256 k	1/k	−3.2256

Trials 4 and 5 show that the difference has reversed. That is, if $\omega^2 = 3.50$ k/m, then the final difference is −0.3125; while if $\omega^2 = 3.60$ k/m, then the final difference is 0.7696; It shows that the true value lies somewhere in between these two values. The correct value is $\omega^2 = 3.532$ k/m. It corresponds to mode 4.

Trial 6: Let us assume $\omega^2 = 2.35\dfrac{k}{m}$ and $\phi_1 = 1.0$

The calculations are shown in Table 10.6.
At the end of the 4th row calculations, it is found that

$$\phi_s = \phi_4 - \frac{1}{k}\sum m_i\omega^2\phi_i$$

or, $\qquad \phi_s = 1.5346 - 1.5440 = -0.01 \approx 0$ $\qquad$ Hence OK

TABLE 10.6 $\quad \omega^2 = 2.35$ k/m

S. No	mass	$m\omega^2$	ϕ	$m\omega^2\phi$	$\sum m_i\omega^2\phi_i$	$\dfrac{1}{k}$	$\dfrac{1}{k}\sum m_i\omega^2\phi_i$
1	m	2.35 k	1.0	2.35 k	2.35 k	1/k	2.35
2	m	2.35 k	−1.35	−3.1725 k	−0.8225 k	1/k	−0.8225
3	m	2.35 k	−0.5275	−1.2396 k	−2.062 k	1/k	−2.062
4	m	2.35 k	1.5346	3.6063 k	1.544 k	1/k	1.544

Frequency and mode shapes are as follows:

$$\{\omega^2\} = \begin{Bmatrix} 0.12 \\ 1 \\ 3.532 \\ 2.35 \end{Bmatrix} \frac{k}{m}$$

Or, re-arranging the frequencies in increasing order,

$$\{\omega\} = \begin{Bmatrix} 0.346 \\ 1 \\ 1.53 \\ 1.88 \end{Bmatrix} \sqrt{\frac{k}{m}}$$

The mode shapes are arranged column-wise as follows:

$$[\Phi] = \begin{bmatrix} 1 & 1 & 1 & 1 \\ 0.88 & 0 & -1.35 & -2.5 \\ 0.654 & -1 & -0.5275 & 2.75 \\ 0.35 & -1 & 1.5346 & -1.625 \end{bmatrix}$$

The first column represents mode 1, second column represents mode 2, third column represents mode 3 and fourth column represents mode 4. These mode shapes may be normalized with respect to any element in the respective column. Thus, 3rd mode shape is normalized with respect to 1.5346 while 4th mode shape is normalized with respect to 2.75. The final mode shapes are shown in Figure 10.8.

A mode shape can be identified based on how many times it intersects the mean position, that is, the vertical axis. The first mode shape does not intersect at all; the second mode shape intersects only once; the third mode shape intersects twice; and the fourth mode shape intersects three times. Thus, by looking at the numerical sign of the mode shape, its mode can be easily identified.

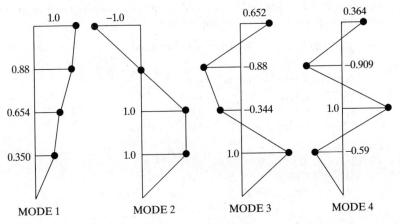

Figure 10.8   Mode shapes.

Let us verify the results using MATLAB.

MATLAB Solution

The mass matrix $M = m \begin{bmatrix} 1 & 0 & 0 & 0 \\ 0 & 1 & 0 & 0 \\ 0 & 0 & 1 & 0 \\ 0 & 0 & 0 & 1 \end{bmatrix}$

The stiffness matrix $K = \begin{bmatrix} k & -k & 0 & 0 \\ -k & 2k & -k & 0 \\ 0 & -k & 2k & -k \\ 0 & 0 & -k & 2k \end{bmatrix}$

>>$[V, D] = \text{eig}(K, M)$ % MATLAB Command

$V =$

$$\begin{matrix}
-0.6565 & -0.5774 & 0.4285 & -0.2280 \\
-0.5774 & -0.0000 & -0.5774 & 0.5774 \\
-0.4285 & 0.5774 & -0.2280 & -0.6565 \\
-0.2280 & 0.5774 & 0.6565 & 0.4285
\end{matrix}$$

$D =$

$$\begin{matrix}
0.1206 & 0 & 0 & 0 \\
0 & 1.0000 & 0 & 0 \\
0 & 0 & 2.3473 & 0 \\
0 & 0 & 0 & 3.5321
\end{matrix}$$

Thus,

$$\{\omega^2\} = \begin{Bmatrix} 0.1206 \\ 1 \\ 2.3473 \\ 3.5321 \end{Bmatrix} \frac{k}{m} \quad \text{or} \quad \{\omega\} = \begin{Bmatrix} 0.346 \\ 1 \\ 1.53 \\ 1.88 \end{Bmatrix} \sqrt{\frac{k}{m}}$$

In this case, the eigenvalues are obtained in increasing order. The mode shapes are available in $[V]$ in the corresponding column.

>>$[V, D] = \text{eig}(M, K)$ % MATLAB Command

$V =$

$$\begin{matrix}
0.1213 & -0.2797 & 0.5774 & 1.8904 \\
-0.3072 & 0.3768 & -0.0000 & 1.6624 \\
0.3493 & 0.1488 & -0.5774 & 1.2339 \\
-0.2280 & -0.4285 & -0.5774 & 0.6565
\end{matrix}$$

$D =$

$$\begin{matrix}
0.2831 & 0 & 0 & 0 \\
0 & 0.4260 & 0 & 0 \\
0 & 0 & 1.0000 & 0 \\
0 & 0 & 0 & 8.2909
\end{matrix}$$

Thus,

$$\{\omega^2\} = \begin{Bmatrix} 1/0.2831 \\ 1/0.4260 \\ 1 \\ 1/8.2909 \end{Bmatrix} \frac{k}{m} \quad \text{or} \quad \{\omega\} = \begin{Bmatrix} 1.88 \\ 1.53 \\ 1 \\ 0.346 \end{Bmatrix} \sqrt{\frac{k}{m}}$$

In this case, the eigenvalues are obtained in decreasing order. The mode shape are available in $[V]$ in the corresponding column. □

Example 10.5

Mass and stiffness matrices for a three-DOF system are as follows:

$$[M] = \begin{bmatrix} 2m & 0 & 0 \\ 0 & 3m & 0 \\ 0 & 0 & 2m \end{bmatrix} \quad \text{and} \quad [K] = k\begin{bmatrix} 1 & -1 & 0 \\ -1 & 3 & -2 \\ 0 & -2 & 4 \end{bmatrix}$$

Calculate the coefficient matrix of the standard eigenvalue problem and show if it is a unsymmetric matrix or a symmetric matrix.

Solution

(i) The standard eigenvalue problem is given as follows:

$$A\phi = \lambda\phi$$

where

$$[A]_{n\times n} = [M]^{-1}_{n\times n}[K]_{n\times n} \quad \text{and} \quad \lambda = \omega^2$$

Let us find $[M]^{-1}_{n\times n}$

$$[M]^{-1}_{n\times n} = \frac{1}{m}\begin{bmatrix} 0.5 & 0 & 0 \\ 0 & 0.333 & 0 \\ 0 & 0 & 0.5 \end{bmatrix}$$

Thus,

$$[A]_{n\times n} = [M]^{-1}_{n\times n}[K]_{n\times n}$$

$$[A] = \frac{1}{m}\begin{bmatrix} 0.5 & 0 & 0 \\ 0 & 0.333 & 0 \\ 0 & 0 & 0.5 \end{bmatrix} \times k\begin{bmatrix} 1 & -1 & 0 \\ -1 & 3 & -2 \\ 0 & -2 & 4 \end{bmatrix}$$

or,

$$[A] = \frac{k}{m}\begin{bmatrix} 0.5 & -0.5 & 0 \\ -0.333 & 1 & -0.666 \\ 0 & -1 & 2 \end{bmatrix}$$

It can be seen that the coefficient matrix is unsymmetric.

(ii) The coefficient matrix can also be written as follows:

$$[A]_{n\times n} = [K]^{-1}_{n\times n}[M]_{n\times n} \quad \text{and} \quad \lambda = \frac{1}{\omega^2}$$

Let us find $[K]_{n \times n}^{-1}$

$$[K]_{n \times n}^{-1} = \frac{1}{k} \begin{bmatrix} 2 & 1 & 0.5 \\ 1 & 1 & 0.5 \\ 0.5 & 0.5 & 0.5 \end{bmatrix}$$

Thus,

$$[A]_{n \times n} = [K]_{n \times n}^{-1} [M]_{n \times n}$$

$$[A] = \frac{1}{k} \begin{bmatrix} 2 & 1 & 0.5 \\ 1 & 1 & 0.5 \\ 0.5 & 0.5 & 0.5 \end{bmatrix} \times m \begin{bmatrix} 2 & 0 & 0 \\ 0 & 3 & 0 \\ 0 & 0 & 2 \end{bmatrix}$$

$$[A] = \frac{m}{k} \begin{bmatrix} 4 & 3 & 1 \\ 2 & 3 & 1 \\ 1 & 1.5 & 1 \end{bmatrix}$$

It can be seen that the coefficient matrix is again unsymmetric.

(iii) The coefficient matrix can also be written as follows:

$$By = \lambda y$$

where,

$$B = M^{-1/2} K M^{-1/2}$$

$$y = M^{1/2} \phi$$

$$\lambda = \omega^2$$

Let us first find $M^{1/2}$

$$M^{1/2} = \begin{bmatrix} 1.4142 & 0 & 0 \\ 0 & 1.7321 & 0 \\ 0 & 0 & 1.4142 \end{bmatrix}$$

$$M^{-1/2} = \begin{bmatrix} 0.7071 & 0 & 0 \\ 0 & 0.5774 & 0 \\ 0 & 0 & 0.7071 \end{bmatrix}$$

$$B = M^{-1/2} K M^{-1/2}$$

$$M^{-1/2} K = \begin{bmatrix} 0.7071 & -0.7071 & 0 \\ -0.5774 & 1.7321 & -1.1547 \\ 0 & -1.4142 & 2.8284 \end{bmatrix}$$

$$B = M^{-\frac{1}{2}} K M^{-\frac{1}{2}} = \begin{bmatrix} 0.5 & -0.4082 & 0 \\ -0.4082 & 1 & -0.8165 \\ 0 & -0.8165 & 2 \end{bmatrix}$$

It can be seen that the coefficient matrix B is a symmetric matrix. $\square$

Example 10.6

In a previous problem, the following mass matrix and stiffness matrix were employed. The corresponding eigenvalues and eigenvectors are also shown.

$$[M] = m\begin{bmatrix} 2 & 0 & 0 \\ 0 & 3 & 0 \\ 0 & 0 & 2 \end{bmatrix} \text{ and } [K] = k\begin{bmatrix} 1 & -1 & 0 \\ -1 & 3 & -2 \\ 0 & -2 & 4 \end{bmatrix}$$

$$\{\omega^2\} = \begin{Bmatrix} 2.4782\beta \\ 0.8665\beta \\ 0.1552\beta \end{Bmatrix} \quad [\Phi] = \begin{bmatrix} 0.5195 & -0.4741 & 0.0734 \\ 0.3582 & 0.3476 & -0.2902 \\ 0.1942 & 0.3066 & 0.6069 \end{bmatrix}$$

Check if the eigenvectors are orthogonal and orthonormal.

Solution   In mathematics, two vectors v_1 and v_2 are said to be orthogonal if their dot product is zero, that is,

$$v_{1_{1 \times n}}^T v_{2_{n \times 1}} = 0$$

In the dynamics of structures, two mode shapes are said to be orthogonal, if the following relation is satisfied:

$$[\Phi]^T [M][\Phi] = \text{A diagonal matrix} \tag{i}$$

or,

$$\phi_r^T M \phi_s = 0 \text{ for } \omega_r \neq \omega_s \tag{ii}$$

Similar relations exist for stiffness matrix.

Let us check using the dynamics of structures and carry out the following operation:

$$[\Phi]^T [M][\Phi] \tag{i}$$

On substituting the values of Φ and M in Equation (i), we get a diagonal matrix which happens to be an identity matrix.

$$\begin{bmatrix} 1 & 0 & 0 \\ 0 & 1 & 0 \\ 0 & 0 & 1 \end{bmatrix}$$

The orthogonality of mode shapes with respect to mass matrix is proved.
Similarly, consider the following operation:

$$[\Phi]^T [K][\Phi] \tag{iii}$$

On substituting the values of Φ and M in Equation (iii), we get a diagonal matrix.

$$\begin{bmatrix} 0.1552 & 0 & 0 \\ 0 & 0.8665 & 0 \\ 0 & 0 & 2.4782 \end{bmatrix}$$

The orthogonality of mode shapes with respect to stiffness matrix is proved.
Now, consider the first two eigenvectors

$$\phi_1 = \begin{Bmatrix} 0.5195 \\ 0.3582 \\ 0.1942 \end{Bmatrix} \text{ and } \phi_2 = \begin{Bmatrix} -0.4741 \\ 0.3476 \\ 0.3066 \end{Bmatrix}$$

Therefore, if ϕ_1 and ϕ_2 are orthogonal, then,

$$\phi_1^T M \phi_2 = 0 \tag{iv}$$

On substituting the values of mode shapes, we do get a zero.
Similarly, if ϕ_2 and ϕ_3 are orthogonal, then,

$$\phi_2^T M \phi_3 = 0 \tag{v}$$

It again gives a zero.
Similarly, if ϕ_1 and ϕ_3 are orthogonal, then,

$$\phi_1^T M \phi_3 = 0 \tag{vi}$$

It again gives a zero.
It can be concluded that the eigenvectors in the present case are orthogonal.
Similar results are obtained with respect to stiffness matrix.

Check vector norm
The first norm of a vector is denoted by $\|x\|$ and is defined as follows:

$$\|x\| = \sqrt{x^T x} = \left[\sum_1^n (x_i)^2 \right]^{1/2}$$

For eigenvector ϕ_1

$$\|\phi_1\| = \left[\sum_1^n (\phi_i)^2 \right]^{1/2}$$

or,

$$\|\phi_1\| = \sqrt{0.5195^2 + 0.3582^2 + 0.1942^2} = 0.6596$$

Eigenvector ϕ_1 can be normalized as follows:

$$1 = \|\phi_1\| = \phi_{11} \sqrt{0.5195^2 + 0.3582^2 + 0.1942^2} = \phi_{11} 0.66$$

or,
$$\phi_{11} = 1/0.66$$

or,
$$\phi_{10} = \frac{1}{0.66} \begin{Bmatrix} 0.5195 \\ 0.3582 \\ 0.1942 \end{Bmatrix}$$

This vector ϕ_{10} is called as orthonormal since it was already an orthogonal vector. Now it has also been normalized.
Similarly, eigenvector ϕ_2 can be normalized as follows:

$$1 = \|\phi_2\| = \phi_{21} \sqrt{-0.4741^2 + 0.3476^2 + 0.3066^2} = \phi_{21} 0.662$$

or,
$$\phi_{21} = 1/0.662$$

or,
$$\phi_{20} = \frac{1}{0.662} \begin{Bmatrix} -0.4741 \\ 0.3476 \\ 0.3066 \end{Bmatrix}$$

Similarly, eigenvector ϕ_3 can be normalized as follows:

$$1 = \|\phi_3\| = \phi_{31} \sqrt{(0.0734)^2 + (-0.2902)^2 + 0.6069^2} = \phi_{31} 0.676$$

or,
$$\phi_{30} = \frac{1}{0.676} \begin{Bmatrix} 0.0734 \\ -0.2902 \\ 0.6069 \end{Bmatrix}$$

Vectors ϕ_{10}, ϕ_{20} and ϕ_{30} are orthonormal vectors.   □

Example 10.7

Consider a two storey steel frame as shown in Figure 10.9. The dead load at the roof girder is 10 kN/m² and that at the first floor girder is 15 kN/m². The dead load due to walls lumped at the top columns is 35 kN each and that lumped at the lower columns is 70 kN each. The bent spacing is 5 m c/c. Determine its frequencies and mode shapes.

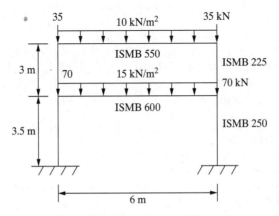

Figure 10.9 Two storey portal frame.

Solution

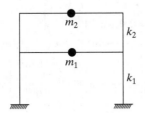

Figure 10.10(a) Idealized lumped mass system.

The properties of the ISMB steel sections used in this frame are as given in Table 10.7.

TABLE 10.7 PROPERTIES OF STEEL SECTIONS

Section	Moment of inertia cm⁴	Stiffness I/L	Least radius of gyration, cm	Slenderness ratio L/r
ISMB 225	3441	11.47	9.31	32.2
ISMB 250	5131	14.66	10.39	33.7
ISMB 550	64893	108.15	22.16	27.1
ISMB 600	91813	153.0	24.24	24.75

It can be seen that the girders are very rigid as compared to columns with respect to I/L ratio. Let us determine the storey lateral stiffness. It can be determined by using the basic principles of stiffness method of structural analysis. First, the first floor is held against translation and a unit displacement is given to the roof. Alternatively, an arbitrary load, say 10 kN, is applied at the roof level and the lateral displacement of roof is determined. Next, roof is held against translation, and a unit displacement is given to the first floor. Alternatively, an arbitrary load, say 10 kN, is applied at the floor level and the lateral displacement of the floor is determined. This can be done using any manual method or any computer program for matrix analysis.

It is important to mention here that this method gives better results when the beams are taken as rigid. The ratio of I/L of the beams and columns of a given storey is about 10 in the present case which shows that the beams are very rigid.

Storey Stiffness
Case 1 – First floor is held against translation
The displaced shape of the frame is shown in Figure 10.10(b). The roof displacement is 1.96 mm due to a 10 kN lateral load.

$$\text{Storey stiffness } k_2 = \frac{10}{1.96} = 5.10 \text{ kN/mm}$$

Case 2 – Roof is held against translation
The displaced shape of the frame is shown in Figure 10.10(c). The support lateral reactions are also shown. The floor displacement is 0.98 mm due to a 10 kN lateral load.
Lateral forces in the storeys are shown in Figures 10.10(d) and (e). Net storey shear in second storey is $V_2 = 5.01$ kN.

$$\text{The second storey stiffness } k_2 = \frac{V_2}{\Delta} = \frac{5.01}{0.98} = 5.10 \text{ kN/mm}$$

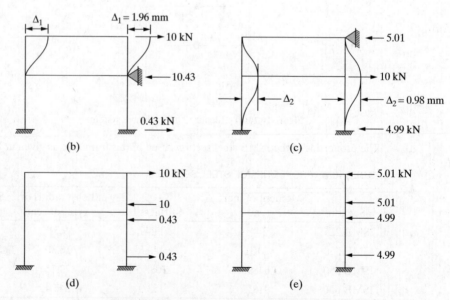

Figure 10.10(b-e) Storey stiffness calculations.

This is the same value as obtained in the earlier case.

Net storey shear in first storey is $V_1 = 4.99$ kN.

The first storey stiffness $k_1 = \dfrac{V_1}{\Delta} = \dfrac{4.99}{0.98} = 5.09$ kN/mm ≈ 5.10 kN/mm

Mass Calculations

Mass of the second storey can be lumped at the roof while that of the first storey can be lumped at the first floor.

$$\text{Mass } m_2 = \frac{35 + 35 + 10 \times 5 \times 6}{g} = \frac{370}{9.81} = 37.7 \approx 38 \frac{\text{kNs}^2}{\text{m}}$$

$$\text{Mass } m_1 = \frac{70 + 70 + 15 \times 5 \times 6}{g} = \frac{590}{9.81} = 60.14 \approx 60 \frac{\text{kNs}^2}{\text{m}}$$

The mass matrix is

$$[M] = \begin{bmatrix} 60 & 0 \\ 0 & 38 \end{bmatrix}$$

and stiffness matrix is

$$[K] = \begin{bmatrix} k_1 + k_2 & -k_1 \\ -k_1 & k_2 \end{bmatrix} = \begin{bmatrix} 10.2 & -5.1 \\ -5.1 & 5.1 \end{bmatrix}$$

Now the frequency and mode shapes can be determined by the methods discussed earlier.

$$\omega = \begin{Bmatrix} 6.618 \\ 16.137 \end{Bmatrix} \text{rad/sec} \quad \text{Period T} = \begin{Bmatrix} 0.95 \\ 0.39 \end{Bmatrix} \text{sec}$$

Mode shapes are given by

$$\Phi = \begin{bmatrix} 0.674 & -0.94 \\ 1 & 1 \end{bmatrix}$$

Mode shapes are shown in Figure 10.11.

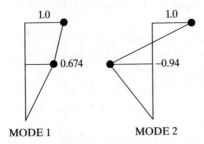

MODE 1   MODE 2

Figure 10.11   Mode shapes.

Let us check their orthogonality

$$\phi_1^T M \phi_2 = \{1 \quad 0.674\} \begin{bmatrix} 38 & 0 \\ 0 & 60 \end{bmatrix} \begin{Bmatrix} 1 \\ -0.94 \end{Bmatrix} = 0.0136 \approx 0 \qquad \text{OK}$$

Let us find the mode participation factors

$$\Gamma_r = \frac{\sum m_i \phi_i}{\sum m_i \phi_i^2}$$

For mode 1: $\Gamma_1 = \dfrac{60 \times 0.674 + 38 \times 1}{60 \times 0.674^2 + 38 \times 1^2} = \dfrac{78.44}{65.256} = 1.20$

For mode 2: $\Gamma_2 = \dfrac{60 \times (-0.94) + 38 \times 1}{60 \times 0.94^2 + 38 \times 1^2} = \dfrac{-18.4}{91} = -0.20$

It shows that the participation of the first mode is much higher than that of second mode in the present case. The sign in the mode participation factors does not have any significance.   □

Example 10.8

Consider a two bay × three storey RC frame as shown in Figure 10.12(a). The floor is rigid. The mass at the first floor girder, second floor girder and roof is 75, 75 and 50 kN-s²/m, respectively. The column sizes from top are: 300 × 300 mm, 300 × 350 mm, 300 × 400 mm. Determine the storey stiffness, frequencies and mode shapes. Grade of concrete is M25. Also, compute storey shears and floor forces using an elastic response spectra.

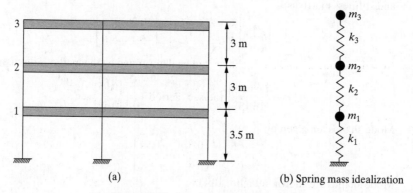

(a)   (b) Spring mass idealization

Figure 10.12   Two bay-three storey frame.

Solution   It may be noted that the DOF may be numbered either from top or from bottom. In the present case, these have been numbered from bottom. The equations of motion will change accordingly.

Modulus of elasticity of concrete $E_c = 5000\sqrt{fck} = 5000 \times 5 = 25000$ MPa

or, $E_c = 2500$ kN/cm²

Moment of inertia of top storey column = $\dfrac{bD^3}{12} = \dfrac{30 \times 30^3}{12} = 67500$ cm⁴

Moment of inertia of middle storey column = $\dfrac{bD^3}{12} = \dfrac{30 \times 35^3}{12} = 107200$ cm⁴

Moment of inertia of bottom storey column = $\dfrac{bD^3}{12} = \dfrac{30 \times 40^3}{12} = 160000$ cm⁴

Lateral stiffness of one column $k = \dfrac{12EI}{L^3}$

Lateral stiffness of top storey column $k = \dfrac{12EI}{L^3} = \dfrac{12 \times 2500 \times 67500}{300^3} = 75$ kN/cm

Lateral stiffness of middle storey column $k = \dfrac{12EI}{L^3} = \dfrac{12 \times 2500 \times 107200}{300^3} = 119$ kN/cm

Lateral stiffness of bottom storey column $k = \dfrac{12EI}{L^3} = \dfrac{12 \times 2500 \times 160000}{350^3} = 112$ kN/cm

The total lateral stiffness of top storey $k_3 = 3\,k = 22500$ kN/m
The total lateral stiffness of middle storey $k_2 = 3\,k = 35700$ kN/m
The total lateral stiffness of bottom storey $k_1 = 3\,k = 33600$ kN/m
Now a three DOF mass-spring model of the building can be developed as shown in Figure 10.12(b). Mass and stiffness matrices can be determined as follows:

$$[M] = \begin{bmatrix} m_1 & 0 & 0 \\ 0 & m_2 & 0 \\ 0 & 0 & m_3 \end{bmatrix} \quad [K] = \begin{bmatrix} k_1 + k_2 & -k_2 & 0 \\ -k_2 & k_2 + k_3 & -k_3 \\ 0 & -k_3 & k_3 \end{bmatrix}$$

$$[M] = \begin{bmatrix} 75 & 0 & 0 \\ 0 & 75 & 0 \\ 0 & 0 & 50 \end{bmatrix} \text{ and } [K] = \begin{bmatrix} 69300 & -35700 & 0 \\ -35700 & 58200 & -22500 \\ 0 & -22500 & 22500 \end{bmatrix}$$

$$\{\omega\} = \begin{Bmatrix} 10.30 \\ 25.42 \\ 37.38 \end{Bmatrix} \text{ rad/sec and } [\Phi] = \begin{bmatrix} 0.445 & 0.748 & -2.118 \\ 0.763 & 0.436 & 2.105 \\ 1.0 & -1.0 & -1.0 \end{bmatrix}$$

Mode shapes are shown in Figure 10.13.

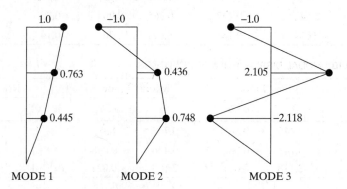

MODE 1   MODE 2   MODE 3

Figure 10.13   Mode shapes.

Let us find the mode participation factors

$$\Gamma_r = \frac{\sum m_i \phi_i}{\sum m_i \phi_i^2}$$

This can be done in a tabular form for convenience as shown in Table 10.8.

TABLE 10.8   MODE PARTICIPATION FACTORS

Floor	m_i	Mode 1			Mode 2			Mode 3		
		ϕ_i	$m_i\phi_i$	$m_i\phi_i^2$	ϕ_i	$m_i\phi_i$	$m_i\phi_i^2$	ϕ_i	$m_i\phi_i$	$m_i\phi_i^2$
Bottom	75	0.445	33.37	14.85	0.748	56.1	41.96	-2.118	-158.85	336.45
Middle	75	0.763	57.22	43.66	0.436	32.7	14.26	2.105	157.87	332.33
Top	50	1.0	50	50	-1.0	-50	50	-1	-50	50
Σ			140.59	108.51		38.8	106.22		-50.98	718.78

Mode participation factor in mode $1 = 140.59/108.51 = 1.30$
Mode participation factor in mode $2 = 38.8/106.22 = 0.365$
Mode participation factor in mode $3 = -50.98/718.78 = -0.071$
Two observations can be made from these factors:

1. The participation factor is maximum for mode 1 and thereafter it decreases very rapidly.
2. It may be positive or negative. Negative participation factor has no physical significance.

Let us read the spectral acceleration for 5% damping from Housner's average spectra given in Figure 8.16(b) as shown in Table 10.9.
Let us calculate the floor displacements in different modes, storey displacements and storey shears knowing the storey stiffness as shown in Table 10.10, Table 10.11 and Table 10.12, respectively.

TABLE 10.9   SPECTRAL VALUES

Mode	Frequency ω	Period T sec	MPF	S_a/g	$S_d = \dfrac{S_a}{\omega^2}$ cm	MPF $\times S_d$
1	10.30	0.61	1.30	0.15	1.39	1.81
2	25.42	0.247	0.365	0.20	0.30	0.11
3	37.38	0.168	-0.071	0.20	0.14	-0.01

TABLE 10.10   MODAL DISPLACEMENTS OF FLOORS

Mode	First Floor		Middle Floor		Roof	
	ϕ_i	$\phi_i\Gamma S_d$	ϕ_i	$\phi_i\Gamma S_d$	ϕ_i	$\phi_i\Gamma S_d$
1	0.445	0.805	0.763	1.38	1	1.81
2	0.748	0.082	0.436	0.048	-1	-0.11
3	-2.118	0.021	2.105	-0.021	-1	0.01

TABLE 10.11   MODAL DISPLACEMENTS OF STOREYS

Mode	Ground Storey		Middle Storey		Top Storey	
	$\phi_1\Gamma S_d$	$|x_1|$	$(\phi_2 - \phi_1)\Gamma S_d$	$|x_2|$	$(\phi_3 - \phi_2)\Gamma S_d$	$|x_3|$
1	0.805	0.805	1.38 – 0.805	0.575	1.81 – 1.38	0.43
2	0.082	0.082	0.048 – 0.082	0.034	-0.11 – 0.048	0.16
3	0.021	0.021	-0.021 – 0.021	0.042	-0.01 + 0.021	0.03

TABLE 10.12   STOREY SHEAR

	Abs Max value		SRSS Value	
Storey	Storey Displacement, cm	Storey Shear kN	Storey Displacement, cm	Storey Shear kN
Top	$0.43 + 0.16 + 0.03 = 0.62$	140	$SQRT(0.43^2 + 0.16^2 + 0.03^2) = 0.46$	104
Middle	$0.575 + 0.034 + 0.042 = 0.65$	232	$SQRT(0.575^2 + 0.034^2 + 0.042^2) = 0.57$	204
Ground	$0.805 + 0.082 + 0.021 = 0.91$	306	$SQRT(0.805^2 + 0.082^2 + 0.021^2) = 0.81$	272

TABLE 10.13   MODAL FORCES

	First Floor		Middle Floor		Roof	
Mode	ϕ_i	$\phi_i \Gamma S_a m_i$	ϕ_i	$\phi_i \Gamma S_a m_i$	ϕ_i	$\phi_i \Gamma S_a m_i$
1	0.445	64	0.763	110	1	96
2	0.748	41	0.436	23	−1	−36
3	−2.118	22	2.105	−22	−1	7

TABLE 10.14   LATERAL FORCES AND STOREY SHEARS

	Abs Max Value kN		SRSS Value kN	
Floor	Force F_i	Shear V_i	Force F_i	Shear V_i
Roof	$96 + 36 + 7 = 139$	139	$SQRT(96^2 + 36^2 + 7^2) = 103$	103
Middle	$110 + 23 + 22 = 155$	294	$SQRT(110^2 + 23^2 + 22^2) = 115$	218
First	$64 + 41 + 22 = 127$	421	$SQRT(64^2 + 41^2 + 22^2) = 79$	297

Let us determine the modal forces in various modes using the S_a/g values computed in Table 10.9 and again determine the storey shears as shown in Tables 10.13 and 10.14. The SRSS values of the floor forces and storey shears are shown in Figure 10.14. Two observations can be made in Tables 10.12 and 10.14:

1. The absolute value of the storey shears in Table 10.14 are quite different than those obtained in Table 10.12 using the floor displacement approach.
2. The SRSS storey shears are quite close to those obtained in Table 10.12 using the floor displacement approach.   □

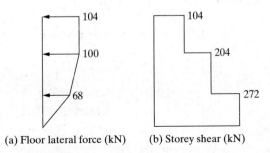

(a) Floor lateral force (kN)   (b) Storey shear (kN)

Figure 10.14   Lateral force distribution.

Example 10.9

Consider the two storey frame shown in Example 10.7. Determine its undamped free response if the initial conditions are as follows:

$$\{x(0)\} = \begin{Bmatrix} 1 \\ -1 \end{Bmatrix} m \quad \text{and} \quad \{\dot{x}(0)\} = \begin{Bmatrix} 0 \\ 0 \end{Bmatrix}$$

Solution   Let us find $\{y(0)\}$ and $\{\dot{y}(0)\}$ using Equation (10.52)

$$y_r(0) = \frac{\phi_r^T[M]\{x(0)\}}{\phi_r^T M \phi_r} \quad \text{and} \quad \dot{y}_r(0) = \frac{\phi_r^T[M]\{\dot{x}(0)\}}{\phi_r^T M \phi_r}$$

The mass matrix is

$$[M] = \begin{bmatrix} 60 & 0 \\ 0 & 38 \end{bmatrix}$$

Frequency and mode shapes are as follows:

$$\omega = \begin{Bmatrix} 6.618 \\ 16.137 \end{Bmatrix} \text{rad/sec}$$

Mode shapes are given by

$$\Phi = \begin{bmatrix} 0.674 & -0.94 \\ 1 & 1 \end{bmatrix}$$

Initial conditions in normal coordinates are given by:

$$y_1(0) = \frac{\phi_1^T[M]\{x_1(0)\}}{\phi_1^T M \phi_1} \qquad y_1(0) = \frac{\{1 \quad 0.674\} \begin{bmatrix} 60 & 0 \\ 0 & 38 \end{bmatrix} \begin{Bmatrix} 1 \\ -1 \end{Bmatrix}}{\{1 \quad 0.674\} \begin{bmatrix} 60 & 0 \\ 0 & 38 \end{bmatrix} \begin{Bmatrix} 1 \\ 0.674 \end{Bmatrix}} = 0.445$$

$$y_2(0) = \frac{\{1 \quad -0.94\} \begin{bmatrix} 60 & 0 \\ 0 & 38 \end{bmatrix} \begin{Bmatrix} 1 \\ -1 \end{Bmatrix}}{\{1 \quad -0.94\} \begin{bmatrix} 60 & 0 \\ 0 & 38 \end{bmatrix} \begin{Bmatrix} 1 \\ -0.94 \end{Bmatrix}} = -0.26$$

The initial velocity vector $\{\dot{y}(0)\}$ will be nil as $\{\dot{x}(0)\}$ is also nil.
The solution can be written as Equation (10.54):

$$y_r(t) = y_r(0)\cos\omega_r t + \frac{\dot{y}_r(0)}{\omega_r}\sin\omega_r t$$

or,

$$\{y(t)\} = \begin{Bmatrix} y_1(t) \\ y_2(t) \end{Bmatrix} = \begin{Bmatrix} 0.45\cos(6.618t) \\ -0.26\cos(16.137t) \end{Bmatrix}$$

and

$$X_{2\times1}(t) = \Phi_{2\times2} Y_{2\times1}(t)$$

$$X_{2\times1}(t) = \begin{bmatrix} 0.674 & -0.94 \\ 1 & 1 \end{bmatrix} \begin{Bmatrix} 0.45\cos(6.618t) \\ -0.26\cos(16.137t) \end{Bmatrix}$$

or,

$$X_{2\times1}(t) = \begin{Bmatrix} 0.30\cos(6.618t) + 0.25\cos(16.137t) \\ 0.45\cos(6.618t) - 0.26\cos(16.137t) \end{Bmatrix}$$ □

10.12 RAYLEIGH DAMPING

Consider Equation (10.47)

$$\Phi^T M \Phi \ddot{Y} + \Phi^T C \Phi \dot{Y} + \Phi^T K \Phi Y = \Phi^T P(t) \tag{10.47a}$$

$$C_n = \Phi^T C \Phi \tag{10.47b}$$

The square matrix given by Equation (10.47b) may or may not be a diagonal matrix depending upon the nature of matrix C. If C is diagonal, then Equation (10.47a) represents N uncoupled differential equations in normal coordinates. The system possesses the same natural modes as those of the undamped system. The system is said to have *classical damping*. If C is not diagonal matrix, then Equation (10.47a) cannot be uncoupled. The undamped natural modes are not the modes of the damped system. Such a damping is called *nonclassical damping*. Such a system cannot be solved using modal analysis.

Let us consider mass and stiffness proportional damping as follows:

$$C = a_0 M \quad \text{and} \quad C = a_1 K \tag{10.74}$$

In both cases, Equation (10.74) will be a diagonal matrix in view of orthogonal properties of the mode shapes. Thus, Equation (10.74) represents *classical damping*. Let us relate the modal damping ratios for a system with mass proportional damping to the coefficient a_0. The generalized damping for the nth mode is

$$C_n = a_0 M_n$$

We know for a SDOF system,

$$c = 2\, m\omega\xi$$

∴

$$C_n = 2 M_n \omega_n \xi_n \tag{10.75}$$

∴

$$\xi_n = \frac{a_0}{2\omega_n} \tag{10.76}$$

The coefficient a_0 can be determined using the specified damping in any mode i

$$a_0 = 2\omega_i \xi_i \tag{10.77}$$

Knowing a_0, damping in any other mode can be obtained using Equation (10.76).

Similarly, the modal damping ratio for a system with stiffness proportional damping can be related to the coefficient a_1 as follows:

$$C_n = a_1 K_n = a_1 \omega_n^2 M_n$$

also,

$$C_n = 2M_n \omega_n \xi_n \qquad (10.75)$$

$\therefore$

$$a_1 \omega_n = 2\xi_n$$

or,

$$\xi_n = \frac{a_1 \omega_n}{2} \qquad (10.78)$$

The coefficient a_1 can be determined using the specified damping in any mode i

$$a_1 = \frac{2\xi_i}{\omega_i} \qquad (10.79)$$

Thus, modal damping in any mode can be determined using Equation (10.78).

Both mass proportional damping and stiffness proportional damping given by Equation (10.74) are not suitable for use in a MDOF system. The results are not consistent with those obtained experimentally. Therefore, there is a need to develop another formulation called *Rayleigh Damping* given as follows:

$$C = a_0 M + a_1 K \qquad (10.80)$$

The damping ratio for the nth mode is given by

$$\xi_n = \frac{a_0}{2\omega_n} + \frac{a_1 \omega_n}{2} \qquad (10.81)$$

The coefficients a_0 and a_1 can be determined knowing the damping ratios in any two modes i and j.

Thus,

$$\xi_i = \frac{a_0}{2\omega_i} + \frac{a_1 \omega_i}{2} \qquad \xi_j = \frac{a_0}{2\omega_j} + \frac{a_1 \omega_j}{2}$$

These two relations can be written as:

$$\begin{Bmatrix} \xi_i \\ \xi_j \end{Bmatrix} = \frac{1}{2} \begin{bmatrix} \dfrac{1}{\omega_i} & \omega_i \\ \dfrac{1}{\omega_j} & \omega_j \end{bmatrix} \begin{Bmatrix} a_0 \\ a_1 \end{Bmatrix} \qquad (10.82a)$$

The coefficients a_0 and a_1 can be determined. In case, any two modes have equal damping ratios, the coefficients are as follows:

$$a_0 = \frac{\omega_i \omega_j}{\omega_i + \omega_j} \xi \qquad (10.82b)$$

and

$$a_1 = \frac{2\xi}{\omega_i + \omega_j} \qquad (10.82c)$$

The two modes i and j should be chosen to ensure reasonable values of damping ratios in all other modes contributing significantly to the overall response. The variation of Rayleigh damping is shown in Figure 10.15.

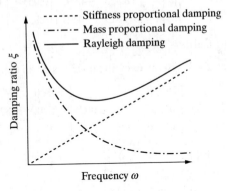

Figure 10.15   Rayleigh damping vs frequency.

Example 10.10

Consider the three storey moment resistant frame of Example 10.8. If the Rayleigh damping in the first two modes is 5% each, determine the damping in the third mode.

Solution   The mass matrix, stiffness, frequency and mode shapes were determined as follows:

$$[M] = \begin{bmatrix} 75 & 0 & 0 \\ 0 & 75 & 0 \\ 0 & 0 & 50 \end{bmatrix} \text{ and } [K] = \begin{bmatrix} 69300 & -35700 & 0 \\ -35700 & 58200 & -22500 \\ 0 & -22500 & 22500 \end{bmatrix}$$

$$\{\omega\} = \begin{Bmatrix} 10.30 \\ 25.42 \\ 37.38 \end{Bmatrix} \text{ rad/sec and } [\Phi] = \begin{bmatrix} 0.445 & 0.748 & -2.118 \\ 0.763 & 0.436 & 2.105 \\ 1.0 & -1.0 & -1.0 \end{bmatrix}$$

For any two modes

$$\frac{1}{2} \begin{bmatrix} 1/\omega_i & \omega_i \\ 1/\omega_j & \omega_j \end{bmatrix} \begin{Bmatrix} a_0 \\ a_1 \end{Bmatrix} = \begin{Bmatrix} \xi_i \\ \xi_j \end{Bmatrix}$$

or,

$$\frac{1}{2} \begin{bmatrix} 1/10.30 & 10.30 \\ 1/25.42 & 25.42 \end{bmatrix} \begin{Bmatrix} a_0 \\ a_1 \end{Bmatrix} = \begin{Bmatrix} 0.05 \\ 0.05 \end{Bmatrix}$$

This equation is of the form

$$[A]\{x\} = \{b\} \text{ or } \{x\} = [A]^{-1}\{b\}$$

where,

$$[A] = \begin{bmatrix} a_{11} & a_{12} \\ a_{21} & a_{22} \end{bmatrix}$$

$$\therefore \quad [A]^{-1} = \frac{1}{(a_{11} \times a_{22} - a_{21} \times a_{12})} \begin{bmatrix} a_{22} & -a_{12} \\ -a_{21} & a_{11} \end{bmatrix}$$

$$\left\{ \begin{array}{c} a_0 \\ a_1 \end{array} \right\} = 2 \begin{bmatrix} 12.323 & -4.993 \\ -0.019 & 0.0471 \end{bmatrix} \left\{ \begin{array}{c} 0.05 \\ 0.05 \end{array} \right\} = \left\{ \begin{array}{c} 0.733 \\ 0.0028 \end{array} \right\}$$

Damping matrix $[C] = a_0[M] + a_1[K]$

Or, for the three-DOF system, damping matrix is given by:

$$[C] = 0.733 \begin{bmatrix} 75 & 0 & 0 \\ 0 & 75 & 0 \\ 0 & 0 & 50 \end{bmatrix} + 0.0028 \begin{bmatrix} 69300 & -35700 & 0 \\ -35700 & 58200 & -22500 \\ 0 & -22500 & 22500 \end{bmatrix}$$

$$[C] = \begin{bmatrix} 249 & -100 & 0 \\ -100 & 218 & -63 \\ 0 & -63 & 99.65 \end{bmatrix}$$

Damping ratio

$$\xi_3 = \frac{a_0}{2} \frac{1}{\omega_3} + \frac{a_1}{2} \omega_3$$

or,

$$\xi_3 = \frac{0.733}{2} \frac{1}{37.38} + \frac{0.0028}{2} \times 37.38 = 0.0621$$

or,

$$\xi_3 = 6.21\% \text{ in the third mode.} \qquad \square$$

PROBLEMS

10.1 Consider a five-DOF undamped lumped mass system having equal mass 'm' and spring stiffness 'k' as shown in Figure P10.1. Determine its fundamental frequency and mode shape using (i) Holtzer method and (ii) Power method.

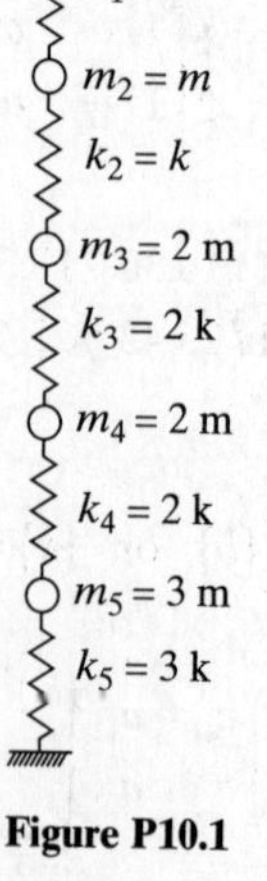

$m_1 = m$
$k_1 = k$
$m_2 = m$
$k_2 = k$
$m_3 = 2\,m$
$k_3 = 2\,k$
$m_4 = 2\,m$
$k_4 = 2\,k$
$m_5 = 3\,m$
$k_5 = 3\,k$

Figure P10.1

10.2 In Problem 10.1,

(a) Determine all frequency and mode shapes using (i) solution of the characteristic polynomial equation, and (ii) using the power method with matrix deflation.

(b) Check if the eigenvectors are orthogonal?

(c) Verify the eigenvalues using the Rayleigh's quotient.

(d) Verify the results using MATLAB.

10.3 Consider the following coefficient matrix:

$$\begin{bmatrix} 10 & 5 & 0 & 0 \\ 5 & 20 & 5 & 0 \\ 0 & 5 & 20 & 5 \\ 0 & 0 & 5 & 30 \end{bmatrix}$$

Determine its highest and lowest eigenvalues and eigenvectors only using (i) power method and (ii) inverse iteration method with shift = 5 and 30. You may carry out the calculations in MS-EXCEL. Verify the results using MATLAB.

(Hint: Operate on A^{-1} to get its highest eigenvalue or the lowest eigenvalue of A.)

10.4 In a three-DOF system, the mass matrix and stiffness matrix are as follows:

$$[M] = \begin{bmatrix} 5 & 0 & 0 \\ 0 & 10 & 0 \\ 0 & 0 & 15 \end{bmatrix} \text{ and } [K] = \begin{bmatrix} 2 & -1 & 0 \\ -1 & 4 & -2 \\ 0 & -2 & 6 \end{bmatrix}$$

Calculate its frequencies, mode shapes, mode participation factors and modal mass.

10.5 In Problem 10.4, show that the eigenvectors are orthogonal. Normalize each mode so that modal mass is unity.

10.6 (a) A three-storey shear frame is shown in Figure P10.2. The flexural rigidity of beams and columns is shown. The masses are lumped at the floor. Using the mass and stiffness influence coefficients, write the equations of motion. Neglect the axial deformations in all members.

(b) If mass $m = 5000$ kg and $I = 67,500$ cm^4, grade of concrete = M30 and storey height is 3.5 m, determine the frequencies, mode shapes, mode participation factors and modal mass.

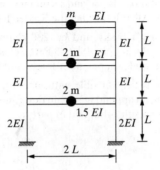

Figure P10.2

10.7 Consider a two bay × three storey RC frame as shown in Figure P10.3. The floor is rigid. The mass at the first floor girder, second floor girder and roof is 50, 50 and 40 kN-s^2/m, respectively. The column sizes from top are: 300 × 400 mm, 300 × 500 mm, 300 × 600 mm. Determine the storey stiffness, frequencies and mode shapes. Grade of concrete is M30.

Also, compute storey shears and floor forces using elastic response spectra for 5% damping of El Centro earthquake of May 1940 given in Chapter 8.

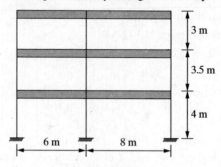

Figure P10.3

10.8 Consider the three-storey frame shown in Problem 10.7. Determine its undamped free response if the initial conditions are as follows:

$$\{x(0)\} = \begin{Bmatrix} 0.1 \\ -0.1 \\ 0.1 \end{Bmatrix} m \quad \text{and} \quad \{\dot{x}(0)\} = \begin{Bmatrix} 0 \\ 0 \\ 0 \end{Bmatrix}$$

10.9 (a) A four storey frame has its mass and storey stiffness from top as follows:

$$[M] = \begin{Bmatrix} 10 \\ 15 \\ 15 \\ 15 \end{Bmatrix} \times 100 \text{ kg} \quad K = \begin{Bmatrix} 150 \\ 150 \\ 200 \\ 200 \end{Bmatrix} \text{ kN/m}$$

Assemble the mass matrix and stiffness matrix of the frame and determine its frequency and mode shapes.

(b) Determine the mode participation factors and modal mass. Check if sum of total modal mass at each floor is equal to the respective mass.

(c) If damping in first mode is 5% and second mode is 7%, determine the damping in the other two modes. Also, determine the Rayleigh damping.

10.10 (a) In Fig. P10.1, if m = 1500 kg, and k = 200 kN/m, determine lateral forces and storey shears at each level using the IS:1893 Part 1 elastic response spectra for 5% damping on hard soil. Plot mode shapes, floor forces and storey shears.

(b) If the top storey is very flexible with mass m_1 = 30 kg and stiffness k_1 = 700 N/m only, representing an appendage, again determine lateral forces and storey shears and compare with the results obtained in part (a).

11 | Systems with Distributed Mass and Elasticity

11.1 INTRODUCTION

In the previous chapters, we have discussed the dynamics of discrete single degree of freedom (SDOF) and two-DOF systems. There are situations when it is required to determine the vibration characteristics of a system with distributed mass and elasticity or a continuum system such as a chimney or a flexure member having different boundary conditions. The mass and elasticity or stiffness of such systems are distributed along their length. The variation of mass and stiffness may be uniformly distributed or uniformly varying. The dynamic behaviour of a rod, tightly held across a length L, and having a uniform mass, is the simplest example of such a problem. Such a system has infinite degrees of freedom. Now the question arises how to analyze it. Such a system cannot be modeled as a MDOF system in view of infinite DOF, which are very difficult to identify. Moreover, all the DOF may not be necessary to understand its dynamic behaviour. One possible solution is to lump its mass at pre-determined locations along its length and thus discretizing it as a finite MDOF system. If its mass is lumped at three locations, it becomes a three-DOF system; if its mass is lumped at ten locations, it becomes a ten-DOF system. The solution of such a problem is discussed in detail in physics at the higher secondary level of education to create awareness about frequencies and mode shapes. The question arises how to select at how many points its mass should be lumped to get an accurate result? In order to avoid such a situation, it has to be treated as a continuum system or a distributed mass and stiffness system. A general distributed mass and stiffness system can vibrate in different modes, such as axial mode, shear mode, torsional mode or flexural mode. In civil engineering domain, flexural mode is more significant.

This chapter deals with the dynamic behaviour of flexure members having distributed mass and stiffness with different boundary conditions. Rayleigh's method for determining the fundamental frequency of vibration of such systems is also discussed.

11.2 DISTRIBUTED MASS AND STIFFNESS SYSTEMS

Consider forced vibration of a flexure member, that is a beam shown in Figure 11.1(a) subjected to a force $p(x, t)$ varying in space and time. Such a member will undergo transverse vibrations, that is vibrations normal to its length. The free body diagram of its small element is shown in Figure 11.1(b).

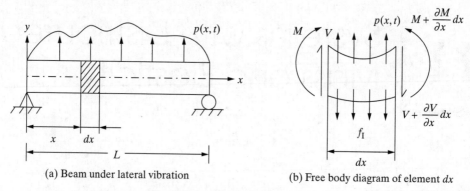

(a) Beam under lateral vibration   (b) Free body diagram of element dx

Figure 11.1   Forced vibrations in a beam.

The equation of dynamic equilibrium in the y-direction can be written as follows:

$$\Sigma F_y = 0$$

or,

$$-\left[V + \frac{\partial V}{\partial x} dx\right] + V + p(x,t)\,dx - f_I\,dx = 0 \tag{11.1}$$

but

$$f_I\,dx = (m\,dx)\frac{\partial^2 w}{\partial t^2}$$

$\therefore$

$$\frac{\partial V}{\partial x} = p(x,t) - f_I = p(x,t) - m\frac{\partial^2 w}{\partial t^2} \tag{11.2}$$

where, $w(x,t)$ = vertical deflection at any section
$m(x)$ = mass per unit length
$EI(x)$ = flexural stiffness
f_I = inertia force $(= m\ddot{w})$
$V(x,t)$ = shear force
$M(x,t)$ = bending moment

Here vertical deflection w, shear force V, bending moment M and the external force p, each of these parameters is a function of position x and time t. It means each of these parameters vary along the length of the flexure member as well as time t. Mass m and moment of inertia I are functions of position x only. For clarity, these parameters will be used without specifying x or t in the subsequent derivations.

The second equilibrium equation is obtained by summing moments about the elastic axis at the right-hand face of the segment, that is,

$$\Sigma M = 0$$

or,

$$M + V\,dx - \left\{M + \frac{\partial M}{\partial x} dx\right\} = 0$$

or,

$$\frac{\partial M}{\partial x} = V \tag{11.3}$$

we know

$$M = -EI\frac{\partial^2 w}{\partial x^2}$$

or,
$$M = EI \frac{\partial^2 w}{\partial x^2} \tag{11.4}$$

This is standard relationship for a long slender beam also known as Euler–Bernoulli beam. All the assumptions used in the derivation of Equations (11.3) and (11.4) for the static solution are valid in dynamics too. These are:

1. Beam is uniform along its length and is slender
2. It consists of linear, homogeneous, isotropic and elastic material
3. A cross-section remains plane before and after the application of the force
4. A beam vibrates along the plane of symmetry so that rotation and translation vibrations are decoupled
5. Rotatory inertia and shear deformations can be neglected

It may be noted that the distributed lateral force $p(x, t)$ makes only a second-order contribution to moment. Inertia force does not contribute to the moment equilibrium. Differentiating Equation (11.3) with respect to x gives

$$\frac{\partial^2 M}{\partial x^2} = \frac{\partial V}{\partial x}$$

and substituting in Equation (11.2) gives:

$$\frac{\partial^2 M}{\partial x^2} + m \frac{\partial^2 w}{\partial t^2} = p(x,t) \tag{11.5}$$

In this case due to sign convention

$$\frac{\partial^2}{\partial x^2} \left(EI \frac{\partial^2 w}{\partial x^2} \right) + m \frac{\partial^2 w}{\partial t^2} = p(x,t) \tag{11.6a}$$

In Equation (11.6a), the flexural stiffness EI is also a function of x, that is it is a distributed stiffness.

or,
$$EI \frac{\partial^4 w}{\partial x^4} + m \frac{\partial^2 w}{\partial t^2} = p(x,t) \tag{11.6b}$$

In Equation (11.6b), the flexural stiffness EI is taken as constant.

This is the equation of motion for undamped forced vibrations of a system with distributed mass and elasticity. The equation for free vibrations is as follows:

$$EI \frac{\partial^4 w}{\partial x^4} + m \frac{\partial^2 w}{\partial t^2} = 0 \tag{11.7}$$

As stated earlier, the transverse deflection w is a function of position x and time t. It means the deflection varies along the length of the beam as well as at any given section, it also varies with time. The solution of Equation (11.7) will require four boundary conditions and two initial conditions in terms of deflection $w(x,t)$, slope $\theta(x,t)$, shear force $V(x,t)$, bending moment $M(x,t)$ and initial conditions displacement and velocity at time $t = t_0$. This solution becomes very tedious. Therefore, the solution of Equation (11.7) is obtained by using separation of variables techniques available in differential calculus.

Let
$$w(x, t) = \phi(x) \, Y(t) \tag{11.8}$$

where, $\phi(x)$ gives the deflected shape and depends only upon the position variable x, and $Y(t)$ gives the displacement and depends only upon at time t. It means at a given time t, the position of the deflected shape of the beam along its length remains constant.

Substituting Equation (11.8) in Equation (11.7) gives,

$\therefore$
$$Y(t)\,EI\,\frac{\partial^4\phi(x)}{\partial x^4} + m\phi(x)\,\frac{\partial^2 Y(t)}{\partial t^2} = 0$$

or,
$$\frac{EI}{m\phi(x)}\frac{\partial^4\phi(x)}{\partial x^4} = -\frac{1}{Y(t)}\frac{\partial^2 Y(t)}{\partial t^2} = \text{constant}$$

$$\frac{1}{\phi(x)}\frac{\partial^4\phi(x)}{\partial x^4} = (-)\frac{m}{EI\,Y(t)}\cdot\frac{\partial^2 Y(t)}{\partial t^2} = a^4 \quad \text{say}$$

or,
$$\frac{\partial^4\phi(x)}{\partial x^4} - a^4\,\phi(x) = 0 \tag{11.9a}$$

and
$$\frac{\partial^2 Y(t)}{\partial t^2} + \frac{a^4\,EI}{m}Y(t) = 0 \tag{11.9b}$$

Let
$$\omega^2 = a^4\,\frac{EI}{m}$$

or,
$$\frac{\omega^2 m}{EI} = a^4 \tag{11.10}$$

$\therefore$ Equation (11.9a) becomes

$$\phi^{IV}(x) - a^4\,\phi(x) = 0 \tag{11.11a}$$

This is a fourth-order differential equation in $\phi(x)$ and requires four boundary conditions for its solution.

and Equation (11.9b) becomes:

$$\ddot{Y}(t) + \omega^2\,Y(t) = 0 \tag{11.11b}$$

This equation is similar to that of an undamped SDOF-free vibration.

For solving Equation (11.11a)

Let
$$\phi(x) = Ce^{sx} \tag{11.12}$$

$\therefore$ Equation (11.11a) gives,

$$(s^4 - a^4)\,Ce^{sx} = 0$$

or,

$$s = +a, +ia$$

Hence solution is,

$$\phi(x) = c_1\,e^{iax} + c_2\,e^{-iax} + c_3 e^{ax} + c_4 e^{-ax} \tag{11.13a}$$

or, alternatively,

$$\phi(x)=A_1 \sin ax + A_2 \cos ax + A_3 \sinh ax + A_4 \cosh ax \qquad (11.13b)$$

For solving Equation (11.11b)

Let
$$Y(t)=A \sin \omega t + B \cos \omega t$$

or,
$$Y(t)=\frac{\dot{Y}(0)}{\omega} \sin \omega t + Y(0) \cos \omega t \qquad (11.14)$$

where, $Y(0)$ and $\dot{Y}(0)$ represent initial conditions of displacement and velocity at time $t = t_0$.

The complete solution for a given continuum system requires the solution of Equations (11.10), (11.13) and (11.14) with the help of expressions for displacement, slope, moment and shear at the two ends. These relations will yield three constants in terms of the fourth constant and will also yield a frequency equation from which ω can be evaluated. The fourth coefficient expressing amplitude of vibration would require knowledge of the initial conditions of motion.

In the preceding derivation of the equation of motion for the transverse vibration of a beam, the effects of rotational inertia and shear deformation were ignored.

11.3 SIMPLY SUPPORTED BEAM

Let us consider a simply supported beam. The four boundary conditions for this beam are as follows:

At one end, $x = 0$,

$$\text{Deflection } \phi(0) = 0 \qquad \text{(i)}$$

$$\text{Bending moment M}(0) = \text{EI } \phi''(0) = 0 \qquad \text{(ii)}$$

at other end, $x = L$,

$$\text{Deflection } \phi(L) = 0 \qquad \text{(iii)}$$

$$\text{Bending moment M}(L) = \text{EI } \phi''(L) = 0 \qquad \text{(iv)}$$

The general solution is given by Equation (11.13b)

$$\phi(x)=A_1 \sin ax + A_2 \cos ax + A_3 \sinh ax + A_4 \cosh ax \qquad (11.13b)$$

Let us substitute the boundary conditions (i) and (ii) in Equation (11.13b),

$$\phi(0)=A_1 \sin 0 + A_2 + A_1 \sin 0 + A_4 =0$$

or, $$A_2 + A_4 = 0 \qquad \text{(v)}$$

$$\phi''(0)=a^2 (-A_1 \sin 0 - A_2 \cos 0 + A_3 \sinh 0 + A_4 \cosh 0)=0$$

or, $$-A_2 + A_4 = 0 \qquad \text{(vi)}$$

$\therefore$ Equations (v) and (vi) give, $A_2 = A_4 = 0$

Similarly, let us substitute the boundary conditions (iii) and (iv) in Equation (11.13b),

$$\phi(L) = A_1 \sin aL + A_3 \sinh aL = 0$$

and

$$\phi''(L) = a^2 (-A_1 \sin aL + A_3 \sinh aL) = 0$$

or,

$$A_3 = 0$$

$\therefore$

$$\phi(L) = A_1 \sin aL = 0 \qquad \text{(vii)}$$

A non-trivial solution exists if,

$$\sin aL = 0 \qquad \text{(viii)}$$

This is known as the *frequency equation or characteristic equation.*

Its solution gives,

$$aL = n\pi$$

or,

$$a = \frac{n\pi}{L}$$

where, $n = 0, 1, 2, \ldots, \infty$

The sine function vanishes when its argument is 0 or any integer multiple of π. There is one solution of the characteristic equation for each value of $n = 0, 1, 2\ 3, \ldots$. Hence, there exists infinite number of values of 'a' that satisfy the condition (viii). Thus, 'a' can be replaced with the notation 'a_n' as follows:

$$a_n = \frac{n\pi}{L} \quad \text{where } n = 1,2,3,\ldots$$

The solution at $n = 0$ is ignored because it means zero solution.

but

$$a^4 = \frac{\omega^2 m}{EI} \qquad (11.10)$$

or,

$$\omega_n^2 = \left(\frac{n\pi}{L}\right)^4 \frac{EI}{m}$$

or,

$$\omega_n = n^2 \pi^2 \sqrt{\frac{EI}{mL^4}} \qquad (11.15)$$

The mode shape is given by Equation (11.13b).

Because $A_2 = 0 = A_3 = A_4$

$$\phi_n(x) = A_1 \sin \frac{n\pi}{L} x \qquad (11.16)$$

Different values of n will give different values of frequency and mode shapes for different modes. First three mode shapes are shown in Figure 11.2.

$$\omega_1 = \pi^2 \sqrt{\frac{EI}{mL^4}} \quad \text{and} \quad \phi_1 = \sin \frac{\pi x}{L}$$

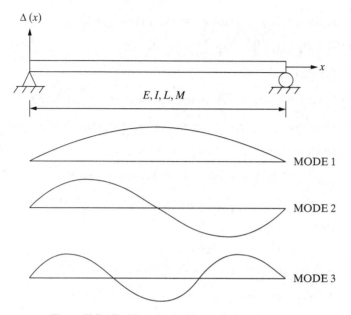

Figure 11.2 Simply supported beam and mode shapes.

$$\omega_2 = 4\pi^2\sqrt{\frac{EI}{mL^4}} \quad \text{and} \quad \phi_2 = \sin\frac{2\pi x}{L}$$

$$\omega_3 = 9\pi^2\sqrt{\frac{EI}{mL^4}} \quad \text{and} \quad \phi_3 = \sin\frac{3\pi x}{L} \tag{11.17}$$

It will be seen that the first mode is one-half sine wave, second mode is one-full sine wave and third mode is one and one-half sine wave.

11.4 CANTILEVER BEAM

Let us consider a cantilever beam fixed at $x = 0$.
Boundary conditions are:

at $\qquad\qquad\qquad x = 0$ (Fixed end)

$$\text{Deflection } \phi(0) = 0 \quad \text{and} \quad \text{slope } \phi'(0) = 0 \tag{i}$$

at $\qquad\qquad\qquad x = L$ (Free end)

$$\text{Moment } M = EI\,\phi''(L) = 0 \quad \text{and} \quad \text{shear } V = EI\,\phi'''(L) = 0 \tag{ii}$$

$$\phi(x) = A_1\sin ax + A_2\cos ax + A_3\sinh ax + A_4\cosh ax \tag{11.13b}$$

Introducing the boundary conditions in Equation (11.13b),

$$\phi(0) = A_2 + A_4 = 0 \quad \text{or} \quad A_2 = -A_4 \tag{iii}$$

$$\phi'(0) = a(A_1 + A_3) = 0 \quad \text{or} \quad A_1 = -A_3 \tag{iv}$$

$$\phi''(L) = a^2(-A_1 \sin aL - A_2 \cos aL + A_3 \sinh aL + A_4 \cosh aL) = 0 \tag{v}$$

$$\phi'''(L) = a^3(-A_1 \cos aL - A_2 \sin aL + A_3 \cosh aL + A_4 \sinh aL) = 0 \tag{vi}$$

Substituting Equations (iii) and (iv) in (v) and (vi),

$$0 = A_1 (\sin aL + \sinh aL) + A_2 (\cos aL + \cosh aL)$$

and

$$0 = -A_1 (\cos aL + \cosh aL) + A_2 (\sin aL - \sinh aL)$$

In matrix form,

$$\begin{bmatrix} \sin aL + \sinh aL & \cos aL + \cosh aL \\ \cos aL + \cosh aL & \sin aL - \sinh aL \end{bmatrix} \begin{Bmatrix} A_1 \\ A_2 \end{Bmatrix} = \{0\} \tag{vii}$$

For non-trivial solution, determinant must be zero, that is:

$$\begin{vmatrix} \sin aL + \sinh aL & \cos al + \cosh aL \\ \cos aL + \cosh aL & \sin aL - \sinh aL \end{vmatrix} = 0$$

or,

$$(\cos aL + \cosh aL)^2 - (\sin^2 aL - \sinh^2 aL) = 0$$

or,   On simplification,

$$1 + \cos aL \cosh aL = 0 \tag{11.18a}$$

This is a transcendental equation and gives the value of aL. It must be solved numerically or graphically to get the frequency of vibration. It gives

$a_n L = 1.875, 4.694, 7.855$ and 10.996 for $n = 1, 2, 3$ and 4.
Mode shapes are given by Equation (vii), that is,

$$A_2 = -\left[\frac{\sin aL + \sinh aL}{\cos aL + \cosh aL}\right] A_1 \tag{viii}$$

Substituting Equations (iii), (iv) and (viii) in Equation (11.13b) gives:

$$\phi(x) = A_1 \left[\sin ax - \sinh ax + \frac{\sin aL + \sinh aL}{\cos aL + \cosh aL}(\cosh ax - \cos ax)\right] \tag{11.18b}$$

This gives mode shapes.
The solution of Equation (11.18a) gives,

$$\omega_n = \frac{(aL)^2}{L^2}\sqrt{\frac{EI}{m}} \tag{11.19}$$

$$\omega_1 = (1.875)^2 \sqrt{\frac{EI}{mL^4}}$$

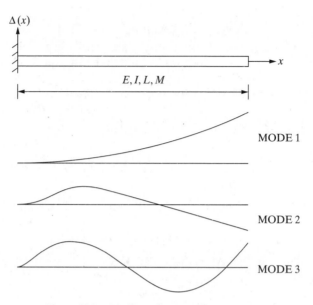

Figure 11.3   Cantilever beam and mode shapes.

$$\omega_2 = (4.694)^2 \sqrt{\frac{EI}{mL^4}}$$

$$\omega_3 = (7.855)^2 \sqrt{\frac{EI}{mL^4}} \qquad (11.20)$$

First three mode shapes are shown in Figure 11.3.

Similarly, it is possible to write the expressions for frequency and mode shapes for systems with distributed mass and elasticity having different boundary conditions.

11.5   RAYLEIGH'S PRINCIPLE: CONSERVATION OF ENERGY

The energy in a freely vibrating system must remain constant if no damping forces act to absorb it. That is,

Total potential energy + total kinetic energy = constant   (11.21)

For a SDOF system

$$x = x_0 \sin \omega t$$

or,
$$\frac{dx}{dt} = \dot{x} = x_0\, \omega \cos \omega t$$

Potential energy = strain energy of the spring

$$PE = \int_0^L kx\, dx$$

$$= \frac{1}{2}k\,x^2 = \frac{1}{2}k\,x_0^2 \sin^2 \omega t \tag{i}$$

= work done on the system by the applied loading.

Kinetic energy of the mass $= \frac{1}{2}m\dot{x}^2 = \frac{1}{2}m\,x_0^2\,\omega^2 \cos^2 \omega t$ \hfill (ii)

$$\therefore \qquad \frac{1}{2}kx_0^2 \sin^2 \omega t + \frac{1}{2}mx_0^2\omega^2 \cos^2 \omega t = \text{constant} \tag{iii}$$

$$\text{Max. PE} = \frac{1}{2}kx_0^2 \qquad \text{and} \quad KE = 0 \ (\text{at } t = T/4) = \pi/2\omega \tag{iv}$$

$$\text{Max. KE} = \frac{1}{2}mx_0^2\omega^2 \quad \text{and} \quad PE = 0 \ (\text{at } t = T/2) = \pi/\omega \tag{v}$$

If total energy in a vibrating system remains constant,

then $\qquad\qquad\qquad$ Max. PE = Max. KE

or, $$\frac{1}{2}kx_0^2 = \frac{1}{2}mx_0^2\omega^2$$

or, $$\omega = \sqrt{k/m} \tag{11.22a}$$

This equation can be applied to any structure, which can be represented as a SDOF system through the use of an assumed displacement shape function ϕ of the *fundamental mode*. Even though the assumed mode shape is approximate, the *Rayleigh method* gives fairly accurate value of the fundamental frequency. The best first estimate of the fundamental mode shape is produced by the dead weight or the gravity forces of the structure. Most international building codes specify Rayleigh method to estimate the fundamental frequency of the building as follows:

$$T = 2\pi \sqrt{\frac{\displaystyle\sum_{i=1}^{n} w_i x_i^2}{g \displaystyle\sum_{i=1}^{n} F_i x_i}} \tag{11.22b}$$

where

x_i = elastic horizontal displacements at i^{th} level due to lateral forces F_i ignoring the effect of torsion.

w_i = weight at the ith floor

The lateral force F_i can be taken in proportion to the weight of the ith floor.

11.6 MULTI-DEGREE OF FREEDOM SYSTEM

Consider a flexure member which has infinite numbers of DOF. It is desired to determine its fundamental frequency of vibration. It can be determined by treating it as a continuum system and solving Equation (11.13b). It is convenient to solve this equation

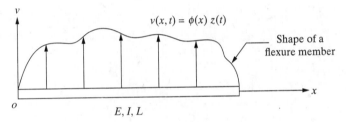

Figure 11.4   Assumed deflected shape in fundamental mode.

for simpler cases. In many practical applications, a member may have a continuously varying cross-section along its length. In such cases, it is convenient to estimate the fundamental frequency of vibration using the Rayleigh's principle. It is necessary to assume the shape which the flexure member will take in its fundamental mode of vibration (Figure 11.4).

Let
$$v(x, t) = \phi(x) Z(t) \tag{11.23a}$$

or,
$$v(x, t) = \phi(x) Z_0 \sin \omega t \tag{11.23b}$$

This equation assumes that shape of the vibrating beam does not change with time. Only the amplitude of motion does, and it varies harmonically in a free vibration condition. $\phi(x)$ is referred to as the *shape function* or *Ritz function,* which represents the ratio of the displacement at any point x to the *generalized coordinate* $Z(t)$. This assumption of the shape function *effectively reduces* the beam *to a SDOF system.* Thus, the frequency of vibration can be found by equating the maximum strain energy developed during the motion to the maximum kinetic energy.

Strain energy of the flexural system

$$U = \frac{1}{2} \int \frac{M^2 dx}{EI} \tag{11.24a}$$

Potential energy

$$U = \frac{1}{2} \int_0^L EI(x) \left(\frac{\partial^2 v}{\partial x^2} \right)^2 dx \tag{11.24b}$$

Substituting the assumed mode shape and letting the displacement amplitude take its maximum value leads to

$$PE_{max} = \frac{1}{2} Z_0^2 \int_0^L EI(x)[\phi''(x)]^2 \, dx \tag{11.25}$$

Kinetic energy of non-uniformly distributed mass is

$$KE = \frac{1}{2} \int_0^L m(x) \, (\dot{v})^2 \, dx$$

Equation (11.23b) is differentiated with respect to time to obtain the velocity, and amplitude is allowed to take its maximum value,

$$KE_{max} = \frac{1}{2} Z_0^2 \, \omega^2 \int_0^L m(x)[\phi(x)]^2 \, dx \tag{11.26}$$

Equating the maximum energies, $\text{PE}_{\text{max}} = \text{KE}_{\text{max}}$

$$\text{Rayleigh frequency } \omega^2 = \frac{\int_0^L EI(x)[\phi''(x)]^2\, dx}{\int_0^L m(x)[\phi(x)]^2\, dx} \tag{11.27}$$

or,

$$\omega^2 = \sqrt{\frac{k^*}{m^*}} \tag{11.28a}$$

where,

$$m^* = \int_0^L m(x)[\phi(x)]^2\, dx \tag{11.28b}$$

$$k^* = \int_0^L EI(x)[\phi''(x)]^2\, dx \tag{11.28c}$$

In Equation (11.27), the numerator is merely the generalized stiffness of the beam k^* for this assumed displacement shape, while the denominator is its generalized mass m^*. This equation is referred to as the standard Rayleigh frequency equation. The accuracy of the estimation of frequency depends upon the selection of the shape function for its fundamental mode of vibration.

11.7   IMPROVED RAYLEIGH METHOD

A better approximation of the frequency can be made by computing the potential energy from the work done in deflecting the structure by the inertia force associated with the assumed deflection. The distributed inertia force is given by

$$p(t) = m\ddot{x}(t) = m(x)\ddot{x}(t) \tag{11.29a}$$

As a first approximation,
    Let

$$v^{(0)}(x,t) = \phi^{(0)}(x)Z^{(0)}(t)$$

or,
$$v^{(0)}(x,t) = \phi^{(0)}(x)Z_0^{(0)} \sin \omega t$$

where,

$$Z^{(0)}(t) = Z_0^{(0)} \sin \omega t$$

$Z_0^{(0)}$ = amplitude of generalized coordinate $Z^{(0)}(t)$

The inertia force can be expressed as

$$p^{(0)}(t) = \omega^2 m(x)v^{(0)}(x,t) \tag{11.29b}$$

$$= \omega^2 m(x)\phi^{(0)}(x)Z^{(0)}(t)$$

The deflection produced by this inertia loading may be written as

$$v^{(1)}(x,t) = \omega^2 \frac{v^{(1)}(x,t)}{\omega^2} = \omega^2 \phi^{(1)}(x) \frac{Z_0^{(1)}(t)}{\omega^2}$$

$$v^{(1)} = \omega^2 \frac{v^{(1)}}{\omega^2} = \omega^2 \phi^{(1)} \frac{Z_0^{(1)}}{\omega^2}$$

or,
$$v^{(1)} = \omega^2 \phi^{(1)} \bar{Z}_0^{(1)} \qquad (11.30)$$

where ω^2 is the unknown frequency. The term ω^2 has been brought in so as to determine its value.

$v^{(1)}$ is a better approximation than $v^{(0)}$.

The potential energy of strain produced by this loading is given by

$$PE_{max} = \frac{1}{2} \int_0^L p^{(0)} v^{(1)} dx \qquad (11.31)$$

$$= \frac{Z_0^{(0)} \bar{Z}_0^{(1)}}{2} \omega^4 \int_0^L m(x) \phi^{(0)} \phi^{(1)} dx \qquad (11.32)$$

$$KE_{max} = \frac{1}{2} Z_0^2 \omega^2 \int_0^L m(x) [\phi(x)]^2 dx \qquad (11.26)$$

It can be written as

$$KE_{max} = \frac{1}{2} Z_0^{(0)2} \omega^2 \int_0^L m(x) \left(\phi^{(0)}(x) \right)^2 dx \qquad (11.26a)$$

Equating maximum potential energy to the maximum kinematic energy gives

$$\omega^2 = \frac{Z_0^{(0)} \int_0^L m(x) \left(\phi^{(0)} \right)^2 dx}{\bar{Z}_0^{(1)} \int_0^L m(x) \phi^{(0)} \phi^{(1)} dx} \qquad (11.33)$$

Equation (11.33) gives a better estimation of the fundamental frequency than that of Equation (11.27). It is because this relation avoids the curvature term, which is poorly estimated by differentiation than the shape function $\phi(x)$, which involves no derivative.

11.8 GENERALIZED SDOF SYSTEMS

A system with distributed mass and elasticity can be treated as a SDOF system if a suitable displacement shape can be assumed that satisfies its boundary conditions. This approach can be conveniently used to estimate the forces generated in such a system during an earthquake excitation. The generalized force produced due to earthquake needs to be computed. Let us consider a cantilever system with rigid base subjected to an earthquake in the lateral direction as shown in Figure 11.5.

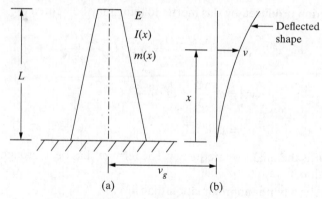

Figure 11.5 Generalized SDOF system.

The equation of motion can be written as follows:

$$f_I(x,t) + f_D(x,t) + f_S(x,t) = 0 \tag{11.34}$$

The displacement can be expressed in terms of separation of variables $\phi(x)$ and $Z(t)$, that is

$$v(x,t) = \phi(x)\, Z(t) \tag{11.23a}$$

Using the principle of virtual work, $\delta v = \phi(x)\delta Z$, leads to the equation of dynamic equilibrium

$$f_I^* \delta Z + f_D^* \delta Z + f_S^* \delta Z = 0 \tag{11.35}$$

where,

$$f_I^* = \int_0^L f_I(x,t)\phi(x)\,dx$$

$$f_D^* = \int_0^L f_D(x,t)\phi(x)\,dx \tag{11.36}$$

$$f_S^* = \int_0^L f_S(x,t)\phi(x)\,dx$$

where,

$$f_D^* = c^*\dot{Z}$$

and

$$f_S^* = k^*Z$$

The inertia force depends upon the total acceleration, that is

$$f_I(x,t) = m(x)\ddot{v}^t(x,t)$$

Since,

$$v^t(x,t) = v(x,t) + v_g(t) = \phi(x)Z(t) + v_g(t)$$

where, $v^t(x,t)$ = total displacement

The generalized inertia force can be written as

$$f_I^* = \ddot{Z}(t)\int_0^L m(x)(\phi(x))^2\,dx + \ddot{v}_g\int_0^L m(x)\phi(x)\,dx \tag{11.37}$$

Substituting all the generalized force expressions in Equation (11.35) gives the modal equation of motion.

$$m^*\ddot{Z}(t) + c^*\dot{Z}(t) + k^*Z(t) = -\bar{m}\ddot{v}_g(t) \tag{11.38}$$

where,

$$m^* = \int_0^L m(x)[\phi(x)]^2\,dx \tag{11.28b}$$

$$k^* = \int_0^L EI(x)[\phi''(x)]^2\,dx \tag{11.28c}$$

$$c^* = \int_0^L c(x)[\phi(x)]^2\,dx \tag{11.39a}$$

$$\bar{m} = \int_0^L m(x)\phi(x)\,dx \tag{11.39b}$$

$\bar{m}$ = extent to which an earthquake motion excites the response in an assumed mode shape $\phi(x)$

By analogy of the analysis of a lumped mass system, Equation (11.38) can be written as

$$\ddot{Z} + 2\omega\xi\dot{Z} + \omega^2 Z = -\frac{\bar{m}}{m^*}\ddot{v}_g(t)$$

The solution of the modal equation of motion, that is response $Z(t)$ can be obtained by any procedure discussed earlier.

$$Z(t) = \frac{\bar{m}}{m^*\omega}V(t) \tag{11.40a}$$

where, $V(t)$ = velocity response at time t.

Its peak response can be estimated using

$$Z_0 = \frac{\bar{m}}{m^*\omega}S_V \tag{11.40b}$$

The local displacement at any section x at time t is given by

$$v(x,t) = \phi(x)\,Z(t) \tag{11.23a}$$

or,

$$v(x,t) = \frac{\phi(x)\bar{m}}{m^*\omega}V(t) \tag{11.40c}$$

11.9 ILLUSTRATIVE EXAMPLES

Example 11.1

Estimate the fundamental frequency of vibration of a simply supported beam using the Rayleigh's principle. EI = constant, m = constant

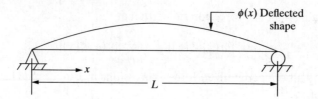

Figure 11.6 Simply supported beam.

Solution
Let us consider a simply supported beam as shown in Figure 11.6.

(i) Let us consider the shape function

$$\phi(x) = \frac{x}{L}\left(\frac{x}{L} - 1\right) \tag{i}$$

It satisfies the boundary conditions with respect to deflection. Let us differentiate it twice.

$$\therefore \qquad \phi'(x) = \frac{2x}{L^2} - \frac{1}{L} \tag{ii}$$

$$\therefore \qquad \phi''(x) = \frac{2}{L^2} \tag{iii}$$

Maximum potential energy

$$PE_{max} = \frac{1}{2} Z_0^2\, EI \int_0^L \left(\frac{2}{L^2}\right)^2 dx = \frac{1}{2} Z_0^2 \frac{4EI}{L^3}$$

and maximum kinetic energy

$$KE_{max} = \frac{1}{2} Z_0^2\, \omega^2\, m \int_0^L \left[\frac{x}{L}\left(\frac{x}{L} - 1\right)\right]^2 dx$$

$$= \frac{1}{2}\, Z_0^2\, \omega^2\, \frac{mL}{30}$$

Equating the maximum energies gives,

$$\omega^2 = \frac{120\, EI}{mL^4} \tag{iv}$$

(ii) Let us consider an improved shape function.

$$\phi(x) = \sin(\pi x/L) \tag{v}$$

Let us differentiate it twice

$$\therefore \qquad \phi'(x) = \frac{\pi}{L} \cos\left(\frac{\pi x}{L}\right) \tag{vi}$$

$$\therefore \qquad \phi''(x) = (-)\frac{\pi^2}{L^2}\left(\sin\left(\frac{\pi x}{L}\right)\right) \tag{vii}$$

Equating the maximum PE and maximum KE and using Equation (11.27)

$$\omega^2 = \frac{\displaystyle\int_0^L EI\left(\frac{\pi^2}{L^2}\right)^2 \sin^2\left(\frac{\pi x}{L}\right) dx}{\displaystyle\int_0^L m \sin^2\left(\frac{\pi x}{L}\right) dx}$$

or,
$$\omega^2 = \frac{\pi^4 EI}{mL^4} = \frac{97.408\, EI}{mL^4} \qquad \text{(viii)}$$

The second shape function is a much better approximation since it gives a lower value. It also happens to be the true frequency. The mode shape is also a sine curve.   □

Example 11.2

A RC chimney 200 m high has a uniform hollow section with 15 m outer diameter and wall thickness 1 m in M30 grade. Estimate the peak displacement, shear force and bending moment due to earthquake motion. It is located in Greater Noida on hard soil.

Solution

Let us consider a chimney as shown in Figure 11.7.

Area of cross-section $A = \dfrac{\pi}{4}\left(15^2 - 13^2\right) = 43.96 \text{ m}^2$

Moment of inertia $I = \dfrac{\pi}{64}\left(15^4 - 13^4\right) = 1083 \text{ m}^4$

Density of concrete = 25 kN/m³, mass of chimney $m = 43.96 \times 25/g = 1099/g$ kN/m

Let us assume its deflected shape in the first mode $\phi(x) = 1 - \cos\dfrac{\pi x}{2L}$

Generalized mass

$$m^* = \int\limits_0^L m(x)[\phi(x)]^2\, dx$$

$$= \int\limits_0^L m\left(1 - \cos\frac{\pi x}{2L}\right)^2 dx = 0.227 mL$$

Generalized stiffness

$$k^* = \int\limits_0^L EI(x)[\phi''(x)]^2\, dx$$

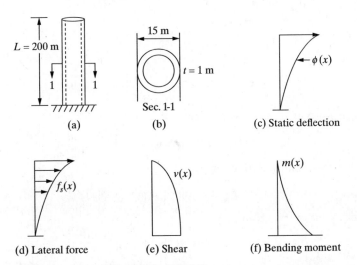

L = 200 m

15 m

t = 1 m

Sec. 1-1

$\phi(x)$

(a)

(b)

(c) Static deflection

$f_s(x)$

$v(x)$

$m(x)$

(d) Lateral force

(e) Shear

(f) Bending moment

Figure 11.7   R.C. Chimney.

$$k^* = EI \int_0^L \left(\frac{\pi}{2L}\right)^4 \cos^2\frac{\pi x}{2L} dx = 3.04\frac{EI}{L^3}$$

$$\bar{m} = \int_0^L m(x)\phi(x)dx$$

$$\bar{m} = m\int_0^L \left(1 - \cos\frac{\pi x}{2L}\right)dx = 0.363mL$$

Fundamental frequency

$$\omega_n = \sqrt{\frac{k^*}{\bar{m}}} = \frac{3.66}{L^2}\sqrt{\frac{EI}{m}}$$

Modulus of elasticity $E = 5000\sqrt{f_{ck}} = 5000\sqrt{30} = 27390$ MPa $= 27390 \times 10^3$ kN/m^2

$$\omega_n = \frac{3.66}{200^2}\sqrt{\frac{27390 \times 10^3 \times 1083}{1099/9.80}} = 1.46 \text{ rad/sec}$$

$$T = \frac{2\pi}{\omega_n} = 4.30 \text{ sec}$$

Horizontal seismic coefficient is given by clause 16 of IS:1893-part 4 as follows:
        Zone factor for zone IV = 0.24, Importance factor $I = 1.50$, Response reduction factor $R = 1.50$

S_a/g for $T = 4.30$ sec on hard rock = $1/T = 0.23$

$$\alpha_h = \frac{Z}{2}\frac{I}{R}\frac{S_a}{g} = \frac{0.24 \times 1.5 \times 0.23}{2 \times 1.50} = 0.0276$$

Base shear $V_B = 0.0276$ W

$$= 0.0276 \times 1099 \times 200 = 6066 \text{ kN}$$

Spectral displacement

$$S_d = \frac{S_a}{\omega_n^2} = \frac{0.23 \times g}{1.46^2} = 1.056 \text{ m}$$

Peak value of displacement

$$Z(t) = Z_0 = \text{MPF } S_d = \frac{\bar{m}}{m^*}S_d$$

$$Z_0 = \frac{0.363mL \times 1.056}{0.227mL} = 1.69 \text{ m}$$

Displacement at any section x is given by

$$v(x) = \text{MPF } S_d \phi(x) = 1.69\left(1 - \cos\frac{\pi x}{2L}\right)$$

Equivalent static force is given by

$$f_s(x,t) = kv(x,t) = \omega_n^2 m(x)\phi(x)Z(t)$$

Peak value of force is given by

$$f_{s,\max}(x) = m(x)\phi(x)\omega_n^2 Z_0$$

$$f_{s,max}(x) = m(x)\phi(x)\text{MPF } S_a$$

$$= \frac{1099}{g} \times \left(1 - \cos\frac{\pi x}{2L}\right) \times 1.60 \times 0.23 \text{ g}$$

$$= 404.4 \times \left(1 - \cos\frac{\pi x}{2L}\right) \text{ kN/m}$$

Shear force at any section can be determined using statics

$$\text{Shear } V(x) = \int_0^x f_s(x)dx$$

$$= \text{MPF } S_a \int_0^x m(x)\phi(x)dx$$

Shear at base is given by integrating it from 0 to L.

$$V(0) = \frac{\bar{m}}{m^*}S_a\bar{m} = \frac{\bar{m}^2}{m^*}S_a = \frac{\bar{m}^2}{m^*}\omega_n S_v$$

$$= 1.60 \times 0.363mL \times 0.23 \text{ g}$$

$$= 1.60 \times 0.363 \times (1099/g) \times 200 \times 0.23 \times g = 29360 \text{ kN}$$

Similarly, base moment can be determined using statics

Moment $\qquad M(x) = \int_0^x f_s(x)xdx$

$$= \text{MPF } S_a \int_0^x m(x)\phi(x)xdx$$

The code specified base shear is only 6066 kN, whereas the structural dynamics gives a base shear of 29360 kN. It means the codal base shear is 20% of that of dynamic consider-ations. It is important to note that:

1. The codal base shear is for the design basis earthquake.
2. The code requires ductile detailing of the chimney.
3. The analytical base shear does not consider the effects of factors Z, I and R.   □

11.10 LUMPED MASS SYSTEM: SHEAR BUILDINGS

It is possible to extend the principle of virtual displacement to discrete lumped mass systems. Let us consider a multi-storey framed building having n-DOF as shown in Figure 11.8. The floor displacements are $x_1, x_2, x_3, x_4, \ldots x_n$. The floor displacements rela-tive to ground can be expressed as follows:

$$x_i(t) = \phi_i Z(t) \qquad i = 1, 2, 3, \ldots n \tag{11.41a}$$

where, $\quad x_i(t)$ = displacement of ith floor
$\qquad \phi_i$ = mode shape of ith floor
$\qquad Z(t)$ = generalized displacement as a function of time t

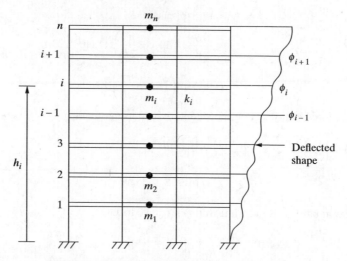

Figure 11.8   Deflected shape of a shear building.

It can be expressed in vector form as follows:

$$\{x(t)\}_{n\times1} = \{\phi\}_{n\times1} Z(t)$$ (11.41b)

where, $\{\phi\}$ = assumed shape vector

A shear building is defined as a building having rigid axial and flexure stiffness and flexible columns. Shear in any i^{th} storey is the sum of shears in all the columns of the storey. The storey shear is related to the storey drift through the storey stiffness as follows:

Storey drift $\Delta_i = x_i - x_{i-1}$ (11.42a)

Storey shear $V_i = \Delta_i k_i$ (11.42b)

where,

Storey stiffness $k_i = \sum \dfrac{12EI}{L^3}$ (11.42c)

The summation sign extends over all the columns in a storey.

It can be shown by proceeding as in the previous case that the natural frequency of the shear building is given by

$$\omega^2 = \frac{k^*}{m^*}$$ (11.43)

where generalized properties are as follows:

$$k^* = \sum k_i (\phi_i - \phi_{i-1})^2$$ (11.44a)

and

$$m^* = \sum m_i \phi_i^2$$ (11.44b)

The equation of motion of an undamped discrete mass spring model under earthquake motion is given by

$$[M]\{\ddot{X}\}+[K]\{X\}=\{P(t)\}=-[M]\{\ddot{y}_g(t)\}$$

We had earlier defined

$$\{x(t)\}_{n\times1}=\{\phi\}_{n\times1}Z(t)$$

n = number of storeys

or,

$$x_i(t)=\phi_i z(t)$$

∴ Equation of motion can be written as:

$$m^*\ddot{z}+k^*z=-\bar{m}\ddot{y}_g(t) \tag{11.45}$$

where,

$$\bar{m}=\{\phi\}^T[M]=\sum m_i\phi_i$$

m_i, k_i, and ϕ_i are properties of the ith storey

It is assumed that the shear building deflects in a shape defined by the shape function ϕ in a given mode. This simplification is best suited for the fundamental mode of vibration as it is difficult to define or assume a shape function for higher modes. This equation can be easily extended to damped shear systems by assuming a modal damping ratio ξ.

Example 11.3

Consider a four-storey shear building as shown in Figure 11.9. Assuming that the floor displacements vary linearly with height, determine its fundamental frequency of vibration.

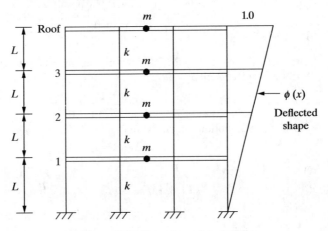

Figure 11.9   Four storey shear building.

Solution Let us determine the generalized properties of the shear building:

$$m^* = \sum m_i \phi_i^2$$

$$k^* = \sum k_i (\phi_i - \phi_{i-1})^2$$

Let us assume that the top floor displacement is 1.0. The displacements at lower floors can be estimated by linear variation. Thus, the shape function can be written as follows:

$$\{\phi\} = \begin{Bmatrix} 1.0 \\ 0.75 \\ 0.50 \\ 0.25 \end{Bmatrix}$$

Thus,

$$m^* = m(1^2 + 0.75^2 + 0.50^2 + 0.25^2) = 1.875\ m$$

$$k^* = k(0.25^2 + 0.25^2 + 0.25^2 + 0.25^2) = 0.25k$$

where,

$$k = \text{total lateral stiffness of a storey}$$

Natural frequency

$$\omega = \sqrt{\frac{0.25k}{1.875m}} = 0.365\sqrt{\frac{k}{m}} \qquad \square$$

Example 11.4

Consider the four-storey shear building of Example 11.3. Its mass $m = 4000$ kg, stiffness $k = 1000$ kN/m and storey height $= 3$ m. Determine the peak displacements, storey shears and floor overturning moments when it is subjected to the average response spectra shown in Figure 8.16(b). Take 5% damping.

Solution

Natural frequency $\omega = 0.365\sqrt{\dfrac{k}{m}}$

$$\omega = 0.365\sqrt{\frac{1000 \times 1000}{4000}} = 5.77\ \text{rad/sec}$$

Period $T = \dfrac{2\pi}{5.77} = 1.09$ sec

The spectral acceleration for 5% damping is given as $0.1\ g = 0.1 \times 981 = 98.1$ cm/sec^2.
Spectral displacement $S_d = S_a / \omega^2$

$$S_d = \frac{98.1}{5.77^2} = 2.95\ \text{cm}$$

$\therefore$ Equation of motion can be written as:

$$m^* \ddot{z} + k^* z = -\bar{m} \ddot{y}_g(t) \tag{11.45}$$

where,

$$\bar{m} = \{\phi\}^T [M] = \sum m_i \phi_i$$

$$\bar{m} = m(1 + 0.75 + 0.50 + 0.25) = 2.5m = 2.5 \times 4000 = 10000$$

$$\Gamma = \frac{\bar{m}}{m^*} = \frac{10000}{1.875m} = \frac{10000}{1.875 \times 4000} = 1.33$$

∴ Peak displacement = 1.33 × 2.95 = 3.93 cm
∴ Peak floor displacements are given by:

$$\{x\} = \begin{Bmatrix} 3.93 \\ 2.95 \\ 1.97 \\ 0.98 \end{Bmatrix} cm$$

Lateral force at each floor is given by:

$$f_i = \Gamma m_i \phi_i S_a = 1.33 \times 4000 \times \phi_i \times \frac{98.1}{100} = 5218\phi_i N$$

The floor forces, storey shear and overturning moment calculations are shown in Table 11.1.

TABLE 11.1   LATERAL FORCES AND STOREY SHEARS

Floor	Mode shape, ϕ_i	Floor force, N	Storey shear N	Overturning moment, N-m
Roof	1.0	5218	5218	$5218 \times 3 = 15654$
Third	0.75	3913	9131	$5218 \times 6 + 3913 \times 3 = 43047$
Second	0.50	2610	11741	$5218 \times 9 + 3913 \times 6 + 2610$ $\times 3 = 78270$
First	0.25	1305	13046	$5218 \times 12 + 3913 \times 9 + 2610$ $\times 6 + 1305 \times 3 = 117400$

The base shear = 13046 N
   Or, base shear = 13046/(4 × 4000 × 9.81) = 0.083 W
   It means the base shear is 8.3% of the weight of the building.   □

PROBLEMS

11.1 Calculate the natural frequencies and mode shapes of a flexural member clamped at both ends and plot the first three mode shapes using MATLAB.

11.2 Calculate the natural frequencies and mode shapes of a flexural member hinged at both ends and plot the first three mode shapes using MATLAB.

11.3 Compare the natural frequencies of two identical flexural members made of steel and aluminium each, having boundary conditions as: fixed-free, fixed-hinged and hinged-roller.

11.4 Compare the natural frequency of a SDOF system having a concentrated mass M at its free end with that of a distributed cantilever system having a total mass M along its length L.

11.5 Estimate the fundamental frequency of vibration of a fixed ended beam using Rayleigh's principle. Its mass and elasticity are uniformly distributed along the length. Compare the fundamental frequency with the first natural frequency obtained with the exact standard solution.

11.6 Estimate the fundamental frequency of vibration of a fixed-hinged beam using Rayleigh's principle. Its mass and elasticity are uniformly distributed along the length. Compare the fundamental frequency with the first natural frequency obtained with the exact standard solution.

11.7 Compare the first three mode shapes of a cantilever beam with those of a fixed-hinged beam using MATLAB graphics.

11.8 A beam of length L having uniformly distributed mass and elasticity can be idealized as a five-degree of freedom system by lumping m/5 mass at the centre of each L/5 segment. Determine the first five frequencies and mode shapes by treating it as a discrete system using MATLAB and compare them with those obtained from the exact solution. Take boundary conditions as (i) fixed-fixed and (ii) fixed-hinged.

11.9 A RC chimney 250 m high has a tapered hollow section with 15 m outer diameter at the base and 7.5 m at the top; wall thickness 1m uniform throughout in M35 grade. Assume the shape function

$$\phi(x) = 1 - \cos\frac{\pi x}{2L}$$

where, L is height of the chimney and x is measured from the base. The modulus of elasticity of concrete is given by $5000\sqrt{f_{ck}}$ MPa, where f_{ck} is the characteristic strength of concrete. Unit weight of concrete is 25 kN/m³. Damping may be taken as 5%.

Estimate the peak displacement at its top, shear force and bending moment at its base due to earthquake motion. It is located in Coimbatore, TN, on medium soil. Use the design spectrum specified in IS:1893-part 4.

11.10 A steel chimney 150 m high has a tapered hollow section with 10 m outer diameter at the base and 5 m at the top; wall thickness is 0.25 m uniform throughout. Assume the shape function.

$$\phi(x) = \frac{3}{2}\frac{x^2}{L^2} - \frac{1}{2}\frac{x^3}{L^3}$$

where, L is height of the chimney and x is measured from the base. The modulus of elasticity of steel is 200 GPa. Unit weight of steel is 79kN/m³. Damping may be taken as 2%.

Estimate the peak displacement at its top, shear force and bending moment at its base due to earthquake motion. It is located in Itanagar, Arunachal Pradesh, on soft soil. Use the design spectrum specified in IS:1893-part 4.

REFERENCE

IS:1893:2013 (Part 4) Criteria for Earthquake Resistant Design of Structures, Part 4: Industrial and Stack-like Structures, Bureau of Indian Standards, New Delhi.

PART 3

APPLICATION TO EARTHQUAKE ENGINEERING

12 Analysis of Buildings for Earthquake Force

12.1 INTRODUCTION

A force is defined as the product of mass and acceleration. During an earthquake, the mass is imparted by the building, whereas the acceleration is imparted by the ground disturbance. In order to have a minimum force, the mass of the building should be as low as possible. There can be no control on the ground acceleration, being an act of God! The point of application of this inertial force is the centre of gravity of the mass on each floor of the building. Once there is a force, there has to be an equal and opposite reaction to balance this force. The inertial force is resisted by the building and the resisting force acts at the centre of rigidity at each floor of the building or shear centre of the building at each storey. An earthquake may be classified into one of the three general categories along with the desired behaviour and controlling parameter in a building as shown in Table 12.1. It is referred to as the seismic design criteria for buildings.

It was shown in Chapter 8 that the lateral force computed using the codal response spectra are much lower than those actually recorded during real earthquakes. This is intentional. Depending upon the probability of occurrence of an earthquake in a given region, it is desirable to design the building for a much lesser force and allow the building to undergo inelastic deformations. In the event of a stronger earthquake, the ductility provided at all possible locations in the elements of the building will help dissipate energy hysteretically while undergoing (relatively) large inelastic deformations. The intention is to design an economical, affordable and safe structure. Seismic requirements provide minimum standards for use in building design to

TABLE 12.1 SEISMIC DESIGN CRITERIA

Earthquake	Desired Behaviour	Controlling Parameter
Small	No damage to structural components	Control deflection by providing *stiffness*
Moderate	No significant structural damage, minor cracks in beams and columns, Response should be predominantly elastic	Avoid yielding of members or permanent damage by providing *strength*
Large, catastrophic	No collapse of the system which could cause loss of life	Allow structure to enter into inelastic range and absorb energy by providing *ductility*

maintain public safety in a major earthquake. These requirements safeguard against major failures and loss of life. They are not intended to necessarily limit damage, maintain function or provide for easy repair.

This chapter describes structural systems and irregularity in buildings. How to estimate the seismic force using Indian Standard Code IS:1893-Part 1 in buildings using static and dynamic methods including torsion as well as how to analyze them are explained in detail?

12.2 WHAT IS A BUILDING?

It is very important to know as to what is a building before beginning any discussion on the analysis of buildings. Does the term 'building' cover a residential building, or a commercial building, or an auditorium building, or a stadium, or a bridge or a tower and so on? Neither clause 3 of IS:1893 on terminology for earthquake engineering nor clause 4 terminology for earthquake engineering of buildings defines the term 'building'. Clause 6 covers general principles and design criteria for any structure. However, Clause 7 covers only 'buildings' but without defining it. The terms 'structure' and 'building' are being used interchangeably in analysis and design by engineers. There may not be any difference in these two terms for a layman. But this term is causing confusion among many designers in India. The trouble arises in the estimation of the earthquake force which in turn makes use of the fundamental period of vibrations. Clause 7 of IS:1893 gives the empirical formula for estimation of fundamental period of buildings. This formula is being applied for non-buildings as well leading to wrong estimation of the force. Clause 11.2 of ASCE 7-2007 defines building as follows:

BUILDING: *Any structure whose intended use includes shelter of human occupants.*

If this definition is used, then there will be no confusion. The term building in this context includes commercial or office buildings, hospitals, multistorey shopping malls, etc. but excludes auditorium, stadium, bridge or a tower etc. The scope of the present chapter covers only buildings.

12.3 STRUCTURAL SYSTEMS

The purpose of a structural system is to transfer all loads, vertical as well as lateral, to the soil below without any distress anywhere. Different systems may be employed in a building to carry vertical and lateral loads. A structural system is to be conceived depending upon the functional, architectural, structural and geotechnical requirements. Based on the occupancy and functional requirements, different systems may be required. The following buildings will have different requirements:

(a) Residential building
(b) Office building
(c) Hotel building
(d) Car parking garage

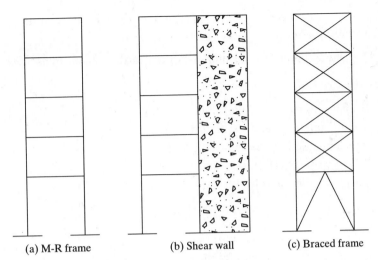

(a) M-R frame   (b) Shear wall   (c) Braced frame

Figure 12.1   Basic structural systems.

There are basically three types of structural systems for RC and steel buildings (Figure 12.1):

1. Moment-resistant frames
2. Shear wall frames
3. Braced frames

By using innovative combinations of these systems, more systems can be evolved such as:

1. Tubular system
2. Dual system
   (a) Frame with shear wall
   (b) Frame with braces

Tubular System   The idea behind a tubular system is to increase the lateral and torsional stiffness of a building so as to control its lateral deflections and vibrations due to severe wind and earthquake forces. The columns are placed at the outer periphery at a very close spacing, say 1 m to 2 m, clear in order to permit placement of doors and windows. The intention is to let light and air inside the building. This system behaves as a continuous wall around its periphery in plan, that is as a box with very high moment of inertia, and therefore, stiffness. This system was developed for the 411 m high World Trade Center twin towers, New York, in the 1970s that were later destroyed in a terrorist attack on 11 September 2001 (*9/11 attack*).

Dual System   There are two structural systems to resist seismic forces: primary system and a secondary system. The former consists of a braced frame or a shear wall frame. In case of failure of the primary system, secondary system resists the lateral forces. For a dual system, the moment frames shall be capable of resisting at least 25% of the design seismic forces. The total seismic force resistance is to be provided by the combination of the moment frames and the shear walls or braced frames in proportion to their rigidities.

Depending upon their detailing, they are further classified as follows.

Reinforced Concrete Buildings

   (a) Ordinary moment-resistant frames
   (b) Intermediate moment-resistant frames
   (c) Special ductile moment-resistant frames
   (d) Ordinary shear wall frames
   (e) Special ductile shear wall frames

Steel Buildings

   (a) Ordinary moment-resistant frames
   (b) Special moment-resistant frames
   (c) Ordinary concentrically braced frames
   (d) Special concentrically braced frames
   (e) Ordinary eccentrically braced frames
   (f) Special eccentrically braced frames

A braced frame is essentially a vertical truss designed to resist lateral forces. The basic concentric and eccentric-braced configurations are shown in Figures 12.2 and 12.3. Bracing members are pin-ended and can be used in the façade to give aesthetic look to buildings as done in the John Hancock building in Chicago built in the early 1970s. The inverted V configuration in Figure 12.2(a) is also known as *K-brace*. In the concentrically braced frame, the centre lines of the bracing members meet the horizontal beam at a single point or beam–column joint. In the eccentrically braced frame, the braces are deliberately designed to frame into a beam a short distance from a beam–column joint or from another diagonal brace. The configuration shown in Figure 12.2(b) is highly undesirable as they may lead to inelasticity in columns and thus collapse of the building. In the eccentric frame, the short piece of beam between the ends of the braces is called a *link beam*. The purpose of the *link beam* is to develop plastic hinges

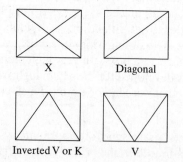

X   Diagonal

Inverted V or K   V

Figure 12.2(a)   Concentric-braced configurations.

Diamond   Split Column

Figure 12.2(b)   Undesirable concentric-braced configurations.

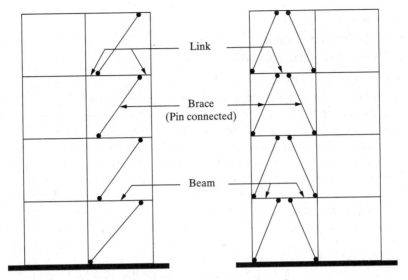

Figure 12.3   Eccentric-braced configurations.

at its ends due to large shear and dissipate energy. Thus, this link beam will help protect rest of the structure. Typical failure mode of an eccentrically braced frame is shown in Figure 12.4.

A bracing member is generally designed to carry only axial forces. In a concentric system, a brace is expected to buckle and start dissipating energy. This is how safety of the main frame is ensured. In an eccentric system, a brace is designed to remain elastic and force the formation of plastic hinge in the link beam due to very high shear. It leads to very fat and stable hysteresis loops. This is how safety of the main frame is ensured. In a concentric braced frame, only probable locations of plastic hinges are known. While in an eccentric braced frame, the locations of plastic hinges are well defined.

There is a unique advantage with steel structures over concrete structures because of the flexibility available in designing their connections. In steel frames, the connections can be as follows:

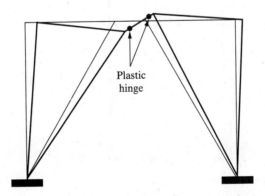

Figure 12.4   Deformations in eccentrically braced frame.

(a) Simple connection

(b) Semi-rigid connection

(c) Moment-resistant connection

Simple connections in steel structures are designed to carry only shear force, only axial force or both. A moment-resistant connection may carry axial force, shear force in addition to a moment. In concrete frames, in general, all connections are moment resistant. In the structural system shown in Figure 12.5(a), all connections are simple or pin-connected. The columns are continuous. Under lateral loads, such a frame acts as a vertical cantilever and each member carries only axial force. Such a system is very economical and popular especially in less severe earthquake zone. In Figure 12.5(b), all beam to column connections are moment resistant while all braces are connected through simple or pin-connections. The beams carry bending moment, columns carry axial force and bending moment, while braces carry only axial forces. The column bases can be pin-connected that will relieve the foundation from bending moment and transfer it to the superstructure.

Dual systems, tubular or box structural systems, and tube-in-tube structural systems are essentially subsets of the three types of systems described for both RC buildings and steel buildings. In choosing the structural system for a building, large dissimilarities in the stiffness and ductile characteristics of framing systems in the orthogonal directions should be avoided. For example, a moment-resisting ductile frame in one direction and reinforced masonry wall in the other direction would be unsuitable, whereas RC ductile flexural walls and RC walls with nominal ductility in orthogonal directions would be acceptable. The reason for this recommendation is that seismic displacements induced in flexible framing systems would probably cause failure in the relatively brittle and weak directions of the elements that resist the load in orthogonal directions. Choice of a structural system depends upon the building configuration, height, loads and geotechnical considerations. It may have to be evolved for a given building. For example, Burj-al-Arab and Burj-al-Khalifa, Dubai, employed innovative structural systems to meet the specific requirements.

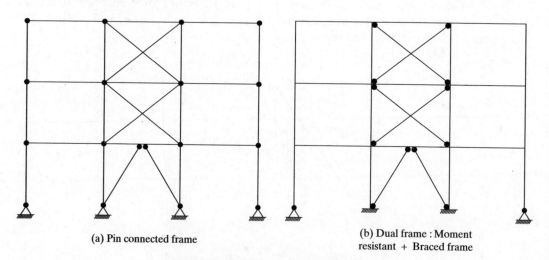

(a) Pin connected frame

(b) Dual frame : Moment resistant + Braced frame

Figure 12.5   Connections in steel frames.

12.4 CONCRETE FRAME AND SHEAR WALLS

Consider a wall system with different degrees of openings in Figure 12.6. A solid RC wall is shown in Figure12.6(a), whereas a wall with very large opening is shown in Figure12.6(c). The wall section is shown below the sectional elevation in each frame. The frame in Figure 12.6(a) is a shear wall frame, whereas the frame in Figure 12.6(c) can be said to be a moment resistant frame. The middle frame with intermediate openings can be said to be a coupled shear wall frame.

The moment resistant frame and shear wall frame deform in different modes under lateral loads as shown in Figure 12.7. A wall deflects in flexure mode, whereas a frame deflects in shear mode. Therefore, in literature, a shear wall is now referred to as a *flexure wall* rather than a *shear wall*.

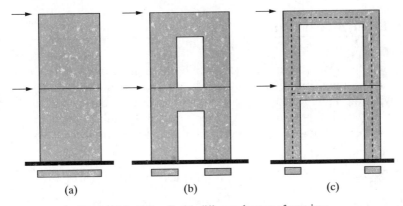

(a)   (b)   (c)

Figure 12.6   RC wall with different degrees of openings.

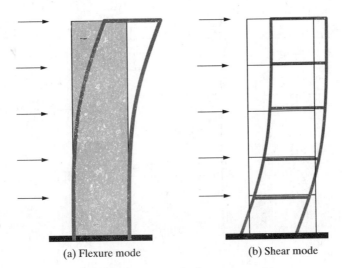

(a) Flexure mode   (b) Shear mode

Figure 12.7   Deflection modes.

Moment-resistant Frame

- Deforms predominantly in a shear mode
- Lateral resistance is due to rigidity of beam–column/slab joints

Shear Wall

- Deforms essentially in bending mode
- Only low shear walls with H/W ratio <1 fail in shear
- Behave mostly like a slender vertical cantilever
- Designed to resist the combined effect of axial, shear and bending about strong axis

12.5 MEMBER PROPORTIONS

One of the most difficult decisions while designing a building is how to proportion the various members relatively. Each beam and column can be designed only after knowing the member forces from analysis after considering various load combinations. However, there is a need to keep a watch on their relative proportions. It may lead to the following two situations in a moment resistant frame (Figure 12.8(a)):

1. Strong beam–weak column proportions (Figure 12.8(b))
2. Weak beam–strong column proportions (Figure 12.8(c))

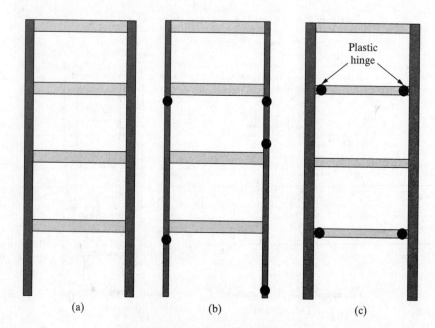

(a)   (b)   (c)

Figure 12.8   Member proportions.

A frame with strong beam–weak column proportions will develop plastic hinges in columns first in the event of a severe force. Inelasticity even in a few columns may eventually lead to early collapse of the whole frame. A frame with weak beam–strong column will develop plastic hinges in beams first. Inelasticity in a beam will eventually lead to a local failure in that bay only. Thus, it is a local failure, whereas, it is a global failure in the former case. Obviously, a local failure is always preferred over a global failure.

12.6 IRREGULARITY IN CONFIGURATIONS OF BUILDINGS

The simplest form of a building is cubical, that is symmetric about each of its three axes. It is easy to analyse, design, construct and has a much better performance in the event of severe loadings. It is called a regular building. However, architects prefer to be innovative and come up with all kinds of configurations leading to unsymmetry in the plan, elevation or both. These irregularities may also be in the mass distribution or stiffness distribution in the building. An irregularity leads to stress concentration in certain areas and torsion about the vertical axis of the building. Both these factors influence the performance of a building in the event of a severe earthquake, besides making the analysis and design quite complicated. A regular building vibrates in translational mode, whereas an irregular building vibrates in translational and torsional mode. Many structures collapsed due to irregularity during the past earthquakes in various parts of the world. A torsional mode imposes a very high ductility demand on the flexible side columns of the building which generally exceeds the ductility capacity and leads to immediate collapse. Some of the worst irregularities are as follows (Figures 12.9 and 12.10):

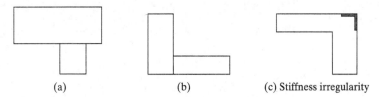

(a)   (b)   (c) Stiffness irregularity

Figure 12.9   Typical plan irregularity—re-entrant corners.

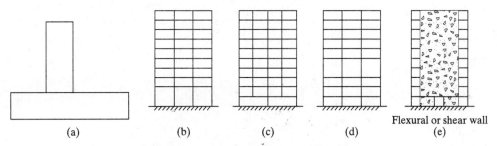

Flexural or shear wall

(a)   (b)   (c)   (d)   (e)

Figure 12.10   Vertical irregularity—stiffness.

(a) Re-entrant corners
(b) Soft and weak storeys
(c) Discontinuous shear walls
(d) Variations in perimeter strength and stiffness

Detailed diagrams for different types of irregularities are available in IS:1893-Part 1-2002. The term *irregularity* gives rise to two new terms: *centre of mass* (CM) and *centre of stiffness or rigidity* (CR). These are defined for each floor of a building in each of the two orthogonal directions. Centre of mass is defined as the centre of gravity of all the masses acting on a floor. It includes 50% of the mass above and below the floor under consideration acting through the columns or walls. Similarly, centre of rigidity is defined as the centre of gravity of stiffness of all the lateral load resisting elements on a floor. The distance between the centre of mass and centre of rigidity on a given floor is called *eccentricity*. A regular building is expected to have a nearly zero eccentricity.

The terms *re-entrant corner, soft storey* and *weak storey* are defined as follows (IS:1893-Part 1):

- Plan configurations of a structure and its lateral force resisting system contain re-entrant corners where both projections of the structure beyond the entrant corner are greater than 15% of its plan dimension in the given direction.
- A soft storey is one in which the lateral stiffness is less than 70% of that in the storey above or less than 80% of the average lateral stiffness of the three storeys above.
- A weak storey is one in which the storey lateral strength is less than 80% of that in the storey above. The storey lateral strength is the total strength of all seismic force resisting elements sharing the storey shear in the given direction.

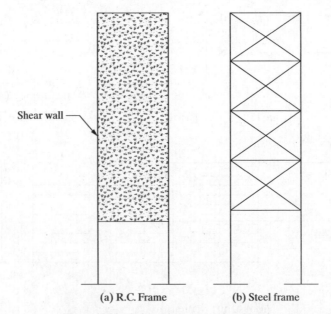

(a) R.C. Frame   (b) Steel frame

Figure 12.11   Soft/weak storey—ground level.

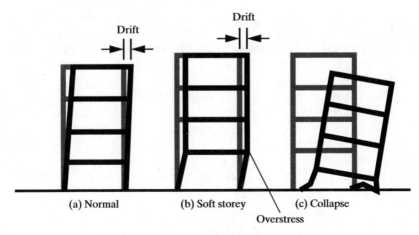

Figure 12.12   Failure mechanism in a soft storey.

Different situations of soft and or weak storey are shown in Figures 12.10(b), (c), (d) and Figure 12.11 where storey heights are significantly different, or a column, shear wall or bracing members are discontinued. The mechanism of failure in a soft storey is shown in Figure 12.12. It deflects essentially in sway mode leading to stress concentration at the upper ends of the columns of the corresponding storey and thus complete collapse.

A regular building configuration provides the following advantages:

(a) Uniform strength and stiffness distribution

(b) Minimum eccentricity between centre of mass and centre of stiffness thus minimizing torsion

(c) Minimum stress concentration

(d) Continuous load path up to the foundation

(e) Ease in design and construction of beams, columns, bracing members and shear walls.

12.7 MODELLING OF A BUILDING

A building is a space structure and consists of any of the various kinds of structural systems. The term *modelling of a building* means how to idealize a building for convenience in analysis and design? There are two kinds of elements in any building: structural elements and non-structural elements. Non-structural elements do not participate in the load carrying mechanism. These elements need to be identified and removed from the building for the purpose of analysis. Only their self-weight needs to be considered. The modelling will depend upon the shape, size, configuration, loads, proposed structural system and geotechnical conditions. A building may be modelled as a series of 2D plane frames in two orthogonal directions. In each plane frame, masses may be lumped at the floor levels, with each mass having one degree of freedom, that of lateral displacement in the direction under consideration. At each floor, 50% of the mass of the storey above this floor and 50% of the mass from the storey below this floor under consideration is lumped at this floor. Similarly, on each vertical frame, 50% of the mass is lumped from the adjoining frame on its left, and 50% of the mass is lumped from the adjoining frame on its right.

A building may be modeled as a 3D space frame with each floor having three degrees of freedom—two orthogonal translations and one rotation—all in the horizontal plane. A building may also be modelled as a space frame with six degrees of freedom at each node or joint. In case, soil is weak, soil-structure interaction also needs to be considered. Choice of a model will depend essentially upon the judgement and experience of the designer. The following salient features of modelling must be kept in mind:

1. A building may be considered to consist of a number of vertical and lateral load resisting systems connected by horizontal diaphragms. The diaphragm may be rigid or flexible in a given case and should be modelled suitably.

2. The model must adequately represent the distribution of mass and stiffness so that all significant mode shapes and inertia forces are properly accounted.

3. The model should account for the contribution of joint regions to the deformability of the building, for example the end zones in beams or columns of frame type structures. These end zones are also modelled as rigid links. The rigid links become critical in case the frame has shear walls also.

4. The mass and stiffness of non-structural elements such as in-fill walls, which may significantly influence the response of the structure, should also be modelled.

5. When the floor diaphragms of the building are taken as being rigid in their own planes, the masses at each floor may be lumped at the centre of gravity (CM).

6. In concrete buildings and in composite steel-concrete buildings, the stiffness of the load bearing elements should, in general, be evaluated taking into account the effect of cracking. Such stiffness should correspond to the initiation of yielding of the reinforcement.

7. In the absence of more accurate information, the elastic stiffness properties of concrete elements may be taken equal to one-half of the corresponding stiffness of the uncracked elements. It is also usual to consider the effect of floor slab in the stiffness of beams by taking the width of the beam as two times its original width.

12.8 BASE SHEAR IN A BUILDING

In the event of an earthquake, the seismic waves travel in all directions inside earth and thus shake it. It is, therefore, natural that an earthquake force is determined at the base of a building in the form of base shear. The base shear is given by the following equation (IS1893-Part 1):

$$V_b = \alpha_h W \tag{12.1a}$$

TABLE 12.2 ZONE FACTOR

Zone	II	III	IV	V
Zone Factor	0.10	0.16	0.24	0.36

TABLE 12.3 IMPORTANCE FACTOR

Structure	Importance Factor
Important service and community centres—hospital, power house, schools, water tanks, telephone exchange, TV station, assembly halls, etc.	1.50
Other buildings, but I/R .LE. 1	1.0

$$\alpha_h = \frac{Z}{2} \frac{I}{R} \frac{S_a}{g}$$ (12.1b)

where α_h = horizontal seismic coefficient

Z = zone factor for MCE condition, Table 12.2

I = importance factor, Table 12.3

R = response reduction factor

S_a = spectral acceleration depending upon the period of vibration and damping

g = acceleration due to gravity

W = seismic weight of building

The zone factor depends upon the seismicity of a given area. The important factor of a building depends upon its post-earthquake utility, that is consequence of its collapse on the rescue and rehabilitation programme of the community, as well as on its safety and life. Response reduction factor in discussed later in this chapter.

The ordinates for the response spectra were given in Chapter 8. Equation (12.1) is applicable to any structure—building or a non-building. However, the rest of the treatment of the subject in the following sections is applicable to buildings only.

Seismic Weight of Floors The seismic weight of each floor is its full dead load plus appropriate amount of imposed load. While computing the seismic weight of each floor, the weight of columns and walls in any storey is equally distributed to the floors above and below the storey.

Seismic Weight of Building The seismic weight of the whole building is the sum of the seismic weights of all the floors. Further, any weight supported in between storeys is distributed to the floors above and below in inverse proportion to its distance from the floors.

It is known that an earthquake force is essentially an inertia force. The reasoning behind considering only a part of the imposed load present on a floor is that only the mass that is fixed to the floor contributes to the inertia term $(m\ddot{x})$. The imposed load by definition is a live load whose magnitude and location on a floor will change with time. Therefore, it is quite logical to consider only a part of the total imposed load contributing to the inertia force. The code requires that for imposed loads up to 3 kN/m^2, consider only 25% load and above that only 50% of the total load. Imposed load present on the roof is ignored. It should be remembered that any load that is fixed to the floor or columns or walls must be considered 100%.

12.9 FUNDAMENTAL PERIOD OF VIBRATION

The fundamental period of any building may be determined either by frequency analysis or eigenvalue problem using any commercially available software. The fundamental period of vibration of a structure can also be determined using the Rayleigh method.

$$T = 2 \pi \sqrt{\frac{\sum_{i=1}^{n} w_i x_i^2}{g \sum_{i=1}^{n} F_i x_i}} \tag{12.2}$$

where, x_i = elastic horizontal displacements at i^{th} level due to lateral forces F_i ignoring the effect of torsion

w_i = weight at the ith floor

This equation gives fairly reasonable estimate of the period because it takes account of mass and stiffness distribution in the building. The eigenvalue analysis may not give a correct fundamental period of a building because of modelling issues. It is a general practice not to model non-structural elements, that is in-fill masonry walls. Thus, the model considers mass of such walls but ignores their stiffness. This results in a longer period of vibration leading to a lower estimation of the spectral acceleration (S_a/g) from the elastic response spectrum. Therefore, most building codes put a restriction on the period or frequency estimated from the eigenvalue analysis to take care of modelling lacuna.

IS:1893-2002 Part 1 requires that period of a building must also be determined by the following empirical relation:

$$T = 0.075 \, H^{0.75} \quad \text{for a RC moment-resistant building} \tag{12.3a}$$

$$T = 0.085 \, H^{0.75} \quad \text{for a steel moment-resistant building} \tag{12.3b}$$

where, T = fundamental period of the building (in first mode) in seconds

H = height of the building in meter. This excludes the basement storeys where basement walls are connected with the ground floor deck or fitted between the building columns.

The fundamental period of a RC framed building with masonry in-fill walls or RC shear walls may be determined by the following empirical relation:

$$T = \frac{0.09H}{\sqrt{D}} \tag{12.3c}$$

where, D = depth of building in meter in the direction of the earthquake force.

It should be noted that Equations (12.3) are not applicable to an auditorium building, industrial building, metro station, stadium or aircraft hangar etc. The period of vibration in such cases need to be estimated using the eigenvalue problem as discussed in Chapter 10.

These equations were intended to give a quick estimate of the period. These are based only upon the height and plan dimensions of a building. Equations (12.3a) and (12.3b) were based on a number of tests carried out on real RC and steel buildings in the USA. The period so computed varies between ±20% of the actual period of a building. The empirical computation of period of structures is quite debatable. There is considerable difference of opinion among different codes. Let us first look at some of the other international code stipulations.

ASCE 7-2007   Clause 12.8.2.1 requires that approximate period may be calculated from the following equation:

$$T_a = C_t H_n^x \tag{12.4}$$

where,   the constant C_t and exponent x are given in Table 12.4.
    H_n = total height of a building above the basement

The fundamental period of the structure, T, in the direction under consideration should be established using the structural properties and deformational characteristics of the resisting elements in a properly substantiated analysis. It has also provided a table for another coefficient C_u for different design spectral acceleration parameter S_{D1}. It requires that the fundamental period, T, shall not exceed the product of the coefficient for upper limit on calculated period (C_u) and the approximate fundamental period, T_a, is determined in accordance with Equation (12.4). Alternatively, it is permitted to use the approximate building period, T_a directly.

Alternatively, for RC or steel buildings up to 12 stories high whose average storey height is at least 3 m, the approximate fundamental period can also be calculated using the following equation:

$$T_a = 0.1 N \tag{12.5}$$

where, N = number of storeys above the base

Equation (12.5) was one of the earliest empirical equations to estimate the period of a building. It is no doubt the simplest equation and gives a fairly reasonable estimate. No strings are attached to this equation except that it should not be used for buildings beyond 12 stories.

TABLE 12.4   APPROXIMATE PERIOD CALCULATION COEFFICIENTS

	Constant C_t	Exponent x
Steel M-R frames	0.0724	0.80
Concrete M-R frames	0.0466	0.90
Eccentrically braced steel frames and Steel buckling restrained frames	0.0731	0.75
All other structural systems	0.0488	0.75

The approximate fundamental period, T_a, for masonry or concrete shear wall structures is permitted to be determined from Equation (12.6a) as follows:

$$T_a = \frac{0.0019}{\sqrt{C_w}} H_n \tag{12.6a}$$

$$C_w = \frac{100}{A_B} \sum_{i=1}^{x} \left(\frac{H_n}{H_i}\right)^2 \frac{A_i}{\left(1+0.83\left(\frac{H_i}{D_i}\right)^2\right)} \tag{12.6b}$$

where A_B = area of base of structure, m^2
A_i = web area of shear wall i in m^2
D_i = length of shear wall i in m
H_i = height of shear wall i in m
x = number of shear walls in the building effective in resisting lateral forces in the direction under consideration

EUROCODE 1998-Part 1   Clause 4.3.3.2.2 of EC8-Part 1 2004 permits the use of the Rayleigh method (Equation (12.2)) for the determination of the fundamental period of vibration for a building.

Alternatively, for a RC moment-resistant building and eccentrically braced steel frames

$$T = 0.075\ H^{0.75} \tag{12.7a}$$

For a steel moment-resistant building

$$T = 0.085\ H^{0.75} \tag{12.7b}$$

$$T = 0.050\ H^{0.75}\ \text{for other buildings} \tag{12.7c}$$

where, H = Height of the building from the foundation or from top of a rigid basement, in m

However, the total height of buildings for use in Equations (12.7) is restricted to 40 m.
Alternatively, for structures with concrete or masonry shear walls, the approximate fundamental natural period of vibration (T_a) in seconds may be estimated by the empirical expression:

$$T_a = \frac{0.075}{\sqrt{A_c}} H^{0.75} \tag{12.8a}$$

where, $$A_c = \sum_{i=1}^{N_w} \left\{ A_i \times \left(0.2 + \left(\frac{L_{wi}}{H}\right)^2 \right) \right\} \tag{12.8b}$$

A_c = total effective area of shear walls in the first storey of the building in m^2
A_i = effective cross-sectional area of the shear wall i in the direction considered in the first storey of the building in m^2

l_{wi} = length of the shear wall i in the first storey in the direction parallel to the applied forces, in m, with the restriction that l_{wi}/H should not exceed 0.90

N_w = number of shear walls in the first storey

Equation (12.3c) gives very low period for buildings. This may result in increase in the earthquake force by a factor of at least two or more. Most of the other international codes have discontinued it.

12.10 EARTHQUAKE FORCE

There are two methods to determine the earthquake force in various members of a building once the base shear has been determined:

(a) Seismic coefficient method or static method

(b) Response spectrum method or modal analysis method or dynamic method

The seismic coefficient method is generally applicable to buildings up to 40 m in height and those are more or less symmetrical in plan and elevation. In other words, the eccentricity between the centre of mass (CM) and centre of rigidity (CR) should be nearly zero. The response spectrum method is a general method which is applicable to all kinds of buildings. The seismic coefficient method is a static method of analysis and does not account for mass and stiffness distribution in a building. Response spectrum method is a dynamic method which accounts for mass and stiffness distribution throughout the building. Thus, the response spectrum method has a wider applicability.

There is yet another method called as the time-history method of analysis but it requires one or more accelerograms for the specific site under consideration. It is usually chosen for a major project as it involves seismological studies at the site and development of site specific accelerograms or an ensemble of acelerograms. It involves time and money. IS:1893-2002 Part 1 does not cover the time-history analysis method. But ASCE 7 and Eurocode 1998-Part 1 cover and give detailed requirements for time-history analysis.

In nearly each building code, it is assumed that the earthquake force acts along any one orthogonal axis in the horizontal plane of the building at a time. Thus, two analyses are required—one along each of the two axes. If it is desired to apply the earthquake force in more than one direction simultaneously, then the code gives combination rules. In case, a building has a non-orthogonal plan, an appropriate combination rule can be applied. The kind of seismic analysis and design procedure for different types of buildings is listed in Table 12.5.

In order to account for strength and stiffness degradation and estimate ductility requirements, performance of a building in a severe earthquake, a non-linear time-history analysis with appropriate hysteresis models and damping properties needs to be carried out as discussed in Chapter 13.

TABLE 12.5   EARTHQUAKE ANALYSIS AND DESIGN PROCEDURES

Method of Analysis	Material Behaviour	Type of Configuration	Design Philosophy
Static analysis—linear	Elastic	Regular	Limit state design for serviceability
	Inelastic	Regular	Limit state design for collapse
Dynamic analysis—linear	Elastic	Regular or irregular	Limit state design for serviceability
	Inelastic	Regular or irregular	Limit state design for collapse
Dynamic analysis— nonlinear time-history	Inelastic—reversed cyclic using hysteresis behaviour	Regular or irregular	Limit state design for collapse

12.10.1 Seismic Coefficient Method

Once the fundamental period of vibration has been estimated using the IS code or eigenvalue analysis, it is possible to estimate the base shear using Equation (12.1). The next step is to distribute this base shear along the height of the building and then laterally to the various frames arranged in the horizontal x- and y-directions.

Vertical Distribution of Base Shear   The lateral force at each floor can be estimated using Equation (12.9), which assumes a parabolic distribution of the force along the height of the building:

$$Q_i = \frac{w_i h_i^2}{\displaystyle\sum_{j=1}^{n} w_j h_j^2} V_b \qquad (12.9)$$

where, Q_i = lateral force at the ith floor

h_i, h_j = height of ith floor or j^{th} floor measured above the base

w_i, w_j = seismic weight of the ith or j^{th} floor

n = total number of storeys

Horizontal Distribution of Shear   The lateral force estimated at a given floor now needs to be distributed to the various frames of the building in proportion to their rigidities considering rigidity of the diaphragm. It is assumed that the floor is very rigid in its own plane. Thus,

$Q_{ik} \propto$ distance of the frame from the centre of gravity of the mass at a floor

where, Q_{ik} = lateral force in k^{th} frame at the ith floor

In other words, the frames farthest from the centre of gravity will carry the maximum lateral force. It is a very time consuming and laborious procedure if carried out manually. Therefore, it is much more convenient to make use of a software. There are many user-friendly softwares with very powerful graphical user interface (GUI) both for pre-processing and post-processing of data. Only the base shear parameters including period, the level of top of the rigid basement or foundation and top of the building need to be specified along with the computer model, and rest of the calculations are done by the software.

12.10.2 Response Spectrum Method

2D Analysis   The plane frame analysis was carried out until the 1990s. Now with the availability of very powerful software, the data preparation is GUI based, very easy and fast. Therefore, a 3D space frame dynamic analysis has become a common practice. The plane frame analysis is essentially meant for learning and understanding the process. The basic steps are as follows:

1. Idealize and isolate a 2D plane frame out of the 3D building.
2. Compute lumped mass at each floor level of the plane frame. The spacing of frames right angles to the direction of the earthquake force must be known.
3. Carry out an undamped-free vibration analysis to evaluate eigenvalues and eigenvectors, that is natural periods of vibration and the corresponding mode shapes. Apply a check on the natural period as per the code.
4. Determine the base shear.
5. Distribute the base shear along the height of the frame using Equation (12.9).
6. Analyse the frame using any method of structural analysis—either manually or using a programme.
7. Carry out modal superimposition of member forces for the desired number of modes.
8. Analyse the frame for gravity loads—dead load and live load.
9. Superimpose the member forces using appropriate load combinations as per IS:456-2000 for a RC building or IS:800-2007 for a steel building.
10. Check the lateral deflections in the frame.

It is not possible to account for torsion in a plane frame. It can be done by placing all the 2D plane frames at their locations in 3D and carrying out a detailed manual calculation by locating centre of mass (CM) and centre of rigidity (CR). It is a very laborious procedure. Therefore, it is best to carry out a 3D dynamic analysis.

3D Analysis   It is important to know the point of application of the earthquake force in a building. It acts at the centre of mass (CM) of each floor. However, there may be some unsymmetry in a building in the plan leading to torsion about the vertical axis of the building. Torsion in a building is a very undesirable force and may lead to partial or complete collapse of the building in the event of a strong earthquake as experienced in the past several earthquakes all over the world. Therefore, it needs to be taken very seriously. The earthquake force is applied at the centre of mass to account for torsion. Most building codes give a pair of equations to define design eccentricity e_d:

$$e_{da} = \alpha e + \beta b \qquad (12.10a)$$

$$e_{db} = \delta e - \beta b \qquad (12.10b)$$

where e = structural eccentricity, that is distance between the centre of mass (CM) and centre of stiffness (CR) at a floor

b = maximum dimension of the building perpendicular to the direction of earthquake under consideration

α and δ = dynamic magnification factors

β = accidental eccentricity factor

The eccentricity e is to be measured both along x-and y-direction in a building at each floor. In case of a symmetric building, eccentricity e is zero. Even then this building will be analysed for accidental eccentricity. The purpose of dynamic magnification factors is to account for the possibility of the increase in in-plane torsion due to dynamic effects. These are prescribed when a static analysis is performed for torsion. The accidental eccentricity intends to take into account unforeseeable differences between computed and actual values of stiffness, yield strength and dead load masses, uncertainties in the unfavorable distribution of live load mass and rotational components of earthquake motion about a vertical axis. The accidental eccentricity is applicable in both static and dynamic analyses.

IS:1893-Part1   The eccentricity of the applied force is given by the following equations:

$$e_{da} = 1.5e + 0.05b \qquad (12.11a)$$

$$e_{db} = e - 0.05b \qquad (12.11b)$$

where, e_{da}, e_{db} = design eccentricity

e = computed eccentricity between the centre of rigidity and centre of mass at each floor

Again, different codes account for torsion differently. The physical interpretation of Equations (12.11) is illustrated in Figure 12.13. The earthquake force acts through the CM while the building resists it through equal and opposite force through CR. It develops a twisting moment $T = Ve_{da}$ or Ve_{db}. In columns and shear walls farthest from the centre of rigidity, the demand on strain becomes very critical due to torsion as seen in Figure 12.13(c) and may lead to complete collapse of the building.

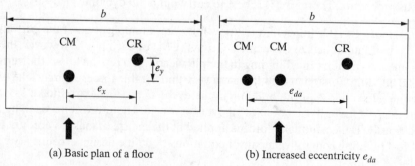

(a) Basic plan of a floor   (b) Increased eccentricity e_{da}

Figure 12.13   Design eccentricities in a floor plan in x-direction.

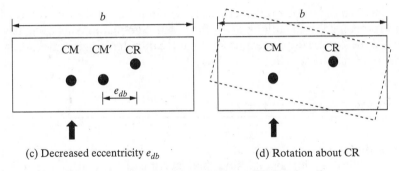

(c) Decreased eccentricity e_{db} (d) Rotation about CR

CM = computed centre of mass; CM′ = modified centre of mass

Figure 12.13 (Continued)

If the direction of earthquake reverses, the building will twist in the opposite direction.

ASCE 7-2007 Clause 12.8.4.2 of ASCE 7 specifies that a building with rigid diaphragm will be subjected to an accidental eccentricity of ±5% of the dimension of the building perpendicular to the direction of the applied forces.

$$e_a = e + 0.05b \tag{12.12a}$$

$$e_b = e - 0.05b \tag{12.12b}$$

A set of three dynamic analyses of a building is carried out in each of the two orthogonal directions: the force applied at the centre of mass, then the mass is shifted by +/– 0.05b on either side of the C.M. Finally, envelope is taken of the forces produced by these three dynamic analyses.

Clause 4.3.2 of the Eurocode 1998-Part 1 also makes use of Equation (12.12).

Orientation of Lateral Load Resisting Elements in a Building When the lateral load resisting elements are oriented along orthogonal horizontal direction, the structure shall be designed for the effects due to full design earthquake load in one horizontal direction at a time. When the lateral load-resisting elements are not oriented along the orthogonal horizontal directions, the structure shall be designed for the effects due to full design earthquake load in one horizontal direction plus 30% of the design earthquake load in the other direction. For instance:

$$\pm EL_x \pm 0.30\, EL_y \quad \text{or} \quad \pm 0.30\, EL_x \pm EL_y \tag{12.13}$$

When response from the three earthquake components are to be considered, the response due to each component may be combined using the assumption that when the maximum response from one component occurs, the responses from the other two components are 30% of their maximum. All possible combinations of the three components (EL_x, El_y and EL_z) including variations in sign (plus or minus) should be considered, Thus, the response due earthquake force (EL) is the maximum of the following three cases:

$$\pm EL_x \pm 0.30\, EL_y \pm 0.30\, EL_z$$

$$\pm 0.30\, EL_x \pm EL_y \pm 0.30\, EL_z$$

$$\pm 0.30\, EL_x \pm 0.30\, EL_y \pm EL_z \tag{12.14}$$

The entire process of design eccentricity, modal analysis, mode superimposition, non-orthogonal combinations and other load combinations as specified in a given design code is carried out seamlessly by the computer programmes. Only the appropriate data is to be supplied through GUI.

12.11 RESPONSE REDUCTION FACTOR

The capability of a structure to absorb energy within acceptable deformations and without failure is a highly desirable characteristic of any earthquake resistant design. Let us consider a typical base shear versus roof displacement curve of a structure subjected to a given earthquake motion until failure in plastic state as shown in Figure 12.14. The dots represent formation of plastic hinges as the base shear increases. The base shear level V_E represents elastic force, V_Y represents fully or significant yield force and V_D represents specified design force. The displacements D_D, D_E and D_Y represent displacement under the specified design force, under the elastic force, and fully yield design force, respectively. Thus, two force ratios can be defined:

$$R_1 = \frac{V_E}{V_D} > 1.0 \tag{12.15a}$$

$$R_2 = \frac{V_E}{V_Y} > 1.0 \tag{12.15b}$$

R_1 represents the ratio of elastic force to the specified design force for a given design earthquake motion. It is always greater than 1.0. R_2 represents the ratio of elastic force to the fully plastic or significant yield force. One more factor can be defined which is known as over strength factor as follows:

$$R_3 = \frac{V_Y}{V_D} > 1.0 \tag{12.15c}$$

Over strength is introduced in a structure by various means such as increase in size, reinforcement or material strength, etc. over their design values. The structure is

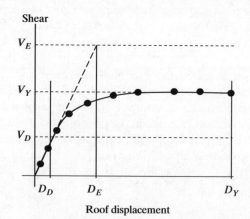

Figure 12.14 Base shear vs. roof displacement.

designed for a force level that is always lower than V_E. The level of significant yield force always exceeds the prescribed design force. Thus, a structure is forced to enter into the inelastic state and make use of its available reserve energy. This reduction in design force is possible due to the following reasons:

(a) As the structure begins to yield and deform inelastically, the effective period of response of the structure tends to lengthen, which for many structures results in a reduction in strength demand. It can be verified from the shape of the response spectrum curves for S_a/g.

(b) The inelastic action results in a significant amount of energy dissipation also known as *hysteretic damping.*

(c) Presence of over strength in a structure

Thus, a response reduction factor R_1 can be expressed as follows:

$$R_1 = R_2 R_3 \tag{12.16}$$

The combined effect, which is also known as the *ductility,* explains why a properly designed structure with a fully yielded strength that is significantly lower than the elastic seismic force demand is expected to provide a satisfactory performance under the design earthquake motion.

The question is how to assign a value to response reduction factor R for a given structural system, such as an ordinary RC frame, ductile M-R frame, shear wall frame, concentrically braced frame or eccentrically braced frame. It can be done based on experimental evidence on reversed cyclic loading on such frames and plotting their hysteresis loops as seen in Figure 12.15. A nonlinear analysis of a SDOF system having this hysteretic characteristics can be carried out under different earthquakes and estimating the available ductility. Thus, response reduction factors for different structural systems having different ductile detailing and therefore, hysteretic characteristics, can be estimated.

The Indian Code IS:1893-Part 1-2002 also includes calibration factor in R value between the previous edition of 1984 so that there is no significant change in the base

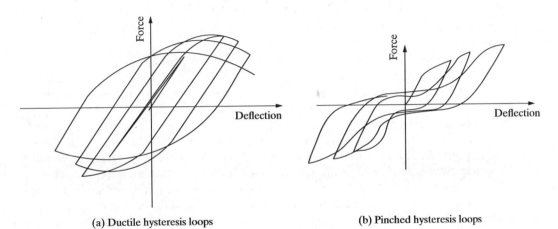

(a) Ductile hysteresis loops   (b) Pinched hysteresis loops

Figure 12.15   Hysteresis behaviour for different systems.

TABLE 12.6   RESPONSE REDUCTION FACTOR *R*

S. No.	Lateral Load Resisting System	R
Framed Building		
1.	RCC moment-resisting frame—ordinary	3
2.	RCC moment-resisting frame—special, that is, with ductile detailing	5
3.	Ordinary moment-resistant steel frame	4
	Ordinary steel frame with	
	(a) Concentric braces	4
	(b) Eccentric braces	4.5
4.	Special moment-resisting steel frame	5
	Special steel frame with concentric braces	4.5
	Special steel frame with eccentric braces	5
Building with Flexural (Shear) walls		
5.	Load bearing masonry wall building	
	(a) Unreinforced	1.5
	(b) Reinforced with horizontal bands	2.5
	(c) Reinforced with both vertical steel and horizontal bands	3
6.	RC flexural wall—ordinary	3
7.	RC flexural wall—ductile	4
Dual System		
8.	Ordinary flexural wall with ordinary M-R frame	3
9.	Ordinary flexural wall with ductile M-R frame	4
10.	Ductile flexural wall with ordinary M-R frame	4.5
11.	Ductile wall with ductile M-R frame	5

shear. The values of factor *R* are given in Table 12.6 for buildings. These factors are not unique across different international building codes. Different international codes deal with this aspect differently.

The minimum design and detailing requirements for RC buildings are given in IS:456-2000 and IS:13920-1993. The existence of alternate load paths or redundancy of a structural system is a desirable characteristic in a structural system. It increases the locations where energy can be dissipated and reduce the risk of collapse when individual members should fail or become severely damaged. Typical failures in 12-storey RC buildings during the Bhuj earthquake of 26 January 2001 are shown in Figures 12.16 and 12.17. Members and connections in such systems must therefore be detailed to accommodate these deformations in a ductile manner. The intention is to encourage a designer to provide ductile detailing and design it for a smaller earthquake force. Currently, there are no guidelines for ductile detailing for steel buildings in India. Therefore, a reference may be made to the AISC requirements or any other specialist literature.

Figure 12.16   Collapse of a 12-storey Mansi Tower,
Ahmedabad, January 2001.

Figure 12.17   12-storey Shikhar Tower,
Ahmedabad, January 2001.

12.12 BUILDING ON STILTS

It is a common practice to design a multi-storey building with parking at the ground floor. Thus, there are usually no walls in the ground floor but only columns. This is a perfect example of a soft storey (loss of stiffness). It may also be a case of weak storey (loss of storey shear strength). The building on soft storey or on stilts needs special precaution in order to avoid the formation of sway mechanism and, therefore, collapse. It should be possible to provide shear walls or diagonal braces in one or both directions at certain locations so that there is no hindrance to the movement of vehicles and at the same time there is no soft storey.

Several buildings having soft storeys have collapsed during earthquakes. The collapse of the Olive View Hospital building in San Fernando Earthquake 1971 is widely reported. Buildings still being built on stilts in the Himalayan hills are shown in Figure 12.18.

(a)   (b)

Figure 12.18 Buildings on stilts in Himalayan Hills (Uttarakhand).

12.13 DEFLECTION AND SEPARATION OF BUILDINGS

Lateral deflection of a structure should be calculated in accordance with accepted practice and based on the loads and requirements given in the code. The design of earthquake force was reduced by factor R in order to push the structure in inelastic region. Next, a linear elastic analysis is carried out to determine member forces and lateral displacements. These lateral deflections obtained from an elastic analysis should be multiplied with the same factor R to give realistic values of the anticipated deflections in the event of collapse. The non-structural components should be designed so as not to transfer to the structural system any forces unaccounted for in the design.

Adjacent structures may vibrate in phase or out of phase with each other during an earthquake depending upon their individual characteristics. If they vibrate out of phase, then there is a chance that they may pound on each other. This pounding effect has been observed in many earthquakes where the adjacent buildings are at arm length, for example in Mexico City during 1985 earthquake. Adjacent structures should either be separated by at least the sum of their individual deflections or should be connected to each other. The method of connection should take into account the mass, stiffness, strength, ductility and anticipated motion of the connected building and the character of the connection. The connected buildings should be assumed to have the lowest R value of the building connected unless the use of a higher value can be justified by rational analysis.

$$\text{Seismic gap} \geq R \times (\Delta_1 + \Delta_2)_{max} \tag{12.17}$$

where, Δ_1 and Δ_2 are maximum absolute elastic lateral deflections of the two adjacent buildings.

12.14 ILLUSTRATIVE EXAMPLES

Example 12.1

A 10-storey moment-resistant RC residential building has a plan dimension 20 m × 30 m and has 32 m height above the ground. It is located in Lucknow. Estimate the fundamental period of vibration and base shear coefficient if it is supported on medium soil.

Solution The fundamental period of vibration can be estimated using the empirical equation given in IS:1893-Part 1-2002 code.

$$T = 0.075 \, H^{0.75}$$

$$= 0.075 \times 32^{0.75} = 1 \text{ sec}$$

For a moment-resistant building, the empirical period of vibration is independent of its plan dimensions. Therefore, it will have the same period in both the horizontal directions. Lucknow is located in seismic zone III. The spectral acceleration value S_a/g for 5% damping and 1 sec period can be estimated from the IS:1893–2002 spectra given in Figure 8.25, Chapter 8.

Seismic zone $Z = 0.16$, $I = 1.0$, and $S_a/g = 1.36$

If the response reduction factor is taken as 5 for a ductile M-R frame building, then

$$\alpha_h = \frac{Z}{2} \frac{I}{R} \frac{S_a}{g} = \frac{0.16}{2} \times \frac{1}{5} \times 1.36$$

or,

$$\alpha_h = 0.02176 \qquad \square$$

Example 12.2

If the building in Example 12.1 has a period of vibration of 0.6 sec and 0.15 sec in second and third modes of vibrations, estimate the seismic coefficient in these modes.

Solution The spectral acceleration value S_a/g for 5% damping and 0.6 sec and 0.15 sec periods can be estimated from the IS:1893–2002 spectra (Figure 8.25):

$$S_a/g = 1.36/T = 1.36/0.6 = 2.27 \quad \text{for} \quad T = 0.6 \text{ sec}$$

and

$$S_a/g = 2.50 \quad \text{for} \quad T = 0.15 \text{ sec}$$

The seismic coefficient α_h in the 2nd mode is 0.036 and the 3rd mode is 0.04. ☐

Example 12.3

Find the period of vibration of the shear wall buildings and framed building shown in Figures 12.19(a) and 12.19(b) using the ASCE 7, Eurocode 8 and IS 1893 codal provisions.

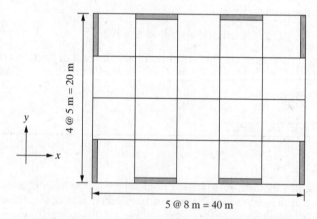

Figure 12.19(a) Shear wall building in plan (wall thickness = 30 cm).

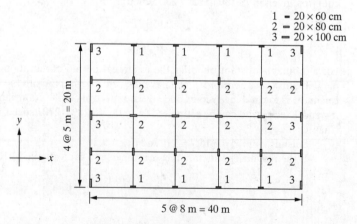

Figure 12.19(b) Framed building in plan.

Solution   In building A, there are 4 shear walls in each direction. In building B, there are large numbers of elongated columns in each direction. These elongated columns fall outside the geometric definition of a column. IS:13920 requires that in a column, the ratio of shortest cross-sectional dimension to the perpendicular dimension is not less than 0.4. In the present case, in building B, the width of each column = 200 mm.

$$\therefore \qquad D < 200/0.4 = 500 \text{ mm.}$$

$\therefore$ All elongated columns are to be treated as shear walls in the present case.

ASCE Formula

$$T_a = \frac{0.0019}{\sqrt{C_w}} H_n \tag{12.6a}$$

$$C_w = \frac{100}{A_B} \sum_{i=1}^{x} \left(\frac{H_n}{H_i}\right)^2 \frac{A_i}{\left(1+0.83\left(\frac{H_i}{D_i}\right)^2\right)} \tag{12.6b}$$

If height of both the buildings is 30 m and height of all walls and columns is also 30 m, the periods in the *x*-direction are given as follows:

Building A
$H_n = 30$ m, $H_i = 30$ m, $D_i = 8$ m, $A_B = 40 \times 20 = 800$ m², $A_i = 0.3 \times 8 = 2.4$ m²
$x = 4$
$C_w = 0.095$ and $T = 0.608$ sec

Building B
$H_n = 30$ m, $H_i = 30$ m, $A_B = 40 \times 20 = 800$ m²
$A_i = 0.2 \times 0.6 = 0.12$ m², $D_i = 0.6$ m, $x = 8$ walls
$A_i = 0.2 \times 0.8 = 0.16$ m², $D_i = 0.8$ m, $x = 4$ walls
$C_w = 0.00013$ and $T = 16.637$ sec Too high!

Apparently, the ASCE formula does not envisage such elongated columns in a building. Let us use Equation (12.4)

$$T_a = 0.0488 \times 30^{0.75} = 0.625 \text{ sec}$$

Eurocode EC8

$$T_a = \frac{0.075}{\sqrt{A_c}} H^{0.75} \tag{12.8a}$$

where,

$$A_c = \sum \left\{ A_i \times \left(0.2 + \left(\frac{l_{wi}}{H}\right)^2\right) \right\} \tag{12.8b}$$

Building A
$H = 30$ m, $l_{wi} = 8$ m, $A_i = 0.3 \times 8 = 2.4$ m², no. of walls in *x*-direction = 4
$A_c = 2.603$, $T = 0.596$ sec

Building B
$H = 30$ m, $l_{wi} = 0.6$ m, $A_i = 0.2 \times 0.6 = 0.12$ m², no. of walls in *x*-direction = 8
$H = 30$ m, $l_{wi} = 0.8$ m, $A_i = 0.2 \times 0.8 = 0.16$ m², no. of walls in *x*-direction = 4
$A_c = 0.32$, $T = 1.70$ sec

I.S. Code

$$T = \frac{0.09H}{\sqrt{D}} \qquad (12.3c)$$

Building A
$H = 30$ m, $D = 40$ m, $T = 0.427$ sec

Building B
$H = 30$ m, $D = 40$ m, $T = 0.427$ sec

A comparison of all the three equations for these two buildings is shown in Table 12.7.

TABLE 12.7   COMPARISON OF PERIODS, sec

	ASCE 7	EC 8	IS:1893-Part 1
Building A	0.608	0.596	0.427
Building B	16.637/0.625	1.70	0.427

The computation of fundamental period of buildings using the empirical equations given in the codes need to be carried out carefully. The IS Code gives the lowest period for both buildings. The Eurocode gives highest period for Building B.   ☐

Example 12.4

A 4-storey building having moment-resistant frame with in-fill walls is located in Srinagar, J&K and has the following data:

Floor	Seismic Weight, kN	Storey Height, m
Roof	5500	3.25
3rd	7250	3.25
2nd	7800	3.25
1st	6500	3.75

Its plan dimensions are 15×20 m. Determine the base shear if it is located on soft soil and has a special ductile detailing. Also, determine the lateral force acting at each floor.

Solution
Base shear

$$V_B = \alpha_h W$$

$$\alpha_h = \frac{Z}{2} \frac{I}{R} \frac{S_a}{g}$$

Fundamental period

$$T = \frac{0.09H}{\sqrt{D}}$$

Along the short direction, $T_1 = \dfrac{0.09 \times 13.50}{\sqrt{15}} = 0.314$ sec

Along the long direction, $T_2 = \dfrac{0.09 \times 13.50}{\sqrt{20}} = 0.272$ sec

In case the period of vibration is estimated using Equation (12.7c),

$$T = 0.05\, H^{0.75} = 0.05 \times 13.50^{0.75} = 0.352 \text{ sec}$$

$\therefore\ S_a/g = 2.5$ in both directions since $0.10 \le T \le 0.67$ sec for soft soil

For seismic zone V, $Z = 0.36$, $I = 1.0$, total seismic weight $W = 25250$ kN

Base shear $\qquad V_B = \dfrac{0.36}{2} \times \dfrac{1}{5} \times 2.5 \times 25250 = 2272.5$ kN

The vertical distribution of base shear can be determined using the following equation:

$$Q_i = \frac{W_i h_i^2}{\sum_{j=1}^{n} W_j h_j^2} V_B$$

The distribution of earthquake force on different floors is shown in Table 12.8.

TABLE 12.8   LATERAL FORCES AND STOREY SHEARS

Floor	W_i kN	h_i m	$W_i h_i^2$	F_i kN	V_i kN
Roof	5500	13.50	1002375	1017.97	849.74
3rd	7250	10.25	761703	773.55	1737.6
2nd	7800	7.0	382200	388.15	2165.97
1st	6500	3.75	91406	92.83	2272.5
			2237684	2272.50	

The lateral force and storey shear distributions are shown in Figure 12.20.   □

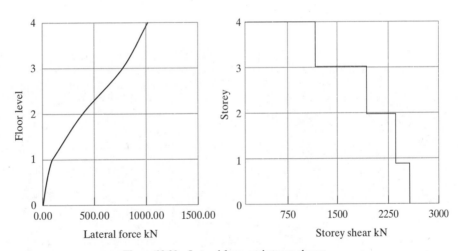

Figure 12.20   Lateral force and storey shears.

Example 12.5

An industrial steel building (Category 2 as per IS:1893-Part 4) is located in Bhopal on hard rock. Its seismic weight is 15000 kN and period from dynamic analysis is 0.7 sec. Estimate its base shear.

Solution   Since this is an industrial building, IS:1893-Part 4 is applicable and not Part 1. However, the basic principles of estimating the base shear remain unchanged. Thus, this example has been chosen.

Bhopal is located in seismic zone II. $Z = 0.10$

As per the frequency analysis, its period is 0.7 sec. It satisfies clause 9.3.

$$\therefore \qquad S_a/g = 1/T = 1.428$$

Clause 8 of IS:1893-Part 4 defines a Category 2 structure as follows:

Structures whose failure can cause conditions that can lead to direct or indirect serious fire threat or extensive structural damage within the plant complex. Structures, which are required to handle emergencies immediately after an earthquake, also are included.

Table 4 requires that a Category 2 structure be designed for MCE shaking as per Clause 7.3.2.

Table 6 requires that importance factor for Category 2 structure should be taken as 1.5.

Clause 9.4 requires that damping for a steel structure under MCE condition should be taken as 7%.

Table 9 gives the multiplying factor for 7% damping as 0.90.

For MCE shaking, the design horizontal seismic coefficient α_h shall be estimated as:

$$\alpha_h = ZI\frac{S_a}{g} = 0.10 \times 1.5 \times 1.428 \times 0.90 = 0.19 \text{ or } 19\%$$

Table 5 of IS:1893-Part 4 requires that an industrial building located in seismic zone II must be designed for a minimum lateral force of 1.5% of its seismic weight.

$$\text{Base shear} = 0.19\,W > 0.015\,W \quad \text{OK} \qquad \qquad \square$$

Example 12.6

A single-storey building is shown in Figure 12.21(a). There are two M-R frames along grid lines A and D with lateral stiffness k and there are two shear walls along grid lines 1 and 4 with lateral stiffness $5k$. Estimate the lateral forces if the earthquake force acts in y-direction.

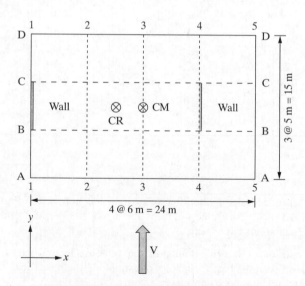

Figure 12.21(a) Plan of a single-storey building.

Solution   By inspection, it can be seen that the centre of mass of the building will be at the c.g. of the building on grid 3, while centre of stiffness will be midway between grids 1 and 4, and A and D.

$\therefore$ Eccentricity $e = 3$ m along x-direction from its c.g.

Consider the lateral force in y-direction. Design eccentricities are given as follows:

$$e_{da} = 1.5\,e + 0.05\,b \qquad\qquad (12.11a)$$

$$e_{db} = e - 0.05\,b \qquad\qquad (12.11b)$$

$$b = 24 \text{ m}$$

$\therefore$

$$e_{da} = 1.5 \times 3 + 0.05 \times 24 = 5.7 \text{ m}$$

$$e_{db} = 0.5 \times 3 - 0.05 \times 24 = 0.3 \text{ m}$$

Shear due to torsion along each axis resisted by a particular element is proportional to the lateral stiffness of the element relative to the total torsional stiffness of the storey and its distance from the centre of rigidity. The total torsional stiffness of the storey I_p about the centre of rigidity is given by

$$I_p = \sum K_{yi} x_i^2 + \sum K_{xi} y_i^2$$

where K_{xi} is lateral stiffness of element i along x-direction (about y-axis)

K_{yi} is lateral stiffness of element i along y-direction (about x-axis)

I_p is similar to polar moment of inertia of a rivet group about its centroid.

Polar moment of inertia I_p calculation in y-direction

Line	K_y	x, m	$K_y x^2$
1-1	5 k	−9	405 k
4-4	5 k	+9	405 k
			$\Sigma 810$ k

x is measured from CR to the c.g. of the wall.

Polar moment of inertia I_p calculation in x-direction

Line	K_x	y, m	$K_x y^2$
A-A	k	−7.5	56.25 k
D-D	k	+7.5	56.25 k
			$\Sigma 112.5$ k

y is measured from CR to the c.g. of the wall.

$\therefore$ Polar moment of inertia $I_p = 810 + 112.5 = 922.5$ k

Consider the frames in the x-direction due to earthquake shear in y-direction:

Additional shear on any frame or column line due to torsion T is given by

$$V'_{xj} = \frac{T K_{xj} y_j}{I_p}$$

where $T = V \times e_x = V \times e_{da} = 5.7\,V$ anti-clockwise

It should be remembered that the earthquake shear V will act through the centre of mass, whereas the resisting shear, equal and opposite to V, will act through the centre of rigidity. The torsion will change its direction with the change in the direction of earthquake. At the centre of rigidity, there is a net force V and an anti-clockwise moment 5.7 V.

Consider Frame A-A, $e_{da} = 5.7$ m

$$V'_{xA} = \frac{V \times 5.7 \times k \times (-7.5)}{922.5k} = -0.046 \ V$$

and on Frame D-D

$$V'_{xD} = \frac{V \times 5.7 \times k \times (7.5)}{922.5k} = 0.046 \ V$$

Now consider frames in y-direction due to earthquake shear in y-direction:

Additional shear due to torsion $T = Ve_{da}$ is given by

$$V'_{yj} = \frac{TK_{yj}x_j}{I_p}$$

∴ Net shear

$$V_{yj} = \frac{VK_{yj}}{\sum K_{yj}} \pm V'_{yj}$$

Consider Frame 1-1

$$V_{y1} = \frac{V\,5k}{10k} - \frac{V \times 5.7 \times 5k \times 9}{922.5k} = (0.50 - 0.278) \ V = 0.222 \ V$$

Frame 4-4

$$V_{y4} = (0.50 + 0.278)V = 0.778 \ V$$

Thus, wall 4–4 carries maximum shear.

Direction of the shear acting on various lateral load-resisting elements
The earthquake direction is reversible. Therefore, the torsion can be assumed to be either clockwise positive or negative. It would not make any difference. The additional shear due to torsion is computed as $\pm 0.278 \ V$. Thus, under an anti-clockwise torsion, the forces on the Frames 1-1 and 4-4 will look as shown in Figure 12.21(b), and under a clockwise torsion, the forces will look as shown in Figure 12.21(c). In any case, Frame 4-4 will continue to carry more shear, that is equal to 0.778 V.

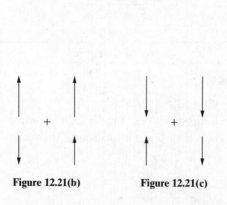

Figure 12.21(b)   **Figure 12.21(c)**   **Figure 12.21(d)**   Total lateral shears on frames/walls.

The total shears on each of the four lateral force resisting elements are shown in Figure 12.21(d) under an anti-clockwise torsion.

Similarly, calculations for $e_{db} = 0.3$ m can be made.   □

Example 12.7

A single-storey RC frame building is shown in Figure 12.22. It is enclosed with 230 mm thick brick masonry walls on three sides up to 3 m high and 16 no. RC columns 230×230 mm and 3.9 m high. There are 230×450 mm deep beams along A-A, B-B, C-C and D-D. The slab thickness is 125 mm and water proofing layer is 100 mm thick over the slab. A section x-x through the wall is shown in Figure 12.22(b). Analyse the building for torsion and short column effects in seismic zone IV assuming ductile RC frames. The building is resting on hard soil.

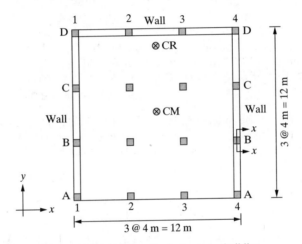

Figure 12.22(a)   Plan of a single-storey building.

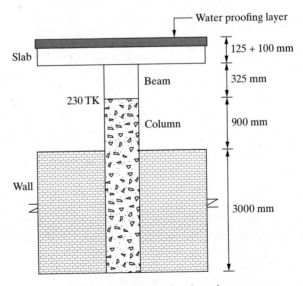

Figure 12.22(b)   Section through x-x.

Solution   There are two main features of this building:

(a) It is unsymmetric in plan about x-axis, therefore, it carries torsion when the earthquake force acts along x-direction.

(b) The columns along the periphery will act as short column of 0.9 m height because they are restrained by the masonry walls.

Let us estimate the forces in these columns by taking the effect of torsion and short column effect.

Dead load

Density of brick masonry = 20 kN/m³

Density of concrete = 25 kN/m³

Density of water proofing material = 20 kN/m³

Dead load of roof = 0.125 × 25 + 0.10 × 20 = 5.125 kN/m²

∴ Total dead load of roof = 5.125 × 12 × 12 = 738 kN

Weight of 230 mm wall = 0.23 × 12 × 3 × 20 = 165.6 kN

∴ Total weight of 3 walls = 3 × 165.6 = 497 kN

Beams, 4 no. = 0.325 × 0.23 × 12 × 25 × 4 = 89.7 kN

3.9 m high columns, 6 no. = 0.23 × 0.23 × 3.9 × 25 × 6 = 31 kN

0.9 m high columns, 10 no. = 0.23 × 0.23 × 0.9 × 25 × 10 = 11.9 kN

∴ Total weight of building = 1370 kN

Although all the 16 columns are in RCC and 9.3 m high, the weight of 10 columns enclosed within the masonry is included in the weight of the walls. There will be slight error on account of difference in material density but it can be ignored.

Seismic weight = 738 + 0.5 × 497 + 89.7 + 11.9 + 0.5 × 31 = 1200 kN

Period of building = 0.1 sec

Base shear
$$V_B = \frac{Z}{2} \frac{I}{R} \frac{S_a}{g} W_{\text{effective}}$$

For zone IV, $Z = 0.24$, $I = 1.25$, $R = 4$ for ductile M-R frame although the code permits $R = 5$.

For 5% damping, $S_a/g = 2.5$

∴   Base shear = $\dfrac{0.24}{2} \times \dfrac{1.25}{4} \times 2.50 \times 1200 = 112.5$ say 120 kN

Let us consider earthquake force along y-axis.

The building is symmetric about the y-axis. Hence, lateral force on each frame along 1-1 and 4-4 will be 60 kN each as shown in Figure 12.22(c).

By visual inspection, the centre of mass CM will be at the centre of gravity of the building while the centre of rigidity CR will lie at mid centre of D-D.

Thus, eccentricity e = 6 m. Let us take it as a design eccentricity also for the purpose of this example.

If the earthquake force acts along x-axis, there will be a torsion equal to 120 × 6 = 720 kNm

It will be resisted by the three masonry walls being very stiff. The equilibrium of forces is shown in Figure 12.22(c). Now member forces in Frame D-D can be computed manually or by using any software for the forces shown in Figure 12.22(d).

Area of cross-section of a column = 0.23 × 0.23 = 0.0530 m²

Moment of inertia of a column I = 2.33 × 10⁻⁴ m⁴

Area of cross-section of a beam = 0.23 × 0.45 = 0.1035 m²

Moment of inertia of a beam I = 17.46 × 10⁻⁴ m⁴

Modulus of elasticity $E = 5000\sqrt{25} = 25000$ MPa for M25 concrete

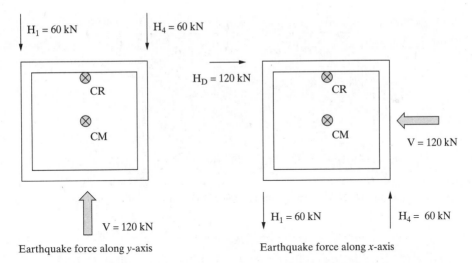

Earthquake force along y-axis   Earthquake force along x-axis

Figure 12.22(c)   Earthquake shear and equilibrium forces.

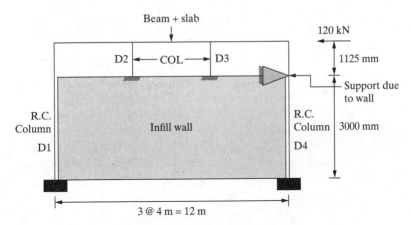

Figure 12.22(d)   Frame D-D in elevation.

Moment of inertia of slab (width = 3 Depth) $I = (12.5 \times 3) \times 12.5^3/12 = 6100 \text{ cm}^4$

or, $I = 0.61 \times 10^{-4} \text{ m}^4$

Frame D1-D4 as shown in Figure 12.22(d) can be analysed using the above data. It should be noted that the wall will offer a restraint to the column D4 when the frame wants to deflect along x-direction. There will be no such restraint to column D1.

The shear force in columns is shown in Figure 12.22(e).

Now if the same frame D1-D4 is analysed by ignoring the masonry walls, the member forces are shown in Figure 12.22(f). The shear force in column D3 with masonry restraint is 50.8 kN and without restraint is 31.6 kN. The increase in shear due to short column effect is 61%. Similarly, the short column effect due to the masonry walls on frame A4-D4 as shown in Figure 12.22(g) can be estimated.

The short column effect in earthquakes is a very common form of failure in buildings in most earthquakes all over the world.   □

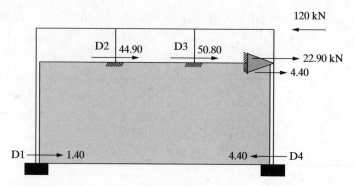

Figure 12.22(e) Forces acting on Frame D-D with short column action.

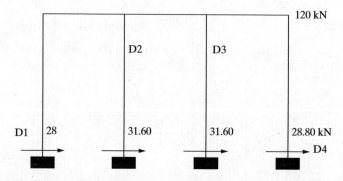

Figure 12.22(f) Forces acting on Frame D-D – without short column action.

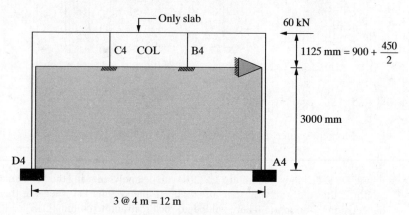

Figure 12.22(g) Frame D-A.

Example 12.8

A 4-storey steel frame is shown in Figure 12.23. It is located in seismic zone V on soft soil. The super imposed dead load SIDL on each floor is 10 kN/m and on the roof is 5 kN/m. Determine the member forces due to earthquake using dynamic analysis in IS:1893-2002 code.

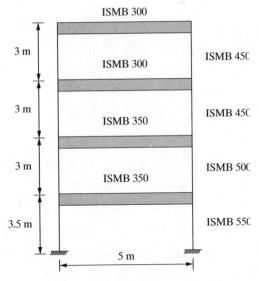

Figure 12.23   Steel frame.

Solution   Moment of inertia of columns $I = \begin{Bmatrix} 30390 \\ 30390 \\ 45218 \\ 64893 \end{Bmatrix}$ cm^4

Modulus of elasticity of steel $= 200$ GPa $= 200000$ MPa

Mass calculation
Let us first consider mass of the top floor

Beam – ISMB 300 – Area $= 5.626 \times 10^{-3}$ m^2, weight density $= 76.97$ kN/m^3
Column – ISMB 450 – Area $= 9.227 \times 10^{-3}$ m^2, weight density $= 76.97$ kN/m^3
SIDL $= 5$ kN/m

The span of beam is 5 m, and there are two columns of 3 m height. However, only 1.5 m height will contribute towards mass on the roof.
Contribution of mass from ISMB 300 $= 5.626 \times 10^{-3} \times 76.97 \times 5/9.81 = 0.22$ kN-s^2/m
Contribution of mass from ISMB 450 $= 9.227 \times 10^{-3} \times 76.97 \times (3/2) \times 2/9.81 = 0.22$ kN-s^2/m
Contribution of mass from SIDL $= 5 \times 5/9.81 = 2.548$ kN-s^2/m
Total mass on roof $= 2.988 \approx 3.0$ kN-s^2/m
Similarly, mass on other floors can be calculated.

Mass $\{M\} = \begin{Bmatrix} 3.0 \\ 6.0 \\ 6.0 \\ 6.0 \end{Bmatrix}$ kN-s^2/m

Now the stiffness matrix of the frame can be assembled using the procedure described in Example 1.6, Chapter 1. It has four lateral degrees of freedom, that is one translation per floor. Node numbers in the frame are shown in Figure 12.24. Its frequency and mode

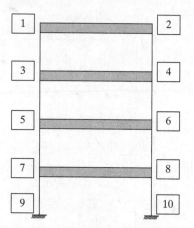

Figure 12.24   Node numbers.

shapes can be determined using the procedure explained in Chapter 10. Alternatively, the frame can be analysed using a stiffness matrix-based software. The mode shapes are shown in Figures 12.25.

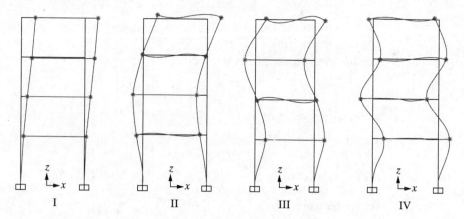

Figure 12.25   Mode shapes.

$$\text{Period } \{T\} = \begin{Bmatrix} 0.39 \\ 0.12 \\ 0.06 \\ 0.038 \end{Bmatrix} \text{ sec} \quad \text{Mode shapes } \Phi = \begin{bmatrix} 1 & 1 & 1 & 1 \\ 0.769 & -0.099 & -1.011 & -1.700 \\ 0.464 & -0.749 & 0.168 & 2.723 \\ 0.177 & -0.490 & 0.966 & -2.698 \end{bmatrix}$$

Clause 7.6.1 of IS:1893-Part 1 for moment resistant steel buildings gives,

$$T = 0.085 \; H^{0.75}$$

$$T = 0.085 \times 12.5^{0.75} = 0.565 \text{ sec}$$

The eigenvalue analysis is giving a lower period of vibration as compared to that of the empirical formula. In many other cases, it has been noted that the empirical formula gives a lower period. Let us calculate its modal mass, mode participation factors and spectral acceleration for 2% damping using the IS:1893-Part 1 response spectra.

Mode participation factor $\quad\quad \Gamma_r = \dfrac{\sum m_i \phi_i}{\sum m_i \phi_i^2}$

This can be done in a tabular form for convenience. The calculations are shown in Table 12.9.

$Z = 0.36$, $R = 5.0$ for a special M-R frame, $I = 1.0$, damping factor $= 1.40$

$$\alpha_h = \frac{Z}{2}\frac{I}{R}\frac{S_a}{g} = \frac{0.36}{2} \times \frac{1}{5} \times \frac{S_a}{g} = 0.036 \frac{S_a}{g}$$

Mode participation factor in mode $1 = 11.47/8.03 = 1.4274$
Mode participation factor in mode $2 = -5.04/7.87 = -0.6396$
Mode participation factor in mode $3 = 3.74/14.89 = 0.2509$
Mode participation factor in mode $4 = -7.05/108.54 = -0.065$

$$\text{Modal mass} = \frac{\left(\sum_{i=1}^{n} m_i \phi_i\right)^2}{\sum_{i=1}^{n} m_i \phi_i^2}$$

Modal mass in mode $1 = (11.47)^2/8.03 = 16.37$
Modal mass in mode $2 = (5.04)^2/7.87 = 3.22$
Modal mass in mode $3 = (3.74)^2/14.89 = 0.937$
Modal mass in mode $4 = (7.05)^2/108.54 = 0.458$
Total modal mass $= 20.99 =$ Total mass of the frame $\quad\quad$ OK

Corresponding to periods of vibration in different modes, the values of spectral accelerations are obtained from the response spectra of IS:1893-Part 1 for 2% damping and shown in Table 12.10.

$$\alpha_0 = \Gamma \alpha_h 1.4g = 0.036(S_a/g)\Gamma 1.4g \quad \text{can be computed for each mode.}$$

Now modal forces at each floor can be computed for each mode as shown in Table 12.11.

These floor modal forces are shown in Figure 12.26 for each mode for a clear understanding of the magnitude and direction of forces. A static analysis of the frame is carried out in each mode and the member forces are determined using a software. These member forces are shown in Table 12.12.

Next, SRSS values of member forces are computed by combining the member forces in each mode for each force component individually. SRSS values for bending moment in beams and columns are shown in Table 12.12. The moment in right-hand columns of the frame can be obtained by anti-symmetry in each mode. The SRSS values in right-hand side columns will be the same as on the left-hand side columns of the frame.

Next, the gravity load member forces are combined with those of the earthquake forces as shown in Table 12.13. The earthquake force is reversal. Therefore, each member will be designed for both maximum sagging and maximum hogging forces.

The following observations can be made in the various results presented in this problem:

1. The role of dynamic analysis is to determine the frequency and mode shapes of the structure and then estimate spectral accelerations in each mode. Modal forces can be computed in each mode.

2. Now onwards, the remaining analysis is purely static. Static analysis of the frame is carried out for each mode and member forces are determined. The floor forces are to be applied in appropriate directions. The static equilibrium of forces is satisfied at each joint in each mode.

TABLE 12.9 MODAL MASS AND MODE PARTICIPATION FACTORS

Floor	m_i	Mode 1			Mode 2			Mode 3			Mode 4		
		ϕ_i	$m_i\phi_i$	$m_i\phi_i^2$	ϕ_i	$m_i\phi_i$	$m_i\phi_i^2$	ϕ_i	$m_i\phi_i$	$m_i\phi_i^2$	ϕ_i	$m_i\phi_i$	$m_i\phi_i^2$
Top	3	1.00	3.00	3.00	1.00	3.00	3.00	1.00	3.00	3.00	1.00	3.00	3.00
3rd	6	0.77	4.62	3.55	−0.10	−0.60	0.06	−1.01	−6.06	6.13	−1.70	−10.20	17.34
2nd	6	0.46	2.79	1.29	−0.75	−4.50	3.37	0.17	1.01	0.17	2.72	16.34	44.51
1st	6	0.18	1.07	0.19	−0.49	−2.94	1.44	0.97	5.79	5.59	−2.70	−16.19	43.69
Σ			11.47	8.03		−5.04	7.87		3.74	14.89		−7.05	108.54

TABLE 12.10 SPECTRAL VALUES

Mode	Period T sec	S_a/g	MPF = Γ	$\Gamma \times S_a/g$	$\alpha_0 = \Gamma \times \alpha_h \times 1.4 \times g$
1	0.39	2.5	1.42	3.550	1.755
2	0.12	2.5	−0.64	−1.600	−0.791
3	0.06	1.9	0.25	0.475	0.235
4	0.038	1.57	−0.065	−0.102	−0.051

$g = 9.81$ m/s²

TABLE 12.11 MODAL FORCES

		Mode 1		Mode 2		Mode 3		Mode 4	
Floor	m_i	ϕ_i	$\phi_i \alpha_0 m_i$	ϕ_i	$\phi_i \alpha_0 m_i$	ϕ_i	$\phi_i \alpha_0 m_i$	ϕ_i	$\phi_i \alpha_0 m_i$
Roof	3	1.000	5.27	1.000	−2.37	1.000	0.70	1.000	−0.15
3	6	0.769	8.10	−0.099	0.47	−1.011	−1.42	−1.700	0.51
2	6	0.464	4.89	−0.750	3.56	0.168	0.24	2.724	−0.82
1	6	0.178	1.87	−0.491	2.33	0.965	1.36	−2.698	0.82

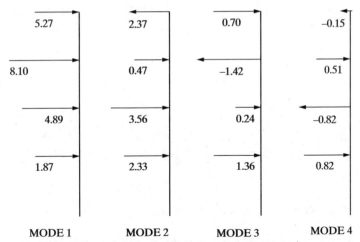

MODE 1	MODE 2	MODE 3	MODE 4
5.27	2.37	0.70	−0.15
8.10	0.47	−1.42	0.51
4.89	3.56	0.24	−0.82
1.87	2.33	1.36	0.82

The direction of modal floor forces in a given mode will always
correspond to the respective mode shape.

Figure 12.26 Floor modal forces (kN).

TABLE 12.12 BENDING MOMENT IN MEMBERS AT NODE I

Member ID		Node	Mode 1	Mode 2	Mode 3	Mode 4	SRSS Value
Beam	1–2	1	7.61	−1.72	0.28	−0.04	7.81
	3–4	3	11.23	−1.67	0.02	0.04	11.35
	5–6	5	19.16	−0.19	−0.33	−0.02	19.17
	7–8	7	15.69	1.44	0.03	−0.02	15.75

(*Continued*)

TABLE 12.12   (CONTINUED)

Member ID		Node	Mode 1	Mode 2	Mode 3	Mode 4	SRSS Value
Column	1–3	1	7.61	–1.72	0.28	–0.04	7.81
		3	–0.20	1.84	–0.83	0.21	2.04
	3–5	3	11.03	0.17	–0.81	0.25	11.06
		5	–9.13	3.07	0.32	–0.37	9.65
	5–7	5	10.03	2.89	–0.01	–0.38	10.44
		7	–17.34	0.37	0.74	0.39	17.37
	7–9	7	–1.66	1.81	0.77	0.38	2.60
		9	–36.92	–5.27	–0.85	–0.33	37.30

+ve moment: Clockwise; –ve moment: anti-clockwise.

TABLE 12.13   FINAL BENDING MOMENT IN MEMBERS, kNm

Member Number		Node	SIDL	SRSS Value ±	Net Moment SIDL+SRSS	Net Moment SIDL–SRSS
Beam	1–2	1	–9.70	7.81	–1.90	17.52
	3–4	3	–20.00	11.35	–8.72	31.43
	5–6	5	–19.90	19.17	–0.75	39.08
	7–8	7	–20.0	15.75	–4.26	35.77
Column	1–3	1	9.70	7.81	–1.90	17.52
		3	10.0	2.04	12.06	–7.98
	3–5	3	10.0	11.06	1.01	21.12
		5	8.98	9.65	18.64	0.66
	5–7	5	10.93	10.44	–0.48	21.37
		7	10.38	17.37	27.74	6.99
	7–9	7	9.64	2.60	–7.04	12.24
		9	4.09	37.30	41.39	33.22

Moments due to dead load of the frame are also to be tabulated.

3. The contribution of higher modes in member forces keeps decreasing depending upon the mode participation factors.

4. SRSS value is computed for each force component in each member. Each SRSS value is absolute. Similarly, SRSS value is also computed for each displacement component.

5. Since earthquake force is reversible, the SRSS values are added and subtracted from the gravity forces to get a set of two forces for each member. The static equilibrium of joints gets lost at this stage because of mode superposition.

6. The shape of bending moment diagram for the frame in each mode depends upon the relative stiffness of the various members.

7. The absolute bending moment, shear force and axial force in each member due to earthquake force depend upon the contributory area of each frame from the earthquake point of view. Larger the contributory area, larger will be the member forces and the displacements. The frame may require special considerations in order to limit the lateral displacements.

8. The storey shears can be estimated from the corresponding column shears in each mode and then superimposed.

9. Appropriate load combinations must be considered as per the relevant codal provisions. Also, for limit state design, appropriate partial safety factors must be considered.

10. Each member must be designed for the worst set of forces.   □

Example 12.9

A 20-storey office building has a floor plan as shown in Figure 12.27(a) and basement plan as shown in Figure 12.27(b). It is symmetric in both directions in plan as well as in elevation. It has two basements as shown in Figure 12.27(c). Determine the points of application of the earthquake force.

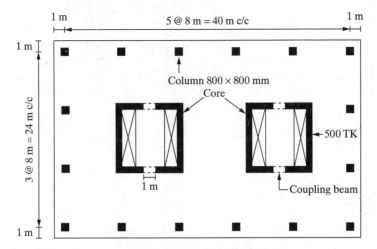

Figure 12.27(a)   Building plan.

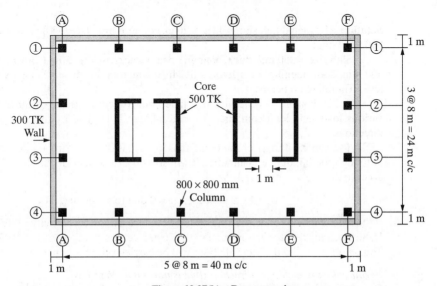

Figure 12.27(b)   Basement plan.

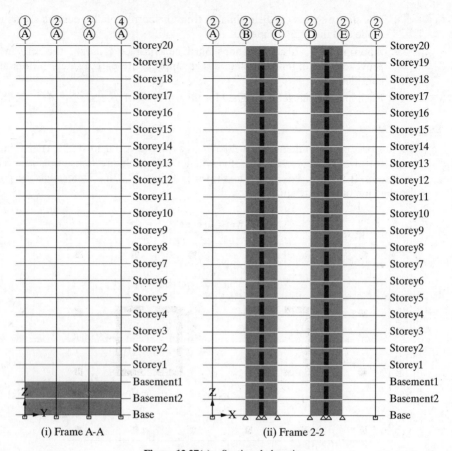

Figure 12.27(c)   Sectional elevation.

Solution   Its plan dimension = 42 m × 26 m, columns are placed @ 8 m c/c. Column size = 800 × 800 mm.

Slab size = 250 mm thick; coupling beam thickness = 1.25 m, Core wall thickness = 500 mm, door opening = 1 m, storey height = 4 m, total height = 80 m above the ground level. There are no beams.

A 3D dynamic analysis will be carried out to determine the member forces under various loads and load combinations. Lateral load is resisted by the core walls in both directions.

The centre of mass of the building is at its axis of symmetry about both directions. Although the building is symmetric, it will still experience accidental torsion. The design eccentricity is given by

$$E_d = \pm 0.05b \text{ because } e = 0 \text{ due to symmetry.}$$

If the earthquake force acts normal to the 42 m face, design eccentricity = 0.05 × 42 = 2.1 m
If the earthquake force acts normal to the 26 m face, design eccentricity = 0.05 × 26 = 1.3 m
Thus, a set of six 3D dynamic analyses will be carried out as follows:

Earthquake force along x-direction (that is normal to 26 m face)
Case 1: No change in the centre of mass and carry out the response spectrum analysis

Case 2: Shift the centre of mass along y-direction by +1.3 m and carry out the response spectrum analysis

Case 3: Shift the centre of mass along y-direction by −1.3 m and carry out the response spectrum analysis

Earthquake force along y-direction (that is normal to 42 m face)

Case 1: No change in the centre of mass and carry out the response spectrum analysis

Case 2: Shift the centre of mass along x-direction by +2.1 m and carry out the response spectrum analysis

Case 3: Shift the centre of mass along x-direction by −2.1 m and carry out the response spectrum analysis

Carry out the load combination analysis with appropriate load factors as per the relevant code (IS:456, IS:800, IS:1893). Get member forces from all load combinations. The worst load combination for each member will govern its design.   □

Example 12.10

Determine the lateral forces in the 20-storey office building shown in Figure 12.27 as per IS:1893-Part 1-2002 if it is situated in seismic zone III. Assume hard soil.

Solution Floor slab thickness = 250 mm

Column size = 800 × 800 mm

Basement wall thickness = 300 mm

Superimposed dead load on each floor = 2.5 kN/m²

Live load = 3 kN/m²

Lateral load resisting system along x-direction = core walls and coupling beams

Lateral load resisting system along y-direction = core walls only

Typical floor area = 26 × 42 = 1092 m²

Total area of columns = 0.8 × 0.8 × 16 no. = 10.24 m²

Coupling beam size = 0.5 m wide × 1.25 m deep × 1 m long

Core wall thickness = 500 mm

Area of core walls = 8 × 8 × 0.5 − 4 × 1 × 0.5 = 30 m²

Grade of concrete = M30

Item	Dead Load, kN	Live Load, kN
Floor slab	1092 × 0.25 × 25 = 6825	1092 × 3 = 3276
Columns	10.24 × 4 × 25 =1024	
Core walls	30 × 4 × 25 = 3000	

Total dead load per floor = 6825 + 1024 + 3000 + 1092 × 2.5 (SIDL) = 13579 kN

Total live load on roof = nil

Total live load per floor = 1092 × 3 = 3276 kN

Floor	Elevation, m	Load, kN
Roof	80	13579 (DL)
Floors 2 to 19	4 to 76	13579 + 3276 = 16855 (DL + LL)
Ground floor	0	13579 + 3276 = 16855 (DL + LL)
Basement 1	−4	13579 + 3276 = 16855 (DL + LL)
Basement 2	−8	

Seismic weight $W = 13579 + 13579 \times 19 + 3276 \times 19 \times 0.25 = 287141$ kN (only 25% of live load)

Zone factor $Z = 0.16$, importance factor $I = 1.0$, Response reduction factor $R = 3$ assuming it to be an ordinary shear wall framed building.

Period of vibration $T = \dfrac{0.09H}{\sqrt{D}}$

Along x-direction, $T_x = \dfrac{0.09 \times 80}{\sqrt{42}} = 1.11 \text{ sec}$; $S_a/g = 0.9$

Along y-direction, $T_y = \dfrac{0.09 \times 80}{\sqrt{26}} = 1.412 \text{ sec}$; $S_a/g = 0.708$

Seismic coefficient along x-direction, $\alpha_{hx} = \dfrac{0.16}{2} \times \dfrac{1}{3} \times 0.9 = 0.024$

Seismic coefficient along y-direction, $\alpha_{hy} = \dfrac{0.16}{2} \times \dfrac{1}{3} \times 0.708 = 0.0188$

Base shear in x-direction $V_{bx} = 0.024 \times 287141 = 6890 \approx 6900 \text{ kN}$
Base shear in y-direction $V_{by} = 0.0188 \times 287141 = 5398 \approx 5400 \text{ kN}$

A 3D dynamic analysis was carried out and the periods of vibrations in the first 12 modes are as shown in the table.

Mode	1	2	3	4	5	6	7	8	9	10	11	12
Period, sec	2.642	2.62	1.023	0.45	0.445	0.321	0.178	0.176	0.175	0.116	0.102	0.101

The lateral force in the x- and y-directions is shown in Figures 12.28(a), and storey shears are shown in Figure 12.28(b). The contribution of each mode in the total base shear is shown in Figure 12.28(c).

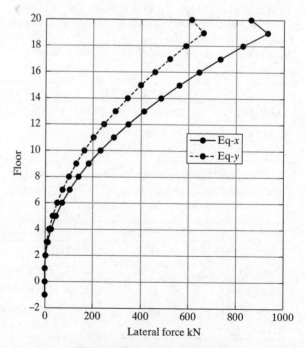

Figure 12.28(a) Lateral forces, kN.

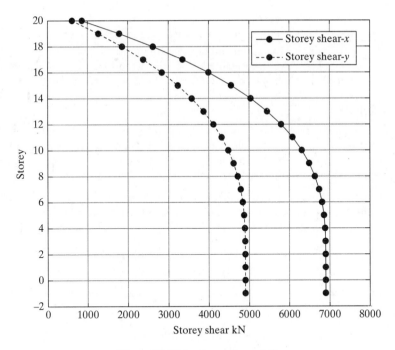

Figure 12.28(b) Storey shears, kN.

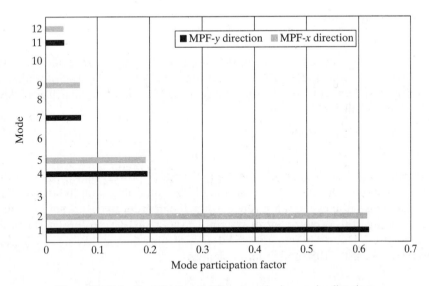

Figure 12.28(c) Contribution of different modes in x- and y-directions.

There are four important observations:

1. The contribution of basements that are underground is not considered in the calculation of seismic weight.

2. Only 25% contribution of live load is considered if it is less than or equal to 3 kN/m²

3. The seismic base shear computed at the ground floor must be transferred to the lowest basement floor and thereby to the foundation

4. The periods of vibration are too close in modes 1–2, 4–5, 7–8 and 11–12. These will qualify for closely spaced modes. Therefore, mode superposition in dynamic analysis must be carried out using CQC method rather than SRSS method. ☐

Example 12.11

A 30-storey building has a total height of 100 m above the ground level. There are two such blocks to be built adjacent to each other. The storey drifts in each block is within 0.4%. What should be the minimum clear gap between these two blocks from earthquake considerations? The response reduction factor was considered as 5.0.

Solution The maximum lateral displacement at roof level = $100 \times 0.004 = 0.4$ m
If the floors in these two blocks are at the same levels, then minimum clear gap between these two blocks is given by

$$\text{Seismic gap} \geq (\Delta_1 + \Delta_2) \times 0.50\, R \quad \text{(IS:1893-Part 1)}$$
$$\geq (0.4 + 0.4) \times 0.5 \times 5 = 2 \text{ m}$$

In case the floors in these two blocks are not at the same levels, then minimum clear gap between these two blocks is given by

$$\text{Seismic gap} \geq (\Delta_1 + \Delta_2) \times R$$
$$\geq (0.4 + 0.4) \times 5 = 4 \text{ m} \qquad ☐$$

12.15 SPECIAL DEVICES

Nowadays with increasing challenges to improve the performance and life of buildings and other structures after a strong earthquake, there is increasing trend to fit them with special devices to absorb the energy or reduce the base shear. These devices are classified as follows:

- Passive Control Devices
- Active Control Devices

Passive control devices do not need any source of power supply, whereas the active control systems do require. It is absolutely essential to guarantee the availability of power even in the event of a severe earthquake in order to ensure smooth and desired functioning of the active control system. Therefore, passive control systems are being widely used. Details of analysis and design of such systems are available in ASCE 7, FEMA 450, 451, P1050 and other documents.

12.15.1 Passive Control Systems

Various passive control systems are as follows:

- Seismic Base Isolation Devices
  - o Elastomeric bearing
  - o Sliding bearing

- Energy Absorbing Devices
  - Viscous dampers
  - Metallic dampers
  - Tuned mass dampers (TMD)

12.15.1.1 Objectives of seismic base isolation devices

- Enhance performance of structures at all hazard levels by minimizing interruption of use of facility
- Reducing the base shear or acceleration response
- Reducing damaging deformations in structural and non-structural components by cutting off the transmission of base excitation to superstructure. In other words, the entire deformation is absorbed by the base isolation system. Nothing is transferred to the superstructure. The superstructure undergoes rigid body displacements under controlled conditions.

The principle of seismic isolation system is illustrated in Figures 12.29(a) through (d). There is a shift in the period of a structure supported on base isolation devices as shown in Figure 12.29(c). It helps reduce the acceleration and therefore base shear. However, this increase in period is beneficial if the structure is supported on hard soil rather than on soft soil as shown in Figure 12.29(d). The effect of base isolation on the mode shapes and period of a single-storey building is shown in Figure 12.30. The base isolation system increases the lateral degree of freedom by one. The storey drift in a building without base isolation is quite large, whereas it is negligible in a building with base isolation. Here lies the advantage of base isolation.

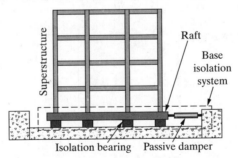

Figure 12.29(a)   A building supported on seismic isolation system (adapted from FEMA 451).

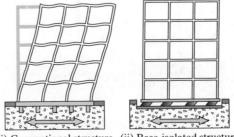

(i) Conventional structure (ii) Base-isolated structure

Figure 12.29(b)   Response of a building without and with base isolation (adapted from FEMA 451).

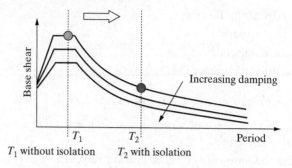

Figure 12.29(c) Shift in period of a base isolated structure to reduce base shear.

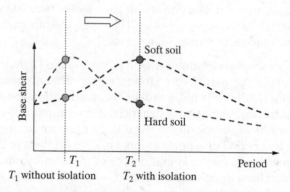

Figure 12.29(d) Effect of soil on the shift of period and therefore base shear.

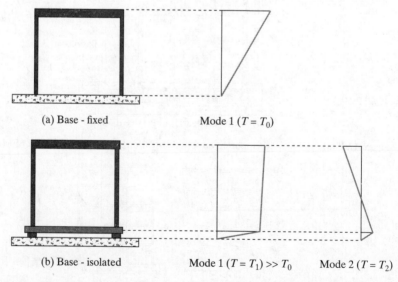

Figure 12.30 Effect of base isolation on mode shapes and period of a single-storey building.

Base isolation may be achieved through bearings of different types:

- Elastomeric bearings
  - Laminated lead rubber bearings
  - High damping laminated rubber bearings
  - Low damping laminated rubber bearings
- Friction sliding bearings
  - Flat sliding bearing
  - Friction pendulum bearing
  - Spherical sliding bearing
- Roller bearings

The concept of base isolation is equally applicable to bridges as depicted in Figure 12.31.

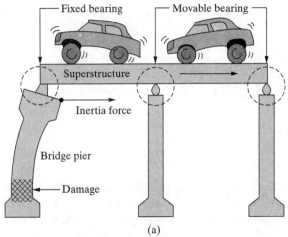

(a)

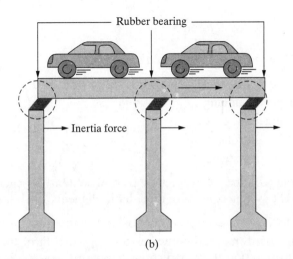

(b)

Figure 12.31 Response of a bridge without and with base isolation (rubber bearings).

Elastomeric isolators act as follows:

- Adds flexibility to the structure and thus lengthens natural period
- Imparts energy dissipation through damping
- Re-centers the structure when ground motion due to earthquake ceases
- May be used to provide necessary rigidity under low service loads, e.g., wind, braking, etc.
- Perform under all service loads and slow displacements due to thermal action and secondary effects, offering moderately low resistance

The hysteresis behaviour of elastomeric bearings of different types is illustrated in Figure 12.32. It is discussed in more detail in Chapters 13 and 14.

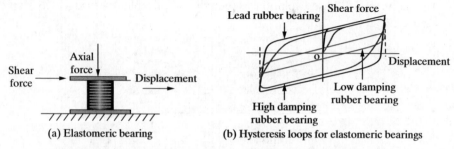

(a) Elastomeric bearing   (b) Hysteresis loops for elastomeric bearings

Figure 12.32   Hysteresis behaviour of elastomeric bearing of different types.

12.15.1.2 Energy Dissipating Devices

Different types of dampers used for dissipating the seismic energy are discussed in Chapter 13. More details are available in ASCE 7 and FEMA P1050. The nonlinear seismic analysis of structures fitted with these special devices can be conveniently carried out using commercial software such as ANSYS, SAP2000 and ETABS.

12.15.2 Active Control Systems

Active control systems can be classified as follows:

- Active control systems (Dynamic Intelligent Building)
  - o Active mass damping
  - o Active bracing
- Semi-active control systems
- Hybrid control systems

The basic configuration of an active control system is schematically shown in Figure 12.33. The system consists of three basic elements:

- Sensors to measure external excitation and/or structural response
- Computer hardware and software to compute control forces on the basis of observed excitation and/or structural response
- Hydraulic actuators to provide the necessary control forces

Thus, an active system has to necessarily have an external energy input to drive the actuators and the control system. On the other hand, passive systems do not required external energy and their efficiency depends on tunings of system to expected excitation and structural behaviour. As a result, the passive systems are effective only for the modes of the vibrations for which these are tuned. The advantage of an active system lies in its much wider range of applicability since the control forces are worked out on the basis of actual excitation and structural behaviour. In the active system, when only external excitation is measured system is said to be in open-looped. However, when the structural response is used as input, the system is in closed loop control. In certain instances, the excitation and response both are used, and it is termed as open-closed loop control. The solution of such systems can be obtained with the help of linear control theory, MATLAB, and direct integration techniques. A detailed discussion on the active control system is beyond the scope of the present text book.

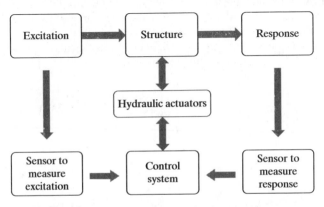

Figure 12.33   Basic configuration of active control system.

PROBLEMS

12.1 (a) Discuss the structural systems for RC buildings for carrying vertical loads and lateral loads with neat sketches. What is the most desirable configuration of lateral load resisting elements?

(b) Discuss the structural systems for steel buildings for carrying vertical loads and lateral loads with neat sketches. Explain the concentric and eccentric bracing systems.

(c) Which is the most suitable system for a low rise building and also for a very tall building in steel?

12.2 Explain the various vertical and horizontal irregularities in buildings with neat sketches. Discuss the ASCE 7, IS 1893 and Eurocode 1998 provisions.

12.3 What do you understand by a dual frame system? Explain with sketches.

12.4 Explain the terms MCE and DBE as adopted in IS-1893-Part 1, ASCE-7 and Eurocode 1998-Part 1.

12.5 A single-storey 3.5 m high RC building is pulled at the roof level with a lateral force of 75 kN and undergoes a lateral displacement of 10 mm. It has a net weight of 30 kN. It is situated in Chennai on medium soil. Estimate its natural frequency, natural period and base shear if damping is 5% and response reduction factor $R = 3$.

How will the base shear change if its damping is (i) 2% and (ii) 10%?

12.6 A 15 m high overhead water tank on RC shaft has an effective weight of 1000 kN and is situated in seismic zone V on soft soil. It is pulled at the top with a lateral force of 100 kN and undergoes a lateral displacement of 35 mm. Estimate its period of vibration and base shear if the response reduction factor is 3.5. Also, determine the shear and overturning moment along the height of the shaft.

12.7 A four-storey steel building has a plan dimension of 20 m × 10 m and each storey is 3.5 m high. It is situated in Kolkata on soft soil. The dead load per floor is 20 kN/m² and live load is 6 kN/m². It is symmetrically braced along the short direction only. Estimate its period of vibration and base shears in both the lateral directions. Also, plot the lateral force distribution along the height.

12.8 A single-storey building has a plan as shown in Figure P12.1. There are two RC walls 200 mm thick each along 1-1 and A-A grids. There are three RC columns 200 × 200 mm at B-1, B-2 and A-2. There are two beams 200 × 450 mm deep along 2-2 and B-B. Estimate the lateral force on the walls and the frames due to earthquake force along the two directions. Assume 4.5 m height and a uniform load on the roof.

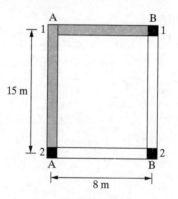

Figure P12.1

12.9 A 10-storey RC building has a moment-resistant frame with 5 bays @ 6 m c/c. The height of the first storey is 4.5 m c/c while rest of the storeys are 3.5 m c/c. The columns are 300 × 500 mm and beams are 300 × 600 mm. The slab thickness is 125 mm including the finish. Imposed load on the floors is 4.5 kN/m² and the lateral spacing of the frames is 5 m c/c. The building is located in seismic zone IV on soft soil.

(a) Determine the fundamental period of vibration using the Rayleigh method.

(b) Determine the period of vibrations in the first 3 modes and the corresponding mode shape.

(c) Analyse the frame in each mode and determine the column shears. Thus, estimate the storey shears, base shears and their SRSS values.

(d) Determine the lateral floor forces along the height in each mode and display graphically.

Hint: Use any software to determine the displacements and member forces, etc. Use MS-EXCEL to estimate the storey shears.

12.10 A 15-storey building plan is shown in Figure P12.2. The width of the shear walls is 200 mm each. Each wall continues up to the roof. The height of first storey is 4.5 m and subsequent storeys are 3.5 m high. Column size is 500 × 500 mm, beam size is 300 × 500 mm and slab thickness is 125 mm. Column is placed at each intersection of grid. Estimate the period of vibration in each direction using the IS 1893-Part 1, ASCE-7 and Eurocode 1998-Part 1 codes.

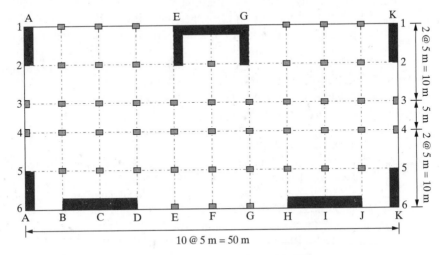

Figure P12.2 Plan of a 15-storey building.

REFERENCES

Agarwal, J. (2001) Earthquake Response of Buildings Fitted with Vibration Isolators, M Tech Thesis, I.I.T. Roorkee.

AISC 341 (2010) Seismic Provisions for Structural Steel Buildings, American Institute of Steel Construction, Chicago.

ASCE 7 (2010) Minimum Design Loads for Buildings and Other Structures, American Society of Civil Engineers, Reston, Virginia.

Eurocode 8-1 (2004) Design of Structures for Earthquake Resistance – Part 1: General Rules, Seismic Actions and Rules for Buildings, incorporating corrigendum 2013, European Committee for Standardization, Brussels.

FEMA 356 (2000) Pre-standard and Commentary for the Seismic Rehabilitation of Buildings, Federal Emergency Management Agency, Washington, DC.

FEMA 451B (2006) 2003 NEHRP Recommended Seismic Provisions – Design Examples, Federal Emergency Management Agency, Washington, D.C.

FEMA 464 (2006) Designing for Earthquakes: a Manual for Architects, Washington. D.C.

FEMA P-749 (2010) Earthquake-Resistant Design Concepts, An Introduction to the NEHRP Recommended Seismic Provisions for New Buildings and Other Structures, Federal Emergency Management Agency, Washington, DC.

FEMA P-750 (2009) NEHRP Recommended Seismic Provisions for New Buildings and Other Structures, Federal Emergency Management Agency, Washington, DC.

FEMA P-1050 (2015) 2015 NEHRP Recommended Seismic Provisions for New Buildings and Other Structures, Federal Emergency Management Agency, Washington, DC

IS:1893-Part 1 (2002) Criteria for Earthquake Resistant Design of Structures, Part 1, General Provisions and Buildings, Bureau of Indian Standards, New Delhi.

IS:1893-Part 2 (2014) Criteria for Earthquake Resistant Design of Structures, Part 2, Liquid Retaining Tanks, Bureau of Indian Standards, New Delhi.

IS:1893-Part 3 (2014) Criteria for Earthquake Resistant Design of Structures, Part 3, Bridges and Retaining Walls, Bureau of Indian Standards, New Delhi.

IS:1893-Part 4 (2013) Criteria for Earthquake Resistant Design of Structures, Part 4, Industrial and Stack-Like Structures, Bureau of Indian Standards, New Delhi.

IS:13920 (1993) Ductile Detailing of Reinforced Concrete Structures Subjected to Seismic Forces, Bureau of Indian Standards, New Delhi.

Naeim, F. and Kelly, J. M. (1999) Design of Seismic Isolated Structures: From theory to practice, John Wiley & Sons, New York.

NZS 1170-5 (2004) Structural Design Actions – Part 5: Earthquake Actions – New Zealand, Standards New Zealand, Wellington.

NZS 1170-5 (S1) (2004) Structural Design Actions – Part 5: Earthquake actions – New Zealand, Commentary, Standards New Zealand, Wellington.

PEER 5 (2010) Seismic Design Guidelines for Tall Buildings, Pacific Earthquake Engineering Research Center (PEER), Berkeley.

Rafael Sabelli, R., Roeder, C. W. and Hajjar, J. F. (2013) Seismic Design of Steel Special Concentrically Braced Frame Systems, A Guide for Practicing Engineers, U.S. Dept. of Commerce National Institute of Standards and Technology Engineering Laboratory, Gaithersburg, MD.

Satyanarayana, J. (2003) Dynamic Behaviour of Base Isolated Buildings, M Tech Thesis, I.I.T. Roorkee.

Willford, M., Whittaker, A. and Klemencic, R. (2008) Recommendations for the Seismic Design of High-Rise Buildings, The Council on Tall Buildings and Urban Habitat, Chicago.

13 | Nonlinear Analysis of Structures

13.1 INTRODUCTION

The concept of nonlinear behaviour of structures and the availability of considerable energy in the post-elastic region is more than a century old. Although the linear elastic analysis and design methods are well established, nonlinear inelastic analysis techniques and their application to design are still evolving. Why do we need a nonlinear analysis? The answer lies in the fact that under an extreme probable loading, it is no longer advisable to keep the structure elastic due to economical considerations. It is expected that a lot of cross-sections in various beams, columns and walls will yield and may develop plastic hinges and dissipate energy. A nonlinear analysis requires a clear understanding of the following:

- Stress–strain curves of all the materials used in a structure
- Inelastic behaviour of the materials—strength and deformation response of components and system
- Failure criteria of components and system
- Definition of collapse, that is capacity in different failure modes
- Nonlinear analysis techniques

It is very difficult to define the above parameters theoretically. There is a need to carryout extensive experimental programs on materials, components and systems to cover vast cases encountered in practice across the globe. The term *components* includes axial members, beams, columns and walls; whereas, the term *system* includes moment-resistant building frame, shear wall frame, concentrically braced steel frame or eccentrically braced steel frame or any other structural system. It may consist of reinforced concrete, steel or a composite material. A considerable amount of research on steel beams, columns and joints were carried out under *static loading* at the Imperial College, London, UK, and Lehigh University, Bethlehem, USA in the 1960s. This experimental program was carried out under static loads and led to the development of *ultimate load theory* or *load and resistance factor design* method for the design of steel and reinforced concrete structures. With the availability of more test data and better understanding of the inelastic behaviour of materials, structural elements and structures, *limit state design philosophy* for the design of reinforced concrete and steel structures evolved. It was clearly understood that *limit states* need to define and control both forces and deformations.

A nonlinear analysis needs to be carried out under *reversed dynamic loading* when a structure undergoes substantial inelastic cyclic excursions. Such a loading is likely to occur under an extreme earthquake, due to a nuclear blast or missile impact. This scenario would require definition of models that capture the force-deformation behavior of structural elements and structural systems based on expected strength and stiffness degradations and large deformations under reversed cyclic loading. A reinforced concrete structure is expected to undergo cracking, spalling and yielding of steel besides significant loss of strength, stiffness and anchorage, whereas a steel structure will undergo yielding and local buckling. This requires sophisticated models that are validated against physical tests to capture the highly nonlinear response approaching collapse. The results of nonlinear analyses are sensitive to the assumed input parameters and types of models used to simulate the inelastic response of members. Since the uncertainties in calculating the demand parameters increase as the structure becomes more nonlinear, the acceptance criteria should limit deformations to regions of predictable behavior where sudden strength and stiffness degradation do not occur. A nonlinear analysis can be carried out in the following situations:

- To identify locations of inelastic deformations in various members.
- To characterize the deformation demands of yielding elements and force demands in non-yielding elements.
- To strengthen and retrofit existing buildings.
- To design new buildings that employ structural materials, elements, systems or other features that do not conform to current building code requirements, for example use of base isolation techniques and various damping devices.
- To assess the performance of buildings for site specific requirements, for example risk assessment in order to determine its insurance liability.

The objective of this chapter is to introduce nonlinear models used to simulate the inelastic response of elements, nonlinear response of a SDOF system and inelastic response spectra. Special purpose nonlinear energy dissipating devices such as a viscous damper and ADAS (*added damping and stiffness*) device used to mitigate the effects of earthquake are discussed. A gap element is also discussed to model expansion gap in a bridge superstructure. The intent is to provide basic knowledge to understand and appreciate nonlinear response of simple structures under earthquake loading.

13.2 OVERVIEW OF NONLINEARITY

The principal object of nonlinear analysis is to arrive at a satisfactory design, which is judged to be the one which limits the maximum ductility demands to the value intended and produces a reasonably uniform distribution of nonlinearity throughout the structure. Nonlinearity is caused due to one or more of the following reasons:

- Change in stiffness due to change in material properties
- Change in stiffness due to change in geometric properties
- Change in damping in dynamic problems

The first two sources of nonlinearity are common to structures under both static and dynamic loading. The third source is specific to structures under dynamic loading only. Nonlinearity, which is based on the material properties, is known as *material nonlinearity*. Nonlinearity, which is based on large deformations, is known as *geometric nonlinearity*. Fortunately, in building frames (both steel and RCC) geometric nonlinearity (P-Delta) is of little importance and may be ignored unless these are either very tall frames or have some unusual geometry. In building frames, the effect of P-delta on forces is restricted to about 5% only. In earthquake-resistant structures, the trend is growing towards making use of energy dissipating devices and introducing artificial damping in the structure and protecting the key elements of the structure from any damage. These devices make use of damping which may be proportional to displacement or velocity. A nonlinear analysis may be carried out as follows:

- Pushover analysis or monotonic analysis under static loads
- Reversed cyclic analysis under dynamic loadings

In the pushover analysis, the building frame is subjected to static lateral forces applied gradually at different floor levels till the building/frame collapses. The distribution of the lateral forces along the height may be the same as given by any building code for static analysis. The total base shear is usually magnified by some factor to cause collapse. In case the user wants to study the response of a frame or a building under a given earthquake time-history, then reversed cyclic loading analysis is carried out. The user has to choose between the nonlinear static and nonlinear dynamic analysis to be performed. Either nonlinear analysis will determine the ductility required in the various beams/columns or other elements for the specified loading.

The most difficult aspect of this analysis is the determination of the *change in stiffness* or *damping properties* to be used during a time increment on the basis of the deformation state developed at the end of the preceding increment in a step-by-step time-history analysis. It is important to define *loading and unloading rules* during the entire reversed cyclic loading from its various branches for different structural elements undergoing nonlinear excursions. There are two major approaches:

- Finite element method
- Discrete element method or stiffness matrix method

In the finite element method, the stiffness is derived from the stress–strain curve. It requires suitable yield criteria under reversed cyclic loading. This method is more suitable for continuous systems rather than framed structures. In the discrete element method or stiffness matrix method, the stiffness is derived directly from the slope of the hysteresis model at a given deformation. The hysteresis model is generally based on the experimental data and, therefore, more reliable. Both these methods require time-history solution. Stiffness matrix method is preferred for discrete systems such as buildings.

13.2.1 Measure of Nonlinearity: Ductility

A typical force-deformation curve is shown in Figure 13.1. Nonlinearity is measured in terms of *ductility*. It is defined as the ratio of maximum deformation to the yield deformation. The deformation may be strain, curvature, rotation or displacement.

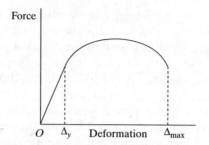

Figure 13.1   Force-deformation behaviour.

Strain ductility	$\mu = \dfrac{\varepsilon_{max}}{\varepsilon_y}$	(13.1a)
Curvature ductility	$\mu = \dfrac{\phi_{max}}{\phi_y}$	(13.1b)
Rotational ductility	$\mu = \dfrac{\theta_{max}}{\theta_y}$	(13.1c)
Displacement ductility	$\mu = \dfrac{\Delta_{max}}{\Delta_y}$	(13.1d)

where $\mu =$ ductility

The curvature ductility depends upon the properties of a cross-section, that is width, depth and amount of reinforcement in tension and compression faces. The rotational ductility depends upon the member properties including its length and boundary conditions at its two ends. The displacement ductility depends upon the properties of the entire structure.

     Different definitions of ductility are being used in practice. Therefore, there is a need to carefully interpret results of a nonlinear analysis.

13.3 MODELING FOR NONLINEAR ANALYSIS

Let us become familiar with some of the terms used in nonlinear analysis of structures.

Monotonic Loading   A structural element or structure is subjected to a constantly increasing force or deformation statically and pushes it well into inelastic region. The response is called *monotonic response*.

Monotonic Curve   The force–deformation data curve obtained from monotonic loading of an element or structural assembly.

Backbone Curve   Relationship between the generalized force and deformation (or generalized stress and strain) of a structural element or assembly that is used to characterize response in a nonlinear analysis model. It is obtained by pushing the system under monotonic loading in one direction and again in opposite direction but on a separate virgin identical specimen.

Strength Degradation   Reduction in strength measured at a given displacement loading cycle due to reduction in yield strength and stiffness that occurs during repeated cyclic loading.

Stiffness Degradation   Reduction in stiffness measured at a given displacement loading cycle due to reduction in yield strength and stiffness that occurs during repeated cyclic loading.

Hysteresis Behaviour   Inelastic behaviour of a structural element under reversed cyclic loading obtained experimentally under repeated cycles.

Hysteresis Model   Idealized multi-linear or curvilinear model of a structural element or structural system to simulate its hysteresis behaviour, that is strength and stiffness degradation and other similar characteristics under different cycles.

Let us examine the nonlinear behaviour of structural elements such as a steel brace, steel and concrete beam and column based on experimental results.

13.3.1 Steel Brace

A steel brace is very strong in axial tension and is likely to buckle in axial compression depending upon its slenderness ratio. Initially, it was thought that:

- Compressive strength of a steel member can be taken as zero to be on the conservative side. Such a member was called *tension-only* member.
- A steel member will not be able to dissipate energy in the post-buckling region.

Later, several improvements were made:

- An axial member will carry substantial strength both in tension and compression.
- An axial member will dissipate energy in the tension region only.
- An axial member will dissipate energy both in tension and post-buckling regions in the first cycle. In the subsequent cycles, it will dissipate very low energy in the post-buckling region.
- The energy dissipation capacity in post-buckling region in subsequent cycles should also be taken into consideration.

Typical hysteresis models for a steel bracing member are shown in Figures 13.2(a)–(e).

13.3.2 Steel Beam

Consider a cantilever beam shown in Figure 13.3. It is convenient to visualize its behaviour under a varying point load applied statically at its free end. A plastic hinge will develop at the fixed end in flexure where the bending moment is maximum. Although length of the plastic hinge is finite, it is usually taken as a point for convenience. Under a monotonic loading, increasing from zero to maximum, its force-displacement response can be easily traced. There are two options: plot force and displacement both at the free end or plot moment and rotation both at the fixed end. In

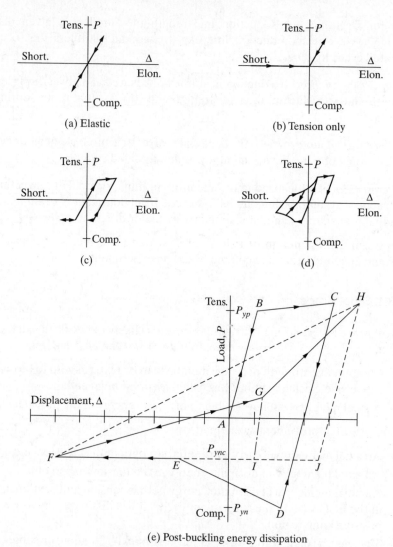

(a) Elastic

(b) Tension only

(c)

(d)

(e) Post-buckling energy dissipation

Figure 13.2   Hysteresis models for a steel brace.

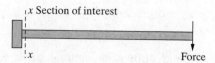

Figure 13.3   Cantilever beam.

flexure members, it is convenient to generate its moment-curvature curve at a given cross-section using the basic principles of static equilibrium. It helps in keeping track of formation of plastic moment and ductility requirements.

The true response is curvilinear and can be represented by Ramberg–Osgood relation as shown in Figure 13.4(a).

$$\frac{x}{x_y} = \frac{P}{P_y}\left(1 + \alpha\left(\frac{P}{P_y}\right)^{r-1}\right)$$ (13.2)

where, α = constant
r = exponent
P = force; P_y = yield force
x = displacement, x_y = yield displacement

The exponent r controls shape of the curve.

It can be replaced by a multi-linear model: an elastic-perfectly plastic model or an elasto-plastic model as shown in Figure 13.4(b) and (c). In an elastic-perfectly plastic curve, the post-yield slope is zero, whereas, in an elasto-plastic curve, the post-yield slope is not zero. Many times, both these curves are referred to as *elasto-plastic*.

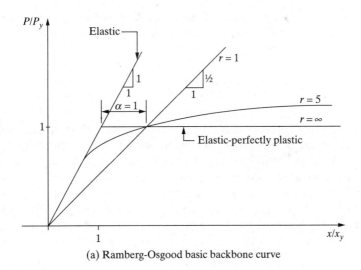

(a) Ramberg-Osgood basic backbone curve

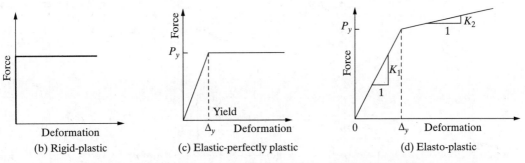

Figure 13.4   Force-deformation models for beams (monotonic loading).

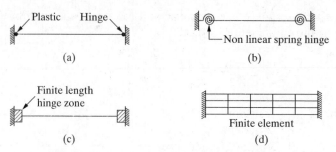

Figure 13.5 Assumptions for plasticity in beams.

This curve or model is also known as a strain-softening model. In a continuous beam, plastic hinges will develop at its ends in each span where the bending moment is maximum and later at its midspan where the sagging moment is maximum.

Subsequently beams were analysed using finite element method. Plasticity was assumed to be concentrated or distributed as shown in Figure 13.5. A model with concentrated plasticity is most convenient and popular for both steel and concrete beams.

A cantilever beam is subjected to a cyclic reversed static loading as shown in Figure 13.6. The load is *increased* from zero to maximum positive (P_{max}) and a hogging moment is developed at its fixed end as shown in Figure 13.6(a). At this instant, the *hogging plastic moment capacity* of the section is reached. If the load is further increased ($P > P_{max}$), the moment remains constant while the beam undergoes more deformation. An essential condition for reaching the plastic moment capacity is that there should be no prior local buckling or lateral torsional buckling. Now, if the direction of the load is reversed and its magnitude is *reduced* from maximum positive to zero to maximum negative (P_{max} to zero and zero to P_{min}) such that a sagging moment is developed at its fixed end (Figure 13.6(b)). At this instant, the *sagging plastic moment capacity* of the section is reached. If the load is further increased ($P > |P_{min}|$), the moment remains constant while the beam undergoes more deformation. Again, if the direction of the load is reversed and its magnitude is reduced from maximum negative to zero (P_{min} to zero), the beam does not return to its original initial position but there remains a residual deflection (Figure 13.6(c)).

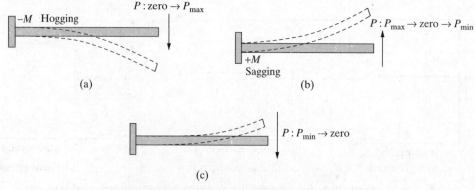

Figure 13.6 A beam under reverse cyclic loading.

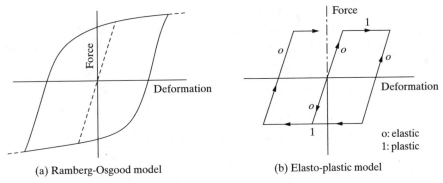

(a) Ramberg-Osgood model   (b) Elasto-plastic model

Figure 13.7   Hysteresis models for a beam.

The cyclic force-deformation behaviour of this beam is shown in Figure 13.7(a). It is a curvilinear curve also referred to as Ramberg–Osgood hysteresis curve. It is idealized as a multi-linear curve similar to those shown in Figures 13.4(b) and (c). If slope of the curve at the yield level is zero, it is referred to as elastic-perfectly plastic curve (Figure 13.7(b)) otherwise as elasto-plastic curve. The unloading from maximum positive displacement takes place along a path parallel to the initial elastic slope. Similarly, reloading from maximum negative displacement takes place along a path parallel to the initial elastic slope. At yield level, the displacement keeps increasing at constant force with zero slope. In Figure 13.7(b), label '0' shows elastic stiffness k, while label '1' shows plastic stiffness, which is zero.

In dynamic analysis, the system undergoes increasing displacement until the velocity is positive (i.e., $\dot{x}(t) > 0$); the displacement decreases, that is unloading takes place along the elastic slope when the velocity is negative (i.e., $\dot{x}(t) < 0$).

13.3.3 Steel Column

A column is the most critical element in a building. It is highly undesirable that there should be any kind of inelasticity in any column. It is well-known that flexural capacity of a column depends upon its axial load. The axial force–moment interaction needs to be taken in consideration while designing a column as shown in Figure 13.8. It is usually modelled as an elastic element. While designing a steel building, care is taken to ensure that the maximum compressive axial force in a column does not exceed about 50% of its buckling strength or yield strength in order to keep sufficient margin against drop in moment capacity due to increase in axial force in the event of a severe earthquake. A column can also be modelled with a plastic hinge at its ends just like in a beam along with P-M3 interaction curve in 2D and with P-M3-M2 curve in 3D. M2 and M3 are bending moment in a column about its local 2 and 3 axes.

$$\frac{P}{P_y} + \frac{M}{M_P} \leq 1.0 \tag{13.3a}$$

$$\frac{P}{P_y} + \frac{M_2}{M_{2P}} + \frac{M_3}{M_{3P}} \leq 1.0 \tag{13.3b}$$

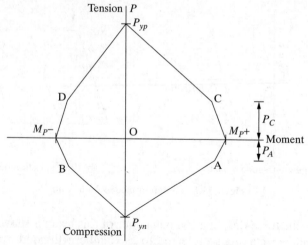

P_{yp} = yield strength of column in axial tension

P_{yn} = yield strength of a column in axial compression or its buckling strength

M_p+ = sagging moment capacity

M_p- = hogging moment capacity

Figure 13.8   P–M interaction curve for a steel column.

13.3.4 Concrete Beam

A most difficult part of seismic response analysis of reinforced concrete structures is the modelling of inelastic material behaviour. Cyclic tests on R.C. beam–column connections show that members loaded beyond their ultimate moment capacity suffer deterioration in strength and stiffness. The hysteresis behaviour of reinforced concrete members depends on many factors such as:

- Extent of cracking in concrete
- Opening and closing of cracks
- Yielding and Bauschinger effect in steel
- Shear deformations due to high shear forces
- Effectiveness of bond and anchorage

The strength and stiffness goes on degrading with each cycle and eventually the beam will collapse. Pinching-in effect is another salient feature of a RC beam. A neck is formed in the hysteresis behaviour near very low force (moment) when reversing from the yield levels due to slippage of reinforcement and closer of cracks. Clough's stiffness degrading model as shown in Figure 13.9 was proposed in the early 1970s and became very popular due to its simplicity and reasonably good results.

Two hysteresis models for reinforced concrete beams were proposed by Takeda, Sozen and Nielsen (1970) as shown in Figure 13.10:

- Bilinear backbone model
- Trilinear backbone model

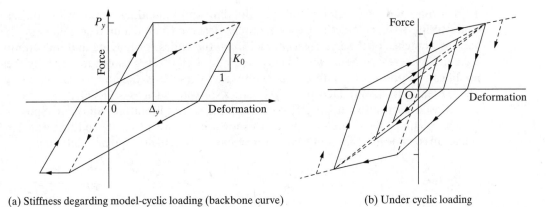

(a) Stiffness degarding model-cyclic loading (backbone curve)   (b) Under cyclic loading

Figure 13.9   Clough stiffness degrading model.

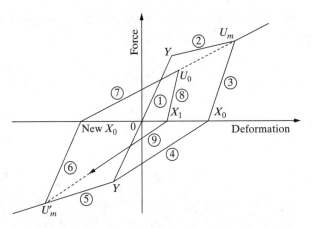

Figure 13.10(a)   Takeda's bilinear backbone model–①–②.

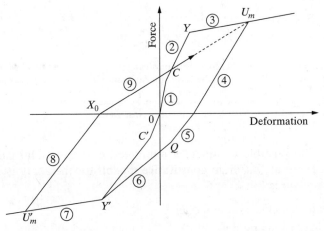

Figure 13.10(b)   Takeda's trilinear backbone model–①–②–③.

They formulated very detailed rules for loading and unloading in various branches while trying to simulate the experimentally observed behaviour. The numbers on various branches of the hysteresis model show the codes for loading and unloading. Takeda's hysteresis models were incorporated in SAKE (1975) software to study the nonlinear response of reinforced concrete plane frames subjected to earthquakes. Subsequently, they were incorporated in other software such as SAP2000.

Based on the extensive test data available in the literature, different types of hysteresis curves have been proposed as shown in Figure 13.11 depending upon the constitutive materials, amount of reinforcement and ductile design and detailing.

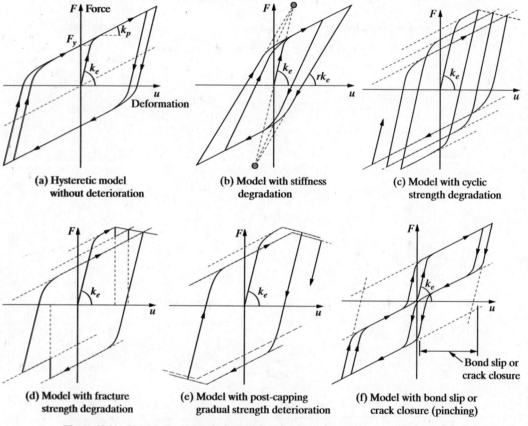

(a) Hysteretic model without deterioration

(b) Model with stiffness degradation

(c) Model with cyclic strength degradation

(d) Model with fracture strength degradation

(e) Model with post-capping gradual strength deterioration

(f) Model with bond slip or crack closure (pinching)

Figure 13.11   Hysteresis models (Adapted from Deierlein, Reinhorn and Willford 2010). (k_e-elastic stiffness, k_p-plastic stiffness)

It is also possible to model a reinforced concrete beam using finite element approach. There are different constitutive models for the analysis of concrete at low confining pressures:

- Smeared crack concrete model
- Brittle cracking model
- Concrete-damaged plasticity model

The *smeared crack concrete model* is intended for applications in which the concrete is subjected to essentially monotonic straining and a material point exhibits either tensile cracking or compressive crushing. Plastic straining in compression is controlled by a 'compression' yield surface. Cracking is assumed to be the most important aspect of the behaviour, and the representation of cracking and post-cracking anisotropic behaviour dominates the modelling.

The *brittle cracking model* is intended for applications in which the concrete behaviour is dominated by tensile cracking and compressive failure is not important. The model includes consideration of the anisotropy induced by cracking. In compression, the model assumes elastic behavior.

The *concrete-damaged plasticity model* is based on the assumption of scalar (isotropic) damage and is meant for applications in which the concrete is subjected to cyclic loading. The model takes into consideration the degradation of the elastic stiffness induced by plastic straining both in tension and compression. It also accounts for stiffness recovery effects under cyclic loading.

Apparently, the finite element modelling is computationally very expensive and is not suitable for studying the nonlinear behaviour of reinforced concrete buildings. It is best suited for studying the behaviour of small components under cyclic loading.

13.3.5 Concrete Column

The P–M interaction curve of a reinforced concrete column is different than that of a steel column because of the inherent difference in their behaviour. Concrete is very strong in compression but very weak in tension, whereas steel is very strong in tension but weak in compression. This difference reflects in their P–M interaction curve as shown in Figure 13.12. Similar to a steel column, a concrete column is designed so as to remain elastic under a severe seismic loading.

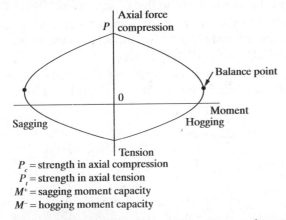

P_c = strength in axial compression
P_t = strength in axial tension
M^+ = sagging moment capacity
M^- = hogging moment capacity

Figure 13.12   P–M interaction curve for a concrete column.

13.3.6 Nonlinear Behaviour of Frames

The study of nonlinear behaviour of frames posed additional challenges. There are different kinds of frames and structural systems with different member proportions.

- Steel Building Frames
  - o Member proportions
  - o Structural system
    - Moment-resistant (M-R) frames
    - Concentrically braced frames
    - Eccentrically braced frames
- Reinforced Concrete Frames
  - o Member proportions
    - Ordinary RC frames
    - Ductile M-R frames
    - Ordinary shear wall frames
    - Ductile shear wall frames
- Building Frames with Other Systems

A ductile frame or ductile shear wall means it has been detailed for ductility, that is concrete has been suitable confined at all possible locations of plastic hinges. Apparently, the problem becomes very complicated at the building frame level. Beam–column joints and shear walls pose serious challenge. Several small scale tests were performed on beam–column joints and 2D and 3D building frames in several universities across the world. Based on the numerous tests carried out by various researchers, some of the broad conclusions can be drawn as follows:

- Frames must be designed using weak girder-strong column proportions.
- M-R frames and eccentrically braced frames in steel were highly ductile with repeatable and stable loops as shown in Figure 13.11(a).
- Concentrically braced steel frames exhibit a less ductile behaviour as shown in Figure 13.13(a) as compared to that of eccentrically braced frames.
- Ductile-reinforced concrete frames and ductile-reinforced concrete shear wall frames produced hysteresis loops with considerable energy dissipation as shown in Figures 13.11(b), (c), (d) and 13.13(a).
- Ordinary reinforced concrete frames produced poor hysteresis behaviour with much less energy dissipation as shown in Figure 13.13(b).

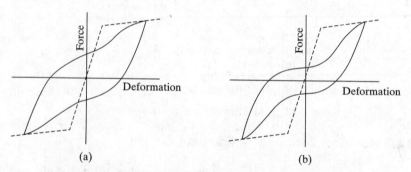

Figure 13.13 Hysteresis models showing poor energy dissipation.

Mathematical Modeling   A mathematical model of the structure should represent the spatial distribution of mass and stiffness throughout the structure. A 3D model incorporating a minimum of three-DOF consisting of translation in two orthogonal plan directions and rotation about the vertical axis through the centre of rigidity at each level of the structure should be used. The hysteretic behavior of structural elements should be modelled consistent with experimental test data and must account for all significant yielding, strength degradation, stiffness degradation and pinching-in effects. Strength of elements should be based on expected values considering strain hardening, over-strength and strength degradation. A flexure beam element is assumed to develop point plastic hinges at its ends as shown in Figure 13.14. Each plastic hinge is embedded with a hysteresis model as applicable. The moment-rotation or moment-curvature curves at each end are computed separately and assigned to each plastic hinge. Similarly, a column is represented with a plastic hinge at its ends along with P–M3 interaction curve in 2D and P-M3-M2 hysteresis surface in 3D. The structure may be assumed to be fixed at the base. Alternatively, it is permitted to model the soil and foundation consistent with detailed geotechnical investigations.

Beam–column joints may be treated as rigid. A wall is modelled as a beam-column. A shear hinge may also be introduced at its mid-height to simulate a plastic hinge due to shear force. For elastic portions, in beam, column and wall, cracked stiffness are assigned which may be 50% of their gross stiffness.

Selection of Ground Motion   Selection of ground motions for carrying out a nonlinear analysis is another challenge. Some international building codes do specify how to select a ground motion and number of such accelerograms for a given site. It is usual to generate a set of accelerograms compatible with the site-specific design response spectrum with suitable probability and return period. Detailed requirements for carrying out nonlinear modeling and analysis are available in the literature (ASCE 7 (2010), AISC 341 (2010), AISC 356 (2010), EC8-1(2004), FEMA 356 (2000), FEMA 440 (2005), PEER /ATC-72-1 (2010), NEHRP Technical Note 4 (2010), and NZS1170-5(2004)).

Figure 13.14   Flexure element with point hinges.

13.4 NONLINEAR ANALYSIS

The implicit direct integration methods discussed in Chapter 7 are capable of carrying out nonlinear analysis of buildings under earthquake loading. Kannan and Powell (1973) developed a very powerful software called DRAIN-2D, with the option to add more element libraries by other researchers. The author (1978) developed two hysteresis elements for steel members subjected to cyclic buckling or cyclic end moments and buckling (EL9 and EL10) for use with DRAIN-2D. Later, Prakash, Powell and Campbell (1994) developed DRAIN-3DX for 3D nonlinear analysis of buildings. The

Pacific Earthquake Engineering Research Center (PEER) has developed an *Open System for Earthquake Engineering Simulation,* OpenSees for short, as a software platform for research and application of simulation for structural and geotechnical systems with realistic models of nonlinear behavior. It is an open source code and developers are welcome to contribute.

In any nonlinear problem, the nonlinearity may be confined within a certain length at the ends of a member. It requires tracking of change in stiffness at all such locations in a building. This necessitates the requirement to modify the member stiffness as and when stiffness changes at one or both of its ends. Let us write the equation of motion at time *t*:

$$m\ddot{x}(t) + c\dot{x}(t) + f(x) = p(t) \tag{13.4}$$

or, at i^{th} step
$$m\ddot{x}_i(t) + c\dot{x}_i(t) + f(x_i) = p_i \tag{13.5a}$$

and at $i+1$ step

$$m\ddot{x}_{i+1}(t) + c\dot{x}_{i+1}(t) + f(x_{i+1}) = p_{i+1} \tag{13.5b}$$

The change over these two steps is

$$m\Delta\ddot{x}_i + c\Delta\dot{x}_i + \Delta f_i = \Delta p_i \tag{13.6}$$

where,
$$\Delta f_i = f(x_{i+1}) - f(x_i) \cong (k_i)_T \Delta x_i \tag{13.7}$$

The force $f(x)$ represents resisting force which depends upon the member stiffness and deformations. The tangent stiffness is a function of displacement and would not be constant in a nonlinear problem. Within any time step, increments in node displacements are computed and hence there are increments in member deformation. It is necessary to compute the increments in the element forces corresponding to these deformation increments taking into account change in stiffness of the element. This is the *state determination phase* of the calculation because the new state of force and deformation in each element is determined. The relationship between element force and deformation can be represented by piecewise linear curve as shown in Figure 13.15. Each change of slope corresponds to change in stiffness at a new point or unloading at a previously yielded point and will be termed an *event*. In general, several events may occur for any element within a single time step. For inelastic structures, the element deformation is usually more important than the element force because deformation

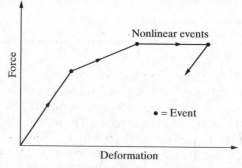

Figure 13.15   Definition of event.

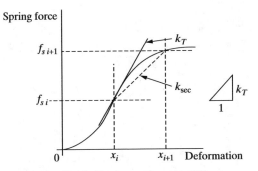

Figure 13.16   Tangent and secant stiffness.

gives direct indication of the ductility demand on the structure. There is a need to keep track of displacement and velocity at each time increment. A *zero or negative velocity* indicates a change in the direction of loading or unloading.

The tangent stiffness k_T and secant stiffness k_{sec} at any instant '*t*' are shown in Figure 13.16. In the step-by-step numerical integration for a nonlinear problem, three situations are encountered as discussed earlier and shown in the various hysteresis models:

- Change from elastic to plastic state (loading)
- Continue in the plastic state (loading)
- Change from plastic to elastic state (unloading)

Change of state (Figures 13.17(a) and (b))   At the beginning of a time step, say at point '*a*', the tangent stiffness at point '*a*' is assumed and the numerical analysis will lead to point '*b*'. It should have led to point *b'* which is the correct answer. Obviously, a tangent stiffness will never lead to the correct point *b'*. The point *b'* is unknown at this stage and can be located by iteration.

$$\Delta f_i - (k_i)_T \Delta x_i = \Delta R_i \tag{13.8}$$

where, Δf_i = true resisting force

$(k_i)_T \Delta x_i$ = approximate resisting force based on tangent stiffness

ΔR_i = residual or unbalanced resisting force

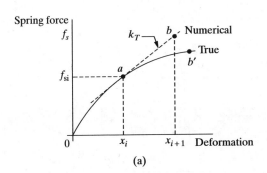

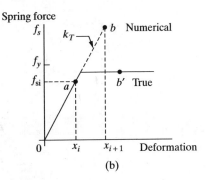

(a)

(b)

Figure 13.17   Change from elastic to plastic state.

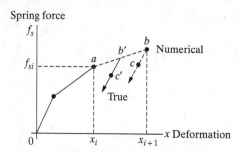

Figure 13.18   Change from plastic to elastic state.

Continue in plastic state (Figure 13.17(b))   Upon further loading, the member may continue to plastify, that is there will be no increase in its resistance but it will keep on deforming.

Change of state (Figure 13.18)   At the beginning of a time step, say at point 'a', the stiffness at point 'a' is assumed and the numerical analysis will lead to point 'b'. In case the velocity at point 'b' is negative or zero, it means the system is now under unloading. Upon unloading from point b, the analysis will lead to point 'c'. Both the points, b and c, are incorrect. The velocity at the beginning of the time step at point 'a' was positive and somewhere in between 'a' and 'b', the velocity has become zero, say at point b'. It means the true unloading will begin at point b' and should lead to point c' which will be the true behaviour. Point b' can be located either by iteration or by choosing a very small time step between points 'a' and b'.

There are different numerical techniques for the solution of nonlinear problems depending upon the complexities involved in the nonlinear behaviour.

13.4.1 Newmark β Method: *With Iterations*

The Newmark β method for linear systems was discussed in Chapter 7. It can be extended to nonlinear systems by making use of the Newton–Raphson technique. The salient features of this step-by-step method for nonlinear systems can be explained with the help of a force–deformation curve as shown in Figure 13.19. Let us first recall the Newmark β method for linear systems in incremental form derived in Chapter 7.

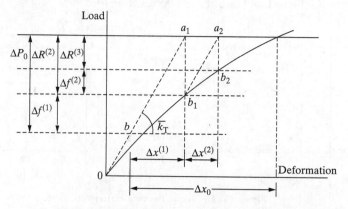

Figure 13.19   Modified Newton–Raphson method.

$$\bar{k} = \frac{\Delta \bar{p}}{\Delta x_i} \tag{7.53}$$

where
$$\bar{k} = k + \frac{\gamma}{\beta \Delta t} c + \frac{1}{\beta (\Delta t)^2} m \tag{7.54}$$

and
$$\Delta \bar{p}_i = \Delta p_i + \left(\frac{1}{\beta \Delta t} m + \frac{\gamma}{\beta} c \right) \dot{x}_i + \left[\frac{1}{2\beta} m + \Delta t \left(\frac{\gamma}{2\beta} - 1 \right) c \right] \ddot{x}_i \tag{7.55}$$

In the nonlinear analysis, tangent stiffness k_T is used instead of k

$$\bar{k} = k_T + \frac{\gamma}{\beta \Delta t} c + \frac{1}{\beta (\Delta t)^2} m \tag{13.9}$$

where $(k_i)_T$ = tangent stiffness which is a function of force–displacement relation of a member.

In static load case, there are no mass and damping terms. The nonlinearity is caused due to stiffness of k_T alone. Therefore, its effect is quite severe. In dynamic systems, the coefficients of mass and damping terms in $\bar{k}$, $\frac{1}{\beta (\Delta t)^2}$ and $\frac{\gamma}{\beta \Delta t}$ are much larger than k_T for usual values of β and Δt. Therefore, the severity of nonlinearity is reduced.

In Figure 13.19, corresponding to a force Δp_0, the correct deflection is x_0. For a force Δp_0, the linear analysis will give a deflection Δx_1 corresponding to point b_1 which is obviously incorrect.

$$\bar{k}_T \Delta x_0 = \Delta p_0 \tag{13.10}$$

This will lead to a deflection $\Delta x^{(1)}$ instead of Δx_0.

$\Delta x^{(1)}$ is the first approximation to the true Δx_0. Corresponding to $\Delta x^{(1)}$, the true force is $\Delta f^{(1)}$ which is less than Δp_0. The residual or unbalanced force is defined by

$$\Delta R^{(2)} = \Delta p_0 - \Delta f^{(1)} \tag{13.11}$$

The additional displacement due to this residual or unbalanced force is given as

$$\bar{k}_T \Delta x^{(2)} = \Delta R^{(2)} = \Delta p_0 - \Delta f^{(1)} \tag{13.12}$$

This additional displacement is used to find a new value of the unbalanced force, and the process is continued until the solution has converged. This iterative process is referred to as the *modified Newton–Raphson* method because the same initial stiffness is used throughout.

The algorithm can be written as follows:

Step 1: For the given system parameters, initialize the Newmark's constants a_0 to a_7 and compute the initial acceleration $\ddot{x}_0$.

Step 2: For each time step i ($i = 0, 1, 2, 3, ...$)

(a) Compute $\bar{k}_{Ti}$ and $\Delta \bar{p}_i$

(b) Set $\Delta R^{(i)} = \Delta \bar{p}_i$ and $x_{i+1}^{(0)} = x_i$ to begin the iteration.

(c) Carry out Newton–Raphson iterations within a time step:

(d) Solve the equilibrium equation for deflection Δx:

$$\bar{k}_T \Delta x^{(j)} = \Delta R^{(j)} \tag{13.13}$$

$$\Delta f^{(j)} = f_s^{(j)} - f_s^{(j-1)} + \left(\bar{k}_T - k_T\right)\Delta x^{(j)} \tag{13.14}$$

$$\Delta R^{(j+1)} = \Delta R^{(j)} - \Delta f^{(j)} \tag{13.15}$$

$$x_{i+1}^{(j)} = x_{i+1}^{(j-1)} + \Delta x^{(j)} j = 1, 2, 3,... \tag{13.16}$$

where, the term $\left(\bar{k}_T - k_T\right)$ corresponds to the contribution of mass and damping terms in the equivalent stiffness.

(e) The acceleration increment and velocity increment can be estimated from the equations developed earlier for the Newmark's method.

$$\Delta \ddot{x}_i = \frac{1}{\beta(\Delta t)^2}\Delta x_i - \frac{1}{\beta \Delta t}\dot{x}_i - \frac{1}{2\beta}\ddot{x}_i \tag{7.51}$$

$$\Delta \dot{x}_i = \frac{\gamma}{\beta \Delta t}\Delta x_i - \frac{\gamma}{\beta}\dot{x}_i + \Delta t\left(1 - \frac{\gamma}{2\beta}\right)\ddot{x}_i \tag{7.52}$$

(f) Finally, when the iterative process has converged, the total incremental displacement is given by,

$$\Delta x_0 = \Delta x^{(1)} + \Delta x^{(2)} + \Delta x^{(3)} +... \tag{13.17}$$

In this method, *initial stiffness matrix* is used for all iterations. The *triangularization* operation of the stiffness matrix is carried out only once. Here lies the advantage, especially in large systems. In this iterative scheme, the convergence is very slow. Yet, in certain problems involving mild nonlinearities, this proves less expensive on the whole.

Convergence Criteria   In any iterative scheme, there has to be a convergence criterion to stop the process. Either $\Delta R^{(j)}$ or $\Delta x^{(j)}$ may be chosen smaller than a limiting value. Another option is to check the ratio $\Delta R^{(j)}/\Delta \bar{p}$ or $\Delta x^{(j)}/\Delta x$ to be sufficiently small. The total increment Δx will not be known till the iteration process is complete, therefore, $\Sigma \Delta x^{(j)}$ may be used in place of Δx.

A better convergence is achieved by using the *current tangent stiffness* in place of the *initial stiffness*. It requires greater computational efforts because of the assembly of tangent stiffness matrix and, therefore, triangularization of such a matrix for each iteration. This iterative scheme is known as the *Newton–Raphson* method as shown in Figure 13.20.

13.4.2 Newmark β Method: *Without Iterations*

It is based on the premise that the step size is very small, therefore, response at the end of the step can be taken as acceptable. If during loading a change of state is encountered, the unbalanced force (residual force) is computed and is applied in the next step for maintaining the equilibrium. If unloading is encountered, the numerical displacement

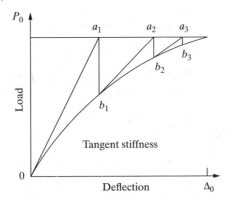

Figure 13.20   Newton–Raphson method.

is accepted without introducing appreciable error. The stiffness is modified in the next step. This algorithm was used by Kanaan and Powell (1973) in DRAIN-2D.

The algorithm can be written as follows:

Step 1: For the given system parameters, initialize the Newmark's constants a_0 to a_7 and compute the initial acceleration $\ddot{x}_0$. The value of β may be taken as 1/4 or 1/6.

Step 2: For each time step i (i = 0, 1, 2, 3, ...)

  (a) Compute $\Delta \bar{p}_i$

  (b) Compute $\bar{k}_i$

  (c) Compute $\Delta x_i = \dfrac{\Delta \bar{p}_i}{\bar{k}_i}$

   Check for change of state. If during loading, yielding occurs, calculate unbalanced force and apply it in the next step. If unloading occurs, accept the numerical displacement.

   The next cycle is carried out using the modified stiffness of the system. $k_i = k$ for elastic state, and $k_i = 0$, for plastic state

  (d) Compute velocity increment using Equation (7.52), and total displacement and total velocity.

  (e) Compute the updated resisting force:

  $$(f_s)_{i+1} = (f_s)_i + k_i \Delta x_i \tag{13.18}$$

  (f) Compute the updated total acceleration

  $$\ddot{x}_{i+1} = \frac{p_{i+1} - c\dot{x}_{i+1} - (f_s)_{i+1}}{m} \tag{13.19}$$

A computer program SDOF-NON was developed for single degree-of-freedom systems based on the above algorithm in FORTRAN. A similar program could be easily written in MATLAB. It included the following hysteresis models:

- Elastic model
- Elasto-plastic model
- Stiffness degrading model

13.5 ILLUSTRATIVE EXAMPLES

Example 13.1

A SDOF elasto-plastic system has a mass 2.5 kg, tangent stiffness 250 N/m and viscous damping of 5%. Its yield strength is 5 N. It was subjected to a dynamic loading and its response at 2.20 sec and 2.34 sec was as shown in the table. The step size was 0.02 sec and load increment was 0.1 N. Find the response at (i) 2.22 sec and (ii) 2.36 sec using the Newmark β method.

Time	Displacement	Velocity	Acceleration	Spring Force	Load
Sec	m	m/s	m/s²	N	N
2.20	0.01825	0.2205	−1.8455	4.5625	0.5
2.34	0.0346	0.01470	−3.3147	5	−3.25

Solution   Natural frequency $\omega = \sqrt{\dfrac{250}{2.5}} = 10$ rad/sec

Period = 0.628 sec, step size = 0.02 sec

Damping coefficient $c = 2m\omega\xi = 2 \times 2.5 \times 10 \times 0.05 = 2.5$ Ns/m

Factors $\beta = 1/4$ and $\gamma = \frac{1}{2}$.

$$\bar{k} = k + \frac{\gamma}{\beta \Delta t} c + \frac{1}{\beta(\Delta t)^2} m$$

$$\bar{k} = 250 + \frac{0.5}{0.25 \times 0.02} c + \frac{1}{0.25 \times (0.02)^2} m$$

$$\bar{k} = 250 + 100c + 10000m = 25500 \text{ N/m}$$

Effective load increment is given by

$$\Delta \bar{p}_i = \Delta p_i + \left(\frac{1}{\beta \Delta t} m + \frac{\gamma}{\beta} c \right) \dot{x}_i + \left[\frac{1}{2\beta} m + \Delta t \left(\frac{\gamma}{2\beta} - 1 \right) c \right] \ddot{x}_i$$

$$\Delta \bar{p} = \Delta p + \left(\frac{2.5}{0.25 \times 0.02} + \frac{0.5 \times 2.5}{0.25} \right) \dot{x} + \left(\frac{2.5}{2 \times 0.25} + 0.05 \left(\frac{0.5}{0.5} - 1 \right) 2.5 \right) \ddot{x}$$

$$\Delta \bar{p} = \Delta p + 505 \dot{x} + 5 \ddot{x}$$

(i) At time step 2.20 sec,

$$\Delta \bar{p} = \Delta p + 505 \dot{x} + 5 \ddot{x} = 102.225$$

$$\Delta x_i = \frac{\Delta \bar{p}}{\bar{k}} = \frac{102.225}{25500} = 0.004009$$

Velocity increment is given by

$$\Delta \dot{x}_i = \frac{\gamma}{\beta \Delta t} \Delta x_i - \frac{\gamma}{\beta} \dot{x}_i + \Delta t \left(1 - \frac{\gamma}{2\beta} \right) \ddot{x}_i$$

$$\Delta \dot{x} = \frac{0.50}{0.25 \times 0.02} \Delta x - \frac{0.50}{0.25} \dot{x} + 0 = 100 \Delta x - 2\dot{x} = -0.0401$$

Spring force is given by

$$f_{i+1} = f_i + \Delta f = 4.5625 + 250 \times 0.004009 = 5.5648 \ngtr 5 \text{ N}$$

It shows that between the load step 2.20 and 2.22 sec, the spring has yielded. There is a need to step back and find the displacement corresponding to the yield force 5 N.

Change of State
Consider Figure 13.21

$$\Delta x = \Delta x_1 + \Delta x_2$$

Let

$$\Delta x_1 = \psi \Delta x, \text{ and } f_i + bc = f_y$$

$$bc = \psi \Delta x \, k_T,$$

∴

$$\psi = \frac{(f_y - f_i)}{\Delta x \, k_T}$$

$$\psi = \frac{5 - 4.5625}{0.004009 \times 250} = 0.4365,$$

∴

$$\Delta x_1 = 0.001750$$

Again in Figure 13.21,

$$ab = ac - bc = \Delta f_i - \psi \Delta f_i = (1 - \psi) \Delta f_i$$

Also,

$$\Delta x_0 = \Delta x_1 + \Delta x_p$$

The plastic deformation Δx_p in the element is given by

$$\overline{k} \Delta x_p = (1 - \psi) \Delta \overline{p} \text{ similar to Equation (13.10)}$$

where $\overline{k} = 25250$ because $k_T = 0$ at yield
or,

$$\overline{k} \Delta x_p = (1 - 0.4365) \times 102.225 \quad \text{or} \quad \Delta x_p = 0.002281$$

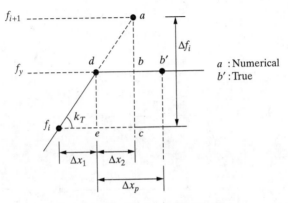

Figure 13.21   Change of state-loading.

Total displacement at the end of this step

$$x_{i+1} = x_i + \Delta x_1 + \Delta x_p = 0.01825 + 0.001750 + 0.002281 = 0.02228 \text{ m}$$

Velocity increment is given by

$$\Delta \dot{x} = 100\Delta x - 2\dot{x} = -0.0379 \text{ m/s}$$

Velocity at the end of the time step is given by

$$\dot{x}_{i+1} = \dot{x}_i + \Delta \dot{x} = 0.1826 \text{ m/s}$$

Acceleration at the end of the time step can be found from the equation of motion, that is

$$\ddot{x}_{i+1} = \frac{p_{i+1} - c\dot{x}_{i+1} - (f_s)_{i+1}}{m}$$

$$\ddot{x}_{i+1} = \frac{0.6 - 2.5 \times 0.1826 - 5}{2.5} = -1.9426 \text{ m/s}^2$$

(ii) At time step 2.34 sec

Given, $x = 0.0346$ m, $\dot{x} = 0.0147$ m/s, and $\ddot{x} = -3.3147$ m/s^2

Since, $f_s = 5N = f_y$, stiffness $k_T = 0$

$$\Delta \bar{p} = \Delta p + 505\dot{x} + 5\ddot{x} = -0.1 + 505 \times 0.0147 + 5 \times (-3.3147) = -9.25$$

$$\Delta x_i = \frac{\Delta \bar{p}}{k} = \frac{-9.25}{25250} = -0.0003663 \text{ m}$$

Velocity increment is given by

$$\Delta \dot{x} = 100\Delta x - 2\dot{x} = -0.0660 \text{ m/s}$$

Total velocity is given by

$$\dot{x}_{i+1} = \dot{x}_i + \Delta \dot{x} = -0.05133 \text{ m/s}$$

Since velocity is negative, it means somewhere in between this step, the velocity has become positive to zero and the direction of loading has changed from loading to unloading.

Change of State
Consider Figure 13.22
    Setting total velocity $= 0$,

$$\Delta x = \Delta x_1 + \Delta x_2 \quad \text{numerical}$$
$$= \Delta x_1 + \Delta x_2 \quad \text{true}$$

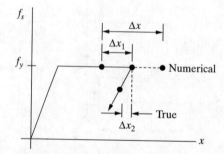

Figure 13.22   Change of state-unloading.

$$\dot{x}_{i+1} = \frac{2}{\Delta t}(\psi \Delta x) - \dot{x}_i = 0 \quad \text{or} \quad \psi = -0.4013$$

$$\Delta x_1 = \psi \Delta x = 0.000147 \text{ m}$$

also,

$$\bar{k}\Delta x_2 = (1-\psi)\Delta \bar{p} \quad \text{similar to Equation (13.10)}$$

where, $k_T = 250$ because unloading is always elastic

$$\therefore \quad \Delta x_2 = \frac{(1-\psi)\Delta \bar{p}}{\bar{k}} = \frac{(1+0.4013)\times(-9.25)}{25500} = -0.0005083 \text{ m}$$

Total displacement increment in the time step

$$\Delta x = 0.000147 - 0.0005083 = -0.0003613 \text{ m}$$

Displacement at the end of the time step

$$x_{i+1} = x_i + \Delta x = 0.0346 - 0.0003613 = 0.03424 \text{ m}$$

Velocity at the end of the time step

$$\dot{x}_{i+1} = \dot{x}_i + \Delta \dot{x} = 100\Delta x - \dot{x}_i = 100\times(-0.0003613) - 0.0147 = -0.05083 \text{ m/s}$$

Similarly, acceleration at the end of the time step can be computed from the equation of motion.

Resisting force at the end of the time step

$$f_{i+1} = f_i + k_T\Delta x_2 = 5 + 250\times(-0.0005083) = 4.8729 \text{ N}$$

Acceleration at the end of the time step

$$\ddot{x}_{i+1} = \frac{p_{i+1} - c\dot{x}_{i+1} - (f_s)_{i+1}}{m}$$

$$\ddot{x}_{i+1} = \frac{-3.15 - 2.5\times(-0.05083) - 4.8729}{2.5} = -3.1583 \text{ m/s}^2$$

Comments
In any hysteresis model such as those shown in Figures 13.2, 13.9, 13.10 and 13.11, a series of control points are identified at the end of each loading or unloading branch. These control points essentially represent a state of transition. The stiffness at each control point is based on experimental data. A specific computer code can be written for each control point to model loading and unloading states and compute displacement and force increments as illustrated in this example.   □

Example 13.2

A damped SDOF system has a mass of 4900 N, stiffness of 20 kN/m and damping 5%. It is subjected to a ground motion as shown in table. The initial displacement and velocity are zero. Its hysteresis behaviour is shown in Figure 13.23. Determine the displacement time-history assuming:

(a) elastic response
(b) elasto-plastic response with yield strength = ±250 N

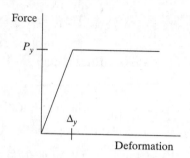

Figure 13.23   Force-deformation behaviour.

| Acceleration | 0 | −0.1 g | 0 | 0 |
| time sec | 0 | 0.3 | 0.6 | 1.0 |

Solution   Mass $m = 4900/9.80 = 500$ kg; stiffness = 20 kN/m
Period of vibration = 0.993 sec
Strain-hardening ratio = nil
Mass proportional damping = 5%;

$$\therefore c = 2\xi\omega m = 316 \text{ Ns/m}$$

Step size = 0.1 sec
         The linear analysis was carried out using the Newmark β method illustrated in Chapter 7. Factor β was taken as 1/4 and γ was taken as 1/2. The nonlinear analysis was carried out using yet another algorithm based on Newmark method – without corrections in force or displacement. Only stiffness was modified in the next step. The calculations were carried out in an Excel sheet as shown in Table 13.1.

$$\Delta x_i = \frac{\Delta \bar{p}}{\bar{k}} \tag{7.55}$$

where

$$\bar{k} = k + \frac{\gamma}{\beta \Delta t} c + \frac{1}{\beta(\Delta t)^2} m \tag{7.56}$$

and

$$\Delta \bar{p}_i = \Delta p_i + \left(\frac{1}{\beta \Delta t} m + \frac{\gamma}{\beta} c \right) \dot{x}_i + \left[\frac{1}{2\beta} m + \Delta t \left(\frac{\gamma}{2\beta} - 1 \right) c \right] \ddot{x}_i \tag{7.57}$$

$$\Delta \dot{x}_i = \frac{\gamma}{\beta \Delta t} \Delta x_i - \frac{\gamma}{\beta} \dot{x}_i + \Delta t \left(1 - \frac{\gamma}{2\beta} \right) \ddot{x}_i \tag{7.54}$$

$$\ddot{x}_{i+1} = \frac{p_{i+1} - c\dot{x}_{i+1} - (f_s)_{i+1}}{m} \tag{13.19}$$

The results of elastic and elasto-plastic analysis are shown in Figure 13.24.
Yield displacement = $F_y/k = 250 \times 100/20000 = 1.25$ cm
Displacement ductility = Maximum displacement/yield displacement = 4.34/1.25 = 3.47.

□

TABLE 13.1 NEWMARK β METHOD WITHOUT NEWTON–RAPHSON ITERATIONS

t_i	x_i	$\dot{x}_i$	f_{si}	$\ddot{x}_i$	p_i	$\Delta\bar{p}_i$	k_i	$\bar{k}_i$	Δx_i	$\Delta\dot{x}_i$	x_{i+1}	$\dot{x}_{i+1}$	f_{si+1}	$\ddot{x}_{i+1}$	t_i
s	m	m/s	N	m/s²	N	N	N/m	N/m	m	m/s	m	m/s	N	m/s²	s
(1)	(2)	(3)	(4)	(5)	(6)	(7)	(8)	(9)	(10)	(11)	(12)	(13)	(14)	(15)	(1)
0	0.0000	0.0000	0.0000	0.0000	0.0000	163.3300	20000.00	226320.00	0.0007	0.0144	0.0007	0.0144	14.4335	0.2887	0
0.1	0.0007	0.0144	14.4335	0.2887	163.3300	749.8038	20000.00	226320.00	0.0033	0.0374	0.0040	0.0518	80.6940	0.4592	0.1
0.2	0.0040	0.0518	80.6940	0.4592	326.6700	1691.8210	20000.00	226320.00	0.0075	0.0459	0.0115	0.0977	230.2010	0.4579	0.2
0.3	0.0115	0.0977	230.2010	0.4579	490.0000	2309.8685	20000.00	226320.00	0.0102	0.0088	0.0217	0.1064	250.0000	0.0861	0.3
0.4	0.0217	0.1064	250.0000	0.0861	326.6700	2118.8818	0.00	206320.00	0.0103	-0.0075	0.0320	0.0990	250.0000	-0.2359	0.4
0.5	0.0320	0.0990	250.0000	-0.2359	163.3300	1642.4005	0.00	206320.00	0.0080	-0.0387	0.0399	0.0603	250.0000	-0.5381	0.5
0.6	0.0399	0.0603	250.0000	-0.5381	0.0000	705.1104	0.00	206320.00	0.0034	-0.0522	0.0434	0.0081	250.0000	-0.5051	0.6
0.7	0.0434	0.0081	250.0000	-0.5051	0.0000	-338.0876	0.00	206320.00	-0.0016	-0.0490	0.0417	-0.0409	250.0000	-0.4742	0.7
0.8	0.0417	-0.0409	250.0000	-0.4742	0.0000	-13173750	20000.00	226320.00	-0.0058	-0.0347	0.0359	-0.0755	133.5830	-0.2194	0.8
0.9	0.0359	-0.0755	133.5830	-0.2194	0.0000	-1778.1313	20000.00	226320.00	-0.0079	-0.0060	0.0280	-0.0816	-23.5513	0.0987	0.9
1	0.0280	-0.0816	-23.5513	0.0987	0.0000	-1584.6174	20000.00	226320.00	-0.0070	0.0231	0.0210	-0.0584	-163.5846	0.3641	1

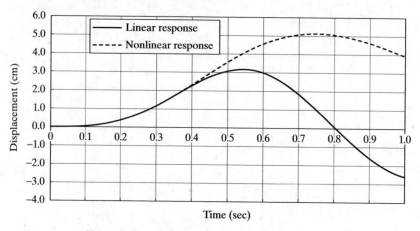

Figure 13.24   Elastic and elasto-plastic displacements.

Example 13.3

Solve Example 13.2 again using Newmark method with Newton–Raphson iterations within a time step.

Solution   The calculations were carried out in an Excel sheet using the Newmark β method with iterations as discussed. Whenever there is a change in state from elastic to plastic, Newton–Raphson iterations were carried out within the time step until the unbalanced load was zero. The results are shown in Table 13.2.

At 0.3 sec, the elastic force reaches yield level. The tangent stiffness needs to be set equal to nil and iterations are required between 0.3 sec and 0.4 sec time step. The details are shown as follows.

Initialize

$$x_{i+1}^{(0)} = x_i = 0.0115, \qquad f_s^{(0)} = 230.2010$$

$$\Delta R^{(1)} = \Delta \bar{p}_i = 2309.8684, \qquad \bar{k}_T = 226320.0$$

Cycle 1

$$\Delta x^{(1)} = 0.0102$$

$$x_{i+1}^{(1)} = x_{i+1}^{(0)} + \Delta x^{(1)} = 0.0217$$

$$\Delta f^{(1)} = f_s^{(1)} - f_s^{(0)} + \left(\bar{k}_T - k_T\right)\Delta x^{(1)}$$

$$\Delta f^{(1)} = f_s^{(1)} - f_s^{(0)} + \left(\frac{1}{\beta(\Delta t)^2}m + \frac{\gamma}{\beta\Delta t}c\right)\Delta x^{(1)} = 2125.5433$$

$$\Delta R^{(2)} = \Delta R^{(1)} - \Delta f^{(1)} = 184.3251$$

TABLE 13.2 NEWMARK β METHOD WITH NEWTON–RAPHSON ITERATIONS

t_i	x_i	$\dot{x}_i$	f_{si}	$\ddot{x}_i$	p_i	$\Delta \bar{p}_i$	k_i	$\bar{k}_i$	Δx_i	$\Delta \dot{x}_i$	x_{i+1}	$\dot{x}_{i+1}$	f_{si+1}	$\ddot{x}_{i+1}$	t_i
s	m	m/s	N	m/s²	N	N	N/m	N/m	m	m/s	m	m/s	N	m/s²	s
(1)	(2)	(3)	(4)	(5)	(6)	(7)	(8)	(9)	(10)	(11)	(12)	(13)	(14)	(15)	(1)
0	0.0000	0.0000	0.0000	0.0000	0.0000	163.3300	20000.000	226320.000	0.0007	0.0144	0.0007	0.0144	14.4335	0.2887	0
0.1	0.0007	0.0144	14.4335	0.2887	163.3300	749.8038	20000.000	226320.000	0.0033	0.0374	0.0040	0.0518	80.6940	0.45920	0.1
0.2	0.0040	0.0518	80.6940	0.4592	326.6700	1691.821	20000.000	226320.000	0.0075	0.0459	0.0115	0.0977	230.2010	0.4579	0.2
0.3	0.0115	0.0977	230.2010	0.4579	490.0000	2309.8685	20000.000	226320.000	0.0102	0.0088	0.0217	0.1243	250.0000	0.0748	0.3
						184.3251			0.0008	0.0163					
						16.2889			0.0001	0.0014					
						1.4395			0.0000	0.0001					
						0.1272			0.000001	0.0000					
0.4	0.0226	0.1243	250.0000	0.0748	326.6700	2476.2177	0.000	206320.000	0.0120	-0.0086	0.0346	0.1157	250.0000	-0.2465	0.4
0.5	0.0346	0.1157	250.0000	-0.2465	163.3300	1977.8446	0.000	206320.000	0.0096	-0.0397	0.0442	0.0760	250.0000	-0.5480	0.5
0.6	0.0442	0.0760	250.0000	-0.5480	0.0000	1020.0038	0.000	206320.000	0.0049	-0.0531	0.0491	0.0229	250.0000	-0.5145	0.6
0.7	0.0491	0.0229	250.0000	-0.5145	0.0000	-42.4858	0.000	206320.000	-0.0002	-0.0499	0.0489	-0.0270	250.0000	-0.4829	0.7

Cycle 2

$$\Delta x^{(2)} = 0.0008$$

$$x_{i+1}^{(2)} = x_{i+1}^{(1)} + \Delta x^{(2)} = 0.0225$$

$$\Delta f^{(2)} = f_s^{(2)} - f_s^{(1)} + \left(\overline{k}_T - k_T\right)\Delta x^{(2)} = 168.0362$$

$$\Delta R^{(3)} = \Delta R^{(2)} - \Delta f^{(2)} = 16.2889$$

Cycle 3

$$\Delta x^{(3)} = 0.0001$$

$$x_{i+1}^{(3)} = x_{i+1}^{(2)} + \Delta x^{(3)} = 0.0226$$

$$\Delta f^{(3)} = f_s^{(3)} - f_s^{(2)} + \left(\overline{k}_T - k_T\right)\Delta x^{(3)} = 14.8494$$

$$\Delta R^{(4)} = \Delta R^{(3)} - \Delta f^{(3)} = 1.4395$$

Cycle 4

$$\Delta x^{(4)} = 0.00001$$

$$x_{i+1}^{(4)} = x_{i+1}^{(3)} + \Delta x^{(4)} = 0.0226$$

$$\Delta f^{(4)} = f_s^{(4)} - f_s^{(3)} + \left(\overline{k}_T - k_T\right)\Delta x^{(4)} = 1.3123$$

$$\Delta R^{(5)} = \Delta R^{(4)} - \Delta f^{(4)} = 0.1272$$

Cycle 5

$$\Delta x^{(5)} = 0.000001$$

$$x_{i+1}^{(5)} = x_{i+1}^{(4)} + \Delta x^{(5)} = 0.0226$$

$$\Delta f^{(5)} = f_s^{(5)} - f_s^{(4)} + \left(\overline{k}_T - k_T\right)\Delta x^{(5)} = 0.1160$$

$$\Delta R^{(6)} = \Delta R^{(5)} - \Delta f^{(5)} = 0.0112$$

These results are substituted in the table below the same time step, and the procedure is continued till another change of state is encountered.

At 0.7 sec

At 0.7 sec, the velocity is positive but at 0.8 sec, the velocity is negative. It means there is a change in state between 0.7 and 0.8 sec. It indicates unloading. The tangent stiffness needs to be restored to 20000 N/m. Here, a different strategy will be required as discussed in Figure 13.18 and Example 13.1, Figure 13.22.

Setting total velocity = 0,

$$\Delta x = \Delta x_1 + \Delta x_2 \quad \text{numerical}$$

$$= \Delta x_1 + \Delta x_2 \quad \text{true}$$

$$\dot{x}_{i+1} = \frac{2}{\Delta t}(\psi \Delta x) - \dot{x}_i = 0$$

or, $$\frac{2}{0.1}(\psi(-0.0002) - 0.0229) = 0,$$

$$\psi = -5.725$$

$$\Delta x_1 = \psi \Delta x = 0.001145 \text{ m}$$

also,

$$\overline{k}\Delta x_2 = (1-\psi)\Delta\overline{p}$$

where, $k_T = 20000$ because unloading is always elastic

$$\therefore \qquad \Delta x_2 = \frac{(1-\psi)\Delta\overline{p}}{\overline{k}} = \frac{(1+5.725)\times(-42.4858)}{226320} = -0.001262 \text{ m}$$

Total displacement increment in the time step

$$\Delta x = 0.001145 - 0.001262 = -0.000117 \text{ m}$$

Displacement at the end of the time step

$$x_{i+1} = x_i + \Delta x = 0.0491 - 0.000117 = 0.04898 \text{ m}$$

Velocity increment

$$\Delta\dot{x}_i = \frac{\gamma}{\beta\Delta t}\Delta x_i - \frac{\gamma}{\beta}\dot{x}_i + \Delta t\left(1-\frac{\gamma}{2\beta}\right)\ddot{x}_i$$

or,

$$\Delta\dot{x}_i = \frac{0.50}{0.25\times0.1}\Delta x - 2\dot{x}$$

Velocity at the end of the time step

$$\dot{x}_{i+1} = \dot{x}_i + \Delta\dot{x} = 20\Delta x - \dot{x}_i = 20\times(-0.000117) - 0.0229 = -0.02524 \text{ m/s}$$

Similarly, acceleration at the end of the time step can be computed from the equation of motion.

Resisting force at the end of the time step

$$f_{i+1} = f_i + k_T\Delta x_2 = 250 + 20000\times(-0.001262) = 247.66 \text{ N}$$

Acceleration at the end of the time step

$$\ddot{x}_{i+1} = \frac{p_{i+1} - c\dot{x}_{i+1} - (f_s)_{i+1}}{m}$$

$$\ddot{x}_{i+1} = \frac{0 - 316\times(-0.02524) - 247.66}{500} = -0.4794 \text{ m/s}^2$$

Knowing the updated values at 0.8 sec, rest of the calculations can be carried out as usual.

□

Example 13.4

Illustrate the influence of different hysteresis models on the inelastic response of a SDOF system.

Solution   Let mass = 1, stiffness = 39.5, Period = 1 sec, Damping = 0%, step size = 0.02 sec It is subjected to first 10 sec of the North–South component of El Centro earthquake of May 1940. Two hysteresis models are selected: elasto-plastic model and stiffness degrading model.

The elastic response gives the maximum force applied on the system. Yield force is computed corresponding to a reduction factor R = 4, 8 and 16. The concept of reduction factor R was discussed in Chapters 8 and 12. The inelastic response is shown in Figures 13.25(a) and 13.25(b). The maximum ductility demands are as follows:

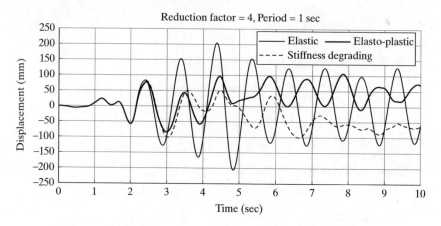

Figure 13.25(a)   Effect of hysteresis models on inelastic response, $R = 4$.

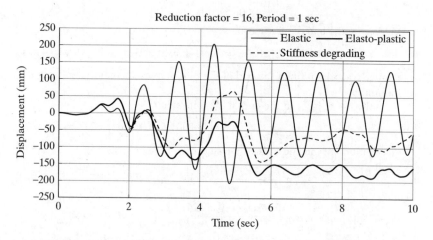

Figure 13.25(b)   Effect of hysteresis models on inelastic response; $R = 16$.

For elasto-plastic model
For reduction factor = 4, maximum ductility demand = 2.1;
For reduction factor = 8, maximum ductility demand = 4.70;
For reduction factor = 16, maximum ductility demand = 14.95;

For stiffness degrading model
For reduction factor = 4, maximum ductility demand = 1.98;
For reduction factor = 16, maximum ductility demand = 11.20;

The SDOF system with period = 0.5 sec. is again analysed using the elasto-plastic model.

The maximum ductility demands are as follows:
For reduction factor = 4, maximum ductility demand = 2.92;
For reduction factor = 8, maximum ductility demand = 4.94;
For reduction factor = 16, maximum ductility demand = 12.10;

The effect of reduction factors on a SDOF system having a period = 0.5 sec and = 1.0 sec are shown in Figures 13.26(a) and (b).

The following significant observations are made in these results:

- The elastic response oscillates about the mean position while the inelastic response tends to sway on either side of the mean position once the system becomes inelastic.
- The displacement is maximum in the elastic case while it remains within a range with the increase in reduction factor. The maximum displacements (mm) in SDOF system in different cases are as follows:

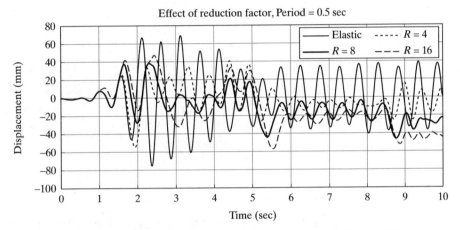

Figure 13.26(a)   Effect of reduction factors on inelastic response; Period = 0.5 sec
(Elasto-plastic model).

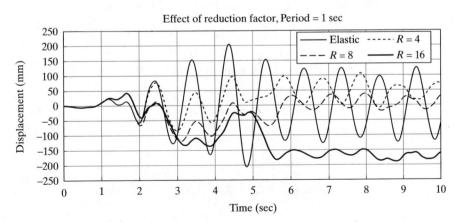

Figure 13.26(b)   Effect of reduction factors on inelastic response; Period = 1 sec
(Elasto-plastic model).

	Displacement, mm	
Reduction Factor	Period = 0.5 sec	Period = 1 sec
R = 1 (elastic)	75 mm	205 mm
R = 4	55	106
R = 8	46	119
R = 16	57	189

- The choice of a hysteresis model has a significant influence on the displacement response of the SDOF system.
- The elastic as well as inelastic response depend on the period of the SDOF system.

□

13.6 INELASTIC RESPONSE SPECTRA

The inelastic response spectra for a SDOF system can be generated by carrying out nonlinear analysis using an appropriate hysteresis model. In case of elasto-plastic system, the maximum force in the spring is given by

$$Q_y = m\omega^2 x_y = kx_y \tag{13.20a}$$

where

Q_y = yield force
x_y = yield displacement

For bilinear and stiffness degrading systems with strain hardening slope k_s the maximum force in the spring is given by

$$Q_{max} = m\omega^2 x_y \left[1 + k_s (\mu - 1)\right] \tag{13.20b}$$

where μ = displacement ductility

The equation of motion of a SDOF nonlinear system is given as follows:

$$m\ddot{x}(t) + c\dot{x}(t) + Q(t) = p(t) = -m\ddot{y}(t) \tag{13.21}$$

where, $Q(t)$ = restoring force

Equation (13.21) can be written as follows:

$$\frac{\ddot{x}(t)}{x_y} + 2\omega\xi \frac{\dot{x}(t)}{x_y} + \frac{Q(t)}{mx_y} = -\frac{\ddot{y}(t)}{x_y} \tag{13.22}$$

Let

$$\mu = \frac{x(t)}{x_y} \tag{13.23a}$$

$$\frac{Q(t)}{mx_y} = \frac{k}{k}\frac{Q(t)}{mx_y} = \frac{k}{m}\frac{Q(t)}{kx_y} = \omega^2 \frac{Q(t)}{Q_y} = \omega^2 \rho(t) \tag{13.23b}$$

$$\frac{\ddot{y}(t)}{x_y} = \frac{k}{k}\frac{\ddot{y}(t)}{x_y} = \frac{\omega^2 m\ddot{y}(t)}{Q_y} \tag{13.23c}$$

and

$$\beta = \frac{Q_y}{m\ddot{y}_{max}} \tag{13.23d}$$

Equation (13.22) can now be written as follows:

$$\ddot{\mu}(t) + 2\omega\xi\dot{\mu}(t) + \omega^2\rho(t) = -\frac{\omega^2}{\beta}\frac{\ddot{y}(t)}{\ddot{y}_{max}} \tag{13.24}$$

Alternatively, structures with seismic resistance coefficient α_y can be defined as:

$$Q_y = \alpha_y W = \alpha_y mg \tag{13.25}$$

$$\beta = \frac{Q_y}{m\ddot{y}_{max}} = \frac{\alpha_y mg}{m\ddot{y}_{max}} = \frac{\alpha_y}{\ddot{y}_{max}/g} \tag{13.26}$$

The following set of spectra was generated by Pal, Dasaka and Jain (1987) for different earthquakes:

(a) Constant strength spectra
(b) Constant ductility spectra
(c) Constant reduction factor spectra
(d) Inelastic yield displacement response spectra (IYDS)
(e) Inelastic acceleration response spectra (IAS)

The inelastic response spectra can be plotted on a tripartite logarithmic graph similar to that used in the elastic response spectra. Period is plotted on the x-axis while pseudo velocity ωx_y is plotted on the y-axis. In the IYDS, the yield deformation x_y necessary to limit the maximum deformation of the system to a specified multiple of the yield deformation itself, $x_{max} = \mu x_y$ is plotted on the displacement axis. The spectral acceleration $\omega^2 x_y$ multiplied by mass m gives the yield resistance which in the case of elasto-plastic system is the maximum force in the system as given by Equation (13.20a). For bilinear and stiffness degrading systems with strain hardening slope k_s, the maximum force in the spring is given by Equation (13.20b). Alternatively, in instances where it is desirable to deal directly with maximum forces, it is possible to plot Q_{max}/m on the acceleration axis to obtain inelastic acceleration spectra (IAS) for systems with strain hardening. For elasto-plastic systems inelastic displacement spectra and inelastic acceleration spectra are identical.

Constant Strength Response Spectra   This is a plot of maximum displacement ductility ratio μ as a function of period T for a constant value of the strength factor β and a constant value of the viscous damping ξ for a given hysteresis model and ground motion. Strength factor β is the ratio of the yield resistance to the maximum inertial force of the given system.

Constant Ductility Response Spectra   For plotting inelastic response spectra, one is usually interested in response associated with pre-determined values of the ductility ratios. A graph was plotted for strength factors as a function of period for desired ductility ratios. This graph is known as *constant ductility response spectra*.

Reduction Factor Spectra It is desirable to establish a relationship between elastic and inelastic behaviour so that a nonlinear system may be approximated by an equivalent linear system for the purpose of analysis and design. In constant ductility spectra, the curves for a ductility of 1.0 correspond to an elastic case. The strength factor ordinate of this curve is divided by the corresponding ordinates of the curve of desired ductility for different periods. These factors are known as *yield strength reduction factors* (R) as these relate the strength levels of elastic and inelastic response spectra for a given value of period and ductility. The reduction factors so obtained may be applied either to elastic pseudo velocity spectra or elastic pseudo acceleration spectra to obtain IAS. Alternatively, for a given ductility ratio, IYDS is obtained by interpolation between yield displacement corresponding to upper and lower ductility ratios computed earlier. This gives IYDS. Among these different formats of the inelastic spectra, the most useful format is the reduction factor spectra. The New Zealand code NZS1170-5(2004) provides seismic design coefficients based on the desired ductility level.

Typical spectra are shown in Figures 13.27(a)–(e) for an artificial earthquake B1 (Pal, Dasaka, Jain 1987). Similar plots can be generated for any other earthquake.

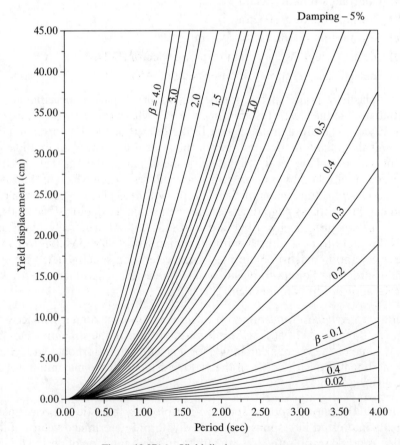

Figure 13.27(a) Yield displacement spectra.

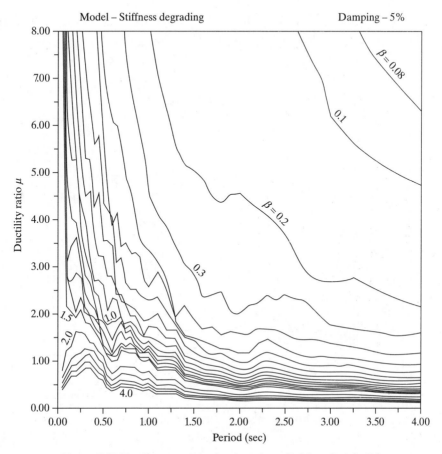

Figure 13.27(b)   Constant strength spectra for artificial earthquake B1.

Though this is a very accurate procedure to generate inelastic response spectra, these are not convenient for design because of zig-zag nature of the curves. Similar problem was faced while generating elastic response spectra as discussed in Chapter 8. There is a need to develop smoothened inelastic response spectra.

13.7 SMOOTHENED INELASTIC RESPONSE SPECTRA

The concept of inelastic response spectra was first introduced by Veletsos, Newmark and Chelapati (1965). By extending the same simplified approach to generate multi-linear elastic response spectra, Newmark and Hall proposed development of multi-linear inelastic response spectra for different ductility ratios. They made use of the following properties of the inelastic systems:

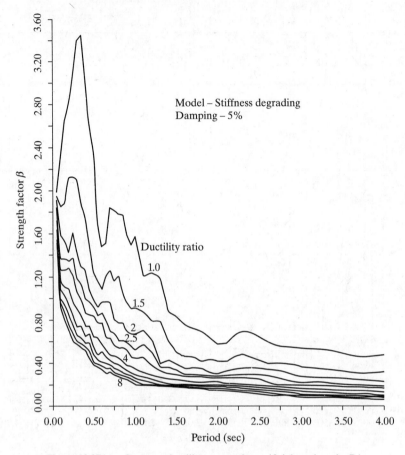

Figure 13.27(c)   Constant ductility spectra for artificial earthquake B1.

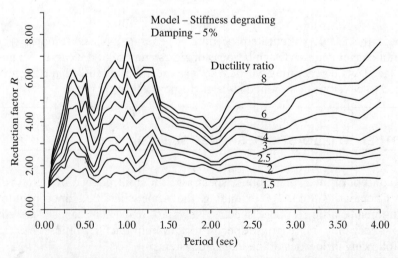

Figure 13.27(d)   Yield strength reduction factor spectra for artificial earthquake B1.

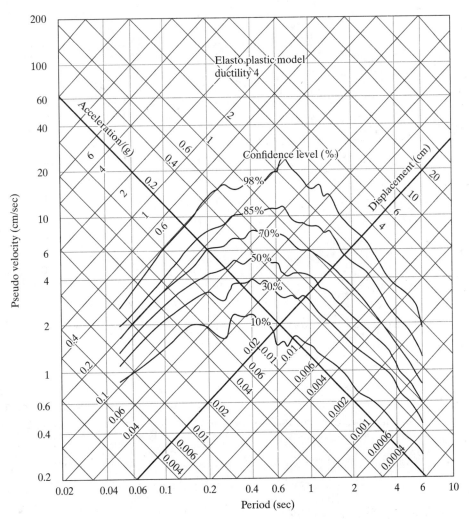

Figure 13.27(e)   Inelastic response spectra for different confidence levels for artificial earthquake B1.

- At low periods of vibration, elastic and inelastic systems have the same force.
- At intermediate periods of vibration, the two systems absorb the same total energy.
- At very high periods of vibration, the two systems have the same total displacement.

Let us consider two identical SDOF systems, elastic and elasto-plastic. Both having the same mass, initial elastic stiffness and damping. Both systems will have the same period. The force-deformation curves for these systems are shown in Figure 13.28.

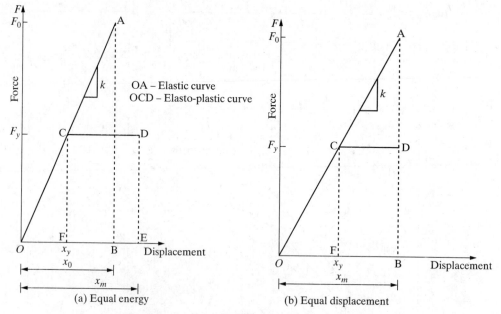

Figure 13.28   Force-displacement response of elastic and inelastic systems.

1. Let us equate the energy in the elastic and inelastic systems.

   Let us consider two equal areas O-A-B and O-C-D-E under the curves (Figure 13.28(a)). It means energy absorption in these two systems is equal.

   The maximum force and displacement in the elastic system are $OA = F_0$ and $OB = x_0$, respectively.

   In the elastic system,

   $$\text{energy } E_1 = \text{area OAB} = \frac{1}{2}x_0 F_0 \tag{i}$$

   In the inelastic system,

   $$\text{energy } E_2 = \text{area OCDE} = \frac{1}{2}x_y F_y + \left(x_m - x_y\right)F_y \tag{ii}$$

   But, $E_1 = E_2$,

   or,

   $$\frac{1}{2}x_0 F_0 = \frac{1}{2}x_y F_y + \left(x_m - x_y\right)F_y$$

   or,

   $$\frac{1}{2}x_0 F_0 = -\frac{1}{2}x_y F_y + x_m F_y \tag{iii}$$

   Also, by similar triangles OAB and OCF,

   $$\frac{F_0}{x_0} = \frac{F_y}{x_y} \quad \text{or} \quad x_0 = \frac{F_0}{F_y}x_y \tag{iv}$$

Substituting Equation (iv) in Equation (iii) gives,

$$\left(\frac{F_0}{F_y}\right)^2 = 2\frac{x_m}{x_y} - 1$$

or,

$$R^2 = 2\mu - 1$$

or,

$$R = \sqrt{2\mu - 1}$$

Thus, the following relation is obtained:

$$\text{Reduction factor } R = \frac{F_0}{F_y} = \frac{kx_0}{kx_y} = \sqrt{2\mu - 1} \tag{13.27}$$

where,

$$\text{Ductility } \mu = \frac{x_m}{x_y} \tag{13.28}$$

2. Let us equate the displacements in the elastic and inelastic systems.

   The force-deformation curves for the same two systems are again shown in Figure 13.28(b) such that the maximum displacements in these two systems are equal.

   Let us equate the displacements O-B under the curves,

   Elastic displacement OB $= x_m$

   also, Inelastic displacement OB $= x_m$

   By similar triangles OAB and OCF,

   $$\frac{F_0}{x_m} = \frac{F_y}{x_y}$$

   or,

   $$\frac{F_0}{F_y} = \frac{x_m}{x_y} = \mu$$

   The following relation is obtained:

   $$\text{Reduction factor } R = \frac{F_0}{F_y} = \frac{kx_m}{kx_y} = \mu \tag{13.29}$$

It is possible to construct constant ductility design spectra from the elastic design spectra discussed in Section 8.8. The yield strength of an elasto-plastic system can be expressed as follows:

$$F_y = \frac{\text{Elastic strength}}{R} \tag{13.30a}$$

or,

$$F_y = kx_y = m\omega_n^2 x_y = mA_y = \frac{w}{g}A_y \tag{13.30b}$$

Now reduction factors can be defined as follows:

$$R = 1 \qquad \text{for} \quad T < T_A \qquad\qquad (13.31a)$$

$$R = (2\mu - 1)^{\gamma/2} \qquad \text{for} \quad T_A < T < T_B \qquad\qquad (13.31b)$$

$$R = (2\mu - 1)^{0.5} \qquad \text{for} \quad T_B < T < T_C' \qquad\qquad (13.31c)$$

$$R = (T/T_C)\,\mu \qquad \text{for} \quad T_C' < T < T_C \qquad\qquad (13.31d)$$

$$R = \mu \qquad \text{for} \quad T > T_C \qquad\qquad (13.31e)$$

The limits for T_A, T_B, T_E and T_F are the same as discussed in Section 8.8 for ground motion on hard soil, that is,

$$T_A = 1/33 \text{ sec}, \ T_B = 1/8 \text{ sec}, \ T_E = 10 \text{ sec and } T_F = 33 \text{ sec}$$

T_C depends on damping ratio ξ. It is the intersection of two lines in the constant acceleration and constant velocity regions and can be obtained as discussed in Section 8.8.

It is now convenient to develop inelastic response spectra for elasto-plastic system in tripartite format. The following needs to be defined in order to plot response spectra for yield deformation and yield strength:

$$D_y = x_y \quad V_y = \omega_n x_y \ \text{ and } \ A_y = \omega_n^2 x_y \qquad\qquad (13.32)$$

where, D_y = yield deformation of the elasto-plastic system

A plot of D_y vs. T for a given ductility μ is called *yield deformation response spectra*. Similarly, plots of V_y vs. T and A_y vs. T are called the *pseudo-velocity response spectra* and *pseudo-acceleration response spectra*, respectively. The definitions of D_y, V_y and A_y for an elasto-plastic system are consistent with the definitions of D, V and A for an elastic system.

The quantities D_y, V_y and A_y can be shown on a tripartite log paper in the same manner as the linear system. These quantities are related and are as follows:

$$A_y = \omega_n V_y \qquad\qquad (13.33a)$$

and

$$V_y = \omega_n D_y \qquad\qquad (13.33b)$$

and

$$A_y = \omega_n^2 D_y \qquad\qquad (13.33c)$$

Similar relationships can be written in terms of natural period.

The inelastic spectra can be schematically developed from the maximum ground parameters as follows:

(a) The peak values of ground acceleration $\ddot{x}_{g0}$, velocity $\dot{x}_{g0}$, and displacement x_{g0} can be shown on the tripartite logarithmic chart. These plots give a polygonal curve representing the maximum ground motion values only.

(b) Get α_A, α_V and α_D magnification factors for a given damping and percentile for acceleration, velocity and displacement, respectively. Using these magnification factors, generate elastic response spectrum as discussed in Section 8.8 and shown in Figure 8.25.

(c) Now generate the inelastic spectrum using the following steps:

$$D' = D/\mu \qquad (13.34a)$$

where D = elastic displacement spectrum ordinate
and μ = desired displacement ductility

$$V' = V/\mu \qquad (13.34b)$$

where V = elastic velocity spectrum ordinate

$$A' = \frac{A}{\sqrt{2\mu - 1}} \qquad (13.34c)$$

where A = elastic acceleration spectrum ordinate

A-B, A'-B', E-F and E'-F' are transition zones. Points A, B, E and F correspond to 1/33 sec, 1/8 sec, 10 sec and 33 sec, respectively. Similarly, points A', B', E' and F' correspond to 1/33 sec, 1/8 sec, 10 sec and 33 sec, respectively. The resulting inelastic response spectrum A_0-A'-B'-C'-D'-E'-F'-F'_0 is shown in Figure 13.29. The points C and

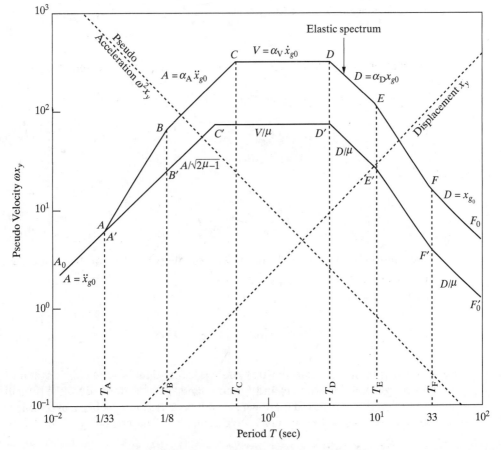

Figure 13.29   Construction of inelastic response spectra.

C' are at different periods because the segments B-C and C-D use different reduction factors to get B'-C' and C'-D'. The points D and D' are at the same period because the segments C-D and D-E use the same reduction factor to get C'-D' and D'-E'.

Relation between peak elastic and elasto-plastic deformations (Figure 13.28(a))

It was shown that

$$\frac{F_0}{x_0} = \frac{F_y}{x_y} \quad \text{or} \quad \frac{F_0}{F_y} = \frac{x_0}{x_y} \tag{iv}$$

also,

$$\text{Ductility } \mu = \frac{x_m}{x_y} \tag{13.28}$$

$\therefore$

$$\frac{x_m}{x_0} = \mu \frac{F_y}{F_0} = \frac{\mu}{R} \tag{v}$$

Let us now derive the relations between the peak displacements in the inelastic and elastic regions for different zones:

For $T < T_A$, Reduction factor $R = 1$,

$\therefore$
$$F_y = F_0 \quad \text{and} \quad x_m = \mu x_0 \tag{13.35a}$$

Peak deformation of the elasto-plastic system is higher than that of the elastic system by a factor μ.

For $T_B < T < T_C$, Reduction factor $R = \sqrt{2\mu - 1}$

$\therefore$
$$F_y = \frac{F_0}{R} = \frac{F_0}{\sqrt{2\mu - 1}} \tag{13.35b}$$

and

$$x_m = \frac{\mu}{R} x_0 = \frac{\mu}{\sqrt{2\mu - 1}} x_0 \tag{13.35c}$$

Peak deformation of the elasto-plastic system is higher than that of the elastic system by a factor $\mu / \sqrt{2\mu - 1}$.

For $T > T_C$, Reduction factor $R = \mu$

$\therefore$
$$F_y = \frac{F_0}{\mu} \quad \text{and} \quad x_m = x_0 \tag{13.35d}$$

Peak deformation of the elasto-plastic system is same as that of the elastic system.

Similar relations between F_0 and F_y and x_m and x_0 can be derived for the transition zones. Equation (13.35(a) to (d)) are very useful in developing inelastic acceleration – displacement response spectrum (ADRS) discussed in Chapter 14.

13.7.1 New Zealand Code NZS 1170.5:2004

The New Zealand Code on earthquake actions provides calculations of horizontal design action coefficients based on ductility. There are equations each for ultimate limit state and serviceability limit state for:

- Equivalent static method
- Response spectrum method

Horizontal design action coefficient $S_D(T)$ for seismic coefficient method for ultimate limit state is given by

$$S_D(T) = \frac{S_a(T,\xi)S_p}{f(\mu)} \tag{13.36a}$$

where, $S_D(T)$ = horizontal design action coefficient for given period T

$S_a(T,\xi)$ = spectral ordinate from the elastic response site hazard spectra for a given damping and soil class

S_p = structural performance factor

$f(\mu)$ = a factor depending upon the ductility for structures on different types of soil

For soil classes A, B, C and D

$$F(\mu) = \mu \qquad\qquad \text{for} \quad T_1 \geq 0.7 \text{ sec} \tag{13.36b}$$

$$= \frac{(\mu-1)T_1}{0.7} + 1 \qquad \text{for} \quad T_1 < 0.7 \text{ sec} \tag{13.36c}$$

For soil class E,

$$F(\mu) = \mu \qquad\qquad \text{for} \quad T_1 \geq 1.0 \text{ sec and } \mu < 1.5 \tag{13.36d}$$

$$= (\mu - 1.5)T_1 + 1.5 \quad \text{for} \quad T_1 < 1.0 \text{ sec and } \mu \geq 1.5 \tag{13.36e}$$

where T_1 = fundamental period of vibration

μ = displacement ductility

It needs to be chosen depending upon the capability of the associated detailing based on the appropriate material code.

13.7.2 Eurocode EC8-part 1:2004

The elastic response spectrum of the Eurocode 8 was discussed in Section 8.9.1. Another elastic response spectra has been provided to be used for *capacity design* that provides reduced seismic design forces. This reduction is accomplished by introducing a behaviour factor q. The behaviour factor is an approximation of the ratio of the seismic forces that the structure would experience if its response was completely elastic with 5% viscous damping, to the seismic forces that may be used in the design with a conventional elastic analysis model still ensuring a satisfactory response of the structure. This behaviour factor approach avoids use of explicit nonlinear structural analysis for design.

Each response spectrum curve is divided in four zones and equations are provided to estimate the design seismic coefficient in different soil conditions (Figure 13.30).

Horizontal elastic response spectrum   For the horizontal components of the seismic action, the elastic response spectrum $S_a(T)$ is defined by the following expressions:

$$S_a(T) = a_g S \left[\frac{2}{3} + \frac{T}{T_B} \left(\frac{2.5}{q} - \frac{2}{3} \right) \right] \qquad \text{for} \quad 0 < T < T_B \tag{13.37a}$$

$$S_a(T) = a_g S \frac{2.5}{q} \qquad \text{for} \quad T_B < T < T_C \tag{13.37b}$$

$$S_a(T) = a_g S \frac{2.5}{q} \frac{T_C}{T} \qquad \text{for} \quad T_C < T < T_D \tag{13.37c}$$

$$S_a(T) = a_g S \frac{2.5}{q} \frac{T_C T_D}{T^2} \qquad \text{for} \quad T_D < T \tag{13.37d}$$

where, a_g = design ground acceleration on type A ground

T = period of a linear SDOF system

T_B = lower limit of the period of the constant spectral acceleration branch

T_C = upper limit of the period of the constant spectral acceleration branch

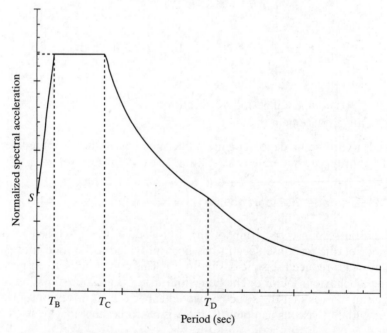

Figure 13.30   Shape of the elastic response spectrum.

T_D = value defining beginning of the constant displacement response range of the spectrum

S = soil factor

Q = behaviour factor

13.8   ILLUSTRATIVE EXAMPLES

Example 13.5

Illustrate the construction of an inelastic response spectrum for a ground motion having peak ground acceleration, peak ground velocity and peak ground displacement as 1 g, 90 cm/sec and 60 cm, respectively. Make use of Newmark–Hall amplification factors for 5% damping and 84.1 percentile.

Solution   First, the elastic design spectrum is generated as per the procedure outlined in Section 8.8. The amplification factors for 5% damping and mean + standard deviation on acceleration, velocity and displacement are 2.71, 2.3 and 2.01, respectively. The elastic spectrum is shown in Figure 13.31(a). Next, inelastic response spectrum is generated for

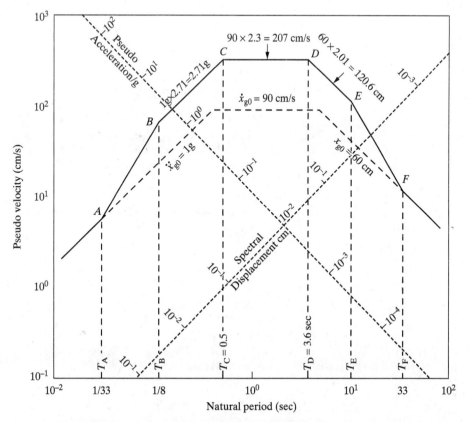

Figure 13.31(a)   Generation of elastic spectrum from peak ground parameters.

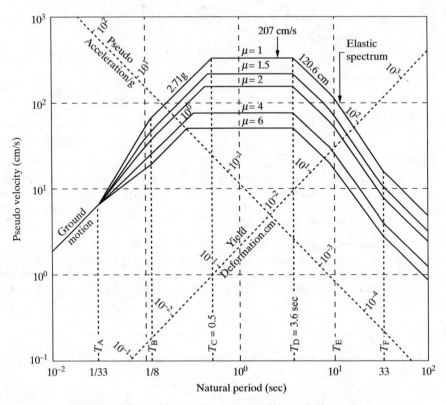

Figure 13.31(b)   Inelastic response spectrum from elastic spectrum.

a ductility of 1.5, 2, 4 and 6 using the procedure outlined in Section 13.7 and Equations (13.34). There is a transition zone between T_A and T_B, and between T_E and T_F. The resulting spectrum on a tripartite graph is shown in Figure 13.31(b).   □

Example 13.6

Develop a spectrum between yield strength reduction factor and period for the ground motion of Example 13.5. Also draw inelastic response spectrum on a log-log scale.

Solution

Ground Motion	
Max. Acceleration	1 g
Max. Velocity	90 cm/s
Max. Displacement	60 cm

Equations (13.30) can be re-written as follows:

$$R = \frac{\text{Elastic strength}}{\text{Yield strength}}$$

The reduction factors for different regions were given by Equation (13.31). From the tripartite spectra generated in Figure 13.31, determine the periods T_C and T_C'. The relation between yield strength reduction factor R and period T for different ductility ratio is shown in Table 13.3 and log-log graph Figure 13.32. The period T_C is 0.5 sec while T_C' values are highlighted in Table 13.3.

Knowing the elastic spectra for $\mu = 1$, the acceleration ordinate for a given ductility can be computed using the following equation:

$$A' = \frac{A}{\sqrt{2\mu - 1}} \tag{13.34c}$$

where A = elastic acceleration spectrum ordinate

TABLE 13.3   RELATION BETWEEN R AND T FOR A GIVEN DUCTILITY μ

	Ductility μ						
$\mu = 1.5$		$\mu = 2$		$\mu = 4$		$\mu = 6$	
R	T	R	T	R	T	R	T
1	0.01	1	0.01	1	0.01	1	0.01
1	0.03	1	0.03	1	0.03	1	0.03
1.41	0.125	1.73	0.125	2.64	0.125	3.31	0.125
1.41	0.45	1.73	0.43	2.64	0.33	3.31	0.28
1.41	0.47	1.8	0.45	3.6	0.45	5.4	0.45
1.5	0.5	2	0.5	4	0.5	6	0.5
1.5	10	2	10	4	10	6	10
1.5	33	2	33	4	33	6	33

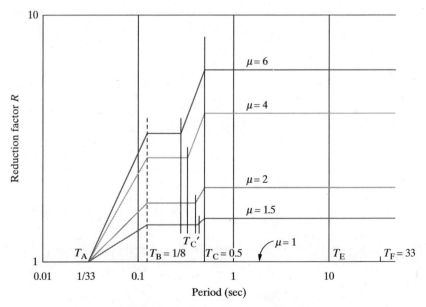

Figure 13.32   Reduction factor spectra.

The relation between acceleration S_a and period T for different ductility μ is shown in Table 13.4 and in log-log graph in Figure 13.33. The values in the table are shown only upto $\mu = 2$. Similar calculations can be done for other values of μ. □

TABLE 13.4 RELATION BETWEEN S_a AND T FOR DIFFERENT DUCTILITY μ

$\mu = 1$			$\mu = 1.5$			$\mu = 2$		
S_a/g	T(sec)	R	S_a/g	T(sec)	R	S_a/g	T(sec)
1	0.01	1	1.00	0.01	1	1.00	0.01
1	0.03	1	1.00	0.03	1	1.00	0.03
2.71	0.125	1.41	1.92	0.125	1.73	1.56	0.125
2.71	0.5	1.41	1.92	0.47	1.73	1.56	0.43
0.38	4	1.5	0.25	4	2	0.19	4
0.05	10	1.5	0.03	10	2	0.03	10
0.003	33	1.5	0.00	33	2	0.00	33

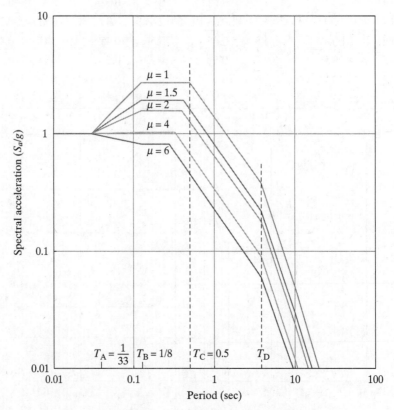

Figure 13.33 Constant ductility inelastic response spectrum.

Example 13.7

(a) Plot the ratio of peak deformation in an inelastic system to that of the peak deformation of the corresponding elastic system for different ductility ratios equal to 1, 1.5, 2, 4 and 6 when this system is subjected to the ground motion of Example 13.5.

(b) A SDOF system has a mass of 100 kg and a period of 0.4 sec. It has 5% viscous damping and exhibits elasto-plastic behaviour in the inelastic region. Determine the maximum deformations for a ductility of 1 and 4 when this system is subjected to the ground motion of Example 13.5.

Solution

(a) The relation between the peak deformations in a SDOF inelastic system and the corresponding elastic system were derived in Equation (13.35). The same are shown in Table 13.5 for different ductility and plotted in Figure 13.34. Although the calculation are shown for period T upto 100 sec, the plot is shown only upto 1 sec for clarity. Similar calculations can be done for other values of ductility.

TABLE 13.5 RELATION BETWEEN MAXIMUM ELASTIC AND INELASTIC DISPLACEMENTS WITH PERIOD T FOR DIFFERENT DUCTILITY μ

	$\mu = 1$			$\mu = 1.5$				$\mu = 2$			
S_a/g	T(sec)	S_{de} (cm)	S_d/S_{de}	R	S_a/g	S_d	S_d/S_{de}	R	S_a/g	S_d	S_d/S_{de}
1	0.01	0.0025	1	1	1	0.0037	1.5	1	1	0.0050	2
1	0.02	0.0099	1	1	1	0.0149	1.5	1	1	0.0199	2
1	0.03	0.0224	1	1	1	0.0336	1.5	1	1	0.0448	2
1.3	0.04	0.0517	1	1.0724	1.2123	0.0724	1.3988	1.1171	1.1637	0.0926	1.7904
1.5	0.05	0.0933	1	1.1321	1.3250	0.1236	1.3250	1.2173	1.2323	0.1533	1.6430
1.8	0.06	0.1612	1	1.1833	1.5211	0.2043	1.2676	1.3058	1.3785	0.2469	1.5317
1.9	0.07	0.2316	1	1.2285	1.5466	0.2828	1.2210	1.3856	1.3713	0.3343	1.4434
2	0.08	0.3184	1	1.2690	1.5761	0.3764	1.1821	1.4587	1.3711	0.4365	1.3711
2.2	0.09	0.4433	1	1.3058	1.6848	0.5092	1.1487	1.5263	1.4414	0.5808	1.3103
2.4	0.1	0.5970	1	1.3396	1.7916	0.6685	1.1197	1.5895	1.5099	0.7512	1.2583
2.6	0.11	0.7825	1	1.3710	1.8964	0.8562	1.0941	1.6489	1.5768	0.9492	1.2129
2.71	0.125	1.0533	1	1.4142	1.9163	1.1172	1.0607	1.7321	1.5646	1.2162	1.1547
2.71	0.13	1.1392	1	1.4142	1.9163	1.2083	1.0607	1.7321	1.5646	1.3155	1.1547
2.71	0.14	1.3212	1	1.4142	1.9163	1.4014	1.0607	1.7321	1.5646	1.5256	1.1547
2.71	0.15	1.5167	1	1.4142	1.9163	1.6087	1.0607	1.7321	1.5646	1.7513	1.1547
2.71	0.16	1.7257	1	1.4142	1.9163	1.8304	1.0607	1.7321	1.5646	1.9926	1.1547
2.71	0.17	1.9481	1	1.4142	1.9163	2.0663	1.0607	1.7321	1.5646	2.2495	1.1547
2.71	0.18	2.1841	1	1.4142	1.9163	2.3165	1.0607	1.7321	1.5646	2.5219	1.1547
2.71	0.19	2.4335	1	1.4142	1.9163	2.5811	1.0607	1.7321	1.5646	2.8099	1.1547
2.71	0.2	2.6964	1	1.4142	1.9163	2.8599	1.0607	1.7321	1.5646	3.1135	1.1547
2.71	0.22	3.2626	1	1.4142	1.9163	3.4605	1.0607	1.7321	1.5646	3.7673	1.1547
2.71	0.24	3.8828	1	1.4142	1.9163	4.1183	1.0607	1.7321	1.5646	4.4834	1.1547
2.71	0.26	4.5569	1	1.4142	1.9163	4.8333	1.0607	1.7321	1.5646	5.2618	1.1547

(Continued)

TABLE 13.5 (CONTINUED)

$\mu = 1$				$\mu = 1.5$				$\mu = 2$			
S_a/g	T(sec)	S_{de} (cm)	S_d/S_{de}	R	S_a/g	S_d	S_d/S_{de}	R	S_a/g	S_d	S_d/S_{de}
2.71	0.28	5.2849	1	1.4142	1.9163	5.6055	1.0607	1.7321	1.5646	6.1025	1.1547
2.71	0.3	6.0668	1	1.4142	1.9163	6.4348	1.0607	1.7321	1.5646	7.0054	1.1547
2.71	0.32	6.9027	1	1.4142	1.9163	7.3214	1.0607	1.7321	1.5646	7.9706	1.1547
2.71	0.33	7.3409	1	1.4142	1.9163	7.7862	1.0607	1.7321	1.5646	8.4765	1.1547
2.71	0.35	8.2576	1	1.4142	1.9163	8.7585	1.0607	1.7321	1.5646	9.5351	1.1547
2.71	0.38	9.7339	1	1.4142	1.9163	10.3243	1.0607	1.7321	1.5646	11.2397	1.1547
2.71	0.4	10.7855	1	1.4142	1.9163	11.4397	1.0607	1.7321	1.5646	12.4540	1.1547
2.71	0.43	12.4640	1	1.4142	1.9163	13.2200	1.0607	1.7321	1.5646	14.3921	1.1547
2.71	0.47	14.8907	1	1.4142	1.9163	15.7940	1.0607	1.8800	1.4415	15.8412	1.0638
2.71	0.49	16.1849	1	1.4700	1.8435	16.5152	1.0204	1.9600	1.3827	16.5152	1.0204
2.71	0.5	16.8523	1	1.5000	1.8067	16.8523	1.0000	2.0000	1.3550	16.8523	1.0000
2.3	0.6	20.5959	1	1.5000	1.5333	20.5959	1.0000	2.0000	1.1500	20.5959	1.0000
1.95	0.7	23.7673	1	1.5000	1.3000	23.7673	1.0000	2.0000	0.9750	23.7673	1.0000
1.77	0.8	28.1775	1	1.5000	1.1800	28.1775	1.0000	2.0000	0.8850	28.1775	1.0000
1.6	0.9	32.2370	1	1.5000	1.0667	32.2370	1.0000	2.0000	0.8000	32.2370	1.0000
1.5	1	37.3114	1	1.5000	1.0000	37.3114	1.0000	2.0000	0.7500	37.3114	1.0000
1	1.5	55.9670	1	1.5000	0.6667	55.9670	1.0000	2.0000	0.5000	55.9670	1.0000
0.7	2	69.6479	1	1.5000	0.4667	69.6479	1.0000	2.0000	0.3500	69.6479	1.0000
0.55	2.5	85.5052	1	1.5000	0.3667	85.5052	1.0000	2.0000	0.2750	85.5052	1.0000
0.45	3	100.7406	1	1.5000	0.3000	100.7406	1.0000	2.0000	0.2250	100.7406	1.0000
0.313	4	124.5702	1	1.5000	0.2087	124.5702	1.0000	2.0000	0.1565	124.5702	1.0000
0.2	5	124.3712	1	1.5000	0.1333	124.3712	1.0000	2.0000	0.1000	124.3712	1.0000
0.139	6	124.4707	1	1.5000	0.0927	124.4707	1.0000	2.0000	0.0695	124.4707	1.0000
0.102	7	124.3214	1	1.5000	0.0680	124.3214	1.0000	2.0000	0.0510	124.3214	1.0000
0.078	8	124.1722	1	1.5000	0.0520	124.1722	1.0000	2.0000	0.0390	124.1722	1.0000
0.062	9	124.9184	1	1.5000	0.0413	124.9184	1.0000	2.0000	0.0310	124.9184	1.0000
0.05	10	124.3712	1	1.5000	0.0333	124.3712	1.0000	2.0000	0.0250	124.3712	1.0000
0.0084	20	83.5774	1	1.5000	0.0056	83.5774	1.0000	2.0000	0.0042	83.5774	1.0000
0.0029	30	64.9218	1	1.5000	0.0019	64.9218	1.0000	2.0000	0.0015	64.9218	1.0000
0.00156	40	62.0861	1	1.5000	0.0010	62.0861	1.0000	2.0000	0.0008	62.0861	1.0000
0.001	50	62.1856	1	1.5000	0.0007	62.1856	1.0000	2.0000	0.0005	62.1856	1.0000
0.0007	60	62.6831	1	1.5000	0.0005	62.6831	1.0000	2.0000	0.0004	62.6831	1.0000
0.00052	70	62.7701	1	1.5000	0.0003	62.7701	1.0000	2.0000	0.0003	62.7701	1.0000
0.00039	80	62.0861	1	1.5000	0.0003	62.0861	1.0000	2.0000	0.0002	62.0861	1.0000
0.00031	90	62.4592	1	1.5000	0.0002	62.4592	1.0000	2.0000	0.0002	62.4592	1.0000
0.00025	100	62.1856	1	1.5000	0.0002	62.1856	1.0000	2.0000	0.0001	62.1856	1.0000

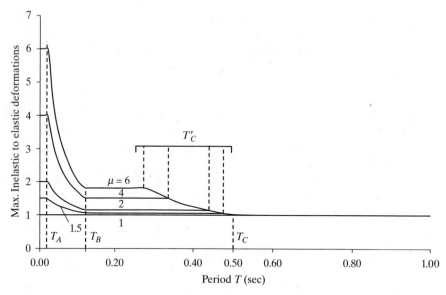

Figure 13.34 Relation between maximum inelastic to elastic deformations with period T for different ductility $\mu = 1, 1.5, 2, 4$ and 6.

(b) For the ground motion of Example 13.5, period $T_C = 0.5$ sec.

$$\therefore \text{ Inelastic acceleration} = \frac{A}{\sqrt{2\mu - 1}} \tag{13.34c}$$

Elastic acceleration $A = 1 \text{ g} \times 2.71 = 2.71 \text{ g}$

$$\therefore \text{ Inelastic acceleration} = \frac{2.71g}{\sqrt{2\mu - 1}}$$

and

Yield strength
$$F_y = \frac{100 \times 2.71g}{\sqrt{2\mu - 1}}$$

Also, the maximum deformation is given by Equations (13.35c) for $T < T_C$.

$$x_m = \frac{\mu}{R} x_0 = \frac{\mu}{\sqrt{2\mu - 1}} x_0 \tag{13.35c}$$

Maximum elastic deformation $x_0 = \dfrac{A}{\omega^2} = \left(\dfrac{T}{2\pi}\right)^2 A$

$$\therefore \qquad x_m = \frac{\mu}{\sqrt{2\mu - 1}} \left(\frac{T}{2\pi}\right)^2 A$$

$$= \frac{\mu}{\sqrt{2\mu - 1}} \left(\frac{0.4}{2\pi}\right)^2 2.71 \text{ g}$$

$$= \frac{0.1077\,\mu}{\sqrt{2\mu - 1}} \text{ m}$$

The maximum strength and maximum deformation are given as follows:

For $\mu = 1$, maximum strength $= 271\ g = 2658.51$ N, maximum deformation $x_0 = 0.1077$ m

For $\mu = 4$, maximum strength $= 1004.8$ N, maximum deformation $x_m = 0.1628$ m

$\square$

Example 13.8

Plot the peak deformations in a SDOF bilinear system for different ductility ratios equal to 1, 1.5, 2, 4 and 6 when subjected to the same ground motion of Example 13.5.

Solution   The values of maximum deformations in an inelastic SDOF system were shown in Table 13.5. The same data is plotted in Figure 13.35(a) on semi log scale. The portion up to $T = T_C$ is enlarged in Figure 13.35(b) for clarity. Beyond T_C, inelastic and elastic displacements are equal, therefore, all curves for different ductility merge. $\square$

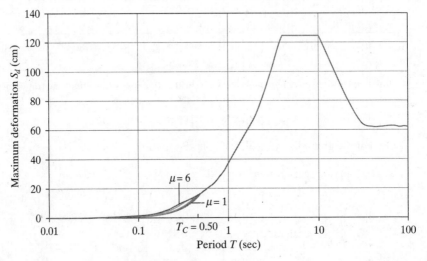

Figure 13.35(a)   Maximum deformation vs. period T for different ductility ratio $\mu = 1, 1.5, 2, 4$ and 6

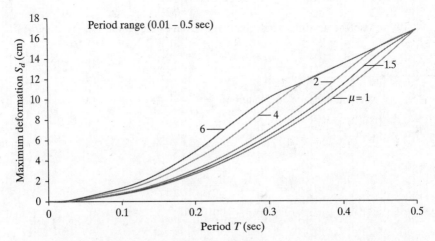

Figure 13.35(b)   Enlarged view of the maximum deformations for period range 0.01–0.5 sec.

13.9 ENERGY DISSIPATION SYSTEMS

In conventional structures, the earthquake-induced energy is dissipated in components of the gravity and lateral-load-resisting system, that is beams, columns and shear walls. The action of dissipating energy through such members produces damage in those components. Moreover, the designer has no control as to which members should plastify and dissipate energy and which members should remain elastic. Repair of such damage after an earthquake may be quite expensive and often may not even be feasible. If the structural engineer can identify where and how the energy can be dissipated within the structural system, without affecting the other parts of the structure, it would be an ideal situation. The objective of adding energy dissipation (damping) devices to new and existing structures is to dissipate much of the earthquake-induced energy in disposable elements only without damaging the other parts or elements. Thus, the designer is able to divert and control energy dissipation through specific elements in a structure while protecting the other elements. The advantage of this approach is to limit or eliminate damage to the protected portion of the structural system. It should be easy to replace or repair the energy dissipating devices after an event while the structure may remain serviceable during this activity. There are two broad categories of such control systems as discussed in Chapter 12:

- Active control systems
- Passive control systems

Active control systems sense and resist building motion, either by applying external force or by modifying structural properties of the active elements. Tuned mass or liquid dampers modify properties and add damping to key building modes of vibration. *Passive control systems* add damping (and sometimes stiffness) to the structure. These devices do not require any external source of energy. Here, we will discuss only passive systems. Applicability of energy dissipating devices is given in Table 13.6 (FEMA 356).

Supplemental damping devices fall into three categories: hysteretic, velocity-dependent and others (FEMA 356). Examples of displacement-dependent or hysteretic dampers include devices based on friction and yielding of metal. Displacement-dependent devices include devices that exhibit either rigid-plastic (friction devices), bilinear (metallic yielding devices), or trilinear hysteresis. Velocity-dependent systems include dampers consisting of viscoelastic solid materials, dampers operating by deformation of viscoelastic fluids and dampers operating by forcing fluid through an orifice.

TABLE 13.6   APPLICABILITY OF ENERGY DISSIPATION SYSTEMS

Performance Level	Applicability of Energy Dissipation Systems
Operational	Limited
Immediate Occupancy	Likely
Life Safety	Likely
Collapse Prevention	Limited

13.9.1 Viscoelasticity

It is the property of materials that exhibits both viscous and elastic characteristics when undergoing deformation. Under stress, viscous materials resist shear flow and strain linearly with time. Elastic materials strain when stretched and quickly return to their original state once the stress is removed. Viscoelastic materials have elements of both of these properties and, as such, exhibit time-dependent strain. Characteristics of the viscoelastic materials are as follows:

- If the stress is held constant, the strain increases with time (creep).
- If the strain is held constant, the stress decreases with time (relaxation).
- The effective stiffness depends on the rate of application of the load.
- If cyclic loading is applied, hysteresis behaviour is exhibited leading to dissipation of mechanical energy.

Depending on the stress versus strain rate inside a material the variation in viscosity can be either linear, nonlinear or plastic.

Constitutive models Viscoelastic materials can be modelled in order to determine their stress or strain interactions, as well as their temporal dependencies. These models, which include the *Maxwell model*, the *Kelvin–Voigt model* and the *Standard Linear Solid Model* or *General Damping Model* are used to predict a material's response under different loading conditions. Viscoelastic behavior has elastic and viscous components modelled as linear combinations of springs and dashpots, respectively. Each model differs in the arrangement of these elements. These models are shown in Figures 13.36(a)–(c).

In the Maxwell model, if the material is put under a constant strain, the stresses gradually relax. When a material is put under a constant stress, the strain has two components. First, an elastic component occurs instantaneously, corresponding to the spring, and relaxes immediately upon release of the stress. The second is a viscous component that grows with time as long as the stress is applied. The Maxwell model predicts that stress decays exponentially with time, which is accurate for most polymers. One limitation of this model is that it does not predict creep accurately. The Maxwell model for creep or constant stress conditions postulates that strain will increase linearly with time. However, polymers for the most part show the strain rate to be decreasing with time.

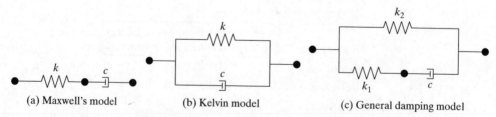

(a) Maxwell's model (b) Kelvin model (c) General damping model

Figure 13.36 Constitutive models for materials.

The Kelvin model represents a solid undergoing reversible, viscoelastic strain. Upon application of a constant stress, the material deforms at a decreasing rate, asymptotically approaching the steady state strain. When the stress is released, the material gradually relaxes to its undeformed state. At constant stress (creep), the Kelvin model is quite realistic. The model is extremely good with modelling creep in materials but is less accurate with regard to relaxation.

The general damping model combines the Maxwell model and another spring in parallel. A viscous material is modelled as a spring and a dashpot in series with each other, both of which are in parallel with a lone spring. Under a constant stress, the modelled material will instantaneously deform to some strain which is the elastic portion of the strain and after that it will continue to deform and asymptotically approach a steady state strain.

13.9.2 Hysteresis Behaviour of Dampers

The hysteresis behavior of displacement-dependent dampers can be represented as shown in Figures 13.4 and 13.9; and that of velocity-dependent systems are shown in Figure 13.37. Other systems have characteristics that fall outside those of these two systems. Examples are dampers made of shape memory alloys, frictional-spring assemblies with re-centering capabilities and fluid restoring force dampers. Hysteresis behaviour of a friction damper is shown in Figure 13.38.

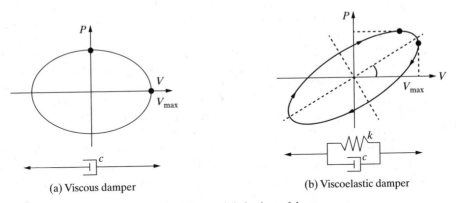

(a) Viscous damper   (b) Viscoelastic damper

Figure 13.37   Hysteresis behaviour of dampers.

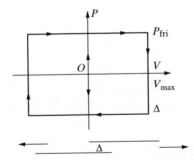

Figure 13.38   Hysteresis behaviour of friction damper.

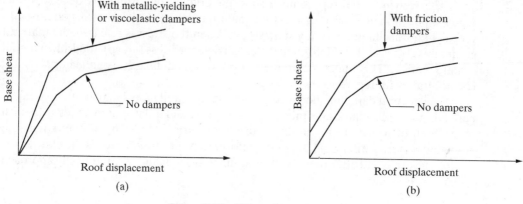

Figure 13.39   Effect of damping devices.

Some supplemental damping systems can substantially change the force–displacement response of a building by adding strength and stiffness. Such influence is demonstrated in Figure 13.39 for metallic yielding, friction and viscoelastic dampers. Ideally, energy dissipation devices dampen earthquake excitation of the structure that would otherwise cause higher levels of response and damage to components of the building. Under favorable conditions, energy dissipation devices reduce drift of the structure by a factor of about two to three (if no stiffness is added) and by larger factors if the devices also add stiffness to the structure. Energy dissipation devices will also reduce force in the structure, provided the structure is responding elastically. However, it would not be expected to reduce force in structures that are responding beyond yield. These special damping devices will be found to be more attractive as a rehabilitation strategy for buildings that have more stringent *rehabilitation objectives*, that is higher levels of performance and more severe levels of earthquake demand.

Models of the energy dissipation system include the stiffness of structural components that are part of the load path between energy dissipation devices and the ground and whose flexibility affects the performance of the energy dissipation system, including components of the foundation, braces that work in series with the energy dissipation devices and connections between braces and the energy dissipation devices.

Displacement-dependent devices   For evaluating the response of a displacement-dependent device from testing data, the force in a displacement-dependent device is calculated as follows (FEMA 356):

$$F = K_{eff}\,D \tag{13.38a}$$

where the effective stiffness k_{eff} of the device is calculated as follows:

$$K_{eff} = \frac{|F^+| + |F^-|}{|D^+| + |D^-|} \tag{13.38b}$$

The force in the device F^+ and F^- is evaluated at displacements D^+ and D^-, respectively.

Velocity-dependent devices—Solid viscoelastic devices Solid viscoelastic devices are modelled using a spring and dashpot in parallel (Kelvin model). The spring and dashpot constants must capture frequency and temperature dependence of the device consistent with fundamental frequency of the rehabilitated building (f_1) and the operating temperature range. The force in a viscoelastic device can be determined as follows (FEMA 356):

$$F = K_{eff}D + C\dot{D} \tag{13.39a}$$

where C = damping coefficient for the viscoelastic device

$\quad\quad D$ = relative displacement between each end of the device

$\quad\quad \dot{D}$ = relative velocity between each end of the device

$\quad\quad f_1$ = fundamental frequency of the building in Hz

$\quad\quad k_{eff}$ = effective stiffness of the device calculated in accordance with Equation (13.38b).

The damping coefficient for the device can be calculated as follows:

$$C = \frac{W_D}{\pi \omega_1 D^2_{avg}} \tag{13.39b}$$

where W_D = area enclosed by one complete cycle of the force-displacement response of the device

$\quad\quad D_{ave}$ = average of the absolute values of displacements D^+ and D^-

$\quad\quad \omega_1 = 2\pi f_1$

Velocity-dependent devices—Fluid viscoelastic devices Fluid viscoelastic devices are modelled using a spring and dashpot in series (Maxwell model). The spring and dashpot constants selected must capture the frequency and temperature dependence of the device consistent with fundamental frequency of the rehabilitated building (f_1) and the operating temperature range. Linear fluid viscous dampers exhibiting stiffness in the frequency range $0.5\ f_1$ to $2.0\ f_1$ shall be modelled as a fluid viscoelastic device. In the absence of stiffness in the frequency range $0.5\ f_1$ to $2.0\ f_1$, the force in the fluid viscous device shall be computed as follows:

$$F = C_0 |\dot{D}|^\alpha\ \text{sgn}(\dot{D}) \tag{13.39c}$$

where C_0 = damping coefficient for the device

$\quad\quad \alpha$ = velocity exponent for the device

$\quad\quad \dot{D}$ = relative velocity between each end of the device

$\quad\quad$ sgn = signum function, in this case defines the sign of the relative velocity term

FEMA 356 provides detailed rules for carrying out linear as well as nonlinear analysis using these devices. FEMA 440 provides detailed rules for carrying out nonlinear static analysis.

13.9.3 ADAS Energy Dissipating System

A metallic-yielding damper known as *added damping and stiffness* (ADAS) element is shown in Figure 13.40. The element is cut in a particular shape to yield at the minimum cross-section and provide a stable hysteresis curve as shown in Figure 13.7.

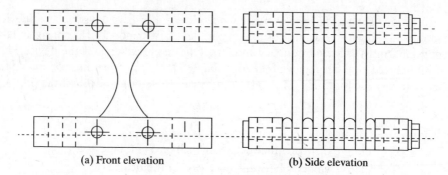

(a) Front elevation (b) Side elevation

Figure 13.40 ADAS element.

The purpose of using an ADAS device is to concentrate the entire nonlinearity in the ADAS element and protect the steel braces and other elements from yielding or buckling. A nonlinear analysis needs to be carried out to study the behaviour of ADAS element in a concentrically braced steel frame.

13.9.3.1 Bouc-Wen Hysteresis Model

The hysteretic response of a system can be found by representing the restoring force in terms of nonlinear plastic Bouc-Wen link as shown in Figure 13.41 (Wen 1976). The restoring force $F(t)$ has two components – elastic $F_{el}(t)$ and hysteretic $F_h(t)$ defined as follows:

$$F(t) = F_{el}(t) + F_h(t) \tag{13.40a}$$

$$F_{el}(t) = a\frac{F_y}{x_y}x(t) \tag{13.40b}$$

$$F_h(t) = (1-a)F_y z(t) \tag{13.40c}$$

The hysteretic part of the restoring force is given by

$$\dot{z}(t) = \frac{1}{x_y}\left[A - |z(t)|^n \left(\alpha + \mathrm{sgn}\left(\dot{x}(t)z(t)\right)\right)\beta\right]\dot{x}(t) \tag{13.40d}$$

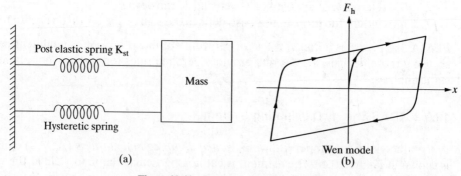

(a) (b)

Figure 13.41 Bouc-wen hysteresis model.

where, F = restoring force
F_y = yield force
F_{el} = elastic force component
F_h = hysteresis force component
x = displacement; x_y = yield displacement
$a = K_{st}/K_i$ = rigidity ratio
K_i = initial stiffness = F_y/x_y; K_{st} = Post-yield stiffness
$z(t)$ = non-dimensional hysteretic parameter that obeys a single nonlinear differential equation with zero initial conditions. It is a fictitious displacement related to the actual displacement.
A, α, β, n are dimensionless quantities controlling the shape and size of the hysteresis model; n may be even or odd
sgn = signum function

Small values of positive exponential parameter n (= 1) corresponds to smooth transition from elastic to post-elastic branch, whereas, for larger values of n (> 15) the transition becomes abrupt approaching that of the bilinear model.

The equation of motion of a SDOF system with hysteretic behaviour can be expressed in terms of Bouc-Wen model as follows:

$$m\ddot{x} + c\dot{x} + kx + z(x, \dot{x}) = p(t) \tag{13.41a}$$

or,

$$\ddot{x} + 2\omega\xi\dot{x} + a\omega^2 x + (1-a)\omega^2 z = u(t). \tag{13.41b}$$

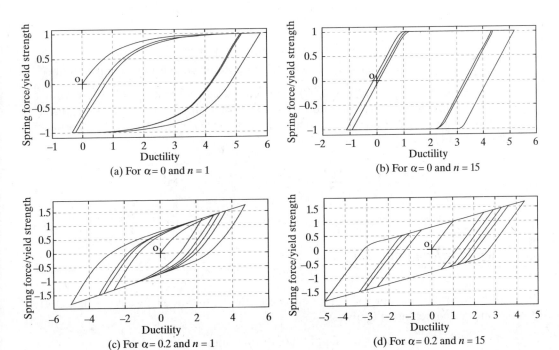

(a) For $\alpha = 0$ and $n = 1$

(b) For $\alpha = 0$ and $n = 15$

(c) For $\alpha = 0.2$ and $n = 1$

(d) For $\alpha = 0.2$ and $n = 15$

Figure 13.42   Hysteresis behaviour of a nonlinear SDOF system for different values of rigidity ratio α and exponent n

and
$$\dot{z} = A\dot{x} - \alpha\dot{x}|z|^{n} - \beta|\dot{x}||z|^{n-1}z \tag{13.41c}$$

where, $u(t)$ = normalized excitation force
Equations (13.41) can be represented in terms of the state space, that is, a set of first order differential equations. Plotting the restoring force against displacement x gives the hysteresis loops. The hysteretic response of a SDOF system given by Equations (13.41) can be found by writing a code in MATLAB. Typical hysteresis response of a nonlinear SDOF system using the Bouc-Wen model subjected to a sinusoidal loading is shown in Figure 13.42 for different values of n and α.

13.10 MODELING OF EXPANSION GAP IN BRIDGES

In multi-span simply supported bridges, there is a need to provide sufficient gap between two adjacent bridge decks to account for expansion and contraction due to change in temperature and due to lateral forces as a result of earthquake. It has been observed in many past earthquakes that the superstructure has fallen off the simply supported bearing in each span in saw-tooth formation. Although the bridge is otherwise intact, it is completely unusable. There is a need to model both superstructure and substructure of a bridge, analyse it under the design earthquake and check if the expansion gap is sufficient. The expansion gap can be modelled using a gap element as shown in Figure 13.43. It is also referred to as the *nonlinear gap-crush element*.

The gap/crush element has the following physical properties:

- The element cannot develop a force until the opening gap x_0 is closed.
- The element can only develop a compression force.
- The crush deformation x_p is always a monotonic decreasing negative number.

The dynamic contact problem between real structural components often does not have a unique solution. Therefore, it is the responsibility of the design engineer to select materials at contact points and surfaces to have realistic material properties that can be predicted accurately.

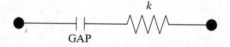

k

GAP

Figure 13.43   Gap element.

13.11 ILLUSTRATIVE EXAMPLES

The following examples illustrate the application of the following devices in real structures using nonlinear analysis:

- A viscous damper in a simply supported bridge
- A ADAS device in a single-storey concentrically braced steel frame
- A gap element in a two span simply supported bridge

These problems have been solved using SAP2000 and ETABS software (CSI, Berkeley).

Example 13.9

A frame has a length of 6 m and height of 3.5 m. Beam size is 30 × 50 cm and column size is 30 × 60 cm. Concrete is of grade M25. Left end of the beam is hinged while the right end has a roller support between the beam and the top of column. A viscous damper is provided between the beam and the right column as shown in Figure 13.44. It is subjected to a sinusoidal ground motion. Plot response of the roller end of the beam, relative displacement with the viscous damper and hysteresis behaviour of the damper.

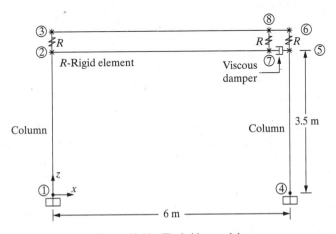

Figure 13.44   The bridge model.

Solution   The frame represents a simply supported bridge. The centre line of the beam is assumed to be 500 mm above the top of column. It is represented through rigid links. It is assumed that there is no lateral pressure on the columns. Period of the frame is 1.9 sec. The hinged end, roller end and viscous damper were simulated using link elements having a finite length in SAP2000.

Boundary conditions:
At a hinge end: nodes 2 and 3
U_1 of node 2 = U_1 of node 3; U_2 of node 2 = U_2 of node 3
U_1 = lateral displacement (along x) and U_2 = vertical displacement (along z)
At a roller end: nodes 5 and 6
U_2 of node 5 = U_2 of node 6
The viscous damper between nodes 5 and 7 was assigned the following properties:
Stiffness = 10^6 kN/m, damping coefficient = 100, damping exponent = 1.0.
Nodes 7 and 8 were connected through a rigid link. Thus, viscous damper was connected between the beam and the column.
Supports 1 and 4 were fixed.
Period of the sinusoidal ground motion was 0.5 sec.
The response of the roller end of the beam and viscous damper are shown in Figures 13.45(a) and (b). The hysteresis behaviour of the viscous damper is shown in Figure 13.45(c).

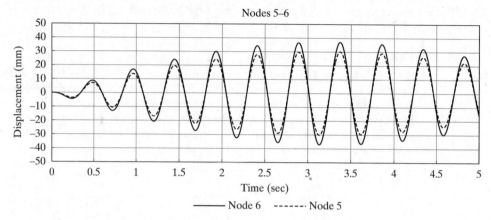

Figure 13.45(a)   Displacement time-history of the right end of the beam (node 6) and top of column (node 5).

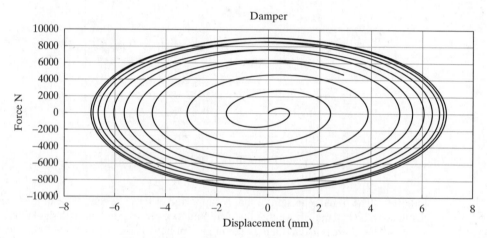

Figure 13.45(b)   Hysteresis behaviour of the damper.

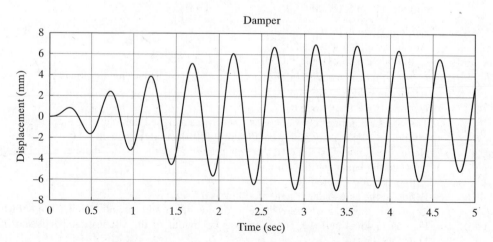

Figure 13.45(c)   Displacement time-history of the damper.

The seismic response of such structures is influenced by the characteristics of the ground motion. It means its response will vary with each different ground motion. In such a situation, it becomes difficult to isolate the effect of the viscous damper from that of the ground motion. The characteristics of a sine curve are well known. Therefore, a sine curve was used as a ground motion in this example for illustration.

The effect of viscous damper is to reduce the maximum lateral displacement of the roller end by 10 mm.   □

Example 13.10

A steel framed building shown in Figure 13.46 is fitted with ADAS device at the junction of braces with the beam. It is subjected to a sinusoidal ground motion. Illustrate the effect of ADAS device.

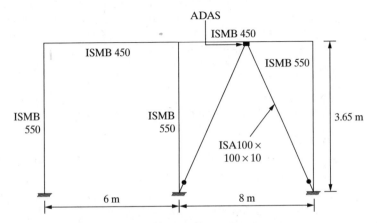

Figure 13.46   Braced steel building with ADAS device.

Solution   In the present example, the frame and the ADAS device were modeled in ETABS (CSI, Berkeley). Period of the frame was 0.1 sec. The ADAS device was modeled using the panel zone between the beam and the brace and assigning a nonlinear plastic Bouc – Wen link. The nonlinear stiffness was taken as 500 kN/m and the yield strength was taken as 10 kN with 5% strain hardening. Yield exponent was taken as 2.0. The frequency of the sinusoidal ground motion was taken as 2 Hz.

The frame was analysed without the ADAS device and again with the ADAS device. The forces in the steel braces and columns are shown in Table 13.7.

TABLE 13.7   FRAME FORCES WITHOUT AND WITH ADAS DEVICE

Particular	Without ADAS Device	With ADAS Device
Lateral displacement (mm)	3.35	11.30
Brace axial force (kN)	174 and 168	11.5 and 3.0
Column shear (kN)	43, 53 and 42 kN	145, 180 and 139 kN
Panel zone shear (kN)	NA	5.5
Panel zone deformation (mm)	NA	11.30

(There are 2 braces and 3 columns)

It can be seen that there is redistribution of forces among columns and braces due to the presence of ADAS device. Steel braces develop little axial force due to ADAS device which helps prevent their buckling. Energy is dissipated by the ADAS device.   ☐

Example 13.11

A two span simply supported bridge is shown in Figure 13.47. The left span is 6 m and the right span is 4 m. Height of piers is 3.5 m. Beam size is 30 × 50 cm and column size is 30 × 60 cm. Concrete is of grade M25. Left end of the beam in each span is hinged while the right end has a roller support between the beam and top of column. A 15 mm expansion gap is provided between the two spans. It is subjected to a sinusoidal ground motion. Plot the response across the gap and displacement and force in the gap element.

Solution   Period of the frame is 1.82 sec. The hinged end, roller end and gap elements were simulated using the link element in SAP2000 (CSI, Berkeley). R represents rigid link and simulates the gap between the center line of the super structure and bridge bearings. *Boundary conditions*

At a hinged end: nodes 2 and 3
U_1 of node 2 = U_1 of node 3
U_2 of node 2 = U_2 of node 3

At a roller end: node 6
Node 6 between rigid elements 5-6 and 6-8 is split in two nodes. A link element having a zero length is introduced across this split node 6. The properties of the link element are set so that:
U_2 of the both the split nodes 6 are same. The link element is represented by B_1.

At a hinged end: node 7
Node 7 between rigid elements 5-7 and 7-11 is split in two nodes. A link element having a zero length is introduced across this split node 7. The properties of the link element are set so that:
U_1 and U_2 of both the split nodes 7 are the same. The link element is represented by B_2.

At a roller end: nodes 13 and 14
U_2 of node 13 = U_2 of node 14
The supports 1, 4 and 12 were fixed.

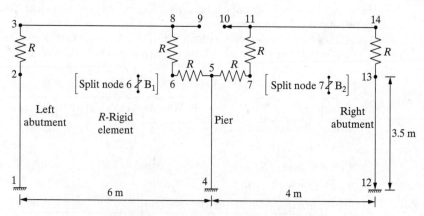

Figure 13.47   Two span simply supported bridge.

The gap element between nodes 9 and 10 was assigned the following properties:
Stiffness = 10^7 kN/m, gap = 15 mm
Frequency of the sinusoidal ground motion was 2 Hz.

The absolute displacement time-history of nodes 8 and 11 are shown in Figure 13.48(a). The displacement time-history of the gap element is shown in Figure 13.48(b). It can be seen that it undergoes a maximum negative displacement (gap closing) of 15 mm, which was the gap, whereas, it undergoes a maximum positive displacement of about 110 mm (gap opening) due to the movement of the piers. The force time-history of the gap element in Figure 13.48(c) shows an impact when the gap is closed. Naturally, there will be no force when the gap is open. This information can be used to design bearing seat size, bearing connectors and stoppers. In real-time situations, the data needs to be assigned very carefully.   ☐

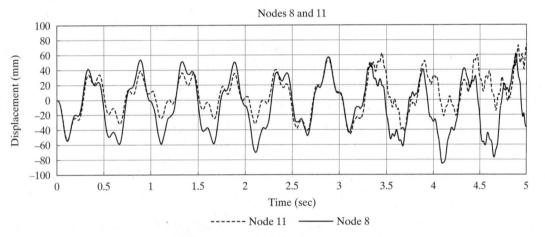

Figure 13.48(a)   Displacement time-history.

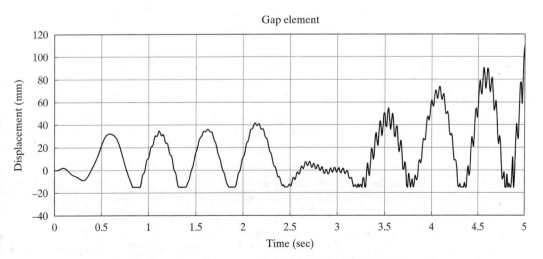

Figure 13.48(b)   Displacement time-history of the gap element.

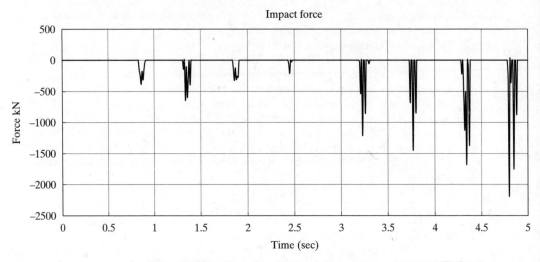

Figure 13.48(c)   Force time-history of the gap element.

PROBLEMS

13.1 What is the need of carrying out a nonlinear analysis of a structure subjected to an earthquake? What kind of differences are expected in the response of linear analysis and nonlinear analysis?

13.2 What do you understand by hysteresis behaviour? Discuss the salient features of hysteresis behaviour of a very ductile structure and a brittle structure.

13.3 Discuss the salient features of hysteresis behaviour of an eccentrically braced steel frame and a concentrically braced steel frame with the help of sketches.

13.4 Discuss the salient features of a reinforced concrete building undergoing reversed cyclic loading with the help of typical hysteresis loops.

13.5 What is ductility? How do you measure it?

13.6 Discuss the salient features of Newton–Raphson method for carrying out a nonlinear analysis.

13.7 Discuss an inelastic response spectra? What do you understand by constant ductility spectra and constant strength spectra? What information do you get from these spectra?

13.8 What is the significance of a reduction factor in inelastic response spectra? Derive it for equal displacement region and equal energy region.

13.9 Discuss the salient features of various energy dissipating devices with suitable sketches. Explain displacement dependent and velocity dependent devices.

13.10 What is viscoelasticity? Discuss the constitutive models.

13.11 A SDOF system has a mass of 5 kg, stiffness of 200 N/m and 3% viscous damping. It is subjected to a ground motion as shown in the table. The spring force–displacement relation is shown in Figure P13.1. Find the inelastic response using the Newton β method (i) with iterations and (ii) without iterations.

Time, sec	0	0.1	0.2	0.3	0.4	0.5	0.6	0.7	1.0
Acceleration/g	0	0.3	−0.2	0.4	−0.1	0.1	−0.3	0.2	−0.1

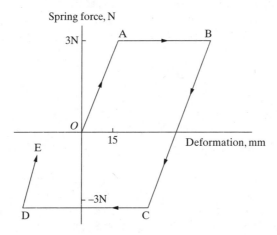

Figure P13.1   Hysteresis Model

13.12 Construct an elastic and an inelastic response spectrum for a ground motion having peak ground acceleration, peak ground velocity and peak ground displacement of 0.5 g, 80 cm/sec and 75 cm, respectively. Make use of Newmark–Hall amplification factors for 84.1 percentile and (i) 2% damping and (ii) 10% damping.

REFERENCES – FURTHER READING

Agrawal, S. and Jain, A.K. (2010) Nonlinear Modeling and Seismic Performance of a Multi-Span Simply Supported Viaduct, Proc, 7th CUEE & 5th ICEE, Tokyo Tech, Tokyo.

AISC 341 (2010) Seismic Provisions for Structural Steel Buildings, American Institute of Steel Construction, Chicago.

AISC 360 (2010) Specification for Structural Steel Buildings, American Institute of Steel Construction, Chicago.

ASCE 7 (2010) Minimum Design Loads for Buildings and Other Structures, American Society of Civil Engineers, Reston, Virginia.

Chopra, A.K. (2007) Dynamics of Structures, 3rd edition, Pearson Education, New Delhi.

CSI (2015) Analysis Reference Manual for SAP2000, ETABS and CSi Bridge, Computers and Structures, Inc. Berkeley, CA.

Deierlein, Gregory G., Reinhorn, Andrei M., and Willford, Michael R. (2010). "Nonlinear Structural Analysis for Seismic Design," NEHRP Seismic Design Technical Brief No. 4, produced by the NEHRP Consultants Joint Venture, a partnership of the Applied Technology Council and the Consortium of Universities for Research in Earthquake Engineering, for the National Institute of Standards and Technology, Gaithersburg, MD.

Eurocode 8-1 (2004) Design of Structures for Earthquake Resistance–Part 1: General Rules, Seismic Actions and Rules for Buildings, incorporating corrigendum 2013, European Committee for Standardization, Brussels.

FEMA 356 (2000) Prestandard and Commentary for the Seismic Rehabilitation of Buildings, Federal Emergency Management Agency, Washington, D.C.

FEMA 440 (2005) Improvement of Nonlinear Static Seismic Analysis Procedures, Federal Emergency Management Agency, Washington, D.C.

Hanson, R. D. and Soong, T. T. (2001) Seismic Design with Supplemental Energy Dissipation Devices, EERI Monograph MNO-8, Earthquake Engineering Research Institute, Oakland, California.

Jain, A.K. and Goel, S.C. (1978) Hysteresis Models for Steel members Subjected to Cyclic Buckling or Cyclic End Moments and Buckling (User's Guide for DRAIN-2D:EL9 and EL10), Research Report UMEE 78R6, The University of Michigan, Ann Arbor.

Jain, A.K. and Goel, S.C. (1980) Seismic Response of Eccentrically Braced Frames, Journal of Structural Division, ASCE, Vol. 106, April, pp. 843–860.

Jain, A.K. (1985) Inelastic Response Spectra, Research Report, Department of Civil Engineering, University of Roorkee, Roorkee.

Jain, A.K. (1985) Seismic Response of R.C. Frames with Steel Braces, Journal of the Structural Division, ASCE, Vol. 111, No. ST10, October, pp. 2138–2148.

Jain, A.K. (1990) Inelastic Response of R. C. Frames subjected to the 1985 Mexico Earthquake, Computers and Structures, Vol. 34, No. 3, pp. 445–454.

Jain, A.K. and Pal, S. (1991) Probabilistic Amplification Factors for Response Spectra, Journal of Structural Engg., ASCE, Vol. 117, No. 8, August, pp. 2464–2476.

Jain, A.K., Redwood, R.G., and Lu, F. (1993) Seismic Response of Concentrically Braced Dual Steel Frames, Canadian Journal of Civil Engineering, Vol. 20, August, pp. 672–687.

Jain, A.K., Sanda, K., and Redwood, R.G. (1996) Design and Behavior of Eccentrically Braced Frames with Flexural Links, Proc., Int. Conf. on Latest Developments in Steel Structures, Hong Kong, Pergamon Press, Dec., pp. 233–237.

Jain, A.K. (2015) Advanced Structural Analysis, 3rd ed, Nem Chand & Bros., Roorkee.

JSCE-SSCS (2010) Standard Specifications for Concrete Structures 2007, Guideline no. 15, Japan Society of Civil Engineers, Tokyo.

Kanaan, A.E. and Powell, G. H. (1973) General Purpose Computer Program for Inelastic Dynamic Response of Plane Structures, Report no. EERC 73-6, University of California, Berkeley.

Lai, S.P. and Biggs, J. M. (1980) Inelastic Response Spectra for Aseismic Design of Buildings, Journal of Structural Div., ASCE, Vol. 106, pp. 1295–1310.

Naiem, F. (1989) The Seismic Design Handbook, Van Nostrand Reinhold Co., New York.

Newmark, N.M. and Hall, W.J., (1969) Design Criteria for Nuclear Reactor Facilities, Proc., 4th World Conference on Earthquake Engg, Santiago, Chile, Vol. 2, pp. B-4, 37–50.

Newmark, N.M. and Hall, W.J., (1973) A Rational Approach to Seismic Design Standards for Structures, Proc., 5th World Conference on Earthquake Engg, Vol. 2, pp. 2266–2275.

Newmark, N.M. and Riddle, R. (1980) Inelastic Spectra for Seismic Design, Proc., 7th World Conference on Earthquake Engg, Istanbul, Vol. 4, pp. 129–136.

NZS 1170–5 (2004) Structural Design Actions – Part 5: Earthquake Actions-New Zealand, Standards New Zealand, Wellington.

NZS 1170–5 (S1) (2004) Structural Design Actions – Part 5: Earthquake Actions-New Zealand, Commentary, Standards New Zealand, Wellington.

Pal, S., Dasaka, S.S., and Jain, A.K. (1987) Inelastic Response Spectra, Computers and Structures, Vol. 25, p. 335–344.

Opensees (2014) Open System for Earthquake Engineering Simulation, Pacific Earthquake Engineering Research Center (PEER), University of California, Berkeley.

Otani, S. (1974) Computer Program for Inelastic Response of R.C. Frames Subjected to Earthquakes, University of Illinois, Urbana-Champaign.

PEER (2008) Guidelines for Nonlinear Analysis of Bridge Structures in California, University of California, Berkeley, California.

PEER (2010) Modeling and Acceptance Criteria for Seismic Design and Analysis of Tall Buildings, Report no. 111, Pacific Earthquake Engineering Research Center, Berkeley, California.

PEER 5 (2010) Seismic Design Guidelines for Tall Buildings, Pacific Earthquake Engineering Research Center (PEER), Berkeley.

Prakash, V., Powell, G.H. and Campbell, S.D. (1994) DRAIN-3DX, NISEE, University of California, Berkeley.

Rafael Sabelli, R., Roeder, C. W. and Hajjar, J. F. (2013) Seismic Design of Steel Special Concentrically Braced Frame Systems, A Guide for Practicing Engineers, U.S. Dept. of Commerce National Institute of Standards and Technology Engineering Laboratory, Gaithersburg, MD.

Saiidi, M. and Sozen, M.A. (1979) Simple and Complex Models for Nonlinear Seismic Response of Reinforced Concrete Structures, University of Illinois, Urbana-Champaign.

Scholl, Roger E. (1993) Design Criteria for Yielding and Friction Energy Dissipaters, Proceedings, ATC-17-1 Seminar on Seismic Isolation, Passive Energy Dissipation, and Active Control, San Francisco, California. Vol. 2, 485–495. Applied Technology Council. Redwood City, CA.

Takeda, T., Sozen, M.A. and Nielsen, N. N. (1970) Reinforced Concrete Response to Simulated Earthquakes, Journal of Structural Div., Vol. 96, ASCE, Dec., pp. 2257.

Veletsos, A.S. and Newmark, N.M. (1960) Effect of Inelastic Behaviour on the Response of Simple Systems to Earthquake Motions, Proc., 2nd World Conference on Earthquake Engineering, Tokyo, p. 895–912.

Veletsos, A.S., Newmark, N.M. and Chelapati, C.V. (1965) Deformation Spectra for Elastic and Elasto-plastic Systems subjected to Ground Shock and Earthquake Motions, Proc., 3rd World Conference on Earthquake Engineering, New Zealand, Vol. 2, pp. 663–680.

Wen, Y.K. (1976) Method for Random Vibration of Hysteretic Systems, Journal of the Engineering Mechanics Division, ASCE, Vol. 102, No. EM2, pp. 249–263.

14 Performance-based Seismic Design of Structures

14.1 INTRODUCTION

The objective of the performance-based seismic design is to verify the seismic performance of the structure and to evaluate its seismic performance for various design limit states. For each limit state, the level of earthquake considered in the design may be determined depending upon the purpose and importance of the structure. The performance-based design (PBD) or performance-based engineering (PBE) is not a new concept. Automobiles, aircrafts and turbines have been designed and manufactured based on this approach for many decades. Generally, in such applications, one or more prototypes of the structure are built and subjected to full scale extensive testing. The design and manufacturing process is then revised to incorporate the lessons learnt from the prototype testing. Once the cycle of design, prototype manufacturing, testing and redesign are successfully completed, the product is manufactured on large scale and sold in the market. In the automotive or aircraft industry, the concept of PBE is very economical. However, in the building industry, the problem is that each building is unique and has a lot of variations in terms of architecture, materials, structural system, layout, etc. It is not feasible to carryout full scale testing on each building and assess its performance. Due to the recent advances in the seismic hazard assessments, PBE methodologies, experimental facilities and computer applications, the PBE is in demand in seismic regions. A detailed study can be carried out with different computer models, and the most efficient system can be chosen. However, in order to utilize the PBE more effectively, one should be aware of the uncertainties involved in both structural performance and seismic hazard estimation. A key requirement of any meaningful PBE is the ability to assess seismic *demands* and *capacities* with a reasonable degree of certainty.

In the prescriptive design as specified in loading and design codes (IS:875-Part 3, IS:1893, IS:456, IS:13920 and IS:800), the code tells the designer what to do at each stage. The final product is expected to respond as desired by the code. The designer need not bother to check the final performance of his/her product. It is presumed that the codes have envisaged without knowing what exactly the codes have desired or intended. The main drawback is that the designer cannot innovate on the design. Whereas in the performance-based design, the code simply tells what performance is expected out of the given component of the structure as well as the structural system. The code does not impose any do's and don'ts. A performance-based seismic code can be expected to be a probabilistic code. The designer has to choose an appropriate option how to design it so as to achieve the specified performance level and probability. The *performance parameters* have to be very specific in terms of *definition*, how to *measure* them, how to *achieve* them and how to *verify* them. The designer has to have a very deep understanding of the behaviour of various structural materials, components and structural systems under different loading conditions, their implications and consequences.

The performance-based seismic design concept can be used for the design of a *new building* as well as for *rehabilitation of an old building*. Many new building codes have detailed stipulations for the PBD of new buildings such as Eurocode 1992 and 1998 and Japan Code on Concrete Structures 2007. The new buildings are designed in accordance with the capacity design method for a given limit state or performance criteria available in the latest building codes taking into account symmetry, regularity and ductile detailing under the specified hazard level. These buildings can be subjected to nonlinear dynamic analysis under a given set of earthquake accelerograms to assess their performance. However the problem lies in the availability of suitable number of accelerograms for the given site. An alternative is to carry out nonlinear static analysis by imposing displacements or lateral loads at various floors.

Decades ago, a number of buildings were designed as per the prevalent practices or codes and available materials. There is a need to preserve and restore them as per the latest specifications and force levels, if possible. Several nonlinear static procedures (NSP) have been developed for the retrofitting and rehabilitation of such buildings. The basic approach of any static nonlinear analysis is to develop an equivalent SDOF system of the MDOF system and try to calculate the inelastic displacement demand for a given representation of the ground motion. ATC 40 (1996) introduced capacity spectrum method, while FEMA 356 (2000) introduced coefficient method. The ATC 40 approach is a form of equivalent linearization. This technique uses empirically derived relationships for the effective period and effective damping as a function of ductility to estimate the response of an equivalent linear SDOF system. The FEMA 356 approach utilizes a displacement modification procedure (Coefficient method) in which several empirically derived factors are used to modify the response of a SDOF model of the structure assuming that it remains elastic. The two approaches are essentially the same when it comes to generating a pushover curve to represent the inelastic force deformation behavior of a MDOF building. They differ in the technique used to calculate the inelastic displacement demand. The problem arises because different methods give significantly different estimates of the displacement demand. An effort was made through FEMA 440 (2005) to identify the source of these differences and to suggest possible solutions. ASCE 41 (2007) suggested further improvements. It was noticed that the results are very sensitive to the modelling of strength degradation when a structure is subjected to earthquake excitation.

The salient features of performance-based seismic design, building performance objectives, rehabilitation objectives, static pushover analysis as applicable to rehabilitation of existing structures based on ASCE 41, FEMA 356 and FEMA 440, and acceleration-displacement response spectra (ADRS) are discussed in this chapter. A moment–curvature relation is necessary in order to define a plastic hinge. It depends on whether the concrete is unconfined or confined. This aspect is discussed in detail. The salient features of nonlinear static and dynamic analyses are illustrated through a 10-storey R.C. framed building.

14.2 PERFORMANCE-BASED SEISMIC DESIGN

The PBD concept makes use of demand and capacity of various elements of the structure. Capacity design is an approach whereby the designer establishes which elements will yield (and need to be ductile) and those which will not yield (and will be designed with sufficient strength) based on the forces imposed by yielding elements. The advantages of this approach are as follows:

- More certainty in how the building will perform under a given set of earthquakes and greater confidence in how the performance can be measured.
- Protection from sudden failures in elements that cannot be proportioned or detailed for ductility.
- Limiting the locations in the structure where expensive ductile detailing is required.
- Reliable energy dissipation by enforcing deformation modes (plastic mechanisms) where inelastic deformations are distributed to ductile components.

Performance Index

The performance index should be selected as appropriate means to quantitatively express the performance of a structure subjected to earthquakes. It may include durability, safety, serviceability, restorability, environmental compatibility, landscape compatibility, etc. Safety means performance of a structure to prevent risk to the users and other people in the vicinity under all expected conditions. Safety includes structural and functional safety of a structure. Restorability means restoring the performance of a structure that has degraded because of accidental loads such as earthquake and making the continued use of the structure possible. It indicates degrees of difficulty in restoring degraded performance of a structure due to accidental loads.

Required Performance Index

The required performance index, PI_R, is defined in terms of *demand* on the member forces and displacement/drift (including member rotations) for each limit state during an earthquake. It is possible to measure the crack width and amplitude of vibrations besides other pertinent parameters under the specified conditions. The PI_R should be computed using appropriate analytical methods.

The performance objectives (*required performance indices PI_R*) are specifically stated in terms of the acceptable risk of casualties, direct economic losses and downtime resulting from earthquake-induced damage. These acceptable risks can be expressed for specific levels of earthquake ground motion intensity, for different scenario earthquakes or for a specific period of time considering all earthquakes that can occur during the life time of the building and the probability of their occurrence.

Possessed Performance Index

The possessed performance index, PI_P, is defined in terms of *capacity* of a member in each failure mode/limit state and displacement/drift (including member rotations) of the structure for a given level of earthquake. The member strength should be computed using the applicable material models. The process of performance assessment (PI_p) is inherently uncertain and complex. It requires that a number of assumptions be made as to the severity and characteristics of earthquake shaking the building, the condition and occupancy of the building at the time an earthquake occurs and response of the structural system in the nonlinear range. It also requires information on the efficiency with which the stakeholders are able to respond and repair the building and restore it to service once damage occurs. The performance assessment process of a building for seismic loads is shown in Figure 14.1.

Once performance objectives for a building have been determined, next step is to design a building so as to allow the building's performance characteristics (*possessed performance indices*) to be determined. This will include identification of the building's site, size and configuration, occupancy, quality and type of non-structural systems, the structural system and estimates of its strength, stiffness, durability and ductility. A series of simulations (analyses of building response to ground shaking) are performed to estimate the possessed performance indices of the building under various design scenario events.

The Indian Standards IS:456, IS:800, IS:875, IS:1893 and IS:13920 are prescriptive codes based on the limit state design philosophy. The concept of PBD is yet to be incorporated.

Demand vs. Capacity

These simulation studies provide statistical data on building drifts, floor accelerations, member forces and deformations, termed *demand parameters* at different levels of ground motions. This demand data from the structural analyses and data on the building configuration is used to calculate the possible distribution of damage to structural and non-structural building components and also the potential distribution in casualty, economic and occupancy losses. The performance assessment produces probability distribution functions for casualties, repair costs and occupancy interruption time. From these distributions, it is possible to extract the expected losses at various confidence levels. Further, it is possible to identify the most significant contributors to these losses, to guide design decisions intended to reduce the severity of assessed losses. The seismic performance of the structure should be verified for each limit state by ensuring that:

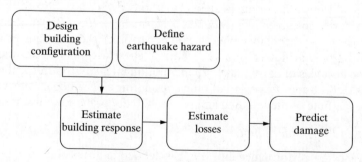

Figure 14.1   Performance assessment process.

$$PI_P > PI_R \qquad (14.1)$$

The seismic performance level of the structure should be evaluated as the ratio of PI_P to PI_R. The higher value of this ratio denotes the higher performance level. Following a performance assessment, the building's possessed performance is compared with the required performance indices. In some cases, it may not be possible to meet the stated PI_R at reasonable cost, in which case, some relaxation of the PI_R may be required. In other cases, it may be found that the building is inherently capable of performance superior to that required by the performance objectives. However, it may not be feasible to reduce its PI_P due to other design considerations. In such cases, the superior performance capability should be documented and accepted.

The difficulty with PBD is as follows:

Quantitative criteria:

- Sometimes difficult to develop
- Often difficult to achieve consensus

Evaluation procedures:

- Measurement is the key—it is essential to find a way to measure (analytically or experimentally) a meaningful quantity

14.3 ACCEPTABLE RISK IN AN EARTHQUAKE

The elements contributing to risk (chance of loss) are shown in Figure 14.2. In simple terms, they are understood as follows:

- *Hazards* physical effects generated in the naturally occurring event,
- *Location* of the hazards relative to the community at risk,
- *Exposure* the value and importance of the various types of structures and lifeline systems in the community, and
- *Vulnerability* of the exposed structures and systems to the hazards expected to affect them during their useful life.

Figure 14.2 Elements of risk.

What is an acceptable risk? It is a million dollar question. Defining acceptable risk is not easy because the risk that is acceptable to one person may be unacceptable to the other. Often a person's perception of an acceptable level of risk depends on whether or not the person believes he or she will be personally affected, and how much loss the person is willing to bear, as well as how much the person is willing to spend to avoid the risk.

ASCE 7 specifies minimum loads along with performance criteria for the design of new structures. It requires that buildings and other structures shall be classified, based on the risk to human life, health and welfare associated with their damage or failure by nature of their occupancy or use for the purposes of applying flood, wind, snow, earthquake and ice provisions. Each building or other structure should be assigned to the highest applicable risk category or categories. All buildings have been classified in four risk categories I (lowest risk), II, III and IV (highest risk). It requires that buildings assigned to risk categories III and IV have minimum strength, respectively, at least 125% or 150% of the strength required for buildings in lower risk categories.

ASCE 41 specifies detailed requirements for seismic rehabilitation of existing buildings. The earthquake hazard levels are shown in Table 14.1.

TABLE 14.1   EARTHQUAKE HAZARD LEVELS (ASCE 41)

Probability of Exceedance	Mean Return Period	Frequency
50%–50 year	72 years ≈ 75	Frequent
20%–50 year	225 years ≈ 250	Occasional
10%–50 year (BSE-1)	474 years ≈ 500	Rare
2%–50 years (BSE-2)	2475 years ≈ 2500	Very rare

Note: BSE Basic Service Earthquake

14.4 REQUIREMENTS FOR SEISMIC REHABILITATION

Requirements for seismic rehabilitation of old buildings are as follows:

1. A seismic evaluation must be performed to identify deficiencies to be rehabilitated
2. Define the rehabilitation objective:
   (a) Earthquake hazard level
   (b) Target building performance level
   (c) Objective classification

14.4.1 Seismic Design Category

The 2009 NEHRP provisions and ASCE 41 have introduced the concept of seismic design category (SDC) to categorize structures according to the seismic risk they could pose. There are six SDCs ranging from A to F with structures posing minimal seismic risk assigned to SDC A and structures posing the highest seismic risk assigned to SDC F. Thus, as the SDC for a structure increases, so do the strength and detailing requirements and the cost of providing seismic resistance. Table 14.2 summarizes the potential seismic risk associated with buildings in the various seismic design categories and the primary protective measures required for structures in each of the categories.

TABLE 14.2   SEISMIC DESIGN CATEGORIES, RISK AND SEISMIC DESIGN CRITERIA

SDC	Building Type and Expected MMI	Seismic Criteria
A	Buildings located in regions having a very small probability of experiencing damaging earthquake effects	No specific seismic design requirements but structures are required to have complete lateral-force-resisting systems and to meet basic structural integrity criteria.
B	Structures of ordinary occupancy that could experience moderate (MMI VI) intensity shaking	Structures must be designed to resist seismic forces.
C	Structures of ordinary occupancy that could experience strong (MMI VII) and important structures that could experience moderate (MMI VI) shaking	Structures must be designed to resist seismic forces. Critical non-structural components must be provided with seismic restraint.
D	Structures of ordinary occupancy that could experience very strong shaking (MMI VIII) and important structures that could experience MMI VII shaking	Structures must be designed to resist seismic forces. Only structural systems capable of providing good performance are permitted. Special construction quality assurance measures are required.
E	Structures of ordinary occupancy located within a few kilometers of major active faults capable of producing MMI IX, or more intense shaking	Structures must be designed to resist seismic forces. Only structural systems that are capable of providing superior performance permitted. Many types of irregularities are prohibited.
F	Critically important structures located within a few kilometers of major active faults capable of producing MMI IX, or more intense shaking	Structures must be designed to resist seismic forces. Only structural systems capable of providing superior performance permitted are permitted.

14.4.2 Building Performance Objectives

A performance objective has two essential parts—a damage state and a level of seismic hazard. Seismic performance is described by designating the maximum allowable damage state (performance level) for an identified seismic hazard (earthquake ground motion). A performance objective may include consideration of damage states for several levels of ground motion and would then be termed a dual or multiple-level performance objective.

It may be further split into *structural performance level* and *non-structural performance level*. These may be specified independently; however, the combination of the two determines the overall *building performance level*. The base shear vs. roof displacement curve for a building is shown in Figure 14.3. It is also referred to as the capacity curve. Also shown on the same figure are the various damage states due to progressive increase in base shear. It is possible to relate these damage states to the performance levels of a building.

Structural performance levels are defined as:

- Immediate occupancy (SP-1): Limited structural damage with the basic vertical and lateral force resisting system retaining most of their pre-earthquake characteristics and capacities.
- Damage control (SP-2): A placeholder for a state of damage somewhere between immediate occupancy and life safety.
- Life safety (SP-3): Significant damage with some margin against total or partial collapse. Injuries may occur with the risk of life-threatening injury being low. Repair may not be economically feasible.
- Limited safety (SP-4): A placeholder for a state of damage somewhere between life safety and structural stability.
- Structural stability (SP-5): Substantial structural damage in which the structural system is on the verge of experiencing partial or total collapse. Significant risk of injury exists. Repair may not be technically or economically feasible.
- Not considered (SP-6): Placeholder for situations where only non-structural seismic evaluation or retrofit is performed.

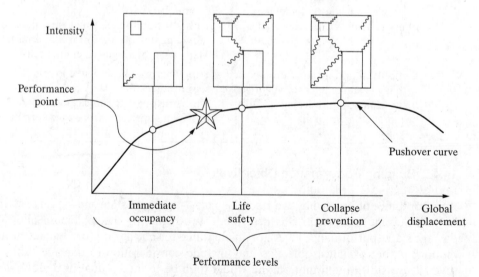

Figure 14.3   Building damage states.

Non-structural performance levels are defined as:

- Operational (NP-A): Non-structural elements are generally in place and functional. Back-up systems for failure of external utilities, communications and transportation have been provided.
- Immediate occupancy (NP-B): Non-structural elements are generally in place but may not be functional. No back-up systems for failure of external utilities are provided.
- Life safety (NP-C): Considerable damage to non-structural components and systems but no collapse of heavy items. Secondary hazards such as breaks in high-pressure, toxic or fire suppression piping should not be present.
- Reduced hazards (NP-D): Extensive damage to non-structural components but should not include collapse of large and heavy items that can cause significant injury to groups of people.
- Not considered (NP-E): Non-structural elements, other than those that have an effect on structural response, are not evaluated.

Combinations of structural and non-structural performance levels to obtain a building performance level are shown in Table 14.3.

TABLE 14.3 BUILDING PERFORMANCE LEVELS (ASCE 41)

Structural	Non-structural	Combined
(1) Immediate occupancy	(A) Operational	(1-A) Operational
(2) Damage control range	(B) Immediate occupancy	(1-B) Immediate occupancy
(3) Life safety	(C) Life safety	(3-C) Life safety
(4) Limited safety range	(D) Hazards reduced	(5-D) Hazards reduced
(5) Collapse prevention	(E) Not considered	

14.4.3 Rehabilitation Objectives

The rehabilitation objectives can be classified as follows:

Basic Safety Objective The basic safety objective (BSO) is a rehabilitation objective that achieves the dual rehabilitation goals of life safety building performance level (3-C) for the BSE-l earthquake hazard level and collapse prevention building performance level (5-E) for the BSE-2 earthquake hazard level. It is applicable to general structures such as an office building.

Enhanced Rehabilitation Objective Rehabilitation that provides building performance exceeding that of the BSO is termed an *enhanced objective*. Enhanced rehabilitation objectives should be achieved using one or both of the following two methods:

- By designing for target building performance levels that exceed those of the BSO at the BSE-I hazard level, the BSE-2 hazard level, or both.
- By designing for the target building performance levels of the BSO using an earthquake hazard level that exceeds either the BSE-I or BSE-2 hazard levels, or both.

It is applicable to emergent facilities.

Limited Rehabilitation Objective   Rehabilitation that provides building performance less than that of the BSO is termed a *limited objective*. It should comply with the following conditions:

- The rehabilitation measures should not result in a reduction in the performance level of the existing building;
- The rehabilitation measures should not create a new structural irregularity or make an existing structural *irregularity more severe*;
- The rehabilitation measures should not result in an *increase in the seismic forces to any component* that is deficient in capacity to resist such forces;
- All new or rehabilitated structural components should be detailed and connected to the existing structure in compliance with the requirements of the code.

It is applicable to other less critical structures.

14.5 NONLINEAR PROCEDURES

A nonlinear analysis of a building can be carried out either statically or dynamically. A set of several earthquake records are required in order to carry out dynamic analysis using the time-history method. It is a very tedious process but it is more accurate. ASCE 7, Eurocode 8-Part 1, NZS 1170 Part 5 and many other codes specify detailed requirements for selecting recorded, simulated or artificial earthquakes for time-history dynamic analysis of structures.

It is convenient to carry out a nonlinear analysis under static conditions which avoids the use of accelerograms. In a nonlinear static procedure (NSP), the basic *demand and capacity* parameter for the analysis is the lateral displacement of the building. It is possible to idealize a MDOF system as an equivalent SDOF system in terms of this *target displacement*. The equal displacement approximation estimates that the inelastic displacement is the same which would occur if the structure remained fully elastic. The target displacement is dependent on the level of seismic activity expected at the site, type of soil, effective mass in the first mode, and amount of viscous damping of the structure. Many methods are available to obtain this target displacement by carrying out a static nonlinear analysis.

An idealized force versus deformation relationship for specifying the force and deformation parameters of nonlinear component models is shown in Figure 14.4(a). These points include: effective yield (point B), peak strength (point C), residual strength (point D) and ultimate deformation (point E). Segment A-B represents elastic region; segment B-C represents strain-hardening region; segment C-D represents loss of strength, which may be sudden or in some cases somewhat gradual; segment D-E represents substantially reduced strength. In some cases, it may be convenient to make use of force–deformation relation as shown in Figure 14.4(a), while in some cases, it may be convenient to use normalized force-deformation curve as shown in Figure 14.4(b). The acceptance criteria for deformation or deformation ratios for

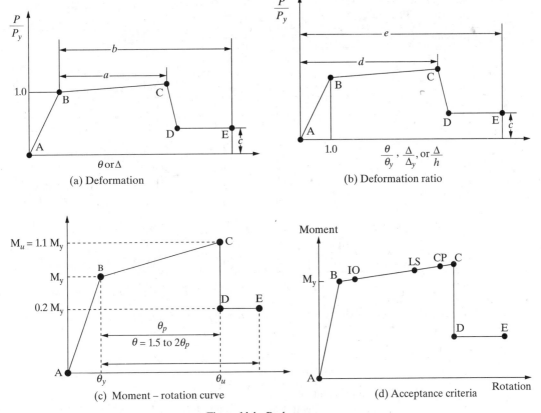

Figure 14.4   Pushover curve.

primary components (P) and secondary components (S) corresponding to the target building performance levels of collapse prevention (CP), life safety (LS) and immediate occupancy (IO) are as shown in Figure 14.4(c) and (d). The coordinates of the control points and details of the acceptance criteria are defined in FEMA 356 and FEMA 440, as well as in ASCE 41 (2007) for various types of structures. Typical values for reinforced concrete beams controlled by flexure are shown in Table 14.4 with respect to Figures 14.4(a) and 14.4(d) in accordance with FEMA 356. The ductility demand classification is shown in Table 14.5.

Some of the idealized hysteresis models shown in Figure 14.5 can be used under monotonic static loading. Figure 14.5(a) represents a ductile material with post-yield residual strength with ability to support gravity loads at point 3. Primary component actions exhibiting this behaviour are classified as deformation-controlled if the strain-hardening or softening range is such that $e \geq 2g$; otherwise they will be classified as force-controlled. Secondary component actions exhibiting this behaviour will always be classified as deformation-controlled, irrespective of e/g ratio. Figure 14.5(b) represents a ductile material without post-yield residual strength without any ability to support gravity loads. Both primary and secondary actions exhibiting this behaviour will be classified as deformation-controlled provided the plastic range is such that

TABLE 14.4 MODELLING PARAMETERS AND ACCEPTANCE CRITERIA FOR RC BEAMS CONTROLLED BY FLEXURE (FEMA 356)

Conditions			Modelling Parameters			Acceptance Criteria		
			Plastic Rotation Angle, Radians		Residual Strength Ratio	Plastic Rotation, Radian Performance Level		
$\dfrac{\rho-\rho'}{\rho_{bal}}$	Trans. Reinf.	$\dfrac{V}{b_w d\sqrt{f'_c}}$	a	b	c	IO	LS	CP
≤ 0	C	≤ 3	0.025	0.05	0.2	0.01	0.02	0.025
≤ 0	C	≥ 6	0.02	0.04	0.2	0.005	0.01	0.02
≥ 5	C	≤ 3	0.02	0.03	0.2	0.005	0.01	0.02
≥ 5	C	≥ 6	0.015	0.02	0.2	0.005	0.005	0.015
≤ 0	NC	≤ 3	0.02	0.03	0.2	0.005	0.01	0.02
≤ 0	NC	≥ 6	0.01	0.015	0.2	0.0015	0.005	0.01
≥ 5	NC	≤ 3	0.01	0.015	0.2	0.005	0.01	0.01
≥ 5	NC	≥ 6	0.005	0.010	0.2	0.0015	0.005	0.005

$C = Conforming,$ within the plastic hinge region, the stirrups are closely spaced,
$NC = Non\text{-}conforming,$ otherwise
ρ = tension steel ratio; ρ' = compression steel ratio; ρ_{bal} = Reinforcement ratio producing balanced strain conditions.

TABLE 14.5 DUCTILITY DEMAND CLASSIFICATION (FEMA 356)

Maximum Value of Displacement Ductility	Ductility Demand
< 2	Low
2 to 4	Moderate
>4	High

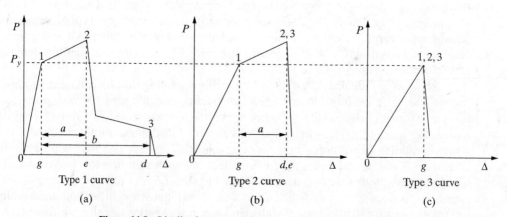

Figure 14.5 Idealized monotonic hysteresis models (ASCE 41-2007).

Figure 14.6   A beam element with point plastic hinges.

$e \geq 2g$; otherwise, they will be classified as force-controlled. Figure 14.5(c) represents a brittle material. They lose strength and ability to support gravity loads beyond point 1. Primary and secondary component actions displaying Type 3 behavior will be classified as force-controlled.

A NSP can be applied either force-controlled or displacement-controlled depending upon the interest in the strain-hardening behaviour. A displacement con- trolled analysis will provide a much better strain hardening response. In modelling the hysteretic properties of actual elements for analysis, the initial stiffness, strength and post-yield force-displacement response of cross-sections should be determined based on principles of mechanics and/or experimental data, considering influences of cyclic loading and interaction of axial, shear and flexural effects. ASCE 41 (2007) pro- vides guidelines for estimation of stiffness, strength and deformation limits in steel and reinforced concrete members; base isolators and energy dissipation components of moment frames, braced frames, shear walls, diaphragms, infills and foundations.

A beam element is modelled as shown in Figure 14.6. The beam–column joint region is modelled as a rigid link. A plastic hinge is modelled as a discrete point. Any of the appropriate hysteresis models discussed so far can be embedded in the point hinge. Moment-rotation or moment-curvature curve properties are computed at each end of a member and assigned to each hinge.

All plastic deformations, whether it be displacement or rotation, occur within the point hinge. It means there is a need to assume a length for the hinge over which the plastic strain or plastic curvature is integrated. There is no easy way to choose this length, although guide lines are available in FEMA356 and other documents. Typically, it is a fraction of the element length and quite often taken as equal to 0.5 D to D of the section or 0.1L. Plastic hinge rotation capacities can be calculated as follows:

First, estimate yield and ultimate curvatures ϕ_y and ϕ_u using the material nonlin- ear stress–strain curves. Then, plastic hinge rotation capacity is given as:

$$\theta_p = (\phi_u - \phi_y)\, l_p \tag{14.2}$$

where l_p is length of plastic hinge.

A column is also modeled in a similar manner. However, an interaction diagram is introduced. Beam-column joints are treated as rigid. Walls are modelled as beam- columns, and a shear hinge may be introduced at its mid height to simulate a shear plastic hinge. For elastic portions, cracked stiffness is assigned.

14.5.1 Performance Point

The generation of a capacity curve as shown in Figure 14.3 or 14.4(a) defines the capacity of the building for an assumed force distribution and displacement pattern. It is independent of any specific seismic shaking demand and replaces the base shear capacity of conventional design procedures. If the building displaces laterally, its response must lie on this capacity curve. A point on the curve defines a specific damage state for the structure because the deformation for all components can be related to the global displacement of the structure. By correlating this capacity curve to the seismic demand generated by a given earthquake, a point can be found on the capacity curve that estimates the maximum displacement of the building the earthquake will cause. This defines the performance point or target displacement. The location of this performance point relative to the performance levels defined by the capacity curve indicates whether or not the performance objective is met. It is presumed that the target displacement would be the actual displacement obtained if the MDOF system was subjected to nonlinear analysis with a real earthquake.

The next step is to estimate the ductility demand and capacity in each element corresponding to this target displacement and assess its state of plastification in accordance with the pushover curve in Figure 14.4(d). This will help decide the need and scheme of strengthening or retrofitting a structure.

14.6 STRESS–STRAIN CURVE FOR CONCRETE SECTION

The stress–strain curve of concrete depends on whether it is unconfined or confined. Different investigators have proposed different stress–strain distributions based on extensive experimental data. Most building codes specify unconfined stress–strain curve for concrete usually up to 0.35% strain. Eurocode 2-Part 1 specifies both unconfined as well as confined stress–strain curves for concrete but without the descending branch.

Kent and Park Curve

The idealized stress–strain curve due to Kent and Park is given in Figure 14.7(a). The various notations are as follows:

ε_0 = strain corresponding to maximum compressive strength in unconfined concrete
= 0.002

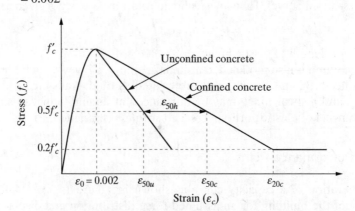

Figure 14.7(a)   Stress–strain curves of concrete for unconfined and confined states—proposed by Kent and Park (1971).

ε_{50u} = strain corresponding to the stress equal to 50% of the maximum concrete strength for unconfined concrete

ε_{20u} = strain corresponding to the stress equal to 20% of the maximum concrete strength for unconfined concrete

f_c' = compressive cylinder strength of unconfined concrete

In this model, the ascending branch is defined as follows:

$$f_c = f_c'\left[\frac{2\varepsilon_c}{\varepsilon_0} - \left(\frac{\varepsilon_c}{\varepsilon_0}\right)^2\right]$$ (14.3)

The post-peak branch was assumed to be a straight line whose slope was given by

$$f_c = f_c'\left[1 - Z(\varepsilon_c - \varepsilon_0)\right]$$ (14.4)

where

$$Z = \frac{0.5}{\varepsilon_{50u} - \varepsilon_0}$$ (14.5)

Mander Curve Mander et al. (1988) proposed stress–strain curves for both unconfined and confined concrete as shown in Figure 14.7(b). The initial ascending curve may be represented by the same equation for both the confined and unconfined model because the confining steel has no effect in this range of strains. As the curve approaches the compressive strength of the unconfined concrete, the unconfined stress begins to fall to an unconfined strain level before rapidly degrading to zero at the spalling strain ε_{sp} (≈ 0.005). The confined concrete model continues to ascend until the confined compressive strength f_{cc}' is reached. This segment is followed by a descending curve depending on the type and arrangement of the confining steel. The ultimate strain ε_{cu} should be the point where strain energy equilibrium is reached between the concrete and the confinement steel.

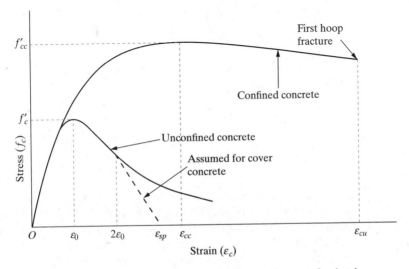

Figure 14.7(b)   Stress–strain curves of concrete for unconfined and confined state—proposed by Mander et. al. (1988).

For unconfined concrete,

$$\frac{f_c}{f_c'} = \frac{n\left(\dfrac{\varepsilon_c}{\varepsilon_0}\right)}{(n-1)+\left(\dfrac{\varepsilon_c}{\varepsilon_0}\right)^n} \tag{14.6}$$

$$n = \frac{E_c}{E_c - E_{sec}} \tag{14.7}$$

$$E_{sec} = \frac{f_c'}{\varepsilon_0} \tag{14.8}$$

where

f_c' = compressive cylinder strength of unconfined concrete
ε_0 = strain at the compressive strength of unconfined concrete, f_c'
ε_{sp} = spalling strain = 0.005

For confined concrete,

$$\frac{f_c}{f_{cc}'} = \frac{n\left(\dfrac{\varepsilon_c}{\varepsilon_{cc}}\right)}{(n-1)+\left(\dfrac{\varepsilon_c}{\varepsilon_{cc}}\right)^n} \tag{14.9}$$

$$E_{sec} = \frac{f_{cc}'}{\varepsilon_{cc}} \tag{14.10}$$

$$f_{cc}' = f_c'\left[2.254\sqrt{1+\frac{7.94 f_l'}{f_c'}} - \frac{2 f_l'}{f_c'} - 1.254\right] \tag{14.11}$$

$$\varepsilon_{cc} = \varepsilon_0\left[5\left(\frac{f_{cc}'}{f_c'} - 1\right)+1\right] \tag{14.12}$$

The effective confining lateral pressure is given by

$$f_l' = f_l k_e \tag{14.13a}$$

$$k_e = \frac{A_e}{A_{cc}} \tag{14.13b}$$

$$A_{cc} = A_c(1-\rho_{cc}) \tag{14.13c}$$

where

f_{cc}' = compressive cylinder strength of confined concrete
f_l' = effective lateral confining pressure
f_l = lateral pressure from the transverse reinforcement assumed to be uniformly distributed over the surface of the concrete core
f_{yh} = yield strength of transverse reinforcement (hoop)
ε_{cc} = strain at the compressive strength of confined concrete, f_{cc}'

ϵ_{cu} = ultimate strain in concrete

E_c = tangent modulus of elasticity of concrete

E_{sec} = secant modulus of elasticity, that is, slope of the line connecting the origin and peak stress on the compressive stress–strain curve

k_e = confinement effectiveness coefficient

A_e = area of effectively confined concrete core

A_{cc} = area of concrete within the centre lines of perimeter spiral or hoop

A_c = area of core of section enclosed by the centre lines of the perimeter spiral or hoop

ρ_{cc} = ratio of area of longitudinal reinforcement to area of core section

For circular ties or hoops (Figure 14.8)

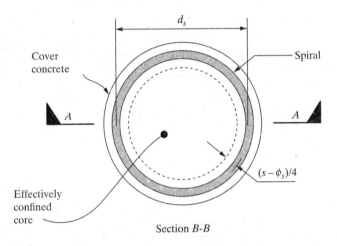

Section B-B

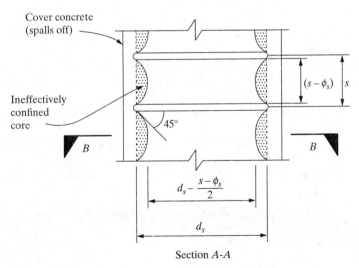

Section A-A

Figure 14.8   Effectively confined core with circular hoop (Mander et al. 1988).

$$A_e = \frac{\pi}{4}\left(d_s - \frac{s-\phi_s}{2}\right)^2 \tag{14.14a}$$

$$A_{cc} = \frac{\pi}{4}d_s^2\left(1-\rho_{cc}\right) \tag{14.14b}$$

or,
$$k_e = \frac{\left(1-\dfrac{s-\phi_s}{2d_s}\right)^2}{1-\rho_{cc}} \tag{14.14c}$$

The effective confining lateral pressure is given by

$$f_l' = f_l k_e \tag{14.13a}$$

where

   d_s = diameter of spiral between bar centres, that is, centre to centre of hoop
   s = spacing of circular hoops along longitudinal direction
   ϕ_s = diameter of ties or hoop

For spiral reinforcement

$$f_l' = k_e \rho_s f_{yh}/2$$

$$k_e = \frac{\left(1-\dfrac{s-\phi_s}{2d_s}\right)}{1-\rho_{cc}} \tag{14.15}$$

$$\rho_s = \frac{(\pi d_s)a_{sp}}{\dfrac{\pi}{4}d_s^2 s} = \frac{4a_{sp}}{d_s s} = \frac{\pi\phi_s^2}{d_s s} \tag{14.16}$$

where ρ_s = ratio of volume of transverse confining steel to volume of confined concrete core in a length s

For rectangular hoops with or without cross-ties (Figure 14.9)

The circular ties and spiral in circular columns provide confinement to the concrete and thereby increases its strength and ultimate strain. The same effect is achieved in rectangular columns by making use of cross-ties in both x- and y-directions of the cross-section.

   The arching action is assumed to act in the form of a parabola with an initial tangent slope of 45°. Arching occurs vertically between layers of transverse hoops and horizontally between longitudinal bars. The area of a parabola containing the ineffectively confined concrete is given by $(w_i')^2/6$.

where w_i' = i^{th} clear distance between adjacent longitudinal bars

   The total plan area of ineffectively confined core concrete at the level of hoops when there are n longitudinal bars is given by

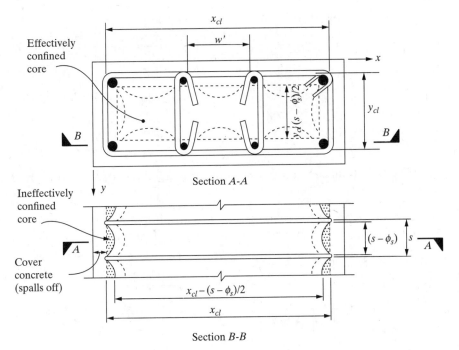

Figure 14.9   Effectively confined core with rectangular hoop (Mander et. al. 1988).

$$A_i = \sum_{i=1}^{n} (w_i')^2 / 6 \tag{14.17}$$

Similarly, the area of effectively confined concrete core at midway between the levels of transverse hoop reinforcement after excluding the ineffective area is given by

$$A_e = (A_{core} - A_i)\left(1 - \frac{s - \phi_s}{2x_{cl}}\right)\left(1 - \frac{s - \phi_s}{2y_{cl}}\right) \tag{14.18}$$

where

x_{cl} = core dimension to centre line of perimeter hoop in x-direction
y_{cl} = core dimension to centre line of perimeter hoop in y-direction

$$A_{core} = x_{cl} \times y_{cl} \tag{14.19}$$

The confinement effectiveness coefficient k_e can be computed using Equations (14.13b), (14.13c), (14.17) and (14.18).

In a rectangular section, it is quite likely that the transverse confining steel in the x- and y-directions is unequal. Thus,

$$p_{tx} = \frac{A_{tx}}{sy_{cl}} \quad \text{and} \quad p_{ty} = \frac{A_{ty}}{sx_{cl}} \tag{14.20}$$

where A_{tx} and A_{ty} = total area of transverse steel along x- and y-directions

The lateral confining stress on the concrete is given by

$$f_l = \frac{\text{total transverse bar force}}{\text{vertical area of confined concrete}}$$

or, along x-direction,

$$f_{lx} = \frac{A_{tx} f_{yh}}{s y_{cl}} = \frac{A_{tx}}{s y_{cl}} f_{yh} = p_{tx} f_{yh} \tag{14.21a}$$

and along y-direction,

$$f_{ly} = p_{ty} f_{yh} \tag{14.21b}$$

The effective lateral confining stress in the x- and $\acute{y}$-directions are given by Equation (14.13a).

Idealized Stress–Strain Curve for Steel   The idealized stress–strain curve for steel is shown in Figure 14.10. The various notations are as follows:

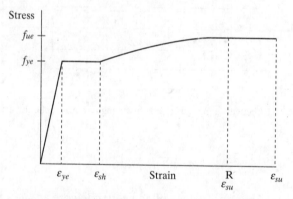

Figure 14.10   Idealized stress–strain curve for steel.

ϵ_y = nominal yield strain
ϵ_{ye} = expected yield strain in steel
ϵ_{sh} = onset of strain hardening
ϵ_{su} = strain at ultimate strength
ϵ_{su}^R = reduced ultimate strain
f_y = specified minimum yield strength
f_{ye} = expected yield strength of steel
f_u = specified minimum ultimate strength
f_{ue} = expected ultimate strength of steel

14.7 MOMENT-CURVATURE CURVE FOR CONCRETE SECTION

A moment-curvature analysis is carried out in order to generate load-deformation behaviour of a cross-section using nonlinear material stress–strain relationship. The procedure is general and can be used to generate the M-ϕ curve for a steel section or a concrete section. Presently, this method is being illustrated for a concrete section, which is more complex. Moment-curvature analysis derives the curvatures associated with a range of moments for a cross-section based on the principles of strain compatibility and equilibrium of forces.

Assumptions

The following assumptions are made:

- The strain diagram is assumed as linear at all stages of loading up to ultimate (*Bernoulli hypothesis*—for plane sections remaining plane).
- It is assumed that there is perfect bond between concrete and steel.
- The strength of concrete in tension is assumed to be zero.
- Axial force, if any, is applied at the centroid of the section.

Let us consider a cross-section of concrete as shown in Figure 14.11. It is assumed that its top face is in compression under the action of bending moment. The nonlinear stress–strain curves for both concrete and steel are known.

Basic steps to generate a moment-curvature curve can be summarized as follows:

Step 1: Divide a cross-section into a number of strips perpendicular to the axis of loading.

Step 2: Compute the area of unconfined cover concrete, confined core concrete and reinforcing steel in each strip.

Step 3: Choose an extreme fibre compression strain in concrete starting with a lowest value, say, $0.0005 < \varepsilon_{cu}$

Step 4: Assume a value for the depth of neutral axis Nd from the extreme compression edge.

Step 5: Find the strain at the centre of each strip in concrete and steel, and thus compute stresses in concrete and steel from their stress–strain curves.

Step 6: Determine the force of compression in concrete and steel and force of tension in steel.

The force in concrete can be evaluated by integrating numerically under the concrete stress-distribution curve. The relationship between concrete compressive stress

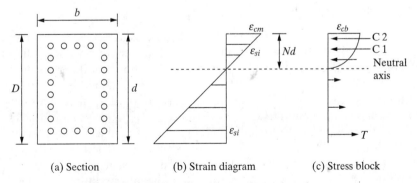

(a) Section   (b) Strain diagram   (c) Stress block

Figure 14.11   Section of concrete under strain and stress.

distribution and concrete strain may be assumed to be rectangular, trapezoidal, parabolic or any other shape that results in prediction of strength in substantial agreement with test results.

$$N = \int \sigma_{cb} b \, dy + \sum \sigma_{si} A_{si}$$ (14.22a)

where

N = axial force in the section

A_{si} = total area of steel in i^{th} strip

Step 7: Check equilibrium of forces, that is,

$$N = 0$$ (14.22b)

or, $N \leq$ acceptable tolerance   (14.22c)

If Equation (14.22) is not satisfied, adjust the depth of neutral axis until the above equilibrium condition is satisfied. This will give the accurate depth of neutral axis.

Step 8: The curvature can be computed as follows:

$$\phi = \frac{\varepsilon_{cm}}{Nd}$$ (14.23)

where

$\in_{cm}$ = maximum strain in extreme fibre of concrete chosen in Step 1

Nd = depth of neutral axis

Step 9: Taking moments of the stress resultants about the centroid of the section

$$M = F_{cb} z_1 + \sum F_{si} z_i$$ (14.24a)

or, $$M = \int \sigma_{cl} b y \, dy + \sum \sigma_{si} A_{si} y_i$$ (14.24b)

where

z_1 = distance of the point of application of the force of compression in concrete from the reference axis

z_i = distance of the point of application of the force in steel in i-layer from the reference axis

Step 10: Increment the extreme fiber compression stain and repeat Steps 1 to 9.
Step 11: This process is continued until the extreme fibre compression strain reaches the ultimate strain in concrete.

The M-ϕ curve can be idealized with an elastic perfectly plastic response to estimate the plastic moment capacity of a member's cross-section. The elastic portion of the idealized curve should pass through the point marking the first reinforcing bar yield. The idealized plastic moment capacity is obtained by balancing the areas between the actual and the idealized M-ϕ curves beyond the first reinforcing bar yield point as shown in Figure 14.12.

In the design of reinforced concrete structures subjected to gravity and earthquake loads, it is essential to make use of strength reduction factors (0.67 and 1.5 on concrete and 1.15 on steel) in order to compute capacity of a section and arrive at a safe design. However, while determining moment–curvature relations in order to

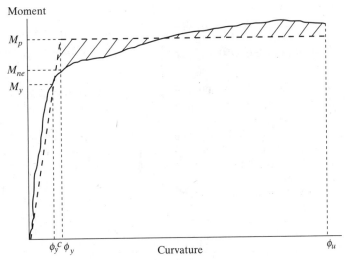

ϕ_y^c = computed curvature at the first yield of a reinforcing bar

Figure 14.12   Estimation of plastic moment capacity.

predict a plastic hinge and inelastic rotation, there is no need to make use of these strength reduction factors. The formation of a plastic hinge and its behaviour will be governed by its true material properties at a given section.

Example 14.1

Generate moment-curvature curve for a reinforced concrete unconfined section is shown in Figure 14.13.

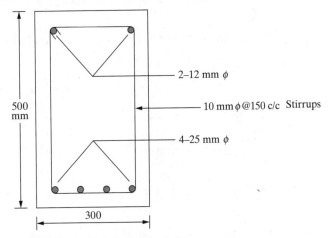

Figure 14.13   R.C. beam section.

Solution   Section properties:
breadth = 300 mm, depth = 500 mm, clear cover to stirrups = 25 mm

Concrete properties:

$$f_{ck} = 30 \text{ MPa}, \ f'_c = 25 \text{ MPa}, \ \varepsilon_0 = 0.002, \ \varepsilon_{cu} = 0.0035 \text{ and } E_c = 27400 \text{ MPa}$$

spalling strain = 0.0050

Reinforcing steel properties (hot rolled steel):
$f_y = 415 \text{ MPa}, E_s = 200000 \text{ MPa}, f_u = 460 \text{ MPa}, \varepsilon_u = 0.12, E_{sh} = 10000 \text{ MPa } (5\% \text{ of } E_s)$, diameter of longitudinal bars $\phi_L = 25$ mm, diameter of stirrups $\phi_T = 10$ mm and stirrup spacing $x = 150$ mm.

The basic relations for generating M-ϕ curve were discussed earlier. These equations were used to derive the moment-curvature curve shown in Figure 14.14. The iterations were done in Excel sheet. The final values of M and ϕ for a given strain level are illustrated in Table 14.6.

Idealized plastic moment = 326 kNm ☐

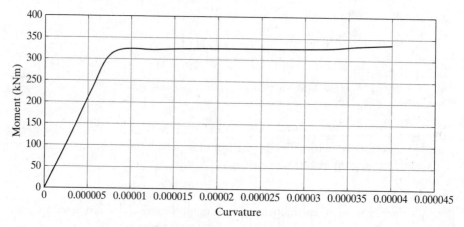

Figure 14.14 Moment-curvature curve.

TABLE 14.6 COMPUTED VALUES OF MOMENT AND CURVATURE

Strain	Depth of Neutral Axis mm	Moment kNm	Curvature
0	0	0	0
0.0005	174	123.3	0.000003
0.001	180	231.1	0.0000055
0.0015	183	315.9	0.000008
0.002	152	322.9	0.000013
0.0025	137	325.7	0.000018
0.003	128	326.2	0.000023
0.0035	123	326.4	0.000028
0.004	122	327.9	0.000033
0.0045	124	332.7	0.000036
0.005	126	336.4	0.00004

Example 14.2

Generate a moment-curvature curve for a concrete section shown in Figure 14.15 using the Mander model for confined concrete.

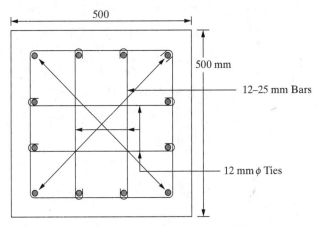

Figure 14.15   Cross section of a R.C. column.

Solution   Axial load in column = 1000 kN (assumed); axial load capacity = 4100 kN

Section properties:

Width = 500 mm, height = 500 mm, clear cover to ties = 40 mm

Concrete properties:

$f_{ck} = 30$ MPa, $E_c = 27400$ MPa

Reinforcing steel properties:

$f_y = 415$ MPa, $E_s = 200000$ MPa, $f_u = 550$ MPa, $\epsilon_u = 0.09$, $\epsilon_{sh} = 0.0105$, $E_{sh} = 10000$ MPa, $f_{yh} = 415$ MPa, diameter of longitudinal bars $\phi_L = 25$ mm, diameter of stirrups $\phi_T = 12$ mm and stirrup spacing $s = 100$ mm.

Mander concrete model

Unconfined strain = 0.002; Unconfined stress = 25 MPa (Cylinder);
Ultimate strain = 0.02051

Ultimate stress = 25 MPa; Spalling strain = 0.005; Confined stress = 35.7 MPa

If A_{shx} is the total amount of lateral reinforcement in a hoop layer crossing a section perpendicular to y-axis, then the maximum effective confining stress that can be developed in that direction is given by

$$f'_{lx} = f_{lx}k_e \tag{14.13a}$$

$$f_{lx} = p_{tx}f_{yh} \tag{14.21a}$$

∴ $$f'_{lx} = p_{tx}f_{yh}k_e \tag{14.25}$$

For the square cross-section considered in this example:
Effective cover to centre line of the tie (hoop) = 40 + 12/2 = 46 mm
Effective cover to centre of longitudinal bars = 40 + 12 + 25/2 = 64.5 mm
$s = 100$ mm c/c

Distance between two longitudinal bars = $(500 - 40 - 12 - 40 - 12 - 25)/3 = 123.7$ mm c/c

$$\therefore \qquad w_i = 123.7 - 25 = 98.7 \text{ mm clear}$$

$$A_i = 12 \times 98.7^2/6 = 19480 \text{ mm}^2$$

$$A_{core} = x_{cl} \times y_{cl} = (500 - 46) \times (500 - 46) = 206116 \text{ mm}^2$$

Net area of concrete $A_{cc} = A_{core} - A_t = 206116 - 12 \times 490 = 200236 \text{ mm}^2$

$$A_e = \left(A_{core} - A_i\right)\left(1 - \frac{s - \phi_T}{2x_{cl}}\right)\left(1 - \frac{s - \phi_T}{2y_{cl}}\right)$$

$$\therefore \qquad A_e = (206116 - 19480) \times (1 - (100 - 12)/(2 \times 454))$$

$$\times (1 - (100 - 12)/(2 \times 454)) = 152240 \text{ mm}^2$$

$$K_e = \frac{A_e}{A_{cc}} = 0.76$$

Total area of lateral steel in x-direction $= 4 \times 113 = 452 \text{ mm}^2$

$$p_{tx} = \frac{A_{tx}}{sy_{cl}} = \frac{452}{100 \times (500 - 46)} = 0.00996$$

The effective confining lateral pressure can be computed using Equation (14.25).

$$f'_{lx} = p_{tx} f_{yh} k_e = 0.00996 \times 415 \times 0.76 = 3.14 \text{ MPa}$$

The M-ϕ curve is shown in Figure 14.16.

Idealized plastic moment = 591 kNm

Yield curvature = 0.0000109; ultimate curvature = 0.000113 □

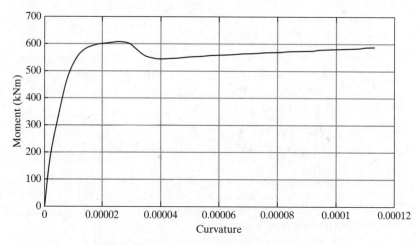

Figure 14.16 Moment-curvature curve.

14.8 AXIAL FORCE–MOMENT INTERACTION CURVES FOR CONCRETE

The axial force–moment interaction curves for a concrete section can be generated using a procedure similar to that used for generating moment–curvature curves. The first five steps remain same. The other steps are as follows:

Step 6: Compute axial force in the section using Equation (14.22a).

Step 7: The moment corresponding to this axial force can be computed using Equation (14.24).

Step 8: Increment the extreme fibre compression strain and repeat steps 1 to 7.

Step 9: This process is continued until the extreme fibre compression strain reaches the ultimate strain of concrete.

The detailed procedure for generating P-M3 or P-M2-M3 curves can be found in any book on reinforced concrete which is required for the design of columns.

14.9 ACCELERATION-DISPLACEMENT RESPONSE SPECTRA (ADRS)

The response spectra discussed in Chapter 8 was plotted in spectral acceleration vs. period format or in a tripartite graph format for a given damping. This response spectra is also referred to as the *demand spectra*. The base shear vs. roof displacement curve for the given structure when subjected to a given set of static forces is referred to as the *pushover curve* or *capacity curve* or *capacity spectra*. Now the question is how to assess demand vs. capacity for the given structure? This can be done only when both the demand and capacity spectra are plotted on a common graph or format. This created a need to develop an alternative format. The concept of tripartite graph provided the hint. It was possible to plot both the demand response curves and capacity (or pushover) curves in the spectral acceleration vs. spectral displacement domain. The curves plotted in this format are known as *acceleration–displacement response spectra* (ADRS) and can be plotted in elastic domain or inelastic domain.

14.9.1 Elastic A–D Response Spectra

Every point on a demand or response spectrum curve has associated with it a unique spectral acceleration S_a, spectral velocity S_v, spectral displacement S_d for a given period T. To convert a demand spectrum from the standard S_a (spectra acceleration) vs. T (period) format (Figure 14.17(a)) found in the building codes to A–D format, it is necessary to determine the value of S_{di} (spectral displacement) for each point on the curve (S_{ai}, T_i) as shown in Figure 14.17. This can be done using the equation:

$$S_{di} = \frac{T_i^2}{4\pi^2} S_{ai} g \tag{14.26}$$

Spectral acceleration and displacement at period T_i are given by:

$$S_{ai} g = \frac{2\pi}{T_i} S_v \quad \text{and} \quad S_{di} = \frac{T_i}{2\pi} S_v \tag{14.27}$$

For a given T_i and S_{ai}, it was possible to compute S_{di} and plot as shown in Figure 14.17(b). The lines radiating from the origin have constant periods. This spectra is known as the acceleration displacement response spectra.

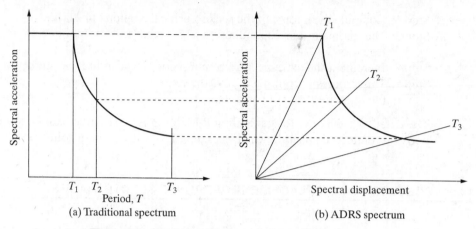

Figure 14.17 Traditional spectrum vs. ADRS spectrum.

Representation of capacity spectrum in A–D format The capacity of a given building and the demand imposed upon it by a given earthquake are not independent. One source of this mutual dependence is evident from the capacity curve itself. As the demand increases, the structure eventually yields and, as its stiffness decreases, its period elongates. As the seismic accelerations depend on period of the structure, the demand also changes as the structure yields. Another source of mutual dependence between capacity and demand is effective damping. As a building yields in response to seismic demand, it dissipates energy with hysteretic damping. Buildings that have large stable hysteresis loops during cyclic yielding dissipate more energy than those with pinched loops caused by degradation of strength and stiffness. This effective damping reduces displacement demand.

The capacity spectrum can be developed from the pushover curve by a point by point conversion to the first mode spectral coordinates. Any point V_i (Base Shear), δ_i (Roof Displacement) on the capacity (pushover) curve is converted to the corresponding point S_{ai}, S_{di} on the capacity spectrum using the equations:

$$V_b = \alpha_h W = \alpha_1 S_{ai} W$$

or,

$$S_{ai} = \frac{V_i / W}{\alpha_1} \qquad (14.28)$$

$$S_{di} = \frac{\delta_{roof}}{MPF_1 \times \phi_{1,roof}} \qquad (14.29)$$

and,

$$T = 2\pi \sqrt{\frac{S_d}{S_a}} \qquad (14.30)$$

where α_1 = modal mass coefficient for the first mode
MPF_1 = modal participation factor for the first mode
δ_i = roof displacement
$\phi_{1,roof}$ = mode shape at roof level in the first mode

The capacity spectrum conversion analogy is shown in Figure 14.18.

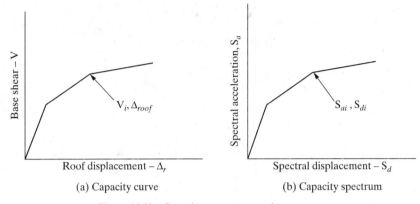

(a) Capacity curve

(b) Capacity spectrum

Figure 14.18   Capacity curve vs. capacity spectrum.

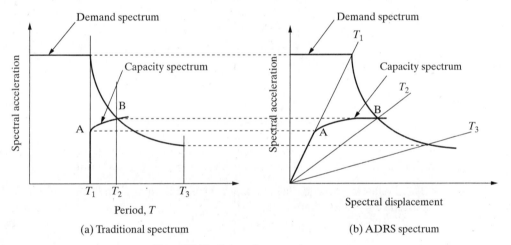

(a) Traditional spectrum

(b) ADRS spectrum

Figure 14.19   Demand vs. capacity spectrum.

The capacity spectrum is superimposed over response spectra in ADRS format in Figure 14.19. The point of intersection of demand spectrum and capacity spectrum is located. This point establishes the performance point or *target displacement*. As stated earlier, there are many methods to locate the target displacement.

14.9.2 Inelastic A–D Response Spectra

The inelastic A–D response spectra can be generated as follows:

Step 1: First generate the elastic response spectrum for a given damping using the Newmark–Hall procedure. This will provide spectral acceleration vs. period response spectrum.

Step 2: The Newmark and Hall procedure suggested reduction factors as a function of ductility for acceleration, or velocity-sensitive regions. These are as follows:

$$R = 1 \qquad \text{for} \quad T < T_A \tag{14.31a}$$

$$R = (2\mu - 1)^{\gamma/2} \qquad \text{for} \quad T_A < T < T_B \tag{14.31b}$$

or,

$$R = \sqrt{(2\mu - 1)^{\gamma}}$$

$$R = (2\mu - 1)^{0.5} \qquad \text{for} \quad T_B < T < T'_C \tag{14.31c}$$

$$R = (T/T_C)\mu \qquad \text{for} \quad T'_C < T < T_C \tag{14.31d}$$

$$R = \mu \qquad \text{for} \quad T > T_C \tag{14.31e}$$

The reduction factor for the transition zone A–B can be computed using the inclined line A–B in Figure 13.29 as given by Equation (14.31b). The exponent γ is given by

$$\gamma = \frac{\log\left(\dfrac{T}{T_A}\right)}{\log\left(\dfrac{T_B}{T_A}\right)} \tag{14.31f}$$

In these equations, the period T_C is the point of intersection of constant acceleration and constant velocity regions in the elastic domain. Equation (14.31c) is applicable where equal energy concept governs, while Equation (14.31e) is applicable where equal displacement concept governs. Using the appropriate reduction factors, spectral accelerations in different period ranges for a given ductility are obtained.

Step 3: The inelastic spectral displacement S_d is obtained using Equation (13.35) derived earlier in Chapter 13:

$$x_m = \mu x_0 \qquad \text{for} \quad T < T_A \tag{13.35a}$$

$$x_m = \mu x_0/R \qquad \text{for} \quad T_B < T < T_C \tag{13.35b}$$

$$x_m = x_0 \qquad \text{for} \quad T > T_C \tag{13.35c}$$

Let us replace the symbols x_0 by $S_{d\,\text{elastic}}$ and x_m by $S_{d\,\text{inelastic}}$ for convenience and re-write these equations. Equations (13.35a) and (13.35b) can be merged as shown in Equation (14.32a), where $R = 1$ for $T < T_A$.

$$S_{d\,\text{inelastic}} = \mu S_{d\,\text{elastic}}/R \qquad \text{for} \quad T < T_C \tag{14.32a}$$

$$S_{d\,\text{inelastic}} = S_{d\,\text{elastic}} \qquad \text{for} \quad T > T_C \tag{14.32b}$$

Step 4: Steps 2 and 3 are repeated for different values of ductility.

This inelastic ADRS can be used to estimate the target displacement for nonlinear pushover analysis.

The Eurocode 8-Part 1 has specified how to obtain target displacement in short period and medium to long period range using the acceleration displacement response spectrum (ADRS) in Appendix B. Unlike the Newmark–Hall approach, it divides the spectrum into two zones only: small period range $T < T_C$ and medium to long period range $T > T_C$.

$$R = (\mu - 1)T/T_C + 1 \qquad \text{for} \quad T < T_C \qquad\qquad (14.33a)$$

$$R = \mu \qquad\qquad\qquad \text{for} \quad T > T_C \qquad\qquad (14.33a)$$

where, T_C = point of intersection of constant acceleration and constant velocity regions of the elastic spectrum.

A schematic representation of nonlinear static procedure – pushover analysis is shown in Figure 14.20.

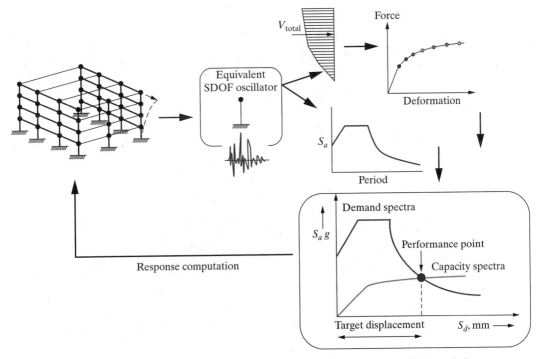

Figure 14.20   Schematic representation of nonlinear static procedure – pushover analysis.

14.9.3 Acceptance Criteria for Nonlinear Procedures

Primary and secondary components in a building must have expected deformation capacities not less than maximum deformation demands calculated at the target displacement. Primary and secondary component demands should be within the acceptance criteria for secondary components at the selected structural performance level. The strength ratio R calculated from the results of the nonlinear analysis must be less than R_{max}, that is,

$$R < R_{max} \tag{14.34}$$

where, R = ratio of elastic strength demand to yield strength demand, it is a measure of system ductility

R_{max} = maximum strength ratio that a building can have up to dynamic instability, it is a measure of system stability

Rehabilitation Options   Once the results of the nonlinear analysis are accepted, the next step is to choose a suitable strengthening or rehabilitation option. It may consist of one or more of the following:

- Addition of new concrete shear walls
- Addition of steel bracing
- Addition of energy dissipating device
  - (i) Fluid viscous dampers
  - (ii) Friction dampers
  - (iii) Tuned mass dampers
- Seismic base isolation
  - (i) Elastomeric bearings
  - (ii) High damping laminated rubber bearings.
- Use of fiber reinforced polymer (FRP) laminates to strengthen masonry, unreinforced clay tile or concrete members

The last option needs to be exercised very carefully after carrying out detailed testing.

14.10 ILLUSTRATIVE EXAMPLES

Example 14.3

Draw the response spectrum curves of IS:1893 code on hard soil for 2% and 5% damping in ADRS format.

Solution   The response spectra of IS:1893-Part 1 was presented in Chapter 8. It can be converted in ADRS format by the procedure outlined earlier using Equation (14.26) for a given damping.

$$S_{di} = \frac{T_i^2}{4\pi^2} S_{ai} g \tag{14.26}$$

Typical calculations are shown in Table 14.7. In the last five columns, spectral displacement has been computed for different periods ($T = 0.5, 1, 1.5, 2$ and 4 sec) corresponding to spectral accelerations for 2% damping. This data is used to plot constant period lines.

TABLE 14.7 CALCULATIONS FOR ADRS FOR IS:1893 SPECTRA

Period (T)	5% damping		2% damping		T = 0.5	T = 1	T = 1.5	T = 2	T = 4
	Acceleration (S_a/g)	Displacement (S_d)	Acceleration (S_a/g)	Displacement (S_d)	Displacement (S_d)	Displacement (S_d)	Displacement (S_d)	Displacement (S_d)	Displacement (S_d)
0	0.000	0.000	0.000	0.000	0	0	0	0	0
0.1	2.500	0.0062	3.500	0.0087	0.1555	0.6219	1.3992	2.4874	9.9497
0.2	2.500	0.0249	3.500	0.0348	0.1555	0.6219	1.3992	2.4874	9.9497
0.3	2.500	0.056	3.500	0.078	0.1555	0.6219	1.3992	2.4874	9.9497
0.4	2.500	0.099	3.500	0.139	0.1555	0.6219	1.3992	2.4874	9.9497
0.5	2.000	0.124	2.800	0.174	0.1244	0.4975	1.1193	1.9899	7.9598
0.6	1.667	0.149	2.333	0.209	0.1036	0.4146	0.9328	1.6583	6.6331
0.7	1.429	0.174	2.000	0.244	0.0888	0.3553	0.7995	1.4214	5.6855
0.8	1.250	0.199	1.750	0.279	0.0777	0.3109	0.6996	1.2437	4.9748
0.9	1.111	0.224	1.556	0.313	0.0691	0.2764	0.6219	1.1055	4.4221
1	1.000	0.249	1.400	0.348	0.0622	0.2487	0.5597	0.9950	3.9799
1.1	0.909	0.274	1.273	0.383	0.0565	0.2261	0.5088	0.9045	3.6181
1.2	0.833	0.298	1.167	0.418	0.0518	0.2073	0.4664	0.8291	3.3166
1.3	0.769	0.323	1.077	0.453	0.0478	0.1913	0.4305	0.7654	3.0614
1.4	0.714	0.348	1.000	0.488	0.0444	0.1777	0.3998	0.7107	2.8428
1.5	0.667	0.373	0.933	0.522	0.0415	0.1658	0.3731	0.6633	2.6533
1.6	0.625	0.398	0.875	0.557	0.0389	0.1555	0.3498	0.6219	2.4874
1.7	0.588	0.423	0.824	0.592	0.0366	0.1463	0.3292	0.5853	2.3411
1.8	0.556	0.448	0.778	0.627	0.0345	0.1382	0.3109	0.5528	2.2110
1.9	0.526	0.473	0.737	0.662	0.0327	0.1309	0.2946	0.5237	2.0947
2	0.500	0.497	0.700	0.696	0.0311	0.1244	0.2798	0.4975	1.9899

(Continued)

TABLE 14.7 (CONTINUED)

Period (T)	5% damping Acceleration (S_a/g)	5% damping Displacement (S_d)	2% damping Acceleration (S_a/g)	2% damping Displacement (S_d)	T = 0.5 Displacement (S_d)	T = 1 Displacement (S_d)	T = 1.5 Displacement (S_d)	T = 2 Displacement (S_d)	T = 4 Displacement (S_d)
2.1	0.476	0.522	0.667	0.731	0.0296	0.1184	0.2665	0.4738	1.8952
2.2	0.455	0.547	0.636	0.766	0.0283	0.1131	0.2544	0.4523	1.8090
2.3	0.435	0.572	0.609	0.801	0.0270	0.1081	0.2433	0.4326	1.7304
2.4	0.417	0.597	0.583	0.836	0.0259	0.1036	0.2332	0.4146	1.6583
2.5	0.400	0.622	0.560	0.871	0.0249	0.0995	0.2239	0.3980	1.5920
2.6	0.385	0.647	0.538	0.905	0.0239	0.0957	0.2153	0.3827	1.5307
2.7	0.370	0.672	0.519	0.940	0.0230	0.0921	0.2073	0.3685	1.4740
2.8	0.357	0.696	0.500	0.975	0.0222	0.0888	0.1999	0.3553	1.4214
2.9	0.345	0.721	0.483	1.010	0.0214	0.0858	0.1930	0.3431	1.3724
3	0.333	0.746	0.467	1.045	0.0207	0.0829	0.1866	0.3317	1.3266
3.1	0.323	0.771	0.452	1.080	0.0201	0.0802	0.1805	0.3210	1.2838
3.2	0.313	0.796	0.438	1.114	0.0194	0.0777	0.1749	0.3109	1.2437
3.3	0.303	0.821	0.424	1.149	0.0188	0.0754	0.1696	0.3015	1.2060
3.4	0.294	0.846	0.412	1.184	0.0183	0.0732	0.1646	0.2926	1.1706
3.5	0.286	0.871	0.400	1.219	0.0178	0.0711	0.1599	0.2843	1.1371
3.6	0.278	0.895	0.389	1.254	0.0173	0.0691	0.1555	0.2764	1.1055
3.7	0.270	0.920	0.378	1.288	0.0168	0.0672	0.1513	0.2689	1.0756
3.8	0.263	0.945	0.368	1.323	0.0164	0.0655	0.1473	0.2618	1.0473
3.9	0.256	0.970	0.359	1.358	0.0159	0.0638	0.1435	0.2551	1.0205
4	0.250	0.995	0.350	1.393	0.0155	0.0622	0.1399	0.2487	0.9950

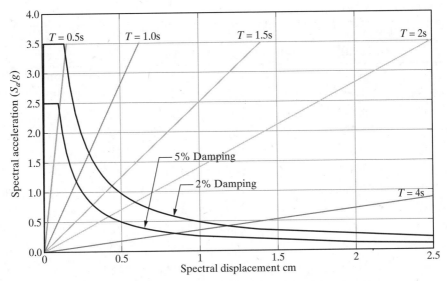

Figure 14.21   IS:1893 spectrum in ADRS format.

The ADRS spectrum curves for 2% and 5% damping are shown in Figure 14.21. The radial lines are constant period lines. ☐

Example 14.4

Construct an ADR spectrum for ductility ratio of 1, 1.5, 2, 4 and 6 for a ground motion having peak ground acceleration, peak ground velocity and peak ground displacement as 1 g, 90 cm/sec and 60 cm, respectively. Make use of Newmark–Hall amplification factors for 5% damping and 84.1 percentile.

Solution   The inelastic response spectra for this ground motion for ductility ratio of 1.5, 2, 4 and 6 were developed in Example 13.5. An alternative format was shown in Example 13.6. The same data was used to develop the ADRS. The reduction factor R depends upon the acceleration or velocity-sensitive regions given by Equation (14.31). The spectral displacements are computed using Equation (14.32). Typical calculations for generating inelastic ADRS are shown in Table 14.8. Similar calculations can be done for other ductility ratios. The double lines in the table show change in reduction factor region. The inelastic ADRS is shown in Figure 14.22. ☐

TABLE 14.8   CALCULATIONS FOR R, S_a AND S_d COORDINATES

$\mu = 1$			$\mu = 1.5$			$\mu = 2$		
S_a/g	$T(\text{sec})$	$S_d(\text{cm})$	R_y	S_a/g	$S_d(\text{cm})$	R_y	S_a/g	$S_d(\text{cm})$
1	0.01	0.002	1.00	1.00	0.00	1.00	1.00	0.00
1	0.03	0.022	1.00	1.00	0.03	1.00	1.00	0.04
2.71	0.125	1.053	1.41	1.92	1.12	1.73	1.56	1.22
2.71	0.2	2.696	1.41	1.92	2.86	1.73	1.56	3.11

(Continued)

TABLE 14.8 (CONTINUED)

S_a/g	$T(sec)$	$S_d(cm)$	R_y	S_a/g	$S_d(cm)$	R_y	S_a/g	$S_d(cm)$
	$\mu = 1$			$\mu = 1.5$			$\mu = 2$	
2.71	0.25	4.213	1.41	1.92	4.47	1.73	1.56	4.86
2.71	0.3	6.067	1.41	1.92	6.43	1.73	1.56	7.01
2.71	0.35	8.258	1.41	1.92	8.76	1.73	1.56	9.54
2.71	0.4	10.785	1.41	1.92	11.44	1.73	1.56	12.45
2.71	0.45	13.650	1.41	1.92	14.48	1.80	1.51	15.17
2.71	0.5	16.852	1.50	1.81	16.85	2.00	1.36	16.85
2.3	0.6	20.596	1.50	1.53	20.60	2.00	1.15	20.60
1.95	0.7	23.767	1.50	1.30	23.77	2.00	0.98	23.77
1.77	0.8	28.178	1.50	1.18	28.18	2.00	0.89	28.18
1.6	0.9	32.237	1.50	1.07	32.24	2.00	0.80	32.24
1.5	1	37.311	1.50	1.00	37.31	2.00	0.75	37.31
1	1.5	55.967	1.50	0.67	55.97	2.00	0.50	55.97
0.7	2	69.648	1.50	0.47	69.65	2.00	0.35	69.65
0.55	2.5	85.505	1.50	0.37	85.51	2.00	0.28	85.51
0.45	3	100.741	1.50	0.30	100.74	2.00	0.23	100.74

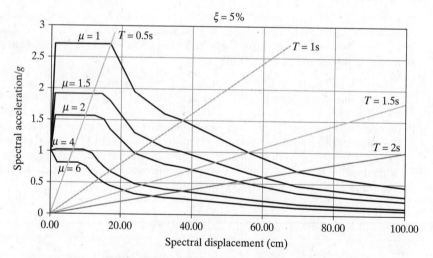

Figure 14.22 Inelastic spectra in ADRS format.

Example 14.5

A SDOF system has the following data:

Mass = 100 kg, Damping = 5%, Yield strength = 175 N
Maximum ground acceleration = 0.25 g
Locate the performance point using the ground motion of Example 14.4, if the period is
0.3 sec and capacity curve is bi-linear.

Solution   For $T = 0.3$ sec, stiffness = 43820 N/m

It is a short period system having $T = 0.3$ sec $< T_C = 0.5$ sec

Spectral acceleration corresponding to the ground motion with peak acceleration 1 g in Example 14.4 was 2.71 g. In the present case, the peak ground acceleration is 0.25 g.

∴ peak spectral acceleration = $0.25 \times 2.71 \times 9.81 = 6.65$ m/sec²

Elastic force = $100 \times 6.65 = 665$ N

Yield displacement = 0.004 m

The steps for locating the performance point are as follows:

Step 1: Plot the elastic spectral acceleration – spectral displacement curve for 5% damping using Equation (14.26) along with radial lines for $T = 0.3$ and 0.5 sec.

Step 2: Next, the capacity curve is plotted. The initial stiffness line is extended up to the demand curve with $\mu = 1$, which meets at point A.

Step 3: Knowing the spectral accelerations in elastic demand and capacity curves, estimate the reduction factor R.

$$R = 6.65/1.75 = 3.79$$

Step 4: The period 0.3 sec lies in the transition zone. Now compute ductility from

$$R = (T/T_C)\mu$$

or,

$$\mu = R/(T/T_C)$$

or,

$$\mu = (T_C/T)R$$

∴

$$\mu = (0.5/0.3)\ 3.79 = 6.32$$

Step 5: Compute R, S_a and S_d coordinates for ductility $\mu = 6.32$ using Equation (14.31) and (14.32). Now plot S_a vs S_d for $\mu = 6.32$. This demand curve will intersect the capacity curve at B. The point of intersection B is the target displacement equal to 0.0253 m. Again, target displacement corresponds to a ductility equal to

$$\mu = 0.0253/0.004 = 6.32 \qquad \text{OK}$$

Step 6: If this point of intersection B is joined with the point of intersection A between the elastic demand curve and period $T = 0.3$ sec as obtained in Step 1, an inclined line is obtained. It confirms that the inelastic and elastic displacements in the short period range are not equal.

Typical calculations are shown in Table 14.9. The double lines in the table show change in reduction factor R region. The performance point B is shown in Figure 14.23.   □

TABLE 14.9   CALCULATION FOR R, S_a AND S_d COORDINATES

$\mu = 1$ (1 g)		$\mu = 1$ (0.25 g)		$T = 0.3$	$T = T_C = 0.5$	$\mu = 6.32$		
S_a/g	T	S_a(m/s²)	S_d(m)	S_d(m)	S_d(m)	R	S_a(m/s²)	S_d(m)
1	0.01	2.45	0.0000	0.0056	0.0155	1.000	2.453	0.000
1	0.03	2.45	0.0001	0.0056	0.0155	1.000	2.453	0.000
2.71	0.125	6.65	0.0026	0.0152	0.0421	3.412	1.948	0.005
2.71	0.2	6.65	0.0067	0.0152	0.0421	3.412	1.948	0.012
2.71	0.3	6.65	0.0152	0.0152	0.0421	3.792	1.753	0.025
2.71	0.4	6.65	0.0270	0.0152	0.0421	5.056	1.315	0.034

(Continued)

TABLE 14.9   (CONTINUED)

| $\mu = 1$ (1 g) | | $\mu = 1$ (0.25 g) | | $T = 0.3$ | $T = T_c = 0.5$ | | $\mu = 6.32$ | |
S_a/g	T	$S_a(\text{m/s}^2)$	$S_d(\text{m})$	$S_d(\text{m})$	$S_d(\text{m})$	R	$S_a(\text{m/s}^2)$	$S_d(\text{m})$
2.71	0.5	6.65	0.0421	0.0152	0.0421	6.320	1.052	0.042
2.33	0.6	5.71	0.0522	0.0130	0.0362	6.320	0.904	0.052
1.83	0.8	4.49	0.0728	0.0102	0.0284	6.320	0.710	0.073
1.5	1	3.68	0.0933	0.0084	0.0233	6.320	0.582	0.093
1	1.5	2.45	0.1399	0.0056	0.0155	6.320	0.388	0.140
0.93	1.6	2.28	0.1481	0.0052	0.0145	6.320	0.361	0.148
0.81	1.8	1.99	0.1632	0.0045	0.0126	6.320	0.314	0.163
0.71	2	1.74	0.1766	0.0040	0.0110	6.320	0.276	0.177
0.55	2.5	1.35	0.2138	0.0031	0.0086	6.320	0.213	0.214
0.45	3	1.10	0.2519	0.0025	0.0070	6.320	0.175	0.252

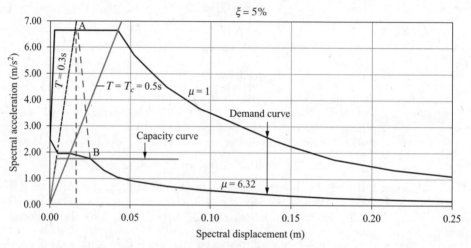

Figure 14.23   Performance point for a SDOF with $T = 0.3$ sec ($< T_c$).

Example 14.6

A SDOF system has the following data:

Mass = 100 kg, Damping = 5%, Yield strength = 197 N

Maximum ground acceleration = 0.25 g.

Locate the performance point using the ground motion of Example 14.4, if the period is 1 sec and capacity curve is bi-linear.

Solution

For $T = 1$ sec, stiffness = 3944 N/m

It is a medium period system having $T > T_c = 0.5$ sec

Spectral acceleration corresponding to the ground motion with peak acceleration 1 g in Example 14.4 was 2.71 g. In the present case, the maximum ground acceleration is 0.25 g.

∴ peak spectral acceleration = $0.25 \times 2.71 \times 9.81 = 6.65$ m/sec²

Elastic force = $100 \times 6.65 = 665$ N

Yield displacement = 0.05 m

The steps for locating the performance point are as follows:

Step 1: Plot the elastic spectral acceleration–spectral displacement curve for 5% damping using Equation (14.26) along with radial lines for $T = 1$ and 0.5 s.

Step 2: Next the capacity curve is plotted. The initial stiffness line is extended up to the demand curve with $\mu = 1$, which meets at point A.

Step 3: From the point of intersection A, draw a vertical. It intersects the capacity curve at B. The point of intersection gives the target displacement equal to 0.0933 m.

Step 4: Knowing the spectral accelerations in elastic and capacity curves, estimate the reduction factor R.

$$R = 3.68/1.97 = 1.87$$

Step 5: The period 1.0 sec lies beyond $T_C = 0.5$ sec. Now compute ductility from

$$R = \mu$$

or, $\qquad \mu = R = 1.87$

Step 6: Compute R, S_a and S_d coordinates for ductility $\mu = 1.87$ using Equation (14.31) and (14.32). Now plot S_a vs S_d for $\mu = 1.87$. This curve will intersect the capacity curve at the same point B as the point of intersection of the vertical line. It confirms that the elastic and inelastic displacements in this period range are equal.

Again, target displacement corresponds to a ductility equal to

$$\mu = 0.0933/0.050 = 1.866 \approx 1.87 \qquad \text{OK}$$

Typical calculations are shown in Table 14.10. The double lines in the table show change in reduction factor R region.

The location of performance point is shown in Figure 14.24. ☐

TABLE 14.10 CALCULATION FOR R, S_a AND S_d COORDINATES

$\mu = 1$ (1 g)		$\mu = 1$ (0.25 g)		$T = 1$	$T = T_C = 0.5$		$\mu = 1.87$	
S_a/g	T	S_a(m/s²)	S_d(m)	S_d(m)	S_d(m)	R	S_a	S_d
1	0.01	2.45	0.0000	0.0622	0.0155	1.00	2.453	0.000
1	0.03	2.45	0.0001	0.0622	0.0155	1.00	2.453	0.000
2.71	0.125	6.65	0.0026	0.1685	0.0421	1.65	4.022	0.003
2.71	0.2	6.65	0.0067	0.1685	0.0421	1.65	4.022	0.008
2.71	0.3	6.65	0.0152	0.1685	0.0421	1.65	4.022	0.017
2.71	0.4	6.65	0.0270	0.1685	0.0421	1.65	4.022	0.030
2.71	0.5	6.65	0.0421	0.1685	0.0421	1.87	3.563	0.042
2.33	0.6	5.71	0.0522	0.1449	0.0362	1.87	3.063	0.052
1.83	0.8	4.49	0.0728	0.1138	0.0284	1.87	2.406	0.073
1.5	1	3.68	0.0933	0.0933	0.0233	1.87	1.972	0.093
1	1.5	2.45	0.1399	0.0622	0.0155	1.87	1.315	0.140
0.93	1.6	2.28	0.1481	0.0578	0.0145	1.87	1.223	0.148
0.81	1.8	1.99	0.1632	0.0504	0.0126	1.87	1.065	0.163
0.71	2	1.74	0.1766	0.0442	0.0110	1.87	0.933	0.177
0.55	2.5	1.35	0.2138	0.0342	0.0086	1.87	0.723	0.214
0.45	3	1.10	0.2519	0.0280	0.0070	1.87	0.592	0.252

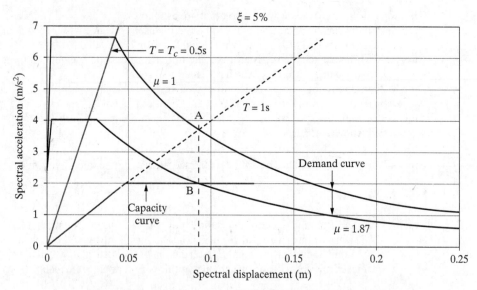

Figure 14.24 Performance point for a SDOF with $T = 1$ sec ($> T_c$).

Example 14.7

Construct an ADR spectrum for ductility ratio of $1, 2, 3, 4, 5$ and 6 for a ground motion having peak ground acceleration, peak ground velocity and peak ground displacement as $1g$, 90 cm/sec and 60 cm, respectively. For elastic response spectrum, make use of Newmark–Hall amplification factors for 5% damping and 84.1 percentile. For constant ductility spectra, make use of reduction factors as specified in the Appendix B, Eurocode 8-Part 1.

Solution

Plot the elastic spectral acceleration-spectral displacement curve for 5% damping using Equation (14.26) along with radial lines for $T = 0.5, 1, 1.5$ and 2 sec as in previous examples. The reduction factors for spectral accelerations specified in Eurocode 8 are as follows:

$$R = (\mu - 1)T/T_c + 1 \qquad \text{for} \qquad T < T_C \tag{14.33a}$$
$$R = \mu \qquad\qquad\qquad \text{for} \qquad T > T_C \tag{14.33a}$$

The spectral displacements are obtained using Equation (14.32). Typical calculations for generating inelastic ADRS are shown in Table 14.11. The double lines in the table show change in reduction factor R region. Similar calculations can be done for other ductility ratios.

The constant ductility ADRS is shown in Figure 14.25.   ☐

TABLE 14.11 CALCULATIONS FOR R, S_a AND S_d COORDINATES

$\mu = 1$ (1 g)			$\mu = 2$			$\mu = 3$		
S_a/g	T	S_d(m)	R	S_a/g	S_d(m)	R	S_a/g	S_d(m)
1	0.01	0.0000	1.0200	0.9804	0.0000	1.0400	0.9615	0.0001
1	0.03	0.0002	1.0600	0.9434	0.0004	1.1200	0.8929	0.0006
2.71	0.125	0.0105	1.2500	2.1680	0.0169	1.5000	1.8067	0.0211

(Continued)

TABLE 14.11   (CONTINUED)

S_a/g	T	$S_d(m)$	R	S_a/g	$S_d(m)$	R	S_a/g	$S_d(m)$
	$\mu = 1$ (1 g)			$\mu = 2$			$\mu = 3$	
2.71	0.2	0.0270	1.4000	1.9357	0.0385	1.8000	1.5056	0.0449
2.71	0.3	0.0607	1.6000	1.6938	0.0758	2.2000	1.2318	0.0827
2.71	0.4	0.1079	1.8000	1.5056	0.1198	2.6000	1.0423	0.1244
2.71	0.5	0.1685	2.0000	1.3550	0.1685	3.0000	0.9033	0.1685
2.33	0.6	0.2086	2.0000	1.1650	0.2086	3.0000	0.7767	0.2086
1.83	0.8	0.2913	2.0000	0.9150	0.2913	3.0000	0.6100	0.2913
1.5	1	0.3731	2.0000	0.7500	0.3731	3.0000	0.5000	0.3731
1	1.5	0.5597	2.0000	0.5000	0.5597	3.0000	0.3333	0.5597
0.93	1.6	0.5922	2.0000	0.4650	0.5922	3.0000	0.3100	0.5922
0.81	1.8	0.6528	2.0000	0.4050	0.6528	3.0000	0.2700	0.6528
0.71	2	0.7064	2.0000	0.3550	0.7064	3.0000	0.2367	0.7064
0.55	2.5	0.8551	2.0000	0.2750	0.8551	3.0000	0.1833	0.8551
0.45	3	1.0074	2.0000	0.2250	1.0074	3.0000	0.1500	1.0074

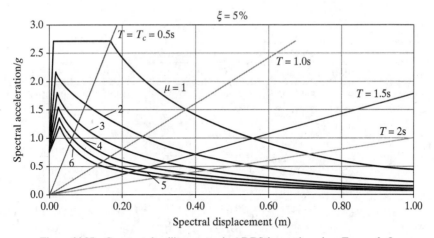

Figure 14.25   Constant ductility spectra in ADRS format based on Eurocode 8.

Example 14.8

Re-do Example 14.5 and locate the performance point using the EC8-Part 1 method.

Solution

For $T = 0.3$ sec, stiffness $= 43820$ N/m

This is a short period system having a period $T < T_C = 0.5$ sec.

The calculations are same up to Step 3 of Example 14.5. The reduction factor $R = 3.79$.

Step 4: The period 0.3 sec lies in the transition zone. Now compute ductility from

$$R = (T/T_c)(\mu - 1) + 1$$

or, $$\mu = (R - 1)/(T/T_c) + 1$$

or, $$\mu = (T_c/T)(R - 1) + 1$$

∴ $$\mu = (0.5/0.3)(3.79 - 1) + 1 = 5.65$$

Step 5: Compute R, S_a and S_d coordinates for ductility $\mu = 5.65$ using Equation (14.32) and (14.33) and plot. This demand curve will intersect the capacity curve at B. The point of intersection B gives the target displacement equal to 0.0226 m. Again, target displacement corresponds to a ductility equal to

$$\mu = 0.0226/0.004 = 5.65 \quad \text{OK}$$

Step 6: If this point of intersection B is joined with the point of intersection A between the elastic demand curve and period $T = 0.3$ sec as obtained in Step 1, an inclined line is obtained. It means the elastic and inelastic displacements are not equal in this range.

Typical calculations are shown in Table 14.12. The double lines in the table show change in reduction factor R region. The location of performance point in the A–D response spectra is shown in Figure 14.26. The ductility curve for 5.65 does pass through the performance point.

TABLE 14.12 CALCULATIONS FOR R, S_a AND S_d COORDINATES

$\mu = 1$ (1 g)		$\mu = 1$ (0.25 g)		$\mu = 5.65$			$T = 0.3$	$T = 0.5$
S_a/g	T	S_a(m/s²)	S_d(m)	R	S_a	S_d(m)	S_d(m)	S_d(m)
1	0.01	2.45	0.0000	1.0931	2.24	0.0000	0.0056	0.0155
1	0.03	2.45	0.0001	1.2792	1.92	0.0002	0.0056	0.0155
2.71	0.125	6.65	0.0026	2.1632	3.07	0.0069	0.0152	0.0421
2.71	0.2	6.65	0.0067	2.8612	2.32	0.0133	0.0152	0.0421
2.71	0.3	6.65	0.0152	3.7918	1.75	0.0226	0.0152	0.0421
2.71	0.4	6.65	0.0270	4.7224	1.41	0.0323	0.0152	0.0421
2.71	0.5	6.65	0.0421	5.6529	1.18	0.0421	0.0152	0.0421
2.33	0.6	5.71	0.0522	5.6529	1.01	0.0522	0.0130	0.0362
1.83	0.8	4.49	0.0728	5.6529	0.79	0.0728	0.0102	0.0284
1.5	1	3.68	0.0933	5.6529	0.65	0.0933	0.0084	0.0233
1	1.5	2.45	0.1399	5.6529	0.43	0.1399	0.0056	0.0155
0.93	1.6	2.28	0.1481	5.6529	0.40	0.1481	0.0052	0.0145
0.81	1.8	1.99	0.1632	5.6529	0.35	0.1632	0.0045	0.0126
0.71	2	1.74	0.1766	5.6529	0.31	0.1766	0.0040	0.0110
0.55	2.5	1.35	0.2138	5.6529	0.24	0.2138	0.0031	0.0086
0.45	3	1.10	0.2519	5.6529	0.20	0.2519	0.0025	0.0070

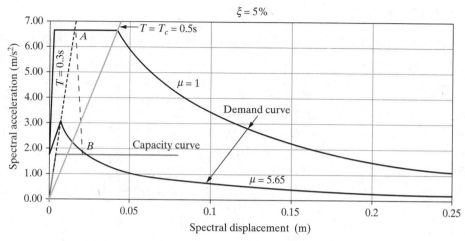

Figure 14.26   Performance point for a SDOF with $T = 0.3$ sec ($< T_C$).

It can be seen that the Newmark–Hall spectra required a ductility of 6.32 and target displacement of 2.53 cm. A slight difference in the two methods is expected.   □

Example 14.9

Re-do Example 14.6 and locate the performance point using the EC8-Part 1 method.

Solution

For $T = 1$ sec, stiffness = 3944 N/m
It is a medium period system having a period $T > T_C = 0.5$ sec
The calculations are same as in Example 14.6. The reduction factor $R = 1.87$ and the ductility demand is also 1.87.

Step 5: Compute R, S_a and S_d coordinates for ductility $\mu = 1.87$ using Equation (14.32) and (14.33). This curve will intersect the capacity curve at the same point B as the point of intersection of the vertical line. The target displacement is 0.0933 m, which is same as obtained by the Newmark–Hall method.

Typical calculations are shown in Table 14.13. The double lines in the table show change in reduction factor R region. The performance point in the A–D response spectra is shown in Figure 14.27.

TABLE 14.13   CALCULATIONS FOR R, S_a AND S_d COORDINATES

$\mu = 1$ (1 g)		$\mu = 1$ (0.25 g)		$\mu = 1.87$			$T = 1$	$T = 0.5$
$S_a(g)$	T	S_a	$S_d(m)$	R_y	S_a	S_d	$S_d(m)$	$S_d(m)$
1.0000	0.01	2.45	0.0000	1.0173	2.408	0.0000	0.0621	0.0155
1.0000	0.03	2.45	0.0001	1.0520	2.329	0.0001	0.0621	0.0155
2.7100	0.125	6.6395	0.0026	1.2165	5.458	0.0040	0.1684	0.0421
2.7100	0.2	6.6395	0.0067	1.3465	4.931	0.0094	0.1684	0.0421
2.7100	0.3	6.6395	0.0152	1.5197	4.369	0.0186	0.1684	0.0421

(Continued)

TABLE 14.13 (CONTINUED)

$\mu = 1$ (1 g)		$\mu = 1$ (0.25 g)		$\mu = 1.87$			$T = 1$	$T = 0.5$
$S_a(g)$	T	S_a	$S_d(m)$	R_y	S_a	S_d	$S_d(m)$	$S_d(m)$
2.7100	0.4	6.6395	0.0269	1.6929	3.922	0.0298	0.1684	0.0421
2.7100	0.5	6.6395	0.0421	1.8662	3.558	0.0422	0.1684	0.0421
2.3300	0.6	5.7085	0.0521	1.8662	3.059	0.0522	0.1447	0.0362
1.8300	0.8	4.4835	0.0728	1.8662	2.403	0.0729	0.1137	0.0284
1.5020	1	3.6799	0.0933	1.8662	1.972	0.0935	0.0933	0.0233
1.0000	1.5	2.45	0.1398	1.8662	1.313	0.1401	0.0621	0.0155
0.9300	1.6	2.2785	0.1479	1.8662	1.221	0.1482	0.0578	0.0144
0.8100	1.8	1.9845	0.1630	1.8662	1.063	0.1634	0.0503	0.0126
0.7100	2	1.7395	0.1764	1.8662	0.932	0.1768	0.0441	0.0110
0.5500	2.5	1.3475	0.2135	1.8662	0.722	0.2140	0.0342	0.0085
0.4500	3	1.1025	0.2516	1.8662	0.591	0.2521	0.0280	0.0070

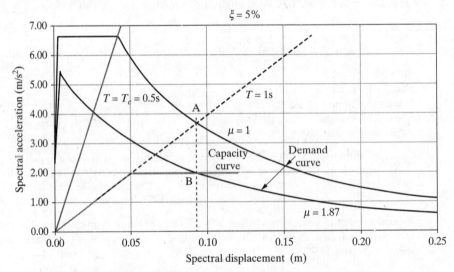

Figure 14.27 Performance point for a SDOF with $T = 1$ sec ($> T_C$).

It can be seen that the Newmark–Hall spectra required a ductility of 1.87 and target displacement of 9.33 cm which are the same as required by the EC8-Part 1. The demand curves for a ductility of 1.87 are different in both the methods. Nevertheless, both the demand curves do intersect at the same performance point.   □

Example 14.10

A 10-storey RC building is shown in Figure 14.28. One of its inner frames is subjected to nonlinear static pushover analysis as well as nonlinear time-history analysis under the El Centro earthquake of May 1940. Determine the target displacement and ductility demands in various members.

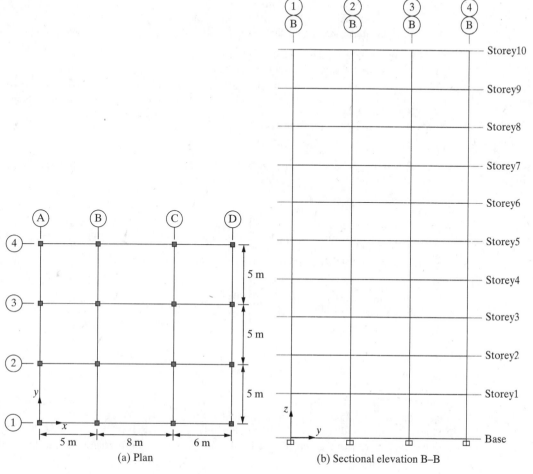

Figure 14.28   10 storey building.

Solution

The major steps in the static pushover analysis are as follows:

Step 1: Choose suitable materials, appropriate loads and sizes for various members of the building.

Step 2: Choose Takeda's hysteresis model for concrete/plastic hinges.

Step 3: Carryout analysis for gravity and lateral loads and carryout ductile design of the beams and columns in the building. Check for weak girder and strong column proportions in both vertical planes of the building.

Step 4: Choose appropriate moment-curvature properties for plastic hinges in beams and columns from the database of the software. Estimate yield moment and yield rotation for each member. In case these properties are not readily available, then derive them from the basic principles on an Excel sheet.

Step 5: Assign the plastic hinges to both ends of each member of the building.

Step 6: Carryout a displacement controlled static pushover analysis. The value of the controlling displacement is assumed to be 4% of the height of the building at the roof level.

Step 7: Generate capacity curve for the building and develop ADRS spectra. Now locate performance points using EL or DM methods.

Step 8: Examine the state of plastic hinges in the building and compute rotational ductility demand in girders and columns. Check with the acceptance criteria.

Step 9: Re-design the building, if necessary.

Steps for nonlinear dynamic analysis are as follows:
The first five steps are same as discussed earlier.

Step 6: Now carry out nonlinear time-history analysis by subjecting the building/frame to the desired accelerogram(s). Compute rotational ductility demand in girders and columns and analyses the results.

Step 7: Re-design the building, if necessary.

Data
A 2D inner frame 2–2 is chosen for the present analysis for convenience. The design and nonlinear static and dynamic analyses were carried out using ETABS.
No. of storeys =10
Ground floor height = 4.5 m; Typical storey height = 3.75 m;
Material-M30 grade concrete; Fe 415 grade steel

Beam sections, 300×500 mm outer beams
300×650 central beams

Column sections
350×600 – 1 to 3 storeys
350×500 – 4 to 6 storeys
350×400 – 7 to 10 storeys
Slab – 120 mm thick concrete
Live load on floor = 1.5 kN/m²
Zone = V
Mass source DL + 0.25 LL
Period of the 2D frame = 1.70 sec
Plastic Hinges with Takeda hysteresis model for concrete
Beams – M3 hinges; Columns – P-M3-M2 hinges
The girder properties are shown in Table 14.14. Similarly, column properties were determined.

TABLE 14.14 GIRDER PROPERTIES

Floor	Girder Size, mm		ϕ_y (rad/mm)	I (crack) mm⁴	M_y (kNm)	Θ_y (rad)
8–10	300×500 (outer)	Positive	7.20E-06	4.31E + 08	66	5.76E-03
		Negative	7.60E-06	5.11E + 08	79	6.08E-03
	300×650 (inner)	Positive	5.44E-06	1.05E + 09	120	5.08E-03
		Negative	5.44E-06	1.05E + 09	120	5.08E-03
4–7	300×500 (outer)	Positive	7.22E-06	5.11E + 08	79	5.78E-03
		Negative	7.32E-06	5.65E + 08	90	5.86E-03
	300×650 (inner)	Positive	5.72E-06	1.05E + 09	122	5.34E-03
		Negative	5.72E-06	1.05E + 09	122	5.34E-03
1–3	300×500 (outer)	Positive	7.28E-06	5.48E + 08	87	5.82E-03
		Negative	7.32E-06	5.62E + 08	90	5.86E-03
	300×650 (inner)	Positive	5.43E-06	1.28E + 09	152	5.07E-03
		Negative	5.43E-06	1.28E + 09	152	5.07E-03

Yield rotation is calculated using $\theta_y = M_y L / 6EI_{crack}$. The member is assumed to deflect in double curvature.

Pushover case
Loads = Acceleration loads in X direction
Monitored displacement = 0.04 times the maximum z coordinate of the building that is, the building was pushed to achieve a roof displacement of $0.04 \times 38.25 = 1.53$ m
Total steps specified = 500
Control node = point at centre of mass at the roof of the building

For each earthquake hazard level, the structure is assigned a seismic coefficient C_A and C_V. The elastic response spectrum for a site is constructed based on C_A and C_V.
C_A – Represents the effective peak acceleration of the ground. A factor of 2.5 C_A represents average value of peak response of a 5% damped short period system in the acceleration domain.
C_V – Represents 5% damped response of a 1-second system, and a factor of C_V/T represents acceleration response in velocity domain.
       Factors C_A and C_V depend seismic zone, soil profile, distance and type of seismic source. Their values were computed using IS:1893-Part 1 and ATC-40 as $C_A = 0.432$ $C_V = 0.576$.

Results–Pushover Analysis
The pushover analysis was terminated after the 23rd step only against maximum specified steps of 500 due to the formation of a plastic mechanism. The maximum roof displacement was 1500 mm for a base shear of 312 kN. The capacity curve is shown in Figure 14.29(a). A tangent is drawn at the origin, and the first point of deviation gives the yield displacement equal to 78 mm. The floor displacements corresponding to this roof displacement are assumed to represent corresponding floor yield displacements. The ratio of the maximum floor displacement to that of the corresponding floor yield displacement gives the displacement ductility. The A–D response spectra obtained using the equivalent linearization method is shown in Figure 14.29(b). The target displacement was 309 mm. The bilinear force-deformation curve is obtained using the displacement modification method

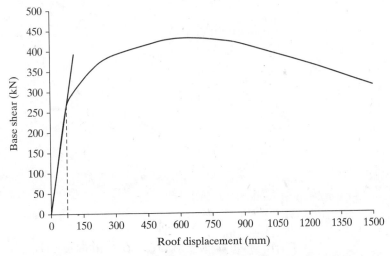

Figure 14.29(a) Base shear vs. roof displacement—capacity curve.

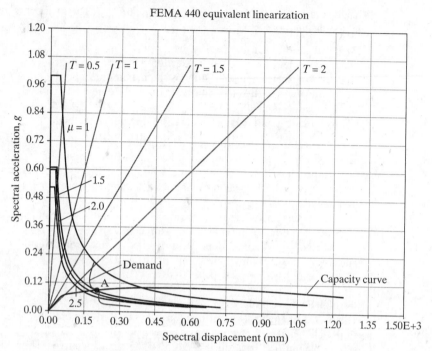

Figure 14.29(b)   Performance point by equivalent linearization method.

and it gives the target displacement as 445 mm. For the same capacity curve, the two methods give different target displacements. It shows that the static monotonic nonlinear pushover analysis is still evolving in modelling the nonlinear response of a MDOF system using SDOF approach.

The frame displacements, storey shears, state of the plastic hinges, rotational ductility in outer and inner girders for sagging and hogging rotations at the performance point (441 mm) are shown on Figures 14.29(c) to 14.29(h). The maximum base shear is 415 kN.

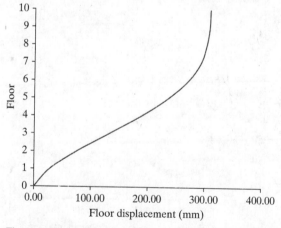

Figure 14.29(c)   Floor displacements at performance point.

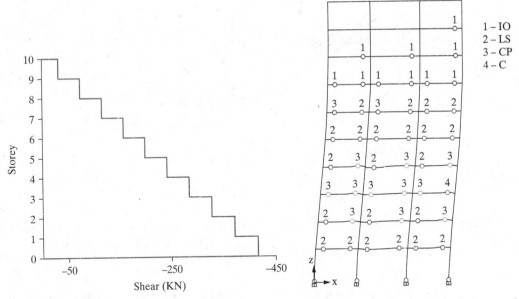

Figure 14.29(d)   Storey shears at performance point.

Figure 14.29(e)   Hinge status at performance point.

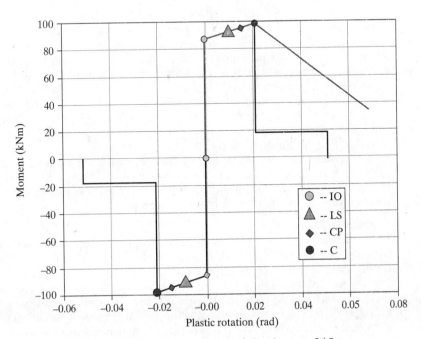

Figure 14.29(f)   State of a plastic hinge in a beam on 3rd floor.

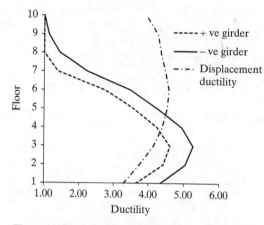

Figure 14.29(g) Maximum rotational ductility—outer girders (+ve sagging, –ve hogging).

Figure 14.29(h) Maximum rotational ductility—inner girders (+ve sagging, –ve hogging).

The maximum rotational ductility in outer girders in hogging and sagging is 5.3 and 4.6, respectively. The maximum rotational ductility in inner girders in hogging and sagging is 5.7 and 5.1, respectively. The maximum displacement ductility is 4.5. There was no inelasticity in any column up to the performance point.

Results–Dynamic Analysis

It was assumed that the N–S component of El Centro accelerogram of May 1040 is a representative accelerogram for the site under consideration in zone V. The frame was subjected to first 10 second of this earthquake. The state of plastic hinges, maximum floor displacements, top floor, time-history, storey shears, rotational ductility in outer and inner girders for sagging and hogging rotations are shown in Figures 14.30(a) to 14.30(f). It can be seen that the maximum roof displacement is 235 mm and maximum base shear is 380 kN. The maximum rotational ductility in outer girders in hogging and sagging is 3 and 2.5, respectively. The maximum rotational ductility in inner girders in hogging and sagging is 3.3 and 2.8, respectively. The maximum displacement ductility is 3.40. There was no inelasticity in any column.

The performance of the frame girders under both static and dynamic analyses are shown in Table 14.15. There are a total of six possible plastic hinges per floor or 12 hinges in any two floors. Most of the inelastic activity was in the lower six floors. The upper four floors remained in IO state that is, immediate occupancy.

Summary of Results

The frame was subjected to the nonlinear static pushover analysis as well as the N–S component of the El Centro accelerogram of May 1940, which is one of the strongest earthquakes ever recorded. The rotational ductility in the girders and the displacement ductility demand due to the El Centro earthquake are less than those demanded by the pushover analysis at the performance point. These results show that the monotonic static loading (pushover) is more severe than a nonlinear dynamic analysis under the El Centro earthquake. The results of both nonlinear static and dynamic analyses need to be interpreted with care. The dynamic analysis is more realistic but requires a very careful selection of the ground motion(s) for a given site. □

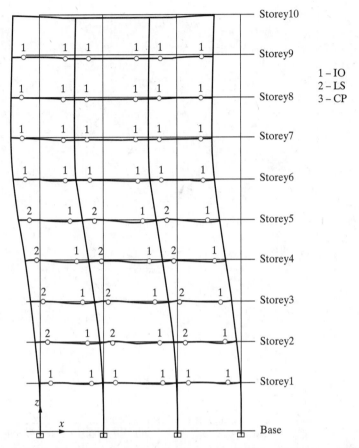

Figure 14.30(a)   Plastic hinges at the end of earthquake loading – El Centro earthquake.

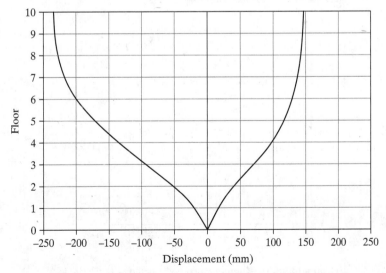

Figure 14.30(b)   Maximum floor displacements under El Centro earthquake.

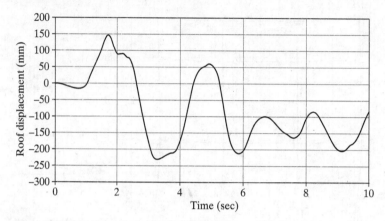

Figure 14.30(c) Roof displacement—time-history under El Centro earthquake.

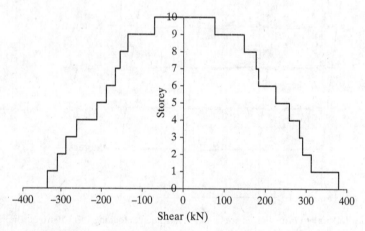

Figure 14.30(d) Maximum storey shears due to El Centro earthquake.

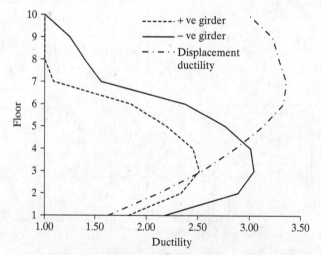

Figure 14.30(e) Maximum rotational ductility—outer girders
(El Centro earthquake). (+ve sagging, –ve hogging)

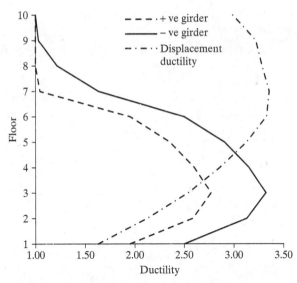

Figure 14.30(f)   Maximum rotational ductility—inner girders
(El Centro earthquake) (+ve sagging, –ve hogging).

TABLE 14.15   PERFORMANCE OF THE FRAME GIRDERS: STATE OF
PLASTIC HINGES

Floor	Pushover Analysis	Dynamic Analysis
9th and 10th floors	IO-1	IO-6
7th and 8th floors	IO-9	IO-12
5th and 6th floors	IO-2 , LS-10	IO-9, LS-3
3rd and 4th floors	LS-3 , CP-8 ,> C-1	IO-6 , LS-6
1st and 2nd floors	LS-9 , CP-3	IO-9 , LS-3

PROBLEMS

14.1 What do you understand by performance-based design? How does it differ with prescriptive design?

14.2 Explain the terms required performance index and possessed performance index.
What is performance objective?

14.3 Explain the terms: Hazard and risk. What are earthquake hazard levels?

14.4 Explain the steps to carry out a nonlinear dynamic analysis on a new building in order to assess its performance.

14.5 What do you understand by seismic design category? How it can be related to the design criteria?

14.6 Discuss the salient features of a static pushover curve for seismic rehabilitation of an existing building. Give the typical values of the control points for a RC moment resistant frame and a steel frame as per ASCE 41-2007.

14.7 Discuss the capacity and demand curves in seismic design.

14.8 What do you understand by ADRS spectra? How do you generate elastic ADRS for different damping?

14.9 How do you generate inelastic ADRS for different ductility ratios? How do you obtain target displacement for short-period and long-period structures?

14.10 Explain the complete process of performance-based design for rehabilitation of existing buildings as detailed in ASCE 41-2007. How does it differ with that of a new building?

14.11 Generate moment-curvature curves for the following sections using Mander's models for concrete. Other data as required may be assumed.

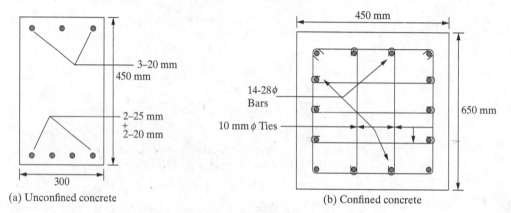

(a) Unconfined concrete

(b) Confined concrete

Figure P14.1

(*Hint:* You may write a program in FORTRAN or MATLAB.)

14.12 Construct an acceleration-displacement response spectrum for ductility ratio of 1, 1.5, 2, 5, 6, 8 and 10 for a ground motion having peak ground acceleration, peak ground velocity and peak ground displacement of 0.5 g, 80 cm/sec and 75 cm, respectively. Make use of Newmark-Hall amplification factors for 2% damping and 84.1 percentile; and Newmark-Hall reduction factors.

14.13 Redo problem 14.12 making use of the Eurocode 8 reduction factors.

REFERENCES – FURTHER READING

Aparna, K.P and Jain, A.K (2016) Performance Evaluation of Multistoreyed R.C Frames, Indian Concrete Journal, Vol. 90, No. 1, January.

AASHTO (2010) LRFD Bridge Design Specifications, Fifth Edition, Washington, D.C.

ASCE 7 (2010). Minimum Design Loads for Buildings and other Structures, ASCE/SEI Standard ASCE 7–10, American Society of Civil Engineers, Reston, VA

ASCE 41 (2007) Seismic Rehabilitation of Existing Buildings, ASCE/SEI Standard 41-06 with supplement 1, American Society of Civil Engineers, Reston, VA

ATC 40 (1996) Seismic Evaluation and Retrofit of Concrete Buildings, Vol. 1, Applied Technology Council, Redwood City, CA.

CALTRANS (2013) Seismic Design Criteria, Ver 1.7, California Department of Transportation, June, Sacramento, CA.

Eurocode 1992–1–1 (2004) Eurocode 2: Design of Concrete Structures — Part 1-1: General Rules and Rules for Buildings, European Standard, Brussels.

Eurocode 1998–1 (2004) Design of Structures for Earthquake Resistance — Part 1: General Rules, Seismic Actions and Rules for Buildings, incorporating corrigendum 2013, European Committee for Standardization, Brussels.

FEMA 356 (2000) Pre-standard and Commentary for the Seismic Rehabilitation of Buildings, Federal Emergency Management Agency, Washington D.C.

FEMA 440 (2005) "Improvement of Nonlinear Static Seismic Analysis Procedures", Federal Emergency Management Agency, Washington D.C.

FEMA 451B (2006) 2003 NEHRP Recommended Seismic Provisions–Design Examples, Federal Emergency Management Agency, Washington, D.C.

FEMA P749 (2010) Earthquake-Resistant Design Concepts — An Introduction to the NEHRP Recommended Seismic Provisions for New Buildings and Other Structures, Federal Emergency Management Agency, Washington, D.C.

FEMA P750 (2010) 2009 NEHRP Recommended Seismic Provisions for New Buildings and Other Structures, Federal Emergency Management Agency, Washington, D.C.

FEMA P752 (2013) 2009 NEHRP Recommended Seismic Provisions–Training and Instructional Materials, Federal Emergency Management Agency, Washington, D.C.

FEMA P1050 (2015) 2015 NEHRP Recommended Seismic Provisions for New Buildings and Other Structures, Federal Emergency Management Agency, Washington, D.C.

IS:15988 (2013) Seismic Evaluation and Strengthening of Existing RC Buildings – Guidelines, Bureau of Indian Standards, New Delhi.

Jain, A. K. (1985) Seismic Response of R. C. Frames with Steel Braces, Journal of the Structural Division, ASCE, Vol. 111, No. ST10, October, pp. 2138–2148.

Jain, A. K. (1990) Inelastic Response of R. C. Frames subjected to the 1985 Mexico Earthquake, Computers and Structures, Vol. 34, No. 3, pp. 445–454.

Jain, A.K. and Mir, R.A. (1991) Inelastic Response of R.C. Frames Under Earthquakes, Indian Concrete Journal, Vol. 65, No. 4, April, pp. 175–180.

JSCE-SSCS (2010) Standard Specifications for Concrete Structures 2007, Guideline no. 15, Japan Society of Civil Engineers, Tokyo.

Kent, D. C. and Park, R. (1971) "Flexural Members with Confined Concrete." Journal of the Structural Division, ASCE, Vol. 97, No. 7, pp. 1969–1990.

Mander, J. B., M.J.N. Priestley, and R. Park (1988) "Theoretical Stress–Strain Model for Confined Concrete," Journal of Structural Engineering, ASCE. Vol. 114, No. 8, 1804–1826.

Mahaney, J. A., Paret, T. F., Kehoe, B. E. and Freeman, S. A. (1993), The Capacity Spectrum Method for Evaluating Structural Response During the Lorna Prieta Earthquake, National Earthquake Conference, Memphis.

Mir, Riyaz A. and Jain, A. K. (1988) Inelastic Seismic Response of R. C. Frames, Vol. 2, Research Report for B.R.N.S., Dept. of Atomic Energy, University of Roorkee, Roorkee.

PEER (2010), "Modelling and Acceptance Criteria for Seismic Design and Analysis of Tall buildings", Pacific Earthquake Engineering Research Center, Report No. 111 California.

PEER (2010), "Guidelines for Performance-Based Seismic Design of Tall Buildings", Pacific Earthquake Engineering Research Center, Report No. 5, Berkeley, California.

Priestley, M J N, Calvi, G. M., and Kowalsky (2007) Displacement Based Seismic Design of Structures, IUSS Press, Italy.

PART 4

WIND LOAD

15 | Wind Load

15.1 INTRODUCTION

Wind is essentially a random phenomenon. In the past, it was considered sufficient to use the mean wind speed that had been recorded at the nearest meteorological station. The corresponding wind pressure was applied statically. This was an erroneous practice since wind loading varies with time. In addition to steady wind, there are effects of gusts which may last for a few minutes. Gust causes increase in air pressure and may affect only part of the building. The increased local pressures may be more than balanced by a momentary reduction in the pressure elsewhere. Because of inertia of a building, short period gusts may not cause any appreciable increase in stress in the main components of the building although the walls, roof sheeting and individual cladding units (glass panels) and their supporting members such as purlins, sheeting rails and glazing bars may be seriously affected. Gust is extremely important for design of structures with high slenderness ratios, that is flexible structures. The design wind speed depends on several factors such as density of obstructions in the terrain, topography, size of gust, return period and probable life of structure. A deterministic approach cannot do justice with wind loading.

The wind loads in IS: 875-1987 (Part 3) are based on two considerations:

1. The statistical and probabilistic approach to the evaluation of wind loads
2. Due recognition to the dynamic component of wind loading and its interaction with the dynamic characteristics of the structure.

These revisions are consistent with the philosophy of limit state design. The pressure coefficients due to wind depend upon the shape and size of a structure, along with direction and angle of attack. It is not possible to estimate these pressure coefficients theoretically. The only way to calculate these coefficients is by conducting experiments in a *boundary layer wind tunnel*. The term *boundary layer* means the region of wind flow affected by friction at the earth's surface, which can extend up to 1 km. Wind is treated as a fluid, and the theory of fluid mechanics is used to estimate the pressure coefficients under different situations and obstructions.

The wind load may be treated as static or dynamic. The dynamic wind load is not the same as the dynamic loads considered in the previous chapters. The wind loads generally do not introduce inertia force in the structure. In the context of wind, the word dynamic means to include the effect of gust. In either case, the wind load is always applied statically. The intensity of wind is mild as compared to other lateral loads except in a storm, cyclone (or hurricane or typhoon) or a tornado. The effect of a severe wind is shown in Figure 15.1. The collapse of a steel tower due to a wind storm is shown in Figure 15.2. The cumulative loss of property in the country due to wind storms and loss of life and property due to a tornado, cyclone or a tsunami in a given year is enormous. Therefore, it is essential to understand the wind phenomenon: how it affects a structure, how to assess wind loads and how to design a structure against wind loads?

Figure 15.1   A severe wind.

(a) Before the storm.

Figure 15.2   Collapse of a 149 m tall steel tower.

(b) After the storm.

(c) Tension failure of main legs of the tower.

(d) Local buckling of an angle section.

Figure 15.2   (Continued)

(e) Bent up portion of the tower after collapse.

(f) The tower platform.

Figure 15.2 (Continued)

This chapter deals with how to compute wind pressure in accordance with IS Code (IS:875-Part 3) on some typical structures in static and dynamic conditions. This code provides several tables and charts and should be referred to obtain the values of various parameters required to calculate the wind load. The highway bridges in India are designed for wind loads as specified in the Indian Roads Congress Code IRC 6 (2014). The salient features of both these codes are explained through illustrations.

15.2 TERMINOLOGY

Angle of Attack   Angle between the direction of wind and a reference axis of the structure.

Breadth   Breadth means horizontal dimension of the building measured normal to the direction of wind.

Note: Breadth and depth are dimensions measured in relation to the direction of the wind, whereas length and width are dimensions related to the plan.

Depth   Depth means the horizontal dimension of the building measured in the direction of the wind.

Developed Height   Developed height is the height of upward penetration of the velocity profile in a new terrain. At large fetch lengths, such penetration reaches the gradient height, above which the wind speed may be taken to be constant. At lesser fetch lengths, a velocity profile of a smaller height but similar to that of the fully developed profile of that terrain category has to be taken, with the additional provision that the velocity at the top of this shorter profile equals that of the un-penetrated earlier velocity profile at that height.

Fastest Mile   Over a specified period (usually the 24 hour observational day), the fastest speed, in miles per hour, of any 'mile' of wind. The accompanying direction is specified also. The fastest mile is the reciprocal of the shortest interval (in 24 hours) that it takes one mile of air to pass a given point. This definition is used in American codes.

Gust   A positive or negative departure of wind speed from its mean value, lasting for not more than, say 2 minutes, over a specified interval of time.

Gust Speed is the highest sustained gust over a three-second period of time. Gust is typically 20% to 25% higher than the fastest mile.

Peak Gust   Peak gust or peak gust speed is the wind speed associated with the maximum amplitude.

Fetch Length   Fetch length is the distance measured along the wind from a boundary at which a change in the type of terrain occurs. When the changes in terrain types are encountered (such as, the boundary of a town or city, forest, etc.), the wind profile changes in character but such changes are gradual and start at ground level, spreading or penetrating upwards with increasing fetch length.

Gradient Height   Gradient height is the height above the mean ground level at which the gradient wind blows as a result of balance among pressure gradient force, Coriolis force and centrifugal force. For the purpose of this code, the gradient height is taken as the height above the mean ground level, above which the variation of wind speed with height need not be considered.

Mean Ground Level   The mean ground level is the average horizontal plane of the area enclosed by the boundaries of the structure.

Pressure Coefficient Pressure coefficient is defined as:

$$= \frac{\text{Pressure acting at a point on the surface} - \text{static pressure of the incident wind}}{\text{Design wind pressure}}$$

where the static and design wind pressures are determined at the height of the point considered after taking into account the geographical location, terrain conditions and shielding effect.

There is an internal pressure coefficient (C_{pi}) and an external pressure coefficient (C_{pe}).

Shielding Effect Shielding effect or shielding refers to the condition where wind has to pass along some structure(s) or structural element(s) located on the upstream wind side, before meeting the structure or structural element under consideration. A factor called 'shielding factor' is used to account for such effects in estimating the force on the shielded structures.

Suction Suction means pressure less than the atmospheric (static) pressure and is taken to act away from the surface.

Solidity Ratio Solidity ratio is equal to the effective area (projected area of all the individual elements) of a frame normal to the wind direction divided by the area enclosed by the boundary of the frame normal to the wind direction. *Solidity ratio is to be calculated for individual frames.*

Velocity Profile The variation of the horizontal component of the atmospheric wind speed at different heights above the mean ground level is termed as *velocity profile*.

Topography The nature of the earth's surface as influenced by the hill and valley configurations.

15.3 WIND LOAD

The wind speed is measured with an instrument called *anemometer*. The wind speed is converted into wind pressure using the principles of fluid mechanics. Wind pressure always acts normal to the surface. The wind load on a structure is calculated as follows depending upon the purpose:

1. Individual structural elements—walls or roof
2. Individual cladding units—sheeting and their fixtures
3. Building as a whole
   (a) with cladding
   (b) without cladding

There are different requirements for each of the above elements. The wind pressure calculation is a common denominator. The main difference lies in the calculation of drag coefficients or pressure coefficients. A pressure coefficient is specified for a given surface or part of a surface depending upon the direction of wind. On any surface, wind causes either *pressure or suction*. Pressure is indicated with a positive sign while suction with a negative sign. A suction is usually a more dangerous condition of wind loading. Every effort is made to ensure that part(s) of the structure under suction is safe, especially the fixtures and sheeting.

Wind load on individual elements

The wind load on individual elements is given as follows:

$$F = \left(C_{pe} - C_{pi}\right) A p_z \tag{15.1}$$

where

C_{pe} = external pressure coefficient
C_{pi} = internal pressure coefficient
A = surface area of structural element or cladding unit exposed to wind
p_z = design wind pressure at height z

The code provides several tables for estimating the pressure coefficients for elements with different shapes and sizes commonly used in practice. Sometimes, it is quite possible that the desired specific situation is not available in the code. In such a case, the option is either to go for wind tunnel test or make a judicious choice based on the available data, if possible. The wind load acts normal to the surface of the individual element.

Wind load on a structure/building

The wind force F on a complete building can be calculated as follows:

$$F = C_f A_e p_z \tag{15.2}$$

where C_f = force coefficient for the building
A_e = effective exposed area at height Z

The force coefficient is essentially a shape factor. It is a non-dimensional quantity which depends on the geometry of the structure and direction of wind. The effect of wind must be considered along both axes of a building taken one at a time. The response of a building to high wind pressures depends not only upon the geographical location and proximity of other obstructions to air flow but also upon the characteristics of the structure itself. The effect of wind on the structure as a whole is determined by the combined action of external and internal pressures acting upon it. The calculated wind loads act normal to the surface.

15.4 STATIC WIND PRESSURE

The design wind speed V_z at any given height and at a given site is expressed as a product of four parameters:

$$V_z = V_b k_1 k_2 k_3 \tag{15.3}$$

where V_b = basic wind speed in meter/sec at 10 m height
k_1 = probability or risk factor
k_2 = terrain, height and structure size factor
k_3 = local topography factor

The basic wind speed represents the extreme value, which is likely to be exceeded on an average only once during a specified return period. It is arrived at by statistical analysis. The wind speed fluctuates with time and can be averaged over any time interval. Typical records of wind under different averages are shown in Figure 15.3. In the Indian Code, it is based on peak gust speed averaged over three second and have been worked out for a 50 year return period. Magnitude of the fluctuating component of the wind speed is referred to as *gust* as shown in Figure 15.4. The value of basic wind speed V_b in India varies between 33 m/s and 55 m/s.

Factor k_1

The probability or risk factor k_1 is based on statistical concepts which take account of the degree of security required and probability of exceedance of the basic wind speed.

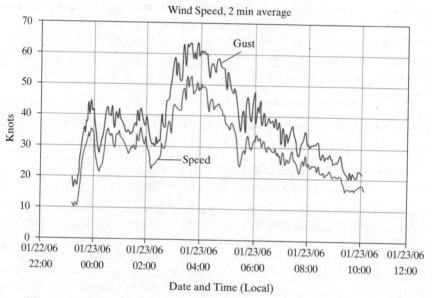

Figure 15.3(a)   A graph of wind speed in knots @ 2 hour interval.

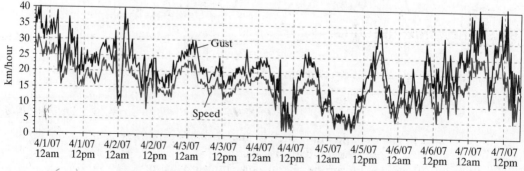

Figure 15.3(b)   A graph of wind speed km/h @ 12 hour interval.

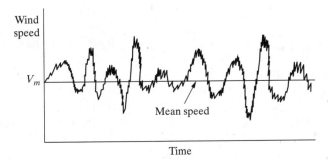

Figure 15.4   Mean and gust wind.

It increases with the increase in mean probable life of a structure. Most buildings are designed for a 50 year mean life. However, it does not mean that the life of a structure is only 50 years.

Factor k_2

The terrain factor k_2 takes due regard to the effect of roughness or height and density of obstructions on the basic wind speed. The wind flows smoothly in the open and calm ocean. Its speed varies smoothly with height and becomes constant beyond a certain height called *gradient height*. This variation of wind speed with height is referred to as the *wind profile*. As the wind hits the sea shore and travels inward, its velocity profile will change depending upon the size and density of obstructions referred to as *the terrain*. Terrains are classified in four categories: open type 1 category to very dense type 4 category as shown in Figure 15.5. The terrain category used in the design of a structure may vary depending upon the direction of wind under consideration.

  Category 1: Exposed open terrain with few or no obstructions and in which the average height of any object surrounding the structure is less than 1.5 m. This category includes open sea coasts and flat treeless plains.

  Category 2: Open terrain with well-scattered obstructions having heights generally between 1.5 and 10 m.

  Category 3: Terrain with numerous closely spaced obstructions having the size of building-structures up to 10 m in height with or without a few isolated tall structures.

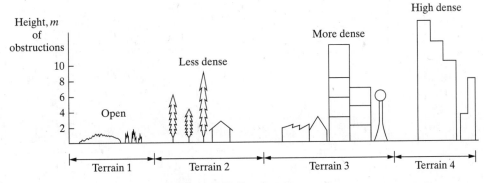

Figure 15.5   Terrain category.

This category includes well-wooded areas and shrubs, towns and industrial areas full or partially developed.

Category 4: Terrain with numerous large high closely spaced obstructions. This category includes large city centres generally with obstructions above 25 m and well-developed industrial complexes.

Usually, the relevant terrain category is the lowest terrain category for the area within a distance of 10 times the height of structure and extending to 20 times the height of structure or 1 km, whichever is greater in the upwind direction.

The wind speed reduces with the increase in density of obstruction but increases with the increase in height. The variation of wind speed with height (wind profile) is given by the power law:

$$\frac{V_z}{V_0} = \left(\frac{z}{z_0}\right)^\alpha \tag{15.4}$$

where

V_z = wind speed at height z above ground
V_0 = basic wind speed at the reference height z_0
α = an exponent depending upon the terrain roughness

Wind velocity profile was measured in different terrains and cities. Based on the data, several different models were proposed. Power law as given by Equation (15.4) has been widely accepted. The value of exponent α may be taken as 0.07, 0.09 0.14 and 0.20 for terrain category 1, 2, 3 and 4, respectively. However, these coefficients vary with the geography of a region. The effect of terrain on the wind profile is shown in Figure 15.6. In this figure, z_g is the gradient height above which the wind speed becomes constant. The values of k_2 factor are tabulated in IS:875-Part 3 at different heights, in each terrain category for different sizes of buildings/structures based on field measurements. The buildings/structures are classified into the following three classes depending upon their sizes:

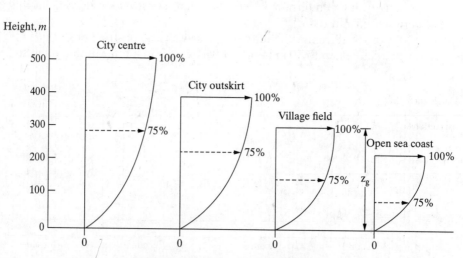

Figure 15.6 Wind profile with terrain.

Class A: structures and/or their components, such as cladding, glazing, roofing, etc., having maximum dimension less than 20 m.

Class B: same as above but having maximum dimension between 20 m and 50 m.

Class C: same as above but having maximum dimension greater than 50 m.

Factor k_3

The wind speed at a given site is also influenced by local topography. For example, wind speed may increase in valleys narrowing towards top or for site on top of steeply sloping hill. Let us first look at different types of topography as shown in Figure. 15.7.

(a) Escarpment

(b) Ridge or embankment

(c) Hill

(d) Valley–steep or shallow

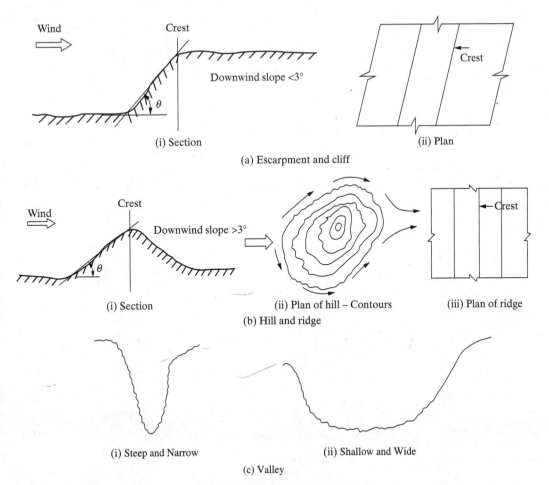

Figure 15.7 Definition of topography.

The flow of wind over different topographies is shown in Figure 15.8.

The effect of topography is considered to extend 1.5 L_e upwind to 2.5 L_e downwind of the summit crest of the feature, where L_e is the effective horizontal length of the hill. It is accounted for through a factor k_3. The definition of local topography for use with k_3 is shown in Figure 15.9. The topography factor is given by the following equation:

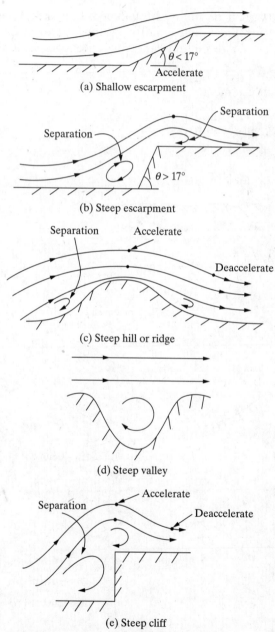

(a) Shallow escarpment

(b) Steep escarpment

(c) Steep hill or ridge

(d) Steep valley

(e) Steep cliff

Figure 15.8   Flow over different types of topography.

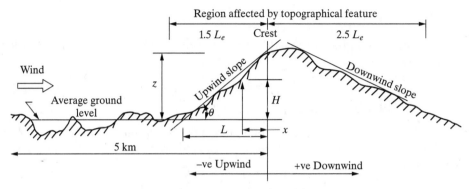

Figure 15.9   Definition of ground feature for k_3.

$$k_3 = 1 + Cs \tag{15.5}$$

where

$s =$ factor depending upon the height under consideration, H above mean ground level, distance x from the crest relative to the effective length L_e.

$C = 0$, if slope of the ground is less than 3°

  $= 0.36$, if slope of the ground is more than 17°

  $(1.2 \times \tan 17 = 1.2 \times 0.30 = 0.36)$

  $= 1.2\, z/L$, if slope of the ground is between 3° and 17°.   (15.6)

15.4.1 Change of Terrain

The velocity profile for a given category does not develop to full height immediately as the wind encounters a new terrain. It takes some time to develop it gradually as shown in Figure 15.10. A relation between the fetch for wind flow over each terrain category and developed height is given in the code.

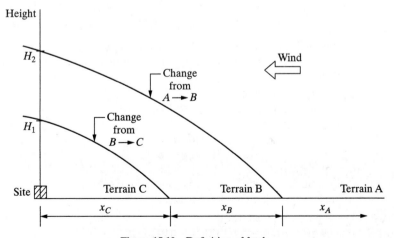

Figure 15.10   Definition of fetch.

15.4.2 Design Wind Pressure

The design wind pressure p_z in N/m² at any height above mean ground level is given by the relation:

$$p_z = 0.6 \, V_z^2 \tag{15.7}$$

where V_z = design wind speed in m/s at height z.

The coefficient 0.6 (in S.I. units) depends mainly on atmospheric pressure and air temperature. This represents an average value of mass density of wind for Indian atmospheric conditions.

15.5 ILLUSTRATIVE EXAMPLES

Example 15.1

A structure is to be located on the top of a hill at 'O' midway as shown in Figure 15.11. Estimate the topography factor k_3. If it is to be located at E on the slope, again estimate the factor k_3.

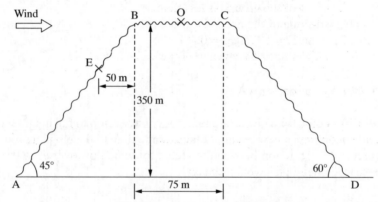

Figure 15.11   Section of a hill.

The topography corresponds to a hill as specified in the question. For the wind direction as shown, point B represents crest. If the direction of wind is reversed, point C will represent crest.

(i) The structure is to be located at O.
The upwind slope θ is more than 17°. The factor $C = 0.36$.
Length $L = 350$ m, $z = 350$ m
∴ effective length $L_e = z/0.3 = 1166.67$ m
$x = +37.5$ m, ∴ $x/L_e = 37.5/1166.67 = 0.0321$
$H = 350$ m, ∴ $H/L_e = 350/1166.67 = 0.30$
∴ The value of s is obtained from Figure 15 of the code $= 0.6$.
∴ The factor $k_3 = 1 + Cs = 1 + 0.36 \times 0.6 = 1.216$

(ii) The structure is located at E.
$x = -50$ m, ∴ $x/L_e = -50/1166.67 = -0.0428$

$H = 300$ m, $\therefore$ $H/L_e = 300/1166.67 = 0.257$

$\therefore$ The value of s is obtained from Figure 15 of the code $= 0.65$.

$\therefore$ The factor $k_3 = 1 + Cs = 1 + 0.36 \times 0.65 = 1.234$ $\square$

Example 15.2

A G + 6 storey building as shown in Figure 15.12 is located in wind zone 3 and terrain type 2. Estimate the wind pressure at various floor levels of the building.

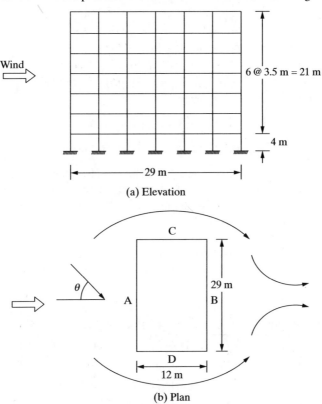

(a) Elevation

(b) Plan

Figure 15.12   Wind on a building.

Solution

Basic wind speed $V_b = 50$ m/s

The risk factor $k_1 = 0.90$ for general buildings with 50 year mean probable design life.

Terrain 2; Building class = B because its maximum dimension is less than 50 m.

Topography factor $k_3 = 1$

The value of factor k_2 is obtained from Table 2 of the code.

Design pressure coefficients for walls

It is assumed that openings are in between 5% and 20%. It means a medium opening. The internal pressure coefficient is taken as +/– 0.5.

$h/w = 25/12 = 2.08$; $1.5 < h/w < 6$

$l/w = 29/12 = 2.42$; $1.5 < l/w < 4$

Table 4 of the code gives the external pressure coefficients for the walls as shown in Table 15.1.

TABLE 15.1 EXTERNAL PRESSURE COEFFICIENT FOR WALLS C_{pe}

	Angle of incidence (degree)	
Wall	0°	90°
Wall A	0.7	-0.5
Wall B	-0.4	-0.5
Wall C	-0.7	0.8
Wall D	-0.7	-0.1

Net pressure coefficient for the walls is as follows:

For longer side walls A, $(C_{pe} - C_{pi}) = 0.7 - (-0.5) = 1.2$ pressure

For shorter side walls C, $(C_{pe} - C_{pi}) = 0.8 - (-0.5) = 1.3$ pressure

Wind speed at height z is given by

$$V_z = V_b k_1 k_2 k_3$$

$\therefore$
$$V_z = 50 \times 0.90 \times k_2 \times 1.0 = 45 k_2$$

The values of k_2 for different heights are obtained from Table 2 of the code. The static wind pressure is computed from Equation (15.7) and shown in Table 15.2.

$$p_z = 0.6\, V_z^2$$

$\square$

TABLE 15.2 WIND PRESSURE AT DIFFERENT FLOORS

Floor level	Height (m)	k_2	V_z (m/s)	p_z (N/m²)	Wind pressure on long face (N/m²)	Wind pressure on short face (N/m²)
R	25	1.075	48.375	1404	1685	1825
6	21.5	1.058	47.61	1360	1632	1768
5	18	1.038	46.71	1309	1571	1702
4	14.5	1.016	45.72	1254	1505	1630
3	11	0.988	44.46	1186	1423	1542
2	7.5	0.98	44.1	1167	1400	1517
1	4	0.98	44.1	1167	1400	1517

Example 15.3

A metro railway platform is covered with a shed as shown in Figure 15.13. Estimate the wind pressure coefficients on the roof.

Solution The angle of roof is 30°. In metro stations, the roof may cover tracks. There is a sudden increase in pressure inside the station due to the arrival of the metro. The current code does not cover the case of a covered roof over the tracks. For preliminary analysis, the coefficients given in Tables 9 and 10 of the code may be used. The correct pressure coefficients should be estimated from a wind tunnel test or from literature. The analysis can be refined once the results of wind tunnel test are available. These tables cover two cases:

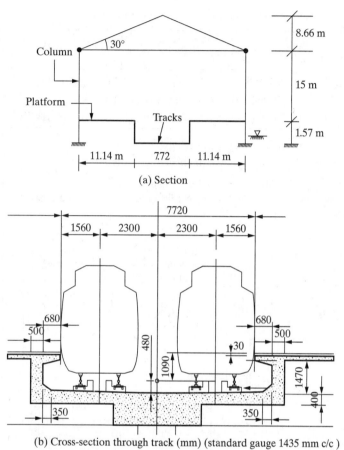

(a) Section

(b) Cross-section through track (mm) (standard gauge 1435 mm c/c)

Figure 15.13 Section of a metro rail platform.

Height of the top of the column = 15 m.
Net pressure coefficient, $C_p = C_p$ (top) $- C_p$ (bottom)

Case 1 – Net pressure coefficient, without the effect of train

	Wind Zone			
Angle of wind	D	E	C'	G'
0°	0.6–(–1.0) = 1.6	–0.5–(–0.9) = 0.4		
45°	0.1–(–0.3) = 0.4	–0.6–(–0.3) = –0.3		
90°	–0.3–(–0.4) = 0.1	–0.3–(–0.4) = 0.1	–0.3–(0.8) = –1.1	0.3–(0.4) = –0.1

For $\theta = 45°$, for region J, $C_p = -1.0 - (-0.2) = -0.8$
For $\theta = 90°$, there will be tangentially acting friction drag,

$$R = 0.05 \, p_z \, b \, d = 0.05 \, p_z \, (30 \times 100) = 150 \, p_z$$
where

$$p_z = 0.6 \, V_z^2 \qquad\qquad (15.7)$$

Case 2 – Net pressure coefficient considering the effect of train

| Angle of wind | Wind Zone | | | |
	D	E	C′	G′
0°	0.1–0.8 = –0.7	–0.7–(0.9) = –1.6		
45°	–0.1–(0.5) = –0.6	–0.8–(0.5) = –1.3		
90°	–0.4–(–0.5) = 0.1	–0.4–(–0.5) = 0.1	–0.3–(0.8) = –1.1	0.3–(–0.4) = 0.7

For $\theta = 45°$, for region J, $C_p = -1.5-(0.5) = -2.0$
For $\theta = 90°$, there will be tangentially acting friction drag,

$$R = 0.05 \, p_d \, b \, d = 0.05 \, p_d \, (30 \times 100) = 150 \, p_d$$

The various zones of the roof shown in Figure 15.14 can be designed for the worst load cases.   □

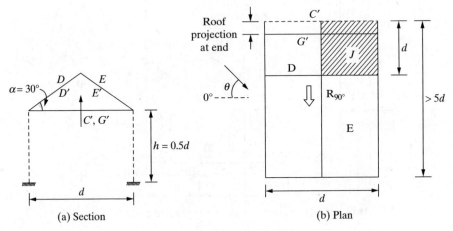

(a) Section   (b) Plan

Figure 15.14   Wind pressure zones for roof.

Example 15.4

Estimate the pressure coefficients for the free standing double sloped roof for a stadium as shown in Figure 15.15. The columns are placed @10 m c/c in the long direction.

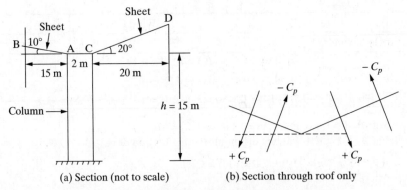

(a) Section (not to scale)   (b) Section through roof only

Figure 15.15   Pitched-free roof for stadium (Continued)

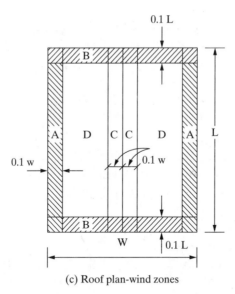

(c) Roof plan-wind zones

Figure 15.15   Pitched-free roof for stadium.

Solution   The free standing double sloped roof shown in Figure 15.15(a), members AB and CD are cantilevers consisting of tapered built-up box sections.

$L = 100$ m, $W = 37$ m, $h = 15$ m;

Basic wind speed = 44 m/s

Coefficient $k_1 = 1.07$

Coefficient $k_3 = 1.21$

Height of the top of the column = 15 m.

Table 8 of the code gives the following pressure coefficients.

$l = 98$ m, $w = 35$ m (dimensions without overhangs)

$L/w = 100/35 = 2.86$; $h/w = 15/35 = 0.43$

For $1/4 < h/w < 1$; $1 < L/w < 3$

The pressure coefficients for different zones of the roof are computed in Table 15.3.

TABLE 15.3   NET PRESSURE COEFFICIENTS IN DIFFERENT ZONES OF ROOF

Roof angle	Overall coeff.		A		B		C		D	
θ	Max	Min	Max	Min	Max	Min	Max	Min	Max	Min
$-10°$	0.4	-0.6	0.8	-1.5	1.4	-1.3	1.1	-0.6	0.6	-0.8
$-20°$	0.7	-0.7	0.6	-1.6	1.6	-1.3	1.7	-0.6	0.8	-0.9

The supporting column will be designed for the net moment due to positive pressure on its left and negative pressure on its right or vice-versa, whichever is critical.   □

Example 15.5

Two panels 39 and 42 of a 150 m TV steel tower are shown in Figure 15.16. The basic wind speed is 47 m/s, terrain is 2 and factor k_3 is 1.25. Estimate the wind force on the panels under parallel and diagonal wind.

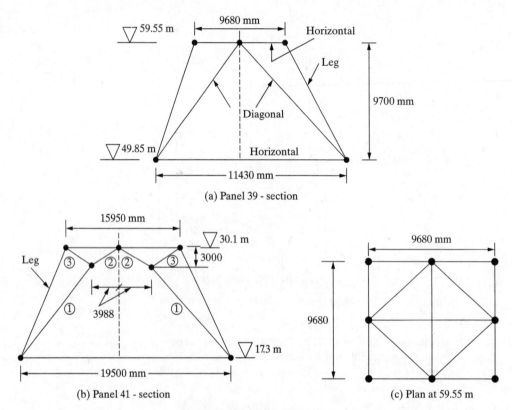

(a) Panel 39 - section

(b) Panel 41 - section

(c) Plan at 59.55 m

Figure 15.16 Panels of TV tower.

Solution Let us calculate the exposed area of each panel to wind as shown in Table 15.4. Box 250 × 28 means a built-up hollow square section having outer dimension as 250 mm and thickness 28 mm steel plate. Similarly, 2L 90 × 8 means 2 no. ISA 90 × 90 × 8 mm section (⌐L) separated by a 8 mm thick (say) gusset.

TABLE 15.4 EXPOSED AREA TO WIND

Panel no.	Member	Section	Flange width (m)	Length (m)	No.	Obstruction area (m²)
39	Main leg	Box 250 × 28	0.25	9.78	2	4.89
	Bracing	2L 90 × 8	0.09	11.29	2	2.032
	Horizontal	2L 65 × 6	0.065	9.68	1	0.629
					Total	7.551
41	Main leg	Box 300 × 28	0.30	13.04	2	7.824
	Bracing 1	2L 100 × 8	0.10	11.36	2	2.272
	Bracing 2	2L 75 × 8	0.075	5.0	2	0.75
	Bracing 3	2L 65 × 6	0.065	5.0	2	0.65
	Horizontal	2L 90 × 8	0.09	15.95	1	1.436
					Total	12.932

Increase panel exposed area by 5% to take care of gusset plates.

$$1.05 \times 7.551 = 7.928 \text{ m}^2; \text{ and } 1.05 \times 12.932 = 13.578 \text{ m}^2$$

Wind pressure is given by Equation (15.7)

$$p_z = 0.6 V_z^2 \qquad\qquad (15.7)$$

where $\qquad\qquad V_z = V_b k_1 k_2 k_3 \qquad\qquad (15.3)$

$V_b = 47$ m/s, $k_1 = 1.07$, $k_3 = 1.25$, terrain 2
The wind pressure is computed at the mid height of a panel.
At 54.70 m, $k_2 = 1.107$
$p_z = 0.60 \times (47 \times 1.07 \times 1.107 \times 1.25)^2 = 2906 \text{ N/m}^2$
At 23.70 m, $k_2 = 1.02$
$p_z = 0.60 \times (47 \times 1.07 \times 1.02 \times 1.25)^2 = 2467 \text{ N/m}^2$
The total wind force in any panel is computed as follows:

Force = exposed area × force coefficient × wind pressure

The computation of wind force is shown in Table 15.5. Half of the total wind load is applied at the top and the remaining half at the bottom of the panel.

TABLE 15.5 COMPUTATION OF WIND FORCE

Panel no.	Height of panel top (m)	Gross area panel (m²)	Exposed area panel (m²)	Solidity ratio	Force coeff.	p_z (N/m²)	Wind load at top of panel: Parallel wind (kN)	Wind load at top of panel: Diagonal wind (kN)
39	59.55	102.37	7.928	0.077	3.8 (4.56)*	2906	87.60	105.10
	49.85							
42	30.1	226.86	13.578	0.060	3.8 (4.56)*	2467	127.30	152.70
	17.3							

Note: * For diagonal wind, the overall force coefficient for parallel case is multiplied by 1.2 as per the code.   □

Example 15.6

The top panel of a 150 m TV steel tower is shown in Figure 15.17. The basic wind speed is 47 m/s, terrain is 2 and factor k_3 is 1.25. Estimate the static wind force on the panels under parallel and diagonal wind.

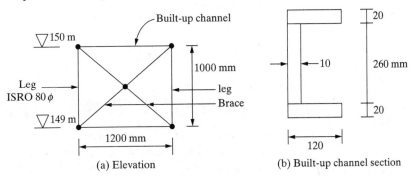

(a) Elevation   (b) Built-up channel section

Figure 15.17 Top panel of tower.

Solution   Let us calculate the exposed area of each panel to wind as shown in Table 15.6. Its main legs consist of solid round section ISRO 80 mm dia. The other members consist of flat-sided members. Therefore, the force coefficients will be calculated based on Clause 6.3.3.3 and 6.3.3.5 of the code.

TABLE 15.6   EXPOSED AREA TO WIND

Panel no.	Member	Section	Flange width (m)	Length (m)	No.	Obstruction area (m²)
1	Main leg	ISRO 80 ϕ	0.08	1.0	2	0.16
	Bracing	2L 50 × 6	0.05	1.562	2	0.156
	Horizontal	Built up channel	0.30	1.20	1	0.36
					Total	0.676

Increase panel exposed area by 5% to take care of gusset plates.

$$1.05 \times 0.676 = 0.71 \text{ m}^2$$

Wind pressure is given by

$$p_z = 0.6 \, V_z^2 \tag{15.7}$$

where

$$V_z = V_b \, k_1 \, k_2 \, k_3 \tag{15.3}$$

$V_b = 47$ m/s, $k_1 = 1.07, k_3 = 1.25$, terrain 2

At 149.5 m, $k_2 = 1.21$

$V_z = 47 \times 1.07 \times 1.21 \times 1.25 = 76$ m/s

$p_z = 0.60 \times (47 \times 1.07 \times 1.21 \times 1.25)^2 = 3470$ N/m²

D $V_z = 0.08 \times 76 = 6.08$ m²/s > 6.0 m²/s

Therefore, it falls in *supercritical flow* region.

Force coefficient for the flat member is 2.1 and for round member is 1.4 based on Tables 30 and 31 of the code. Let

$$A_1 = \frac{\text{exposed area of circular members}}{\text{total exposed area}}$$

$$A_2 = \frac{\text{exposed area of flat members}}{\text{total exposed area}}$$

Overall force coefficient C_f for parallel wind is given by

$$C_f = C_{fR} A_1 + C_{fF} A_2 = 1.4 \times \frac{0.168}{0.71} + 2.1 \times \frac{0.542}{0.71} = 1.94$$

Overall force coefficient C_f for diagonal wind is given by

$$C_f = 1.2 \times 1.94 = 2.32$$

The computation of wind load on the panel is shown in Table 15.7. Half of the total wind load is applied at the top and the remaining half at the bottom of the panel.   □

TABLE 15.7 COMPUTATION OF WIND FORCE

Panel no.	Height of panel top (m)	Gross area panel (m²)	Exposed area panel (m²)	Solidity ratio	Force coeff.				p_z (N/m²)	Wind load at top of panel : Parallel wind (kN)	Wind load at top of panel : Diagonal wind (kN)
					Circular member	Flat member	Overall				
1	150	1.20	0.71	0.59	1.4	2.1	1.94	3470	4.78	5.74
	149		(0.168) round member				(2.32)*			

Note: * For diagonal wind, the overall force coefficient for parallel case is multiplied by 1.2 as per code.

15.6 DYNAMIC WIND PRESSURE

Flexible slender structures and structural elements should be investigated to ascertain the importance of wind-induced oscillations or excitations along and across the direction of wind. Any building or structure which satisfies either of the following two criteria should be examined for dynamic effects of wind.

1. Buildings and closed structures with a height to minimum lateral dimension ratio of more than 5.0.

2. Buildings and closed structures whose natural frequency in the first mode is less than 1 Hz or fundamental period is more than 1 sec.

A designer should be aware of the following three forms of wind-induced motion, which are characterized by increasing amplitude of oscillation with the increase of wind speed.

1. *Galloping* Galloping is transverse oscillations of some structures due to the development of aerodynamic forces which are in phase with the motion. It is characterized by the progressively increasing amplitude of transverse vibration with increase of wind speed. The cross-section which are particularly prone to this type of excitation include the following:

   (a) All structures with non-circular cross-sections, such as triangular, square, polygons, as well as angles, crosses and T-sections,

   (b) Twisted cables and cables with ice encrustations.

2. *Flutter* Flutter is an unstable oscillatory motion of a structure due to coupling between aerodynamic force and elastic deformation of the structure. Perhaps the most common form is oscillatory motion due to combined bending and torsion. A structure may undergo progressively increased amplitude of the oscillatory motion which is a combination of different modes and may collapse eventually. Such energy transfer takes place when the natural frequencies of modes, taken individually, are close to each other (ratio being typically less than 2.0).

   Flutter can set in at wind speeds much less than those required for exciting the individual modes of motion. Long span suspension bridge decks or any member of a structure with large values of d/t (where d is the depth of a structure or structural member parallel to wind stream and t is the least lateral dimension of a member) are prone to low speed flutter. Wind tunnel testing is required to determine critical flutter speeds and the likely structural response.

3. *Ovalling* Thin-walled structures with open ends at one or both ends such as oil storage tanks and natural draught cooling towers, in which the ratio of the diameter of minimum lateral dimension to the wall thickness is of the order of 100 or more, are prone to ovalling oscillations. These oscillations are characterized by periodic radial deformation of the hollow structure.

The design wind pressure at any height Z is given by the following equations:

$$\bar{p}_z = 0.6\,\bar{V}_z^2 \tag{15.8a}$$

where

$$\bar{V}_z = V_b k_1 \bar{k}_2 k_3 \tag{15.8b}$$

$\bar{k}_2$ = hourly mean wind speed terrain factor
The hourly mean wind speed terrain factor $\bar{k}_2$ as given in Table 33 of IS:875 code is used to compute the wind pressures at various heights of the tower.
The along wind force on the building is calculated by modifying Equation (15.2) as follows:

$$F = GC_f A_e \bar{p}_z \tag{15.9}$$

where
G = gust factor = peak load effect/mean load effect

$$G = 1 + g_f r \sqrt{\left[B(1+\phi)^2 + \frac{SE}{\xi} \right]} \tag{15.10}$$

where
g_f = peak factor

$$= \frac{\text{expected peak value}}{\text{root mean value of a fluctuating load}} \tag{15.11}$$

r = roughness factor which depends on the size of the structure relative to ground roughness
For the product $g_f r$, refer to Figure 8 of the code.

B = back ground factor indicating a measure of slowly varying component of fluctuating wind load (refer to Figure 9 of the code)
SE/ξ = measure of resonant component of the fluctuating wind load
S = size reduction factor (refer Figure 10 of code)
E = available energy in the wind stream at the natural frequency of the structure (refer to Figure 11 of the code)
ξ = damping ratio of the material of the structure

For welded steel structure, 1%, for bolted steel structure 2%, and for RC structure 1.6%.

$$\phi = g_f r \sqrt{B} / 4 \tag{15.12}$$

This factor is to be accounted for buildings whose height is less than 75 m in Category 4 and whose height is less than 25 m in Category 3. For all other cases, it is taken as zero. The background factor is computed using a factor λ given by

$$\lambda = \frac{C_y b}{C_z h} \tag{15.13}$$

C_y = lateral correlation constant may be taken as 10 in the absence of any data
C_z = longitudinal correlation constant may be taken as 12 in the absence of any data

b = breadth of the structure normal to wind

h = height of the structure

$$F_0 = \frac{C_z f_0 h}{\overline{V}_z} \tag{15.14}$$

where

f_0 = natural frequency of the structure in Hz

15.7 ILLUSTRATIVE EXAMPLES

Example 15.7

Estimate the gust factor for a 300 m TV tower at Mumbai. The basic wind speed for Mumbai is 44 m/sec. It is a class C structure and terrain category is taken as 3.

Solution   The mean hourly wind speed at 300 m height is computed as follows:

$$\overline{V}_z = V_b k_1 \overline{k}_2 k_3$$

The various parameters are as follows:

Fundamental frequency of vibration = 0.36 Hz

V_b = 44 m/s; k_1 = 1.07 for 100 years mean life

$\overline{k}_2$ = 0.93 (Table 33 of the code); k_3 = 1.0

h = 300 m

$$\overline{V}_z = 44 \times 1.07 \times 0.93 \times 1 = 43.78 \text{ m/s}$$

A TV tower has varying width with height. The code does not clarify how to estimate its width. In the absence of any clarity, the width b is taken at mid height of the tower.

b = 16.5 m

C_y = 10; C_z = 12 as per the code

$$\lambda = \frac{C_y b}{C_z h} = \frac{10 \times 16.5}{12 \times 300} = 0.0458$$

$g_f r$ = 0.74 (Figure 8) ; and $L(h)$ = 2050 (Figure 8 of the code)

$$\frac{C_z h}{L(h)} = \frac{12 \times 300}{2050} = 1.756, \quad \therefore \text{background factor } B = 0.58$$

$$F_0 = \frac{C_z f_0 h}{\overline{V}_z} = \frac{12 \times 0.36 \times 300}{43.78} = 29.60$$

Size reduction factor S = 0.082 (Figure 10 of the code)

$$\frac{f_0 L(h)}{\overline{V}_h} = \frac{0.36 \times 2050}{43.78} = 16.86$$

Gust energy factor E = 0.085 (Figure 11 of the code)

The gust factor is computed as follows:

$$G = 1 + g_f r \sqrt{\left[B(1+\phi)^2 + \frac{SE}{\xi} \right]}$$

$$G = 1 + 0.74 \times \sqrt{0.58 + \frac{0.082 \times 0.085}{0.02}} = 1.71$$

The wind pressure at 300 m is given by:

$\therefore p_h = 0.6 \times 43.78^2 = 1150$ N/m² or 1.15 kN/m²

With a gust factor of 1.71, the dynamic wind pressure is 1.97 kN/m²   □

Example 15.8

A 100 m tall building has a width of 30 m and storey height is 3 m. Compare the static and dynamic wind pressures if it is located in (i) terrain 2 and (ii) terrain 4. Given $V_b = 44$ m/s, $k_1 = 0.91$ and $k_3 = 1.21$.

Solution   The storey height is 3 m. Its period of vibration in the first mode is 3.5 sec. Let us compute the terrain and height factor k_2 @ 9 m interval.

It is a class C building because height H is more than 50 m.

Static Pressure

$$V_z = V_b k_1 k_2 k_3$$

$\therefore$
$$V_z = 44 \times 0.91 \times k_2 \times 1.21 = 48.45\, k_2$$

The values of k_2 for different heights are obtained from Table 2 of the code.
The static wind pressure is computed in each category from:

$$P_z = 0.6\, V_z^2$$

Dynamic Pressure

$$\bar{V}_z = V_b k_1 \bar{k}_2 k_3 = 44 \times 0.91 \times \bar{k}_2 \times 1.21 = 48.45\, \bar{k}_2$$

The values of $\bar{k}_2$ for different heights are obtained from Table 33 of the code.
At 100 m,

(i) in Category 2, $\bar{k}_2 = 0.92 \therefore \bar{V}_z = 44.58$ m/s

(ii) in Category 4, $\bar{k}_2 = 0.57 \therefore \bar{V}_z = 27.62$ m/s

(i) *Gust Factor in Terrain Category 2*

The width of the building $b = 30$ m

Fundamental frequency $f_0 = 1/3.5 = 0.285$ Hz

$C_y = 10; C_z = 12$ as per the code

$$\lambda = \frac{C_y b}{C_z h} = \frac{10 \times 30}{12 \times 100} = 0.25$$

$g_f r = 0.95$ (Figure 8) and $L(h) = 1750$ (Figure 8 of the code)

$$\frac{C_z h}{L(h)} = \frac{12 \times 100}{1750} = 0.68, \therefore \text{background factor } B = 0.7$$

$$F_0 = \frac{C_z f_0 h}{\bar{V}_z} = \frac{12 \times 0.285 \times 100}{44.58} = 7.67$$

Size reduction factor $S = 0.21$ (Figure 10 of the code)

$$\frac{f_0 L(h)}{\bar{V}_h} = \frac{0.285 \times 1750}{44.58} = 11.2$$

Gust energy factor $E = 0.11$ (Figure 11 of the code)
The gust factor is computed as follows:

$$G = 1 + g_f r \sqrt{\left[B(1+\phi)^2 + \frac{SE}{\xi} \right]}$$

$$G = 1 + 0.95 \times \sqrt{0.70 + \frac{0.21 \times 0.11}{0.02}} = 2.30$$

(ii) *Gust Factor in Terrain Category 4*

The width of the building $b = 30$ m
Fundamental frequency $f_0 = 1/3.5 = 0.285$ Hz
$C_y = 10$; $C_z = 12$ as per the code

$$\lambda = \frac{C_y b}{C_z h} = \frac{10 \times 30}{12 \times 100} = 0.25$$

$g_f r = 1.85$ (Figure 8) and L(h) = 1250 (Figure 8 of the code)

$$\frac{C_z h}{L(h)} = \frac{12 \times 100}{1250} = 0.96, \quad \therefore \text{ background factor } B = 0.6$$

$$F_0 = \frac{C_z f_0 h}{\bar{V}_z} = \frac{12 \times 0.285 \times 100}{27.62} = 12.38$$

Size reduction factor $S = 0.11$ (Figure 10 of the code)

$$\frac{f_0 L(h)}{\bar{V}_h} = \frac{0.285 \times 1250}{27.62} = 12.90$$

Gust energy factor $E = 0.10$ (Figure 11 of the code)
The gust factor is computed as follows:

$$G = 1 + g_f r \sqrt{\left[B(1+\phi)^2 + \frac{SE}{\xi} \right]}$$

$$G = 1 + 1.85 \times \sqrt{0.60 + \frac{0.11 \times 0.10}{0.02}} = 2.98$$

The dynamic wind pressure is computed from

$$\bar{p}_z = 0.6 \, G \bar{V}_z^2$$

The static and dynamic wind pressures are shown in Figures 15.18 and 15.19 for terrain Category 2 and 4, respectively. It is to be noted that the dynamic pressures are more than the static wind pressures in terrain Category 2, while the dynamic pressures are less in terrain Category 4. □

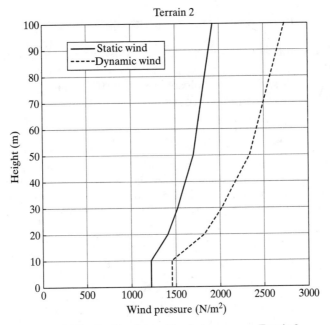

Figure 15.18 Static and dynamic wind pressures – Terrain 2.

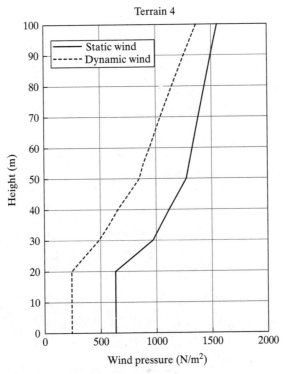

Figure 15.19 Static and dynamic wind pressures – Terrain 4.

15.8 WIND LOAD ON A TRUSS BRIDGE

The loads on a highway bridge are computed by using Indian Roads Congress Code IRC 6–2014. This code gives all kinds of loads including wind load on different types of highway bridges. The basic philosophy of the IRC code for wind loads is same as in the IS:875 code. The computation of wind load on a 40 m steel truss bridge is illustrated in Example 15.9.

Example 15.9

A 40 m (8 panels @ 5 m c/c) steel bridge as shown in Figure 15.20 is to be built near Srinagar, Garhwal. It is located in a terrain with obstructions, and the mean height of the bridge above water level is 15 m. It is to be designed for Class A loading. There are two trusses 5.5 m c/c apart. Height of the truss is 7 m between the top and bottom chords.

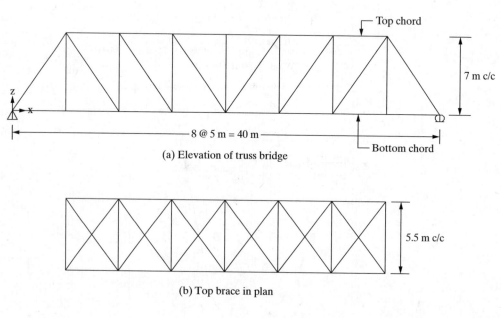

(a) Elevation of truss bridge

(b) Top brace in plan

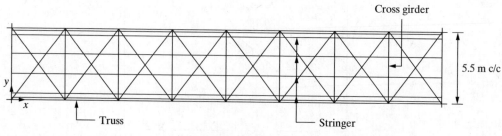

(c) Deck level plan

Figure 15.20   Truss steel bridge.

The exposed height of the bottom chord, cross-girder, stringers and RC deck with kerb is 0.9 m. The width of the carriage way is 5 m and clear height is 6.15 m. Estimate the wind load on the bridge.

Solution   It is assumed that one-half height of a panel is shared by top chord and the remaining by the bottom chord. The exposed area of a panel is computed as shown in Table 15.8(a).

TABLE 15.8(a)   EXPOSED AREA OF A PANEL

Exposed area of one panel of top chord			
Top chord	2 ISMC 250	$0.25 \times 5 = 1.25$	m²
Vertical	4 ISA 75 × 75 × 8	$2 \times 0.075 \times 2 \times 3.5 = 1.05$	m²
Diagonal	4 ISA 100 × 100 × 10	$2 \times 0.10 \times 4.3 = 0.86$	m²
		Total area $= 3.16 \times 1.10 = 3.476$	
Exposed area of one panel of bottom chord			
Bottom chord	2 ISMC 250	$0.90 \times 5 = 4.50$	m²
Vertical	4 ISA 75 × 75 × 8	$2 \times 0.075 \times 2 \times 3.5 = 1.05$	m²
Diagonal	4 ISA 100 × 100 × 10	$2 \times 0.10 \times 4.3 = 0.86$	m²
		Total area $= 6.41 \times 1.10 = 7.051$	

The exposed area of each chord is increased by 10% to take care of the extra area of gusset plates.

Total exposed area $= 3.476 + 7.051 = 10.527$ m²

Total panel area $= 5 \times 7 = 35$ m²

∴ Solidity ratio $= 10.527/35 = 0.3$

Drag coefficient $C_D = 1.7$ for built up section (Appendix C)

Truss spacing ratio $= 5.5/7 = 0.8$, ∴ shielding factor $= 0.8$

Corresponding to basic wind speed of 33 m/s, the hourly mean wind speed @ 15 m above the water surface $= 19.6$ m/s for the bridge situated in terrain with obstructions.

The corresponding wind pressure $= 0.6 \, V_z^2 = 0.6 \times 19.6^2 = 230$ N/m²

The bridge falls in wind zone having a basic wind speed of 39 m/s.

∴ Revised pressure $= 230 \times \left(\dfrac{39}{33} \right)^2 = 321.25$ N/m²

The topography at the site is such that it creates a tunneling effect.

∴ Increased pressure $= 1.2 \times 321.25 = 385.5$ N/m²

The gust factor for a bridge $= 2$ as per IRC 6
The wind force is given by:

$$F = p_z A_e C_D G$$

Wind load without Class A load on the bridge
The wind load calculations without live load on the bridge for one panel are shown in Table 15.8(b).

TABLE 15.8(b) WIND LOAD

Location	Wind Force, N
Top chord of windward truss	$F = 385.5 \times 3.476 \times 1.7 \times 2 = 4556$ N
Top chord of leeward truss	$F = 385.5 \times 3.476 \times (0.8 \times 1.7) \times 2 = 3645$ N
Bottom chord of windward truss	$F = 385.5 \times 7.051 \times 1.7 \times 2 = 9242$ N
Bottom chord of leeward truss	$F = 385.5 \times 7.051 \times (0.8 \times 1.7) \times 2 = 7394$ N

Total load at a panel point at top chord = 4556 + 3645 = 8200 N
Total load at a panel point at bottom chord = 9242 + 7394 = 16636 N

Wind load with Class A load on the bridge
Length of one Class A vehicle = 20.3 m head to tail and clear space between two Class A vehicles = 18.5 m
Total no. of vehicles on the bridge = 1 at a time
Height of vehicle for the purpose of wind load (as per the code) = 3 m above the roadway surface
Drag coefficient = 1.2 for vehicle
Wind on vehicle

$$F = p_z A_e C_D G$$
$$F = 385.5 \times (3 \times 5) \times 1.2 \times 2 = 13878 \text{ N}$$

Height of the truss is 6.75 m c/c of the chords
The height of the kerb above the road surface = 0.3 m
The height of the road way above the bottom of the bottom chord is 0.9 − 0.30 = 0.60 m.
Exposed height of the bridge above the vehicle = 7 − 0.9 + 0.3 − 3.0 = 3.4 m
The exposed area calculation of a panel is shown in Table 15.9(a).

TABLE 15.9(a) EXPOSED AREA OF A PANEL

Exposed area of one panel of top chord			
Top chord	2 ISMC 250	$0.25 \times 5 = 1.25$	m²
Vertical	4 ISA 75 × 75 x 8	$2 \times 0.075 \times 2 \times 3.4 = 1.02$	m²
Diagonal	4 ISA 100 × 100 × 10	$2 \times 0.10 \times 4.2 = 0.84$	m²
		Total area = $3.11 \times 1.10 = 3.42$	
Exposed area of one panel of bottom chord			
Bottom chord up to kerb		$0.90 \times 5 = 4.50$	m²
		Total area = $4.50 \times 1.10 = 4.95$	

The wind load calculations with live load on the bridge are shown in Table 15.9(b).

TABLE 15.9(b) WIND LOAD

Location	Wind Force, N
Top chord of windward truss	$F = 385.5 \times 3.42 \times 1.7 \times 2 = 4283$ N
Top chord of leeward truss	$F = 385.5 \times 3.42 \times (0.8 \times 1.7) \times 2 = 3586$ N
Bottom chord of windward truss	$F = 385.5 \times 4.95 \times 1.7 \times 2 = 6488$ N
Bottom chord of leeward truss	$F = 385.5 \times 4.95 \times (0.8 \times 1.7) \times 2 = 5190$ N

Total load at a panel point at top chord = 4283 + 3586 = 7869 N
Total load at a panel point at bottom chord = 13878 + 6488 + 5190 = 25556 N
In the same manner, wind load at other panel points can be estimated. The live load (Class A vehicle) should be placed at different positions on the bridge to get the critical condition for each member. The bridge should be designed for the governing load case.   □

15.9 RESPONSE OF STRUCTURES TO WIND LOAD

The wind loads are estimated based on static and dynamic considerations as discussed so far. The higher of these loads are applied statically on the structure, and analysis is carried out in the usual manner. In certain aerodynamically sensitive structures such as tall buildings, chimneys and cooling towers, there are two additional considerations:

- Across wind response
- Wind interference due to adjoining structures

A treatment of these topics is beyond the present scope.

During strong winds, the accelerations of top floors of multistoried buildings may increase significantly causing discomfort to the occupants. Typical qualitative values of discomfort are shown in Table 15.10. The floor acceleration should be controlled by proper structural detailing.

TABLE 15.10 HUMAN RESPONSE TO WIND-INDUCED
VIBRATIONS IN MULTISTORIED BUILDINGS

Degree of discomfort	Acceleration % g
Imperceptible	< 0.5 %
Perceptible	0.5 % – 1.5 %
Annoying	1.5 % – 5 %
Very annoying	5 % – 15 %
Intolerable	> 15 %

PROBLEMS

15.1 What do you understand by the terms: (i) velocity profile, (ii) fetch length, (iii) shielding factor and (iv) gust.

15.2 Determine the wind pressure on the walls and roof of a building shown in Figure P15.1. It is located in Chennai in Terrain 2. Assume (i) a high permeability and (b) zero permeability. Consider all wind directions in the plan. The basic wind speed is 44 m/s. Assume suitable data as required.

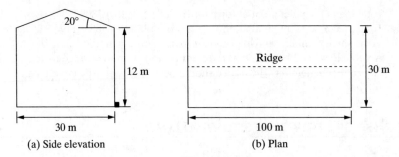

(a) Side elevation   (b) Plan

Figure P15.1

15.3 Determine external and internal wind pressure coefficients for the roof of a stadium whose section is shown in Figure P15.2.

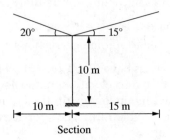

Section

Figure P15.2

15.4 A section of an aircraft hangar is shown in Figure P15.3. It is located at Cochin. Find the wind pressure on its roof in various zones.

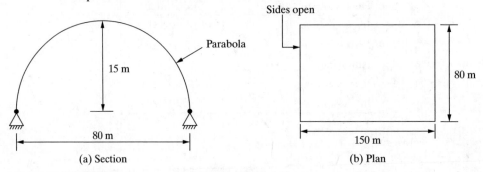

(a) Section   (b) Plan

Figure P15.3

15.5 A 150 m tall moment resistant RC building has a width of 30 m, ground storey height of 3.75 m and other storey height is 3.25 m. In plan it is 30 × 60 m with 5 m spacing between frames. Compare the static and dynamic wind pressures if it is located in (i) Terrain 3 and (ii) Terrain 4. Given V_b = 50 m/s, k_1 = 0.90 and k_3 = 1.15.

15.6 (a) A structure is located at 'P' in Terrain 4 as shown in Figure P15.4. Find the velocity profile up to 150 m height @ 10 m interval. Assume class B structure. Given V_b = 50 m/s, k_1 = 0.90 and k_3 = 1.10.

     (b) A structure is located at 'Q' in Terrain 2 as shown in Figure P15.4. Find the velocity profile if the direction of wind is reversed.

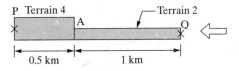

Figure P15.4

15.7 A structure is located at 'P' in Terrain 2 as shown in Figure P15.5. Find the velocity profile up to its gradient height @ 10 m interval. Assume class C structure. Given $V_b = 44$ m/s, $k_1 = 1.07$ and $k_3 = 1$.

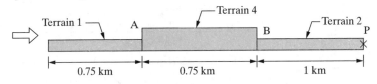

Figure P15.5

15.8 In Figure P15.6 find the factor k_3, if (i) a 50 m high building is located at 'B' and (ii) a 100 m high MW tower is located at 'D'. Wind direction is reversible.

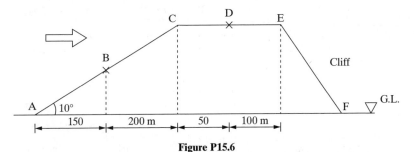

Figure P15.6

15.9 A chimney 270 m high has 22 m external diameter at the base and 12 m at the top. Its fundamental period of vibration is 3.25 sec. It is situated in terrain type 2, and basic wind speed is 39 m/s. Calculate the gust factor and dynamic wind pressure along its height. Take $k_3 = 1.08$.

15.10 Two panels 35 and 40 of a 150 m TV tower are shown in Figure P15.7. The basic wind speed is 47 m/s, terrain is 2 and factor k_3 is 1.25. Estimate the static wind force on the panels under parallel and diagonal wind.

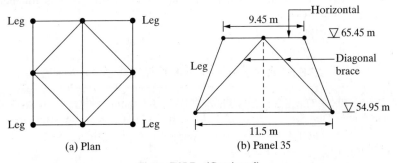

(a) Plan   (b) Panel 35

Figure P15.7 (Continued)

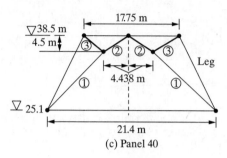

(c) Panel 40

Figure P15.7

		Panel 35		
	Leg	Horizontal	Brace	
	Box 300×32	2 ISA 75×8	2 ISA 100×10	

		Panel 40		
Leg	Horizontal	Brace 1	Brace 2	Brace 3
ISRO 125	2 ISA 110×12	2 ISA 130×10	2 ISA 75×8	2 ISA 65×8

15.11 The top panel of a 175 m TV tower is shown in Figure P15.8. The basic wind speed is 47 m/s, terrain is 2 and factor k_3 is 1.1. Estimate the static wind force on the panels under parallel and diagonal wind.

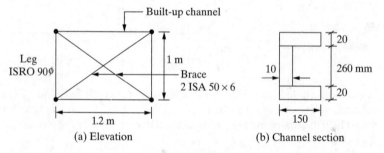

(a) Elevation   (b) Channel section

Figure P15.8

15.12 Estimate the gust factor for a 300 m TV tower at Amritsar. Its width at mid height may be taken as 18 m. Its fundamental period of vibration is 2.75 sec. It is situated in Terrain 2. Assume suitable data.

REFERENCES – FURTHER READING

Cook, N. J. (1985) The Designer's Guide to Wind Loading of Building Structures, Part 1: Background, Damage survey, Wind data and Structural Classification, Butterworths, London.

Cook, N. J. (1989) The Designer's Guide to Wind Loading of Building Structures, Part 2: Static Structures, Butterworths, London.

Eurocode 1-4 (2005) Actions on Structures – Part 1-4: General actions – Wind actions, European Committee for Standardization, Brussels.

Gould, P. L. and Abu-Sitta, S. H., (1980) Dynamic Response of Structures to Wind and Earthquake Loading, Pentech Press, London.

Holmes, J. D. (2001) Wind Loading of Structures, Spon Press, London.

Houghton, E. L. and Cerruthers, N. B. (1976) Wind Forces in Building and Structures, Edward Arnold Ltd. London.

IRC 6 (2014) Standard Specifications and Code of Practice for Road Bridges, Indian Roads Congress, New Delhi.

IS:875-Part 3 (1987) Design Loads (other than Earthquake) for Buildings and Structures, BIS, New Delhi.

IS:4998-Part 1 (1992) Design of Reinforced Concrete Chimneys, BIS, New Delhi.

IS:15498 (2004) Guidelines for Improving Cyclonic Resistance of Low Rise Houses and other Buildings, BIS, New Delhi.

Lawson, T. V. (1980) Wind Effects on Buildings, Vol 1 and 2, Applied Science Publication, Essex, U.K.

Sachs, P. (1978) Wind Forces in Engineering, Pergaman Press, London.

Scruton, C. (1981) An Introduction to Wind Effects on Structures, Engineering Design Guide 40, British Standard Institution, Oxford University Press, London.

Simiu, E. and Scanlan, R. H. (1996) Wind Effects on Structures – Application to Design, John Wiley and Sons, 2nd Ed., New York.

A1 | Measuring Earthquakes: Magnitude and Intensity

Once an earthquake occurs, it is important to know where the seismic event took place, how intense it was and its impact on the built environment, that is buildings, transportation structures, utilities and communication lines. Magnitude refers to the total energy released. Intensity refers to the extent of damage and loss of life.

A1.1 MAGNITUDE

Earthquake magnitude is typically measured by the Richter Scale, which is based on the maximum ground amplitude at a location 100 km from the epicenter. The Richter Scale was developed by Charles F. Richter in 1935 to measure the magnitude of an earthquake. It is a logarithmic measurement of the amount of energy released by an earthquake. Earthquakes with a magnitude of at least 4.5 are strong enough to be recorded by sensitive seismographs all over the world. An increase of 1 point means a 10-fold increase in the characteristic amplitude and an approximately 31-fold increase in the energy released.

In India, several hundred shocks of varying sizes occur annually. Some of the major earthquakes in the world are listed in Table A1.1.

TABLE A1.1 MAJOR WORLD EARTHQUAKES

S. No.	Earthquake	Date	Magnitude
1	Chile	22 May 1960	9.5
2	Great Alaska, USA	28 March 1964	9.2
3	Northern Sumatra	26 Dec 2004	9.2
4	Honshu, Japan	11 March 2011	9.0
5	Assam, India	15 Aug 1950	8.6
6	Sichuan, China	12 May 2008	7.9
7	Kathmandu, Nepal	25 April 2015	7.8
8	Tangshan, China	28 July 1976	7.5

A1.2 INTENSITY

Modified Mercalli Intensity scale (MMI) measures the intensity or impact of an earthquake on people and the built environment. The intensity of a quake is evaluated according to the observed severity of the quake at specific locations. The Mercalli scale rates the intensity on a Roman numeral scale that ranges from I to XII.

In some countries, the comprehensive scale also called MSK 64 proposed by UNESCO is also used.

TABLE A1.2   MODIFIED MERCALLI INTENSITY SCALE

MMI Scale	Summary Damage description	Full Description
I		Not felt. Marginal and long period effects of large earthquakes.
II		Felt by persons at rest, on upper floors, or favorably placed.
III		Felt indoors. Hanging objects swing. Vibration like passing of light trucks. Duration estimated. May not be recognized as an earthquake.
IV		Hanging objects swing. Vibration-like passing of heavy trucks; or sensation of a jolt like a heavy ball striking the walls. Standing motor cars rock. Windows, dishes, doors rattle. Glasses clink. Crockery clashes. In the upper range of IV, wooden walls and frame creak.
V	Picture move	Felt outdoors; direction estimated. Sleepers wakened. Liquids disturbed, some spilled. Small unstable objects displaced or upset. Doors swing, close, open. Shutters, pictures move. Pendulum clocks stop, start, change rate.
VI	Object fall	Felt by all. Many frightened and run outdoors. Persons walk unsteadily. Windows, dishes, glassware broken. Knickknacks, books, etc., off shelves. Pictures off walls. Furniture moved or overturned. Weak plaster and masonry D cracked. Small bells ring (church, school). Trees, bushes shaken (visibly, or heard to rustle).
VII	Nonstructural damage	Difficult to stand. Noticed by drivers of motor cars. Hanging objects quiver. Furniture broken. Damage to masonry D, including cracks. Weak chimneys broken at roof line. Fall of plaster, loose bricks, stones, tiles, cornices (also unbraced parapets and architectural ornaments). Some cracks in masonry C. Waves on ponds; water turbid with mud. Small slides and caving in along sand or gravel banks. Large bells ring. Concrete irrigation ditches damaged.
VIII	Moderate damage	Steering of motor cars affected. Damage to masonry C; partial collapse. Some damage to masonry B; none to masonry A. Fall of stucco and some masonry walls. Twisting, fall of chimneys, factory stacks, monuments, towers, elevated tanks. Frame houses moved on foundations if not bolted down; loose panel walls thrown out. Decayed piling broken off. Branches broken from trees. Changes in flow or temperature of springs and wells. Cracks in wet ground and on steep slopes.

(Continued)

TABLE A1.2   (CONTINUED)

MMI Scale	Summary Damage description	Full Description
IX	Heavy damage	General panic. Masonry D destroyed; masonry C heavily damaged, sometimes with complete collapse; masonry B seriously damaged. (General damage to foundations.) Frame structures, if not bolted, shifted off foundations. Frames racked. Serious damage to reservoirs. Underground pipes broken. Conspicuous cracks in ground. In alluvial areas sand and mud ejected, earthquake fountains, sand craters.
X	Heavy damage	Most masonry and frame structures destroyed with their foundations. Some well-built wooden structures and bridges destroyed. Serious damage to dams, dikes, embankments. Large landslides. Water thrown on banks of canals, rivers, lakes, etc. Sand and mud shifted horizontally on beaches and flat land. Rails bent slightly.
XI	Extreme damage	Rails bent greatly. Underground pipelines completely out of service.
XII		Damage nearly total. Large rock masses displaced. Lines of sight and level distorted. Objects thrown into the air.

Masonry A: Good workmanship, mortar and design; reinforced, especially laterally and bound together by using steel, concrete, etc.; designed to resist lateral forces.

Masonry B: Good workmanship and mortar; reinforced but not designed in detail to resist lateral forces.

Masonry C: Ordinary workmanship and mortar; no extreme weaknesses like failing to tie in at corners but neither reinforced nor designed against horizontal forces.

Masonry D: Weak materials, such as adobe; poor mortar; low standards of workmanship; weak horizontally.

TABLE A1.3A   COMPREHENSIVE SCALE MSK 64 – TYPE OF STRUCTURE

Type of Structure – Building	
Type A	Building in field-stone, rural structures, unburnt brickhouses, clay houses.
Type B	Ordinary brick buildings, buildings of large block and pre-fabricated type, half-timbered structures, buildings in natural hewn stone,
Type C	Reinforced buildings, well-built wooden structures

TABLE A1.3B   COMPREHENSIVE SCALE MSK 64 – DEFINITION AND CLASSIFICATION OF DAMAGE

Definition of Damage	
Single, few	About 5%
Many	About 50%
Most	About 75%

(Continued)

TABLE A1.3B (CONTINUED)

Classification of Damage to Buildings		
Grade 1	Slight damage	Fine cracks in plaster: fall of small pieces of plaster
Grade 2	Moderate damage	Small cracks in plaster: fall of fairly large pieces of plaster: pantiles slip off cracks in chimneys parts of chimney fall down
Grade 3	Heavy damage	Large and deep cracks in plaster: fall of chimneys
Grade 4	Destruction	Gaps in walls: parts of buildings may collapse: separate parts of the buildings lose their cohesion: and inner walls collapse
Grade 5	Total damage	Total collapse of the buildings

TABLE A1.3C COMPREHENSIVE SCALE MSK 64 – INTENSITY SCALE

Scale	Brief Description	Detailed Description
1	Not noticeable	The intensity of the vibration is below the limits of sensibility: the tremor is detected and recorded by seismograph only.
2	Scarely noticeable (very slight)	Vibration is felt only by individual people at rest in houses, especially on upper floors of buildings.
3	Weak, partially observed only	The earthquake is felt indoors by a few people, outdoors only in favorable circumstances. The vibration is like that due to the passing of a light truck. Attentive observers notice a slight swinging of hanging objects. Somewhat more heavily on upper floors.
4	Largely observed	The earthquake is felt indoors by many people, outdoors by few. Here and there people awake, but no one is frightened. The vibration is like that of the passing of a heavily loaded truck. Windows, doors and dishes rattle. Floors and walls crack. Furniture begins to shake. Hanging objects swing slightly. Liquid in open vessels are slightly disturbed. In standing motor cars, the shock is noticeable.
5	Awakening	(i) The earthquake is felt indoors by all, outdoors by many. Many people awake. A few run outdoors. Animals become uneasy. Buildings tremble throughout. Hanging objects swing considerably. Pictures knock against walls or swing out of place. Occasionally pendulum clocks stop. Unstable objects overturn or shift. Open doors and windows are thrust open and slam back again. Liquids spill in small amounts from well-filled open containers. The sensation of vibration is like of heavy objects falling inside the buildings. (ii) Slight damages in buildings of Type A are possible. (iii) Sometimes changes in flow of springs.

(Continued)

TABLE A1.3C   (CONTINUED)

Scale	Brief Description	Detailed Description
6	Frightening	(i) Felt by most indoors and outdoors. Many people in buildings are frightened and run outdoors. A few persons lose their balance. Domestic animals run out of their stalls. In few instances, dishes and glassware may break, and books fall down. Heavy furniture may possibly move and small steeple bells may ring. (ii) Damage of Grade 1 is sustained in single buildings of Type B and in many of Type A. Damage in few buildings of Type A is of Grade 2. (iii) In few cases, cracks up to widths of 1 cm possible in wet ground in mountains occasional landslips: change in flow of springs and in level of well water are observed.
7	Damage of buildings	(i) Most people are frightened and run outdoors. Many find it difficult to stand. The vibration is noticed by persons driving motor cars. Large bells ring. (ii) In many buildings of Type C, damage of Grade 1 is caused: in many buildings of Type B damage is of Grade 2. Most buildings of Type A suffer damage of Grade 3, few of Grade 4. In single instances, landslides of roadway on steepslopes: crack inroads; seams of pipelines damaged; cracks in stone walls. (iii) Waves are formed on water and is made turbid by mud stirred up, Water levels in wells change and the flow of springs changes. Some times dry springs have their flow resorted and existing springs stop flowing. In isolated instances parts of sand and gravelly banks slip off.
8	Destruction of buildings	(i) Fright and panic; also persons driving motor cars are disturbed, Here and there branches of trees break off. Even heavy furniture moves and partly overturns. Hanging lamps are damaged in part. (ii) Most buildings of Type C suffer damage of Grade 2 and few of Grade 3, Most buildings of Type B suffer damage of Grade 3. Most buildings of Type A suffer damage of Grade 4. Occasional breaking of pipe seams. Memorials and monuments move and twist. Tombstones overturn. Stone walls collapse. (iii) Small landslips in hollows and on banked roads on steep slopes; cracks in ground up to widths of several centimetres. Water in lakes become turbid. New reservoirs come into existence. Dry wells refill and existing wells become dry. In many cases,change in flow and level of water is observed.
9	General damage of buildings	(i) General panic; considerable damage to furniture. Animals run to and fro in confusion and cry. (ii) Many buildings of Type C show damage of Grade 3 and a few of Grade 4. Many buildings of Type B show a damage of Grade 4 and a few of Grade 5. Many buildings of Type A suffer damage of Grade 5. Monuments and columns fall. Considerable damage to reservoirs; underground pipes partly broken, In individual cases, railway lines are bent and roadway damaged.

(Continued)

TABLE A1.3C   (CONTINUED)

Scale	Brief Description	Detailed Description
		(iii) On flat land overflow of water, sand and mud is often observed. Ground cracks to widths of up to 10 cm, on slopes and river banks more than 10 cm. Furthermore, a large number of slight cracks in ground; falls of rock, many landslides and earth flows; large waves in water. Dry wells renew their flow and existing wells dry up.
10	General destruction of buildings	(i) Many buildings of Type C suffer damage of Grade 4 and a few of Grade 5. Many buildings of Type B show damage of Grade 5. Most of Type A have destruction of Grade 5. Critical damage to dykes and dams. Severe damage to bridges. Railway lines are bent slightly. Underground pipes are bent or broken. Road paving and asphalt show waves.
		(ii) In ground, cracks up to widths of several centimetres, sometimes up to 1 m, Parallel to water courses occur broad fissures. Loose ground slides from steep slopes. From river banks and steep coasts, considerable landslides are possible. In coastal areas, displacement of sand and mud: change of water level in wells; water from canals, lakes, rivers, etc. thrown on land. New lakes occur.
11	Destruction	(i) Severe damage even to well built buildings, bridges, water dams and railway lines. Highways become useless. Underground pipes destroyed.
		(ii) Ground considerably distorted by broadcracks and fissures, as well as movement in horizontal and vertical directions. Numerous landslips and falls of rocks. The intensity of the earthquake requires to be investigated specifically.
12	Landscape changes	(i) Practically all structures above and below ground are greatly damaged or destroyed.
		(ii) The surface of the ground is radically changed. Considerable ground cracks with extensive vertical and horizontal movements are observed. Falling of rock and slumping of river banks over wide areas, lakes are dammed; waterfalls appear and rivers are deflected. The intensity of the earthquake requires to be investigated specially.

A2 | MATLAB Basics

A2.1 MATLAB BASICS

MATLAB provides several standard functions. In addition, there are several toolboxes or collections of functions and procedures available as part of the MATLAB package. MATLAB offers the option of developing customized toolboxes. Many such tools are available worldwide. MATLAB is case sensitive, so the commands and programming variables must be used very carefully. It means A + B is not the same as $a + b$. The MATLAB prompt (>>) will be used to indicate where the commands are entered. Anything written after this prompt denotes user input (i.e., a command) followed by a carriage return (i.e., the "enter" key).

A2.1.1 Help Command

MATLAB provides help on any command or topic by typing the help command on the prompt:

```
>> help help
```

HELP Display help text in Command Window. HELP, by itself, lists all primary help topics. Each primary topic corresponds to a directory name on the MATLAB PATH.

```
>> help sum   % It provides help on the command sum
>> help paren % It provides help on different types of parenthesis;
   ( ); { }; [ ]
>> help arith % It provides help on all arithmetic operators
```

Comment   It can be seen that on any command line, any information typed after the "%" sign is treated as a comment and is ignored by the MATLAB.

The MATLAB also provides a very exhaustive documentation along with the software for each toolbox. In addition, more information on various aspects is available on MATLAB user groups on the web.

A2.1.2 Parenthesis

In MATLAB, parenthesis ( ); braces { }; and brackets [ ] have specific meanings which is not so in FORTRAN or visual C++.

( ) Parentheses are used to indicate precedence in arithmetic expressions and to enclose arguments of functions in the usual way. They are used to enclose subscripts of vectors and matrices in a manner somewhat more general than the usual way. Parenthesis can also enclose logical (or 0–1) subscripts.

For example:

$$X = [4 \quad -5 \quad 2.50 \quad 10]$$

(i) X(3)　　　It is the third element of X.

(ii) X([1 2 3])　It is the first three elements of X.

```
ans =

    4.0000    -5.0000    2.5000
```

(iii) If X has N components, X(N:–1:1) reverses them. Thus, X(4:–1:1) gives

```
ans =

    10.0000    2.5000    -5.0000    4.0000
```

(iv) X(X > 2.0) returns those elements of X that are greater than 2.0.

```
ans =

    4.0000    2.5000    10.0000
```

{ } Braces are used to form cell arrays. Braces are also referred to as the curly brackets. They are similar to brackets [ ] except that nesting levels are preserved. Braces are also used for content addressing of cell arrays. They are similar to parentheses in this case except that the contents of the cell are returned.

[ ] Brackets are used in forming vectors and matrices. It is also referred to as the square brackets.

```
A = [2 4 0]              %A is a row vector
B = [ -4 10 SQRT(-5)]    %It is a vector with three elements
```

A2.1.3 Defining Variables

The basic variable types in MATLAB are scalar, vector and matrix. Variables are defined by typing the name of the variable followed by an equal sign and the value of the variable. The values of a vector or matrix are enclosed by square brackets, and rows of matrices are separated by semicolons.

For example:

```
A = 1                    % A is a scalar
```

Vectors

(i) Let us define a row vector

```
>>X = [4 -5 2.50 -10]
X =

    4.0000 -5.0000    2.5000 -10.0000
```

Note that an equal sign was used for assigning the variable name 'X' to the vector, square brackets to enclose its entries and spaces to separate them. It was possible to use commas (,) instead of spaces to separate the entries or even a combination of the two.

There is one more observation. MATLAB repeats what was typed in after processing the command. Quite often, we do not think the need to 'see' the output of a specific command. This output can be suppressed by using a semicolon (;) at the end of the command line.

(ii) Let us define a column vector

To create a column vector, either use semicolons (;) to separate the entries or first define a row vector and then take its *transpose* to obtain a column vector. Let us define a column vector D with entries (10 15 −12 0   0.50) using both techniques.

Case (a)

```
>>D= [10; 15; -12;0;0.50]          % It defines a column vector
D =
        10
        15
       -12
        0
        0.50
```

Case (b)

```
>>D = [10, 15, -12, 0,0.50]        % First define a row vector
D =
10 15 -12 0 0.50
>>D'                               % Now take transpose of vector D
ans =
        10
        15
       -12
        0
        0.50
```

Case (c)

```
>>E = transpose (D) % it will give the same result as
above.
```

A single quote is used to take the *transpose* of a vector (or a matrix).

A2.1.4 Define a Matrix

```
C = [1 2 3; 4 5 6; 7 8 9]          % C is a 3 × 3 matrix
C =
```

$$\begin{bmatrix} 1 & 2 & 3 \\ 4 & 5 & 6 \\ 7 & 8 & 9 \end{bmatrix}$$

You can extract the numbers from the matrix using the convention A(*row #, col #*).

```
Try
>>C(1,3)                % Element at first row and third column
ans
        3.0000
>>C(3,2)                % Element at third row and second column
ans
        8.0000
```

You can also assign values of individual array elements

```
>>C(1,2) =100
```

Matrices with regularly increasing or decreasing values can be created as follows:

```
F = [1:6]           % create a vector with entries 1  2  3  4  5  6
G = [1:0.1:2]       % create a vector with entries from 1 to 2
                       incremented by 0.1
```

We can build a matrix from row vectors

```
row1 = [1 2 3]; row2 = [4 5 6]; row3 = [7 8 9];
C = [row1; row2; row3]
```

or from column vectors.

```
column1 = [1; 4; 7]; column2 = [2; 5; 8]; column3 = [3; 6; 9];
D = [column1 column2 column3]
```

Serveral matrices can be joined to create a larger one.

```
M = [A B; C D]
```

Displaying Data in a Matrix   The values of a variable can be displayed by simply typing the variable name. In matrix case, a specific element, row or column of a matrix can be examined separately. A single element of a matrix can be addressed by typing the name of the matrix followed by the row and column indices of the element in parentheses. To address an entire column or row, a colon can be substituted for either index. For example:

```
A(1,1)          display the element in the 1st row, 1st column of A
A(:,1)          display the 1st column of A
A(2,:)          display the 2nd row of A
```

A2.1.5 Special Matrices

There are some short-cuts for creating special matrices. Try the following:

```
>>B = ones(1,8)             and,   >> B = ones(8)
>>C = eye(6,8)              and,   >> eye(8)
>>D = zeros(3,4)            and,   >> zeros(4)
>>E = diag([1  2  3])       % create a matrix whose diagonal is 1 2 3
```

The 'eye' command creates the 'identity matrix' – this is the matrix version of the number 1.

A2.1.6 Variable Name "ans"

MATLAB automatically assigns the variable name "ans" to anything that has not been assigned a name. The variable "ans", however, gets re-cycled each time a command is entered without assigning a variable name, and "ans" gets that value.

A2.1.7 Who and Whos Commands

Sometimes it is necessary to keep track of which variables have been defined and occupy the workspace. MATLAB does it for us through the command "who" or "whos" that give all sorts of information on which variables are active.

```
>>who        % List current variables only
>>whos       % Lists more information about each variable
```

A2.1.8 Operators

The operators in MATLAB are arithmetic operators, relational operators and logic operators.
The relational operators are as follows:

```
<        less than
>        greater than
<=       less than or equal
>=       greater than or equal
= =      equal
~ =      not equal
```

Note that "=" is used in an assignment statement while "= =" is used in a relation. Relations may be connected or quantified by the logical operators

```
&        and    xor
|        or     all
~        not    any
```

A2.1.9 Functions

Scalar functions Certain MATLAB functions operate essentially on scalars but operate element-wise when applied to a matrix. The most common functions are as follows:

```
sin    asin   exp                  abs    round
cos    acos   log (natural log)    sqrt   floor
tan    atan   rem (remainder)      sign   ceil
```

Vector functions MATLAB functions operate essentially on a vector (row or column) but act on a m-by-n matrix ($m \geq 2$) in a column-by-column fashion to produce a row vector containing the results of their application to each column. Row-by-row action can be obtained by using the transpose; for example mean(A')'.

A few of these functions are:

```
max      sum      median     any
min      prod     mean       all
sort     std
```

Matrix functions   Much of MATLAB's power comes from its matrix functions. Some of the useful ones are as follows:

det	determinant
size	size
norm	1-norm, 2-norm, F-norm, ∞-norm
cond	condition number in the 2-norm
rank	rank
chol	cholesky factorization
svd	singular value decomposition
inv	inverse
lu	LU factorization
qr	QR factorization
hess	hessenberg form
expm	matrix exponential
sqrtm	matrix square root
poly	characteristic polynomial
eig	eigenvalues and eigenvectors; solution of $[A]\{X\} = \lambda \{X\}$; where λ is eigenvalue and $\{X\}$ is eigenvector.

Matrix building functions   Convenient matrix building functions are as follows:

eye	identity matrix
zeros	matrix of zeros
ones	matrix of ones
diag	diagonal matrix
triu	upper triangular part of a matrix
tril	lower triangular part of a matrix
rand	randomly generated matrix
hilb	Hilbert matrix
magic	magic square

Example 1

zeros(m,n) produces a *m*-by-*n* matrix of zeros.

```
>>>>zeros(3,4)
ans =
       0      0      0      0
       0      0      0      0
       0      0      0      0
```

Example 2

If x is a vector, diag(x) is the diagonal matrix with x down the diagonal.

```
>> x=[4 6 8]
```

```
x =
      4      6      8
>>diag(x)
ans =
      4      0      0
      0      6      0
      0      0      8
```
                                                                    □

Example 3

If C is a square matrix, then diag(C) is a vector consisting of the diagonal of C.

```
>> C =[1 2 3;4 5 6;7 8 9]
C =
      1      2      3
      4      5      6
      7      8      9
>>diag(C)
ans =
      1
      5
      9
```

MAGIC – A magic square is an arrangement of numbers (usually integers) in a square grid, where the numbers in each row and in each column, and the numbers that run diagonally in both directions, all add up to the same number. The constant that is the sum of every row, column and diagonal is called the *magic constant or magic sum, S.* Every normal magic square has a unique constant determined solely by the value of size of the matrix n.
                                                                    □

Example 4

```
>>magic(4)
ans =
     16      2      3     13
      5     11     10      8
      9      7      6     12
      4     14     15      1
```

The sum is 34 in each case. It is a magic matrix.
                                                                    □

A2.1.10 Matrix Arithmetic and Functions

MATLAB is able to calculate simple functions.
   For example,

```
det(A)              calculate the determinant of A
inv(A)              calculate the inverse of A
rank(A)             calculate the rank of A
```

The following matrix operations are available in MATLAB:

```
+       addition                e.g. A + B
–       subtraction             e.g. A - B
```

*	multiplication	e.g. A × B
^	power	e.g. A ^ 2
'	transpose	e.g. A'
\	left division or back slash	e.g. A\b
/	right division or slash	e.g. b/A

The matrix division operators "back slash" and "slash" have the following meanings:

X = A\B is the solution of linear simultaneous equations AX = Band,

X = B/A is the solution of XA = B

A is a coefficient matrix, X is unknown matrix, and B is known matrix. Matrix A need not be a square matrix.

In practice, linear equations of the form AX = B occur more frequently than those of the form XA = B. Consequently, the backslash is used far more frequently than the slash.

Example 5

$$[A] = \begin{bmatrix} 24 & 15 & 10 \\ 35 & 20 & 0 \\ 56 & -20 & 45 \end{bmatrix} \qquad [B] = \begin{bmatrix} 34 & -20 & 0 \\ 25 & 45 & -9 \\ 67 & -9 & 22 \end{bmatrix}$$

Using MATLAB, Find
  (i) A + B = C   **(ii)** A − B = C
  (iii) A B = C   **(iv)** AB + B = C

Solution
Matrix Addition

```
>>A = [24    15   10;   35   20    0;   56   -20   45];
>>B = [34   -20    0;   25   45   -9;   67    -9   22];
>>C = A + B
C =
       58    -5    10
       60    65    -9
      123   -29    67
```

Matrix Subtraction

```
>>C = A - B
C =
      -10    35    10
       10   -25     9
      -11   -11    23
```

Matrix Multiplication

```
>>C = A × B
C =
     1861     105      85
     1690     200    -180
     4419   -2425    1170
```

Matrix Multiplication and Addition
```
>>C = A × B + B
C =
     1895       85        85
     1715      245      -189
     4486    -2434      1192
```
□

Example 6

(a) Determine the inverse and determinant of the following matrix using MATLAB.

$$A = \begin{bmatrix} 50 & 20 & 0 \\ 20 & 75 & -10 \\ 0 & -10 & 100 \end{bmatrix}$$

(b) Find the eigenvalues of A.

Solution

(a)
```
>>A = [50      20     0;  20     75     -10;  0     -10     100];
% The matrix A is defined
>>INV(A)    % Find the inverse of A using MATLAB function INV
ans =
      0.0224    -0.0061    -0.0006
     -0.0061     0.0152     0.0015
     -0.0006     0.0015     0.0102
>>det(A)    % Find the determinant of A using MATLAB function
            det

ans =
      330000
```

(b)
```
>>eig(A)    % Find the eigenvalues of A using MATLAB function
            eig

ans =
       38.5225
       81.9673
      104.5102
```
□

Example 7

Determine the solution of the following linear simultaneous equations using MATLAB.

$$A = \begin{bmatrix} 5 & 2 & 3 \\ 4 & 5 & 4 \\ 7 & 0 & 9 \end{bmatrix}, \qquad B = \begin{Bmatrix} 10 \\ 13 \\ 16 \end{Bmatrix}$$

Solution
```
>> A = [5 2 3;4 5 4;7 0 9]    % define matrix A
```

```
A =
        5       2       3
        4       5       4
        7       0       9
>> b = [10 13 16]        % define b vector as a row
b =
        10      13      16
>> A\b'   % find solution by taking transpose of b, that is, column
                vector
ans =
        1.0000
        1.0000
        1.0000
```

It makes use of Gaussian elimination method.   □

A2.1.11 Eigenvalues and Eigenvectors

The command eig(K,M) gives two matrices V and D. Matrix V is for eigenvectors arranged column-wise and matrix D is a diagonal matrix consisting of eigenvalues on the diagonal. The frequencies are obtained as follows:

$$\lambda = \omega^2$$

```
>>[V,D] = eig(K,M)
```

Alternatively, the following command can be given in MATLAB.

```
>>eig(M,K)
```

It again generates two matrices V and D. Matrix V is for eigenvectors arranged column-wise, and matrix D is a diagonal matrix consisting of eigenvalues on the diagonal. The frequencies are obtained as follows:

$$\lambda = 1/\omega^2$$

```
>>[V,D] = eig(M,K)
```

More options for this function are illustrated in Chapter 10.

A2.2 WORKING WITH MS EXCEL FILES

Data between MS Excel file and MATLAB can be easily exchanged using some simple commands. There are two options:

(a) The data can be exchanged using the following commands:

```
xlsfinfo
xlsread
xlswrite
```

For example

```
num = xlsread (filename, sheet)
num = xlsread (filename, sheet, x1Range)
[num, text, raw] = xlsread(filename, sheet, x1Range)
```

The `xlsread` function optionally returns the text fields in cell array·txt, the unprocessed data (numbers and text) in cell array `raw`.

(b) Copy from Excel row or column and paste in MATLAB array

Copy and paste each column from excel sheet to an array in MATLAB.

In MATLAB create an array:

`array =[ ];`

Select the column in excel, choose copy, then go to MATLAB window and place the cursor between the square brackets above.

Then paste the column data.

Repeat above with different array numbers for each column.

You can save all the var in MATLAB as

save filename var name1 var name 2, … .

It will be saved as a mat file named filename.mat.

Example 8

```
filename=' DOS-A2.xlsx';
sheet=2;
x1Range='C2:C7';
Data=xlsread(filename,sheet,x1Range)

% MATLAB will print the EXCEL data as follows:

Data =

    1
    2
   -3
    0
    5
   21
```

□

Example 9

```
filename=' DOS-A2.xlsx';
[num,txt,raw]=xlsread(filename);
xArray=cell(raw(:,1))
yArray=cell(raw(:,2))
```

This EXCEL file contains data in first two columns: A and B. MATLAB will read data from column A in xArray and column B in yArray.

```
xArray
     1
     2
    -3
     0
     5
    21
yArray
     3
     5
     0
    -1
     7
     9
```

It is also possible to specify the cell nos as in the previous example.

Example 10

The EXCEL file DOS_A3.xlsx looks like as follows:

A	B	C	D	E	F
1		JAN	FEB	MAR	APR
2					
3		1	2	3	4
4		5	6	7	8

The MATLAB program is as follows:

```
filename='DOS-A3.xlsx';
sheet=2;
[NDATA,TXT,ALLDATA]=xlsread(filename,sheet)

NDATA =            % numerical data
     1     2     3     4
     5     6     7     8

TXT =              % text data
    'JAN'    'FEB'    'MAR'    'APR'

ALLDATA =          % all data
    'JAN'    'FEB'    'MAR'    'APR'
    [NaN]    [NaN]    [NaN]    [NaN]
[   1]   [   2]   [   3]   [   4]
[   5]   [   6]   [   7]   [   8]
```

Similarly, xlswrite function can be used.

    xlswrite(FILE,ARRAY,SHEET,RANGE) writes to the specified SHEET and RANGE.

A2.3 CONDITIONAL STATEMENTS

Like any other programming language, MATLAB also makes use of the FOR, WHILE and IF conditional statements. The general structure of these statements is illustrated through the flow diagrams shown in Figures A2.1–A2.3.

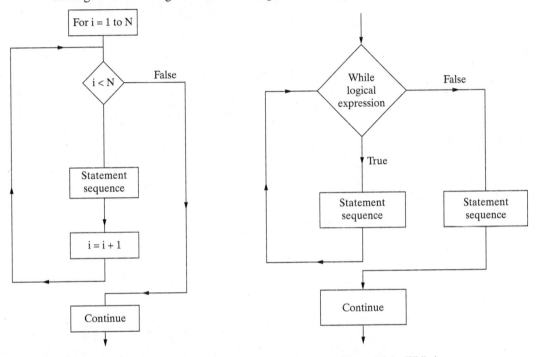

Figure A2.1   For loop

Figure A2.2   While loop

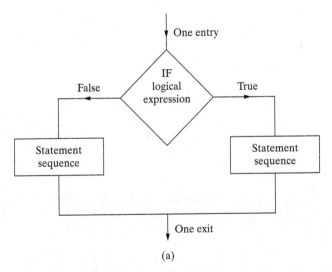

(a)

Figure A2.3   IF loop (Continued)

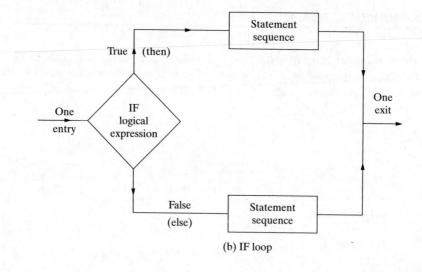

(b) IF loop

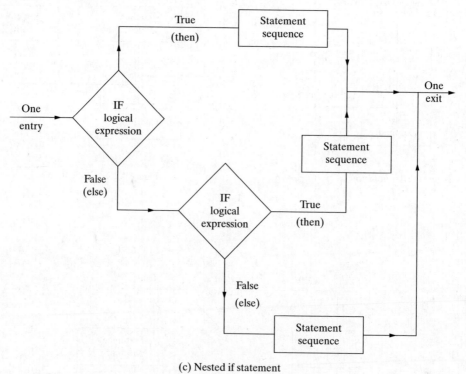

(c) Nested if statement

Figure A2.3   IF loop.

For Statement   For Repeat statements a specific number of times.

The general form of a for statement is:

```
for variable = expr,
statements
        END
```

While Statement   While Repeat statements an indefinite number of times.

The general form of a while statement is:

```
while expression
statements
        END
```

If Statement   If Conditionally execute statements.

The general form of the if statement is

```
if expression
statements
        ELSEIF expression
statements
        ELSE
statements
        END
```

The statements are executed if the real part of the expression has all non-zero elements. The ELSE and ELSEIF parts are optional.

A2.4 BASIC GRAPHING ROUTINES

```
2D plots
>> plot (x,y)
>> plot (t,y(:,1))
>> grid on;
>> grid off;

>> hold ON;      % holds the current plot and all axis properties so
                 that subsequent graphing commands add to the existing
                 graph.
>> hold OFF;     % returns to the default mode whereby PLOT commands
                 erase the previous plots and reset all axis properties
                 before drawing new plots.

>> title ('This is the title')
>> axis ([xmin    xmax    ymin    ymax])    % sets scaling for the x- and
                                           y-axes on the current plot.
>> figure;      % creates a new figure window
```

```
3D plots

mesh    grid      cartesian grid in 2-D/3-D space

create a colored mesh plot:
>> figure; mesh (xx,yy,z1); xlabel ('x'); ylabel ('y'); zlabel ('z');
>> title ('This is the title');

create a colored surface plot:
>> figure; surf (xx,yy,z1); xlabel ('x'); ylabel ('y'); zlabel ('z');
>> title ('This is the title');

create a contour plot:
>> figure; contour (xx,yy,z1); xlabel('x'); ylabel('y'); zlabel ('z');
>> title ('This is the title');

>> clear all
```

A2.5 MATLAB PROGRAMS WITH THIS BOOK

Several programs have been written for this book to perform various calculations. These programs can be stored in any directory and it should be on the path of the MATLAB. The following help command will give a brief description of any program say, DOS2_3:

```
>> help DOS2_3
```

Similarly, help about other programs can be obtained.

MATLAB source codes developed in this text can be obtained by sending an email to the author at dr.ashokkjain@gmail.com or ashokjain_iitr@yahoo.co.in.

Answers to Selected Problems

Chapter 1

1.1 $\omega = 31.30$ rad/sec

1.3 $k_{equ} = \dfrac{k_1(k_2 + k_3)}{(k_1 + k_2 + k_3)}$

1.5 $k_{equ} = k_1 + k_2$, $\omega = \sqrt{\dfrac{k_1 + k_2}{m}}$

1.7(b) $k = \dfrac{16}{3}\dfrac{EI}{L^3}$

1.8 $\omega = \sqrt{\dfrac{\rho Ag}{m}}$

1.11 $k = \dfrac{120}{11}\dfrac{EI}{h^3}$

1.13 $k = 2.8 \times 10^6$ N/m, Force $= 56$ kN

1.15 $k_{col} = 10064$ kN/m, $k_{brace} = 72000$ kN/m, $k_{eq} = 82064$ kN/m

Chapter 2

2.1 $\omega = 4.082$ rad/sec, $T = 1.539$ sec, $x_{max} = 20.915$ mm

2.3 $\omega = 3.158$ rad/sec, initial velocity $= 0.05$ m/s

$$x(t) = \frac{0.05}{3.158} \sin 3.158 t \ (\text{m})$$

2.4 $x(t) = A\cos\omega t + B\sin\omega t + \dfrac{m_2 g}{k}$ the last term is due to shift in the origin

or $x(t) = \dfrac{m_2 g}{k}(1 - \cos\omega t) + \dfrac{m_2\sqrt{2gh}}{(m_1 + m_2)\omega}\sin\omega t$

2.6 $k_{eq} = k_1 + \dfrac{k_2 k_3}{k_2 + k_3} = 3353 \dfrac{\text{N}}{\text{m}}$, $c_c = 2\sqrt{k_{eq}m} = 518 \dfrac{\text{Ns}}{\text{m}}$; $= 0.24$ underdamped

2.8 $k_{col} = 35.55$ kN/mm, $k_{brace} = 25.6$ kN/mm, $k_{eq} = 61.60$ kN/mm

$$x(t) = 12.91\sin \omega t + 50\cos \omega t$$

2.10 $x_F = 5.59$ mm, $\omega = 20.94$ rad/sec, 127.64 mm

2.12 $x_F = 7.35$ mm, $T = 0.444$ sec, comes to rest after 8.5 cycles, -0.1 mm

Chapter 3

3.5 $\omega = 11.55$ rad/sec, (i) $D = 0.498$, (ii) $D = 1.22$

3.6 $\xi = 11.1\%$

3.7 $\xi = 54\%$

3.8 $m = 19.28$ kg, $k = 12180$ N/m

3.9 $\xi_{eq} = 40.2\%$

3.10 $\xi = 4\%$

Chapter 5

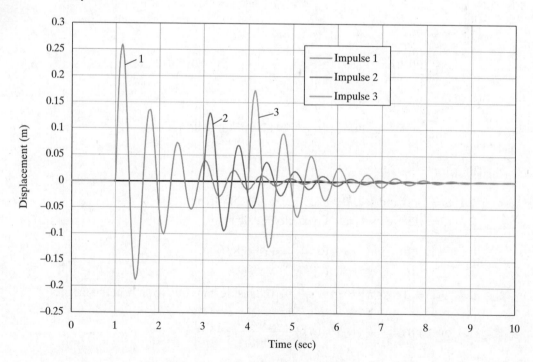

Figure Q5.5(a)   Response due to each impulse.

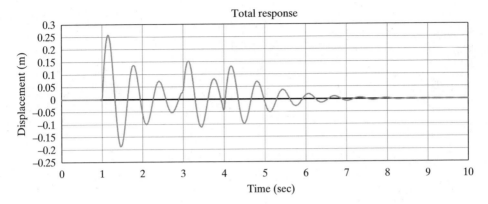

Fig Q5.5(b)   Total response due to all the three impulses.

Chapter 6

6.1 $\omega = 12.18$ rad/sec, $k = 371260$ N/m, $\Delta_{st} = 6.7$ mm

6.2 (a) $k = 9.8 \times 10^6$ N/m, (b) $k = 2.87 \times 10^6$ N/m

6.3 $\xi = 28.8\%$, $c = 17985$ Ns/m

6.4 $\xi = 32\%$

6.6 $x_{max} = 3.63$ mm

Chapter 7

7.1 and 7.3 Period = 1 sec, Step size = 0.1 sec

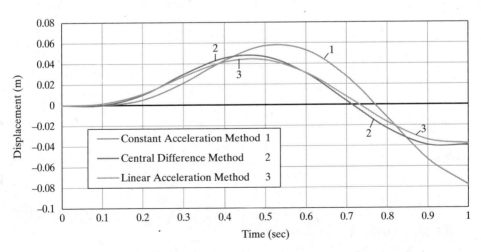

Figure Q7.1(a)   Displacement – time history.

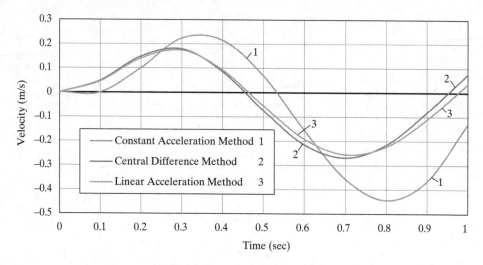

Figure Q7.1 (b) Velocity – time history.

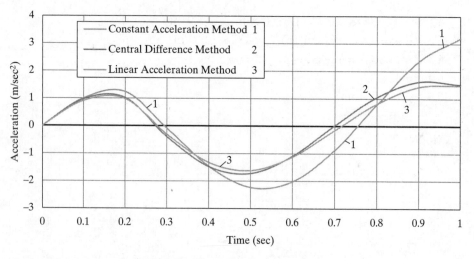

Figure Q7.1 (c) Acceleration – time history.

Chapter 9

9.1 $\omega = \begin{Bmatrix} 0.517 \\ 1.93 \end{Bmatrix} \sqrt{\dfrac{k}{m}}$ $\Phi = \begin{bmatrix} 1 & 1 \\ 0.732 & -2.732 \end{bmatrix}$

9.2 $\omega_2 = 121 \text{ rad/sec}$ $\phi_2 = \begin{Bmatrix} 1 \\ -1.667 \end{Bmatrix}$

9.3 $m_2 = 2.66 \text{ kg}$, $k_2 = 116666 \text{ N/m}$

9.7 $m_2 = 37.5 \text{ kg}$, $k_2 = 7500 \text{ N/m}$

9.10 $\omega = \begin{Bmatrix} 16.456 \\ 36.458 \end{Bmatrix} \text{rad/sec} = \begin{bmatrix} -0.1174 & 0.0789 \\ 0.0644 & 0.0958 \end{bmatrix}$

Chapter 10

10.1 Lowest eigenvalue $\lambda = 16.6264$, or fundamental frequency $\omega = 4.077$ rad/sec,

$$\{\phi\} = \begin{Bmatrix} 0.0147 \\ 0.0128 \\ 0.0094 \\ 0.0065 \\ 0.0028 \end{Bmatrix}$$

10.2 $\omega = \begin{Bmatrix} 4.077 \\ 9.017 \\ 14.26 \\ 18.74 \\ 20.88 \end{Bmatrix}$ rad/sec

$$\Phi = \begin{bmatrix} 0.0147 & 0.0156 & 0.0080 & -0.0108 & 0.0057 \\ 0.0128 & 0.0061 & -0.0042 & 0.0177 & -0.0116 \\ 0.0094 & -0.0071 & -0.0100 & -0.0004 & 0.0096 \\ 0.0065 & -0.0094 & 0.0024 & -0.0083 & -0.0113 \\ 0.0028 & -0.0059 & 0.0111 & 0.0057 & 0.0047 \end{bmatrix}$$

10.3 $\lambda_1 = 7.5576 \ \{\phi\} = \begin{Bmatrix} 0.8813 \\ -0.4305 \\ 0.1900 \\ -0.0423 \end{Bmatrix}$ and $\lambda_4 = 32.4424 \ \{\phi\} = \begin{Bmatrix} 0.0423 \\ 0.1900 \\ 0.4305 \\ 0.8813 \end{Bmatrix}$

10.4 $\lambda = \begin{Bmatrix} 0.184 \\ 0.400 \\ 0.616 \end{Bmatrix} \ \omega = \begin{Bmatrix} 0.4290 \\ 0.6325 \\ 0.7848 \end{Bmatrix} \ \Phi = \begin{bmatrix} 1 & -1 & -1 \\ 1.0801 & 0 & 1.0801 \\ 0.6667 & 0.5 & -0.6667 \end{bmatrix}$

Mode participation factors 1.106, 0.286, and − 0.18; modal mass = 28.527, 0.714, and 0.756

The sum of modal mass = 30 = total mass

10.10(b) $\omega = \begin{Bmatrix} 4.6235 \\ 5.0 \\ 11.55 \\ 15.674 \\ 20.50 \end{Bmatrix}$ and $T = \begin{Bmatrix} 1.358 \\ 1.2565 \\ 0.543 \\ 0.400 \\ 0.306 \end{Bmatrix}$ sec

$$\Phi = \begin{bmatrix} -0.1259 & 0.1321 & -0.0036 & 0.0013 & 0.0003 \\ -0.0106 & -0.0095 & 0.0172 & -0.0122 & -0.0044 \\ -0.0085 & -0.0082 & 0.0000 & 0.0103 & 0.0094 \\ -0.0061 & -0.0060 & -0.0086 & 0.0026 & -0.0134 \\ -0.0027 & -0.0027 & -0.0086 & -0.0099 & 0.0060 \end{bmatrix}$$

Chapter 12

12.5 Mass $m = 30000/9.81$, stiffness $k = 7500000$ N/m
Natural frequency $= 49.52$ rad/sec; period $T = 0.126$ sec

(a) For 5% damping, base shear $= 0.0667$ W
(b) For 2% damping, base shear $= 0.0933$ W
(c) For 10% damping, base shear $= 0.0534$ W

12.6 Mass m $= 101936$ kg, stiffness $k = 2857140$ N/m
Natural frequency $= 5.294$ rad/sec; period T $= 1.186$ sec; base shear $= 108.5$ kN

Chapter 15

15.6 (a) Fetch length for terrain type 4 $= 0.5$ km, developed height $= 95$ m,
(b) Fetch length for terrain type 2 $= 1$ km, developed height $= 45$ m,

The factor k_2 and wind speed are shown in the Table Q15.6 for both cases. The wind profiles are shown in Figure Q15.6(a) and (b), respectively in accordance with Appendix B of IS:875 part 3.

TABLE Q15.6 K_2 FACTOR AND WIND SPEED FOR STRUCTURE LOCATED AT P AND Q

Height	k_2 factor		Wind speed m/s	
m	# 4	# 2	V_z in # 4	V_z in # 2
(1)	(2)	(3)	(4)	(5)
10	0.76	0.98	37.62	48.51
20	0.76	1.05	37.62	51.975
30	0.93	1.1	46.035	54.45
45	1.02	1.138	50.49	56.331
50	1.05	1.15	51.975	56.925
94	1.138	1.212	56.331	59.994
95	1.14	1.213	56.43	60.0435
100	1.15	1.22	56.925	60.39
150	1.2	1.25	59.4	61.875

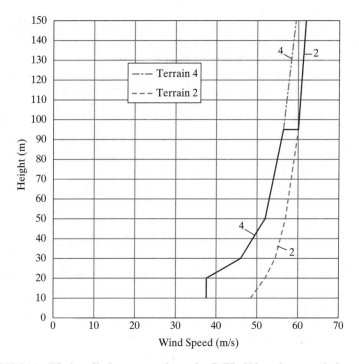

Figure Q15.6 (a)   Wind profile for structure located at P; Wind blows from terrain 2 to terrain 4.

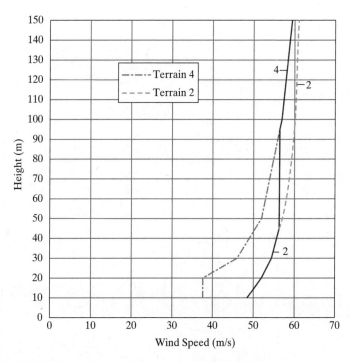

Figure Q15.6 (b)   Wind profile for structure located at Q; Wind blows from terrain 4 to terrain 2.

15.7 The fetch length for terrain type 2 = 1 km (point B), developed height = 45 m. The same k_2 factor (= 1.085) is available in terrain 4 at a height of 135 m.

The fetch length for terrain type 4 = 1.75 km (point A), developed height = 175 m,

The factor k_2 and wind speed are shown in the Table Q15.7. The wind profile is shown in Figure Q15.7 in accordance with Appendix B of IS:875 part 3.

TABLE Q15.7 K_2 FACTOR AND WIND SPEED FOR STRUCTURE LOCATED AT P

Height	k_2 factor			Wind speed in m/s		
m	# 2	# 4	# 1	V_z in # 2	V_z in # 4	V_z in # 1
10	0.93	0.67	0.99	43.7844	31.5436	46.6092
20	1	0.67	1.06	47.08	31.5436	49.9048
30	1.04	0.83	1.09	48.9632	39.0764	51.3172
45	1.085	0.92	1.128	51.0818	43.3136	53.10624
50	1.1	0.95	1.14	51.788	44.726	53.6712
100	1.17	1.05	1.2	55.0836	49.434	56.496
135	1.198	1.085	1.228	56.40184	51.0818	57.81424
150	1.21	1.1	1.24	56.9668	51.788	58.3792
175	1.225	1.115	1.25	57.673	52.4942	58.85
200	1.24	1.13	1.26	58.3792	53.2004	59.3208
250	1.26	1.16	1.28	59.3208	54.6128	60.2624
300	1.28	1.17	1.3	60.2624	55.0836	61.204

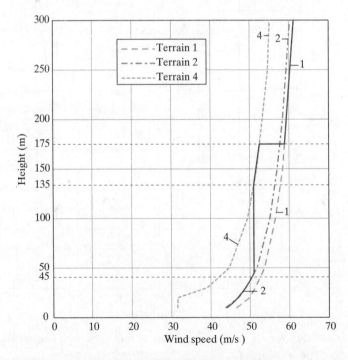

Fig Q15.7   Wind profile for structure located at P; Wind blows from terrain 1 to terrain 4 to terrain 2.

Index